CANADIAN CHILD WELFARE LAW
Children, Families and the State
SECOND EDITION

D1176991

DEDICATION

This book is dedicated to the memories of

the Honourable Mr. Justice John D. Bracco
and
Dr. David R. (Dan) Offord,

colleagues and friends who will be dearly missed.

CANADIAN CHILD WELFARE LAW
Children, Families and the State

SECOND EDITION

Nicholas Bala

Professor of Law, Queen's University, Kingston, Ontario

Michael Kim Zapf

Professor of Social Work, University of Calgary, Alberta

R. James Williams

Justice, Supreme Court of Nova Scotia, Family Division, Halifax, Nova Scotia

Robin Vogl

Lawyer for Muskoka and District Children's Aid Society, Ontario

Joseph P. Hornick

Executive Director, Canadian Research Institute for Law and the Family, Calgary, Alberta

Thompson Educational Publishing, Inc.
Toronto

Information on how to obtain copies of this book is available at:

Website:	www.thompsonbooks.com
E-mail:	publisher@thompsonbooks.com
Telephone:	(416) 766-2763
Fax:	(416) 766-0398

National Library of Canada Cataloguing in Publication

Canadian child welfare law : children, families and the state /
[edited by] Nicholas Bala ... [et al.]. — 2nd ed.

Includes index.
ISBN 1-55077-144-2

1. Parent and child (Law)—Canada. 2. Children—Legal status, laws, etc.—Canada.
3. Social work with children—Law and legislation—Canada. 4. Child welfare—Canada.
I. Bala, Nicholas, 1952—

KE3515.C35 2004   344.7103'27   C2004-902456-6   KF3735.C35 2004

Copy Editing: Elizabeth Phinney
Proofreading: Colborne Communications
Cover Design: Elan Designs

We acknowledge the support of the Government of Canada through the Book Publishing Industry Development Program for our publishing activities. We also acknowledge the support of the Government of Ontario through the Ontario Media Development Corporation Book Initiative.

Printed in Canada.
1 2 3 4 5   08 07 06 05 04

Table of Contents

Foreword

George Thomson

Executive Director, National Judicial Institute, Ottawa, Ontario

The world of child protection proceedings can be confusing, alien and hostile to all — from the children and families involved, to those who work with them, support them, advocate for them and judge them.

This is the second edition of *Canadian Child Welfare Law: Children, Families and the State*, a book which takes readers into the challenging, difficult realm of child protection proceedings from a wide variety of perspectives. The book has been written expressly for lawyers and law students with limited experience in the field, and those from disciplines other than law who are required to perform important roles within the unique environment of the Family Court.

When first published in 1991, this text was one of the only Canadian publications on child welfare law and practice. Traditionally, criminal laws affecting children have received significantly more attention than child welfare laws. Although the amount of analysis and research that now exists is still relatively modest, there is a growing recognition of the importance of the issues at stake in these cases. In large measure, this is the inevitable result of greater public and media discussion of high-profile cases, together with recent, extensive law reform in virtually all parts of the country.

These factors demonstrate why I believe this updated and expanded edition of this book will be a valuable resource for the many new practitioners in the child welfare field. It will also help those with more experience who are still adapting to the major changes in law and procedure introduced over the past decade.

The child welfare field is truly multi-disciplinary, and yet much of the decision making is legally constrained and must be justified within a complex legal environment. This book offers those with a legal background an understanding of the social context of child welfare law. For child welfare workers, professional excellence depends not only on an understanding of the legal framework and the reasons for its existence, but also on a knowledge of practical methods of overcoming the uncertainty, feelings of loss of control and fear that can arise when crossing professional boundaries and justifying one's actions and decisions to lawyers and judges. The challenges of child welfare practice are heightened by the recent trend towards greater public and legal scrutiny of the always fallible decision making in this area.

Updated chapters explain the law and its rationale in a straightforward, pragmatic fashion, taking the reader through the child protection process from initial involvement to final review. Readers will find the chapters which explain the rules of evidence and provide advice on how to prepare to testify in court particularly useful. The legal regime that applies to children in care and to the adoption process is reviewed, along with such important topics as Aboriginal child welfare, the challenges created by the phenomenon of street kids and adolescent prostitution and the confusion caused by parallel civil and criminal proceedings. A chapter — new to this edition — that considers the potential civil and criminal liability of child welfare workers, along with practical strategies for ensuring that one's work meets both legal and professional standards will be of value to all working in this area.

Several new authors have contributed to this edition. As with the authors in the original edition, their writings demonstrate a sincere commitment and dedication to child welfare. The work of all the contributors to this edition speaks to the strong personal beliefs held by those who work in this field. Through this collection, readers will experience the healthy uncertainty and openness to new ideas that characterize the professional lives of those who practice successfully in an area where human tragedy and high-risk decision making are everyday events. Perhaps nowhere in the book is this more apparent than in the chapter where four judges explain their individual approaches to child protection cases and their efforts to cope with the enormous responsibility placed on their shoulders. It is again reflected in the chapter on representation in protection cases, where lawyers who regularly represent children, parents and protection agencies explain the dilemmas and challenges they face in presenting their cases in court. Finally, a new chapter on social work education and practice provides an additional voice, showing the readers how difficult and frustrating and yet how very important is the work done by those who deal with families and children in crisis.

This edition maintains and builds on its predecessor, a book which filled a major gap in the field. It explains — in an easy-to-read manner — a complex, seemingly unintelligible set of legal rules and procedures. The recent major reforms in child welfare law are described, along with some analysis of their impact. Readers will be able to better understand the continuing debate about many difficult issues of law and policy, the answers to which can have a direct impact on the fate of children and families who come before the Family Court. The book — and the unique collection of voices in it — reinforces the human aspects of all decision-making in this field, a place where the role of the state is clearly at issue and the needs and interests of our most vulnerable citizens are at stake.

Preface and Acknowledgements

This book is written for students of law and social work in Canada, and is intended to provide an introduction to child welfare law — one of the most complex, demanding and important areas of law and social work practice, but also one that receives relatively little attention in professional schools and academic journals. The book is also intended to offer practicing professionals in the justice and child welfare systems an introductory text if they have not had the opportunity to study this area during their formal education, and it may serve as a reference work for busy professionals. It does not, however, provide a detailed discussion of all of the legislation or case law in this field, and those doing research in this area should consult one of the print or on-line services, or the texts that are available in law libraries.

This book reflects the law as of March 1, 2004. This book focuses on principles and trends in the law. There are, however, significant variations between provinces and territories in child welfare legislation, and there may be subtle but important variations within jurisdictions in the interpretation and application of legislation. Further, because of the profound effect that child welfare law has on society as a whole, and most particularly on the lives of children and their families, this body of law is subject to challenge and change. Legislatures not infrequently review and revise child welfare statutes, and the case law is constantly evolving.

While this text provides useful information for professionals, those with specific legal problems are urged to obtain appropriate legal advice. For individual professionals working in the child protection field, it is important to know which people within your agency are reliable resources in keeping up to date on legislation and its interpretation.

Completion of this book would not have been possible without the support of numerous individuals. The production of the text was the product of the energy, knowledge and skill of the contributing authors. We were fortunate to secure the expertise of numerous individuals whose experience and knowledge of Canadian child welfare legislation is so diverse and comprehensive. The authors in this second edition each bring their own experiences and perspectives to their work.

The work of authors who contributed to the first edition of this book, but who, for various reasons, are not included in the second edition, is also gratefully acknowledged. In many cases, these authors provided the foundation for the revised chapters. Specifically, we would like to thank the following: Dick Barnhorst, Bernd Walter, Anne Genereux, David A. Cruickshank, Christopher Bagley, Barbara A. Burrows, Carol Yaworski, Heather L. Katarynych, Donna Phillips, Jennifer A. Blishen, Susan G. Himel, and Mary-Jo Maur Raycroft.

We are extremely grateful to Joanne J. Paetsch, Administrator/Research Associate for the Canadian Research Institute for Law and the Family (CRILF), for her administrative support and editorial assistance throughout the life of this project. Thanks are also due to Linda Haggett, Receptionist/Typist for CRILF, for her diligent assistance in the preparation of the manuscript.

The Canadian Research Institute for Law and the Family undertook and supported this entire project. The Institute is supported by a grant from the Alberta Law Foundation.

Nicholas Bala
Michael Kim Zapf
R. James Williams
Robin Vogl
Joseph P. Hornick

May 2004

Editors and Contributors

Editors

- **Nicholas Bala**, Professor of Law, Queen's University, Kingston, Ontario.
- **Joseph P. Hornick**, Executive Director, Canadian Research Institute for Law and the Family, Calgary, Alberta.
- **Robin Vogl**, Lawyer for Muskoka and District Children's Aid Society, Ontario.
- **R. James Williams**, Justice, Supreme Court of Nova Scotia, Family Division, Halifax, Nova Scotia.
- **Michael Kim Zapf**, Professor of Social Work, University of Calgary, Alberta.

Contributors

- **Nicholas Bala**, Professor of Law, Queen's University, Kingston, Ontario.
- **Marvin M. Bernstein**, Director of Policy Development and Legal Support, Ontario Association of Children's Aid Societies, Toronto, Ontario.
- **Cindy Blackstock**, Executive Director, First Nations Child and Family Services Caring Society of Canada, Ottawa, Ontario.
- **Augustine Brannigan**, Professor of Sociology, University of Calgary, Alberta.
- **Carole Curtis**, Lawyer in private practice, Toronto, Ontario.
- **Theodore G. Giesbrecht**, Lawyer in private practice and Adoption Licensee, Kitchener, Ontario.
- **Dan L. Goldberg**, Senior Counsel, Office of the Children's Lawyer, Ministry of the Attorney General, Toronto, Ontario.
- **Thomas J. Gove**, Judge, Provincial Court of British Columbia.
- **Shelley Hallett**, Senior Counsel, Ontario Ministry of the Attorney General, Toronto, Ontario.
- **Wendy van Tongeren Harvey**, Crown Counsel, Ministry of the Attorney General, Vancouver, British Columbia.
- **Mary Jane Hatton**, Justice, Ontario Family Court, Durham Region.
- **Karima Kanani**, Miller Thomson LLP, Toronto, Ontario.

- **Gordon R. Kelly**, Senior Partner with the firm of Blois, Nickerson & Bryson, Halifax, Nova Scotia.
- **Lynn King**, Justice of the Ontario Court of Justice, Toronto, Ontario.
- **Patricia Kvill**, Judge, Family and Youth Division, Provincial Court of Alberta, Edmonton, Alberta.
- **Heino Lilles**, Chief Judge, Territorial Court of Yukon, Whitehorse, Yukon.
- **Bruce MacLaurin**, Assistant Professor, Faculty of Social Work, University of Calgary, Alberta.
- **Cheryl Regehr**, Associate Professor, Faculty of Social Work, and Director of the Centre for Applied Social Research, University of Toronto, Ontario.
- **Kristina J. Reitmeier**, Chief Counsel/Director of Legal Services, Children's Aid Society of Toronto, Ontario.
- **Murray Sinclair**, Justice, Court of Queen's Bench of Manitoba.
- **D.A. Rollie Thompson**, Professor of Law, Dalhousie University, Halifax, Nova Scotia.
- **George Thomson**, Executive Director, National Judicial Institute, Ottawa, Ontario.
- **Erin Gibbs Van Brunschot**, Assistant Professor of Sociology, University of Calgary, Alberta.
- **Robin Vogl**, Lawyer for Muskoka and District Children's Aid Society, Ontario.
- **James C. Wilson**, Judge, Family Court, Nova Scotia.
- **Michael Kim Zapf**, Professor of Social Work, University of Calgary, Alberta.

1

Child Welfare Law in Canada: An Introduction

Nicholas Bala[1]

The Role of the State in the Raising of Children

There is much controversy in Canada over the "best" way to raise children. Parental practices concerning such matters as children's nutrition, discipline, toilet training, day care, schooling, sports, sex education, dating and recreation are all the subject of heated debate among experts and social commentators. However, parents are largely left to make their own decisions about the best way to care for their children, according to their own values, beliefs and experience. This includes the parental right to determine the extent to which their children will be involved in making decisions about their own lives, though inevitably as children grow older they begin to exercise more autonomy.

Parents are human and none are "perfect"; some parents are far from perfect. Many parents may lack the education, understanding, and resources to do what is "best" for their children. Even if parents think they know what is "best" for their children, they may be unwilling or unable to do it. Nevertheless, it is a fundamental premise of our society that coercive government interference in family life should be kept to a minimum.

Many government services and benefits are offered to assist parents on a voluntary basis. For example, Canadian governments support cultural activities and recreational programs for children, but it is generally for parents to decide whether their children will participate in these programs. Parents are required by law to ensure that their children receive an education, and the government spends billions of dollars supporting the public school system, but parents may choose to send their children to private or sectarian schools, or to educate them at home.

There are, however, some situations in which the care parents provide is considered so inadequate that direct interference by the state is justified to protect children from their parents. These are situations where parental care has fallen below the minimum standards that our society will tolerate. State interference in the family and removal of a child from parental care is not legally justified merely because the child might have greater opportunities elsewhere.

---

[1] Nicholas Bala is Professor of Law, Queen's University, Kingston, Ontario.

Rather, state interference through removal of a child from parental care will only be justified if it is proven that there is a significant risk to the child.

This book examines the situations in which the state becomes involved in protecting children from their parents, with a particular emphasis on the role of the legal system. It considers the situations, processes and consequences of involuntary state intervention in the family. The major focus is on the child protection system, where a state agency is involved in trying to directly protect and care for children, but some of the discussion also deals with the criminal justice system — a system that punishes parents who may be guilty of abuse or neglect. The criminal justice system may also indirectly protect children, as the prosecution of abusive or neglectful parents may serve to remind all parents of their responsibilities towards children.

The History of Child Protection in Canada

It has not always been accepted that the state has a duty to protect children. The legal system of ancient Rome recognized the concept of *patria potestas*,[2] which gave a father complete authority over his children, including the lawful authority to sell them into slavery or even put them to death. With the spread of Christianity, the harshest aspects of Roman law were tempered, and by the sixth century A.D. the father's power had been limited to the right of "reasonable chastisement."

The English common law adopted the principle of a parental right of "reasonable chastisement," which in practice gave parents the authority to subject their children to harsh discipline, and the right to sell them into apprenticeship. Through the Middle Ages there was little social recognition of a concept of childhood as a time of special needs, and there was a tendency to treat children as young as seven years of age as miniature adults.[3] While gradually provision was made to care for orphans, first by religious bodies and later by municipal institutions, little was done to protect children from abuse or neglect if they were in the care of a parent or guardian. The criminal law made it an offence to kill or maim a child, and it was an offence to fail to provide a child under one's care with necessities of life. In practice, however, these laws were sporadically enforced, and children were regularly beaten by parents, subjected to sexual exploitation, and forced to work long hours under terrible conditions in mines and factories.

Prompted by the work of such social critics as Charles Dickens, who described the fate of children in institutions in *Oliver Twist*, the nineteenth century was a period of social reform in the United States, Great Britain and Canada. Many developments in this period improved the lot of children. The

---

[2] Latin for "the power of the father."

[3] See L. de Mause, *The History of Childhood* (London: Souvenir Press, 1976). Generally, on the history of child abuse, see M.C. Olmesdahl, "Paternal Power and Child Abuse: A Historical and Cross-Cultural Study" in J. Eekelaar and S. Katz (Eds.), *Family Violence* (Toronto: Butterworths, 1978) at 253.

latter part of the century witnessed the establishment of a publicly funded school system, as well as special courts and corrections facilities to deal with juvenile offenders.

Children's Aid Societies were established in various Canadian municipalities in the last decade of the nineteenth century, with the objective of helping orphaned, abandoned and neglected children. In 1893, reformers persuaded the Ontario legislature to enact *The Children's Protection Act*,[4] which gave these privately controlled societies broad legal powers, including the right to remove neglected or abused children from their homes and become legal guardians for such children.

Child welfare agencies were established throughout Canada by the early years of the twentieth century, and child welfare legislation was enacted in each province. However, the enormous growth and the legalization of the field has only occurred in the last 40 years.

Until the early 1960s, child welfare agencies dealt largely with the most obvious cases of abuse and neglect, and with situations of adolescent unmanageability. Agencies also had responsibility for the placement and adoption of some illegitimate children (i.e., those born out of wedlock) and had considerable responsibility for dealing with delinquent youth as well. While the courts exercised a supervisory function over the removal of children from their homes and over the adoption process, in practice the system tended to operate informally. Historically, most of the judges who sat in the Family Courts and dealt with this type of case lacked legal training, and lawyers rarely appeared in these proceedings. Parents who were involved in the protection process were often poor and poorly educated individuals who lacked the sophistication and resources to challenge the actions of the agencies. Many of the parents whose children were removed from their care were Aboriginal, or members of religious minority groups like the Doukhobors in British Columbia, who were socially marginalized.[5] There was no thought given to notions of children's rights, and children were not overtly involved in the child welfare proceedings where courts made decisions profoundly affecting their futures.

In the last 40 years, enormous changes have occurred in the child welfare field in Canada. An important development was the identification of the battered child syndrome in the early 1960s.[6] Until that time, doctors and social workers

---

[4] S.O. 1893, c. 45.

[5] One of the first reported cases in Canada of parents challenging child protection agency involvement was *Re Perepolkin* (1957), 11 D.L.R. (2d) 417 (B.C.C.A.) where the agency had removed a child from the care of parents who were Doukhobors, a small religious group in British Columbia that was viewed as "outside the mainstream." Hundreds of children were removed from their parents and placed in institutions. A report released in 1999 documented the long-term emotional trauma that these children suffered as a result of their removal from their families. According to a recent report of the British Columbia Ombudsman, almost all of them (the adult survivors of this forceful removal from parental care) still suffer from some form of post-traumatic stress syndrome. See R. Mickelburgh, "Doukhobor children wronged, B.C. told," *Globe and Mail* (9 April 1999) at A3.

[6] A seminal article in the field is by the American pediatrician, H.C. Kempe, "The Battered Child Syndrome" (1962) 181 *Journal of the American Medical Association* 17.

tended to suspect physical abuse only in cases where there was a witness to the abuse, or a child stated that an assault had occurred. But in the 1960s there was a growing recognition that parents often lie about abusing their children, describing injuries they inflicted as the result of "accidents," and that children are often too frightened or too young to disclose the truth to investigators during a single interview. Increased understanding of the problem led to changes in legislation to require professionals and members of the public to report suspected cases of child abuse. Child Abuse Registers were established in many North American jurisdictions in the mid-1960s to help keep track of abusers and abused children, and to facilitate research. Changes in reporting laws and growing professional awareness led to significant increases in the number of reports of physical abuse.

The late 1970s and early 1980s were marked by a "discovery" of child sexual abuse, similar to the earlier uncovering of physical abuse. Researchers learned that children were often too intimidated, guilty or ill-informed to report sexual abuse, and that parents and professionals often ignored reports or symptoms of sexual abuse. Changes in public and professional awareness resulted in enormous increases in the number of reported cases of child sexual abuse in the 1980s, with both children and adult survivors of abuse from previous decades coming forward to disclose what had happened to them in childhood. There were also fundamental changes in how child witnesses are treated in the Canadian criminal justice system, resulting in many more prosecutions of abusers.[7]

While child welfare agencies were dealing with more reports of sexual abuse in the 1980s and 1990s than in previous decades, agency involvement in other areas declined. Illegitimacy no longer bore a great stigma. Single mothers received more social and financial support than in the past. The concept of "family" broadened (and continues to evolve). Although single mothers face real challenges in raising their children alone, many more single mothers are keeping their children, resulting in a major decline in the adoption work of child welfare agencies. When the *Juvenile Delinquents Act* was replaced by the *Young Offenders Act*[8] in 1984, Canadian child protection agencies also ceased to have direct responsibility for delinquent youth. The *Young Offenders Act* was in turn replaced by the *Youth Criminal Justice Act*[9] in 2003, and there has continued to be a formal separation of the child welfare and youth justice systems, though it is not uncommon for adolescents in the care of child welfare agencies to be charged with offences, and there continues to be concerns that some agency wards with behavioural problems are being "dumped" into the youth justice and corrections systems.

---

[7] N. Bala, "Child Witnesses in the Canadian Criminal Court" (1999), 5 *Psychology, Public Policy and Law* 323-354.

[8] R.S.C. 1985, c Y-1.

[9] S.C. 2002, c. 1, in force April 1, 2003.

The Legal Revolution

Related to some of the fundamental changes in the child protection field has been a veritable revolution in the role of law and the courts in Canadian society. Until the last quarter century, the law was primarily concerned with the regulation of economic, commercial and property affairs, and with the control of deviant personal behaviour by means of the criminal law. In the last 25 years, however, the role of law in Canadian society has changed dramatically. Law has become an important social policy tool, affecting virtually every aspect of Canadian public policy. We are living in an increasingly "rights-based" society, in which individuals look to the courts to address a broad range of concerns. For example, the courts have been called upon to deal with such political issues as abortion, same-sex marriage, language rights and native land claims.

Both reflecting and reinforcing the importance of law in defining society was the enactment of the *Canadian Charter of Rights and Freedoms*[10] in 1982. The *Charter* has had a profound effect on Canadian society. While in the first few years that the *Charter* was in effect it had only limited impact on child welfare law, in its 1999 decision in *New Brunswick (Minister of Health) v. G.(J.)*, the Supreme Court of Canada sent a strong message that parents have a vital interest in their relationship with their children, an interest that is entitled to protection under s. 7 of the *Charter* as an aspect of "security of the person." The Court concluded that, pursuant to s. 7 of the *Charter,* a single mother on social assistance whose children had been apprehended by a child welfare agency had the constitutional right to be represented by counsel paid by the government. The provision of counsel is intended to ensure that the temporary wardship proceedings are conducted "in accordance with the principles of fundamental justice." In *G.(J.)* the Supreme Court invoked the constitutional rights of a parent, but was clearly also influenced by a concern for the promotion of the welfare of children. Chief Justice Lamer wrote:[11]

...the interests of fundamental justice in child protection proceedings are both substantive and procedural. The state may only relieve a parent of custody when it is necessary to protect the *best interests* of the child, provided that there is a fair procedure for making this determination ....

The interests at stake in the custody [child protection] hearing are unquestionably of the highest order. Few state actions can have a more profound effect on the lives of both parent and child. Not only is the parent's right to security of the person at stake, *the child's is as well. Since the best interests of the child are presumed to lie with the parent,* the child's psychological integrity and well-being may be seriously affected by the interference with the parent-child relationship....

In light of these factors, I find that the appellant [mother] needed to be represented by counsel for there to have been a fair determination of the children's best interests. Without the benefit of counsel, the appellant would not have been able to participate effectively at the hearing, creating an *unacceptable risk of error in determining the children's best interests* and thereby threatening to violate both the appellant's and her children's s. 7 right to security of the person.

---

[10] Part I of the *Constitution Act*, 1982, being Schedule B of the *Canada Act* 1982 (U.K.), 1982, c. 11.

[11] [1999] 3 S.C.R. 46, 50 R.F.L.(4th) 63 at para 70 and 76; emphasis added. For a fuller discussion, see N. Bala, "The Charter of Rights and Family Law in Canada: A New Era" (2001), 18 *Canadian Family Law Quarterly* 373-428.

It is now clear that when faced with a concrete situation in which parents or children are being subjected to treatment in a child protection proceeding that does not accord with the "principles of fundamental justice," the courts will respond. The *Charter* has also been used by the courts to eliminate unjustified discrimination and has, for example, been invoked to give biological fathers greater rights in the adoption process,[12] and by same-sex partners seeking the right to adopt children.[13] However, as will become clear from the discussion of the *Charter* in this book, the rights that it guarantees are not absolute, but rather are subject (under s. 1) to "such reasonable limits...as can be demonstrably justified in a free and democratic society." The courts are continually struggling to balance concerns about the protection of the constitutional rights of parents and children within the family, with the desire to promote the welfare of children, or at least ensure that children are not endangered by the recognition of their legal rights.

In 2004 the Supreme Court of Canada decided *Canadian Foundation for Children, Youth and the Law v. Canada*, a case that required the Court to carefully balance the rights of children and the rights of parents in deciding on the constitutional validity of s. 43 of the *Criminal Code*, a provision that allows a parent to use force to "correct" a child, provided that the force does not exceed what is "reasonable" under the circumstances. The Court narrowed the scope of this provision by overruling earlier cases that had, for example, held that parents could use a belt or paddle to correct a child. While the Court recognized that children are vulnerable and entitled to special protections, it also recognized that they are not just small adults who should always be given the same rights as adults, but rather generally be viewed in the context of their families. Parents are entitled to a significant degree of authority to raise their children as they see fit, without undue state interference. Chief Justice MacLachlin wrote:[14]

> Children need to be protected from abusive treatment. They are vulnerable members of Canadian society and Parliament [must]...shield children from psychological and physical harm. In so acting, the government responds to the critical need of all children for a safe environment. Yet this is not the only need of children. Children also depend on parents...for guidance and discipline, to protect them from harm and to promote their healthy development within society. A stable and secure family...is essential to this growth process.

The Supreme Court ruled that it was not appropriate to criminalize parents who spank their children, though emphasizing that any parental conduct that injures or degrades child is a crime. While the Court did not advocate the use of corporal punishment, it recognized that the criminal law is a "blunt instrument" for educating parents about appropriate parenting.

---

[12] *MacVicar v. British Columbia Superintendent of Family and Child Services* (1986), 34 D.L.R. (4th) 488 (B.C.S.C.).

[13] *Re K* (1995), 15 R.F.L. (4th) 129 (Ont. Prov. Ct.).

[14] [2004] S.C.J. 6 at para. 58.

The increased emphasis on individual rights has had a strong impact on child protection proceedings in Canada. Over the past quarter century the child protection process has become much more legally oriented. There is a greater recognition of the rights of parents and children; there are greater controls placed on the power of the state to intervene in the family. The child protection system is now premised on the notion that children may only be removed from parental care in accordance with "due process" of law. This reflects fundamental values in our society, as well as ensuring that decisions about state intervention are based on careful consideration of the issues by an impartial arbiter.

Due process is not without costs, monetary and other, however. With the legalization of the child protection system has come an expanded legal aid system to ensure representation for indigent parents and, in some Canadian jurisdictions, legal representation for children. Child protection proceedings have become more complex and hence more costly, not only for legal aid plans, but for child protection agencies and for the court system. More serious than the financial costs of due process are the human costs. Due process takes time. Delays due to the court process can be very stressful for children and families, though sometimes parents can take advantage of delays to improve their parenting skills and relationships with their children.

While due process may ensure fairness and considered decision making, it can make the job of social workers and other child welfare professionals more difficult and complex. The child protection system now has a more sharply adversarial nature than it had in the past, and professionals in that system may have their opinions and decisions challenged in the sometimes hostile environment of the courtroom, by lawyers who may seem insensitive to constraints placed on those who work in the child protection system. It must be recognized that parents and children separated from one another by the child welfare system have always felt a level of hostility towards agency workers. However, it is only with the rise of due process that parents and children have had a forum to effectively challenge decisions that profoundly affect their lives.

Although a key component of Canada's legal system is the adversarial trial, there is a growing recognition that having a trial is an emotionally and financially expensive process that will inevitably strain relations between agency workers and parents. Accordingly, in recent years there has been an emphasis on trying to use mediation, settlement conferences and other methods to try to resolve child welfare cases without a trial.[15] These innovations in alternative dispute resolution are discussed in Chapters 3 and 15.

Balancing Parental Rights and Protection Concerns

One of most significant developments in the child welfare field in Canada in the late 1990s was a growing focus on protecting children from abusive or

---

[15] See e.g., M. Bernstein, "Child Protection Mediation: Its Time Has Arrived" (1999), 16 *Canadian Family Law Quarterly* 73-119.

neglectful home situations, and providing them with permanent, safe homes. There was a concern that there may have been too much effort in the 1980s and early 1990s directed to "family preservation," and not enough attention to the protection of children. These concerns were heightened by some highly publicized, tragic cases where children died in the care of parents, even though child welfare workers were aware of some problems in the home but had not removed the children from parental care. There was also a growing awareness in the 1990s of the potentially devastating effects to a child's well-being from emotional neglect and abuse, that might, for example, result from poor attachment to parent figures in a child's early years or from witnessing parents engaging in spousal abuse.

The perception that agencies were not doing enough to protect children resulted in investigations and inquiries in British Columbia, Quebec, Ontario, Manitoba and New Brunswick in the late 1990s. The British Columbia public inquiry by Family Court Judge Tom Gove into the tragic death of five-year-old Matthew Vaudreuil, who was killed by his mother, provided the most comprehensive study.[16] The 1995 *Gove Report* resulted in new legislation in British Columbia as well as a substantial change in the administration of child welfare services in that province, with a new Ministry for Children and Families being created.

In Ontario, after a series of coroners' inquests, a special committee was appointed by the Ontario government to study the child welfare system and recommend legislative reforms. This committee was also chaired by Family Court Judge Mary Jane Hatton, though the Ontario committee did not hold public hearings, and had a limited budget and little time to produce a report. The Ontario *Report of the Panel of Experts on Child Protection: Protecting Vulnerable Children* was released in 1998, and resulted in significant new amendments to the *Child and Family Services Act*, which came into effect in 2000.[17] This legislation both facilitated earlier intervention in cases of physical abuse or neglect, and broadened the grounds for intervention in cases of emotional abuse or neglect.

In addition to the legislative changes that occurred in some Canadian provinces, most jurisdictions have developed more standardized approaches to the assessment of risk of abuse or neglect. Most jurisdictions in Canada now employ a standardized process for assessing the degree of risk that a child faces in a home situation. For example, in Ontario, the *Child Welfare Eligibility Spectrum* and the *Risk Assessment Model* are used to guide case management by child

---

[16] British Columbia, *Gove Inquiry into Child Protection in British Columbia*, (1995), [1995] B.C.J. 2483 (Q.L.); Ontario Association of Children's Aid Societies, *Ontario Child Mortality Task Force Recommendation: A Progress Report* (1998); R. Seguin, "Horrific child abuse case reveals deep flaws in system: Commission censures Quebec for failing to protect children," *Globe and Mail* (23 April 1998) at A4; K. Cox, "Answers sought on child neglect in New Brunswick," *Globe and Mail* (29 December 1997) at A4; and K. Cox, "Ontario to review child abuse cases," *Globe and Mail* (22 September 1997) at A7.

[17] S.O. 1999, c. 6; in force March 31, 2000. See N. Bala, "Reforming Ontario's Child and Family Services Act: Is the Pendulum Swinging Back Too Far?" (2000), 17 *Canadian Family Law Quarterly* 117-173.

protection workers.[18] These tools are intended to promote a consistent, structured approach to the investigation of cases, and to the making of critical decisions about a case, such as whether to apprehend and remove a child from parental care. While these tools are useful, there is inevitably also a degree of professional judgement involved in the risk and safety assessment process. Their use has produced a more consistent approach to the assessment of risk, but it has not made the process "objective." Although the information that is used in the risk assessment process is admissible in court, a judge is not obliged to accept the assessment of the agency workers based on these instruments. Indeed, the very purpose of the court process is to determine whether the views of the agency are adequately supported by the evidence proven in court and whether they meet the standards of the legislation.

While there were important differences in the approaches to child welfare reform in different North American jurisdictions in the late 1990s, there were common themes of developing more effective measures to remove children from the care of parents who were perceived to be inadequate, and to having "permanent decisions" about children's futures made more quickly once they were in agency care.[19] These changes were intended to increase the protections available to children, but they also reflected the more conservative political attitudes of that period and related efforts to reduce government spending. This was, for example, also a period of major efforts to restructure social assistance; there were greater expectations that the poor would take responsibility for their economic situation, and take steps to become self-supporting by taking training programs or participating in workfare, and if they failed to do so, there was a greater likelihood that they would lose welfare eligibility. In the child welfare field, if parental care was not considered acceptable, parents were more likely to face the prospect of earlier termination of parental rights than under the previous legislative regimes. As a result, there has been less spent on trying to help parents gain the capacity to effectively care for their children. In addition, in the late 1990s there were cuts to many government-funded social programs that had previously been available to assist parents in the community.

In the late 1990s and in the early years of the new century there were very substantial increases in the number of children taken into the care of child welfare agencies in many jurisdictions in North America. While there were

---

[18] *Ontario Child Welfare Eligibility Spectrum* (revised 2000) and *The Risk Assessment Model for Child Protection in Ontario* (revised 2000), available through The Ontario Association of Children's Aid Societies, 75 Front Street East, 2nd Floor, Toronto, Ontario, Canada, M5E 1V9. These tools were developed by the Ontario Association of Children's Aid Societies and are authorized by the Ministry of Community, Family and Children's Services. New child protection workers in the province receive training in their use: see http://www.oacas.org/ programs/ocptp.htm.

[19] In the U.S., the *Adoption and Safe Families Act of 1997*, Pub. L. No. 105-89 had a broadly similar focus, shifting from "a family preservation" approach to one that emphasized "permanency planning." See D. Roberts, "Is There Justice in Children's Rights? The Critique of Federal Family Preservation Policy" (1999), 2 *University of Pennsylvania Journal of Constitutional Law* at 112; and P. Parkinson, "Child Protection, Permanency Planning and Children's Right to Family Life" (2003), 17 *International Journal of Law, Policy and the Family* 147-172.

many causes for these increases, the changes in the law, which were intended to reduce the risk of abuse of children, clearly played a significant role.

Legal Contexts and the Protection of Children

There are a number of different legal contexts in which issues related to the protection of children from abuse, neglect or ill treatment can arise. While the factual issues may be similar, the legal outcome that is being sought varies with the legal context, and there are important procedural differences between these different types of legal proceedings.

Historically, the criminal law was the only legal tool employed to protect children. It still has an important role. It is a criminal offence to sexually abuse or physically assault a child. However, with regard to the use of physical force, caretakers can raise the defence of "using force by way of correction...if the force used does not exceed what is reasonable under the circumstances."[20] It is also an offence for a parent or guardian to fail to provide a child with "necessaries of life" or to abandon a child under the age of 10.[21] While the *Criminal Code* can be used to prosecute those who harm children, it is a blunt tool that is often difficult to employ.

Persons charged with criminal offences are guaranteed a broad set of rights under the *Canadian Charter of Rights and Freedoms*. There is an onus upon the state to prove guilt according to the highest legal standard, "proof beyond a reasonable doubt." Abuse cases can be especially difficult to prove because it is often necessary to rely heavily on the evidence of the child who was the victim of abuse. The traditional rules of evidence and procedure governing criminal cases made it difficult for children to testify, and the courts discounted their evidence. While beginning in the late 1980s legal reforms in Canada and changes in the administration of justice made it easier for children to testify, and resulted in a significant increase in the number of child abuse prosecutions, especially for sexual abuse, it can still be difficult to prove in a criminal proceeding that a particular person has been guilty of abuse and should be punished by the state, for example, by being sent to jail.

Criminal investigations are handled by the police, and the presentation of the case in criminal court is the responsibility of the Crown prosecutor. There are sometimes disagreements between these criminal prosecutorial authorities and child protection agencies about how cases should be handled. In some cases child protection workers are concerned about the effect on a child of prosecuting a parent, and may be opposed to criminal proceedings that the Crown and police want to pursue. In other cases child protection workers may favour a prosecution, but the police or prosecutor may be unwilling to proceed. There have been

---

[20] *Criminal Code*, R.S.C. 1985, c. C-46, s. 43. The constitutional validity of this provision was upheld by the Supreme Court of Canada in *Canadian Foundation for Children, Youth and the Law v. Canada*, [2004] S.C.J. 6.

[21] *Criminal Code*, R.S.C. 1985, c. C-46, ss. 215, 218.

efforts to improve liaison and coordination between child protection agencies and those responsible for criminal prosecutions, and it is now common for local police and child welfare agencies to have a "protocol" or joint policy to guide joint investigations. This improved coordination has resulted in more support for children in the prosecution of cases in the criminal justice system. Even now, however, criminal prosecutions for physical abuse are relatively rare, except in cases involving serious physical injury or death, and overall only a relatively small portion of abuse and neglect cases that child protection agencies are involved with result in criminal prosecutions.

It is generally easier to prove abuse or neglect in a civil child protection proceeding than in a criminal proceeding, even if exactly the same conduct is at issue in both cases. The rules about what types of evidence a court may consider are less restrictive in a civil trial, and the standard of proof is lower, requiring only proof "on the balance of probabilities." While the *Charter of Rights* is applicable to child protection proceedings, the type of rights granted to those alleged to have abused or neglected their children in these civil proceedings is much narrower than the rights afforded to those accused of the same acts in the criminal justice process.

Allegations of parental abuse and neglect are most commonly dealt with as a child protection issue rather than as one requiring criminal prosecution. The child protection case is a civil proceeding in which the state-mandated child protection agency seeks to intervene in the family, either by making the child the subject of court-ordered supervision, or by having the child removed from parental care, on either a temporary or permanent basis.

Sometimes abuse or neglect issues are raised in a civil case involving separated parents who are in a dispute over custody or access to their children. With growing awareness of the problem of child abuse, the number of cases involving this type of allegation has increased.

It is also possible for a child who has been the victim of abuse, or a guardian acting on behalf of the child, to bring a civil suit for monetary damages. However, abusers frequently lack the financial resources to satisfy a judgement and such suits have been rare. Further, children are often reluctant to sue their parents, even after they reach adulthood. However, victims may feel a sense of psychological vindication from recovering an award, and such civil suits are becoming more common. It is also becoming more common for victims of abuse to seek monetary awards from their provincial Criminal Injuries Compensation Board. It is not necessary for there actually to be a criminal conviction for compensation to be granted, though there must be proof that abuse occurred. In theory, the Board may seek reimbursement from an abuser for compensation paid, but in practice the Boards do not pursue abusers if they are without assets or reasonable income.

Complex issues may arise if there is simultaneously more than one type of legal proceeding dealing with allegations of abuse or neglect arising out of a single family situation; for example, it is possible for a criminal prosecution and a child protection application to proceed through different courts at the same time. Although the major focus of this book is on child protection proceedings, Chapter 9 considers parental custody or access disputes in which abuse allegations have been made, and Chapter 10 deals with criminal prosecutions involving child abuse allegations. Children are much more likely to be called upon to testify in court in criminal proceedings than in any other context; Chapter 12 discusses the preparation of children for the experience of testifying as witnesses in court.

The Role of the Child Welfare Agency

In every Canadian jurisdiction there is an agency that has the legal responsibility for investigating reports that a child may be in need of protection and taking appropriate steps to protect children from ill-treatment. The agency may provide services to the child and parents in their home, or may remove the child from the home on a temporary or permanent wardship basis. The child welfare agency may provide services on either a voluntary or an involuntary basis, making use of the legal system to require children and parents to receive services. Child welfare agencies also are responsible for arranging some adoptions, though in most jurisdictions private adoption agencies or licensees are involved in this type of work as well. In some localities child welfare agencies assume other responsibilities related to their principal mandates, such as organizing programs for the prevention of child abuse.

Child welfare agencies are given very significant powers under legislation to search for children who may be in need of protection and, if necessary, to force parents to surrender custody. These agencies receive all or most of their funding from the state. From a conceptual perspective, child welfare agencies are agents of the state, in some cases exercising the coercive power of the state.

In most Canadian jurisdictions, child welfare services are provided by provincial employees serving out of local offices, typically of the Ministry of Social Services. In Manitoba, Nova Scotia and Ontario there are local child welfare agencies, called Children's Aid Societies or Child and Family Service Agencies. These non-profit agencies serve a particular geographical area. In Ontario, a few Children's Aid Societies are denominational, serving only Catholic or Jewish families and children in a particular region. Recently in some provinces child welfare agencies have been established to serve native children exclusively. Even in provinces with these local semi-autonomous child welfare agencies, ultimate statutory and financial responsibility for the agencies rests with the provincial government, and their employees should be viewed in many respects as agents of the state.

While the structure of each child welfare agency or local office is unique, the agencies share certain common features. Agencies have two basic functions: child protection (or family services) and child care. In some agencies workers have both child protection and child care responsibilities. In other agencies, however, workers have a more specialized role.

Child protection workers are responsible for investigating suspected cases of abuse or neglect, and working with children and parents in their homes. Some agencies have intake departments, with a special mandate to deal with initial investigations and crisis situations; in such agencies, if ongoing service is required, the cases are usually transferred to a family service worker after the initial investigation is completed by the intake worker.

Child care workers have responsibility for children who have been taken into care on either a temporary or permanent basis. Typically, children are actually cared for in foster or group homes, and child care workers have a liaison function with foster parents and group home staff. In some agencies, adoption work is done as part of child care while in others it is the responsibility of a separate department.

In some agencies there are specialized workers who are responsible for dealing with specific types of cases such as adolescents living on the streets or child sexual abuse; in others, workers have a more generalized protection caseload. In some localities, particularly in smaller agencies, staff members are responsible for both child protection and child care work.

In Quebec, there are regionalized Social Service Centres with a mandate for providing a broad range of social services to children and adults. Workers in that province may have a mixed caseload including, for example, young offenders, child protection cases and marital counselling cases.

Child welfare agencies are involved with the court system and must have access to adequate legal services. In some localities, especially larger centres, there are staff lawyers who work exclusively in representing agencies in child protection cases. In some locales, Department of Justice lawyers represent agencies. In other places, child welfare agencies hire lawyers in private practice to provide representation in individual cases, typically establishing a relationship with a specific law firm. Use may also be made of court workers; these are employees of child welfare agencies who are not lawyers, but who are familiar with the court system. These workers handle certain cases in court, typically those which are less contentious, leaving the more complex cases to lawyers who are on staff or retained from private practice.

Child welfare agencies provide services in conjunction with other agencies and professionals in private practice. For example, initial reports of suspected abuse or neglect may come from doctors in hospital emergency departments, public health nurses or teachers. When determining how a case should be handled, a child welfare agency may refer a case to a psychologist, psychiatrist or mental health clinic for an assessment, sometimes as part of the court process. If a child is taken into the care of an agency, it may be necessary for agency staff to work with therapists or educators. While some agencies have facilities where their own employees care for children, it is common for agencies to have foster parents or group home operators who are not agency employees provide care for children.

If there is a criminal prosecution, child protection workers will have to maintain contact with the police and Crown prosecutor's office. To be effective, child welfare agencies must have good working relationships with others in the community.

Working for a child welfare agency can be a difficult, stressful job. There tends to be high staff turnover in these agencies. While most workers in this field are quite well educated, having a college diploma or university degree, often in social work, they are relatively young and inexperienced. Young social workers not infrequently start their careers in child welfare agencies and, after gaining experience, move to less stressful work elsewhere in the helping professions.

The stress in the child protection field relates to both the nature of the cases and the nature of the work. There is an inevitable degree of tension, as the role of child protection workers has both supportive and investigative functions. Child protection workers usually try to be supportive to parents and to provide services on an informal, voluntary basis. Indeed, most families that a worker comes into contact with do not end up in court, and in these cases the role of the protection worker can be regarded as similar to that of a therapist or counsellor, or of an educator in parenting skills. However, the role of a child protection worker can also in some ways be viewed as similar to that of a police officer. Protection workers have legal responsibility for investigating allegations of abuse or neglect. Even if their involvement with a family is at one time voluntary, in the event of later difficulties, anything a parent or child has told a worker may be relevant and admissible in a subsequent protection hearing.

Through education and disposition, most child protection workers want to have a therapeutic role, helping children and parents. Large caseloads mitigate against such a role, reducing the time the social worker has for each case. Understandably, however, workers may be viewed with hostility and distrust by parents, who may focus on the investigative role of child protection work. This often makes the job frustrating and contributes to the high turnover rate.

Some would argue that legal constraints make child protection work even more demanding. The law sometimes can make it difficult for child protection staff to take effective measures to protect a child. It is not enough for a worker to feel or believe that a child is at risk and should be removed from parental care. Involuntary removal of a child from parental care can only occur if legal requirements are satisfied and the need for this is documented in court. However, if a child is inappropriately left in parental care and suffers further abuse, the worker will inevitably feel a sense of guilt and moral responsibility.

Further, there is the threat of personal legal liability for taking inappropriate actions. While the likelihood of a social worker facing personal legal responsibility for being either too aggressive in removing a child, or insufficiently protective and leaving a child with a family that subsequently injures the child is low, even the threat of personal liability can make workers apprehensive. The questions of civil and criminal liability for child welfare agencies and their staff are discussed in Chapter 13.

The Law and the Child Protection Process

Child welfare agencies are charged with the legal and moral obligation of protecting children from abuse and neglect, and thereby promoting their welfare. Provincial legislation gives these agencies the legal authority to intervene in the lives of parents and children in order to provide protection. While the legislation varies from one jurisdiction to another, and different judges have conflicting views about how to interpret and apply the legislation, the law clearly presumes that parents are capable of raising their children without state interference. The law places a burden on child welfare agencies to clearly establish the need for intervention.

The nature of this burden was discussed by Judge Stortini in *Re Brown*:[22]

> In attempting to establish what is best for the children, I must accept the realities and accidents of life and refrain from judging the needs of the children and the parents' ability to satisfy them on an unfair or unrealistic basis....
>
> In other words, the community ought not to interfere merely because our institutions may be able to offer a greater opportunity to the children to achieve their potential. Society's interference in the natural family is only justified when the level of care of the children falls below that which no child in this country should be subjected to.

An onus is placed on the agency to establish its case based on the recognition that in some cases, the child protection workers involved will be mistaken in concluding that a child has been a victim of parental abuse or neglect and would benefit from removal from parental care. At least part of the rationale for placing an onus on child welfare agencies to justify their intervention is based on fundamental values of our society. Parents are viewed as having the moral right to raise their children in the manner they see fit; state-imposed restrictions on individual freedom, including the right to bear and raise children, require justification by the state. In *Re Chrysler*, Judge Karswick frankly recognized the potential risk of placing the burden on the Children's Aid Society (C.A.S.) to prove its case:[23]

> It seems to me that...the potential for real and immediate abuse must be clear before the state should be permitted to intervene by removing the child from her parents. If it were otherwise, it would allow a C.A.S. to be the final arbitrator in a so-called child abuse case and would leave the parents and the child with no real recourse to a really independent and impartial court. In adopting this principle, I realize that there is always the danger that some real and even irreparable harm may be inflicted upon the child if the parents are really potential child abusers, but the C.A.S. has not been able to prove that fact because of the unavailability of witnesses who can testify to the alleged abuse and therefore has not been able to meet the standard of proof required by the court.
>
> I think that this risk must still give way to the greater risk of the irreparable harm that can be inflicted upon a child and the danger to society of the serious undermining of the parents and the family if a C.A.S. is permitted to act in an arbitrary way, even though its intentions are motivated by the highest ideals and concerns.

---

[22] (1975), 9 O.R. (2d) 185 at 189 (Ont. Co. Ct.).
[23] (1978), 5 R.F.L. (2d) 50 at 58 (Ont. Prov. Ct. — Fam. Div.).

While placing an onus on child welfare agencies to prove their case creates the risk that in some cases the courts may fail to take appropriate steps to protect children, inappropriate intervention also creates risks for children. Removal of children from their homes by child welfare agencies inevitably involves some risks for the child.[24] At least in the short term, removal of children from their homes is always disruptive and often emotionally traumatic for children, even if the parents are neglectful or abusive. Assessing what will be best for a child is often very difficult: it may be impossible to make an accurate prediction about a child's long-term psychological development in different settings simply by observing child-rearing practices in the home. Determining what will best promote a child's welfare is often an inherently speculative exercise.

Children who are placed in agency care often experience emotionally damaging moves from one placement to another. Placements that are intended to be temporary and short-term often turn out to be long-term, sometimes extending over several years. Parental contact during foster care placements frequently is limited or even nonexistent. It has also been found that the longer children remain in care and the less contact they have with their parents, the more likely that they will never return home.

Child Welfare Legislation in Canada

Every Canadian jurisdiction has child welfare legislation in place to regulate the child protection process. While there are variations in philosophy and approach, all of the legislative regimes deal with the same fundamental issues, and have similar basic features.[25]

Declaration of Principle and the "Best Interests of the Child"

Almost all child welfare statutes in Canada have a statement of principles that is intended to guide the courts and child welfare agencies in the implementation of the law, and a definition of "best interests" that requires consideration of a number of listed factors when making a decision about a child, such as the decision that a court is to make if a child is found to be in need of protection.[26] There is some overlap with the direction provided by the declaration of principles and the definition of "best interests" of the child.

The central themes that appear in these declarations of principles and definitions of the best interests of the child are:

---

[24] See e.g., M. Wald, J. Carlsmith, and P. Leiderman, *Protecting Abused and Neglected Children* (Stanford, CA: Stanford University Press, 1988) at 14.

[25] For a fuller analysis of child welfare laws in Canada, see M. Bernstein et al., *Child Protection Law in Canada* (Toronto: Carswell, 1990 — present, updated looseleaf); and Human Resources Development Canada, *Child Welfare in Canada* — 2000 (Ottawa, 2002); on-line <http://www.hrdc.gc.ca/sp-ps/socialp- psociale/cfs/ rpt2000/ rpt2000e_toc.shtml>. For simplicity, most references in this book are to provincial statutes, but the three territories also have child welfare legislation and policies.

[26] Quebec's *Youth Protection Act* has similar concepts and provisions, though its structure and the concepts employed are somewhat different from those employed in Canada's common law provinces.

- *Respect for family autonomy and support of families*: Most of these statements recognize the importance of respecting the family and the parents' primary responsibility in child rearing. For example, Ontario's *Child and Family Services Act* states that "...while parents often need help in caring for their children, that help should give support to the autonomy and integrity of the family...."[27] Manitoba's *Act* states that: "The family is the basic source of care, nurture and acculturation of children and parents have the primary responsibility to ensure the well-being of their children."[28]

- *Continuity of care*: Most of these statements explicitly recognize the importance of continuity and stability for the child. For example, Manitoba's *Child and Family Services Act* states that: "Children have a right to a continuous family environment in which they can flourish."[29] Quebec's *Youth Protection Act* provides:[30]

  > Every decision made under this Act must contemplate the child's remaining with his family. If in the interest of the child, his remaining with [his family]... is impossible, the decision must contemplate his being provided with continuous care and stable conditions of life...as nearly similar to those of a normal family environment as possible.

These principles emphasize the importance of permanence for children, a preference for children continuing to remain with their own family and, if removal is necessary, the need for a stable foster or adoptive family.

- *Consideration of views of children*: All child welfare statutes in Canada specify that decision makers are to take into consideration the views and wishes of children when making decisions, but it is clear that the preferences of children are not determinative of how child protection cases are to be resolved.

- *Respect for cultural heritage, especially for Aboriginal children*: All of the statutes have statements that recognize the desirability of respecting a child's cultural and religious heritage, and most have a statement that gives particular emphasis on the unique significance in Canada of Aboriginal cultural heritage.

- *The paramountcy of the protection of children from harm*: In some provinces, like Ontario and British Columbia, where there was a concern that too much of an emphasis may have been given to preservation of families or parental rights and as a result children were left in abusive or neglectful home situations where they were died, statements of principle were added to the legislation in the late 1990s that the protection of children from abuse, neglect and harm is to be "a paramount objective."[31]

---

[27] S.1(b), as enacted S.O. 1999, c. 6.

[28] *The Child and Family Services Act*, R.S.M. 1987, c. C80, Declaration of Principles.

[29] R.S.M. 1987, c. C80, Declaration of Principles.

[30] R.S.Q. 1977, c. P-34.1, s. 4, as amended by S.Q. 1984, c. 4, s. 5.

[31] *Child and Family Services Act*, s. 1(a), as amended S.O. 1999, c.6; *Child, Family and Community Service Act*, R.S.B.C. 1996, c.46, s. 2(a) and 4(1).

These statements of principles and definitions may be of some assistance to judges and social workers in making decisions under the legislation, especially when these decision makers are applying the legislation to a particular case and the relevant, specific section does not provide sufficient guidance. Most of these declarations and definitions, however, do not clearly prioritize how different considerations are weighed in individual cases, and hence tend to confer significant discretion on individual decision makers. In practice, child protection workers are more likely to be influenced by professional ethics and government and agency policies, while courts receive more direction from specific provisions of the legislation and from leading judicial precedents than from generalized statements of principles. Tension can develop between agency and legislative policies. The general statutory statements that seem to be most frequently cited by the courts are those which are also reflected in the specific statutory provisions that govern critical decision-making points in the child protection process, or that are reflected in leading precedents.

The "Child in Need of Protection"

Each child welfare statute has a definition of a "child in need of protection" (or an "endangered child"). This is a key legal concept, as only children within this definition are subject to involuntary state intervention under the legislation. While there is some variation in how the concept of the "child in need of protection" is defined, there is a common core of situations of physical and sexual abuse, parental neglect (including failure to provide needed medical treatment) and abandonment that are within the definition in every jurisdiction. Further, in all jurisdictions, a child may be brought into agency care with the consent of the parents. In all jurisdictions there is also provision for finding a child in need of protection in cases of emotional maltreatment or if the child is an adolescent whose parents are having serious difficulties in caring for the child, though there are variations in the statutory definitions for these types of situations. For example, in some jurisdictions like New Brunswick, the fact that a child resides in a home where spousal abuse has occurred is in itself a basis for finding a child in need of protection; in other provinces, such as Ontario, spousal abuse is not a specific ground for establishing that a child is in need of protection, but this could be a contributing factor in determining that a child is at risk of suffering "emotional harm" or physical injury.

The last national survey of child welfare agency files reported that there were an estimated 21.5 child protection investigations per 1,000 children in Canada.[32] About 45% of these investigations were regarded as "substantiated" by the child protection workers involved, 33% were considered unsubstantiated after investigation, and 22% remained suspected but not substantiated within three months of opening the file. These child maltreatment investigations were classified into four categories: physical abuse was the primary subject of 31% of all

---

[32] Health Canada, *Canadian Incidence Study of Reported Abuse and Neglect* (Ottawa, 2001).

investigations; sexual abuse was the primary issue in 10% of investigations; neglect was the primary concern in 40% of investigations, and emotional maltreatment was the primary concern in 19% of investigations.

One significant variation between provinces is in the age of children who may be found to be in need of protection. In most Canadian jurisdictions, the maximum age for an initial finding that a child is in need of protection is a child's eighteenth birthday, while in British Columbia and New Brunswick it is the nineteenth birthday, and in Saskatchewan, Ontario, Nova Scotia and Newfoundland it is the sixteenth birthday. There are provisions in all jurisdictions for providing financial and other support for children taken into care at a younger age until they reach the age of 20 or 21. But even in jurisdictions like British Columbia that have a high maximum age for an initial finding that a child is need of protection, there are significant practical problems in providing involuntary care or assistance for older adolescents and young adults, who may be resistant to agency involvement in their lives. Some of the problems in providing help for older adolescents who are engaging in street prostitution or may be living on the street are discussed in Chapter 5.

Voluntary Involvement

While the main focus of legislation is on involuntary intervention in the lives of children and parents, in most cases a child protection agency is involved with a family with the consent of the parents, and in some cases at the request of the parents. In some cases, the parents may only be "consenting" to agency involvement because the agency is threatening to commence child protection proceedings and the parents may regard "voluntary involvement" as preferable to the involuntary agency involvement that would be the likely result of any court action. In some cases, the parents may lack the financial or emotional resources to litigate, and feel that they have no choice but to "consent" to agency involvement in their lives. In other cases, however, the parents may genuinely appreciate the help and support that the agency and its staff can provide, and they will be truly agreeing to have agency involvement.

In several provinces, including Ontario, there are legislative provisions that govern cases where a parent voluntarily agrees to place a child in care for a temporary period. In all jurisdictions there are statutory provisions that allow for a child to be permanently taken into care with the consent of the parents, as might occur, for example, if a single unmarried mother wants a child welfare agency to take the child and have the child placed for adoption.

Reporting, Apprehension, and Interim Care

Child welfare legislation governs the reporting of child abuse, and every Canadian jurisdiction except the Yukon imposes an obligation on individuals who become aware of possible situations of abuse or neglect to report to their local child welfare agency or the police so that an investigation can be carried out. If a child protection worker has reasonable grounds to believe that a child may be at risk, legislation in all Canadian jurisdictions allows the worker to "apprehend" the child, that is, to immediately take the child into the care of the agency. There must be a court hearing within days to decide whether the child will remain in agency care pending a full hearing.

The reporting of child abuse and issues related to apprehension, voluntary care agreements and interim care are discussed in Chapter 2.

The Child Protection Hearing

When a child protection proceeding has been commenced, either by the apprehension of a child by the agency or by the agency's filing of court documents, it will usually take several weeks or more typically months before a trial can be held. During this period arrangements will be made for the parents, and in some provinces the children, to have access to a lawyer. Many parents who are involved in the child protection process will be unable to afford a lawyer, but will be eligible for legal aid. In preparation for a trial, counsel for parents will have the opportunity to have "disclosure" of documents and records that the agency has acquired during the course of its investigation. The lawyers and agency staff may also be contacting third parties, like a family doctor or relatives, to prepare for the trial, and often to develop a possible "plan of care" that may be put before the court. Outside experts may also be retained to assess the child or the "parenting capacity" of the parents of the child, and ultimately to provide testimony in court.

A child protection trial is held in private, though legislation generally allows for the publication of non-identifying information about child protection proceedings in the relatively rare cases that attract media attention. The judges who decide child protection cases generally have a special expertise in family and children's law. These cases never involve a jury.

At a child protection hearing, the court may determine that a child is not in need of protection, and dismiss the agency application. Most commonly, however, when the agency begins a child protection application, there is some legitimate cause for agency concern, and the court will find that the child is in need of protection. If a child is found to be in need of protection, the court will make a decision that accords with the "best interests" of the child. There are three basic types of orders that can be made: supervision, temporary wardship, or permanent wardship. In some provinces, like Ontario, there may be a formal "bifurcation" or division of the child protection hearing into two stages, the first dealing with the issue of whether the child is in need of protection, and the second stage dealing with the type of order to be made, with somewhat different rules of evidence and procedure at each stage. In most provinces there is usually a single hearing to deal with both issues.

Under a supervision order the child remains at home under parental care, but the agency staff will conduct supervisory visits at the child's home, and the parents may be subject to other conditions, such as a requirement that they attend a parenting effectiveness course. Temporary wards are placed in the care of the protection agency, usually in a foster or group home. Reunification with parents is generally contemplated when a child is made a temporary ward, and parents typically have the right to visit children who are temporary wards. Children made permanent (or Crown) wards are generally expected to be wards of the protection agency until they reach adulthood. Parental access to a child who is a permanent ward may be terminated, especially if the child is young, and the child may be placed for adoption by the agency. If the child is older when made a permanent ward, it is likely that the child will remain in a foster home or group home, and the parents are more likely to be given a continuing right to see their child, though in practice it can be difficult to keep parents involved in the lives of children who are made permanent wards.

Child protection legislation in each jurisdiction provides for court review of prior orders, and may result in the termination, extension or alteration of a prior order. If a permanent ward is placed for adoption, the parents generally lose the right to seek a review.

It is increasingly common when children are made agency wards for the parents to be expected to contribute to the cost of their support, though a significant portion of parents involved in these cases are without the means to make any contribution.

Child protection hearings and the types of disposition orders that can be made as a result of these proceedings are discussed in Chapter 3.

Evidentiary Issues in Child Protection Cases

While the strict laws of evidence that govern criminal cases do not apply in child protection cases, there are rules of evidence that may result in the exclusion of certain types of evidence in child protection cases or may restrict what witnesses can say when testifying. There are, for example, rules about the necessary level of "expertise" that a witness must be able to demonstrate before being permitted to give "expert" or "opinion" testimony in a child protection case. In each province and territory there are also special legislative provisions that deal with some of the evidentiary issues that arise in child protection cases.

Chapter 11 discusses the rules of evidence that are applicable to child protection cases and offers practical advice for professionals who may be called upon to testify in court.[33]

The Child in Care

If a child is made a temporary or permanent ward of a child welfare agency, the agency will have legal guardianship of the child, and subject to any order of the court concerning the child's access to parents or siblings, may determine where the child will reside. Children in state care were historically a very vulnerable population, and were not infrequently subject to exploitation or abuse in foster homes or child welfare institutions. Legislation and programs are

---

[33] See also R. Vogl and N. Bala, *Testifying on Behalf of Children: A Handbook for Canadian Professionals* (Toronto: Thompson Educational Publishing, 2001).

now in place in many Canadian jurisdictions to protect the rights of children in agencies and to give them access to advocates.

An important set of issues relate to the situations in which the agency is obliged to plan for and support efforts of the child to be returned to his or her family. There are also cases in which a court will require that a child is to have contact with siblings who may also be in care.

Chapter 4 discusses some of the legal and social issues that arise when children are in the care of a child welfare agency.

Adoption

In some jurisdictions, such as Ontario, adoption is governed by the same statute as child protection proceedings, as part of a comprehensive child welfare scheme. In other jurisdictions, such as Saskatchewan, adoption is dealt with in a separate statute — though even in these jurisdictions, child welfare agencies are involved in some, though not all, adoptions. Adoption is discussed in Chapter 6.

The Role of the Trial Judge

While trial judges dealing with child protection cases are governed by a statute and bound by appeal court decisions, they also have considerable discretion. Judges have a range of views and attitudes about the child protection process. Some judges tend to emphasize the adversarial nature of the process, and may place relatively high expectations on the state agency that is challenging the integrity of the family unit to justify its position. Other judges may tend to focus a little more on the protection of children, and may interpret the statute and procedural rules somewhat more flexibly. The attitude of the presiding judge can have a significant impact on the manner in which child protection legislation is interpreted and applied. The views of four different judges about the child protection process are found in Chapter 15.

Who Speaks for the Child?

A fundamental question in the child welfare field is: "Who speaks for the child?" It is a question that defies an easy answer. Some would argue that the child welfare agency, with its statutory mandate to protect children, is speaking on behalf of the child. Others would point out that child welfare agencies often have financial, institutional and professional constraints that prevent them from truly advocating what is best for the child. There may also be disagreements between the agency and foster parents or within the agency about how a particular case should be handled. While the agency will have an administrative mechanism for establishing how such disagreements will be resolved, there may still be controversy over what is truly best for the child.

In British Columbia, Alberta, Saskatchewan, Manitoba, Ontario, Quebec and Newfoundland the government has established offices of child advocacy, separate from child welfare agencies, with responsibility to act as advocates for children involved in the protection process or in the legal care of a protection agency.[34] These offices are not intended to provide legal representation for children in court, but rather to act as advocates for them within the context of the child protection system. The establishment of these offices reflects a concern that the bureaucratic nature of child welfare agencies may result in situations where the agencies are not acting in the best interests of children.

Since it is difficult to understand a child separate from his or her community, there can also be situations where the community or its representatives purport to speak for the child; this most commonly occurs with Aboriginal children.

Parents involved in protection cases typically believe that they know and care for their children more than any of the professionals. Parents may thus claim that they speak for their children.

The children who are the subject of a protection case may also have their own views about what they want to have happen. Some children are too young to express their views, and older children are sometimes reluctant or ambivalent about expressing their views. However, many children involved in the protection process have definite ideas about their futures. In most jurisdictions, legislation specifies that courts should consider the "child's views and wishes, if they can be reasonably ascertained."[35] In some jurisdictions, children involved in child protection proceedings can have lawyers who represent them and claim to speak on their behalf. In some cases a psychologist or other mental health professional will interview or assess the child and report the child's views to the court, and in other situations the child may come to court and testify.

In some sense, the judges who decide child protection cases also have a role in acting on behalf of children. Although judges have a responsibility for balancing the rights of the litigants and acting in accordance with the legislation, judges may be regarded as having ultimate responsibility for the protection of children and the promotion of their welfare.

The issue of legal representation for children, parents and agencies in child protection proceedings is discussed in detail in Chapter 8, but the broader questions of who speaks for the child and who truly represents the interests of the child are underlying themes of this book.

Child Welfare in a Social Context

Child abuse and neglect are endemic to all parts of our society, and are not restricted to a particular region, economic or cultural group or race. One of the most infamous cases of physical abuse in North America in the last years of the twentieth century involved a prominent, wealthy New York City lawyer, who was convicted of murdering his foster daughter. The Canadian public has

---

[34] In Quebec, the Commission of the Rights of the Person and the Rights of Youth is an independent agency that monitors human rights violations in a range of contexts, including for children in state care, and has reported to the National Assembly of Quebec and the abuse of children in child welfare and juvenile justice institutions.

[35] See e.g., Ontario's *Child and Family Services Act*, R.S.O. 1990, c. C.11, s. 37(3) 9.

learned that even trusted and respected community members like doctors, teachers and priests can be guilty of sexual abuse.

Despite the widespread nature of child abuse and neglect, child welfare agencies are more likely to be involved with families from disadvantaged economic, social and cultural groups. While child protection workers are typically white, well-educated and from middle-class backgrounds, their clients are generally socially marginalized. The clients of child welfare agencies are often poorly educated, living in or near poverty, and not infrequently members of a racial minority group and living in a family led by a single parent, usually the mother. Many of the clients of child welfare agencies are living on social assistance.

The National Council of Welfare observed that the clients of the child welfare system are "overwhelmingly drawn from the ranks of Canada's poor." In some cases, the personal or emotional problems that result in a life of poverty also may make it difficult to parent adequately. The Council also explained:[36]

> There are two major reasons why poor families are more likely than those with higher incomes to use children's social services. First, low-income parents run a greater risk of encountering problems that reduce their capacity to provide adequate care for their children. Second, poor families are largely dependent upon a single, overburdened source of help — the child welfare system — in coping with their problems, whereas more affluent families enjoy access to a broader and superior range of supportive resources.

> Precisely because they cannot command the resources needed to deal with difficulties before they develop into more serious problems, low-income families' vulnerability is further increased as untreated problems accumulate and compound one another. By the time they come to the attention of a child welfare system, their problems often have become much more difficult to tackle in an effective manner....

The Council further observed:[37]

> Despite what most would consider a more enlightened and compassionate attitude than in the past, our society still stands in judgement on parents who are unable to care for their children. Whether a child is returned home under the supervision of a child welfare agency or sent to a foster home or treatment facility, the implication is the same: his or her parents have failed to perform adequately one of the most important roles of adult life.

> On the face of it, of course, parental inability is the reason underlying any decision to place a child in care. Whether the problem lies with the parent, the child, or both, and whether or not the initiative to remove the child is taken by the parents or by the child welfare authorities, the state can only intervene when it judges parents unable or unwilling to care properly for their children. What is often forgotten, however, is that the term "unable or unwilling to provide care" is nothing more than a convenient administrative label lumping together a wide variety of family problems, many of which stem from inadequate income, unemployment and other factors that cannot fairly be blamed on their victims.

---

[36] National Council of Welfare, *In the Best Interests of the Child* (Ottawa, 1979) at 2-3.
[37] *Ibid.* at 11.

Most judges dealing with child protection cases are aware of the need to be sensitive to the realities of poverty in Canada. In one child protection case, the judge wrote:[38]

> In a hearing such as this there is danger in over-reliance upon any group of witnesses self-conscious respecting their professionalization. I resolved not to fall victim to this specific bias of the profession, the group psychology of the social workers....
>
> It was manifest from the opening that this was a contest between the right of a subsocio-economic family to subsist together and the right of the public, represented by the Children's Aid Society, to insist upon higher standards of parental care than the couple in question were capable of offering. Many witnesses called for the Society were persons of superior education with post-graduate degrees in social work or some other related specialty. One could not listen to their testimony with all the somber implications of this application without resolving that this Court must not be persuaded to impose unrealistic or unfair middle-class standards of child care upon a poor family of extremely limited potential.

Those who work in the child welfare system must be sensitive to problems of poverty. They must also be sensitive to cultural and racial differences between themselves and their clients.

A number of racial minorities and immigrant groups are over-represented in Canada's child welfare system, but probably the most pervasive problems are with Aboriginal children. Aboriginal children are apprehended and taken into care at more than three times the rate of other Canadian children. In some western provinces, more than half the children in care are Aboriginal. Compounding conditions of poverty, chronic underemployment, inadequate housing and poor nutrition, are a history of racial discrimination and insensitivity to different child-rearing values. For many of those Aboriginal people who come to live in cities, culture shock adds another source of stress and instability.

The special problems related to Aboriginal children and the child welfare system are addressed in Chapter 7, along with some of the recent innovations that are intended to increase the sensitivity of the system to the needs of these children and their families.

Like the role of the parent in society, the role of the child protection worker has become a complex and highly demanding one, requiring a unique blend of knowledge, skill and dedication. The personal views of a social worker are presented in Chapter 14. In the context of child protection cases that are resolved by the trial process, agency staff and parents are in an adversarial relationship, each trying to challenge the competence, knowledge or skill of the other. It is, however, also important to appreciate that the majority of parents, even those involved with the child welfare system, have a genuine love for their children and want what is best for them.

---

[38] *Re Warren* (1973), 13 R.F.L. 51 at 52 (Ont. Co. Ct), Matheson J.

2

Initial Involvement: Reporting Abuse and Protecting Children

Robin Vogl and Nicholas Bala[1]

Every Canadian jurisdiction has a child protection service agency which has the legal responsibility for investigating reports that a child may be in need of protection, and for taking appropriate steps to protect children from ill-treatment. Services for the child and parents may be provided in their home, or the child may be removed from the home on a temporary or permanent wardship basis. The agency may provide services either on a voluntary basis or an involuntary basis, seeking a court order to require families to receive services.

Child protection intervention usually begins with a report to the agency that a child may be in need of protection. Reports are often made by professionals who have contact with the family, such as a family physician or emergency physician, but they may also be made by a neighbour, a relative or even a parent. Almost every jurisdiction in Canada has legislation requiring the reporting of suspected abuse or neglect.

Once a report is made, a child protection worker begins an investigation. If a worker believes that the child has been abused or neglected, and that the child is in need of protection services, then the agency may become voluntarily involved with the family in the provision of support or even in providing care for the child, or there may be court-based involuntary intervention. Court-based interventions involve a range of responses from providing supervision and support to the family to immediate apprehension by removing the child from parental care, and placing the child in another setting ranging from extended family to foster care.

This chapter discusses the issues that arise in the reporting and investigation of suspected abuse or neglect, and the initial decisions about provision of child protection agency services or placement of the child. Both voluntary and involuntary agency involvement are discussed.

Reporting Abuse and Neglect

The Obligation to Report Suspected Child Abuse

Most child protection cases begin when someone contacts the agency to report concerns about possible child abuse or neglect. Child protection agencies

---

[1] Robin Vogl is a lawyer for Muskoka and District Children's Aid Society, Ontario. Nicholas Bala is Professor of Law, Queen's University, Kingston, Ontario.

rely on members of the public and professionals who work with children to report situations appearing to involve abuse or neglect of children, so that the agency can investigate and take appropriate steps to protect children.

In every Canadian province and territory there is legislation that imposes a duty on members of the public and professionals to report cases where they have reasonable grounds to suspect that a child is being maltreated by a parent, caregiver or guardian.[2] Based on limited observation or interaction with a child, it may be difficult for a person to know whether the child is actually suffering from abuse or neglect, and the law emphasizes that there is an obligation to report *suspected* cases, leaving it to the child protection agency to determine the validity of the allegation.

There is some variation in the details of the provincial and territorial reporting laws.[3] The primary purpose of the reporting laws is educational, rather than punitive. The maximum penalties for failing to report range as high as $10,000 and a year in jail, but prosecutions are relatively rare and the usual sanction for a conviction for a failure to report is a fine. To encourage reporting, these statutes all provide for civil immunity for individuals who in good faith make a report that proves unfounded, so that a parent who feels maligned by an unfounded report cannot sue for defamation if the reporter was acting in good faith.

In Ontario and New Brunswick, professionals who fail to report may be prosecuted under the reporting laws, but there is no statutory sanction for members of the public who fail to report; this more limited type of legislation reflects a policy concern that members of the public may be less aware of their obligation to report, and that in cases involving maltreatment of one family member by another, there may be great pressure not to report. However, in cases where one parent is aware of serious abuse or neglect being perpetrated by the other parent, there is the possibility of prosecution under the *Criminal Code* for failing to provide adequately for the child, or perhaps for being a party to abuse being perpetrated by the other parent.

Historically many professionals failed to report child abuse or neglect in cases where they should have done so, sometimes with fatal consequences for the child. These cases may in part have reflected a lack of awareness of the signs of abuse and neglect, as well as ignorance of the legal obligation to report. Many professionals are ordinarily bound by a duty of confidentiality, and reporting to

---

[2] The Yukon is the only jurisdiction in North America without a mandatory requirement for the reporting of child abuse, though legislation in that Territory grants civil immunity for those who report in good faith, and policies governing such professionals as teachers require the reporting of suspected child abuse: see *Children's Act*, R.S.Y. 2002, c. 31, s. 115.

[3] For a review of child abuse reporting legislation and policies in all Canadian provinces and jurisdictions, see R. Bessner, *The Duty to Report Child Abuse* (Ottawa: Justice Canada, 2002); on-line <http://canada.justice. gc.ca/en/index.html>.

a state agency is contrary to their usual professional practices.[4] Increasingly, however, education programs for professionals like doctors, nurses and teachers are dealing with child abuse and neglect, providing information about signs of parental abuse and neglect, and emphasizing the legal and moral obligation to report.

In addition to the possibility of prosecution under reporting laws, professionals who fail to report cases that should have been reported may also face discipline proceedings that might result in suspension of their professional practice privileges for a period of time. Further, the Canadian courts have held that if a professional like a doctor fails to report a case that should have been reported and the child remains in parental care and then suffers additional injury, the professional may have civil liability for the injury that could have been prevented. In one Alberta case a radiologist failed to report to the local child welfare agency the injuries of a three-month-old child that should have given rise to suspicions of "shaken baby syndrome." As a result, after receiving medical treatment, the baby was returned to the care of her parents, where she suffered much more severe and permanent injuries. Even though the father actually caused the severe injuries that occurred after the child was returned to parental care, and there was a possibility that the child might have been returned to the parents notwithstanding a report of abuse by the doctor, the doctor's failure to report was considered to be professional negligence and he was held 50% liable for the injuries in a civil suit brought on behalf of the child.[5]

Often those who report abuse will have had only limited contact with the child and family, and will genuinely be uncertain of whether the child has been abused or neglected. When a report of suspected child abuse or neglect is received, the agency is required to conduct an immediate investigation to determine whether the child is endangered.

It can be very challenging for agency investigators to ascertain whether a child has been abused or neglected. In some cases the investigation reveals clear and convincing evidence that a child is in danger and the child will be immediately taken into care. Quite frequently, however, the investigation reveals concerns and suspicions, but not conclusive proof of abuse or neglect. Abuse and neglect typically occur in private. Parents and relatives may be very guarded in their conversations with agency investigators, or may actually lie to cover up what has occurred. Children, if old enough to be interviewed, may be subjected

---

[4] In every jurisdiction except Newfoundland, the reporting legislation specifically maintains "solicitor-client privilege." Thus if a client tells her or his lawyer about a situation of abuse or neglect, and perhaps admits to having abused a child, the lawyer is not obliged to report the abuse. It is, however, generally accepted that a lawyer does not act unethically in reporting a situation where there is a real risk that a client *will* cause further harm to a child. See e.g., Law Society of Upper Canada, *Rules of Professional Conduct*, Rule 2.03(3). Other professionals who work with adults who may admit abuse, such as a priest hearing confession or a psychiatrist treating a pedophile, have a legal obligation to report if they learn of a situation that may be exposing a child to risk of abuse or neglect, even though that information may have been disclosed to them in confidence.

[5] *Brown v. University of Alberta Hospital*, [1997] A.J. 298 (Q.B.).

to parental pressure or threats, or may have feelings of guilt, and may not disclose what has occurred to agency investigators.

Complicating the investigation process, in some cases the reporter may have ulterior motives for reporting child protection concerns, such as an animosity towards the parent who is accused of abusing or neglecting the child. Some of these reports may prove to be unfounded, and may be made maliciously. However, the mere fact that a reporter has negative feelings towards a parent and *might* have a reason for making a malicious and unfounded report does not necessarily mean that the information is exaggerated or untrue.

In one Ontario inquest, a coroner's jury found that a child had died while in the custody of the father and stepmother, despite repeated reports from the biological mother to the local child protection agency.[6] The concerns of the biological mother were discounted by the agency because she had a number of personal problems that interfered with her own ability to parent, and displayed a negative attitude towards her former husband. The inquest revealed the danger of discounting information from one parent solely because the informant herself is not a capable parent. As a result of these concerns, the *Child Welfare Eligibility Spectrum*[7] now used in Ontario does not distinguish concerns based upon the source of the information, but rather the *nature of the information itself* is the determinant of the requisite action.

Most reports to child protection agencies of suspected abuse or neglect are received by telephone. However, it is important for agency workers to ensure that any information received by a child protection agency, no matter what form it takes, is responded to quickly and appropriately. For example, a member of the public may choose to attend personally at the offices of the child protection agency to detail concerns.

Not all cases are reported by outside professionals or family members. Parents or children (especially adolescents) themselves may approach a child protection agency either for assistance or when placement outside the family is necessary. In these cases, help is usually provided on a voluntary basis.

Sometimes estranged spouses embroiled in a dispute over the care of a child may send or deliver affidavit material, photos, audio or videotapes, or CDs to a protection agency, requesting that they be reviewed to ascertain whether there are abuse or neglect concerns. Intake workers may be reluctant to review such material, because of the form it takes and the large amount of irrelevant information that is usually contained. However, the material may contain specific allegations of a child protection concern (e.g., contents of an affidavit describing an incident in which a child was harmed by a caregiver) or may itself constitute such a concern (e.g., child pornography), which may warrant investigation. In

---

[6] *Inquest Into the Death of Kasandra Hislop Shepard*, Peel County Court House, April-July 1997, presiding coroner: Dr. Bonita Porter, Deputy Chief of Inquests for Ontario, 26 Grenville Street, Toronto, Ontario, M7A 2G9.

[7] *Ontario Child Welfare Eligibility Spectrum*, Revised 2000, Ontario Association of Children's Aid Societies, 75 Front Street East, 2nd Floor, Toronto, Ontario, Canada M5E 1V9, tel. (416)366-8115, fax (416)366-8317.

such cases it is appropriate to ask the person providing the material to identify the parts of the materials that reveal abuse or neglect concerns.

Not infrequently when parents are separated, one parent will report a wide range of concerns that may be relevant to the issues in the family law arena, but only some or none of which are child protection concerns. As an example, one parent may be concerned about the absence of bedtime routines, or the exposure to violent videos at the home of the other parent. Workers need to acknowledge the concerns as potentially valid in regard to the child's development, but should redirect parents to their lawyers, and explain that the mandate for child protective services is much narrower than the broader "best interests of the child" test that is applied in litigation between parents. It is understandable that members of the public would assume *child welfare* to include all aspects of a child's well-being, but in law the agency's mandate is much narrower.[8]

One of the most frustrating situations for child protection professionals is the repeat caller with a history of reporting unsubstantiated concerns. The decision not to proceed with an investigation is one to be taken with great care, however, and only after careful consultation. At times, the worker may feel that the investigation itself, including repeated interviews or examinations of the child, may be psychologically abusive to the child. In some cases, where police have been consulted and have concluded that the informant is acting in bad faith, the individual may be warned about the possibility of "public mischief" charges being laid.[9] Like the boy who cried wolf, however, there is always the nagging fear that this complaint, unlike the past complaints, may prove to be based upon fact.

Reporting a situation to child protection authorities can require courage. A family member may suffer guilt for exposing the parent, and other family members may be very hostile as a result of the report, even if it is justified. Likewise, a neighbour who expresses concern about a child can face open hostility from an angry parent.

The fact that a person who reports may have an angry or vengeful attitude towards the parent does not necessarily mean that the information is inaccurate. It is often during a relationship breakdown that previously held confidences are disclosed because there is no relationship left to protect. On the other hand, it is during conflict that the temptation to make false or exaggerated complaints is greatest. Information gleaned from more objective sources, such as teachers, daycare professionals, and doctors can be of considerable assistance to the investigation process. Despite a thorough and professional investigation, however, there will still be cases in which it is impossible to determine whether a child has been maltreated.

While the vast majority of reports of child abuse and neglect are made in good faith, in the most recent national study of child protection investigations in

---

[8] See Chapter 9, "Abuse and Neglect Allegations in the Context of Parental Separation."

[9] *Criminal Code*, s. 140.

Canada,[10] only 45% of these investigations were regarded as "substantiated" by the child protection workers involved, while 33% were considered unsubstantiated after investigation, and 22% remained "suspected" but not substantiated within three months of opening the file. Only 4% of the total number of reports were considered by the investigating workers to be "unsubstantiated and maliciously made."

Confidentiality of Reporters

It is possible for individuals to report concerns of child abuse or neglect without identifying themselves, much like the "tips" about crimes received by police departments. The fact that callers refuse to identify themselves does not obviate the need to conduct an appropriate investigation, provided sufficient information is given to identify the child involved and to justify a child protection concern warranting investigation. If the information provided is substantiated upon investigation, the identity of the caller is not needed. However, if the investigation does not yield any evidence to support the caller's concerns, it is obviously impossible to obtain further details that might assist in the ongoing investigation.

Some callers will identify themselves, but request that their name not be revealed to the child's parent due to fear of retaliation or because of a concern about straining the relationship between the reporter and the parent. These are realistic concerns in many cases, and requests for anonymity should be honoured whenever possible. However, callers should be cautioned that the nature of the complaint itself may identify the source to the parent, and attempts to protect the identity of the caller may be of no practical effect. Further, the informant's identity may ultimately be revealed to the parents if a judge orders the name to be disclosed, though there is a basis in case law for arguing that such information is "privileged" and should not be disclosed.[11] Despite the possibility of protection of the identity of a caller, if the investigation yields neither objective evidence nor an admission and the informant observed direct evidence of abuse or neglect, it may still be necessary to summons the reluctant informant to come to court to testify in child protection or criminal proceedings.

---

[10] N. Trocmé, B. MacLaurin, B. Fallon, J. Daciuk, D. Billingsley, M. Tourigny, M. Mayer, J. Wright, K. Barter, G. Burford, J. Hornick, R. Sullivan, and B. McKenzie, *The Canadian Incidence Study of Reported Child Abuse and Neglect* (Ottawa: Ministry of Public Works and Government Services Canada, 2001).

[11] In Quebec and Prince Edward Island legislation prohibits the disclosure of the identity of a reporter of child abuse, while New Brunswick, Manitoba, Alberta, and British Columbia legislation only allows the disclosure of the identity of a reporter with the consent of a court or a government official. In *D. v. National Society for the Prevention of Cruelty to Children*, [1977] 1 All E.R. 589 (H.L.) it was held that as a matter of common law, the courts should not allow the disclosure of the identity of a person who reported child abuse, even though the report was not substantiated in the subsequent investigation.

Jurisdiction to Investigate and Intervene

Protection of the Unborn

A child's age is critical in determining whether the agency has the legal mandate to investigate and protect the child. The provinces and territories have varying age ranges for the involvement of child protection agencies in the lives of children and their parents. On the low end of the age continuum is the issue of protecting the unborn. With growing awareness of the harm that maternal drug or alcohol abuse during pregnancy can cause a child, it is not surprising that the justice system has had to face the issue of "abuse and neglect" of the "unborn child." Cases before the courts have generally involved drug abuse or alcohol abuse, or lack of physical self-care by the mother, especially immediately prior to expected delivery. Agencies have been concerned about risk to the child and mother during the birth process, as well as about risks to the unborn child prior to birth.

The issue of protecting the unborn child has found its way to the courtroom in jurisdictions where the definition of child does not indicate whether the legislation applies to the unborn. For example, in a 1987 Ontario case, a child protection agency brought an application for the "apprehension" of a "child" where the agency had concerns about a woman in late stages of pregnancy who was leading a nomadic life and sleeping in an underground parking lot.[12] The agency believed that the woman was mentally unstable and about to deliver, and that her living conditions would place the unborn child at risk during the birthing process as she did not intend to go to a hospital. The court held that there was jurisdiction to make an order to protect an unborn child and ordered that "the child" was to be made a temporary ward prior to its birth. The judge simultaneously ordered that the mother be detained for assessment under the provincial mental health legislation.

In 1997 in *Winnipeg Child and Family Services v. G.(D.F.)*, the Supreme Court of Canada decided that, in the absence of explicit legislation, child welfare agencies and the courts have no jurisdiction to intervene to protect an unborn child.[13] The case involved a woman who was five months pregnant with her fourth child. She was addicted to glue sniffing, which might damage the nervous system of the developing fetus. As a result of her addiction, two of her previous children were born disabled and had been made permanent wards. The director of Child and Family Services applied to have the woman detained in a health centre for treatment until the birth of her child. While the superior court judge who first heard the case was prepared to make this order, based on the

---

[12] *Children's Aid Society of Belleville v. Linda T. and Gary K.* (1987), 7 R.F.L. (3d) 191 (Ont. Prov. Ct. – Fam. Div.). But see contra, *Re Baby R.* (1988), 15 R.F.L. (3d) 225 (B.C.S.C.).

[13] *Winnipeg Child and Family Services v. G.(D.F.)*, [1997] 3 S.C.R. 925.

court's inherent *parens patriae* jurisdiction,[14] the Supreme Court held that in the absence of an explicit legislative authority, a court cannot make such an order. The majority of the Supreme Court emphasized that the law of Canada does not recognize the unborn child as a "legal person" possessing rights or status. Any right that a fetus may have remains "inchoate" or incomplete until the child's birth.[15] The Supreme Court ruled that in the absence of explicit legislation, no court has the power to interfere with the freedom of a pregnant woman with the objective of protecting her unborn child. Although the Supreme Court did not find it necessary to rule on any of the *Charter of Rights* issues raised in argument, writing for the majority of the Court, Justice McLachlin noted that any legislation that might be enacted to protect the unborn "would have to be assessed against the provisions of the *Charter.*"

Only in New Brunswick does child protection legislation specifically refer to the "unborn child" in its definition of "child" for protection purposes.[16] In theory, this would impose a reporting obligation on all those who have reasonable grounds to suspect that a pregnant woman is abusing or neglecting her unborn child, and would allow for a child protection order to be made in regard to an unborn child. However, other than the mention of the "unborn child" in the definition section of the legislation, there are no specific provisions that indicate how child protection law is to apply to the unborn.

In a 1996 case, the New Brunswick Court of Queen's Bench held this vague legislative scheme could not be invoked to make a "supervision order" for an unborn child, as the law violated the constitutional rights of pregnant women.[17] In the case before the court, the woman was 22 years of age, in the third trimester of her pregnancy, and she did not intend to have an abortion. She was of "average intellectual potential" but had a "severely restricted emotional development and [was] emotionally very immature" due to childhood abuse. She had consumed drugs and alcohol during two prior pregnancies, and both of those children had been permanently removed from her care. The child welfare

---

[15] The *parens patriae* jurisdiction refers to the residual inherent power of the superior courts in Canada to make orders to promote the "best interests" of children in cases where there is no specific legislation that regulates the manner in which children's interests are to be protected. This jurisdiction derives from the power exercised by the ancient Court of Equity to act as *parens patriae* [Latin for "parent of the country"], protecting the interests of children, mental incompetents, and others who may lack the capacity to protect themselves. In Canada, only federally appointed judges have this residual *parens patriae* power; provincially appointed judges, who often deal with child welfare matters, do not have this power and can only exercise jurisdiction specifically conferred by statute.

[15] One type of an "inchoate" right of a fetus is the right to inherit property. For example, if property is left by will or intestacy to a man's "child," that property may pass to a child born after his death, but the "child" only acquires rights after birth.

[16] *Family Services Act*, S.N.B. 1980, c. F-2.2, s. 1(a). While the Yukon does not specifically include the "unborn child," its *Children's Act* includes a provision allowing the Director of Child Welfare to apply for a court order for supervision if a pregnant woman subjects herself to addictive or intoxicating substances which might endanger her fetus (R.S.Y. 2002, c. 31, s. 133). That legislation has also been held to be in violation of the *Charter of Rights*, s. 7; see *Joe v. Director of Family & Children's Services* (1986), 5 B.C.L.R. (2d) 267 (Yk. Sup. Ct.).

[17] *New Brunswick (Minister of Health and Community Services) v. N.H.*, [1996] N.B.J. 660 (Q.B., Fam. Div.), per Young J.

agency was concerned about how she would care for herself during the last stages of pregnancy and whether she would get appropriate care for the delivery of the child. The agency, with the support of the "potential father" and some professionals who had been working with the woman, sought a "supervision order" that would have required the woman to have mental health care and follow the directives of medical staff in regard to the delivery. The court recognized that there might be risk to the child in this type of situation. However, the court held that in the absence of explicit legislative direction authorizing this type of highly intrusive order and specifying how the rights of a pregnant woman are to be balanced by a court against concerns for the unborn child, to restrict the freedom of a pregnant woman would be a violation of the *Charter*, which guarantees that no person shall be deprived of "liberty and security of the person except in accordance with the principles of fundamental justice." The statement in the child welfare statute that applies to an "unborn child" was considered too vague in itself to allow for this type of highly intrusive order.

The New Brunswick legislature has not responded to this type of situation by enacting such legislation, nor has any other Canadian legislature responded by enacting legislation to explicitly allow for the apprehension of "unborn children." While there is no doubt that by abusing drugs or alcohol during pregnancy a woman can cause enormous damage to her child and impose great long-term costs on society, there are real concerns about the effectiveness of a legal response to this problem. Beyond the issue about whether such laws may unduly infringe the freedoms of women and violate their constitutional rights, there is a concern that the threat of legal intervention may make vulnerable pregnant women reluctant to seek medical or other help for fear of being reported and perhaps detained. Further, there are concerns about the potentially discriminatory application of any legal regime, with Aboriginal, visible minority and low-income women being at greater risk of apprehension than higher-status women who may have equally serious drug or alcohol addiction problems.

Even though the law does not permit intervention prior to birth, it is not uncommon for doctors or nurses to contact a child protection agency when a woman comes to a hospital to deliver a baby and appears drug or alcohol addicted or otherwise unable to care for a child. If there are serious concerns about the woman's ability to care for the child, the agency may apprehend the child immediately after birth. The courts have held that a mother's prenatal exposure of her child to drugs may constitute "abuse" that justifies such an apprehension.[18]

While child protection agencies may not have a legal mandate to provide involuntary intervention prior to the birth of a child, agencies commonly provide voluntary help to pregnant women, especially young unwed mothers,

---

[18] See e.g., *Superintendent of Family and Child Service v. M.(B) and O.(D)*, [1982] B.C.D. Civ. 1568-06 (B.C.S.C.), Proudfoot J.

and can help to find them accommodation and support during pregnancy. Agencies may be involved in providing counselling about whether the woman should keep the child or have the child placed for adoption, though a final decision about such an issue can only be made after the child is born.

Maximum Age

The upper age limit of child protective services varies across Canada. In Ontario, Nova Scotia, Newfoundland, and Saskatchewan, the upper age limit for the making of an order is the child's 16th birthday, with the qualification that in Ontario and Nova Scotia, if proceedings are commenced before a child attains the age of 16, an order can be made or extended after the child turns 16 years of age. In Alberta, Quebec, Manitoba, Prince Edward Island, the Northwest Territories, Nunavut and the Yukon, the upper age limit is the 18th birthday, while British Columbia and New Brunswick have upper age limits of 19 years of age for child protective services.

When a report is received concerning a youth or young adult beyond the legal age mandate of a child protection agency, it is important to direct the involved individual or family to an appropriate agency for voluntary services.[19]

Investigation and Apprehension

Initial Investigation of a Report

The initial investigation of a case reported to a child protection agency is one of the most significant and sensitive stages of an investigation. Often faced with time pressures and limited information, the child protection worker who is responsible for agency intake needs the skills, knowledge and experience to assess the urgency of a report and determine an appropriate initial response. For example, a caller may initially characterize a situation as one of neglect, but upon further questioning, it may be more appropriately classified as abuse.

Several jurisdictions have adopted tools to help evaluate the seriousness and urgency of a report that a child may be in need of protective services. The *Eligibility Spectrum*[20] in Ontario is an example of an instrument that helps workers to determine an appropriate response. The *Eligibility Spectrum* provides "descriptors" of various child protection situations. Depending on the facts reported, a case may fall over or below the "intervention line." If the report appears to place the case "over the intervention line," it will warrant a full, immediate investigation, whereas other situations do not necessarily call for a full investigation. While professional judgement can never be replaced with

---

[19] If a child has been made a ward of a child welfare agency while within the age jurisdiction of eligibility for protective services, financial and other support can be provided into young adulthood, for example to support attendance at a post secondary educational institution, but once the age of wardship termination has passed, there is no basis for an involuntary intervention in the life of the former ward by the child protection agency.

[20] *Ontario Child Welfare Eligibility Spectrum* (revised 2000) and *The Risk Assessment Model for Child Protection in Ontario* (revised 2000), available through The Ontario Association of Children's Aid Societies, 75 Front Street East, 2nd Floor, Toronto, Ontario, Canada, M5E 1V9.

such tools, they do assist in structuring the approach to a given case, and allow for a more consistent approach from worker to worker and from agency to agency.[21]

Most provinces and territories have established policies or guidelines to regulate the investigation process. This may involve the use of risk assessment tools, such as in New Brunswick and Ontario, or the application of government standards. Most jurisdictions impose time frames for an investigation, based upon the urgency of the situation from a child-safety perspective (often referred to as a "Safety Assessment"). Time frames range from immediate action, to days, and sometimes weeks, where, for example, the concerns are historical and no child is currently at risk of harm. In addition to time frames, most jurisdictions also impose procedures for the investigation of protection concerns. The written procedures are helpful in ensuring that investigations are thoroughly and consistently carried out.

In some jurisdictions, such as Ontario, a computerized recording package has been designed to prompt workers in addressing the focus of the risk assessment process in their written records. Prior to the standardization of recording expectations, it was not uncommon for workers to have subjective narratives; the computer programs require the worker to document specific protection concerns, risk factors and strengths of the families under investigation.

Despite the efforts by agencies to improve the process of reporting and investigation, the rate of non-substantiated cases is high. For example, a recent Canada-wide study on the incidence of reports of child abuse found that investigating workers reported that after completing the initial investigations, 64% of child maltreatment investigations were closed (without further action).[22] Of the remaining open cases, 65% were substantiated and 23% remained suspected. Rates of substantiated cases varied by type of abuse ranging from a low of 51% of open cases for physical abuse to 79% for multiple maltreatment.

---

[21] For example, "sexual activity" includes "extreme sexual abuse, sexual intercourse, sexual molestation, sexual exhibitionism, sexual harassment and sexual suggestiveness." Examples of "Extremely Severe" behaviours include: sexual abuse by a prime caregiver; sexual abuse by someone other than the prime caregiver, but with the full knowledge of the prime caregiver; and sexual abuse by a family member who was in a caregiving role (e.g., grandfather) and has regular access to the child. "Moderately Severe" behaviours include: a child sustaining abusive sexual activity at the hands of someone outside the family in a caregiving role, where the prime caregiver did not have knowledge or did not allow it to occur; where the child displays physical indicators of abusive sexual activity (e.g., sexually transmitted disease) but no specific perpetrator is identified; where the child exhibits unexplained sexual behaviour indicative of knowledge/experience beyond his/her age and development (e.g., simulated intercourse) and where no specific abuse allegation has been made; and where the child has sustained harmful sexual activity at the hands of a family member not in a caregiving role (e.g., sibling) and the caregiver has not condoned the behaviour, but has not been able to protect the child. All behaviours described thus far would fall "above the intervention line," i.e., warranting a full and immediate investigation by the society. Below that line, and therefore not *necessarily* demanding a full investigation, are listed "Minimally Severe" concerns such as questionable sexual activity (e.g., adults being indiscreet in having sexual relations in the presence of a child); adults continuing to bathe with older children; adults sharing a bed with older children, etc., and sexual harm by an individual who is neither a family member nor a caregiver, without knowledge and consent of caregiver. "Not Severe" are situations where there has been no abusive sexual activity, but there was exposure to inappropriate sexual material, such as showing a young child sexually pornographic videotapes.

[22] *Supra*, note 10.

The high rates of non-substantiated cases have led a number of jurisdictions in the United States and more recently in Canada to adopt a "Differential Response System" for potential child welfare cases. This approach involves the provision of early assessment and support services to lower-risk children and families who voluntarily co-operate. For cases where the risk to children is higher, or where the family will not address their needs voluntarily, a child protection services investigation is conducted to determine whether a child may be in need of mandatory services.[23]

Alberta is the first Canadian jurisdiction to formally adopt the Differential Response System — referred to in that province as the Alberta Response Model. The objectives of this model are as follows:

1. Stronger community-based partnerships and linkages that work together to improve outcomes for children, youth and families.

2. Increased utilization rate of effective community-based supports for children, youth and families in "at-risk" circumstances.

3. Increased permanent placement in families for children who have Permanent Guardianship Status.

4. Decrease in the number of children and youth requiring child protection services and increase in child, youth and family well-being.

5. Systemic changes to child protection and community-based delivery systems.[24]

In Alberta, unless there is an apparent urgency or high risk, the investigation is usually preceded by a screening procedure that does not necessarily involve direct contact with the child, and only "positive screen" cases are investigated. After the investigation is completed, a decision is made regarding whether the report was substantiated and the child is in need of protection, or not substantiated and the child is not in need of protection. There is also a "third option" in Alberta, which is "substantiated" but with "no need for protection services" (e.g., the child is no longer in need of protection services because the perpetrator no longer has access to the child).

Interagency Investigation Protocols

One of the most significant developments of the 1980s and 1990s in the child abuse investigation field was the introduction of interagency protocols (or guidelines) that set out how child protection agencies and other community partners are to coordinate their efforts. The first investigation protocols in Canada were intended to facilitate joint child protection and police investigations, in particular for sexual abuse cases involving the potential of criminal charges. The protocols were designed to meet the differing needs of both agencies, while maintaining the focus on minimizing the trauma for the child.

---

[23] *Alberta Response Model: Building on Successful Practice and Transforming Outcomes for Children* (see <http://www.child.gov.ab.ca>).

[24] *Ibid.*

These protocols are now often reflected in government policies, as well as in agency policies, and have expanded beyond application in sexual abuse cases to any case in which a criminal charge might result from harm to a child.

Protocols have also been useful in assisting child protection agencies to work cooperatively with schools and hospitals in developing procedures that respect the mandates of different agencies and professions.

The Investigation

When a concern is reported with respect to a child, an initial assessment is made to determine whether a child may be in need of protective services. If so, the worker usually searches the agency records to see if there is any history of child protection involvement. Where a provincial Child Abuse Register or "fast-track" computer information systems exist, as in Ontario, there is a routine expectation that there will be a records search. A prior history of child protection involvement may help to direct a current investigation, though of course the absence of such a record may not be significant and does not lessen the urgency of a current investigation.

Together with a supervisor, a worker will decide on a plan for the investigation that may involve interviews with family members, teachers, doctors, daycare or other community members, or viewing a home environment and meeting the child. Any protocols that have developed between the agency and police should be reflected in the development of an investigation plan. The speed of commencing an investigation will depend on the degree of risk suggested by the report and on any known prior history of abuse or neglect. Best practice standards require that at an early stage of the process, a worker who is investigating suspected abuse or neglect should see the child and any other children in the family, without the parents being present, though this does not always happen.

While the right to apprehend a child believed to be in need of protection is clearly set out in the statutes of all provinces, there is little statutory guidance for how to conduct an investigation of suspected abuse or neglect. Sometimes parents are unwilling to allow a protection worker into their home, or to allow their children to be seen or examined by a protection worker. Some jurisdictions have legislation that expressly allows for the apprehension of a child solely for the purpose of a medical examination. In every jurisdiction child protection workers can obtain the assistance of police to allow forced entry to a dwelling to search for a child believed to have been abused or neglected. Such steps may seem highly intrusive if the investigation process requires only an opportunity to interview the child or view the child. Where a parent offers, for example, to have an examination of the child by the family doctor and a report prepared by the physician, this may be an alternative to an interview or observation by a child protection worker.

In one Ontario case, a child protection agency sought a court order to allow the local Health Unit and Building Inspector to have access to a home for purposes of an inspection to determine whether there were child neglect concerns. Justice Schnall refused to make the order, comparing the situation to the criminal context where an individual would have the right to deny entry to the police in the absence of a warrant. While acknowledging that the order requested by the agency was relatively non-intrusive as compared with the other statutory options, the judge, nevertheless, found that such a step would be a breach of the privacy rights of the family. In scrutinizing the justification for such a step, the court was critical of the information given by the person who reported concerns to the child protection agency, describing the source as "biased" and vague as to time frames and specifics of neglect. The judge was unable to conclude that the observations were reliable, and therefore denied the agency the order sought.[25] However, in another later decision, Justice Schnall was asked to answer a number of questions concerning the right of a child protection agency in conducting an examination.[26] The case involved allegations of physical abuse by parents who were members of a church that encouraged the use of corporal punishment with an object, like a switch or belt. Among other questions, the court was asked to consider:

- Do child protection workers have the right to question parents during the course of their investigation of alleged abuse?

- Are the parents who are being questioned by child protection workers during an investigation of suspected abuse or neglect compelled to answer their questions, in the sense that their failure or refusal to answer will attract an adverse inference against them?

- Are child protection workers empowered to interview children without the consent of their parents or a court order during an investigation?

Justice Schnall made clear that an investigation by child protection workers into suspected abuse or neglect is legally quite different from an investigation by police into a suspected crime. She concluded that child protection workers are "empowered to speak to the children and examine them, where there are allegations of abuse. The [agency workers do]...not require the parents' consent to examine and interview the children."

Occasionally, particularly where there is a criminal investigation proceeding at the same time as the child protection investigation, a parent or parents will refuse to co-operate in any manner with the investigation. Criminal legal counsel often advise parents not to meet with the investigating child protection worker, because that worker is obliged to share any information with the police. It is not uncommon for an investigation under these circumstances to be concluded without an interview of one or both parents, as they have a right to remain silent under the *Charter*.

---

[25] *Children's Aid Society of Huron County v. R.B. and J.B.*, 1999 Carlswell Ont 4557 (Ont. Ct. J.).

[26] *Family and Children's Services of St. Thomas and Elgin v. W.F.*, [2003] O.J.717, per Schnall J.

Justice Schnall observed that where allegations of abuse or neglect are made, the agency is normally expected to question the parents in the course of its investigation. While parents are not legally obliged to answer the questions during the course of an investigation, the agency workers may draw an adverse inference from a parental failure to answer questions and address agency concerns. Although the agency "must have reasonable and probable grounds to believe that there is a risk of harm, or the children have been harmed, in order to begin its investigation," it may not be unreasonable for the concerns of agency workers to be heightened by a parental failure to answer questions during the course of an investigation,[27] and these concerns may justify apprehension of the children.

Sometimes agency workers believe that information is required from sources such as schools, doctors, daycare staff, hospital records, treatment providers or other sources. In some cases parents who are under investigation by a child protection agency will consent to the disclosure of information about themselves and their children. Where the consent of family members to disclosure of information and records is not forthcoming, it may be possible to obtain a court order for access to records related to the child, and in some cases for records related to a parent or other caregiver. In Ontario, for example, s. 74 of the *Child and Family Services Act* allows a child protection agency to apply for a court order for the release of information contained in a record that is "relevant to investigate an allegation that a child is or may be in need of protection." Such an order may be obtained without notice to the parents and prior to the commencement of child protection proceedings, as simply an "investigative tool," or it can be sought after proceedings have been commenced.

While the focus of an investigation is to protect children from the possibility of harm, it is recognized that these investigations can be highly intrusive and very stressful for families. Child protection investigations are governed by legislation and policies that attempt to ensure a thorough, objective investigation while respecting the rights of parents and children. Adherence to "best practice" procedures helps to ensure that the agency is not perceived as biased against a particular parent and also ensures that similar cases are dealt with in a similar manner.

Child Abuse Registers

A number of Canadian jurisdictions have Child Abuse Registers. Some provinces, such as Manitoba, Nova Scotia and Ontario have Child Abuse Registers mandated by statute. In the jurisdictions where abuse registers are used, child

---

[27] Further, no person can be compelled to answer questions in a *criminal* trial in which they are charged with an offence, and in practice it is not uncommon for a person who refuses to testify to be acquitted of a criminal charge. As a matter of law, a parent can be required to attend and testify in a *civil* child protection case; as a practical matter, if a parent fails to testify in a child protection proceeding, it is inconceivable that a judge will place a child in that parent's care.

protection agencies are required to report "verified" cases of abuse to the centralized register, though the concept of verification differs from one jurisdiction to another.

The Ontario Child Abuse Register is intended to help identify cases where there has been a history of child abuse. The Register may be useful in cases where parents are moving around the province and their children have been identified by different local child welfare agencies as being in need of services. In Ontario, parents' names are to be placed on the Child Abuse Register by local agencies if there is merely "credible evidence" that they have abused a child. While individuals are notified that their names have been placed on the Register and can apply for a hearing to determine whether their names should be removed from the Register, this is a low standard of proof. Because of the low standard for placing names on the Ontario Register, it is not to be used as a screening device for employees or volunteers who are seeking positions working with children.

In all Canadian provinces, organizations that serve children can require that potential employees or volunteers have a criminal record check in order to ascertain whether they have a record of committing offences that should disqualify them from holding such a position. The criminal standard of proof, "proof beyond a reasonable doubt," is a high one, and some individuals who have a known history of abuse may not have a criminal record as a conviction could not be obtained.

In Manitoba and Nova Scotia, the Child Abuse Registers may be used for screening of potential employees or volunteers who will have positions of responsibility for children, and for tracking families with a history of abuse or neglect who may be moving around the province. In these provinces names of abusers are placed on the Register if they have been found guilty in criminal court of abuse or neglect of a child; names are also placed on these Registers if there has been a civil proceeding in which the individual has been found to have abused or neglected a child. In these two provinces there is also the possibility for child protection authorities to have a name placed on the Child Abuse Register and available for job screening, even if there has been no other legal proceeding in which there was a finding of abuse or neglect. The individual must receive notice of the fact that his or her name is on the Register, and has the right to a hearing to have their name removed, at which the agency must establish on the civil standard of proof, on "the balance of probabilities," that the person has abused or neglected a child.

The Manitoba and Nova Scotia Registers, by allowing for screening of individuals who are seeking positions of responsibility for children, afford greater protection for children, and by allowing for a civil review process provide significant legal protections for those whose names are on the Register. The Ontario Register, however, cannot be used for screening and has much less utility. Although access to the Register is restricted, the fact that a government agency has such a "list," based on a relatively subjective determination process, also raises protection of privacy and civil liberties concerns.[28] The usefulness of the Ontario Register has come into serious question, especially since in the late 1990s the government established a province-wide "fast-track" computerized information system to enable all Children's Aid Societies in the province to have access to information concerning any families and children who had been investigated by other child protection agencies in Ontario. The Ontario Child Abuse Register provides less meaningful data to investigators than the "fast-track" system, and there are plans to abolish the Ontario Child Abuse Register.[29]

Even where there is no formal Child Abuse Register, most provinces and territories now give child protection investigators access to jurisdiction-wide child protection records, which helps workers to identify and investigate cases when a family with a history of child abuse or neglect moves from one part of the jurisdiction to another. Given the mobility of Canadian families, it would be useful for child protection investigators to have access to a nation-wide system that would allow access to information about whether a parent or child has been the subject of an abuse or neglect investigation or has received child protection services in another jurisdiction. There are discussions ongoing between provincial officials about the establishment of such a system, but there are issues of cost and protection of privacy, as well as difficulties due to variations in record-keeping policies and computer standards.

Involuntary and Voluntary Involvement

While the primary focus of child protection legislation and the court process is on involuntary involvement of child protection agencies in the lives of children and families, in all jurisdictions legislation and policy encourage child protection agencies to become involved with families on a cooperative, voluntary basis if at all possible. In fact, most protection workers have caseloads with a significant number of cases where the family has either voluntarily approached the agency for service, or was referred by an individual or outside agency and agreed to the involvement of the protection agency. However, it is possible for a case to move from a voluntary status to become an involuntary case with an apprehension of the child and the commencement of court proceedings if at any point increased protection concerns should arise or the parents seem uncooperative.

The distinction between voluntary and involuntary involvement is often quite subtle, and frequently there are situations where a family will reluctantly agree to work "voluntarily" with the agency. Given the authority of the child protection agency to remove children if necessary, it is not surprising that families sometime may not realize their right to decline the "voluntary offer" of services

---

[28] N. Bala et al., *Review of the Ontario Child Abuse Register* (Ontario Ministry of Community and Social Services, 1988).

[29] Section 75 of the Ontario *Child and Family Services Act* governs the Ontario Register. This section was repealed in 1999, by S.O. 1999, c. 2, s. 27, but this part of the amending legislation has not been proclaimed in force, so the Register continues to operate.

of the child protection agency. As a practical matter, in many cases the "right" to decline services may be somewhat illusory, given the agency's mandate to ensure the protection of children through the court process, if necessary. It is only with legal advice that parents can know whether the agency would have the legal authority to intervene even without their "consent." It is important for a protection worker to respect and encourage use of the parents' right to seek legal or other advice at any stage of involvement.

Without parental consent, a child protection agency can only provide services to a family or take a child into its custody if the agency is in the process of commencing court proceedings, or has a court order. The outcome of child protection proceedings may be:

- supervision of the child and parents in the home by the child protection agency;
- placement of the child in the temporary care of the agency (called temporary or Society wardship); or
- permanent placement of the child in the care or guardianship of the agency (called permanent or Crown wardship); this alternative may ultimately result in the termination of all parental rights and placement of the child for adoption, though in some cases the child may be a permanent ward and still remain in contact with members of his or her biological family.

To bring a child protection case before the court, a child protection agency will normally follow one of the following routes:

- application to court without apprehending the child (sometimes called a "simple application");
- apprehension of the child with a warrant or court order; or
- apprehension of the child in the absence of a warrant or court order.

Applying for a Protection Order without Apprehending the Child

All jurisdictions except Saskatchewan and the Northwest Territories allow for the commencement of a child protection proceeding without the necessity of apprehending the child. This approach may be particularly useful where the ultimate goal is not the removal of the child, but rather an order for agency supervision of the child and parents in the family home.

In some cases the agency may not believe that there is a sufficiently imminent risk of harm to the child to justify apprehension, and a court application without immediate removal may be a more appropriate option. In most jurisdictions a child protection application may be commenced with the agency serving the parents with a "notice to produce" the child, which in theory means that the parents are required to produce the child in court, though in practice this is usually effected by the appearance of the parents in court with their agreement to turn the child over to the care of the child protection agency if so ordered by the court. Given the emotional trauma to a child of an unnecessary removal from parents, consideration should be given to the "simple" application, where the safety and well-being of a child is not unduly compromised by leaving the child at home, pending a full court hearing.

Apprehension

The "apprehension" of a child is the exercise by a child protection worker of the power to immediately remove a child from the care of the parents or guardian, based on the worker's assessment that this is necessary to prevent harm to the child, before a court hearing has established that removal is necessary. While concerns about the protection of children from harm may justify immediate removal of children from parental care, this process represents a dramatic exercise of state power and is subject to legal regulation and control.

One of a child protection worker's most difficult professional decisions (and in all but the most urgent or extreme cases a decision requiring consultation with a supervisor) is whether to remove a child against the wishes of a parent or caregiver, i.e., whether to apprehend a child. If a child is able to disclose abuse and articulate the wish to be cared for outside the home, the decision to remove may be easier for everyone involved. Other situations are also quite clear, as in the case of an abandoned infant, or a teenager who is out of the parents' control and agrees to be removed from the home. However, if the child is too young to communicate or wishes to stay home despite the risk to health and safety posed by the home situation, the decision to remove a child becomes more difficult for everyone.

As noted by an American law professor:[30]

Removals can be terrifying experiences for children and families. Often they occur at night. Parents have little or no time to prepare children for separation. The officials conducting the removal, as well as the adults supervising the placement, are usually complete strangers. Children are thrust into alien environments, separated from parents, siblings and all else familiar, with little if any idea of why they have been taken there.

Apprehension should not be used to punish unco-operative families. It is an extreme step that should only be taken to ensure the health and safety of a child. The right to apprehend a child is considered by some to be the most far-reaching state power that exists. Not surprisingly, the exercise of such a power is viewed as a very serious step by child protection agencies, and is subject to judicial scrutiny.

It is impossible to define exhaustively all situations that might warrant apprehension of a child. In a case where there has been a series of "accidental" injuries to a child, removal may be appropriate. One of the "accidents," seen in isolation, might not justify such a radical step, but in the context of repeated injuries, the most recent injury may raise questions about the possibility of physical abuse or serious chronic neglect. In other situations, a single incident

---

[30] P. Chill, "Burden of Proof Begone: The Pernicious Effect of Emergency Removal in Child Protection Proceedings" (2003), 41 *Family Court Review* 457.

with clear evidence of abusive behaviour may be sufficient to warrant removal of a child. For example, cigarette burns, burns resulting from direct contact of a child's buttock with a burner on a stove, or medical evidence of sexual abuse might justify immediate removal.

In some cases, a child's removal is made necessary by a lack of information about the risk of further injury to the child. In cases of suspected child abuse, there is often a frustrating absence of convincing information from parents or caregivers about how the injuries occurred. In some cases, parents may face the possibility of criminal charges and refuse to answer questions by invoking their constitutional right to silence. From the child protection perspective, it then becomes impossible to ascertain what happened in the family, what risks the child faces in the home, and what steps, if any, might reduce the risk to the child. In these situations, apprehension of the child may be necessary to ensure the safety of the child.

Provincial laws do not require that a child actually suffer harm before the child is apprehended, only that there is a substantial risk of harm that cannot be addressed without removal of the child. Removal may be the only practical alternative if parents have a history of violence towards children or are suffering from a condition that places their children at significant risk (e.g., addiction to drugs or alcohol, or severe mental illness) and support is unavailable to reduce the risks to a tolerable level. In the absence of evidence that abuse or neglect has already occurred, courts are reluctant to sanction removal of children solely to prevent the possibility of future harm; yet the law does allow for this, and a child protection worker needs to consider whether preventative removal is justified by the significant risks that a child's home situation creates for the child. The age of the child may be a crucial factor in such a decision, since it is assumed that an older child may be more capable of avoiding harm or reaching out for help.

Legislation in most jurisdictions requires that an agency is only to apprehend a child if a worker has reasonable grounds to believe that (a) a child is in need of protection, and (b) there is imminent risk of harm. In some jurisdictions such as Newfoundland and Labrador, British Columbia, Ontario and New Brunswick, the statute provides that before apprehension is warranted, there must also be a consideration of whether less intrusive options could adequately protect the child. In other jurisdictions, despite the absence of explicit mention, it is common practice before deciding to apprehend a child to consider whether less intrusive options would be adequate to protect the child.

In a number of provinces, including British Columbia, Saskatchewan, Manitoba, Nova Scotia and New Brunswick, there is no requirement for a worker to obtain a warrant (or court order) for the apprehension of a child, even if the situation does not involve an "emergency," as long as the child is in a situation where there is believed to be a "risk of serious harm." In several other jurisdictions, however, the legislation distinguishes between urgent and non-urgent situations. In Ontario, for example, s. 40(7) of the *Child and Family Services Act* allows for a worker to apprehend a child without a warrant, but only if the worker believes that there would be a "substantial risk to the child's health or safety during the time necessary" to obtain a warrant or to bring the case to court. In other situations, the worker is obliged to obtain a warrant (or court order) under s. 40(2) before apprehending a child.

Where a warrant is required, a protection worker appears before a justice of the peace or judge, providing a document known as an "information" (or sworn statement) setting out the reasons for the requested warrant; in some cases the warrant can be obtained at a hearing conducted by telephone. The parent and child are not to be notified of the request for a warrant, so this type of unopposed application is usually granted. Once the warrant is issued by the court, a copy of the warrant is given to the parents at the time of apprehension.

All provinces provide for the apprehension of children without the necessity of a warrant in emergency situations. There has been controversy, however, over the use of apprehension powers without a warrant in "non-emergency" situations. In *Winnipeg Child and Family Services v. K.L.W.*,[31] the Supreme Court of Canada considered the constitutional validity of Manitoba child welfare legislation which permits warrantless apprehensions in situations where there is a risk of serious harm, but there is not an immediate "emergency." The Supreme Court upheld the validity of warrantless apprehensions in such non-emergency situations, even though it would, in theory, be possible without placing the child at risk for a child protection worker in such cases to prepare the documentation and contact a justice of the peace to obtain a warrant to apprehend the child. The Supreme Court accepted the difficulty in distinguishing between emergency and non-emergency situations in child protection cases, and accordingly held that the *Charter* does not require that child protection legislation distinguish between emergency and non-emergency situations. Justice L'Heureux-Dubé stated, however, that apprehension of a child from parental care prior to a full court hearing can only be justified if there is a "situation of harm or a *risk of serious harm* to the child." She wrote:

> Apprehension should be used only as a measure of last resort where no less disruptive means are available...the appropriate minimum s. 7 threshold for apprehension [referring to the *Charter of Rights* protection for "security of the person"] without prior judicial authorization is not the "emergency" threshold. Rather the constitutional standard may be expressed as follows: where a statute provides that apprehension may occur without prior judicial authorization in situations of *serious harm or risk of serious harm* to the child, the statute will not necessarily offend the principles of fundamental justice.[32]

While the *K.L.W.* decision establishes that the *Charter of Rights* does not demand a legislative regime that requires a warrant for non-emergency situations, the Supreme Court does suggest that an apprehension in a situation where there is not a *"serious harm or risk of serious harm* to the child" would be unconstitutional.

---

[31] [2000] 2 S.C.R. 519.
[32] [2000] 2 S.C.R. 519. Emphasis added.

The technical legal requirements of apprehension (whether with or without a warrant) are that a child be physically removed from the care and custody of a parent, without the parent's consent. It is advisable for the worker to clearly tell the parents that a child is being apprehended, for example, by saying: "I am apprehending Johnny." This makes it clear to both the worker and the parents that the child has been involuntarily removed from parental custody, rather than possibly leaving parents with the perception that they were coerced into agreeing to have their child taken from them. Normally an apprehended child will be taken to a "place of safety," which will usually be a foster home or a group home. In many cities there are "receiving homes" operated by child protection agencies to allow the placement of children on very short notice for indeterminate stays.

If a doctor or nurse reports suspicions of abuse or neglect of a child who is being treated at a hospital, the child may be apprehended there. The usual practice in these cases is to leave the child at the hospital for treatment, and provide a letter for hospital staff, to be placed in the child's medical chart, stating that the child has been apprehended and that the agency has lawful custody of the child pending any court hearing and can provide any necessary consents to treatment. The timeline for the first court appearance begins from the time the child is apprehended (i.e., the letter is placed on the chart), and not on the day the child is released from hospital. In the case of a hospital apprehension, it is still important for the protection worker to inform the parents of the apprehension as soon as possible in a face-to-face meeting. Everyone involved should be informed that unless the decision is reversed by the agency or a court, the parents are not entitled to take the child, and that at the time of discharge from the hospital the child will be taken into the physical care of the agency.

In some jurisdictions, legislation allows a child protection worker to apprehend a child for the specific purpose of having the child medically examined, with the possibility of immediate return if there is no need for continuing with a child protection application.

Occasionally, the circumstances that justified apprehension are resolved within days following the apprehension (e.g., the abusive parent is criminally charged and held in custody, leaving the non-offending parent free to care for the child), or alternatively the agency enters into a voluntary agreement with the parent as an alternative to a court application. In such circumstances, the court application may be discontinued.

In most jurisdictions child protection legislation authorizes a protection worker to enter premises, by force if necessary, for the purpose of apprehending a child considered to be in danger. In a situation where a worker anticipates physical violence or extreme verbal abuse by the parents, it is common to request the assistance of the police in the apprehension. In some jurisdictions, police officers also have an explicit statutory authority in child protection legislation to undertake an emergency apprehension, though in practice, the police will usually request that this be effected by child protection personnel, if for no other reason than that foster homes and other child care facilities are usually accessed through the child protection system.

Aboriginal Children

There is a sad history in Canada of the culturally insensitive apprehension of large numbers of Aboriginal children by child protection agencies that resulted in trauma and disruption for many Aboriginal families and their communities. Tragically, some of these children were abused in the care of the child protection system, and larger numbers experienced profound cultural dislocation that has plagued their adult lives.

There is now a recognition that child protection services in Aboriginal communities should be provided in a culturally sensitive fashion, and whenever possible by an Aboriginally controlled child protection agency.[33] Where Aboriginal child protection services are not available, services to children who are identified as having an Aboriginal background should, whenever possible, be provided in a matter that respects their native heritage. This may require notification of the proceedings to the band to which they belong, with the possibility of a plan being put forward by the band for the child's care. As a result, it is important at the earliest opportunity in a child protection case to establish whether a child has an Aboriginal status or heritage.

Appearing in Court

The Post-Apprehension Interim Care Hearing

All jurisdictions in Canada have statutes that require the agency to bring a case to court soon after a child is apprehended from a parent's care, at what is known as an "interim care hearing," a "presentation hearing," or a "temporary custody hearing." The time for having a post-apprehension hearing varies, but in most jurisdictions there must be an initial court appearance within five to ten days of the apprehension. In *Winnipeg Child and Family Services v. K.L.W.*, the Supreme Court of Canada emphasized that parents are entitled to a "fair and prompt" post-apprehension hearing, and suggested that a "two-week delay between apprehension of a child and...an interim care protection hearing would seem to lie at the outside limit of what is constitutionally acceptable."[34]

All provinces and territories require that there must at least be an attempt to serve notice on the parents of the time and place of the interim hearing, though it is not always possible to locate and notify the parents before the initial appearance in court. While it is expected that a protection worker will take all reasonable steps to notify the parents before the first court appearance, if it is not

---

[33] For a fuller discussion of child protection issues related to Aboriginal children, see Chapter 7.

[34] [2000] 2 S.C.R. 519 at 587. In Canada's two most remote jurisdictions, Nunavut and the Northwest Territories, the hearing must be commenced within 45 days. While it may be reasonable in these jurisdictions to have a longer statutory period before an initial court appearance, arguably there may be circumstances in which waiting the full period in these territories would be unconstitutional.

possible to do this, notification must be made as soon thereafter as reasonably possible.

The initial appearance in court in a child protection application is the first opportunity for the parents, and for the child, if old enough, to express their views to the court, and to challenge the agency's decision to intrude into family life by removing the child. The first appearance provides an important "check and balance" in the child protection process, with the child protection agency expected to at least summarily justify its actions.[35]

After the apprehension, there may be an ongoing investigation, with the agency discovering increasing amounts of evidence about the case. Not infrequently, the parents will be quite overwhelmed at this stage of the process. Often the parents will not have obtained legal counsel before their first appearance in court, and they may find it impossible at this initial stage to effectively challenge the agency's decision or present evidence to respond to the agency's allegations. It is not uncommon for parents to consent to the agency having interim care, or at least not to actively oppose an interim order that the agency is to have the care of their children pending trial. In some cases, however, even at this interim stage, the parents may be eager to challenge the agency's action and obtain the return of their children. The interim hearing can be very important for parents and children, for the longer that the children are out of parental care, the harder it may be to maintain their relationship and secure their return.

Interim care hearings are scheduled on short notice, and there is usually only limited court time available for the judge to receive evidence, listen to the arguments of the parties and render a decision. The evidence that the court receives at an interim care hearing is usually based on affidavits and documents such as medical reports, though the judge has discretion to allow oral testimony.

If the parents are not contesting the issue of interim care, the case may be dealt with in a matter of minutes. If the interim care hearing is seriously contested, it may be necessary for the hearing to be adjourned for a few days in order to have sufficient time to complete it. While these interim hearings must be relatively brief and may be based exclusively on documentary and affidavit evidence, it is important to give parents an opportunity to present and challenge evidence. In some cases it may be necessary to adjourn an interim care hearing, either to allow time for the parties to obtain evidence and prepare plans, or to permit all of the evidence to be heard by the court. If the interim hearing is adjourned, when it is recommenced it is important for the court to be informed about changes in circumstances since the last court appearance as the court should make its decision based on its assessment of the situation at the time that the decision is being made. In some cases there may be quite a lengthy time between the initial interim care order and the start of the trial, and there may be a

---

[35] P.C. McVey, *Fundamentals of Child Protection Proceedings: Part I Interim Hearings; Child Protection and the Law* (Child Welfare Program, National Judicial Institute, Ottawa, September 2002).

review of the interim care order, including presentation of new evidence or fresh proposals for interim care of the child.[36]

In Nova Scotia and Ontario the legislation specifies that the court may rely on evidence that is considered "credible and trustworthy" at the interim hearing, which gives the court some discretion to consider evidence that might not be admissible in a child protection trial. In jurisdictions without explicit legislative guidance for this hearing, it is common practice for judges to consider documents, letters and other evidence that might not be admissible at trial. It is, however, important for the court to be aware of the source of information and documents that are being put before the court, and that the evidence that is tendered is fair. For example, in a decision at a contested interim care application at which the court returned a two-month-old infant to his mother's care, Justice Katarynch was critical of much of the evidence that the agency filed with the court, expressing concern about such matters as the introduction of evidence that the mother, who was a young adult, had herself been a Crown ward. The judge commented:[37]

> A sheaf of paper reciting snippets of comment from a variety of named individuals who had come into contact with this mother…does not become credible and trustworthy "evidence" by simply attaching that sheaf of paper to a child protection worker's affidavit. Credibility and trustworthiness does not spring full blown from a simple recitation of the information. A concern, absent a factual underpinning, remains an allegation….

> Just dealing places at the beginning of the affidavit — not buried somewhere within pages of historical information culled from the society's files — the society's account of what prompted the intervention, why less disruptive steps to the child were not taken, what has been learned to date in the investigation. It is not the parent's entire life that is on parade in an interim custody motion.

> Just dealing requires a respect for the rules of evidence. At the risk of stating the obvious, what is evaluated in this [interim care] motion…is evidence. Supposition, conjecture, speculation, leaps of hyperbole, innuendo, gossip, unqualified opinion where qualified opinion is required — all have no place in an affidavit….

In several jurisdictions, including Alberta, Manitoba, Newfoundland, Prince Edward Island and British Columbia, child protection legislation does not give the court clear direction about how to weigh the evidence or reach a conclusion about what type of interim order to make. In Ontario and Nova Scotia, the legislation requires a form of "risk assessment," specifying that the child is only to be in the interim care of the agency if the court is satisfied that the child cannot be adequately cared for by the parents pending the hearing, with or without agency supervision. Ontario amended its statute in 1999, to make it clear the agency is *not* required to establish a "*substantial* risk of harm" if the child is left in parental care at this interim stage. Rather the present Ontario law provides that the court is to order that a child is to be returned to the care of his or her parents,

---

[36] See *Children's Aid Society of Halifax v. D.(T.J.)* (1999), 47 R.F.L. (4th) 293 (N.S.S.C. Fam. Div.) where Williams J. refers to interim care as a "revolving issue" that the court can revisit at any stage of the interim proceedings, and pointing out that one judge may review and vary an order made earlier by another judge if there is new evidence or circumstances change.

[37] *Children's Aid Society of Toronto v. A.M.*, [2002] O.J. 1432 (Ont. Ct. Just.) at paras. 54 and 68-70.

perhaps with agency supervision, unless the court is satisfied that "there are reasonable grounds to believe that there is a risk that the child is likely to suffer harm and the child cannot be adequately protected" by supervision at home.[38] In *C.A.S. of Ottawa-Carleton v. T.*, Justice Blishen wrote that this test requires the child protection agency to

> ...establish, on credible and trustworthy evidence, reasonable grounds to believe that there is a real possibility that if the child is returned to his parents, it is more probable than not that he will suffer harm. Further, the society must establish that the child cannot be protected by terms and conditions of an interim supervision order.[39]

If the child is placed in the interim care of the child protection agency, an important issue for the court to address is the access or contact that the parents will have with their children pending final resolution of the case. The courts will usually order that the parents are to have some form of regular contact with their children. If there are concerns about possible abuse, intimidation of the children or their removal from the jurisdiction, as is commonly the case after apprehension, it is likely that the agency will have to supervise the visits, which means that the visits are likely to be limited to a couple of hours per week. Since the proceedings may drag on for months before there is a trial, the amount of contact that parents have may be very important, as without significant contact, their relationship with their child may start to atrophy. If the child is young, the child may not remember who the parents are without frequent contact. Agencies, however, may have real concern about the administrative burdens that they face in arranging and supervising contact between the parents and their child.

In *Children's Aid Society of Toronto v. A.M.*, Justice Katarynch discussed the importance of contact between a two-month-old infant and his parents during the period of interim care:[40]

> The Society had been providing twice weekly visits in its offices for a one-hour period.... Society counsel indicated that the Society had not been able to carry out...more generous access...because of administrative difficulties....
>
> As a matter of common sense, no infant of this age and stage of development can sustain a relationship with a parent with the frequency of access provided by the Society in this case. The Society can be taken to know that a young child is rooting himself in his primary care-giver and losing connection from his family of origin with every day in foster care. The court is regularly faced with cases in which young children have drifted in "interim" society foster care for so long and with so sparse an "interim" access to their parents that their parents have become strangers to them. The Society then points to the "lack of attachment" as a reason to abandon any hope of successfully reuniting the family.
>
> It is fundamentally unfair at the earliest stages of a court case to provide a level of access that in its effect sets the child on the path to a loss of his family.... The Society's apprehension of the child from his mother's care had already disrupted a process of parent-and-child attachment that had barely begun. The uncertainty of outcome makes it particularly important that the society arrange parent-and-child access in a manner that does not create an ever-widening chasm between the child and his family.

---

[38] Ontario *Child and Family Services Act*, s. 51(3), as enacted by S.O. 1999, c.2, s.13.

[39] [2000] O.J. 2273 (Ont. Sup. Ct.).

[40] [2002] O.J. 1432 (Ont. Ct. Just.) at para. 24.

The results of an interim care hearing can be profoundly important for parents and children. Contested interim care hearings can be very challenging for judges, who must assess evidence that may be conflicting, unreliable and untested by cross-examination. The parents and child may be traumatized by an unjustified separation if the child is not returned to parental care. But there is also the danger that a child may be returned to the very situation of risk that prompted the initial apprehension, and that the initial apprehension may prompt the family to keep its abusive or neglectful conduct better hidden from agency view once the child is returned.

Disclosure of the Agency's Case

Child protection agencies have struggled for a long time to reconcile the obligation to respect confidentiality with the rights of a parent to information contained in the agency's files. While disclosure of information about the investigation beyond a minimum may not be desirable or required during the initial stages of a child protection proceeding, the agency has a duty to disclose to parents before trial the information that it has collected in the course of its investigation.

In 1991, the Supreme Court of Canada, in *R. v. Stinchcombe*, ruled that the Crown prosecutor in a criminal case is obligated to provide full disclosure to the accused of all evidence gathered by the police during their investigation, whether the evidence tends to prove the guilt or the innocence of the accused, subject to the exception of evidence that might be "privileged," such as the identity of a police informer.[41] Prior to this decision, disclosure of information by Crown prosecutors and child protection agencies was somewhat "hit and miss," with widely divergent practices in different places. Since *Stinchcombe*, however, the obligation on Crown prosecutors is clear. Further there have been growing expectations that child protection agencies will also provide disclosure of all information that they have gained in the course of an investigation and involvement with a family. Since the Supreme Court has also held that child protection proceedings must be conducted "in accordance with the principles of fundamental justice,"[42] child protection agencies must provide disclosure of information that they have collected to ensure that parents can prepare adequately for trial. Disclosure of information to parents can impose a burden on agencies, but it is necessary in order that fair trials can fully explore the needs and interests of the children involved.

In a 2002 decision of the Alberta Court of Queen's Bench, *S.D.K. v. Alberta*, Justice Bielby ruled that s. 7 of the *Charter* requires a child protection agency to provide full disclosure of "all relevant information in [its] possession."[43] The only material that can be withheld is information relating to the identity of persons who have made an initial confidential report of abuse, and information

[41] [1991] 3 S.C.R. 326.

[42] See e.g., *New Brunswick (Minister of Health) v. G (J.)*, [1999] 3 S.C.R. 46.

[43] [2002] A.J. 70 (Alta. Q.B.).

which in the opinion of the agency "may potentially harm a child's physical, mental or emotional health to a degree that such harm outweighs the entitlement of his or her parents to disclosure." Any material that the agency decides to withhold is to be specifically listed by the agency and a court may be asked by parents' counsel to rule upon whether or not the agency is justified in withholding it. The court's decision also required the agency to seek out information and documents that are not in its files, but to which it is entitled (in this case, the notes of a psychologist who conducted tests on the child), and share it with the parents.

While it may be argued that the decision is not strictly binding outside of Alberta, the principles enunciated in the *S.D.K. v. Alberta* decision are increasingly reflected in rules and practice directions governing child protection matters throughout Canada.

As a practical matter, counsel for parents often delays a request for disclosure of the agency file until such time as a contested trial appears imminent, as counsel are reluctant to review what is often a daunting amount of documentation unless it is clear that a trial is inevitable. Many child protection agencies now request as a condition to orders or agreements about disclosure a solicitor's "undertaking" (a solemn promise by a lawyer, with professional consequences for non-compliance), similar to those available when a file is produced in criminal proceedings as in s. 278.3 of the *Criminal Code*. These undertakings may provide, for example, that the file material is to be kept in a secure and confidential location, that copies are not to be made, and that the material is to be returned or destroyed at the conclusion of the hearing.

In addition to information regarding the identity of informants and information deemed as potentially harmful to the child, protection agencies also routinely withhold (often with judicial approval) information that may identify potential adoptive parents, or, upon request, foster parents. Occasionally, disclosure is delayed where the release of information may interfere with the integrity of an ongoing investigation. For example, a child's taped interview may be temporarily withheld from an alleged abuser until such time as the police have had an opportunity to complete their questioning of the suspect. Such a delay, however, is unlikely to be lengthy, and the information must usually be provided to the parent within a reasonable period and, in any event, prior to the child protection trial.

Disclosure of videotapes of interviews with children is often treated in a different manner from disclosure of copies of documents in the child protection file. Where the videotape (or a copy) is in the possession of the agency, counsel are often requested to attend at the agency offices to view the tape. Where a court requires the release of the tape to counsel, an "undertaking" will be appropriate, prohibiting release or further duplication of the tape.

The *S.D.K. v. Alberta* decision requires (as do the Rules of Court Procedure in most other jurisdictions), that the agency is obliged to produce not only information that is in its possession, but also information that can be accessed by the agency. An example might be obtaining a videotape that is in the possession of the police as part of a joint investigation, or the counselling records of a child, or police records or psychological reports about the child. This suggests that the agency may be required to take proactive steps to obtain information at the request of a parent's counsel, even where such information has not been gathered in the child protection investigation.

There are a number of practical issues related to a child protection agency's disclosure obligations. The files in question are often voluminous. The time required to review the file for possible information that should arguably be withheld can be significant, and the cost of photocopying the entire file may be substantial. In many cases, there is information that must be removed (the telephone or address of a foster parent who has requested not to be identified, for example) prior to copying, a tedious task at best. While some of the costs can legitimately be passed on to the litigants (for example, the prevailing legal aid rate for photocopies), this amount is only a portion of the true costs borne by the agency in providing disclosure. Another difficulty is that in addition to providing disclosure, if the matter proceeds to trial, the agency will be required to compile trial document briefs for the judge and all parties, usually containing the same or significant portions of the material already provided to counsel by way of disclosure. In some cases, counsel for parents are prepared to co-operate by returning disclosed material so that the same copies can be organized, bound and returned to them in preparation for trial.

The unrepresented or "self-represented" parent poses challenges to the agency in the disclosure process. Unlike for counsel, who may be sanctioned by the Law Society for unprofessional conduct for failure to honour an undertaking, an undertaking about the use of disclosed documents has no real practical consequences for the non-lawyer. It may be necessary to have a court order imposing any requested conditions upon the parent. Even so, the fact that the documentation released to a parent will not be stored in a professional setting may raise concerns that the information will not be kept as confidential as if in the care of a lawyer. On the other hand, the self-represented parent should have no fewer rights than the represented parent to "know the case she/he has to meet."

Voluntary Arrangements

While child welfare legislation primarily deals with involuntary intervention, in many cases child protection agencies provide services on a voluntary basis without court involvement. Indeed, in some cases the agency will initially become involved because the parents are seeking the agency's help and support.

When protection concerns have been identified, most agencies discuss with parents the objectives of agency involvement, and ascertain whether the parents are prepared to address the agency's concerns. For example, in cases where the agency has concerns about excessive discipline, if the parents agree to take an effective parenting course and have a child management worker provide help, this may obviate the need for a protection proceeding.

It is a common practice for agencies to expect parents who are willing to have voluntary involvement with the agency to sign a written agreement setting out what the parents and agency are agreeing to do, so that the agency and the parents can be clear about the intervention goals. While most cases of voluntary involvement with a child protection agency do not end up in court, if the parents fail in a significant way to carry out their part of the plan, this failure may be an important piece of evidence in justifying the need for court-ordered intervention. The preparation of such an agreement not only represents cooperative planning with a family, it also anticipates the possibility of later court involvement.

Homemakers

In some jurisdictions, child protection agencies may provide temporary homemakers for the family if a parent is absent from the home or prevented from assuming normal parental duties by a temporary illness or disability. This option is contained in the legislation of several jurisdictions, but it is only a practical option if there is an existing program to support it. Where a homemaker is used, the child protection agency is obliged to obtain a judge's order if the placement exceeds a few days. Use of a homemaker minimizes disruption to the children, but is clearly only a short-term solution to a family problem, and this service is often unavailable even in jurisdictions where legislation allows for this.

Placement with a Relative or Friend

When an alternative to parental care is required, it is best for the agency worker to discuss the options with the parent (and the child, if appropriate). Individuals such as grandparents, aunts, uncles or family friends can often provide the short- or long-term care needed by the children. Informal family plans, "customary care," or "kinship care" arrangements are particularly common with Aboriginal children.

In some cases, a custodial parent may discourage a worker from considering a plan of care with a non-custodial parent or other family member because of feelings of anger or resentment. A parent experiencing difficulties may also feel guilty or embarrassed about revealing the situation to the other parent or a relative. However, from the child's perspective, if voluntary arrangements with a known and trusted adult are feasible, they are usually a far better option than care by strangers, such as a foster parent, especially if the period of care is anticipated to be of short duration.

If the custodial parent has objections to placement with a particular individual (such as the other parent following separation or divorce), these concerns must be carefully addressed. As a general rule, whenever there is an apparent conflict between a parent and the protection agency, it is advisable to bring the matter before a court to protect the rights of all parties. This includes situations where a custodial parent wants a third party to provide care for the child, but the access parent does not agree.

Where an agency is concerned about care being provided by a single parent, placement with the other parent can only be arranged with the consent of the parent with legal custody or by a court order. While a transfer of the child to the care of the parent without legal custody is a useful option to consider, there are concerns that if child welfare agencies do this too frequently there may be many more questionable allegations of abuse or neglect being made by non-custodial parents hoping that this will result in a transfer of custody.

A voluntary placement of a child with relatives is a possible response to situations where there are concerns about the care being provided by biological parents. In many cases the agency will consider it preferable that such placements be arranged pursuant to a court order which makes the child a temporary ward of the agency, though the agency may still make the placement with a relative rather than in a foster home with strangers. If the child is a ward and placed with relatives by the agency, the agency will have a clear legal mandate to supervise the placement and remove the child if there are any concerns, and the agency may be in a better position to provide financial assistance to the relatives who are caring for the child.

Care by Agreement

Sometimes parents cannot care for their children and voluntary placement with a friend or relative is inappropriate or impossible. If it then becomes necessary to use a foster care or a group home, placement may be authorized by a signed written agreement between the parent and the child protection agency without the need for court proceedings. A child who is old enough to understand the nature and consequences of the proposed agreement may need to participate in the decision. In some jurisdictions, a specific age is identified (e.g., 12 years of age in Ontario) as triggering the requirement of the child's consent. It is important that agency staff review the contents of the agreement with the family in some detail before they are asked to sign. A parent being asked to enter an agreement for care should be given an opportunity to consult a lawyer before signing. In Ontario, s. 4(2) of the *Child and Family Services Act* sets out certain requirements for a valid temporary care agreement:

- the parent or guardian must have the mental capacity to understand the agreement;
- the person signing must be informed as to the nature and consequences of the agreement and alternatives to it;
- the agreement must be voluntary; and
- the person signing must have a reasonable opportunity to obtain independent advice. (Note: while there must be an opportunity to obtain advice, it is not necessary for legal advice to be obtained.)

The maximum period for any voluntary care agreement varies across the country. Most agreements provide for an early termination if one of the parties wishes to end the placement, as long as the required notice is provided to the other parties. Some agreements provide that the parents retain certain rights and responsibilities concerning their children, such as the right to make decisions about medical treatment, even though the children are in the agency's care. In other cases, parents may specifically authorize the agency to make decisions related to the child's care, such as routine medical or dental care.

The agreements may include a regular financial contribution to be paid by the parents for the support of the child in care, if the parents are able. Increasingly, agencies are looking to parents for contribution to the costs of their children in care. Most temporary care agreements include a financial contribution (nominal where a parent is, for example, in receipt of social assistance) in accordance with their ability to pay.

In most cases, an agreement can be extended after an initial period. However, some jurisdictions such as Ontario (12 months), Saskatchewan and the Yukon have limited the total period of time a child can be kept in care under temporary agreements. In some cases, a child over 16 may enter into an agreement directly with the protection agency for the provision of services or care, without the involvement of a parent.

Agreement for Adoption Placement

A parent may wish to relinquish a child with the intention of adoption placement. Most jurisdictions have this option available without the necessity of a court application. Because of the profound consequences of such a decision, such agreements generally contain a prescribed period within which a parent has an absolute right to change his or her mind. It is also imperative that a child protection agency placing a child for adoption on this basis obtain all necessary consents so that any subsequent adoption placement is legally valid.[44] For a fuller discussion of adoption, see Chapter 6.

---

[44] In *Re N.P.*, [2001] O.J. 441 (Sup. Ct.), the agency obtained an order for substituted (alternative) service for a father whose whereabouts were described as "unknown" by the agency worker in the supporting affidavit. That service was effected by newspaper advertisements which the father never actually saw. After the newspaper ads appeared, the father's rights were terminated by a Crown wardship order and the child was placed for adoption. The father subsequently learned that the baby had been placed in an adoptive home. In seeking to overturn the Crown wardship order, the father established that the maternal grandmother had previously told the worker that the father's parents lived in a small town, which she had identified, and that the paternal grandparents telephone number could have been easily found. In setting aside the permanent wardship order, Justice J. MacKinnon was highly critical of the agency worker for providing a "deficient" and "misleading" affidavit in the application for substituted service. The same issues might arise in the context of adoption consents, where the consent of only one parent is obtained, and the affidavit of a worker is submitted for dispensing with the consent of the other parent.

3

The Child Protection Hearing

Marvin M. Bernstein and Kristina J. Reitmeier[1]

Child protection legislation in different Canadian jurisdictions has the same basic structure. There are, however, some significant variations in the approach to some issues in different jurisdictions, reflecting in part different balances between a child's entitlement to grow up in a safe environment and the family's right to live without interference by the state. Not only is there variation in approach between jurisdictions, but there have been changes in approach and legislative amendments within provinces over the course of time.

In many jurisdictions in North America there was a move in 1990s towards having legislation that places a greater emphasis on children's safety. In Ontario, for example, a panel of experts, chaired by Family Court Judge Mary Jane Hatton, was established in 1997 to consider how the government should respond to a number of highly publicized deaths of children while in the care of their parents, but under the supervision of child protection agencies. In its report, the panel observed:

> The recent deaths of Ontario children while receiving child welfare services have raised concerns about child protection practices, policies and legislation in Ontario. The Child Mortality Task Force and Coroners' juries which examined these deaths raised specific concerns as to whether or not the legislation adequately protected children from abuse and neglect. The task force and individual juries recommended amendments to the legislation that governs child protection, the *Child and Family Services Act.*[2]

This report resulted in amendments in 2000 to Ontario's *Child and Family Services Act*, which placed a greater emphasis on child safety and facilitated intervention by child protection agencies.[3]

It is understandable that politicians and bureaucrats feel a need to respond to highly publicized abuse or deaths, whether while children are in the care of parents or in the care of state agencies (the issue of institutional abuse is explored in the next chapter). It would, however, be preferable for legislative reform and systemic change in the child welfare field to take place as a

---

[1] Marvin M. Bernstein is Director of Policy Development and Legal Support, Ontario Association of Children's Aid Societies. Kristina J. Reitmeier is Chief Counsel/Director of Legal Services, Children's Aid Society of Toronto.

[2] M.J. Hatton et al., *Report of the Panel of Experts on Child Protection* (Toronto: Ontario Ministry of Community and Social Services, 1998) at 3.

[3] S.O. 1999, c. 2. See discussion in Bala, "Reforming Ontario's Child and Family Services Act: Is the Pendulum Swinging Back Too Far?" (1999), 17 *Canadian Family Law Quarterly* 121-172.

consequence of thoughtful policy and legislative analysis, in a context of careful research, and not simply as a reaction to tragic individual cases.

Forum and Jurisdiction

Forum

There is significant variation both between and within jurisdictions as to which courts and judges deal with child protection cases. In most places, especially in larger centres, judges who deal with child welfare cases also deal with other types of family law cases, but in some places, especially in less populated areas, the judges may deal with a broader range of cases. In most places in Canada provincially appointed judges are given jurisdiction to deal with child protection proceedings, but in some places, especially where there are Unified Family Courts, child protection cases are dealt with by federally appointed judges. The courts with jurisdiction over child protection cases are:

- Alberta — Provincial Court;[4]
- British Columbia — Provincial Court or Supreme Court, depending on location;[5]
- Manitoba — Court of Queen's Bench (Family Division) or the Provincial Court (Family Division), depending on location;[6]
- New Brunswick — Court of Queen's Bench;[7]
- Newfoundland and Labrador — Unified Family Court or Provincial Court, depending on location;[8]
- Northwest Territories and Nunavut — Supreme Court or the Territorial Court;[9]
- Nova Scotia — Family Court (Provincial) or Supreme Court (Family Division), depending on location;[10]
- Ontario — Court of Justice (provincially appointed) or the Family Court of the Superior Court of Justice, depending on location;[11]

---

[4] Alberta, *Child Welfare Act*, R.S.A. 2000, c. C.12, s. 1(1)(h). [Hereafter this statute cited in this chapter as, "Alberta".]

[5] British Columbia, *Child, Family and Community Service Act*, R.S.B.C. 1996, c. C.46, s. 1(1). [Hereafter this statute cited in this chapter as "British Columbia".]

[6] Manitoba, *Child and Family Services Act*, C.C.S.M. 1985, c. C.80, s. 1. [Hereafter this statute cited in this chapter as "Manitoba".]

[7] New Brunswick, *Family Services Act*, S.N.B. 1980, c. F-2.2., s. 1. [Hereafter this statute cited in this chapter as "New Brunswick".]

[8] Newfoundland and Labrador, *Child, Youth and Family Services Act*, S.N. 1998, c. C.12.1, s. 2(1)(g). [Hereafter this statute cited in this chapter as "Newfoundland".]

[9] Northwest Territories, *Child and Family Services Act*, R.S.N.W.T. 1997, c. 13, s. 4. [Hereafter this statute cited in this chapter as "Northwest Territories".]

[10] Nova Scotia, *Children and Family Services Act*, S.N.S. 1990, c. 5, s. 3(1)(k). [Hereafter this statute cited in this chapter as "Nova Scotia".]

[11] Ontario, *Child and Family Services Act*, R.S.O. 1990, c. C.11, s. 3(1). [Hereafter this statute cited in this chapter as "Ontario".]

- Prince Edward Island — Supreme Court;[12]
- Quebec — Court of Quebec (provincially appointed);[13]
- Saskatchewan — Provincial Court or the Court of Queen's Bench, depending on location;[14] and
- Yukon Territory — Territorial Court.[15]

Court Jurisdiction

The provincial courts, which generally have jurisdiction over child protection matters, are "statutory courts," and derive their authority to act exclusively from the governing statutes.[16] Where child protection legislation gives a federally appointed judge (usually called a "superior court judge"[17]) jurisdiction over a child protection case, the judge, in addition to exercising statutory powers, also has a relatively narrow inherent "*parens patriae*" jurisdiction to do what the best interests of the child may require, provided that the legislation does not explicitly deal with an issue.[18]

Any court can invoke the *Charter of Rights* to give relief within its scope of jurisdiction if there is a violation of the *Charter* in the case before the court.

Jurisdictional Relationship with Other Legislation

From time to time, there are conflicts between the provisions of provincial child protection legislation and other provincial or federal statutes. Where such a conflict arises, there is the issue of which statute should have priority.

---

[12] Prince Edward Island, *Family and Child Services Act*, R.S.P.E.I. 1988, c. F-2, s. 1(1)(h). [Hereafter this statute cited in this chapter as "Prince Edward Island".]

[13] Quebec, *Youth Protection Act*, R.S.Q. 1991, c. P-43.1, as amended, s. 1(g). [Hereafter this statute cited in this chapter as "Quebec".]

[14] Saskatchewan, *Child and Family Services Act*, S.S. 1989-90, c. C-7.2, s. 2(1)(e). [Hereafter this statute cited in this chapter as "Saskatchewan".]

[15] Yukon Territory, *Children's Act*, R.S.Y. 2002, c. 31 s. 104. [Hereafter this statute cited in this chapter as "Yukon".]

[16] *M.(R.) v. M.(S.)* (1994), 20 O.R. (3d) 621 (Ont. C.A.).

[17] The term "superior court" refers to a court which has federally appointed judges, appointed under s. 96 of the *Constitution Act*, 1867; these judges have an inherent residual *parens patriae* jurisdiction to deal with issues not dealt with explicitly by legislation, if this is necessary to promote the best interests of a child. The names that are used to refer to the superior court in each province include the Court of Queen's Bench (Q.B.), and the Supreme or Superior Court. Only superior court judges can grant divorces or deal with matrimonial property issues, or deal with civil cases involving significant sums of money.

The term "inferior court" is technically used in contrast to the "superior courts." The "inferior court" judges are appointed by provincial or territorial governments, and do not have a residual inherent jurisdiction. The term "inferior" is unfortunate, but the reality is that superior court judges have a higher status within the legal profession and higher salaries, and in some cases a superior court judge may hear an appeal from an "inferior court" judge. It is a sad comment on Canadian society that the judges who most frequently make decisions about the future of children who are abused or neglected are sitting in the "inferior courts," while judges who deal with significant financial issues have a higher position in the judicial hierarchy. Increasingly in Canada, however, "Unified Family Courts" are being established, which are superior courts (federally appointed judges) with jurisdiction over child welfare issues as well as other family law matters, and that generally have a range of support services affiliated with the court.

[18] *Beson v. Director of Child Welfare for Newfoundland* (1982), 30 R.F.L. (2d) 438 (S.C.C.); *Re A.* (1991), 28 R.F.L. (3d) 288 (Ont. U.F.C.); *Winnipeg Child & Family Services (Northwest Area) v. G.(D.F.)*, [1997] 3 S.C.R. 925 (S.C.C.).

Although it is generally accepted that a parent whose child has been appre-hended by a child protection agency can only seek relief under provincial child protection laws, there are different judicial approaches to the relationship between general domestic relations legislation and child protection legislation when a foster parent or family member seeks a custody or access order under general domestic legislation in respect of a child who is a ward of the child protection agency.

There is one line of cases which views child protection legislation as a comprehensive code dealing with the care and custody of children in need of protection.[19] Representative of this judicial approach is the Ontario Court of Appeal decision of *W.(C.G.) v. J.(M.)*, where the court dismissed a birth mother's application under the general domestic relations statute, the *Family Law Reform Act* [now the *Children's Law Reform Act*] for access to her birth child, who was previously a permanent agency ward and had been adopted just one month prior to her access application:[20]

> The *Ontario Child Welfare Act*, 1978 [now the *Child and Family Services Act*] deals specifically, by way of special provisions, with the care and protection of neglected, abused and abandoned children. It establishes a comprehensive and exhaustive code for the supervision, custody, access, wardship and adoption of such children to en-sure that their best interests and welfare are protected and forwarded. The very title of the act defines its purpose. Such children are not to be "dealt with" by the general provisions of another statute which are not directly concerned with them, unless of course, the provisions of that statute say so in specific terms...

In most provinces, including Ontario, it has been held that where child protection proceedings have been commenced, any order under child protection legislation takes priority over a custody order made under the provincial *Children's Law Reform Act*[21] or the federal *Divorce Act*,[22] regardless of the sequence of the orders and the level of courts making the orders. For example, in *Re J.D.*, Judge Fisher stated:[23]

> ...the Provincial Court (Family Division) has a special jurisdiction over children in need of protection, notwithstanding a custody order, no matter where or when ob-tained, based on the difference in subject matter. This court has jurisdiction the mo-ment the child is apprehended and continues to exercise that jurisdiction until its orders are exhausted. Any prior or parallel custody order continues in existence but cannot take effect until the jurisdiction under the *Child Welfare Act* [now *Child and Family Services Act*] ceases.

While the dominant approach is to treat the child welfare statute as creating an exhaustive code, there is a line of cases which takes a more integrated

---

[19] See e.g., *Fortowsky v. Roman Catholic Children's Aid Society for Essex (County)*, [1960] O.W.N. 235, 23 D.L.R. (2d) 569 (Ont. C.A.); *Perfect v. British Columbia (Superintendent of Family and Child Services)* (1988), 48 D.L.R. (4th) 469 (B.C.C.A.); *G.(C.) v. Catholic Children's Aid Society of Hamilton-Wentworth* (1998), 161 D.L.R. (4th) 466 (Ont. C.A.).

[20] (1981), 24 R.F.L. (2d) 342, 34 O.R. (2d) 44 (Ont. C.A.) at 348, 349.

[21] R.S.O. 1990, c. C.12.

[22] R.S.C. 1985, c. 3 (2nd Supp.).

[23] (1978), 8 R.F.L. (2d) 208 (Ont. Prov. Ct.) at 220.

jurisdictional approach, and allows, in some situations, for an application to be made for custody or access under general family law legislation even if a child has been made a child welfare ward. Representative of this judicial interpretation is the Saskatchewan Queen's Bench decision of *H.(C.) and H.(R.) v. G.(D.) and Saskatchewan (Minister of Social Services)*, where the court agreed to rescind a long-term child welfare order made pursuant to the *Child and Family Services Act* in favour of a custody order granted to the applicant foster parents pursuant to the *Children's Law Act*:[24]

> The *Child and Family Services Act* and the *Children's Law Act* and other similar and related enactments together form part of a comprehensive scheme of legislation dealing with children and their care and well-being. In that scheme each separate statute deals with a different aspect relating to child care.
>
> The *Child and Family Services Act* deals with those children in need of protection....
> The *Children's Law Act* deals primarily with the custody of children and the access to them by their...parents or such other persons having in the opinion of the court a sufficient interest in their well-being. In each instance the primary consideration of these acts is to ensure the welfare of a child or children.
>
> Both enactments under consideration bear upon some aspect of conduct relating to the best interests of a child or children and can, and indeed ought to, be read together as forming one comprehensive regime touching upon the best interests of children.
>
> Where several statutes deal with different aspects of the same subject matter, the enactments will, where possible, be read together as parts of one whole scheme.

Where courts allow an application for custody or access to be made for a child who is already subject to a child welfare order, this jurisdiction is used sparingly, for example, to give rights to individuals who do not have clearly defined rights under the relevant child welfare statute, such as foster parents. Biological parents are generally restricted to exercising rights under child welfare statutes.

On the other hand, as is more fully discussed in Chapter 6, even in jurisdictions that accept that the child welfare statute creates an exhaustive code for making custody or access applications in regard to children who are subject to child protection orders, there may be some scope for making access orders under other legislation when a child is subject to the adoption process.

Age of the Child

In all provinces and territories, the age of the child is critical to the jurisdiction of the court to make an order under a child protection statute. As the following list indicates, the definition of "child" for child protection law purposes varies in terms of the maximum age limit:

---

[24] (1996), 147 Sask. R. 230 (Sask. Q.B.) at paras. 10-25. Saskatchewan *Children's Law Act*, S.S. 1990-91, c. C 8.1. See also *F.(M.A.) v. Southeast Child and Family Services*, [2000] 10 W.W.R. 479, 147 Man. R. (2d) 192 (Q.B.); the Saskatchewan *Child and Family Services Act*, S.S. 1989-90, c. C-7.2, s. 33(3), which provides: "If a protection hearing is stayed pending the determination of a custody application pursuant to the *Children's Law Act*, the time for a determination and order pursuant to subsection (1) does not include the period of the stay of proceedings."

- Nova Scotia,[25] Saskatchewan;[26] and Newfoundland[27] — a person under the age of 16;
- Ontario,[28] the Northwest Territories and Nunavut[29] — a person under the age of 16 when an initial order is made, though for a child already the subject of an order there may be further orders made until the child reaches the age of 18;
- Alberta,[30] Manitoba,[31] New Brunswick,[32] Prince Edward Island,[33] Quebec[34] and the Yukon Territory[35] — a person under the age of 18 years when the order is made; and
- British Columbia — a person under the age of 19.[36]

For a child protection court to have jurisdiction over a child, generally that child must be under the stipulated maximum age limit both at the time of apprehension and at the time of the hearing,[37] although in Ontario, it is sufficient if the child was under the age of 16 "when the proceeding was commenced or when the child was apprehended."[38] Age is usually established by a child's birth certificate, though some children, such as those who are immigrants or refugees from war-torn countries, do not have a birth certificate, and it may be necessary to establish a child's age based on other less reliable documents or testimony, or even based on their appearance.

The age of maximum jurisdiction is a contentious policy issue. It is difficult to make effective orders regarding older adolescents, who may be "runners" and will leave any placement that is not locked. However, older adolescents may engage in high risk and self-destructive behaviour, and may well be in need of child welfare services. In Ontario, in 1998 the Panel of Experts on Child Protection recommended that the definition of child for child protection purposes should be changed to include children aged 16 and 17,[39] but this recommendation was not incorporated into the 2000 legislative amendments, in part because of government concerns about the costs of providing services to these children.

---

[25] Nova Scotia, s. 3(1)(e).

[26] Saskatchewan, s. 2(1)(d).

[27] Newfoundland, s. 2(1)(d).

[28] Ontario, ss. 3(1), 37(1).

[29] Northwest Territories, s. 1.

[30] Alberta, s. 1(1)(d).

[31] Manitoba, s. 1.

[32] New Brunswick, s. 1.

[33] Prince Edward Island, s. 1(1)(e).

[34] Quebec, s. 1(c).

[35] Yukon, s. 104.

[36] British Columbia, s. 1(1).

[37] See *R. v. Allcock* (1975), 25 R.F.L. 84 (B.C.S.C.); *Re Lakeman and Andreychuk* (1978), 6 R.F.L. (2d) 389, 90 D.L.R. (3d) 158 (Sask. Q.B.). But see: *Re Moe* (1979), 18 B.C.L.R. 311 (B.C.S.C.).

[38] Ontario, *Child and Family Services Act*, R.S.O. 1990, c. C.11, s. 47(3).

[39] *Report of the Panel of Experts on Child Protection* (Toronto: Ontario Ministry of Community and Social Services, 1998) at 52. For a further discussion of issues related to the provision of child welfare services to older adolescents, see Chapter 5.

The Stages of a Proceeding

Conceptually a child protection proceeding can be divided into several distinct stages:

- apprehension and interim care (discussed in Chapter 2);
- finding that a child is in need of protection;
- disposition: supervision, temporary wardship or permanent wardship; and
- status review.

These stages are all governed by the same statute, and many of the same general principles apply to all of them. Further, in practice in some cases there may be some blurring between the stages, and decisions made at one stage may have a profound influence on later stages. It is, however, important to keep these distinct stages in mind, as different procedural, substantive and evidentiary rules apply at each stage.

The Threshold Finding of Need for Protection

Standard for State Intervention

The fundamental premise underlying all child protection legislation in Canada is that the state has a legitimate interest in ensuring that children receive certain minimal standards of parental care. Where the care given to the child falls below the minimally acceptable standards, then the state-mandated child protection agency is empowered to intervene in the family to supervise the care of that child and, if necessary, to remove the child to a place of safety.

In the 1975 Ontario County Court decision of *Re Brown*, Justice Stortini commented on the limits of appropriate state intervention: [40]

> ...the community ought not to interfere merely because our institutions may be able to offer a greater opportunity to the children to achieve their potential. Society's interference in the natural family is only justified when the level of care of the children falls below that which no child in this country should be subjected to.

In *Re D.(M.G.L.)*, the Ontario Court of Appeal made a similar pronouncement: [41]

> The standard is the minimal standard that society will tolerate. The community ought not to impose a standard of lesser or greater opportunity to achieve a child's potential. The standard is a given, and it is the one obtaining in the home of the natural family. Interference will only take place when the level of care as defined in the *Child Welfare Act* falls below the minimum to which all children are entitled.

In all provinces and territories, child protection statutes define the child's need for protection on the basis of prescribed criteria, which authorize state intervention into the family unit. In this chapter, the phrase "child in need of

---

[40] (1975), 9 O.R. (2d) 185 at p. 189 (Ont. Co. Ct.). See also: *Children's Aid Society of Kingston v. Reeves* (1975), 23 R.F.L. 391 (Ont. Prov. Ct); and *Children's Aid Society of Winnipeg (City) v. M.* (1980), 15 R.F.L. (2d) 185 (Man. C.A.).

[41] (1984), 41 R.F.L. (2d) 176 at 186 (Ont. C.A.).

protection"[42] will be used generically to denote the relevant statutory definition, which lists a series of protection grounds. It is also referred in different jurisdictions by such terms as a child "in need of protective services,"[43] a child "in need of protective intervention"[44] or whose "security or development may be in danger."[45] In Quebec, the statute uses a similar concept, authorizing child protective intervention where "the security or development of a child is considered to be in danger."[46]

Although there is variation in the exact definitions, there is in practice very significant overlap, with the legislation intended to permit intervention when a child has been physically, sexually or emotionally abused, or has been physically or emotionally neglected. These statutes also allow for intervention when there is a serious risk that such harm will occur in the future, even if it has not occurred to this child in the past, thus allowing an agency to apprehend a child at birth if there is strong evidence of future risk. In every jurisdiction the definition also allows for intervention if the parents are refusing to provide needed medical care, such as if Jehovah's Witness parents are refusing to consent to a blood transfusion after a child has been involved in a serious accident. Further, in every jurisdiction, the definition allows for intervention if a child is abandoned or the parents are deceased and there is no caregiver, as well as allowing for a court order to be made based on a parental acknowledgment that they are unable to care for a child.

One area of difference between jurisdictions is in regard to treatment of domestic violence, where in some jurisdictions, like New Brunswick, the statute explicitly states a "child living in a situation where there is domestic violence" is a child in need of protection.[47] In other jurisdictions, like Ontario, there is no similar provision, but the fact that there is domestic violence may, depending on the circumstances, be a factor in establishing physical or emotional abuse.

In Ontario and Manitoba, the agents of the state, who can initiate child protection proceedings in order to obtain a finding that a "child is in need of protection" are local Children's Aid Societies or mandated Aboriginal agencies, while in most other jurisdictions, such proceedings are commenced by provincial directors of Child Welfare or agents of the Minister responsible for social services.[48] In Nova Scotia there are both kinds of agencies (local Children's Aid Societies and offices of the Minister of Community Services). For purposes of this chapter, the generic term "child protection agency" will be used to refer to these various entities.

---

[42] Manitoba, s. 17(1); Ontario, s. 37(2); Prince Edward Island, s. 1(2); Saskatchewan, s. 11; Yukon, s. 116(1).

[43] Alberta, s. 1(2); Nova Scotia, s. 22(2).

[44] Newfoundland, s. 14.

[45] New Brunswick, s. 31(1).

[46] Quebec, s. 38.

[47] New Brunswick, s. 31(1)(f).

[48] As discussed in Chapter 7, in a number of jurisdictions Aboriginal child welfare agencies are mandated to provide child protection services.

Statements of Principle

Almost every child protection statute explicitly outlines the philosophical bases or principles within which that statute is to be interpreted. This takes the form of either a relatively elaborate Declaration of Principles[49] or a concise Statement of Purpose.[50] A common element, although the express language may differ, is a cogent statement that the "best interests" of the child are the paramount consideration.

These Declarations of Principles or Statements of Purpose, including the statement of the "best interests" of children as being the paramount consideration, are intended to govern the application of the whole of each statutory scheme. In *Children's Aid Society of the County of Bruce v. T.R.*, the court was dealing with a decision about whether to make an interim care order following apprehension, and discussed the overall Ontario statutory framework in the following terms:[51]

> The court has to determine what is in the best interests of the children. This is mandated by the paramount purposes set out in section 1 of the *Child and Family Services Act* and is implicit in all of the sections that have to be considered when making a decision in a child protection matter.
>
> .... To a large extent, the risks have been reduced, but they remain in place and, in my view, are of a substantial nature. A substantial risk means an actual or real risk. It is not something that is imagined or speculative. The risk is to be weighed in light of the purposes of the *Child and Family Services Act* and specifically the paramount objective to promote the best interests, protection and well-being of the children....

It should, however, be appreciated that the concept of "best interests" of the child in a protection proceeding has a different and more restricted meaning than the term has in other contexts. When parents separate, legislation like the *Divorce Act*[52] s. 16 also states that decisions are to be made on the basis of the "best interests" of the child, but in the context of parental separation there is no presumption in favour of either party, and the court is truly making a decision about the very "best" option available for the child. In child protection proceedings, the statutory statements of principle and the definitions of "best interests" of the child acknowledge the importance of a child's family and cultural heritage, especially Aboriginal heritage, thus creating *a presumption that it is in a child's best interests to be in the care of his or her family*. While the term "best interests" of the child is used in statements of principle and elsewhere in child protection statutes, it has been consistently interpreted by the courts in a way that places a significant onus on the state agency to justify removal of a child from his or her family. The nature of the onus placed on child protection agencies is further discussed below, though in general there is a clearer onus on

---

[49] See Alberta, s. 2; British Columbia, s. 2; Manitoba, Declaration of Principles; Northwest Territories, Preamble; Newfoundland, s. 7; Ontario, s. 1.

[50] See Nova Scotia, s. 2; Prince Edward Island, s. 2; Saskatchewan, s. 3; Yukon, s. 1; Quebec, ss. 2.2, 2.3.

[51] [2001] O.J. 5571(Ont. Ct. J.), per Brophy J. at para. 50-54.

[52] R.S.C. 1985, c. 3 (2nd Supp.).

the agency at the stage of making a finding of whether a child is in need of protection, and more of a focus on the best interests of the child at the disposition stage.

The Relevant Date for the Determination of a Finding

In almost all jurisdictions in Canada, the date that is relevant for the determination of whether a child is in need of protection is established through case law. One exception is Nova Scotia, where subs. 40(4) of the *Children and Family Services Act* provides that "[t]he court shall determine whether the child is in need of protective services as of the date of the protection hearing...."[53]

There is some case law which has established that the operative date for the determination of the issue of a child's need for protection is the date of apprehension or commencement of the application.[54] There is, however, a more persuasive line of case law which holds that the protection finding is to be based upon the circumstances in existence at the time of the protection hearing, as well as the circumstances existing at the time of the child's apprehension.[55] This latter interpretation is taken in British Columbia, where it has been held that a court is not limited to considering only the circumstances existing at the precise moment of apprehension, but "should look at all the evidence up to, and including, the date of the hearing."[56] In the British Columbia decision in *Re J.(D.M.)*, Justice Meiklem stated:[57]

> Assessing the need of protection involves, as a component consideration (not as a separate consideration) assessing the risk of future abuse or neglect on inferences to be taken from all that has transpired up to the date of the hearing.

In the Ontario case of *Children's Aid Society of Hamilton-Wentworth v. R.(K.)*, Justice Czutrin made a compelling argument in favour of a more flexible approach to the issue of the relevant date for the determination of a child's need for protection, emphasizing the need for the court to base its decision on up-to-date information:[58]

> [For a court to] refer only to the start [apprehension] date is to interpret the Act in a manner that would undermine the purposes of the *C.F.S.A.* If under the *C.F.S.A.* the only time that can be considered when determining protection is the start date, it might result in the court returning a child to a person even if the court came to the conclusion the child was in need of protection at the time of the hearing as opposed to

---

[53] Nova Scotia, s. 40(4).

[54] *Central Winnipeg Child and Family Services v. H.(L.L.)*, [1987] W.D.F.L. 1963 (Man. Q.B.); *Children's Aid Society (Pictou) v. P.(L.)* (1987), 10 R.F.L. (3d) 217 (N.S. Co. Ct.); *Children's Aid Society for the Region of Peel v. C.(V.)*, [1989] W.D.F.L. 1152 (Ont. Prov. Ct.).

[55] See e.g., *Re MacKinnon* (1975), 20 R.F.L. 57 (Ont. Prov. Ct.); *F.(L.) v. Children's Aid Society of Halifax* (1984), 40 R.F.L. (2d) 403 (N.S. Co. Ct.); *Re H.(R.M.)* (1984), 40 R.F.L. (2d) 100 (Alta. C.A.); *Awasis Agency of Northern Man. v. A.(M.J.)* (1986), 44 Man. R. (2d) 222 (Q.B.), affirmed (1987), 48 Man. R. (2d) 241 (Man. C.A.).

[56] *British Columbia (Superintendent of Family & Child Services) v. Gilmour*, (May 14, 1986) Doc. Vancouver CC85-1987 (B.C. Co. Ct.).

[57] (March 30, 1992), Doc. Prince George 21831 (B.C.S.C.).

[58] [2001] O.J. 5754 (Ont. Sup. Ct. J.) at para. 49.

the date of apprehension. This could potentially put a child in need of protection and potentially at risk, and would require a new apprehension after return. This cannot be in the best interests of a child. The legislation emphasizes the need to avoid having children in limbo. It cannot be in the child's best interests to create such a scenario....

...the court should be free to consider whether the child is in need of protection at the commencement of the proceedings or at the hearing date, or for that matter some other date, depending on the circumstances. There cannot be an absolute rule as to the relevant date.

In some cases the apprehension may have been justified at the time that it occurred, but by the time of trial the circumstances may have changed and the child is no longer in need of protection. In most jurisdictions the courts will simply dismiss the child protection application in such cases, and have the child returned to his or her previous caregiver. In Ontario the same result is achieved by the court making a finding that the child is in need of protection and then granting a "no order" disposition.[59]

The Burden of Proof

In a few jurisdictions, the child protection legislation addresses either or both the nature of the proceeding and the onus to be discharged. For example, the child protection proceeding is described as being "civil" in nature in British Columbia and Newfoundland.[60] In the Yukon, subs. 168(1) of the *Children's Act*[61] sets out the nature of the standard of proof:

In proceedings under this Act...the standard of proof shall be proof on the balance of probabilities, and that standard is discharged if the trier of fact is satisfied of the existence of the fact to be proven on evidence sufficient to establish that the existence of the fact is more probable than its non-existence.

In most jurisdictions, child protection legislation does not deal explicitly with the nature of these proceedings, but the courts have clearly recognized that child protection hearings are "civil" in nature, both in terms of procedure and evidentiary onus. Thus, child protection agencies are *not* required to meet the high standard of proof that applies in criminal proceedings, "proof beyond a reasonable doubt," when attempting to establish that a child has been abused or neglected.

There are, however, differing judicial opinions as to the degree of proof required to discharge this civil evidentiary burden in child protection proceedings.[62] Some judges hold that the burden on a child protection agency at the "protection finding" or "adjudication" stage is the ordinary civil onus,[63] while other judges hold that there is a "heavy" or "demanding" civil onus on a child

---

[59] Ontario, s. 57(9).

[60] British Columbia, s. 66(1)(a); Newfoundland, s. 50(1)(a).

[61] Yukon, s. 168(1).

[62] See J. Wilson, *Wilson on Children and the Law* (Toronto: Butterworths, 1995) at 3.6.

[63] See e.g., *Re B. and Children's Aid Society of Winnipeg* (1975), 64 D.L.R. (3d) 517 (Man. C.A.); *Children's Aid Society of Halifax (City) v. Lake* (1981), 45 N.S.R. (2d) 361, 86 A.P.R. 361 (N.S.C.A.); *S.(B.) v. British Columbia (Director of Child, Family and Community Services)* (1998), 38 R.F.L. (4th) 138 (B.C.C.A).

protection agency when it is seeking to establish that a child is in need of protection.[64] This disagreement in the case law was explained by the Ontario County Court in *P.(S.) v. Catholic Children's Aid Society of Metropolitan Toronto:*[65]

> I was referred to a number of decisions in respect to the question of onus, and I adduced from them that there is some conflict as to whether, given the fact that this is a civil and not a criminal proceeding, with an onus on the balance of probabilities based on credible evidence, is there a more demanding onus, as seems to be the feeling...in the decisions of *Re Chrysler...*and *Caldwell v. Children's Aid Society of Metropolitan Toronto...*or the normal civil onus as in the *Children's Aid Society of Winnipeg v. Forth...*or alternatively, the heavy onus on the Children's Aid Society in establishing that the child is in need of protection under...[now s. 37(2) of the *Child and Family Services Act*] and without reference and deference to the second issue of placement of the Child under...[now s. 57(1) of the *Child and Family Services Act*], as was discussed in *D. v. Children's Aid Society of Kent....*

In a paper prepared for the Law Society of Upper Canada, Judge R.J. Abbey attempted to reconcile the two lines of authorities as both supporting the normal civil standard of the balance of probabilities, having regard to the seriousness of the issues to be determined:[66]

> In applying the civil standard and in reaching required findings of fact, however, the court should...take into account the severity of the allegations and the gravity of the consequences which would flow from the finding which is sought. Such matters are simply considerations which have a bearing upon the question as to whether a particular matter has been proved to the reasonable satisfaction of the court on the test of the balance of probabilities....

While there may be only limited practical significance to the exact verbal formulation that a judge chooses to use to describe the nature of the onus on the agency in a child protection proceeding, the divergence in approaches to this issue are emblematic of a tension that exists in much of the case law and judicial practice that governs specific substantive, procedural and evidentiary issues in child protection cases. All judges operate within the same statutory framework, and on some issues there is considerable consistency in how judges apply the law. There are, however, also issues for which there is considerable difference in judicial approach. Some judges tend to have a more flexible approach to these proceedings, for example, tending to give the agency a little more leeway in admitting evidence. Other judges tend to focus more on the adversarial and intrusive nature of these proceedings, and, for example, take a stricter view of how to apply the rules of evidence, and place a higher onus on the agency to prove its case.

---

[64] See e.g., *D. v. Children's Aid Society of Kent* (1980), 18 R.F.L. (2d) 223 (Ont. Co. Ct.); *Re Chrysler* (1978), 5 R.F.L. (2d) 50 (Ont. Prov. Ct.); *W.(N.) v. Prince Edward Island (Director of Child Welfare)* (1997), 153 D.L.R. (4th) 20, 33 R.F.L. (4th) 323 (P.E.I.C.A).

[65] Unreported, October 26, 1982, (Ont. Co. Ct.) at 4-5.

[66] Judge R.J. Abbey, *"Child and Family Services Act* — Section 37(2): "A Child in Need of Protection" in Law Society of Upper Canada CLE Program on *Representing Parents in Child Protection Cases* (Toronto, 9 May 1989) at E-11.

Grounds for a Finding that a Child is "In Need of Protection"

Before a child protection agency can intervene to protect a child through the courts, other than on an interim basis, a "finding" must be made that the "child is in need of protection." Generally, such a finding can only be made where the evidence satisfies the court on the basis of one or more grounds listed under the relevant definition of "child in need of protection" that there is a sufficient basis for state intervention.

Although the grounds for finding a child in need of protection vary from one jurisdiction to another, the definitional variations of "child in need of protection" in all jurisdictions include the following:

- physical, sexual or emotional abuse, or risk thereof;
- abandonment;
- orphanhood;
- parental failure to meet the health needs of the child;
- inadequate parental care, supervision or control; and
- absence of the parent in circumstances that endanger the child's safety or well-being.

In most jurisdictions, neglect[67] and exposure to domestic violence[68] also constitute protection grounds. In the Yukon,[69] there is an interesting provision which attempts to delineate the factors that would cause a court to determine that the level of physical discipline has been unreasonable or excessive, thereby rendering the child "in need of protection":

> The mere subjection of a child to physical discipline does not bring the child within the definition of child in need of protection, but the child may be in need of protection where the force is unreasonable or excessive, having regard to:
>
> a)   the age of the child,
>
> b)   the type of instrument, if any, employed in corporal punishment,
>
> c)   the location of any injuries on the child's person,
>
> d)   the seriousness of the injuries, which resulted, or which might reasonably have been expected to result, to the child, and
>
> e)   the reasons for which it was felt necessary to discipline the child and any element of disproportion between the need for discipline and the amount of force employed.

In Ontario, there was a significant broadening of the definition of "child in need of protection" with the 2000 amendments to s. 37(2) of the *Child and Family Services Act*. One significant amendment was the change in statutory language in ss. 37(2)(b), (2)(d), (2)(g) and (2)(g.1) of the Ontario Act, which

---

[67] See: Alberta, s. 1(3)(ii)(B); British Columbia, s. 13(1)(d); Manitoba, s. 17(2)(b)(ii); New Brunswick, s. 31(1)(e); Nova Scotia, s. 22(2)(j); Ontario, ss. 37(2)(a), (2)(b), (2)(f), (2)(g); Prince Edward Island, s. 1(2)(c); Yukon, s. 116(1)(j).

[68] See: Alberta, s. 1(3)(ii)(c); Manitoba, s. 17(2)(b)(iii); New Brunswick, s. 31(1)(f); Nova Scotia, s. 22(2)(i); Prince Edward Island, s. 1(2)(i); Saskatchewan, s. 11(a)(vi).

[69] Yukon, s. 116(2).

now includes among children who are in need of protection those who are "likely" to suffer future physical, sexual or emotional harm. This new language was interpreted by Madam Justice Blishen in *Children's Aid Society of Ottawa-Carleton v. T.*, a decision that is widely cited[70] in Ontario:[71]

> In my view, the word "likely" suggests at least more probable than not. The *Concise Oxford Dictionary* (10th edition)...defines "likely" as "such as well might happen or be true." Therefore, the harm must be more than possible. It must be more probable than not.

> ...Therefore, the test in my view is as follows: The Children's Aid Society must establish...that there is a real possibility that if the child is returned to his parents, it is more probable than not that he will suffer harm....

The Ontario approach to the risk of future harm may be contrasted with the decision of the British Columbia's Court of Appeal in *S.(B.) v. British Columbia (Director of Child, Family & Community Services)*, where the court gave a broader interpretation to similar language in the British Columbia legislation, placing a somewhat lower onus on the child protection agency:[72]

> ...[W]here the assertion being made is that there is a risk that an event will occur in the future, then it is the *risk of the future event and not the future event itself* that must be shown by the weight of the evidence to be more probable than not. That is the case with a consideration of future harm.

> The result is that in considering past abuse, the degree of certainty that it has occurred will be more than is required in considering whether abuse will occur in the future....

> ...Generally speaking, a risk sufficient to meet the test might well be described as a risk that constitutes "a real possibility."

> ...I would adopt the views expressed...[in *Re H.*, [1996] A.C. 563 (H.L.)] that the word "likely" has a primary meaning of "more probable than not," but a recognized secondary meaning of "a real possibility," and that the secondary meaning captures the intent of Parliament in the use of the word "likely" in relation to the possibility of a child suffering harm in the future.

Amendment of Grounds Pleaded

In most jurisdictions, the *Rules of Civil Procedure* or *Family Law Rules*[73] provide for the amendment of "pleadings" (the documents that parties file with the court and serve on each other setting out the nature of their case). These rules allow, in appropriate cases, for the agency (or the parents) to amend these documents as more is learned about the case or circumstances change. If an amendment is not allowed, a party may be restricted to proving the matters alleged in those documents as originally drafted and basing its case on those grounds. The courts are somewhat more flexible about allowing amendments in child protection cases than in ordinary civil litigation, reflecting the fluid nature of child

---

[70] See e.g., *Re A.C.M.*, [2001] O.J. No. 548 (Ont. S.C.J.); *Re D.S.* (2001), 14 R.F.L. (5th) 414 (Ont. S.C.J.); *Children's Aid Society of Ottawa-Carleton v. K.D.*, [2002] O.J. No. 2408 (Ont. S.C.J.).

[71] [2000] O.J. 2273 (Ont. S.C.J.) at para. 7 and 8.

[72] *S.(B.) v. British Columbia (Director of Child, Family & Community Service)* (1998), 38 R.F.L. (4th) 138 (B.C.C.A.) at 150, 151.

[73] See, for example, Ontario *Family Law Rules*, O. Reg. 114/99, Rule 11 (2.1), where the parties may, without the court's permission, serve and file amended "pleadings ... if a significant change relating to the child happens after the original document is filed."

protection cases and a desire to make a decision that truly meets the child's needs.

Often in child protection proceedings, a child protection agency will plead multiple grounds for alleging that a named child is in need of protection. Where, however, the child protection agency fails to plead a relevant protection ground, that omission will not be fatal to the success of the application if the courts allow an amendment. The courts are quite flexible in allowing a child protection agency to amend the grounds in its protection application, in order to determine the real issues between the parties,[74] notwithstanding errors or inadequacies in the pleadings, so long as no injustice is thereby done to another party.[75] One method of preventing such injustice is for the court to grant an adjournment in order to enable the respondents to reply to the amended protection grounds. A court might, in rare cases, make an order that the agency compensate the parents for additional legal costs incurred as a result of the amendment.

There is generally similar, or even greater, flexibility, shown by the courts in allowing parents to amend their court documents. In some cases, however, courts will refuse to allow amendments to court documents and will restrict parties to proving the matters raised in those documents, such as where the application for an amendment comes at a late date before trial (or during the trial) and allowing an amendment would unduly delay the trial and making a decision about the child.

The Legal Framework of Protection Proceedings

Privacy and Exclusion of the Media

All Canadian jurisdictions have, to a greater or lesser degree, legislation that provides for the privacy of child protection proceedings and the exclusion of the media.[76] Ontario has the most comprehensive legislation relating to the protection of privacy and the exclusion of the media, with the *Child and Family Services Act* stipulating that the protection hearings must be held separately from criminal proceedings and must be conducted in private, unless the court orders that the hearing be held in public.[77] Not more than two media representatives, selected either by their choice or if they cannot agree, selected by the court, are permitted to attend, unless the court orders otherwise.[78] The court is also given the discretion to ban media representatives from the hearing where it

---

[74] *Re Wanda S.* (1980), 3 F.L.R.R. 70 (Ont. Prov. Ct.); *Catholic Children's Aid Society of Metropolitan Toronto v. W.(D.)* (1981), 8 A.C.W.S. (2d) 114 (Ont. Prov. Ct.).

[75] *Re Milner* (1975), 23 R.F.L. 86, 13 N.S.R. (2d) 378, 58 D.L.R. (3d) 593 (N.S.S.C.). See also *Re M.T.*, (1984), 36 R.F.L. (2d) 386 (Ont. Prov. Ct.) and in *Children's Aid Society of Algoma v. A.(B.)*, [2001] O.J. 2754 (Ont. C.J.), where the flexible judicial approach was also recommended.

[76] Alberta, s. 25(1); British Columbia, s. 66(1)(c); Ontario, s. 75; Manitoba, s. 75; New Brunswick, s. 10; Newfoundland, s. 50; Northwest Territories, ss. 84 and 87; Nova Scotia, ss. 93 and 94; Prince Edward Island, ss. 31, 47 and 49; Quebec, ss. 82 and 83; Saskatchewan, s. 26; Yukon, s. 172.

[77] Ontario, s. 45(3) and (4).

[78] *Ibid.*, ss. 45(5), (6).

concludes that such presence would cause harm to a child who is involved in the hearing.[79] Further, there is a prohibition on the publication of any information "that has the effect of identifying" any child, parent, family member or foster parent involved in a proceeding.[80] The court also has the authority to make an order prohibiting publication of any information about a hearing, but only if the court is satisfied that such publication would cause emotional harm to a child involved in a proceeding.[81]

The Nature of the "Hearing" and Summary Judgement

While legislation in every jurisdiction requires a hearing before a child protection order is made, none of the statutes define the term "hearing." In Ontario, which has perhaps the most detailed and rights-oriented child protection statute in Canada, the courts have accepted that an agency can make a motion for "summary judgement," asking the court to dispose of a child protection application on the basis of affidavits and documents that the agency files with the court without the need for an oral hearing and calling witnesses to testify.

In the Ontario case of *Catholic Children's Aid Society of Toronto v. B.(D.)*,[82] Madam Justice Jones had occasion to consider the statutory requirement for a "hearing" set out in subs. 47(1) of the *Child and Family Services Act*:[83]

> ...Subsection 47(1) of the Act imposes on the court the duty to conduct a "hearing" to determine whether a child is in fact in need of protection and then to make an order under section 57.

> ...The Act does not define the term "hearing." The Court of Appeal...confirmed the jurisdiction of the court to give summary relief in a protection hearing, and that a hearing need not always take the form of a trial, although that would be desirable in most cases.

> The manner in which the court conducts the necessary inquiry or "hearing" contemplated by section 47 would depend on a number of factors. A "hearing" might take the form of a summary judgement motion on affidavit evidence, the admission of an agreed statement of facts or a viva voce trial [a trial with witnesses testifying].

This approach has now been codified in the Ontario *Family Law Rules*, which specifically provide for motions for summary judgement, though requiring a court to be satisfied that there is "no genuine issue for trial" as a condition of

---

[79] *Ibid.*, 45(7).

[80] *Ibid.*, 45(8).

[81] Ontario, s. 45(7)(c). See *Family & Children's Services of St. Thomas and Elgin v. F.(W.)*, unreported, June 28, 2002 (Ont. S.C.J.), where Granger J., on appeal, set aside a trial court's publication ban under s. 45(7) stating that "...[since] the required evidentiary foundation (i.e., would there be emotional harm as set out in s. 45(7) and *Daginais v. CBC, R. v. M...., CAS v. L.(T.)* to support a publication ban) is lacking in this case, a trial judge is not at liberty to make such a ban based on speculation. In addition, there is no rule that would prohibit such publishing of these proceedings including the evidence on a *voir dire* in a judge alone trial, even if such testimony is eventually ruled inadmissible, unless such publication ban can be founded on s. 45(7) criteria."

[82] [2002] O.J. 2318 (Ont. C. J.) at para. 7-10.

[83] R.S.O. 1990, c. C. 11.

granting the request for summary judgement. In *B.(F.) v. G.(S.)*, Justice Himel summarized the law applicable to summary judgement:[84]

> In a ruling on a motion for summary judgement, the court is not to assess credibility, weigh evidence, or find the facts. The court's role on such a motion is narrowly limited to assessing the threshold issue of whether a genuine issue exists requiring a trial..... The court, however, has the duty to take a hard look at the merits of an action at this preliminary stage....

Accordingly, the material submitted on a motion for summary judgement "must clearly and indisputably support a convincing *prima facie* case for the relief sought" and clearly justify the conclusion reached, as well as demonstrate that a trial would be a waste of judicial resources, and contrary to the interests of the child.[85]

For example, in *R.A. v. Jewish Child and Family Services*, Justice Lane granted the agency's motion for summary judgement where the father pled guilty to sexually assaulting his 11-year-old daughter and taking sexually provocative naked pictures of her, and it was established that these acts occurred in the presence of the mother.[86] The court concluded that there was "no triable issue" related to either whether the child was in need of protection or what was in her best interests, and made the child a permanent ward without access to the parents, based on the agency's plan of having the child adopted.

Summary judgement motions need not be dealt with on an "all-or-nothing" basis, and can be invoked solely for purposes of making a finding that a child is in need of protection, or for disposition, or for some corollary orders such as access. To the extent that there are "no genuine issues for trial," child protection cases may be disposed of, in whole or in part, on a motion for summary judgement.

While a summary judgement motion may seem like an extreme remedy in child protection cases, it can be a very effective device in selected cases and can expedite the decision-making process, thereby promoting the welfare for vulnerable children. These motions are not uncommon in Ontario, though they appear to be used rarely in child protection cases in other jurisdictions.

Bifurcated Hearings

There are two distinct stages to a child protection application. The first stage is the "protection finding" or "adjudication" stage, where the court must determine whether the child is in need of protection under the defined grounds set out in the applicable child protection legislation. Only if the court is satisfied that the child is in need of protection will the court proceed to the "disposition" stage, where the court must decide what dispositional order will serve the "best interests."

---

[84] (2001), 16 R.F.L. (5th) 237 (Ont. S.C.J.) at 247, 248.

[85] *Children's Aid Society of Peel (Region) v. O.(W.)*, [2002] O.J. No. 1099 (Ont. C.J.).

[86] [2001] O.J. 47 (Ont. Sup. Ct.).

Since a child protection proceeding involves a contest between the state and the family, it is fundamentally different than a child custody dispute between parents, and thus, at the adjudication stage of a child protection proceeding, the court is precluded from intervening solely on the basis of a "best interests" concern for the child.[87] This separation of issues and stages was the subject of a decision by the Nova Scotia Court of Appeal in *Re Sarty*:[88]

> Having regard to the evidence as a whole, it seems to me that the learned Family Court Judge directed his attention solely to the issue as to what he thought on balance was in the best interests of the child, as opposed to also determining whether the mother was unable or unfit to properly care for the child. Under the Act, one can only determine that a child is in need of protection when the latter question has been determined affirmatively. In my view, the Administrator failed to establish that the child was in need of protection.

In both Ontario and Nova Scotia, the relevant child protection legislation requires not only a conceptual division of the "adjudication" and "disposition" stages, but also an actual two-stage hearing, where the court is precluded, at the adjudication stage, from receiving evidence relating only to disposition.[89] Thus there will normally be two distinct stages to a hearing, though at the second stage, the disposition, the court may consider evidence that was introduced at the earlier adjudication stage.

The Nova Scotia *Children and Family Services Act* makes it clear that the prohibition against the admission of solely dispositional evidence at the adjudication stage can be waived where "all parties consent to the admission of such evidence or consent to the consolidation of the protection and disposition hearings"[90] and that "[t]he evidence taken on the protection hearing shall be considered by the court in making a disposition order."[91] Although not explicitly dealt with in the Ontario statute, as a matter of practice some judges are, with the consent of the parties, also prepared to receive evidence on both issues at one hearing.

In Ontario, subs. 50(2) of the *Child and Family Services Act* has been interpreted as setting out a restriction "with respect to evidence that goes only to the disposition, not evidence that has an element of both finding and disposition."[92] While one judge has held that courts should be cautious about admitting evidence at the first stage that relates solely to disposition,[93] another judge has

---

[87] *Re Sarty* (1974), 19 R.F.L. 315 (N.S.C.A.); see also e.g., *Hansen v. Children's Aid Society of Hamilton-Wentworth* (1976), 27 R.F.L. 289 (Ont. S.C.); *Re D.(M.G.L.)* (1984), 41 R.F.L. (2d) 76 (Ont. C.A).

[88] (1974), 19 R.F.L. 315 (N.S.C.A.) at 325.

[89] Ontario, s. 50(2); Nova Scotia, s. 40(2).

[90] Nova Scotia, s. 40(2).

[91] Nova Scotia, s. 41(2).

[92] *Children's Aid Society of Hamilton-Wentworth v. R.(K.)*, (November 26, 2001), Doc. Hamilton FC-97-001604-C, (Ont. S.C.J.) at 17.

[93] *Ibid.* at 17.

interpreted this provision as being "merely a practice requirement whose violation would result in a procedural irregularity rather than a substantive nullity."[94]

In *Children's Aid Society of Algoma v. A.(B.)*[95] the court considered the intent and operation of subs. 50(2) of the Ontario Act:

> I should note that part of the reason for subsection 50(2) is to avoid dealing with disposition until a finding is made, as a finding is a condition precedent to any disposition under section 57. However, if a finding is made in a case, the Act does not, by subsection 50(2), require a repetition of any evidence that may apply to both finding and disposition that has already been adduced. Such evidence is already before the court. A bifurcated proceeding is still only one proceeding. Subsection 50(2) does not purport to exclude any evidence that is relevant to disposition; it merely provides for an order of precedence of presentation of evidence in a child protection case.

Court-Ordered Assessments

Opinions from various professionals about the capacities of the parents and the needs of children are often central to child protection cases. One of the contentious issues in child protection proceedings is the extent to which social workers employed by the agency should be permitted to express opinions about the issues before the court. A major concern of some judges is the apparent lack of independence of some expert witnesses. In *C.A.S. of Niagara Region v. D.M.*, Justice Quinn expressed this concern and refused to permit an agency social worker to express an opinion about the adoptability of a child, remarking:[96]

> It surprises me that the Society routinely adduces expert evidence from its own employees. This is not what I would call "independent assistance to the court."

In contested cases, some judges will rule that, unless specially qualified as "expert witnesses," child protection agency staff social workers are ordinarily not permitted to testify about their opinions related to such "ultimate issues" as whether a child is in need of protection. There is clearly a potentially important role for *qualified* social workers and other mental health professionals in providing expert opinions in child protection cases, and the fact that a person is a employee of a child protection agency does not preclude that person from being qualified as an "expert."[97]

Increasingly psychologists in private practice are being retained to assess parents in child protection cases to determine their "parenting capacity" or "competence." A "parenting capacity" assessment is typically based on the results of a number of psychological tests, interviews and observations. Some of these assessments are conducted by trained, multidisciplinary teams that conduct a multi-source, interdisciplinary assessment of parenting capacity, considering both the strengths and weaknesses of a parent. In other cases,

---

[94] *Catholic Children's Aid Society of Metropolitan Toronto v. O.(L.M.)* (December 15, 1995), affirmed on other grounds (1996), 139 D.L.R. (4th) 534 (Ont. Gen. Div.), further affirmed at (1997), 149 D.L.R. (4th) 464 (Ont. C.A.).

[95] [2001] O.J.2754 (Ont. C.J.).

[96] [2002] O.J. 1421 (Ont. Sup. Ct.).

[97] See the discussion in Chapter 11 on expert evidence.

however, a single professional with limited training may conduct an assessment.[98] These assessments can be very helpful to agencies in their planning for how to deal with a case, and may be very influential in court.

While it is appropriate to admit opinion evidence from a qualified psychologist or team of assessors about "parenting capacity,"[99] it should be appreciated that this is merely an opinion, and not definitive "scientific" proof of a person's capacity to care for a child. Although there is literature that describes the use of psychological testing and assessments in child welfare proceedings, as with other tests and concepts used in assessments, there is a lack of rigorous scientific research about the concept of "parenting capacity."[100] There is a concern that some tests or assessments may tend to over-predict the likelihood of parental abuse or focus too much on parental incapacity. A leading expert in the field of parenting capacity assessments for child protection proceedings, Dr. Karen Budd, cautions that:[101]

> ...the standards for evaluating parental fitness are not well defined or agreed upon, so applying a minimum parenting criterion can be difficult.... Another set of challenges in evaluating parental fitness concerns the dearth of appropriate measures. Traditional psychological instruments were not designed to measure parenting adequacy.... A related challenge in conducting assessments of minimum parenting adequacy concerns the difficulty in predicting future behaviour.

Some of the issues of institutional bias that arise with agency employees may arise with a psychologist in private practice if a significant portion of his or her professional practice is based on referrals from the local child protection agency.[102]

Most child protection statutes make express provision for court-referred or court-ordered assessments of children, parents and others proposing to care for a child. Generally these provisions are very broad, once again the exception being Ontario, where an assessment can only be ordered after a determination that the child is in need of protection has been made.[103]

The completion of an assessment and preparation of a report can be a lengthy process, sometimes further exacerbated by waiting lists or a shortage of

---

[98] For a study describing the great variation in approach, see K. Budd, L. Poindexter, E. Felix and A. Naik-Polan, "Clinical Assessment of Parents in Child Protection Cases: An Empirical Analysis" (2001), 25 *Law and Human Behavior* 93-109.

[99] See e.g., *C.A.S. of Sudbury v. P.M.*, [2002] O.J. 1217 (Ont. Ct. J.).

[100] See e.g., American Psychological Assoc., Committee on Professional Practice and Standards, *Guidelines for Psychological Evaluation in Child Protection Matters* (Washington D.C., 1998); see also L.O. Condie, *Parenting Evaluations for Court in Care and Protection Matters* (New York City: Kluwer Publishing, 2003); R. Otto and J. Edens, "Parenting Capacity," chapter 7 in T. Grisso, *Evaluating Competencies: Forensic Assessments and Instruments*, 2nd ed. (New York: Plenum, 2003), 229-307.

[101] K. Budd, "Assessing Parenting Competence in Child Protection Cases: A Clinical Practice Model" (2001), 4 *Clinical Child and Psychology Review* 1-18 at 2-3. See also S. Azar and L. Cote, "Sociocultural Issues in the Evaluation of the Needs of Children in Custody Decision Making: What Do Our Current Frameworks for Evaluating Parenting Practices Have to Offer" (2002), 25 *International Journal of Law and Psychiatry* 193-217.

[102] *Re R.A.*, [2002] Y.K. 48 (Terr. Ct.) at paras. 224-234.

[103] Ontario, s. 54.

assessors. The need for an assessment should be explored at an early stage in the proceeding to minimize delay if one is to be prepared. The need for a particular subject-area expertise and the benefits of an independent and objective clinical look at the circumstances are common reasons for ordering an assessment. Effective judicial case management can assist in identifying not only the need for an assessment, but also in narrowing the issues to be assessed.

A complete parenting capacity assessment can be very expensive, and the provincial legal aid plan may or may not contribute pursuant to its tariff or an arrangement with the Ministry responsible for child protection services. In *C.A.S of Toronto v. Kemi O. and Bruce L.*, Justice Spence held that as the legislation gives a court the authority to order an assessment, it "must be necessarily implied" that there is the power to order one or both parties to pay, and ordered the child protection agency to pay the full cost for an independent assessment in a child protection case.[104]

In Ontario, s. 54 of the *Child and Family Services Act* only allows a court to order an assessment of the child or parent by a psychologist or other expert after there has been a finding that the child is in need of protection. While one party, most commonly the agency, may obtain an assessment of the child without a court order prior to a finding, a court-ordered assessment under s. 54 may have greater weight since it is performed by a court-appointed expert who, because of this independent status is most likely to have the co-operation of all of those involved and hence will be able to provide the most complete report. Since this assessment can only be ordered after a finding that a child is in need of protection, this may further emphasize the bifurcation of the protection proceeding, and may result in a significant delay between the two stages as it may take time to have an assessment performed.

Time Limits for Court Decisions and Delay

There are understandable concerns about how long it can take for the court system to make decisions about children, and the disruption that children experience while left "in limbo."[105] A number of jurisdictions have provisions in their child protection legislation prescribing time limits within which a child must be found to be in need of protection or for a disposition to be made in a case. While it is clearly desirable to have decisions made expeditiously, the reality of the court system is that all too often these time limits are not met, leaving judges to decide what is an appropriate remedy.

In Nova Scotia, where an application is made to the court to determine whether a child is in need of protection, the statute provides that "the court shall,

---

[104] [2003] O.J. 5090 (Ont. Ct. J.); see also *C.A.S. of Huron City v. C.P. and M.T.*, [2002] O.J. 176 (S.C.).

[105] See, e.g., W. McTavish, *Report on Delay Within the Administration of Justice in Proceedings Involving the Care, Custody and Access of Children* (Toronto: Ontario Ministry of the Attorney General, 1995); Sparrow Lake Alliance, *Children In Limbo: Report of the Children In Limbo Task Force of the Sparrow Lake Alliance* (Toronto, 1996).

not later than 90 days after the date of the application, hold a protection hearing to determine whether the child is in need of protective services."[106] Similarly, in Saskatchewan, there is a requirement that the court make a determination of whether a child is in need of protection "within 60 days of the day on which the protection hearing commences unless the court does not have sufficient evidence on which to make an order."[107] Where, however, the court is unable to hear all the evidence and does not sit again within the prescribed time period, "the protection hearing shall be adjourned to the next available court day."[108]

In Ontario, where a protection application is commenced and there has been no determination as to whether the child is in need of protection within three months after the commencement of the proceeding, the court "shall by order fix a date for the hearing of the application...[which] may be the earliest date that is compatible with the just disposition of the application."[109] In Ontario, there are also procedural rules, as in other jurisdictions, which require specific steps according to a prescribed timetable, so that the protection hearing must occur within 120 days from the start of the case.[110] Rule 33(3) of the same *Family Law Rules* stipulates that "[t]he court may lengthen a time shown in the timetable only if the best interests of the child require it."

In a few provinces there is also a time limit within which a dispositional order must be made in a proceeding. In Nova Scotia, there is a specific requirement that a dispositional hearing be held and a dispositional order made not later than 90 days after the finding of need for protection.[111]

In cases in which a court has been unable to conclude a proceeding within the statutory deadline, it may have to decide whether the consequence is a loss of jurisdiction over the case, or whether the court simply deals with the case on a delayed basis. While the impact of delay and litigation limbo upon young children is a significant concern, it would invariably be contrary to the interests of children to dismiss an application because the time limits were not met.

In *Children's Aid Society & Family Services of Colchester County v. W.(H.)*,[112] the Nova Scotia Court of Appeal ruled that the trial judge did not lose jurisdiction where there was a breach of the 90-day requirement for making a disposition, because the trial judge was guided by the best interests of the subject children:

> ...what this appeal illustrates, is that the time limits, which give effect to the concern expressed in the Preamble, are sometimes in conflict with the best interests of the child. When that occurs, the legislation must be given a construction consistent with

---

[106] Nova Scotia, s. 40(1).

[107] Saskatchewan, s. 33(1).

[108] Saskatchewan, s. 33(2).

[109] Ontario, s. 52.

[110] *Family Law Rules*, O. Reg. 114/99 under the *Courts of Justice Act*, Rule 33(1).

[111] Nova Scotia, s. 41(1).

[112] (1996), 25 R.F.L. (4th) 82 (N.S.C.A.) at p. 90. See also *Children's Aid Society of Halifax v. B.(T.)* (2001), 194 N.S.R. (2d) 149 (N.S.C.A.), where the court affirmed the jurisdiction to grant time extensions beyond the statutory time limits in exceptional cases.

the best interests of the child. In my view the ordinary meaning of the legislation creating the time limits cannot be ascertained from looking at the sections containing those specific provisions standing alone, they must be read in light of the Preamble and s. 2 [statement of principles].

The alternative loss of jurisdiction which nullifies all proceedings prior to the infringement of the time limit, may not only be contrary to the best interests of the child but to the concern addressed in the Preamble, and to the intent of the time limits themselves....

I would consider the time limits provisions to be not mandatory but strongly directory, to be obeyed to the fullest extent possible consistent with the best interests of the child....

It is also important for the courts and the litigants to be mindful of the timelines set out in *Family Law Rules* or other procedural rules and to ensure compliance, wherever possible. However, it is equally important to apply common sense and fairness to the manner in which they are interpreted. A concern about delay ought not to override the child's best interests and a concern about a technical breach of procedural rules by the adults should not be used to penalize a vulnerable child. In *Catholic Children's Aid Society of Toronto v. T.S.*, Justice Katarynych encouraged a rational and flexible approach to the *Family Law Rules*: "rules governing practice and procedure in the courts are *guidelines* for action, to be used in furtherance of procedural justice. They are not inflexible 'iron rails.'" [113]

The Ontario Court of Appeal also concluded that a breach of the timelines for resolving a case in the *Child and Family Services Act* does not cause a court to lose jurisdiction, provided that the order granted is otherwise consistent with the best interests of the child before the court. In this regard, the court noted:[114]

It is our view, however, that the delay in this case [i.e., 2 years in care without a protection finding] does not bring this matter outside the ambit of the legislation as contended by the appellants... [T]he court does not lose jurisdiction to proceed with a dispositional hearing beyond the stated time limit as long as it is guided in that regard by the best interests of the child... [T]he Act continues to be a complete code although the timelines contemplated by the act are exceeded. Such approach is consistent with the legislative scheme as a whole. When the Act is considered as a whole, it becomes clear that extended periods of care in a foster home, while unfortunate, do not fall outside the ambit of the legislation. What is important is that the time limits under the Act be given a construction consistent with the best interests of the child.

It is not uncommon in child protection cases for parents to consent to adjournments, hoping to use the time to try to deal with personal problems and improve their parenting capacity. But in some cases, the parents may want a trial as quickly as possible in order to have an opportunity to rebut the agency's allegations and regain care of their children. If there is an undue delay, there may be situations in which parents (or a child) may seek to invoke the *Charter*.

---

[113] [2002] O. J. 959 (Ont. C. J.) at para. 20.
[114] *L.(R.) v. Children's Aid Society of the Niagara Region*, [2002] O.J. 4793, 34 R.F.L. (5th) 64 (Ont. C.A.) at para. 46, per Weiler, Charron, Moldaver, JJ.A.

In *Winnipeg Child and Family Services v. K.L.W.*, the Supreme Court of Canada recognized that state intervention must "accord with the principles of fundamental justice." The majority judgement of Justice L'Heureux-Dubé raised concerns about the six-month delay in this case from apprehension to trial, suggesting that if the delay had not been with the mother's consent, for a newborn child such as in this case, a six-month delay "would have constituted an unacceptable violation" of the mother's *Charter* rights.[115] The Court was clearly concerned about the problem of systemic delay in child protection cases. Generally the appropriate *Charter* remedy for delay would be an expedited hearing, perhaps with an order for costs. It is submitted that the remedy of returning the child to parental care, perhaps under agency supervision, would only be appropriate if the court is satisfied that there is not a "serious risk of harm" from this course of action.[116]

The comments of Justice L'Heureux-Dubé in *K.L.W.* could also be used to argue that if a parent regains custody at trial, there is a strong claim for expecting the child to be returned to parental care (probably under agency supervision) pending any appeal by the child protection agency. While the Supreme Court accepted that the apprehension of a child without a warrant is a restraint on parental rights that can be justified by the need to protect children from the possible risk of abuse, there is no advantage to a child from delays in the court system that frustrate the right of parents and the interests of children to obtain a timely hearing about the child's future. Indeed, children often suffer as their cases "drift" through the court system.

Finding That a Child Is Not in Need of Protection

Dismissal of Protection Proceedings

If after hearing all of the evidence the court does not find that the child is "in need of protection," then the child protection proceeding must be dismissed.[117] In Ontario, where the child is found not to be in need of protection, then the court's single responsibility in the protection proceedings is to record that determination. If there is a dispute between the parents as to which one should be entitled to the return of the child, the Ontario Court of Justice, as a provincially constituted court without any inherent jurisdiction, would have no jurisdiction under the *Child and Family Services Act* to determine the issue of custody

---

[115] *Winnipeg Child and Family Services v. K.LW.*, [2000] 2 S.C.R. 519.

[116] See *obiter* comments in *J.W v. M.E.S.*, [2000] B.C.J. 371 (S.C.) about the possibility of interim return of a child to parental care if there is not clear evidence of risk to child.

[117] While several jurisdictions have child protection legislation authorizing a court to make a finding that a child is "not" in need of protection, only Nova Scotia, Saskatchewan and British Columbia explicitly refer to the possibility of a "dismissal": Nova Scotia, s. 40(5); Saskatchewan, s. 36(3); British Columbia, s. 40(2)(b). Where the relevant provincial child protection statute does not confer the explicit authority to dismiss protection proceedings, such authority is implied under other more general legislation or rules of court, which empower a court to control its own process, or alternatively, by invoking its *"parens patriae"* jurisdiction; in Ontario, see *Courts of Justice Act* R.S.O. 1990, c. C.43, s. 146. See *Catholic Children's Aid Society of Metropolitan Toronto v. B.(A.)* (1989), 22 R.F.L. (3d) 145 (Ont. Prov. Ct. — Fam. Div.).

between "parents."[118] However, in places where child protection cases are dealt with by a federally appointed judge in a Unified Family Court, such as Ontario's Family Court, a Judge may by virtue of the court's inherent *"parens patriae"* jurisdiction be able to make such a custodial determination at the same time as the dismissal of the child protection agency's protection application.

In those jurisdictions without specific direction as to what is supposed to happen to a child's placement subsequent to a finding that a child is not in need of protection or a dismissal of a protection application, it is presumed that the child would have to be returned to the person who last had custody of the child prior to the child protection agency's intervention, unless that arrangement has been supplanted by a contrary custody order. This is essentially the direction given, with minor variations, in the child protection legislation of Alberta, British Columbia, Newfoundland and Labrador, Prince Edward Island, Saskatchewan and the Yukon.[119]

Withdrawal and Discontinuation of Protection Proceedings

In the absence of clear statutory language to the contrary, it would seem that a child protection agency can unilaterally withdraw its protection application after apprehension but before the first court appearance. However, once the court has made an interim order and is "seized" with jurisdiction,[120] the child protection agency must bring a motion to seek a court order discontinuing or permitting the withdrawal of the protection proceedings, if the agency no longer wishes to obtain a protection finding.[121] The courts have held that they have an ongoing responsibility to supervise the discontinuance of a protection case. This ensures that there is a degree of agency accountability, and may, for example, allow the parents to seek an order that the agency reimburse them for legal costs as part of the discontinuance.

There must be proper evidence, usually filed in written form with the court, to support the discontinuation order; the material should explain why the child is not in need of protection. The consent of the parties alone is technically not sufficient to justify the granting of a discontinuance order, although such consent is likely to be significant.[122]

---

[118] *Courts of Justice Act*, R.S.O. 1990, c. C.43, s. 146. See also *Re A.B.D.* (1973), 10 R.F.L. 381 (Ont. Prov. Ct.).

[119] Alberta, s. 21(11); British Columbia, s. 40(2)(a); Newfoundland, s. 34(3); Prince Edward Island, s. 34(1); Saskatchewan, s. 36(3); Yukon, s. 126(2).

[120] The concept of a court being "seized" of a case refers to a court having the exclusive possession or responsibility for a case. A related but distinct notion is that a specific judge within a court may become "seized" of a case. For example once that judge has started to hear evidence in a trial, no other judge in that court may deal with that case until the trial is complete; if the judge who is "seized" with the case should be unable to complete the trial, another judge will need to restart the trial.

[121] *Re J.H.* (1983), 5 F.L.R.R. 153 (Ont. Prov. Ct.); *Weechi-it-te-win Child and Family Services v. M.(D.)*, [1992] 3 C.N.L.R. 165 (Ont. Prov. Div.). But see *Re S.P.* (1982), 5 F.L.R.R. 96 (Ont. Prov. Ct. — Fam. Div.), where the court ruled that a child protection agency can withdraw its request for a show cause hearing as well as a protection finding without the court's sanction.

[122] *Weechi-it-te-win Child and Family Services v. M.(D.)*, [1992] 3 C.N.L.R. 165 (Ont. Prov. Div.).

Only British Columbia, the Northwest Territories, Newfoundland and Saskatchewan have child protection legislation that explicitly provides for the "withdrawal" of a protection proceeding.[123] While most child protection legislation is silent as to the court's jurisdiction to allow a withdrawal or discontinuation of protection proceedings, such authority is implied[124] in more general legislation or rules of court, which enable a court to control its own process. In the Ontario case of *Catholic Children's Aid Society of Metropolitan Toronto v. B.(A.)*,[125] Judge Felstiner ruled as follows:

> With reference to s. 92 [now s. 146] of the *Courts of Justice Act*, and considering the failure of the *Child and Family Services Act* to provide for these normal, though occasional situations, I am of the opinion that the Provincial Court (Family Division) possesses a discretionary power to control its own process by permitting applications in child welfare matters to be discontinued or withdrawn....

> ...On a discontinuance it would not be up to the court to determine who would have custody of the child. Such a situation disturbs me in that it could leave the child immediately open to another contest over her custody, this one arising under the Ontario *Children's Law Reform Act*....

Dispositional Stage

In most child protection cases, the court, after hearing the evidence and arguments, will make a finding that a child is in need of protection. It is rare that the child protection agency does not have sufficient evidence to cross this threshold for a finding that the child meets the definitional requirements of being a child in need of protection. If this threshold is crossed, the court must determine, in accordance with the considerations set out in the statute, what dispositional order serves the child's "best interests." This is the aspect of child protection proceedings referred to as the disposition hearing or dispositional stage.

In Ontario, where a judge makes a finding of need for protection in respect of a child, that same judge is not seized for dispositional purposes, so long as the finding of need for protection was made without a trial (e.g., on consent or by motion for summary judgement).[126]

The types of dispositional orders that are available are set out in the legislation governing child protection in the province or territory. There are three basic types of dispositional orders available to protect a child:

- a supervision order;
- a temporary wardship order placing the child in the custody of the child protection agency for a limited period of time; or
- a permanent wardship order, placing the child "permanently" under the guardianship of the child protection agency.

---

[123] British Columbia, s. 48; Northwest Territories, s. 13(2); Newfoundland and Labrador, s. 47; Saskatchewan, *s. 25*.

[124] See discussion under "Dismissal of Protection Proceedings," above, p. 82.

[125] (1989), 22 R.F.L. (3d) 145 (Ont. Prov. Div.) at 150.

[126] Ontario, *Family Law Rules*, Rule 17(25).

Although the specific provisions which the court applies in making a dispositional order vary across jurisdictions, the basic issues are the same. The court must consider:

- the over-arching purposes of the legislation or statement of principles;
- the "best interests of the child," often defined in the legislation;
- any pre-conditions or statutory principles, including maximum duration of temporary orders; and
- the plans of care proposed by each party.

An initial disposition order is made following a finding that the child is in need of protection. Further dispositional orders may also be made in a subsequent proceeding for review of the child's status, which may take the form of an application for extension, variation or termination of protective intervention.

Types of Disposition Orders

Supervision Orders

A supervision order is the least intrusive form of child welfare intervention. A supervision order provides the least amount of disruption for the child and, where the child remains with his or her parents or previous caregivers, preserves the greatest degree of autonomy for the family.

A supervision order may place the child with parents, or with other relatives, like grandparents, who are willing to care for the child. The key to a supervision order is that the child protection agency "supervises" the placement of the child. Terms are generally attached to the order, and it is these specific conditions that serve to protect the child and to ensure that the child's needs are met. Any terms and conditions must be consistent with the plan of care for the child, and should support that plan.

Provincial statutes vary in the degree of detail they provide regarding orders of supervision. Generally speaking, conditions of a supervision order serve one or more of the following purposes:

- enabling the child protection agency to monitor the child's safety and well being through visits to the child's home and the receipt of information from others providing services;
- requiring the parents or caregivers to obtain specific services for themselves, and quite possibly for the child, with the goal of remedying the circumstances that resulted in the child being in need of protection; and
- ensuring or preventing contact with the child by a named person, or facilitating an assessment or the completion of an investigation.

Legislation in several jurisdictions explicitly states that a supervision order authorizes the child protection agency to enter the home where the child resides.[127] Where there is no specific statutory provision regarding the right of

---

[127] See, e.g., Manitoba, s.41(6) and Nova Scotia, s.43(2).

entry, it may be helpful to address the issue by way of a specific condition in the order, particularly if the evidence indicates a history of reluctance to co-operate on the part of the family. Although it may be implied by the court that "supervision" must of necessity include the ability to monitor the child's care, a parent upon whom the involvement of the child protection agency has been imposed may not find it so obvious, so the order should be explicit about the supervision and monitoring that is to occur.

The consequences of a breach of a condition of the terms of supervision will depend not only on the nature of the condition that was breached, but also on the result of the breach for the child. If the agency worker considers that the breach is relatively minor and does not endanger the child, the worker may caution the parent, and make a note of the breach for possible use in future court proceedings. If the worker considers that the breach is serious and that the child is at risk, the worker may apprehend the child and commence an application for judicial review of the supervisory order, with the objective of having it made into a wardship order.[128]

Supervision orders are generally limited to a maximum duration that ranges from six to twelve months, depending on the jurisdiction, though in many provinces an extension of a supervision on expiry of the initial order is possible. In British Columbia, the total period during which a child is under the director's supervision must not exceed twelve months, including the periods during which the child was under the director's supervision before being removed,[129] but this time limit does not apply when the child is in the custody of a person other than the parent.[130]

In a few provinces, including Ontario, legislation allows for a court to make an order for temporary wardship to the child protection agency to be followed immediately by a period of supervision.[131] This combination or "piggyback" order is used infrequently since it is rare that the parties or the court would have sufficient certainty about the happening of anticipated future events to predicate a court order on their occurrence.

Temporary Wardship Orders

Each province and territory has provisions for the temporary committal of a child in need of protection to the care of the child protection agency. These orders are variously called temporary care, temporary wardship, temporary custody or guardianship, and in some jurisdictions, Society wardship. The order removes the child from the care of his or her parents for a fixed period of time, with the expectation that, at the expiry of the order, the situation that required the child to come into care will have changed sufficiently to permit a return home or,

---

[128] There are explicit legislative provisions that deal with breach in British Columbia, s.42 and Manitoba, s.38(7). In B.C. the child protection agency may apprehend the child for breach of a condition only if such a condition is attached to the supervision order in the first instance.

[129] British Columbia, s. 44(3.1).

[130] *Ibid.*, s. 44(4).

[131] See, e.g., Ontario, s. 57(1)4; British Columbia, s. 41(1.1); and Nova Scotia, s. 42(1)(e).

in the alternative, more permanent planning for the child outside the family will be undertaken. This recognized need for stability and permanency planning for a child, particularly a young child, has led to the introduction of increasingly restrictive limits on the length of time children may be subject to temporary custody orders.

Statutory provisions set strict limits on the maximum length of each temporary custody order, ranging from three months[132] to twelve months,[133] and even to twenty-four months.[134] The length of the order that is made should be consistent with the plan of care for the child. From a practical standpoint, the order should be long enough to accomplish the purpose of the order, whether that be assessment or treatment for the child, or rehabilitation of the parents, but not so long as to result in drift or the creation of a status quo that is too difficult to overcome. Regular review by the court is important to ensure the plan is being carried out by the parents, as well as the child protection agency.

In some provinces, legislation explicitly allows a court to impose conditions on parents in a temporary custody order, for example requiring them to undertake drug or alcohol counselling.[135] In most provinces there is no statutory authority for placing conditions on parents while the child is not in their care, except in relation to the exercise of access, but the judge will often make clear that unless the parents take specified remedial steps to address their problems, when the matter comes back to court to be reviewed at the expiration of the temporary order, the court is unlikely to return the child to parental custody.

As discussed in Chapter 4, a child who is in the temporary custody of a child protection agency may be placed in a foster home or a group home, or even in some type of children's institution. It is also becoming increasingly common for agencies to try to find suitable relatives who can provide "kinship foster care" for temporary wards.

Permanent Wardship

The most intrusive order available, permanent wardship, removes a child from his or her family "permanently," or more accurately, for an indefinite period.[136] The label for this status varies, including permanent guardianship and Crown wardship. The intent of a permanent wardship order is to recognize that, if the parents are not willing or able to make and carry out a long-term plan to address the child's needs, the child protection agency must do so.

The effect of a permanent order is essentially that the state, through the child protection agency, becomes the legal guardian to the child. Upon the making of a permanent order, most parental rights and responsibilities for the child are

---

[132] For very young children in Nova Scotia, Newfoundland, and British Columbia, for example.

[133] For children of all ages in Ontario, s. 57(1) and Alberta, s. 28.

[134] For children of the age of 12 years or more in Manitoba, s. 38.

[135] For example, Newfoundland, s. 34(3).

[136] The order is not in reality "permanent," since all provinces have a mechanism for review of the "permanent" order, often at the instance of the child or access parent. See the section of this chapter on Status Reviews.

transferred to the child protection agency. This includes, for example, the right to consent to an adoption, and the right to make decisions about medical treatment.[137]

Permanency planning, especially for young children, is often achieved through adoption, and a permanent wardship order can be a vehicle for making a child available for adoption. In most Canadian jurisdictions, adoption is only possible if the court has also terminated the birth parents' right to access to the child.

For the child who is not adopted, and unless terminated earlier by the court, permanent wardship continues until the child reaches a defined age: 18 years in most jurisdictions, 19 years in others, 16 years in Newfoundland. Generally, the making of a permanent wardship order does not affect inheritance rights. Parents, particularly those with access orders or agreements, may also retain certain rights[138] and in particular the right to apply for a review or termination of the permanent guardianship.[139]

In some jurisdictions, a permanent wardship order may be a pre-requisite to the child being eligible to continue receiving service and financial support from the child welfare authorities into early adulthood.[140]

On a practical level, a permanent order is made when:

- the circumstances that require the child to be removed from the family are unlikely to change in the reasonable future; or

- the statutory time limits on temporary "in care" orders have already been exhausted.

In all jurisdictions permanent guardianship is intended to be the response of "last resort," though it is also clear that this order can be made at an initial hearing. Child protection statutes use various forms of language to direct the court to consider whether less restrictive or disruptive alternatives would be appropriate. However, this does not mean that other temporary orders must always have been attempted before a court imposes a permanent wardship.

Selecting the Dispositional Order

"Best Interests" of the Child

Legislation requires that a court make a decision about which disposition to order based on the "best interests of the child." The concept of "best interests" has a specific meaning in the context of protection proceedings, and does not

---

[137] In most provinces, the court may reserve the authority to consent to medical treatment to the parents during a temporary custody order, but not in the case of a permanent wardship.

[138] For example, rights to information or to participate in reviews of the plan of care for the child.

[139] See discussion of Status Reviews, below.

[140] In Ontario, a former Crown ward may continue to receive agency financial support and services to age 21, although the wardship itself terminates on the eighteenth birthday [Ontario, s. 71(2)]. Similar provisions exist in Prince Edward Island [s.37(7)], Saskatchewan [s.56] and British Columbia, [s.72] where the care and maintenance can continue to age 24 if the youth continues in school.

simply mean what is best for the child in absolute terms, but rather based on a balancing of rights, opportunities, values and the child's needs.

"Best interests of the child" is a concept that is not easily defined. Using this phrase has great political and symbolic appeal, but in practice it tends to give decision-makers a significant amount of discretion.[141] Most child protection statutes list factors that the court or any other decision maker is required to consider in making a determination "in the best interests" of a child.[142] The lists of considerations end with the catch-all: "any other relevant circumstance," or other language indicating that the list is not exhaustive. As noted by Justice L'Heureux-Dubé, writing for the Supreme Court of Canada in the 1994 decision in *Catholic Children's Aid Society of Metropolitan Toronto v. M.(C.):*[143]

> The wide focus of the best interests test encompasses an examination of the entirety of the situation and thus includes concerns arising from emotional harm, psychological bonding, and the child's desires....

Although the considerations that constitute "best interests" vary in the precise statutory language used across the country, there is more similarity than difference in essential areas. Child protection legislation in most jurisdictions makes reference to the following factors as constituting the "best interests" of the child:

- the child's level of development and needs, and the appropriate care to meet them;
- the child's cultural and religious background or ties;
- the child's family relationships;
- the importance of continuity for the child and the effect of disruption of that continuity; and
- the child's views and wishes.

Many provinces and territories explicitly require the decision-maker to consider the merits of the plans proposed by the child protection authority and the parents or others in making best interests decisions.[144] Even where legislation is silent, the reality is that a best interests decision is comparative: a judge is not permitted to develop the "best" possible plan for the child, but is limited to choosing between the plans put forward by the agency and the other parties.

Legislation in Ontario, Alberta and Nova Scotia explicitly includes consideration of the risk of harm to the child if the child remains with, is removed from, or is returned to the family, and in British Columbia and Newfoundland the child's "safety" is an explicit "best interests" factor. Even where legislation is

---

[141] See N. Bala, "The Best Interests of the Child in the Post-Modern Era: A Central but Paradoxical Concept," in H. Niman and G. Sadvari (Eds.), *Family Law: The Best Interests of the Child — Special Lectures 2000* (Toronto: Law Society of Upper Canada, 2001), 1-77.

[142] The factors to be included in considering "best interests" are set out in the following provisions: Alberta, s. 2; British Columbia, s. 4(1); Manitoba, s. 2; New Brunswick, s. 1; Newfoundland, s. 9; Northwest Territories, s. 3; Nova Scotia, s. 3(2); Ontario, s. 37(3); Prince Edward Island, s. 1(1)(d); Saskatchewan, s. 4; Yukon, s. 30.

[143] *Catholic Children's Aid Society of Metropolitan Toronto v. M.(C.),* [1994] 2 S.C.R. 165, para. 38.

[144] Alberta, Manitoba, New Brunswick, Nova Scotia, Ontario, Saskatchewan, Yukon, and Northwest Territories.

not explicit, consideration of risk and safety are important factors in making best interests decisions in child protection cases.

The question of which of the factors are relevant, and how they will be weighed, depends on the circumstances of each child and family. The balancing of the various factors takes place within the broader context of the principles or purposes section of the legislation. In 1994 the Supreme Court of Canada in *M.(C.)* observed:[145]

> Equal competition between parents and the Children's Aid Society is not supported by the construction of the Ontario legislation. Essentially...the Act has as one of its objectives the preservation of the autonomy and integrity of the family unit and that the child protection services should operate in the least restrictive and disruptive manner, while at the same time recognizing the paramount objective of protecting the best interests of children....

The Ontario legislation was amended in 2000[146] to emphasize that the paramount purpose of the *Act* is to promote the best interests, protection and well-being of children, and that the other stated purposes (supporting the autonomy and integrity of the family unit, considering options that are least disruptive for the child, and providing services on the basis of mutual consent where possible, for example) exist only insofar as they "are consistent with the best interests, protection and well being of children."[147] The legislation in New Brunswick has also been amended in recent years to place less emphasis on family preservation and ensure that the focus is on the best interests of the child.[148]

While these legislative changes remind social workers and judges of the importance of protecting the safety of children, there continues to be an onus on child protection agencies to establish their case, and the application of the "best interests" test continues to require consideration of the importance of a child's family ties and cultural heritage.

Maximum Duration of Temporary Care

In addition to the best interests test, in most jurisdictions there are statutory time limits which restrict the time that a child can be in "temporary care," and require that, after a certain time, the court make a decision to return the child to family care or make the child a permanent ward. The time limits recognize the need for permanency planning for children, and are intended to ensure that children do not "drift" indefinitely in temporary care with no clear direction for their future. Across North America, one of the trends in child welfare law in the

---

[145] *Catholic Children's Aid Society of Metropolitan Toronto v. M.(C.)*, [1994] 2 S.C.R. 165 at para. 36.

[146] *Child and Family Services Amendment Act (Child Welfare Reform)*, S.O. 1999, c.12.

[147] Ontario, s. 1, as amended.

[148] In *New Brunswick Minister of Health and Community Services v. J.F. and D.E.*, [1999] N.B.J. 591 (N.B.Q.B.) Justice Athey wrote: "In child protection proceedings the court must place above all other considerations the best interests of the child." See s. 53(2) of the *Family Services Act*. That principle has been bolstered by a recent amendment to the Preamble and the repeal of s. 2, which formerly read: "This Act shall be liberally construed to the end that the integrity of the family will be protected and family breakdown averted."

1990s was the enactment of laws that shortened the duration of time that children could spend in temporary care, with a view to having permanent decisions made sooner.[149]

As noted in the 1998 Ontario *Report of the Panel of Experts on Child Protection*:[150]

> The younger the child, the more urgent is the need for permanence. Experts in the field advise that it is vital for children to form a meaningful, long-term relationship with at least one person. If children do not do so, they are likely to suffer serious developmental harm. Therefore, it is imperative that young children are placed in a permanent setting as soon as possible.

This report resulted in Ontario reducing the maximum duration in temporary care for children under the age of six years from 24 months to 12 months in order to ensure that decisions for infants could be made at an early stage in their lives, allowing them to bond with permanent caregivers.[151] While the imposition of shorter time limits has advantages in terms of permanency planning for children, it has also meant that parents have had to address their problems, like drug addiction, much more quickly if they are to have a hope of regaining custody of their children. This can be very challenging for parents, especially in an environment in which many social service and treatment supports that can assist parents in dealing with their problems have lengthy waiting lists.

All provinces and territories have a statutory limit on the length of time a child can be subject to temporary orders. The provisions vary, and in this regard no two jurisdictions are exactly alike. In many jurisdictions, the limit is on the court's ability to make a temporary wardship order that would result in the child being in the care of the state for a period in excess of the stated maximum.[152]

In some jurisdictions, the time limits are on the total length of time protective intervention orders, including supervision orders, can be in place. For example, in Nova Scotia, the maximum total time permitted for *all* dispositional orders for a child under the age of six at the time of commencement of the proceedings is 12 months; 18 months if the child is between six and twelve years of age when the proceedings are commenced.

Ontario's time limits now not only differentiate between children under the age of six years (12-month maximum temporary wardship) and those six years or older (24-month maximum), but count all periods in care, whether by court order or agreement, on a cumulative basis. The clock is, however, "reset" any time there is a continuous period of five years during which the child has not been in care of a child protection agency.[153]

---

[149] C. Ross, "The Tyranny of Time: Vulnerable Children, 'Bad Mothers,' and Statutory Deadlines in Parental Termination Proceedings" (Dec. 2003), 11 *Virginia Journal of Social Policy & the Law* 176-228.

[150] M.J. Hatton et al., *Report of the Panel of Experts on Child Protection* (Toronto: Ontario Ministry of Community and Social Services, 1998) at 25.

[151] *Child and Family Services Amendment Act (Child Welfare Reform)*, S.O. 1999, c. 2, s. 21.

[152] For example Ontario, New Brunswick, Alberta, and British Columbia.

[153] Ontario, s. 70.

Many, but not all, jurisdictions have a provision permitting the court some discretion to extend the maximum limits on temporary orders "in the best interests of the child." In Ontario, for example, judges have a discretion to extend the maximum statutory periods by six months "if it is in the child's best interests to do so."[154] Further, even in the absence of specific statutory provision, there are cases where a court has extended the statutory time limits by invoking s. 7 of the *Charter of Rights* because it was felt that the "rigidity" of the legislation prevented a decision from being made that was consistent with the "best interests" of the child.[155]

Whatever the statutory limits on duration of temporary custody, it is important to remember that they speak to the *maximum* periods for which temporary orders can be made. Provided that the other dispositional principles are followed, and the child's best interests would be served, a permanent plan not only may, but *should* be made sooner.

Dispositional Principles

Statutory Provisions: Dispositional Guidance or Statutory Pre-Conditions?

In addition to the best interests "test," the over-arching purposes of the legislation, and the limitations on temporary orders which narrow the available options, most provincial and territorial statutes contain other provisions that provide direction for the courts in making a dispositional order. These specific provisions generally require consideration of placements with relatives or in the community before a child is placed in the care of an agency, and are often stated in language that suggests that this type of consideration is a precondition to the making of a more intrusive order.

In British Columbia, for example, the court must not order that the child be placed in the "continuing" (permanent) custody of the director unless:[156]

(a) the identity or location of a parent of the child has not been found after a diligent search and is not likely to be found;

(b) a parent is unable or unwilling to resume custody of the child; or

(c) the nature and extent of the harm the child has suffered or the likelihood that the child will suffer harm is such that there is little prospect it would be in the child's best interests to be returned to the parent.

In Ontario, the court shall not make an order removing the child from the care of the person who had charge of the child immediately before intervention "unless the court is satisfied that alternatives that are less disruptive to the child,

---

[154] For example, Ontario, s. 70(4); British Columbia, s. 45(1.1); Newfoundland, s. 36(2) which makes reference to exceptional circumstances.

[155] *Re R.A.J.*, [1992] Y.J. No. 126 (Y.T. Terr. Ct.); see also discussion in N. Bala, "The Charter of Rights and Family Law In Canada" (2001), 18 *Canadian Family Law Quarterly*, 373 at 413-416.

[156] British Columbia, s. 41(2).

including non-residential services…would be inadequate to protect the child."[157] Further, before making a child a temporary or permanent ward, the court shall consider "whether it is possible to place the child with a relative, neighbour or other member of the child's community or extended family" under a supervision order.[158]

In Nova Scotia the child protection legislation specifies that:[159]

> The court shall not make an order removing the child from the care of a parent or guardian unless the court is satisfied that less intrusive [community based] alternatives, including services to promote the integrity of the family…
>
> (a)   have been attempted and failed;
>
> (b)   have been refused by the parent or guardian; or
>
> (c)   would be inadequate to protect the child.

There are two different judicial approaches to the interpretation of statutory provisions that are intended to encourage the least restrictive alternative intervention with a child. One interpretation is that these provisions are merely "dispositional guidelines" in order to assist the court in making a best interests determination. The other approach to interpretation is that the principles are statutory pre-conditions or "pathways," which must be considered by the court even before it considers the child's "best interests" in an absolute sense.[160]

Consider, for example, the following provision, which appears in both the Ontario and Nova Scotia legislation:

> Where the court decides that it is necessary to remove the child from the care of the person who had charge of him or her immediately before intervention under this part, the court shall, before making an order for Society [temporary] or Crown [permanent] Wardship…consider whether it is *possible* to place the child with a relative, neighbour or other member of the child's community or extended family…with the consent of the relative or other person.[161]

The Nova Scotia Court of Appeal concluded that this provision is only intended to remind judges of the value of placement with relatives or in the child's community, without restricting the court's broad discretion to determine what is in the child's best interests:[162]

> The word "possible" must be read in the context of the whole of the Act and in a fashion consistent with the stated purposes of the Act.…
>
> Extended family as a placement alternative is desirable and consistent with the Act, as is support for families and alternatives that minimize the intrusiveness of these actions. Any placement alternative, however, must be considered in the context of the needs and best interests of the child.

---

[157] Ontario, s. 7(2).

[158] Ontario, s. 57(4).

[159] Nova Scotia, s. 42(2).

[160] M. Bernstein and L. Kirwin, *Child Protection Practice and Procedure* (Toronto: Carswell, 1997) at 100-102.

[161] Ontario, s. 57(3); Nova Scotia, s. 42(3), emphasis added.

[162] Nova Scotia Court of Appeal in *Nova Scotia Minister of Community Services v. C.(D.L.)* (1995), 138 N.S.R. (2d) 241, 395 A.P.R. 241 (C.A.).

Section 3(2) defines security and relationships as a consideration in determining the
child's best interests, not an overriding trump to the child's best interests.

An Ontario appeal court concluded that this same language provides much
greater direction to judges, placing a greater priority on placements with relatives or in the community:

> It is to be observed that the statute mandates and prioritizes the pathway to be fol-
> lowed in keeping with its recognition of the importance of keeping a family unit
> together as a means of fostering the best interests of children. Any deviation from
> this pathway that does not carefully and properly examine and consider the less
> restrictive alternatives preferred...and the extended family or community place-
> ments possible...prior to any consideration of Crown Wardship must be fatal to such
> application.[163]

The Plan of Care

Many jurisdictions require that the child protection agency present a written
"plan of care" for the court to consider before making a dispositional order.[164]
Parents are also encouraged to file a proposal for the care of a child, but they are
not obliged to do so.

Some statutes require that specifically itemized issues be addressed in the
agency plan. In both Ontario and Nova Scotia, the plan filed by the child protection agency must include:[165]

- a description of the services to be provided to the child and parents to help
  remedy the circumstances that caused the child to be found in need of protection;
- the criteria by which the agency will determine when an order will no longer be required;
- an estimate of the time required to achieve the purposes of the intervention; and
- where the child is removed from the care of the parents, the reasons why
  the child cannot be adequately protected in the parents' care; what arrangements will be made to maintain contact; and, if the removal is intended to
  be permanent, what arrangements are being made for the child's long-term
  stable placement.

Making decisions about the "best interests" of a child is an exercise in
predicting the outcome or future consequences of a decision for the child, and
achieving the best disposition requires that the decision maker has available as

---

[163] L.(R.) v. Children's Aid Society of Metropolitan Toronto (1995), 21 O.R. (3d) 724 (Gen. Div.).

[164] Newfoundland, s. 31, requires the child protection agency to file a plan and other parties to prepare a response
or alternate plan; Ontario [s.56] and Nova Scotia [s.41(3)] require that the court consider a written plan from
the child protection agency. In British Columbia, before making a continuing custody (permanent
guardianship) order, the court must consider, inter alia, the plan of care [s.49(6)(b)].

[165] Ontario, s. 56; Nova Scotia, s. 41(3); British Columbia, s. 2 and 3.

much information as possible about the options for the child.[166] A plan of care provides much-needed information to the court, and may help the court understand what the agency is offering the child and family. It also enables the court to hold the agency and parents accountable when a dispositional order is the subject of a later judicial review. Courts have been critical of agency plans of care that are "minimalist documents" or which provide insufficient detail.[167]

Special Considerations Where the Child Is Aboriginal

While a full examination of child protection issues regarding Canada's Aboriginal children is beyond the scope of this chapter, it is important to note that in many jurisdictions there are special provisions that apply to a child who is found to be Indian, native or Aboriginal.[168] These provisions reflect concerns about the very high rate at which Aboriginal children have been taken into care, as well as the unique constitutional and political status of Canada's Aboriginal peoples.

These special provisions affect the dispositional stage in several ways. A number of jurisdictions recognize the unique status of Aboriginal peoples in the statutory statement of principles.[169] Some jurisdictions list as a special factor a child's Aboriginal heritage in the best interests considerations.[170] There may also be specific dispositional considerations in the statute that apply where a child has been found to be Indian or native.[171]

While the establishment of child welfare agencies and programs for Aboriginal families and children has had a profound effect on the practices of child welfare agencies, in cases that are brought before the courts, judges have only given limited weight to a child's Aboriginal heritage, generally concluding that Aboriginal status does not of itself override other "best interests" factors.[172] Considerations of Aboriginal culture and heritage become subsumed in the "best interests test," and are weighed along with all relevant factors, especially for children who have been in care for a significant period of time.

---

[166] B. Walter, J.A. Isenegger, and N. Bala, "Best Interests in Child Protection Proceedings: Implications and Alternatives" (1995), 12 Canadian Journal of Family Law 367-439 at 389.

[167] See e.g., Children's Aid Society of Bruce (County) v. R.(T.), [2001] O.J. 5571 (Ont. Ct. J.), per Brophy J.

[168] Most jurisdictions have provisions for notice to the child's native community or Indian band where a protection proceeding is commenced or an order made, as well as other rights at the interim and protection finding stages. See Chapter 7 for a fuller discussion of the issues raised here.

[169] See, e.g., Ontario, s. 1(2)5.

[170] For example, in Ontario, "Where a person is directed…to make an order or determination in the best interests of a child and the child is an Indian or native person, the person shall take into consideration the importance, in recognition of the uniqueness of Indian and native culture, heritage and traditions, of preserving the child's cultural identity" [s.37(4)].

[171] Ontario, s. 57(5).

[172] See e.g., D.H. v. H.M., [1999] 1 S.C.R. 328, further reasons at 761; Catholic C.A.S. v. A.V.W., [2002] O.J. 1512 (C.A.); Alberta (Director of Child Welfare) v. G.N., [2002] A.J. 1609 (Q.B.); and Algonquins of Pikwakanagan v. C.A.S. of Toronto, [2004] O.J. 1740 (Sup. Ct.).

Ancillary Orders

Access Orders: Temporary Wards

If a child is made a temporary or permanent agency ward, the court will have to make a determination concerning access by or to the child. An access order must always be considered in relation to the persons who were caring for the child prior to intervention, and may also arise in relation to other persons, including siblings.

Implicit in a determination that a temporary custody order is in the child's best interests is the expectation that the child may, upon expiry of the order, return to his or her previous caregivers. Many jurisdictions have therefore legislated a presumption that a child in the temporary care of the child protection agency will have access with the parent. Continued involvement with the family is likely to be important if the child is to be successfully reunited with his or her family, though of course it does not guarantee a return to the care of the family.

While child protection legislation allows for access, and in some jurisdictions creates presumptions about whether access will occur, the legislation does not deal with the sometimes contentious issue of the terms on which access will occur. The agency may, for example, have concerns about the possibility that the parents may intimidate or even abduct the children during a visit, and want any contact between the child and parents to be supervised by a social worker. Supervised access, however, may be quite unnatural and is difficult to arrange, and hence will be for at most a couple of hours a week. Parents will invariably want unsupervised access.

Access visits may be very important for both children and parents, but there can be problems associated with access. Sometimes children will be very much looking forward to seeing their parents, but the parents fail to attend for an arranged visit, or may arrive for the visit obviously intoxicated and the agency staff or foster parents will feel obliged to cancel the visit. In some cases the children will be placed in a foster home far from the parents, and the parents, who may have very limited financial resources, may find that they can only afford the occasional visit.

In some cases the court will simply direct that the agency and parents will work out what access will occur; the parents may have a good relationship with the children and foster parents, and it may be best for the children to have a flexible approach to access. In other cases, however, the parents and agency staff may have a strained relationship, or there may be concerns about parental conduct during access visits, and the court may feel that it is necessary to set out the duration, frequency, location and degree of supervision of visits. In Ontario, it has also been accepted that the court has jurisdiction to make an order for parental access which grants discretion over its terms to the child protection agency.[173]

---

[173] *H.(C.) v. Durham Children's Aid Society*, [2003] O.J. 879 (Ont. Div. Ct.).

A statutory presumption in favour of (or against) access is only a presumption, and the real test for making an access order is the best interests of the child. While it is understandable that children who miss their parents may be upset after an access visit, if access seems frightening or disturbing to a child, a motion may be brought by the agency to terminate access.

Access to Permanent Wards: The Relationship between Access and Adoption

In most provinces there is a statutory presumption that if a child is made a permanent ward, there will not be any access between a child and the birth family. This is because in most jurisdictions, an outstanding order for access to the birth family is a legal impediment to making an adoption order, and adoption is considered the preferred option for a permanent plan of care, especially for young children.

In Alberta, the court shall not make an order for access between the child who is a permanent ward and a parent unless the court "is satisfied that the access provided by the order will not interfere with the adoption of the child."[174] In Manitoba, the child protection agency has discretion over what, if any, access to provide to parents of permanent wards; dissatisfied parents may apply to the court for a determination of access, but no such application can be made where the child has been placed for adoption.[175]

In Nova Scotia, when making an order for permanent guardianship, the court shall not make an order for access unless: [176]

- the child is at least 12 years old and wants to maintain contact with that person;
- the child is placed with a person who does not wish to adopt, permanent placement in a family setting has not been planned or is not possible, and the person's access will not impair the child's future opportunities for such placement; or
- some other special circumstance justifies the making of an access order.

Until 2000, Ontario's child protection statute used language similar to that in Nova Scotia to define the circumstances in which the presumption against access to permanent wards could be rebutted. The focus on adoptability and adoption planning has now been replaced by the statutory direction that the court shall not order access to a permanent ward unless it is satisfied that:[177]

(a) the relationship between the person and the child is beneficial and meaningful to the child; and

(b) the ordered access will not impair the child's future opportunities for a permanent or stable placement.

---

[174] Alberta, s. 35(12).

[175] Manitoba, ss. 39(3), 35(4) and 39(6).

[176] Nova Scotia, s. 47(2).

[177] Ontario, s. 59(2).

Where there is a statutory presumption against access to a permanent ward, the person seeking access bears the onus of rebutting the statutory presumption.[178] Of course, if the child has a close emotional attachment to the parents and the agency does not plan to place a child for adoption, the agency may support permanent wardship with access and, if the agency supports this, the court will invariably accede to this plan.

In British Columbia, where the legislation allows for "open adoption," an outstanding access order does not automatically operate to prevent an adoption order from being made. In some circumstances, a court may make an order for access to a child in the "continuing custody" (permanent wardship) of the protection authorities if access is consistent with the wishes of the child who is 12 years old or more and with the agency's plan of care.[179] New Brunswick also allows for the preservation of a right of access even after adoption.[180]

Access between siblings is an emerging issue in some jurisdictions, particularly where an adoption plan is being considered for one child and not for others in the same family, or when separate adoption plans are in the individual best interests of two or more siblings. In jurisdictions where there is no statutory authority for adoption concurrent with access to the birth family, some judges have engaged in creative interpretations of statutory provisions in well-meaning attempts to give children both a relationship with birth siblings and the permanency of adoptive placement.[181]

In jurisdictions where there is no option that would provide both the permanency of adoption and the opportunity for ongoing court-ordered contact with the birth family, courts increasingly express frustration with the inflexible options provided by the law, which at times requires choosing not so much the "best" option, as the least detrimental alternative. As noted in one Ontario case:[182]

> It is necessary to ask whether the risks of emotional and behavioural difficulties inherent in terminating R's access to his family members outweigh the benefits of placement in a permanent, stable, secure adoptive home. The *Child and Family Services Act* does not permit orders of access to continue after adoption. This is indeed unfortunate for children such as R.

The question of adoption with access and more openness in adoption remains controversial; there have already been significant changes in some jurisdictions,

---

[178] *Catholic Children's Aid Society of Metropolitan Toronto v. M.(C.)*, [1994] 2 S.C.R. 165 at para. 46, interpreting the rebuttable presumption in the Ontario *Child and Family Services Act.*

[179] British Columbia, s. 56(3).

[180] See *Nouveau Brunswick (Ministre de la sante & des services communautaires) v. L.(M.)* (1998), 41 RFL (4th) 339 (S.C.C.).

[181] See *Children's Aid Society of Oxford County and T.M., C.M. and G.B.*, (unreported) October 21, 1999, Schnall, J. (Ontario Court of Justice); also *P.(M.A.R.) (Litigation Guardian of) v. Catholic Children's Aid Society of Metropolitan Toronto* (1998), 40 R.F.L. (4th) 411 (Ont. C.A.).

[182] *Children's Aid Society of Ottawa v. D.K.*, [2002] O.J. 2843 (Ont. Sup. Ct.) per Blishen J. at para. 54.

and there is advocacy for reform in those jurisdictions where the present statutory scheme does not support such openness.[183]

Restraining Orders

Restraining orders (also known in some jurisdictions as "protective intervention" orders) can be made to ensure that a specific person not have contact with a child. Such an order may, for example, be made if there are concerns about a parent contacting a child who is a ward while the child is at school, perhaps upsetting the child or even attempting to pressure the child into retracting allegations of abuse.

Child protection legislation in most Canadian jurisdictions allows for restraining orders to be made.[184] In most jurisdictions such an order may be made at any point in the proceedings, but in Ontario the court may only make such an order after the child has been found in need of protection.[185] A restraining order may prohibit all contact, or may, for example, specify that a parent is to have no contact with the child while the child is in a foster home or at school, but may have supervised visitation at agency offices.

It is an offence under the statute for a person who is the subject of a restraining order to violate the order. Even in the absence of a restraining order, child protection legislation in most jurisdictions specifies that it is an offence for any person to take away a child who is in agency care, or to "harbour" a child in agency care who has run away from a placement. Further, even without a restraining order, a parent or other person who abducts or harbours a child who is in agency care is committing a criminal offence,[186] and the police are likely to be involved in such situations.

Payment Orders

Most child protection statutes also provide for payment (or maintenance) orders to require parents who are able to do so to contribute to the cost of care while the child is in the care of the child protection agency or residing with some other person under a child protection supervision order. Some jurisdictions have a mandatory provision requiring the court to at least consider making an order for payment of support when a temporary custody order is made.[187] In other jurisdictions, there is statutory authority to make payment orders, but no requirement to consider doing so in every case.[188] The statutory provisions generally set out the factors to be taken into account in determining whether to

---

[183] See discussion in Chapter 6.

[184] Alberta, s. 30; British Columbia, s. 98; Manitoba, s. 20; New Brunswick, s. 58; Newfoundland, s. 21; Nova Scotia, s. 30; Ontario, s. 80; Saskatchewan, s. 16. In Prince Edward Island it is an offence to visit or communicate with a child when requested not to by the director or the agency.

[185] Ontario, s. 80.

[186] *Criminal Code*, R.S.C. 1985, chap. C-46, ss. 280-286.

[187] Manitoba, s. 38(3); New Brunswick, s. 55(5).

[188] See, e.g., Prince Edward Island, s. 36(4); Newfoundland, s. 35; Yukon, s. 134; Ontario, s. 60, Nova Scotia, s. 52.

make a payment order, and frequently provide that orders made are enforceable in the same manner as payment orders under the general child support or maintenance legislation applicable in the jurisdiction.

In Ontario, at least, payment orders are not common since most parents in child protection cases have very limited financial resources, and often are on social assistance. Further, if the agency requests such an order, it may exacerbate its relationship with the parents. However, such orders may be sought where parents have sufficient resources, especially if the children are older and it seems that the parents are in effect "dumping" their troubled child into agency care.

Costs Orders

As a general rule in Canada, in ordinary civil litigation, a party who is successful at trial is entitled to an order that the unsuccessful party pay "costs," that is reimburse the successful party for some or even all of the legal fees and expenses incurred. This rule is intended to at least partially reduce the burden on a party who must hire a lawyer and pursue litigation in order to secure its legal rights. The rule also serves to discourage litigation by those who have weak legal claims.

There is some reluctance in courts to award costs in family law disputes between parents, as there is a recognition that parents who cannot agree about their children's future should not be penalized with a costs order for bringing their dispute before a judge to decide what is in their child's best interests. There is even greater reluctance to award costs in child protection cases.

Parents involved in child protection cases are facing the loss of custody and, perhaps, the termination of their relationship with their children, as well as litigation against a state agency with seemingly infinite resources (in comparison to the parents). Given the emotional stakes and the resource imbalance, it is virtually unheard of for a child protection agency in Canada to seek an order for costs against parents, even if the parents take a case to court without any reasonable prospect of success.

It is common for parents to feel that child protection agency actions are unjustified, and if their position is vindicated by a court ruling, to seek compensation for the expenses that they have incurred in securing a judgement. However, child protection agencies in fact have limited resources, and have a duty to take reasonable measures to protect children. As a result, legislation and judicial decisions generally only permit parents to recover costs in cases in which the agency is found to have been unreasonable or unfair in its handling of a case.

Statutory reference to costs orders in relation to child protection proceedings is found only in the legislation of Saskatchewan and the Yukon. In Saskatchewan, the court may order costs in respect of an application to review the status of a child against any party except the child protection agency,[189] presumably in

---

[189] Saskatchewan, s. 39(5).

an effort to forestall frivolous applications. In the Yukon, no order for costs can be made in respect of a child protection proceeding.[190]

In some other jurisdictions the issue of costs may be addressed in the rules of court.[191] In Ontario, for example, the *Family Law Rules* exclude child protection proceedings from the general presumption that costs follow success, yet give the court the discretion to order costs.

The jurisprudence with respect to costs in child protection cases recognizes that neither the child protection agency nor the other parties are ordinary litigants. Agencies have a statutory mandate to protect children, while parents have a right to take a position on whether their children need protection and defend that position in court.[192] Judges have generally been of the view that an award of costs against a child protection agency requires "extraordinary" or "exceptional" circumstances.[193] This is because child protection authorities are required by statute to discharge certain enumerated responsibilities, and there is a general principle that the state is presumed to be acting in good faith. There is also a concern that imposing cost liability may disincline child protection agencies from bringing to court cases where a child may genuinely be at risk but there may be problems in proving this.[194]

In one Ontario case, Justice Katarynch neatly distilled the principles that apply when a court is deciding whether to award costs against a Children's Aid Society:[195]

> The essential test for the appropriateness of an award of costs against the society is *whether the Society should be perceived by ordinary persons as having acted fairly.*
>
> An ordinary person perceives a Society as having acted fairly in the following circumstances:
>
> (a) Before launching a court proceeding, the Society has undertaken a thorough investigation on allegations or evidence of a child's need for protection;
>
> (b) As part of its thoroughness, the Society has recognized and acted on its duty to look beyond an allegation for corroboration or independent evidence of it;
>
> (c) As part of its thoroughness, the Society, mindful of its duty...to ensure that children and parents have an opportunity, where appropriate, to be heard and represented when decisions affecting their interests are made, has interviewed the person who is alleged to have created the need for protective intervention, invited that person to have counsel involved, permitted that person an opportunity to reply to the allegation, and then

---

[190] Yukon, s. 157.

[191] For example, Ontario, *Family Law Rules*, Rule 24.

[192] See *New Brunswick (Minister of Health and Community Services) v. G.(J.)*, [1999] 3 S.C.R. 46.

[193] See *Winnipeg Child and Family Services v. H.(A.M.)* (2002), 24 R.F.L. (5th) 109 (Man. C.A.).

[194] For further discussion of litigation costs in child protection see J. Wilson, *Wilson on Children and the Law*, *supra* note 62 at 3.101–3.107, and M. Orkin, *The Law of Costs*, looseleaf, 2d ed., (Toronto: Canada Law Book Inc., 2001) at 2-87–2-92.

[195] *Children's Aid Society of Waterloo Region v. Z.B.*, [1996] O.J. 4245 (Ont. Prov. Div.) at para. 7.

    weighed the competing versions for their likely reliability and credibility — before the society proceeds to "validate" the allegation and draw the unequivocal conclusion that the need for protection exists;

(d)   The Society has demonstrated its openness to any version of the events that is offered, including the version offered by the person against whom the allegation is made;

(e)   As part of its thoroughness, the Society has been alert to rancour that might reasonably be animating the allegations;

(f)   The Society has reassessed its position as more information becomes available, even if a court hearing is in session at the time; in short, it has continued its investigation up to the time of a final court determination of the alleged need for protection, and done so in a vigorous professional manner;

(g)   The Society has investigated all pieces of relevant information, not just those pieces for which there is uncontroverted proof; and

(h)   The Society's good faith will not relieve it of an award of costs against it. It will, however, preclude an award of costs other than in accordance with the normal tariff.

While it is clear that, where permitted by law, judges may hold child welfare agencies liable in costs, they will only do so when they want to "send a message" that agency staff or their counsel have handled a case poorly.

Status Reviews

Mandatory Review

Although orders for supervision and temporary custody are time-limited in all jurisdictions, only Ontario and Nova Scotia provide for mandatory court reviews before the expiry of these time-limited orders to determine whether the orders should be continued, modified or terminated.[196] The statutory language in all other jurisdictions is permissive ("may" hold a hearing), suggesting that, if those entitled to commence a discretionary review choose not to return the matter to court, the order simply comes to an end once the period of time for which it was made expired.

Most jurisdictions require the child protection agency to bring an application for review where a child who is subject to a supervision order is taken into care by the agency.

Discretionary Review

All jurisdictions provide for access to the court by the child protection agency during the course of a supervision order or a temporary wardship order. There is usually no limit on the agency's ability to bring an application for review, reflecting the child protection agency's statutory duties, including the duty to ensure that children are both safe and in a placement that promotes their best

---

[196] Ontario, s. 64(2)(b); Nova Scotia, s. 46(1).

interests. These mandated duties require an ability to bring matters back before the court as circumstances change.

Most statutes also provide for the ability of parents or caregivers and children to bring the matter back before the court,[197] although generally attaching conditions to the right of these persons to apply for review.[198]

In a number of jurisdictions,[199] the review by the court involves some consideration of whether the child "continues to be in need of protection,"[200] whether the circumstances that caused the child to be in need of protection have changed,"[201] or "whether the child would be in need of protection if returned to the parent or guardian."[202]

On a review, the court generally can make any order that could be made after an initial finding that a child is "in need for protection," subject to the statutory time limits on temporary orders, which may require that if "time has run out" a permanent order is to be made if the child is not returned to parental care. In addition, the court may order that intervention is to be terminated.

The "Test" on Review of a Dispositional Order

The Supreme Court of Canada considered the statutory test on status review applications under the Ontario *Child and Family Services Act* in *Catholic Children's Aid Society of Metropolitan Toronto v. M.(C)*. The case involved a child who was taken into agency care at about the age of two and a half because her mother, who was a single parent suffering from a mental illness, was unable to adequately care for her. The initial four-month temporary wardship order was made with consent. After a period of temporary wardship orders, the agency sought to have a permanent wardship order made with no access to the mother so that the child could be adopted by the foster parents, to whom she had become emotionally attached. The trial judge stated that he was "not concerned with the 'best interests' of the child," but only with whether she continued to be a child in need of protection. The trial judge felt that the mother had sufficiently recovered to the point that she could resume care of the child. The agency appealed, and the case eventually was decided by the Supreme Court of Canada. The child remained in the care of the foster parents throughout the appeal process. By the time the case was resolved by the Supreme Court, the child had spent five years in the care of the foster parents who wanted to adopt her and was closely bonded

---

[197] Prince Edward Island and Newfoundland appear to limit the right to bring an application for review of a supervision order or a temporary custody order to the director.

[198] Alberta: parent or child age 12 or older may apply once during any order; New Brunswick, Nova Scotia, and Ontario: parent or child, after six months has elapsed from making of the order; in Ontario, six months after an order was made or in the event of material non-compliance with the plan of care (s.64).

[199] Review proceedings are referred to by various titles, including "further hearings" in Manitoba and "status review" hearings in Ontario.

[200] Saskatchewan, s. 38.

[201] Alberta, s. 32(2).

[202] Manitoba, s. 40.

with them; she had rarely seen her mother in the previous five years and wanted to be adopted by the foster parents. The Supreme Court concluded:[203]

> The question as to whether the grounds which prompted the original order still exist and whether the child continues to be in need of state protection must be canvassed at the status review hearing.... Equal competition between parents and the Children's Aid Society is not supported by the construction of the Ontario legislation.
>
> ...the examination that must be undertaken on a status review is a twofold examination. The first one is concerned with whether the child continues to be in need of protection and, as a consequence, requires a court order for his or her protection. The second is a consideration of the best interests of the child, an important and, in the final analysis, a determining element of the decision as to the need of protection. The need for continued protection may arise from the existence or the absence of the circumstances that triggered the first order for protection or from circumstances which have arisen since that time.

While the Court held that there must be a new finding that a child is still in need of protection in order for wardship to be continued at a status review hearing, it also ruled that the parent's ability to care for the child at the time of the status review hearing was not the only issue to assess. The court must also consider the potential trauma to the child from separating her from long-term foster parents and returning her to the care of a mother she no longer knew or wanted to live with:[204]

> Among the factors in evaluating the best interests of a child, the emotional well-being of a child is of the utmost importance, particularly where the evidence points to possible long-term adverse consequences resulting from the removal of the child from his or her foster family and the return to his or her birth parents.
>
> On the factors arising on a status review hearing, the need for continued protection in the case at hand seems to be easily established. The determination of whether the child continues to be in need of protection cannot solely focus on the parent's parenting ability, as did [the trial judge]..., but must have a child-centred focus and must examine whether the child, in light of the interceding events, continues to require state protection. The fact that [the girl]...has been in the care of the...Society for such an extended period of time and has exhibited unequivocal resistance to any recent attempt to institute access with her birth mother, in combination with the fact that her birth mother had difficulty in recognizing [the girl's]...emotional and psychological needs and has even reprimanded her for not wanting to see her, together with all circumstances revealed by the evidence is, in my view, sufficient to justify continued state intervention.

Thus, while the Supreme Court held that in principle if a wardship order is to be made at a status review hearing the Ontario statute requires a new finding that the child is in need of protection based on the circumstances at the time of the status review, the parent's capacity to care for the child is not the only issue at this hearing. Rather, the court will consider all of the child's circumstances.

---

[203] *Catholic Children's Aid Society of Metropolitan Toronto v. M.(C.)*, [1994] 2 S.C.R. 165 at para. 37.
[204] [1994] 2 S.C.R. 165 at para. 40-42.

In subsequent cases interpreting different provincial legislation from the Ontario statute considered in *M.(C.)*, some courts have taken a different approach to the question of whether there must again be a finding that a child is in need of protection at a status review hearing. For example, in *Winnipeg Child and Family Services v. F.(J.M.) and H.(R.J.)*,[205] the Manitoba Court of Appeal considered the test to be applied when a matter comes on for "further hearing" under the Manitoba protection legislation. The court held that there is no requirement to make a separate finding of need for protection at the status review, but the court should focus on what order is in the child's best interests at that time.

The approach towards plans for family placements presented at the status review stage is different than on the initial application. The Ontario Court of Appeal has held that the legislation in that province does not give a familial plan presented at the status review stage some priority simply because it proposes care by parents or members of the extended family.[206] The Nova Scotia Court of Appeal was of a similar view, stating:

> Once the maximum time limit is reached, s. 42(3) [which requires the court to consider whether placement with a relative is possible] can no longer be determinative, since temporary placement with a relative, neighbour or other extended family is no longer available.... [O]nce the agency establishes that the child remains in need of protective services, and subject to the court's authority to extend time in the rare circumstances...the determination for the court becomes one of what final or "terminal" order is in the child's best interests. At that stage during such a proceeding, consideration of family relationships is required only because it is one of several factors which are to form part of the child's best interests as defined by s. 3(2) of the Act, not because s. 42(3) continues to require such consideration.[207]

These decisions from different courts interpreting different provincial statutes show that once a child has been in agency care for a significant period of time, it may not be easy for the parents to regain the custody of their children, especially if the children were young when taken into care and have had a stable placement in care. However, if parents maintain regular contact with their children and address the concerns that resulted in their children being taken into care, they stand a good chance of regaining custody, and in these circumstances may well have the support of the agency to return their children to them after a period in temporary care.

Applications to Terminate Permanent Wardship

Applications to terminate permanent wardship orders are generally subject to special provisions, often requiring that the party applying demonstrate a change in circumstances in addition to meeting the best interests test. Such applications are generally prohibited when the child has been placed for adoption.

---

[205] *Winnipeg Child and Family Services v. F.(J.M.) and H.(R.J.)*, 2000 M.B.C.A. 145.

[206] *Children's Aid Society of Peel (Region) v. W.(M.J.)* (1995), 23 O.R. (3d) 174 (C.A.).

[207] *Children's Aid Society of Halifax v. T.B.*, [2001] N.S.J. 225 (C.A.).

If the application is brought by or with the support of the agency, it is very likely to be accepted by the court. However, if a parent or child is seeking to terminate permanent wardship and this is opposed by the agency, it will be necessary to demonstrate that there has been a significant change in circumstances. In a number of jurisdictions, there is a requirement that the applicant must obtain leave (or "permission") of the court to even have a hearing on a termination application.[208] Such requirements are "intended to cull out hearings where the chance of success does not warrant the reopening of the case," and "without being shown a realistic, new, different factor...the permission should not be granted because it will simply end in a rehashing of what has already been gone over at considerable length before."[209]

In Ontario, leave of the court is required to bring a status review application where the child is a Crown (permanent) ward and has been in the same placement continuously for two years or more.[210]

Alternative Dispute Resolution Mechanisms

The use of alternative dispute resolution (ADR) mechanisms, such as mediation and collaborative family law, is widespread in disputes between parents who have separated. Traditional dispute resolution though the court process imposes great strains on the relationship between separated parents, and on the relationship between parents and children. The benefits of mediation and other measures for resolving family law disputes are well documented. ADR may result in a faster, less expensive resolution of a dispute, and can avoid the increase in hostility that often results from a trial. Perhaps most significantly, ADR can result in an arrangement for the child that all parties will endorse and work to implement. A number of provinces have introduced mandatory ADR in ordinary civil cases, and referrals for mediation are frequently made in respect of post-separation disputes between separated parents.

Alternative dispute resolution has not been used as extensively in child protection cases as in other family law cases and in ordinary civil cases,[211] though it can be useful for child protection cases, as it may avoid having parents and child protection workers face one another in the often tense and adversarial atmosphere of the court room. Alternative dispute resolution may make it easier for parents and agency staff to have a positive relationship with one another when the proceedings are over.

Only a few Canadian child welfare statutes contain reference to mediation.[212] In Nova Scotia, Newfoundland and British Columbia, mediation is available to

---

[208] British Columbia, s. 54; Nova Scotia, s. 48(6); Newfoundland, s. 44.

[209] *Re R.R.S.*, [1998] B.C.J. No. 883.

[210] Ontario, s. 64(9).

[211] M. Bernstein, "Child Protection Mediation: Its Time Has Arrived" (1998), 16 *Canadian Family Law Quarterly* 1; and K.B. Olson, "Lessons Learned from a Child Protection Mediation Program" (2003), 41 *Family Court Review* 480.

[212] Newfoundland, Nova Scotia, and British Columbia.

the parties to a child protection proceeding at any time that they agree on the appointment of a mediator. If court proceedings have been commenced, the parties may ask the court to stay proceedings for a period not exceeding three months, and other statutory time limits are suspended or extended as a result.[213] Newfoundland and British Columbia also mention family conferences and other means of alternative dispute resolution. Only in the Yukon Territory is the court expressly granted jurisdiction to make an order for mediation at the request of the parties.[214] Where the legislation is silent, court rules may contain a provision relating to the use of alternative dispute resolution.[215] Even in the absence of legislative provisions or court rules, mediation or other forms of alternative dispute resolution may be tried with the consent of all parties.

Mediation involves the parties meeting with a trained mediator to attempt to settle the case without a trial. In a child protection case, this will typically involve the parents and one or two agency representatives meeting with the mediator for a few sessions to determine whether a mutually acceptable resolution can be achieved that meets the agency concerns for the child's safety as well as the parents' concerns. Adolescent children may be directly involved in the mediation process. Lawyers generally do not attend mediation sessions, but any agreement that is reached is tentative and the parties are urged to get legal advice before signing a mediated agreement.

Although the outcome of mediation is technically not binding on a court charged with making a best interests determination after a "hearing," mediation can assist in narrowing the issues or finding an agreed-upon solution to put before the court, with appropriate supporting evidence. In a child welfare case, the court is not bound by a mediated resolution, but in practice will usually adopt the plan developed by the parties.

Some workable guidelines for the selection of appropriate cases for child protection mediation include:

- the immediate safety of the child is assured;

- the parties have the capacity to participate in the mediation process;

- participation of all parties is voluntary;

- the parties are clear at the outset whether communication during mediation is closed or open (that is whether the results of an unsuccessful attempt at mediation are to be confidential — closed mediation, or shared with the court — open mediation); and

---

[213] Nova Scotia, s. 21; Newfoundland, s. 37; British Columbia, s. 22-23.

[214] Yukon, s. 42.

[215] In Ontario, Rule 17(9) provides that, at a case conference, settlement conference or trial management conference, the judge may, if it is appropriate to do so, on consent, refer any issue for alternative dispute resolution.

- any power imbalance among the parties can be equalized; and the situation provides sufficient time to work through the process from beginning to end.[216]

Some of the issues most amenable to mediation include: parent/teen conflicts; cases involving placement issues; negotiating terms of supervision orders; access issues; long-term care issues; communications issues between protection worker and clients due to client hostility; and any situation where the intervention of a neutral third party may break an impasse.[217]

Family group conferencing is a form of alternative dispute resolution that also involves a trained facilitator who attempts to achieve a resolution of a child protection proceeding without having a judge decide the case. In contrast to mediation, family group conferencing typically involves not just the parties to the litigation (the parents and agency representatives) but also members of the extended family, and often the child himself or herself, and perhaps other community members, all engaged in trying to develop a long-term plan that meets the needs of the child and the family. This process typically goes on for a longer period than mediation, with the expectation of some sort of monitoring and plan adjustment, and may involve sessions where those most involved in the case meet without the facilitator present. The plans that are developed often result in the return of children to their families with some form of supervision or support, or placement with a member of the child's extended family.

Family group conferencing was first developed in Aboriginal communities, but is now used in other communities. Legislative provisions in British Columbia and Newfoundland explicitly permit the use of family conferencing in child welfare cases;[218] demonstration projects in those provinces and elsewhere in Canada have had a high success rate in resolving the cases referred.[219]

Judicially supervised settlement conferences are also used in some Canadian jurisdictions prior to the adjudication of child protection hearings. The parties, their counsel and a judge meet to review the major issues in the case. The judge receives a summary of the evidence that is to be called at trial, but does not hear any witnesses. The settlement conference judge will not preside at the trial. The judge's role in a settlement conference is to explore the possibility of settlement, or at least narrow the range of issues in dispute. The judge at a settlement conference might, for example, suggest how, based on the summary of evidence presented, he or she might decide the case, which might help the parties to settle.

---

[216] From Nova Scotia Department of Community Services, "Child Protection Mediation Policies" (Halifax: 1994), as quoted in M. Bernstein, "Child Protection Mediation: Its Time Has Arrived" (1998), 16 *Canadian Family Law Quarterly* 1. See also S.E. Carrothers, "Mediation in Child Protection and the Nova Scotia Experience" (1997), 35 *Family & Conciliation Courts Review* 102.

[217] J. Wildgoose and J. Maresca, "Mediating Child Protection Cases," *Report on the Centre for Child and Family Mediation, The Fund for Dispute Resolution* (Waterloo, 1994).

[218] See British Columbia, s. 20.

[219] J. Schmid and S. Goranson, "Family Group Conferencing: An Effective Tool in Planning for Children's Safety and Well Being," *Best Practices for the Conduct of a Child Protection File — Part II* (Law Society of Upper Canada, Toronto, March 9, 2004).

It must be recognized that not all child protection cases will benefit from mediation or other ADR. Some cases will never be resolved on consent, particularly ones where the "ultimate" order is sought — severance of the parental relationship through permanent guardianship without access in furtherance of an adoption plan. Some parents simply need the judge to make a decision, and it is important that this be recognized so that the unavoidable trial is scheduled and a decision for the child can be made in a timely way.

Appeals

An appeal is theoretically quite different from a status review since an appeal is based on a claim that the trial judge made an error of law, while a review is based on a claim that there has been a change in circumstances since the original original trial judge made an order. In practice, however, there may be some overlap, since an appeal court in a protection case has the discretion to receive evidence about matters that occurred between the time of trial and the appeal. In "child-centered cases," appellate judges will generally display "flexibility in the admission of new evidence...needed to obtain timely information to inform the decision on the best interests of the child."[220] This evidence will usually be filed in documentary form, for example, by affidavit.

Appeals are governed by provincial child protection legislation; other statutes and the rules of court may also affect the appeal process.[221] In child protection cases, appellate courts are reluctant to reverse the original ruling because trial judges hear extensive testimony enabling them to evaluate the personality of the parents, which is often central to the case. However, if the appeal court finds that there was a legal error, the appeal court may reverse the trial decision and, in order to avoid further delay, whenever possible will make the order that it thinks should be made without remitting the case for a new hearing.[222]

A major concern when appeals are launched is the length of time required for them to be heard. During that time, the plans for the child are in many respects left in limbo. No adoption placement can be made and no steps can be taken towards permanency for the child.

Related to the issue of the delay caused by an appeal is the question of who will care for the child pending the resolution of the appeal. There are statutory provisions that stay (or suspend) the effect of a trial decision as soon as an appeal is launched, and then give an appeal court the jurisdiction to make an order for interim custody and access. There is a tendency for appeal judges to want to maintain stability in a child's life and ensure the safety of children pending an appeal.[223] As a result, if prior to trial the child was in the interim care of the agency, for example living in a foster home, and the trial judge orders that

---

[220] R.A. v. Jewish Family and Child Services, [2001] O.J. 47 at para. 8; see e.g., Ontario, s. 69(6).

[221] See e.g., Ontario. s. 69; and Ontario Family Law Rules, O. Reg. 114/99, Rule 38.

[222] L.(R.) v. Children's Aid Society of Metropolitan Toronto (1995), 21 O.R. (3d) 724 (Gen. Div.).

[223] See e.g., Ontario, s. 69(6).

the child is to be returned to parental care, the appeal court is likely to leave the child in the foster home pending resolution of the appeal. This may seem unfair to the parents, as the child's bonds with the biological family may further weaken while the attachment to the foster parents may increase during the time that the child remains in the care of the agency, making it more difficult for the biological parents to regain care of the child,[224] but this approach is usually most consistent with the best interests of the child.

Where the agency is appealing a trial judge's decision to return a child to the parents, it may be argued that if a stay is granted, the appeal court should ordinarily allow the parents to have significant contact with their child pending the appeal, in the absence of evidence of new circumstances or of a clear error on the part of the trial judge.[225]

Conclusion

This chapter has focused primarily on the law relating to the conduct, process and stages of child protection hearings. While the courts will continue to be the most widely available and appropriate forum for many contested child protection cases, it is not always the venue that provides the most durable solutions to issues involving families and children.

The adversarial system is a blunt instrument that is often costly, results in delay and undermines the importance of continuing relationships. The harmful effects of "litigation limbo" on children have been well documented.[226] As higher expectations are placed on reduced resources in the family justice system as well as in the social services sector, making timely decisions and avoiding delay becomes more challenging.

Achieving more beneficial outcomes in the future will require a careful consideration of an assortment of novel and innovative mechanisms for resolving child protection disputes.

---

[224] See e.g., *Catholic Children's Aid Society of Metropolitan Toronto v. M.(C.)* [1994] 2 S.C.R. 165 (S.C.C.).

[225] See e.g., *C.A.S. of Metro Toronto v. M.(R.)* (1985), 47 R.F.L. (2d) 412 (Ont. Dist. Ct.).

[226] See Sparrow Lake Alliance, *Children in Limbo: Report of the Children In Limbo Task Force of the Sparrow Lake Alliance* (Toronto: Sparrow Lake Alliance, 1996).

4

Children in Care

Bruce MacLaurin and Nicholas Bala[1]

The decision about where to place a child who is in the legal care of a child welfare agency is one of the most complex and challenging decisions that agency staff make. The need for standardized criteria for placement decisions was identified in the early 1960s, but to date no definitive guidelines have been developed.[2] Agency staff have relatively little guidance from legislation in deciding where a child will live for the short or long-term, and in how to find the best match between the resources available to the agency and the needs of children in agency care.

The numbers of children requiring either a temporary or permanent placement away from their families have changed in response to changes in legislation and policy, but over the past few years the numbers have generally increased in Canada. At the end of March 1999, more than 62,000 children were living in care in Canada, a 31% increase since 1992.[3] There continues to be an overrepresentation of Aboriginal children in care in Canada, as estimates suggest that about 40% of Canadian children in care are Aboriginal.[4]

While there are many dedicated individuals who provide care for children whose parents are unable or unwilling to care for them and many children who receive excellent, loving care in the child welfare system, there is also a long history of problems for many children in state care. There have been too many children who have been taken into care only to be abused or neglected by their state-appointed caregivers. Problems such as placement breakdown, discontinuity of relationships with agency staff and school difficulties remain major concerns for children in care, especially among those taken into care after the first few years of life. Adolescents in care experience use of restraints and

---

[1] Bruce MacLaurin is Assistant Professor, Faculty of Social Work, University of Calgary, Alberta. Nicholas Bala is Professor of Law, Queen's University, Kingston, Ontario.

[2] D. Lindsey, *The Welfare of Children*, 2nd Edition (New York: Oxford University Press, 2003); and S.J. Zuravin and D. DePanfilis, "Factors Affecting Foster Care Placement of Children Receiving Child Protective Services" (1997), 21 *Social Work Research* 1, 34-42.

[3] Federal Provincial Working Group on Child and Family Services Information, *Child Welfare in Canada 2000: The Role of Provincial and Territorial Authorities in the Provision of Child Protection Services* (Ottawa: Minister of Supply and Services Canada, 2002).

[4] C. Blackstock, N. Trocmé and M. Bennett, *Child Welfare Response to Aboriginal and Non-Aboriginal Children in Canada: A Comparative Analysis* (2003). Paper presented at the International Symposium on Family Violence, Montreal, QC.

peer-to-peer abuse, and have relatively high rates of charging for minor criminal offences, self-mutilation and suicide.[5]

Effectiveness of Child Welfare Placements

The increased number of children in care has occurred in the midst of an ongoing debate about the value of out-of-home placement relative to family-based approaches. Outcome research suggests that children in the care of child welfare agencies experience disrupted or disjointed sibling and parental connections, high turnover in professional relationships, multiple school moves and difficulty in school, maltreatment in care, adult under-employment and economic instability, teen and adult homelessness, and drug use.[6] Other research, however, suggests there is little evidence to indicate that maltreated children admitted to care experience more negative long-term outcomes than maltreated children who do not enter care but receive agency services in their own families.[7]

While there has been controversy for many years about how the child welfare system is meeting (or failing to meet) the needs of children in agency care, Canadian child welfare systems are now just beginning to use an "outcomes" approach to guide decisions for children and families at risk for maltreatment. An outcomes approach looks to rigorous empirical research to help answer the questions about what type of child care arrangements will best meet the needs of children, and to promote the best long-term outcomes for children. Wald and colleagues clarify the strength of this approach to determine the relative value of foster care when they suggest "the question 'Is home or foster care better?' must be refined by asking further, 'In terms of which aspects of development?' and 'For which children, under what conditions?'"[8]

Understanding the Increase in Child Welfare Placements

It is important to examine the dynamics of the child care system within the larger context of child welfare services in Canada over the past three decades. While the number of children in care has generally increased over this period, this increase largely reflects an increase in the number of family investigations for maltreatment in Canada. For example, child welfare statistics for Ontario indicate that in 1971 there were 28,500 family investigations compared to

[5] See e.g., M. Geigen-Miller, *It's Time to Break the Silence* (Toronto: Defence for Children International — Canada, 2003).

[6] K. Kufeldt, J. Vachon, M. Simard, J. Baker, and T. Andrews, *Looking After Children in Canada* (Ottawa: Social Development Partnerships of Human Resources Development Canada, 2000); R.J. Sawyer and H. Dubowitz, "School Performance of Children in Kinship Care" (1993), 18 *Child Abuse and Neglect* 587-597; and K.S. Smucker, J.M. Kauffman, and D.W. Ball, "School Related Problems of Special Education Foster Care Students with Emotional or Behavioural Disorders: A Comparison to Other Groups" (1996), 4 *Journal of Emotional and Behavioural Disorders* 30-39.

[7] R.P. Barth, "On Their Own: The Experiences of Youth After Foster Care" (1990), 7(5) *Child and Adolescent Social Work* 419-441; T. Festinger, *No One Ever Asked Us...A Postscript to Foster Care* (New York: Columbia University, 1983); and M.S. Wald, J.M. Carlsmith, P.H. Leiderman, C. Smith, and R. deSales-French, *Protecting Abused and Neglected Children* (Stanford: Stanford University Press, 1988).

[8] Wald et al., *supra*, note 7 at 181.

approximately 17,800 children in care — a ratio of .63.[9] This high proportion of family investigations resulting in a placement in care suggests that placement in care was the primary child welfare intervention during the early 1970s. This ratio decreased between 1971 and 1991 from .63 to .08 — thus, a much lower proportion of family investigations resulting in a placement. This period saw an increased reporting of physical and sexual abuse allegations, but also increased concerns about children "drifting" in foster care and a rise in family preservation approaches to child welfare. For much of the 1990s, the number of family investigations increased dramatically, but the ratio of children in care to investigated families remained fairly constant through the early years of the new century. The great increase in reported maltreatment may account for much of the approximately 50% increase in the number of children in care in Ontario between 1998 and 2003.[10]

A second explanation is that the continued increase in the number of children in care is related to the increased duration of placement, which would thus result in an increased number of children included in annual children in care populations. It is also argued that foster care trends in Canada reflect complex dynamics with respect to a changing response to values and professional knowledge, the development of a broader scope of service alternatives, shifts in the dominant values associated with child and family services, and changes in legislation and policy.[11]

Factors Associated with Child Welfare Placement

It is important to appreciate that statistics and research on children in care generally do not distinguish between children who are placed as a result of an involuntary removal from parental care and a child protection proceeding, and those children who are voluntarily placed in care by their parents, pursuant to an agreement or a consent order. In both situations, child welfare agency staff has decided that it is in the best interests of a child to be taken into care.

While a number of variables are identified as being associated with the decision to take a child into care, there is little agreement between studies about the key variables that consistently predict decisions to take children into care or outcomes in care. The review of the literature highlights that the decision to place a child in care is not always clearly or consistently linked to clinical factors related to the best interests of the child (child's vulnerability, severity of harm, parenting capacity), but also is related to factors concerning the size and location of the agency, and the experience and training of the worker.

---

[9] N. Trocmé, B. Fallon, B. Nutter, B. MacLaurin, and J. Thompson, *Outcomes for Child Welfare Services in Ontario* (Toronto: Ontario Ministry of Community and Social Services, Children's Services Branch, 1999).

[10] See website of the Ontario Association of Children's Aid Societies: http://www.oacas.org.

[11] B.J. MacLaurin, N. Trocmé, and B. Fallon, "Characteristics of Investigated Children and Families Referred to Out-of-Home Placement," in K. Kufeldt and B. McKenzie (Eds.), *Child Welfare – Connecting Research Policy and Practice* (Waterloo, ON: Wilfred Laurier Press, 2003).

Child Characteristics

The overrepresentation of Aboriginal and visible minority children in care in many Canadian jurisdictions raises questions about the impact of race and ethnicity on child welfare decisions. The majority of studies that examined race and ethnicity found a significant effect on the decision to place children in foster care.[12] Children with emotional and behavioral problems were frequently cited as requiring placement in foster care.[13] Unusual behaviour or unusual characteristics of a child were related to judgements regarding either the choice of interventions or the decision to place children in care.[14]

Family Characteristics

Most studies indicate that low income is associated with placement in child welfare care, especially related to receipt of social assistance or job loss.[15] Inadequate housing and homelessness were also significant factors in placement decisions.[16] A higher proportion of children in care were admitted from single parent families,[17] and family stress significantly affected case outcomes.[18] Similarly, environmental stress was related to the choice of interventions, in addition to number of family functioning concerns and lack of social supports.[19]

---

[12] Department of Health and Human Services, *National Study of Protective, Preventive, and Reunification Services Delivered to Children and Their Families* (Washington, DC: US Government Printing Office, 1997); A. Hartman and D. Vinokur-Kaplan, "Women and Men Working in Child Welfare: Different Voices" (1985) 64(3) *Child Welfare* 307-315; and S. Jenkins and B. Diamond, "Ethnicity and Foster Care: Census Data as Predictors of Placement Variables" (1985), 55(2) *American Journal of Orthopsychiatry* 267-276.

[13] E. Fernandez, "Factors Associated with the Entry of Children to Care," in J. Mason (Ed.), *Child Welfare Policy: Critical Australian Perspectives* (Sydney, NSW: Iremonger Pty. Ltd., 1993), 51-68; D. Oyserman, R. Benbenishty and D. Ben-Rabi, "Characteristics of Children and Their Families at Entry into Foster Care" (1992), 22(3) *Child Psychiatry and Human Development* 199-211; and W.J. Reid, R.M. Kagan and S.B. Schlosberg, "Prevention of Placement: Critical Factors in Program Success" (1988), 67(1) *Child Welfare* 25-36.

[14] H. Rosen, "How Workers Use Cues to Determine Child Abuse" (1981), 14(8) *Social Work Research and Abstracts* 27-33.

[15] R.P. Barth, M. Courtney, J. Duerr-Berrick, and V. Albert, *From Child Abuse to Permanency Planning* (New York: Aldine de Gruyter, Inc., 1994); R.A. Catalano, S.L. Lind, A.B. Rosenblatt, and C.C. Attkisson, "Unemployment and Foster Home Placements: Estimating the Net Effect of Provocation and Inhibition" (1999), 89(6) *American Journal of Public Health* 851-855; D. Lindsey, "Factors Affecting the Foster Care Placement Decision: An Analysis of National Survey Data" (1991), 61(2) *American Journal of Orthopsychiatry* 272-281; and D. Lindsey, "Decision Making in Child Welfare: Linchpin of the Residual Model" in D. Lindsey (Ed.), *The Welfare of Children* (New York: Oxford University Press, 1994) 127-156.

[16] S. Chau, A. Fitzpatrick, J.D. Hulchanski, B. Leslie, and D. Schatia, *One in Five...Housing as a Factor in the Admission of Children to Care* (Research Bulletin #5) (Toronto: Centre for Urban and Community Studies, 2001); and M. Cohen-Schlanger, A. Fitzpatrick, J.D. Hulchanski, and D. Raphael, "Housing as a Factor in Admissions of Children to Temporary Care: A Survey" (1995), 74(3) *Child Welfare* 547-562.

[17] Barth et al., *supra*, note 15; B. Needell and R.P. Barth, "Infants Entering Foster Care Compared to Other Infants Using Birth Status Indicators" (1997), 22(12) *Child Abuse and Neglect* 1179-1187; and M.H. Phillips, A.W. Shyne, E.A. Sherman, and B.L. Haring, *Factors Associated with the Placement Decision in Child Welfare* (New York: Child Welfare League of America, 1971).

[18] L.P. Groeneveld and J.M. Giovannoni, "Disposition of Child Abuse and Neglect Cases" (1977), 13(2) *Social Work Research and Abstracts* 24-30.

[19] *Supra*, note 14; Department of Health and Human Services, *supra*, note 12; and Phillips et al., *supra*, note 17.

Parental Characteristics

Parental substance abuse problems and parental mental health concerns put children at increased risk of being taken into care.[20] More specifically, the emotional problems of the caretaking parent increased the chances of placement in care,[21] and the majority of placement cases resulting from parental mental illness involved the psychiatric hospitalization of the mother.[22]

Maltreatment Characteristics

Physical abuse, sexual abuse, emotional abuse and neglect by parents are the major factors associated with the decision to take a child into the care of a child welfare agency.[23] The longer and more severe the history of injury, the greater the likelihood of the child being taken into care.[24] Severity of the injury was also consistently related to decisions to place the child in care.

Service and Organizational Characteristics

The lack of community and treatment resources to implement a decision has been found to limit caseworkers' ability to pursue their ideal intervention strategies.[25] A jurisdiction's economic condition has been found to have an impact upon the number of children who entered the child welfare system. Barth et al. maintained that a jurisdiction's economic condition had an impact upon the number of children that entered the child welfare system. Poor labour market conditions, as indicated by increased use of social assistance, were likely to result in an increased number of children entering the child welfare system.[26] Wolock found that caseworker judgements of abuse varied according to the average severity of the caseload handled in the district offices.[27] Researchers have also stressed that child welfare policies and practices were responsible for much of what took place in the child welfare system.[28] Policies that emphasized

---

[20] P. Nair, M.M. Black, M. Schuler, V. Keane, L. Snow, and B.A. Rigney, "Risk Factors for Disruption in Primary Caregiving Among Infants of Substance Abusing Women" (1997), 21(11) *Child Abuse and Neglect*, 1039-1051; D.K. Runyan, C.L. Gould, D.C. Trost, and F.A. Loda, "Determinants of Foster Care Placement of the Maltreated Child" (1981), 6 *Child Abuse and Neglect* 343-352; S. Zuravin and D. DePanfilis, "Predictors of Child Protective Service Intake Decisions: Case Closure, Referral to Continuing Services or Foster Care Placement," in P.A. Curtis, G. Dale and J.C. Kendall (Eds.), *The Foster Care Crisis: Translating Research into Policy and Practice* (Lincoln, Nebraska: University of Nebraska Press and CWLA, 1999); and Zuravin and DePanfilis., *supra*, note 2.

[21] D. Fanshel and E. Shinn, *Children in Foster Care: A Longitudinal Investigation* (New York: Columbia University Press, 1978).

[22] S. Jenkins and E. Norman, *Beyond Placement: Mothers View Foster Care* (New York: Columbia University Press, 1975).

[23] Barth et al., *supra*, note 15; Oyserman et al., *supra*, note 13; Zuravin and DePanfilis, *supra*, notes 20 and 2.

[24] M.H. Katz, R.L. Hamptom, E.H. Newberger, R.T. Bowles, and J.C. Snyder, "Returning Children Home: Clinical Decision Making in Cases of Child Abuse and Neglect" (1986), 56(2) *American Journal of Orthopsychiatry*, 253-262; and *supra*, note 14.

[25] Phillips et al., *supra*, note 17.

[26] Barth et al., *supra*, note 15.

[27] I. Wolock, "Community Characteristics and Staff Judgements in Child Abuse and Neglect Cases" (1982), 18(2) *Social Work Research and Abstracts*, 9-15.

[28] Barth et al., *supra*, note 15.

permanency planning, the priority of placement with relatives as a form of foster care, changes in reporting practices, and alterations in the level of resources allocated for child welfare services had very significant effects on the number of children taken into care by the child welfare system.

Approaches to Child Welfare and Foster Care

One of the challenges in the examination of social problems is to recognize that the current definition of an issue is the result of ongoing evolution and development over time within a context of continual interaction with other social phenomena. Definitions of child maltreatment have changed over time and the response from the state has changed dramatically in response to these shifts in definition. The challenge is to combine the issues of definition, perspective and construction to provide some explanation about how child abuse has been viewed and approached within any given societal context.

There can be no certainty on the correct definition of the state's role with respect to children and families. Different value perspectives suggest very different approaches towards meeting the best interests of the child. As discussed by Spratt, different child welfare orientations will have a critical impact on the decisions that are made and the outcomes for children. Spratt stresses that "the orientation of a particular system is closely related to the prevailing culture, political climate, and ideologies that are underpinning both agency structure and professional practice."[29]

Foster Care Drift and Permanency Planning

The problems in the child care system are not recent:

> As early as the 1920's, there were reports of shortages of foster care placements, of children being moved about from one home to another (foster care drift) and of screening and supervision processes that could not prevent child maltreatment. These problems persist as major challenges in the provision of foster care services today.[30]

By the 1980s, there was a growing body of research documenting that children in care for extended periods of time have a much reduced chance for a permanent placement through adoption or family reunification, and were often "drifting" from placement to placement prior to aging out of the system.[31] In Canada, coroners' inquests into the deaths of children in care clearly identified significant problems in the child care system. The lack of planning and accountability, and the deleterious effects of numerous placement changes were, for

---

[29] T. Spratt, "The Influence of Child Protection Orientation on Child Welfare Practice" (2001), 31 *British Journal of Social Work* 933-954 at 934.

[30] J. Krysik, "Canada," in M. Colton and M. Williams (Eds.), *The World of Foster Care: An International Sourcebook on Foster Family Care Systems* (Brookfield, VT: Ashgate Publishers, 1997) at 44.

[31] A.N. Maluccio, E. Fein, and K.A. Olmstead, *Permanency Planning for Children: Concepts and Methods* (New York: Tavistock Pulications, 1986).

example, documented at the inquest into the suicide death of Richard Cardinal in 1984. He was a Métis youth who moved through many foster placements, keeping a journal that movingly described his lonely existence, before his tragic death in 1984.[32]

A response to many of the problems in the care provided to children by the child welfare system was the development of the concept of *permanency planning*. Permanency planning expects the creation of an individualized, comprehensive plan of action for each child in the care of a child welfare agency. The plan should have clear goals, action plans and specific responsibilities for all partners in the process (agency staff, foster family or group home staff, child and possibly parents). The development of a plan is seen as the first step to providing a clear pathway to a permanent placement, and to reducing the negative effects of drifting in care.[33] Despite the clarity of the necessary direction, the ambitious goals of permanency planning have not yet been fully realized.[34]

Family Preservation Approach

Related to the development of permanency planning in the child welfare field in the 1980s was the move towards a *family preservation approach* to child welfare policy.[35] Family preservation identified the child's relationship with parents and family as a critical element in the child's life; placement in care was seen as a shorter-term arrangement providing the time and space to allow a timely return to the family home.

The family preservation approach to child welfare is related to a *family welfare perspective* to child welfare, which has as a core belief that the natural family is presumptively the best place for a child to be raised, and that coercive state intervention tends to produce harmful results to the child and to the family as a whole. The family welfare perspective considers that state intervention can be a positive step for families. The intervention should be supportive, and whenever possible should maintain the child's contact and involvement with the family, with an emphasis on reunification of children with their families after brief placements in out-of-home care, and the provision of further preventive services to support families and allow children to remain with their families in the community.

The family welfare perspective has been defined by Fox-Harding:[36]

---

[32] R.J. Thomlison, *Case Management Review of Northwest Region, Department of Social Services and Community Health* (Calgary: University of Calgary, 1984); *Richard Cardinal: Cry from a Diary of a Métis Child* (1986) is a documentary movie by the National Film Board that can be viewed at <http://cmm.nfb.ca/E/titleinfo/index.epl?id=16327&recherche=simple&coll=onf>.

[33] *Supra*, note 31.

[34] Barth et al., *supra*, note 15.

[35] H. Altstein and R. McRoy, *Does Family Preservation Serve a Child's Best Interests?* (Washington: Georgetown University Press, 2000); and R.G. Savoury and K. Kufeldt, "Protecting Children Versus Supporting Families" (1998), 65(3) *Social Worker* 146-153.

[36] L. Fox-Harding, *Perspectives in Child Care Policy,* 2nd ed. (London: Longman Publishers, 1997) at 73.

...this viewpoint favours extensive state intervention, but not of the coercive kind. Birth families should be supported in their caring role; children should not enter substitute care except as a last resort or on a "shared care" basis; having entered care, most of them should be kept in touch with their original family and should wherever possible return to it. The state in its child care role pays insufficient attention to upholding birth families; it also operates in a discriminatory way on the basis of social class. Most of the child care problems to which the state responds are attributable to poverty and deprivation.

The family welfare perspective developed in response to what was seen to be the overly intrusive child welfare system on the 1970s, which resulted in the removal of relatively large numbers of children from parental care, and their placement in a child care system where children too often were subjected to abuse and too rarely had their needs met. The family preservation approach sparked the development of family support programs to facilitate keeping children with their families, and reunification programs to support the return of children in care to their families.[37] In most provinces, this policy shift resulted in a substantial reduction in the number of children in the care of child welfare agencies in the 1980s.[38]

The family preservation approach to child welfare is at least in part based on a minimal state involvement perspective on child welfare. This value perspective suggests that state involvement in child and family welfare should be minimal — limited to critical circumstances reflecting danger to the child. The anticipated result of this perspective is stronger families and individuals. This position is debated in the literature on child welfare, and there is a substantial number of authors who adopt this perspective.[39]

Starting in the 1970s, advocates of minimal coercive involvement in the family critiqued the use of the vague provisions in child welfare statutes and laws that relied on a "best interests of the child" approach to decision making for giving too great a latitude to social workers and court judges in decision making.[40] This critique suggested that children should only be removed from their homes when there is substantial risk to their physical health and safety. Critics questioned the ability of the state to ensure that a child's needs can be met in out-of-home placement, both with respect to the stability and the permanence of these out-of-home placements. American child welfare advocates like Michael Wald argued for the need to narrow the scope and focus of state

---

[37] E.S. Morton and R.K. Grigsby, *Advancing Family Preservation Practice* (Newbury Park, CA: Sage Publications, Ltd., 1993); K. Wells and D.E. Biegel (Eds.), *Family Preservation Services: Research and Evaluation* (Newbury Park: Sage Publications, 1991); and J.K. Whittaker, J. Kinney, E.M. Tracy, and C. Booth (Eds.), *Reaching High Risk Families: Intensive Family Preservation in Human Services* (New York: Aldine de Gruyter, 1990).

[38] *Supra*, note 9.

[39] R. Dingwall, J. Eekelaar, and T. Murray, *The Protection of Children: State Intervention and Family Life* (Oxford: Basil Blackwell, 1983); J. Goldstein, A.J. Solnit, S. Goldstein, and A. Freud, *The Best Interests of the Child: The Least Detrimental Alternative* (New York: Free Press, 1996); R.H. Mnookin, "Foster Care in Whose Best Interests" (1973), 43(4) *Harvard Educational Review* 599-638; and Wald et al., *supra*, note 7.

[40] Mnookin, *ibid.*

intervention, specifically with respect to child neglect.[41] According to them, state intervention in cases of child neglect should occur only if the harm is serious, and if there is evidence to suggest that intervention will benefit the child rather than produce additional harm; and it should be the responsibility of the state to identify the likelihood of harm and to determine the beneficial nature of the intervention. It was argued that the child welfare system was overly invasive in the lives of children and families, without producing positive outcomes for children involved with child welfare.

The American psychologist Goldstein and his colleagues identified two key priorities with respect to decision making for children. First, it was argued that the child's needs must be paramount over all other considerations, stressing the child's psychological need for continuity of relations and parenting. If a child has a functioning family, then the family should be entitled to least intrusive state intervention and privacy. Second, they critiqued the ability of the state and the courts to manage family relationships, and questioned the ability of state agencies to determine the long-term impact of the decision to remove a child from their primary caregivers.

> The law, so far as specific individual relationships are concerned is a relatively crude instrument.... Nor does it have the capacity to predict future events and needs that would justify or make workable over the long run any specific conditions it might impose upon the parents or parents with whom the child is placed.[42]

The writings of Goldstein and colleagues have been described as being a commendable effort to formulate laws and family policy on the basis of psychological theory, but a serious flaw is that the work lacked empirical evidence to support their guidelines for the placement of a child.[43]

Some of the academic and policy debates in the 1980s tended to polarize around two extremes of traditional child protection versus family preservation,[44] though there have been significant moves to try to draw on the strengths of each approach and develop differential responses to meet the needs of individual children.[45]

A Shift to Child Safety in the Late 1990s

An ongoing debate has continued regarding the relative benefits of family preservation efforts as a primary alternative to out-of-home care.[46] The balance

---

[41] M.S. Wald, "State Intervention on Behalf of Endangered Children — A Proposed Legal Response" (1982), 6(1) *Child Abuse and Neglect* 3-45.

[42] Goldstein et al., *supra*, note 39 at 47.

[43] M.D.A. Freeman, "Freedom and the Welfare State: Child-rearing, Parental Autonomy and State Intervention," [March 1983] *Journal of Social Welfare Law* 70-91; and D. Katkin, B. Bullington, and M. Levine, "Above and Beyond the Best Interests of the Child: An Inquiry into the Relationship Between Social Science and Social Action" (1974), 8(4) *Law and Society Review* 669-687.

[44] R. Gelles, *The Book of David: How Preserving Families Can Cost Children's Lives* (New York: Basic Books, 1996); and Lindsey, *supra*, note 2.

[45] J. Waldfogel, "Rethinking the Paradigm for Child Protection" (1998), 8(1) *The Future of Children* 104-119.

[46] Alstein and McRoy, *supra*, note 35.

between the benefits of maintaining a child's residence and connection with his or her family versus the risk of further maltreatment or fatality is a critical factor in the decision-making process.

As the family preservation approach gained influence and the rates of children in care declined in the 1990s, there was a growing concern that the child welfare system was not doing enough to protect the children from the dangers of abuse and neglect by their parents. This has been referred to as the development of a *child safety perspective* to child welfare.

In the late 1990s, the Gove Inquiry in British Columbia into the death of a five-year-old boy who died while in his mother's care under agency supervision provided a scathing attack on the focus of family preservation and the entire child welfare system.[47] Fatality reviews in Ontario in the 1990s and a government-appointed task force[48] prompted a swing in child welfare legislation and policy towards a prioritization for child safety as the paramount concern for decision making.[49] This shift in law and policy resulted in the development of new protocols in several provinces for dealing with child abuse and neglect cases.[50]

The child safety perspective supports extensive state intervention to ensure the safety of the children at risk in their parents' care, and clearly identifies that the child's safety is to take precedence to the rights of the parents.[51] This perspective focuses on the child's right to appropriate care and safety rather than a right to self-determination. The threshold for state intervention is lowered to ensure the safety of children, and placement in out-of-home care can occur more readily. A safe, predictable placement with psychological attachment to caregivers is valued more than the preservation of family ties.

The ultimate failure of the child welfare system is a child fatality, and unfortunately this occurrence is frequently the impetus for child welfare reform for legislation, policy and practice resulting from mortality inquests and reviews.[52] A child safety perspective is based on the belief that the state can provide effective and efficient services which will benefit children, and the child safety perspective places trust in the value of the state's services for children. There

---

[47] T.J. Gove, *Report of the Gove Inquiry into Child Protection in British Columbia: Mathew's Legacy — Volume 2* (Victoria: British Columbia Ministry of Services to Children and Families, 1995); and T.J. Gove, *Report of the Gove Inquiry into Child Protection in British Columbia: Mathew's Story Volume 1* (Victoria: British Columbia Ministry of Services to Children and Families, 1995).

[48] Panel of Experts on Child Protection, *Protecting Vulnerable Children* (Toronto: Ontario Ministry of Community and Social Services, 1998).

[49] N. Trocmé, "Staying on Track While the Pendulum Swings: Commentary on Canadian Child Welfare Policy Trends," [Winter 1997] *OACAS Newsmagazine* 13-14.

[50] British Columbia Government, *Child, Family and Community Service Act* (Victoria: Queen's Printer, 1996); Manitoba Government, *Child and Family Services Act* (Winnipeg: Queen's Printer, 1985); and Ontario Government, *Child and Family Services Act* (Toronto: Queen's Printer of Ontario, 1984).

[51] *Supra*, note 36.

[52] T.J. Gove, *Report of the Gove Inquiry into Child Protection in British Columbia: Executive Summary* (Victoria: British Columbia Ministry of Services to Children and Families, 1995); Ontario Child Mortality Task Force, "Ontario Child Mortality Task Force Final Report," [July 1997] *OACAS Journal*, entire issue; and *supra*, note 48.

are, however, continuing concerns that a focus on child safety and removal of children from parental care tends to disregard the potential negative outcomes of state intervention for children taken into state care.[53]

Children's Rights Perspective

The children's rights perspective to child welfare places an emphasis on the child's own viewpoint and identifies the right of the child to be viewed as a separate individual, with rights distinct from those of parents or siblings. Fox-Harding[54] defines the *children's rights perspective* in this way:

> The emphasis is on the child's own viewpoint, feelings, wishes, definitions, freedom, choices rather than attribution by adults of what is best for the child... that children in all spheres should have a greater independent say in what happens to them; and that the provisions of the state should allow for this, in child care law and policy education, health care and other relevant areas. Decisions should not (on the whole) be made over the child's head. Thus children's welfare is (at least partly) for children themselves to define.

There is significant support in the child welfare practice and legal literature for recognizing that children have independent rights, and that the recognition of independent rights for children as they reach adolescence is consistent with child development theory.[55] The *United Nations Convention on the Rights of the Child*, which was ratified by Canada in 1991, recognizes that children have the right to participate in decisions that affect them. Article 12(1) requires that governments "shall assure to the child who is capable of forming his or her own views the right to express those views freely in all matters affecting the child, [and that] the views of the child [are] being given due weight in accordance with the age and maturity of the child."

There are real challenges in operationalizing this declaration, as the *Convention* also recognizes in Article 3 that "the best interests of the child shall be a primary consideration" in all decisions made by governments or child welfare agencies concerning a child. Under the *Convention*, a child has the right to participate in decisions, but not to make the final decision. The *Convention* recognizes that as children mature and gain capacity, their views should be given greater weight, but ultimately, until they reach adulthood they do not have the full right to make decisions for themselves. There is a need to accept differences

[53] National Youth in Care Network, *Creating Positive School Experiences for Youth in Care: Who Will Teach me to Learn?* (Ottawa: National Youth in Care Network, 2000); B. Raychaba, "Canadian Youth in Care: Leaving Home to be on our Own With no Direction from Home" (1989), 11 *Children and Youth Services Review*, 61-73; and Saskatchewan Children's Advocate Office, *Children and Youth in Care Review: Listen to Their Voices* (Regina: Saskatchewan Children's Advocate Office, 2000).

[54] *Supra*, note 36 at 112.

[55] K. Covell and R.B. Howe, *The Challenge of Children's Rights for Canada* (Waterloo: Wilfred Laurier Press, 2001); Freeman, *supra*, note 43; D. Shemmings, "Professionals' Attitudes to Children's Participation in Decision Making: Dichotomous Accounts and Doctrinal Contests" (2000), 5 *Child and Family Social Work*, 235-243; T.J. Stein, "The Adoption and Safe Families Act: Creating a False Dichotomy Between Parents' and Childrens' Rights" (2000), 81(6) *Families in Society: The Journal of Contemporary Human Services* 586-592; and United Nations Committee on the Rights of the Child, *United Nations Convention on the Rights of the Child* (Geneva: Office of the United Nations High Commissioner for Human Rights, 1990).

in development related to the limited capacities of children. In the words of English legal scholar Michael Freeman: "To take children's rights seriously requires us to take seriously [both] 'nurturance' and self-determination.'"[56]

The recognition of rights for children is especially significant and challenging for those children who are in the care of child welfare agencies. These are children who may be especially vulnerable; their parents are often not playing an active role in their lives and they may have no advocates. Especially as they move towards adolescence, it is increasingly difficult to impose decisions on children in care. While many youth in care lack the judgement to make decisions that are in their long-term best interests, if these youth are opposed to the arrangements that have been made for their care, they may end up as "runners," and leave their placements to live on the streets or in other unhealthy environments.

Types of Child Welfare Placements

The child welfare system in Canada consists of a broad spectrum of services and agencies that provide care for children who are in the custody of child welfare agencies. The available services differ by jurisdiction, as resources and provincial and territorial government priorities contribute to how services are defined and coordinated.

Child welfare placements outside the family home can be classified into four broad categories: foster homes, group homes, institutions or residential treatment, and secure treatment.

Foster Homes

Family foster care continues to be the most frequently used form of child welfare placement in Canada. In every province and territory there are more children in foster homes than in all other types of facilities combined.[57] In a foster home, individuals, usually a couple who themselves are parents, agree to take in children who are in the legal custody of a child welfare agency in order to provide substitute parenting in their home. Foster care is premised on the belief that a family setting is usually the best context in which to raise children.

Foster parents are recruited by child protection authorities and go through a screening process that varies by province. Responding to increased professional awareness and media attention to cases of child abuse in foster homes, there have been improvements in the screening of potential foster parents. Information about fostering is provided during information sessions, pre-screening sessions, and during the application process. Those candidates who present with the required skill set for fostering then go through a more formal home study process that examines parenting style, family history, family relationships and methods of interacting. In Ontario, there are regulations and guidelines for the

---

[56] M.D.A. Freeman, "Taking Children's Rights Seriously" (1987), 1(4) *Children and Society* 299-319 at 309.
[57] *Supra*, note 3.

operation and management of foster homes.[58] Generally, foster parents are expected to possess satisfactory mental and physical health, be over the age of 18, if cohabiting with a partner to be in a stable relationship of at least 12 months, and be living within their financial means.

In most provinces there is now also a requirement that foster parents are to undertake some pre-service orientation sessions before receiving children into their homes, as well expectations for some ongoing training. Foster parents accordingly receive some basic education about the special needs of the neglected and abused children who are likely to come into their care, but they are not in any sense trained child care workers.

Most provinces now have different levels of foster care, with relatively limited training expectations for those taking in healthy newborns, and greater levels of experience and training expected for those taking into care older children with greater needs; as well, higher levels of compensation are offered for those taking in children who are often more demanding. While rates vary by province, in most provinces the basic foster care rates are in the range of $20 to $35 a day, providing only minimal financial compensation after foster parents pay for the food and other expenses incurred by having a child in their home. Specialized foster care rates are paid to foster parents with more training who take in children with greater needs; these rates can be as much as two or three times the regular rates, but they provide limited financial rewards for what can be a very demanding round-the-clock responsibility.

Most foster parents have children of their own, as well as the one or more foster children they take in, and they are generally people who truly care about children. For many foster parents, taking children into their homes is an extremely rewarding experience. In recent years, however, with more families with both partners having full-time employment, and more older, demanding children coming into care, it has become increasingly difficult to recruit foster parents.

It is now known that in the past, when there was little screening and supervision of foster parents, some children who were placed in foster care were treated as "second class" members of their foster families, and in some cases were physically or sexually abused by foster parents or foster siblings.[59] While there continue to be cases of abuse and neglect in foster homes, with better screening and monitoring, there are almost certainly fewer than was the case a few decades ago. However, with heightened agency sensibilities to issues of abuse by foster parents, it is now not uncommon for there to be cases of false allegations of abuse against foster parents, made, in particular, by manipulative adolescents who may in fact have been previously abused by parents. Understandably, agencies always investigate and react to any allegations, and immediately move children if an allegation is made against foster parents. Even if the allegation is

---

[58] Ibid.
[59] See e.g., K.L.B. v. British Columbia, 2003 S.C.C. 51.

established as unfounded, this experience can leave foster parents feeling very vulnerable and reluctant to take in any more children. In some of the most unfortunate cases, foster parents have been prosecuted in criminal court for unfounded allegations of abuse; even if eventually acquitted, this is a very draining experience for foster parents;[60] and as stories of false allegations of abuse against foster parents become more widespread, it becomes more difficult to recruit them. While agencies will typically compensate foster parents for damages that a foster child causes to their home, foster parents who are falsely accused of abuse are not always reimbursed for legal expenses arising out of false allegations of abuse.

Foster parents are not the legal guardians of children who are in their care; rather the agency maintains legal custody and is responsible for making decisions about and paying for counselling and medical and dental care. The agency is also responsible for paying for expenses beyond ordinary daily care. Foster parents have a contract to care for children and are not employees of the agency, so the agency is not vicariously (or strictly) liable for any abuse perpetrated by foster parents on children in their care. An agency is only liable for child abuse perpetrated by foster parents if employees of the agency were negligent in screening or supervising a placement.[61]

Kinship Foster Care

Despite the problems with foster care, many foster home placements work out very successfully, especially when younger children are involved.[62] A child may stay many years in the same home, and may eventually be adopted by the foster parents. Unfortunately, for older children, particularly if they have significant behavioural or emotional problems caused by prior abuse or neglect, foster placements are often less successful.

A challenge for this field is the successful recruitment of foster parents who match the social and cultural backgrounds of children being referred to care in Canada. As mentioned previously, children from Aboriginal families are disproportionately represented among children in care, and there are recent efforts to increase the number of Aboriginal foster families. This is also being addressed through the further development of kinship care.

Kinship care is a relatively new program option on the continuum of child welfare care, and it has gained acceptance in many jurisdictions across Canada. Kinship care describes situations where a caregiver who knew the child before placement (a friend, relative or acquaintance to a child at risk) agrees to act as a foster parent and have the child live with their family for an open-ended period

---

[60] See e.g., *D.K. v. Miazga*, [2003] S.J. 830 (Q.B.) where 12 foster parents and their family members were drawn through a lengthy investigation and prosecution; although eventually acquitted, their lives were profoundly disrupted and they were deeply scarred; they recovered significant judgements for malicious persecution.

[61] See e.g., *K.L.B. v. British Columbia*, 2003 S.C.C. 51.

[62] J.A. Silver, B.J. Amster, and T. Haecker (Eds.), *Young Children and Foster Care* (Baltimore: Paul H. Brookes Publishing Company, 1999).

of time. These foster homes are recruited specifically for the child in question, and in many cases these foster parents do not take into care any more children following the child's discharge and are not available for other child welfare placements. Like other foster parents, there is screening, training, supervision and compensation, and the agency retains legal custody of the child.

This form of care is known as *kinship care* in New Brunswick, *specified foster care* in Alberta and Quebec, *special relative and non-relative care* in Nova Scotia, and *restricted family care* in British Columbia. This new resource is growing steadily in many Canadian jurisdictions and more than 9% of all placements in British Columbia are now identified as being restricted family care.[63] The United States has been actively developing kinship foster care homes over the last ten years, and state level estimates suggest that between 30 and 57% of all foster parents in the child welfare system in the USA are now kinship care-givers.[64]

Staffed Group Homes

Staffed group homes are facilities established for the express purpose of caring for children and operated by paid staff. There are generally five to ten children living in a group home with maximum occupancy based on the licensed number deemed appropriate for the design and size of the home. They have more structured programs than foster homes. The amount of training and education of the staff can vary by jurisdiction; however, there is an emphasis on employees having some specialized training in child and youth care leading to a diploma or degree in child and youth care.

There are many different types of group homes. Some have a particular philosophical or psychological approach. Some are operated by a married couple who operate the home as full-time employment, and are often known as group foster homes, while others have staff on rotating shifts. It costs the child welfare authorities much more to keep a child in a group home than in a foster home, but it is possible to place older and more difficult children in these homes. Group homes may be operated directly by the child welfare authorities, though most are privately owned and take children on a contractual basis; some group homes are operated by non-profit corporations.

Some child welfare agencies operate receiving and assessment homes, which are designated for short-term stays immediately following the apprehension of a child, or following a foster care placement breakdown. Both foster homes and group homes are located in the community, and an effort is made to integrate children into the community, by having them attend local schools for example.

In most jurisdictions, there are government regulations and standards for the physical facilities and staffing of group homes. In some provinces like Ontario

---

[63] *Supra*, note 3.

[64] M. Scannapieco, "Formal Kinship Care Practice Models" in R.L. Hegar and M. Scannapieco (Eds.), *Kinship Foster Care: Policy, Practice and Research* (New York: Oxford University Press, 1999).

and Alberta, group homes are screened through a licensing mechanism.[65] The licensing brings greater accountability and scrutiny at the outset. Once licensed a group home is also subject to some monitoring, but the licensee has the right to some form of hearing or review before the licence is removed.[66] As an alternative to licensing, New Brunswick uses a contracting process which also provides for screening and monitoring.[67]

Institutional Care

In the middle of the twentieth century, significant numbers of child welfare wards in Canada lived in relatively large residential facilities or orphanages, often operated by religious or non-profit agencies or by child welfare agencies directly. The number of child welfare wards living in larger residential facilities in Canada declined dramatically over the last three decades of the twentieth century, in part reflecting the decline in numbers of children in care due to an increase in family preservation efforts. There were also growing concerns about abuse of children in large institutions, and more generally about the quality of care provided for children in larger institutions.[68]

While there continue to be concerns about overuse of institutional care,[69] it is generally acknowledged that there will always be a need for some forms of insti-tutionalized residential care for hard-to-serve youth in the care of child welfare agencies.[70] Residential treatment services have increasingly begun to take a more inclusive and collaborative approach to working with the families of children in care.

Today in Canada, residential facilities are typically used for children and adolescents with behavioural or emotional problems; these facilities provide residential treatment for children and youth who pose a high level of concern for community placements. Despite the decreased use of this costly resource, there continues to be a demand for some specialized residential treatment services for hard-to-serve youth. For example, in 1999 in Alberta approximately 6% of child welfare placements in Alberta were designated as residential treatment, compared to approximately 3% for Nova Scotia and Saskatchewan.[71]

---

[65] See, e.g., *Child and Family Services Act*, R.S.O. 1990, c. 11, ss. 192, 23-29.

[66] See, e.g., *Child and Family Services Act*, R.S.O. 1990, c.11, ss. 197-19.

[67] See, e.g., *Family Services Act*, S.N.B. 1980, c. F-2.2, s. 22(4).

[68] M. Harris, *Unholy Orders: Tragedy at Mount Cashel* (Markham ON: Penguin Books Canada Ltd., 1990); R.B. McKenzie, "Rethinking Orphanages: An Introduction" in R.B. McKenzie (Ed.), *Rethinking Orphanages for the 21st Century* (New York: Sage Publications, 1998); and E. Smith, "Bring Back the Orphanages: What Policy Makers of Today can Learn from the Past" (1995), 74(1) *Child Welfare* 115-142.

[69] I. Hoffart and R.M. Grinnell, "Behavioural Differences of Children in Institutional and Group Home Care" (1993), 6(1) *Community Alternatives – International Journal of Family Care* 33-47; K. Wells, "Residential Treatment as Long-Term Treatment: An Examination of Some Issues" (1993), 15 *Child and Youth Services Review* 165-171; and K. Wells and D. Whittington, "Characteristics of Youths Referred to Residential Treatment: Implications for Program Design" (1993), 15 *Children and Youth Services Review* 195-217.

[70] J. Anglin, "Staffed Group Homes for Youth: Towards a Framework for Understanding" in K. Kufeldt and B. McKenzie (Eds.), *Child Welfare: Connecting Research, Policy and Practice* (Waterloo: Wilfred Laurier University Press, 2003).

[71] *Supra*, note 3.

Because of the vulnerability of children in agency care, in some provinces, such as Ontario, there is a special process of approval for placements of children in residential facilities that accommodate ten or more children, with children having the right to seek review of the placement decisions before an administrative tribunal.[72]

Secure Treatment

In most provinces, there is also the possibility for a child welfare agency to place a ward in a secure mental health facility. These facilities are designed to offer highly restricted and supervised care to youth who are at high risk and in need of psychiatric treatment. Many of the youth who are in these facilities are placed directly by their parents, but agencies can also place wards in these facilities. These placements are expensive, and there are often waiting lists for admission. Secure treatment is used only for a relatively small number of child welfare cases. In Alberta, for example, only about 0.5% of all child welfare placements are in secure treatment.[73]

Placement in a secure treatment facility is highly intrusive, and may, for example, result in the administration of psychotropic drugs and the use of restraints. Secure treatment should only be used when less restrictive approaches are not appropriate. Placement in secure treatment should only be used if a child is suffering from a mental or behavioural disorder and poses a danger to self or to others, and it is necessary to confine the child in order to alleviate the disorder. There are concerns that children who are troublesome and have behavioural problems may be inappropriately placed in mental health facilities. Agency wards, who typically do not have parents to act as advocates, may be especially vulnerable to inappropriate placement. A number of provinces, including Alberta and Ontario, now have special legal processes that require court approval or review for placements of agency wards in secure mental health facilities.[74]

The Placement Decision

The formal decision on where a child welfare ward is to be placed is made by child welfare agency staff. When there is a child protection hearing or a status review, the agency generally provides the court with information about the agency's plan for placement. The judge, however, can only make a general order for a committal to agency care and cannot designate a specific type of care or a specific facility or foster home. The maximum length of a placement may be controlled by a court order that limits the length of wardship.

---

[72] *Child and Family Services Act*, R.S.O. 1990, c.11, ss. 26 and 34(6).

[73] *Supra*, note 3.

[74] See, e.g., *Child Welfare Act*, R.S.A. 2000, Chapter C-12, s 44(6); and *Child and Family Services Act*, R.S.O., 1990, c.11, s. 117(1).

Some provinces have balanced the judicial desire to get involved in the placement of children with the administrative need to control those decisions. Ontario and Alberta statutorily require a child service plan to be presented to the court at the time of a wardship application.[75] The requirement for a plan may, in practice, give a judge who is concerned that a child receive a specific placement a certain amount of leverage in making a written recommendation as part of the order. If the placement recommended in the plan is not used without a good reason, when the case comes up for review, the judge may take that departure from the plan into account in deciding whether to continue the wardship. In addition to its function as an accountability device, the child service plan requires the worker to focus on the specific needs of the child and to make an assessment about what is best for the child.

In some jurisdictions there is now legislation to provide general guidance to child welfare workers in the making of placement decisions. The Alberta statute directs that any decision concerning the placement of a child outside the child's family should take into account:

- the benefits to the child of a placement that respects the child's familial, cultural, social and religious heritage;

- the benefits to the child of stability and continuity of care and relationships;

- the benefits to the child of a placement within or as close as possible to the child's home community;

- the mental, emotional, and physical needs of the child and the child's mental, emotional, and physical stage of development; and

- whether the proposed placement is suitable for the child.[76]

While similar criteria are used in policy manuals in other jurisdictions, the value of having guidance in legislation is that it may increase awareness and accountability for placement decisions.

The guidance provided by legislation or policy manuals to agency staff is very general, and in practice the placement decisions involve a balancing of a child's needs with the available placement resources. The placement decisions of front line staff are expected to focus on the needs of the child, though they are reviewed by supervisors who are, of course, aware of funding issues and costs, as well as agency responsibility. Some jurisdictions utilize a placement review committee that assists the worker in determining the needs of children to be placed, and in reviewing available placement resources. The meeting generates a detailed written description for the file, and initiates a bring-forward system to activate a regular review of the placement.

---

[75] See e.g., *Child and Family Services Act*, R.S.O. 1990, c. 11, s. 56.

[76] See e.g., *Child Welfare Act*, R.S.A. 2000, C-12, s. 2(h); and e.g., *Child and Family Services Act*, R.S.O. 1990, c. 11, s. 62(2).

The screening of placement resources may be subject to subsequent court review if a child is abused or neglected in care. A negligence suit for a poor child welfare placement may be brought by an adult survivor of abuse while a child in care, or by a parent or guardian acting on behalf of a child. These suits are not uncommon in the United States, and Canadian courts have accepted that child welfare agencies may be liable to the child for negligence in the screening or monitoring of placements.[77] In deciding whether there was negligence, the courts will consider the accepted standards in the profession at the time when the placement occurred, and ask whether the agency, individual, or care provider met that standard.

Child welfare agencies are increasingly developing clear written standards and procedures for screening and monitoring placement resources. In addition to the agency, the front line workers who make the placement decisions could be personally sued for malpractice. These workers deserve the protection of careful screening and well-enforced standards for placement resources.

The Scope of Wardship and Rights of Parents

A key distinction in provincial legislation concerns the scope of a temporary wardship order compared with a permanent wardship order. Parents have greater rights if a child is a temporary ward as there is an expectation that they will be resuming full care of their children and that they should have as full a role in the lives of their children as is possible. Generally parental rights diminish if the child is made a permanent ward, and are further reduced if their access rights are terminated and permanency planning moves towards adoption.

The scope of permanent wardship is reasonably uniform in Canada. Provincial legislation assigns to the child welfare agency the "care, custody, and control"[78] of a child who is made a permanent ward. This includes the right to decide where the child will live and to make medical care decisions, while leaving the parents certain residual rights, such as a presumptive right to act as guardian of a child's property rights, though that guardianship may be terminated in separate proceedings. Parents may also retain access rights to a permanent ward, and may at some point seek to terminate the wardship if their circumstances change and they are able to resume care of their children. If parental access rights are terminated, a child may be placed for adoption by the agency without the parents having notice or being required to consent.[79]

There is some variation between jurisdictions in the rights and duties of the agency that go with temporary wardship. In most provinces, the legislation is not explicit about the respective rights of the child welfare agency and the parents while the child is a temporary ward. By implication, in these jurisdictions temporary wardship rights include at least physical care and control, and

---

[77] See e.g., *K.L.B. v. British Columbia*, 2003 S.C.C. 51, and discussion in Chapter 13.

[78] See e.g., *Child and Family Services Act*, R.S.O. 1990, c. 11, s. 63(2).

[79] See discussion of adoption in Chapter 6.

the right to make medical decisions, but do not extend to making decisions about such matters as religious upbringing. Clearly, the agency cannot place a child who is a temporary ward for adoption.

Some jurisdictions have legislation that deals more explicitly with the temporary wardship rights of a child welfare authority. There are essentially two types of explicit temporary wardship schemes, though both share the same philosophy — to keep the parents involved while working towards family reunification.

In Ontario, the legislation presumes that access will be granted to parents during temporary wardship (Society wardship), unless a court determines that access is not in the child's best interests.[80] The parents retain the right to consent to marriage of a child under the age 18,[81] and the courts will require that parents with sufficient means contribute to the financial support of their children.[82] If the withholding of medical treatment was not the reason for the protection order, a court can grant the parents the right to give or refuse medical consent during temporary wardship.[83] While the child is in care on a temporary order, the parents will normally have the right to be consulted on major decisions concerning the child, such as in regard to placement and health care, though the agency has the final responsibility for making these decisions.[84] The Ontario approach is to give parents specific rights, as exceptions to the general care, control and custody given to the child protection authorities over their wards.

Alberta has achieved the goal of parental involvement through a more general device. During a temporary guardianship order, the director of Child Welfare becomes a joint guardian with the parents, and may exercise all parental rights except in connection with adoption. The Alberta legislation gives the court discretion to grant parental access, require financial contributions from the parents, and generally set "conditions under which the director shall consult with the guardian on matters affecting the child."[85] This gives the court flexible scope for granting parental input, without allocating specific rights (e.g., consent to medical treatment) to the parents.

Wardship, while the child is in care, has a public interest purpose. It gives the child welfare agency security in its placement planning. Subject to regular court or administrative reviews, the agency knows that the natural parents cannot interfere with the child's stability and upbringing. There is more than administrative convenience behind such a policy. The agency's security is necessary for permanency planning, especially when it applies for permanent wardship.

The developing concept of private guardianship, contrasted to public wardship (or guardianship) by an agency, is helping some jurisdictions find

---

[80] See e.g., *Child and Family Services Act*, R.S.O. 1990, c. 11, s. 61(5).

[81] *Ibid.*, s. 62(4).

[82] *Child and Family Services Act*, R.S.O. 1990, c. 11, s. 60.

[83] *Child and Family Services Act*, R.S.O. 1990, c. 11, s. 62(1)-(3).

[84] *Child and Family Services Act*, R.S.O. 1990, c. 11, s. 61(5) (input on major decisions); and s. 62 (consent to medical treatment).

[85] *Child Welfare Act*, R.S.A. 2000, c. C-12, s. 31.

more options for permanent placements. Manitoba and Alberta have private guardianship provisions in their child welfare legislation.[86] These statutes make it possible for a foster parent or other proposed guardian to apply to court for sole guardianship of a child who is in the permanent care of the child welfare authorities. If an order of private guardianship is made, the public wardship of the child welfare agency ceases and the foster parents (or other applicants) become the sole legal guardians of the person. In addition, private guardianship is reversible upon application to court. In Alberta, legislation permits a guardian (or a parent) whose rights have not been terminated to apply to end private guardianship by another person.[87]

The private guardianship option may, for example, be helpful for disabled children, who are hard to place for adoption. It may also help older children or those who have positive contact with natural parents who are permanently unable to care for them. Private guardianship by a foster parent may be preferable to adoption by some other person, which could disrupt a stable foster care situation, and give the foster parents more control and responsibility while leaving the possibility of government financial support.

Placement Changes

The experience of children in care, especially older children, tends to be characterized by considerable instability, something that is undesirable for any child, especially one who has suffered abuse, neglect or other trauma. Permanency planning is a critical element in child welfare service planning, though it is difficult to achieve for many children referred to care. The number of times that children move while in care has long been viewed as a concern, though there continues to be a need for further research that examines the longitudinal analyses of children's experience in care.[88] In one study, it was discovered that more than one-third of permanent wards lived in three or more placements since becoming permanent wards, and that almost one half had three or more social workers.[89] A review of the foster children involved in the Canadian *Looking After Children Project* indicated that more than 50% of these young people had three or more placements.[90] Aboriginal children in care seem to have more moves than did non-Aboriginal children,[91] while children in kinship care are seen to have fewer placement changes than do children in non-kinship care.[92]

---

[86] See e.g., *Child and Family Services Act*, C.D.S.M. 1987, c. C80, s. 77; and *Child Welfare Act*, R.S.A. 2000, c. C-12, s. 52.

[87] See e.g., *Child Welfare Act*, R.S.A. 1990, c. C-12, s. 57(3).

[88] D. Rosenbluth, "Moving In and Out of Foster Care" in J. Hudson and B. Galaway (Eds.), *Child Welfare in Canada: Research and Policy Implications* (Toronto: Thompson Educational Publishing, Inc., 1995), 233-244; and D. Webster, R.P. Barth and B. Needell, "Placement Stability for Children in Out of Home Care: A Longitudinal Analysis" (2000), 79(5) *Child Welfare* 614-632.

[89] Raychaba, *supra*, note 53.

[90] Kufeldt et al., *supra*, note 6.

[91] Rosenbluth, *supra*, note 88.

[92] Webster et al., *supra*, note 88.

Advocates for a family preservation approach to child welfare often focus on the inability of child welfare agencies to provide children in care with permanent and stable care, pointing out that children in care often experience multiple placement changes, and a turnover in social workers.[93] Placements may break down because the child cannot adjust to the placement offered, or because the people offering the placement find that a child is unmanageable, or the facility is closing. Given the virtually intractable nature of the problems of some of the children in the system and the lack of resources, there will inevitably be serious shortcomings to child welfare placement. Advocates of family preservation argue that when the courts consider how to respond to parents who are providing less than optimal care, it is important that the courts not compare parental care to a hypothetical ideal of parental care, but to the reality of care that the child welfare system is likely to provide. Judges, when considering removing a child from parental care, are usually aware of the fact that committal to care is generally not a magic solution to the problems of a child, and this influences the decisions they make.

It is often a major challenge in the child welfare system to find suitable placements within reasonable proximity of where the parents and children live. In particular, it is often difficult to find placements near communities with relatively large numbers of older children in care. It is not uncommon for children from remote Aboriginal communities to be placed in group homes far from their reserves, and children from downtown inner cities may find themselves placed in group homes in the country. Not only are there issues of cultural shock associated with these placements, but distances from home may make it difficult for these children to maintain contact with their families, and may result in further dislocation when these children return to their communities, as they usually do, at the latest, when their wardship ends. Some jurisdictions will not permit a placement to be changed to a resource outside of the province without special procedures being followed.

The Rights of Children in Care

In 1977, Quebec led the way in Canada towards statutory recognition of the rights of children in the care of child welfare agencies in its *Youth Protection Act*.[94] In 1984, Ontario also enacted a legislative code of rights for children in care, and established a process for children in care to make complaints or allegations of abuse or violations of rights. In addition to the rights granted to children actually in the care of an agency, Ontario has recognized the most extensive set of procedural rights in Canada to children who are the subject of child protection applications. Children may have counsel from the Office of the Children's Lawyer appointed to represent them in any child protection or status review application in court, and a child aged 12 or older is presumptively entitled to

---

[93] Mnookin, *supra*, note 39.
[94] See e.g., *Youth Protection Act*, L.R.Q. 1977, c. P-34.1, ss. 2.4–111.3.

receive notice of and attend at a hearing, can see assessment reports, can consent to the making of an order, and can initiate a review of a placement decision or of a court order.[95] A child of 12 years or older who is in care who objects to the decision of the Children's Aid Society about a placement in a particular group or foster home can ask to have that decision reviewed by an independent board.[96]

The Ontario legislation provides one of the most complete codes of rights for children in care, including the right to:[97]

- private communication with a lawyer and with the Office of Child Advocacy;
- participate in the development of an individual plan of care;
- not be subjected to corporal punishment;
- receive instruction in their religion;
- participate in the development of the child care plan; and
- receive good quality meals, clothing, medical and dental care;
- receive education and recreational activities; and
- be informed of all of their procedural rights under the *Act*.

Further, every licensed service provider, such as a group home, and every child welfare agency must have an internal procedure for hearing alleged violations of the rights of children. Following an internal review, a further complaint can be made to the Minister of Children and Youth Services, who can appoint an independent person to review the complaint and take action. Ontario and most other provinces also have independent offices to receive confidential complaints from children in care about violations of rights or allegations of abuse. The Ontario Office of Child and Family Advocacy, and similar offices in other provinces, do not provide legal representation for children in court proceedings, but rather are authorized to receive complaints and investigate conditions concerning any child in care.[98] These offices have had an important role in dealing with issues of institutional abuse, but even in jurisdictions with these offices, youth may feel intimidated by staff or other youth into not lodging a complaint.[99]

Other jurisdictions in Canada have legislation recognizing the importance of giving explicit statutory rights to children in the care of child welfare agencies, but most provinces have more general statements rather than the more explicit codes found in Quebec and Ontario.[100]

[95] *Child and Family Services Act*, R.S.O. 1990, c. 11, s. 47 (hearings), s. 55 (consent orders), s. 64(6) (status review applications).

[96] *Child and Family Services Act*, R.S.O. 1990, c. 11, s. 34(6).

[97] *Child and Family Services Act*, R.S.O. 1990, c. 11, ss. 99-107.

[98] See *Child and Family Services Act*, R.S.O. 1990, c. 11, s. 102 and ss. 109-110. There are similar offices to investigate complaints from children in care in Alberta, British Columbia, Saskatchewan, Manitoba, Newfoundland and Quebec.

[99] See e.g., M. Geigen-Miller, *It's Time to Break the Silence* (Toronto: Defence for Children International — Canada, 2003).

[100] See e.g., in Alberta, *Child Welfare Act*, R.S.A. 1990, c. C-12: s. 2(b).

The Rights of Foster Parents

Children living with foster parents remain in the legal custody of the child welfare authorities, who have the responsibility for making all major decisions about the child. However, the agency staff who legally make the decisions about a child may see the child relatively infrequently and, due to staff turnover, may not know the child very well. The reality of life for many foster children, especially those who are placed in a foster home at a young age or remain in one home for a significant period of time, is that the foster parents become their true "psychological parents," and the foster parents often know the children much better than the agency staff.

Foster parents traditionally had no legal rights in regard to the children they looked after, and in most jurisdictions in Canada, foster parents still have no legal status in regard to children in their care. Gradually, however, some Canadian legislatures and courts have begun to recognize the profound attachments that many children have to their foster parents, and to afford foster parents limited rights to participate in decisions about children in their care, and in some situations the right to prevent the immediate removal of children from their homes. But there is always a need to appreciate that children come into the care of foster parents under an agreement that creates the expectation that the placement with them will be temporary, and there is a concern that granting rights to foster parents may undermine the rights of biological parents to seek the return of their children.

In some provinces, such as Newfoundland, foster parents have no legal rights in regard to children in their care, and legislation stipulates that a child welfare social worker may remove a child from the care of a foster parent at any time without prior notice.[101] In a British Columbia case, foster parents who cared for a two-year-old special needs child since shortly after his birth went to court to attempt to prevent the transfer of the child to another placement where he could live with some of his siblings. The foster parents argued that the move was contrary to the child's best interests, and two psychologists recommended against the move, as the boy was closely attached to the foster parents. In rejecting the application of the foster parents to prevent the move, Justice Maczko held that the legislation and foster care agreement gave them no standing to challenge the move, observing:[102]

> It is highly probable that foster parents will become attached to the children they care for, particularly when they receive the children immediately after birth. I cannot help but express my admiration for the people who take in needy, handicapped children and care for them as though they were their own.
>
> Unfortunately, the lot of a foster parent is inherently insecure. There are competing interests, such as the interests of biological parents and biological siblings. The legislature anticipated such problems and carefully crafted a statute to ensure that the

---

[101] See e.g., *Child and Family Services Act*, S.N.L. 1998, chap. C-12.1 s 65.

[102] *C.K. v. British Columbia (Ministry of Children and Family Development)*, [2003] B.C.J. 1165 (S.C.), at para. 45-46.

Director has the necessary discretion to act freely in the best interests of the child in care. The...[foster parents] signed a contract with the [Ministry] which contained the following clause:

> A Director may at any time, in his or her sole discretion, retake physical care and control of a child who is receiving services from the Caregiver and revoke any guardianship authority specified or implied, which has been delegated by a Director to the Caregiver.

While most provinces do not grant statutory rights to foster parents, Ontario, Manitoba, and Alberta have given significant legal rights to foster parents, recognizing that foster parents can be important, knowledgeable advocates for the interests of children.

Probably the most important right for foster parents is the ability to challenge removal of the child from their home. Ontario requires that if foster parents have had continuous care of the child for two years, they are to receive notice ten days before a proposed removal.[103] The foster parents can then request an administration review by an official outside the agency, and the child will remain in their care pending the review, unless there is some substantial risk to the child.[104]

Further, Ontario law provides that if foster parents have had the care of a child for at least six months, they are entitled to notice of any child protection hearing or status review hearing in court; they have the right to attend, and may make submissions to the court, though they do not have the right to call evidence or cross-examine witnesses.[105] In practice, in most cases the foster parents will be supporting the position of the child welfare agency in a contested protection hearing. Indeed, not infrequently at a permanent wardship hearing, the agency will argue that it is in the best interests of the child to be adopted by the foster parents, and base part of its case on the close emotional bonds between the foster parents and the child.[106]

Even if the foster parents disagree with the agency position, many of them will be reluctant to take a position contrary to that put forward by the agency. Many foster parents tend to take the view that the decisions of the professional staff at the agency should be respected, and are concerned that if they publicly disagree with the agency, they will not get any more children placed in their homes, depriving them of income from the agency. Further, unlike most biological parents involved in protection proceedings who are low-income individuals and likely to be eligible for legal aid, most foster parents have sufficient resources to make them ineligible for legal aid, and have to pay for counsel if they wish to have a lawyer represent them.

There have, however, been cases in which foster parents have had enough concern for the welfare of a child and enough determination that they have tried to take steps in court to prevent agencies from removing children from their

---

[103] See, e.g., *Child and Family Services Act*, R.S.O. 1990, c. C-11, ss. 61(7).

[104] *Child and Family Services Act*, R.S.O. 1990, c. C-11, ss. 61(7).

[105] *Child and Family Services Act*, R.S.O. 1990, c. C-11, s 39(3).

[106] See e.g., *Catholic Children's Aid Society of Metropolitan Toronto v. M.(C.)*, [1994] 2 S.C.R. 165.

care. Most of the reported cases have involved situations in which the agency plans to remove a child from a long-term foster placement and not to return the child to the care of the biological parents, but rather to place the child in another foster home or with relatives. Some recent Canadian cases have involved Aboriginal children, for whom the agency plan involves placement in an Aboriginal home, or near the child's reserve, but not placement with a parent.

Generally courts have held that foster parents are restricted to the rights that they are afforded under legislation, which usually limits foster parents to seeking a review by an administrative tribunal or board, rather than taking their case to court. There have, however, been cases in which foster parents have persuaded judges that there should be a court hearing to determine whether it is in the interests of the child to be removed from their care.

In the United States there have been a number of decisions in which long-term foster parents have successfully claimed that they were constitutionally entitled to the procedural due process of a court hearing if a child welfare agency plans to move the child to another foster home or to an adoptive placement. On the other hand, at least in situations where a foster parent obtains care of the child through the intervention of an agency, the interests of the foster parents "must be substantially attenuated where the proposed removal from the foster family is to return the child to his natural parents."[107] American courts have indicated that granting foster parents constitutional rights of participation in proceedings about the child is intended to promote the interests of the child, since the foster parents may have important information about the child and a unique understanding of the child's interests.

There have also been occasional cases in Canada in which the courts have been prepared to invoke the *Charter* or their inherent jurisdiction to give long-term foster parents an opportunity for a hearing before a child is removed from their care, generally emphasizing that this is to protect the best interests of the child rather than protecting legal rights that a foster parents may have.[108] Not surprisingly, the courts seem most sympathetic to the position of foster parents in cases where they have had long-term care of children, and the agency decisions have seemed arbitrary and not motivated by any concern about the best interests of the individual child. The courts may also be more inclined to intervene in jurisdictions where there are no provisions for a statutory review process by an administrative board.[109]

---

[107] *Smith v. Organization of Foster Families for Equality and Reform*, 97 S.Crt. 2095 at 2111 (1977), per Brennan J.

[108] *N.P.P. v. Regional Children's Guardian* (1988), 14 R.F.L. (3d) 55 at 78-80 (Alta. Q.B.). See also *Re R.M.S.*, [2001] S.J. 724 (Q.B.), per Smith J.

[109] See e.g. *R.L. v. C.A.S of Niagara*, [2002] O.J. 4793 (C.A.); *K.J. v. Catholic C.A.S of Toronto*, [2003] O.J. 5058 (Div. Ct.); and *C.A.S of Niagara v. K.K.*, [2003] O.J. 837(Ct. J.) where foster parents were not able to persuade judges to invoke their *parens patriae* or statutory jurisdictions to prevent removal of children from their care and placement with biological relatives; the courts declined to take jurisdiction because these were cases where foster parents had a limited right of review by administrative bodies.

Conclusion

Until the last decades of the twentieth century, relatively large numbers of children were in the care of the state, and these children effectively had no rights. We are now learning that tragically large numbers of these children in the care of the state in Canada — in residential schools, in juvenile justice facilities and in the child welfare system — were subjected to physical, emotional and sexual abuse. In the last few decades of the twentieth century, with the greater emphasis on family preservation and on the rights of parents, there were changes in the child welfare system resulting in fewer children coming into care. Further, there has been a greater recognition of the rights and needs of children in care. While the granting of rights to children in care sometimes makes the jobs of those who work in the child welfare system seem frustrating, it has almost certainly contributed to making the system more responsive to the needs of children, and recognizes the fundamental human rights of children.

While the child welfare system was established to provide care for children whose parents are unable to care for them adequately, children in the care of child welfare authorities remain a needy and vulnerable population. Their needs arise from the fact that most of them have been abused or neglected by their parents or relatives, and are suffering from a range of maltreatment. Further, a disproportionately large number of these children have special needs, for example, neurological problems related to maternal drug or alcohol abuse during pregnancy. Many of these children have emotional and behavioural problems that result in some caregivers in the child welfare system finding them "hard to handle."

While the child welfare system undoubtedly provides better care for children than was the case a few decades ago, issues of systemic abuse and neglect are still significant concerns. Children in care are too often subjected to restraint or rough treatment by staff. Further, breakdowns in placements and disruption in relationships between agency staff and children still characterize the lives of children in long-term care. The child care system has improved, but the state is too often still an inadequate "substitute parent."

There continues to be a critical need for debate and research into how to effectively operationalize the "best interests of the child" concept.[110] Almost two decades ago, Michael Wald challenged the professional community to develop an evidence-based approach to child welfare outcomes to determine if foster care is better than parental care. This requires research to determine what the bests interests are for specific children, under which conditions, and for what aspects of development.[111] An eminent Canadian child psychiatrist, the late Dr. Paul Steinhauer, similarly concluded his 1991 text on the least detrimental placement alternative for children by identifying the need for systematic and

---

[110] Goldstein et al., *supra*, note 39; and P.D. Steinhauer, *The Least Detrimental Alternative* (Toronto: University of Toronto Press, 1991).

[111] Wald et al., *supra*, note 7.

controlled research in order for foster care to ensure that child welfare placement decisions are governed by fact rather than fiction, and to establish objective guidelines to determine when this costly placement resource is truly indicated.[112] There continues to be a vital need for sound research in this area if
Canadian society is truly to advance the needs of its most vulnerable citizens.

---

[112] Steinhauer, *supra*, note 110.

5

Juvenile Prostitution and Street Kids: Challenges for Protection Workers and the Justice System

Augustine Brannigan and Erin Gibbs Van Brunschot[1]

For the past two decades in Canada, there appears to have been a significant increase in street prostitution, as well as a growing search for social and legal weapons to fight the activity itself and related harms. Public concern has been expressed over the involvement of youth in prostitution, as well with the broader issue of adolescents "living on the street" and engaging in prostitution, minor crime, drug dealing or begging. The living conditions of these youths place them at great risk of injury, exploitation and disease. A disproportionately large number of these adolescents are from abusive or neglectful home situations, and they are typically distrusting of adult authority figures, such as social workers.

If these children are placed in the care of a child welfare agency, they will often be "runners," leaving the protective, but controlled environment of a group or foster home to return to the excitement and freedom of "the street." While there have been increased efforts in Canada to provide an effective response to these often tragic situations, it can be very challenging to provide appropriate intervention in these cases.

Internationally, particularly in Thailand and the Philippines, there has been great concern with sex tourism and the exploitation of young women and adolescent males and females by men from the industrialized countries. The demise of the Soviet Bloc has also been associated with a sharp rise in the sex trade, and the movement of women and adolescent males in the sex trade from Eastern to Western Europe. In Africa, prostitution appears to have become one of the main vectors for the spread of HIV infection. Prostitution, then, has become a global problem. In this global context, the commercialization of sex has become associated with the exploitation of women by men, the exploitation of children by adults, and the exploitation of the developing world by neo-colonial powers, as well as the spread of one of the most harmful pandemics in recent history.

[1] Augustine Brannigan is Professor of Sociology, University of Calgary, Alberta. Erin Gibbs Van Brunschot is Assistant Professor of Sociology, University of Calgary, Alberta.

At this time in Canada there is widespread concern over violence against sex trade workers by pimps, "johns" and others, including the disappearance and murder of over 50 women involved in street prostitution in Vancouver in the 1990s. Although there may be optimism in social and legal circles that "something can be done" about the prevalence of prostitution and the victimization of prostitutes by making and enforcing appropriate criminal and social welfare laws, the legal objectives of such laws are not always consistent or well defined. The laws that deal with prostitution, especially juvenile prostitution, often have contradictory intentions or effects.

In Canada, the acquisition of sexual services from, and living on the avails of, an adolescent prostitute are viewed as child sexual abuse and can, in theory, be punished with lengthy periods of imprisonment. These laws reflect a desire to limit harm to prostitutes, based on a victimization perspective, but in practice there are few prosecutions under these statutes. Further, reflecting the societal ambivalence about the sex trade in Canada, prostitution *per se* is not a crime, and communication in private between adults is similarly beyond the reach of the law.

In this chapter we describe the extent of adolescent or "pre-adult" prostitution in Canada. We examine the current legal regimes in both the areas of criminal law and child welfare law that are designed to curb juvenile prostitution or abate its adverse social effects. And, finally, we explore some alternative social responses to juvenile prostitution and consider how they might operate to meet specific social objectives.

Prostitution: Nuisance versus Exploitation

Throughout the 1980s, prostitution received considerable attention in urban Canada and elsewhere. The number of charges and convictions for prostitution-related charges jumped significantly. Street activity is believed to have expanded similarly, although the figures for "soliciting for the purposes of prostitution" in public were extremely low after the anti-soliciting law was rendered virtually unenforceable by the Supreme Court of Canada decision in *R v. Hutt* in 1978,[2] which required that the act of soliciting be "pressing and persistent" to qualify as a crime. Since most street prostitutes wasted little time with those uninterested, charges under this law ceased for all practical purposes after 1978. Canadian municipal politicians became so concerned over the street prostitution nuisance that municipal bylaws were enacted in the early 1980s in Calgary, Montreal, Vancouver, Niagara Falls and other cities in attempts to suppress the growing trade in the aftermath of the *Hutt* decision. While these municipal bylaws were eventually ruled unconstitutional,[3] the federal government

---

[2] *R v. Hutt*, [1978] 2 S.C.R. 476.
[3] *Westendorp v. The Queen*, [1983] 1 S.C.R. 43.

responded to the problem of public solicitation in 1985 by enacting a new criminal law, making it an offence to "in any manner communicate with any person...for the purpose of engaging in prostitution" in any public place.[4]

The focus on the nuisance associated with street prostitution soon became overshadowed by the recognition of the involvement of children and adolescents in prostitution, and the need to develop a social and legal response designed to curb their sexual exploitation by adults. Canadian newspapers throughout the 1980s were painting a picture of an epidemic of juvenile prostitution. Rings of juveniles were reported to be working in "trick pads" that were grossing millions of dollars annually. Child advocates and the national press refocused their concerns from the sensationalistic stories of lurid sex on urban strolls to stories of child sexual abuse. The rationale for the suppression of prostitution by adults that had been derived from considerations of public nuisance was superceded by a second orientation. Juvenile prostitution became regarded as a form of pathological conduct among survivors of family abuse, as well as a source of sexual victimization by those who exploited the vulnerability of children and youth for their own sexual gratification. This line of thinking was evident in the 1984 *Badgley Report*,[5] which focused on the involvement of adolescents in prostitution, the role of sexual abuse in the backgrounds of adolescent prostitutes (as well as in the general public), and the medical and psychological consequences of sexual abuse.

The Badgley Committee felt that the law was ill-equipped to ensure the protection of adolescents and argued against censuring adolescent prostitutes under the *Criminal Code*. The Committee believed that juvenile prostitution was less a case of delinquency by young persons, than a case of sexual abuse *of* young persons, and that the focus of criminal law should be to censure the conduct of their "johns." The federal government subsequently revised the age of consent for sexual acts in Canada, created relatively harsh penalties both for those living on the avails of adolescent prostitutes and for procuring adolescents for prostitution, and further made it an offence for any person to purchase or attempt to purchase the sexual services of an adolescent.

As a consequence, Canadian law took two radically different approaches to prostitution. Prostitution (activities associated with communication in *public* for the purposes of buying and selling sex) was prohibited under a federal criminal law designed to curb nuisance. At the same time, federal criminal law intended to prevent the exploitation of adolescents also imposed significant penalties against both the customers and pimps involved with juvenile prostitutes.

---

[4] See *Criminal Code*, s. 213.

[5] *Badgley Report*, known formally as *Report of the Committee on Sexual Offences Against Children and Youth*; the Committee was chaired by Robin Badgley (Ottawa: Department of Supply and Services, 1984), [hereinafter *Badgley Report*].

The Extent of Juvenile Prostitution in Canada

In 1987, the Department of Justice undertook an evaluation of the law enacted in 1985 prohibiting public communication for the purpose of prostitution.[6] Part of this research entailed an examination of adolescent prostitution to determine whether the newly enacted law was having an impact on this aspect of the phenomenon. However, there was (and remains) some controversy about who is defined as adolescent or juvenile. The Badgley Committee defined juvenile prostitutes as those under age 21. In the 1987 national survey, 56% of the 229 "juvenile prostitutes" interviewed were aged 18, 19 or 20, though the criminal law established 18 as the age of consent for engaging in prostitution.

Others effectively confine the concept of juvenile prostitution to those under age 16, particularly in the context of child welfare legislation where, in provinces like Ontario, "children" may be apprehended and brought into custody for their own protection if they pose a danger to themselves, but only if they are under the age of 16.

In Alberta, in 1998 the government defined anyone engaged in prostitution under the age of 18 as "a child,"[7] thereby providing that these children could be apprehended and involuntarily placed in care, even though provincial child welfare law generally accepts persons over the age of 15 as free to decline provincial child welfare assistance.

The debate about age is important, since it is assumed that young persons cannot be permitted to work as prostitutes since their lack of maturity makes their decision uninformed. Further, prior sexual or physical abuse raises the issue of whether the decision to engage in prostitution was made without capacity, since for persons prematurely forced to depart from home due to abuse, the notion of a "free choice" to engage in prostitution is not realistic.

A second definitional problem concerns the kinds of behaviour that count as prostitution. Interviews conducted in five major centers as part of the review of the anti-communication law indicate that when social agencies or members of the media talk about juvenile prostitutes, they are often referring to a broad group of homeless or runaway youths.[8] These "street kids" are sometimes known to exchange sexual encounters for food, lodging, gifts, affection, or even to experiment with their own sexuality. Researchers discovered that young male prostitutes frequently work on the street as a way of "coming out" and meeting other gay males. These young people often do not come to the attention of the law enforcement officials or appear in official statistics as prostitutes. Obviously, the different ages and circumstances associated with these different populations may account for differing definitions of juvenile prostitution and varying official estimates of its frequency.

---

[6] See J. Fleischman, *Street Prostitution: Assessing the Impact of the Law, Synthesis Report* (Ottawa: Federal Department of Justice, 1989).

[7] *Protection of Children Involved in Prostitution Act*, S.A. 1998, c. P-19.3 (the "PCHIP Act" or "Act").

[8] J. Fleischman, *Prostitution in Ontario: An Overview* (Ottawa: Federal Department of Justice, 1984).

In Canada, the data gathered in the evaluation of the 1985 anti-communication law made it possible to devise an estimate of the proportion of persons charged in the various urban centres who were "adolescents" or "juveniles" following a federal criminal criterion. Persons who were prosecuted under the *Young Offenders Act* would by definition be aged 12-17 — excluding persons both older and younger than this age. The police arrest of prostitutes suggested that in the late 1980s some 10% of persons arrested for communicating in public for the purposes of prostitution were under the age of 18. The figure was 13% in Toronto and Winnipeg, 14% in Calgary, and 12% in Vancouver.[9] It is instructive that no figures were reported for Montreal, since in that city police have not viewed the involvement of adolescents in prostitution as a problem of offending that was to be addressed by charging; in Montreal, all cases of adolescents engaging in prostitution are diverted by the police to the control of social services.

The vast majority of prostitution-related charges are for communication in public for the purposes of prostitution. In total, more men than women are charged with prostitution-related offences, largely reflecting the number of customers charged, as well as those living off the avails of prostitution. Among those who are under the age of 18, however, over 80% of those who are charged are female. This may reflect the fact that police use arrest for communication to remove juvenile prostitutes from the "stroll," and that there are substantially more females relative to males working as street prostitutes. In the early 1990s, approximately 300-400 prostitution-related charges per year were laid against those under the age of 18, representing 3-4% of all charges per year. By early in the new century, prostitution-related charges for those under 18 had fallen very substantially to under one hundred a year, reflecting changes in legislation and police approaches to juvenile prostitution.

Legal Approaches to Juvenile Prostitution

An important issue of debate among politicians, policy makers, practitioners and academics centres around how the sale of sex (including both street prostitution and escort services) should be viewed. The way in which it is viewed has major social and legal implications. For example, if any form of prostitution is viewed as a crime, then any attempts to regulate such an activity are misdirected. For others, the sale of sex is best viewed as work. Sex workers then become workers not unlike others in more mainstream, less stigmatized occupations. In Canada, there is profound societal ambivalence towards prostitution. Prostitution itself is not a crime, and escort services operate legally, though without explicit mention of the sexual services that their clientele and workers understand to be part of the "service." On the other hand, public communication for

---

[9] A. Brannigan and J. Fleischman, "Juvenile Prostitution and Mental Health: Policing Delinquency or Treating Pathology?" (1989), 4 *Canadian Journal of Law and Society* 77-98.

the purposes of prostitution (street prostitution) is a criminal offence, and there are various offences related to pimping or the operation of a brothel.

Even in countries like the Netherlands that have very liberal policies towards prostitution, the involvement of juveniles is not legal. In contrast to adult involvement in prostitution, juvenile prostitution is most often seen as a form of victimization. The victimization framework assumes that prostitution activity is the site of victimization and/or the outcome of past victimization experiences such as sexual and familial abuse. The contradiction between viewing participation in juvenile prostitution (or the most common form of it, street prostitution) as a criminal offence and viewing it as victimization has fuelled public debate. There still is little consensus in Canada about how to deal with prostitution in general, and juvenile prostitution in particular.

This quandary — whether the adolescent prostitute ought to be viewed as a rational actor committing a crime, or simply as a victim caught in the web of past and present victimization experiences — is evident in the first major study of adolescent involvement in prostitution in Canada. The 1984 *Badgley Report* was the product of a four-year inquiry into sexual offending against children and youth, and dealt with a range of issues, including the treatment of child victims of sexual abuse in the courts. This report also was the first major national study of juvenile prostitution.

The Badgley Committee advocated both criminalization and treatment of juvenile prostitutes as victims. The Committee concluded that "the amelioration of the tragic plight of juvenile prostitutes lies...chiefly in the implementation of social rather than legal initiatives," but also advocated the creation of a specific criminal offence aimed exclusively at juvenile prostitutes:[10]

> There are no effective means of stopping the demonstrated harms that these children and youths bring upon themselves. For these reasons, the Committee believes that the implementation of criminal sanctions against these children and youths must be made a legal possibility by creating an offence in order that social intervention can take place.

The Committee recommended that social initiatives were to be undertaken with these youths *after* they had been criminally charged, with the youth justice system seen as a route for requiring juvenile prostitutes to have counselling, treatment and social supports.

The recommendations of the Badgley Committee regarding juvenile prostitution were subject to considerable criticism. Lowman argued that by ignoring the literature on the centrality of the family history in the creation of juvenile prostitution, the Badgley Committee "reasserts the sanctity of the family form, and reaffirms the role of specialists in restoring family 'health.'"[11] Brock and Kinsmen observed that the Badgley Committee categorized juvenile

---

[10] *Badgley Report* at 1046.
[11] J. Lowman, "Taking Young Prostitutes Seriously" (1987), 24(1) *Canadian Review of Sociology and Anthropology* 99-116, at 110.

prostitution, pornography, incest, sexual violence and consensual sex into the singular category of sexual abuse, and failed to recognize the differences between consensual and non-consensual sexual activities. By failing to distinguish between the various activities that have been included under the Committee's broad category of "sexual abuse," and obscuring the "social organization of gender differences between male and female young people in its unitary categor[y] of 'child,'" the Committee pathologized the female adolescent prostitute.[12]

The Law and Juvenile Prostitution

The Badgley Committee recommended the creation of a specific criminal offence that would allow the police to arrest and charge juveniles found to be engaging in prostitution. The creation of this type of "status offence" (a criminal offence that could be committed by an adolescent) was inconsistent with the introduction of the *Young Offenders Act* in 1984, a statute that emphasized that youths were to have the same rights as adults, and this recommendation was not accepted by the federal government. There remain real inconsistencies and contradictions in the legal responses to juvenile prostitution. Past and present legislation attempting to deal with young people involved in prostitution fails to resolve the tension between the juvenile prostitute as victim and as offender.

The *Youth Criminal Justice Act* (which replaced the *Young Offenders Act* on April 1, 2003) stresses the responsibility of adolescents for their actions, with the youth assumed to be capable of making rational decisions and exercising legal rights. At the same time, child welfare legislation treats children as victims, and is premised on adolescents lacking the capacity to make rational decisions. As discussed earlier, there is ambivalence in legal attitudes towards prostitution, with public communication for the purpose of engaging in prostitution being a crime, whether as a prostitute or customer, as are certain offences specifically related to juvenile prostitution, but prostitution itself being legal.

At least in theory, the youth criminal justice and child welfare systems both take account of adolescence as a distinct stage of development, giving adolescents greater rights and responsibilities than children, but offering greater protections and in some contexts giving fewer rights than are afforded to adults. For criminal law purposes, a child is someone below the age of 12, who can neither be charged with a criminal offence nor consent to sexual relations. Under the *Youth Criminal Justice Act* and the preceding *Young Offenders Act*, youths 12 through 17 years of age can be charged with committing the same crimes as adults, but they are generally not *as* responsible or *as* accountable as adults.

Starting at age 14, a youth can give a valid consent to engaging in voluntary sexual relations with another youth or an adult, and a youth at the age of 12 can

---

[12] D. R. Brock and G. Kinsmen, "Patriarchal Relations Ignored: An Analysis and Critique of the Badgley Report on Sexual Offenses Against Children and Youth" (1986), 107-126, in J. Lowman, M.A. Jackson, T.S. Palys, and S. Gavigan (Eds.), *Regulating Sex* (Burnaby: School of Criminology, Simon Fraser University, 1986).

consent to having sexual relations with a youth no more than two years older.[13] The criminal law is intended to protect adolescents by creating special offences for adults who may try to engage a youth under the age of 18 in acts of prostitution, and by providing that a youth cannot validly consent to having sexual relations with an adult in a position of "trust or authority" towards the youth. Even if the youth in fact consents, the adult in this situation commits a sexual assault by having sexual relations with the youth.[14]

The age jurisdiction of child welfare legislation varies from one province to another; for example in Ontario, child welfare agencies have no mandate to intervene to protect those who are 16 or older, while in Alberta child welfare agencies can apprehend children up to the age of 18, and in British Columbia adulthood for child welfare purposes only begins at the age of 19. For adolescents over the age of child welfare jurisdiction, child welfare agencies have traditionally had no legal mandate to become involved, even if the child is leading a high-risk life, such as engaging in prostitution or living on the street. Even for adolescents within the age jurisdiction of child welfare agencies, there are great challenges in providing services; many of these adolescents, even if found to be "children in need of protection" and hence legally expected to remain in agency care, are unwilling to remain in agency foster homes or group homes. A significant number of adolescent wards of child welfare agencies will "run" and end up engaged in prostitution or living on the street. Even if the agency has the resources to locate these youth, there are practical, legal and philosophical limitations on how far agencies should go in placing them in secure facilities against their will.

While it is a crime for an adult to engage the services of an adolescent prostitute in any setting or to live off the avails of a prostitute who is under the age of 18,[15] these laws are very difficult to enforce. The offences related to purchasing the services of a juvenile prostitute in theory sanction only the customers, not the juvenile prostitute, treating the adolescent prostitute as a "victim." The process of charging those purchasing the sexual services of youth is seriously impaired by the ethical constraints on police that prevent hiring juveniles to pose as undercover (juvenile) prostitute decoys, and that also preclude passively witnessing an adolescent prostitute engage in prostitution, as there is a duty to intervene to protect these adolescents.[16] It is also very difficult to obtain the co-operation of juvenile prostitutes in prosecuting pimps (those men who may be living off the avails of juvenile prostitutes or procuring them).

---

[13] *Criminal Code*, s. 150.1.

[14] *Criminal Code*, s. 153.

[15] *Criminal Code*, ss. 212(4), 212(2).

[16] A. Brannigan and J. Fleischman, "Juvenile Prostitution and Mental Health: Policing Delinquency or Treating Pathology?" (1989), 4 *Canadian Journal of Law and Society* 77-98 at 95. It is, however, possible for an undercover officer to pose as an underage prostitute and to have a prospective adult customer charged with attempting to procure the services of an underage juvenile prostitute: see *R. v. Lund*, 2000 ABPC 212 (Prov. Ct.).

The involvement of young people in prostitution further exacerbates the already great ambiguity associated with prostitution in Canada. The young person may be considered either a victim or a young offender. Youths may be considered offenders if found to be engaging in "public solicitation," or may be considered as "victims" if an adult is charged with purchasing their services or with procuring their services for another. In practice, the difficulty in "catching" adults buying sex from juveniles or procuring their services for others has often been responded to by "catching" youth involved instead.

Some of the difficulties in using either the criminal justice response or traditional child welfare measures have resulted in new provincial legislative initiatives aimed specifically at juvenile prostitutes. This legislation straddles the victimization and delinquency perspectives, enacted under the provincial child welfare jurisdiction, and allows for relatively short-term detention of juvenile prostitutes even if over the age of traditional child welfare jurisdiction.

Protection of Children Involved in Prostitution Act

Alberta was the first province to enact legislation specifically aimed at juvenile prostitution. A virtually identical statute was enacted in Saskatchewan. Ontario and British Columbia are considering enacting similar laws.[17] Alberta's *Protection of Children Involved in Prostitution Act (PChIP)* came into effect on February 1, 1999. The website of the Government of Alberta states that the *Act* "recognizes that children involved in prostitution are victims of sexual abuse and need protection."[18] In the Preamble to the *Act*, it is further recognized that the Government of Alberta is "committed to assisting children in ending their involvement with prostitution." Under *PChIP* a "child" who is under the age of 18 and is "engaging in prostitution or *attempting* to engage in prostitution" [italics added] may be apprehended without a warrant by a police officer or child protection worker and taken to a "safe house." As originally enacted, the statute provided that an adolescent could be detained for up to three days (since increased to five days) before being taken before a judge for an initial "show cause" hearing where the detention is to be reviewed, and perhaps extended for up to 30 days. During this time in a "safe house," the adolescent receives counselling and support, and the parents are notified of the apprehension. Thereafter the child may be encouraged to return to her or his family, or a normal child protection application may be commenced so that the adolescent may be made a ward and placed in a group home, or if at least 16 years of age the child may be released on his or her own.

---

[17] Saskatchewan, *Emergency Protection for Victims of Sexual Abuse and Exploitation Act*, S.S. 2002, c. E-8.2, in force 1 October 2002. British Columbia, *Secure Core Act*, S.B.C. 2000, c. 28, not yet in force. Ontario, *Rescuing Children from Sexual Exploitation Act*, 2002, S.O. 2002, c. 5, not yet in force. This law is aimed at "children" up to the age of 18, even though in other situations in Ontario the jurisdiction to apprehend "children" believed to be at risk of abuse, neglect, or exploitation ends when they are 16 (unless they were already subject to agency jurisdiction, in which case it extends to 18).

[18] <http://www.child.gov.ab.ca/whatwedo/pchip>.

Hailed by provincial officials as a method of "doing something" about juvenile involvement in prostitution, the *PChIP* is not without its critics. Two of the first adolescent girls apprehended under the *Act* raised a constitutional challenge to the legislation, in a case referred to as *Alberta (Director of Child Welfare) v. K.B.* The girls had been apprehended by the police, who were in the course of looking for stolen property in what was believed to be a "trick pad," with dirty mattresses, drug paraphernalia, and condoms strewn about. The police had concerns for the girls' safety and took them to a "safe house."

At the initial hearing, Judge Karen Jordan of the Provincial Court of Alberta (Family Division) accepted that the law was valid child welfare legislation, intended to protect children and did not intrude into the federal area of responsibility for criminal law.[19] She did, however, rule that the *Act* violated the *Charter of Rights* because it violated the guarantee of s. 7 that no person should be deprived of "liberty" except in "accordance with the principles of fundamental justice," and violated the guarantees for protection against "unreasonable search or seizure" (s. 8) and allowed for adolescents to be "arbitrarily detained or imprisoned" (violating s. 9). The focus of concern for Judge Jordan was that the period of detention prior to court hearing (up to 72 hours) was substantially longer than the period that an adolescent charged with a criminal offence can be detained without a hearing before a judge to review whether the detention is justified.

The decision of Judge Jordan was reversed when Justice John Rooke of the Alberta Court of Queen's Bench, who overturned the lower court ruling and held that the legislation was constitutionally valid.[20] The appeal court held that it is necessary to consider the "context" of legislation when deciding on its constitutional validity, observing that it would be "unlikely that a child would become involved in prostitution on a truly voluntary basis." The appeal court expressed deep concern about the "devastating conditions" that these girls were found in, and observed that due to their condition they slept for most of the three days before they were taken to court to have their detention reviewed. The appeal court ultimately concluded that there was no violation of *Charter* rights, and even if there had been, the law could be constitutionally justified under s. 1 of the *Charter* in light of the importance of the "objective of protecting a vulnerable group...from sexual abuse."

While the courts have accepted the constitutional validity of this law, there remain doubts about the effectiveness of coercive responses to adolescent prostitution. There is a clear need for research into the effectiveness of this type of approach. Do significant numbers of the youths who are apprehended and detained under this law actually stay away from juvenile prostitution, or do they simply return to it after their release? Are juvenile prostitutes being forced

---

[19] *Alberta (Director of Child Welfare) v. K.B.*, [2000] A.J. 876.

[20] *Alberta (Director of Child Welfare) v. K.B.*, [2000] A.J. 1570. For a critical commentary on *PChIP* and the decision of Rooke J., see J. Koshan, "Alberta (Dis)Advantage: The Protection of Children Involved in Prostitution Act and the Equality of Rights of Women" (2003), 2 *Journal of Law and Equity* 210-254.

further away from public view and into greater danger by this law? These are the types of questions that need to be addressed.

Alternative Measures

In this section, possible alternative measures that might be taken by social agencies and law enforcement to minimize danger to juvenile prostitutes are discussed. The difficulty in considering such measures is that the hazards of prostitution are neither simple nor amenable to simple solutions. Young persons who work as prostitutes have generally experienced multiple victimizations in their past and continued risks in their work as prostitutes. The hazards include premature home departure (running away), early school leaving, unplanned pregnancies, suicide attempts, substance dependencies, high health risks and bleak prospects for self-betterment. Aboriginal and visible minority youth disproportionately engage in juvenile prostitution. Street prostitution is one of the last resorts for self-employment among persons with few legitimate opportunities, even though it is, in the words of the Supreme Court of Canada, a "frequently dangerous and dehumanizing trade."[21] Narcotics, alcohol and other mind-numbing substances are occupational props employed by many participants in prostitution to minimize the alienation they experience in engaging in this work. The illicit cash in the prostitution trade flow attracts pimps who exploit the weaknesses of an already vulnerable population, and who actively induct new recruits into its ranks. The illicit sexual opportunities attract normal "johns" for "uncomplicated" sex — as well as predatory males for sexually violent acts. Viewed in this way, the question of alternative measures raises a host of possibilities in respect of different definitions of the sources of danger. Earlier in the chapter we contrasted some of the major conceptual perspectives on prostitution. Public discussions tend to cluster around four ideas.

First is the idea that street prostitution is essentially a *public nuisance* that has to be suppressed to protect neighbourhoods. Section 213 of the *Criminal Code*, creating the offence of communication in public for the purpose of engaging in prostitution, was intended to deal with this problem. Second is the idea that prostitution is an *occupation* in which people exercise rights over their own bodies and over how they propose to earn money with them. Canadian legislation has tended to frown on prostitution *per se*, although the courts have been tolerant in their approach to "exotic dancing," which may be a front for prostitution. Nonetheless, there is no tolerance for the idea that adolescents can "work" legitimately as prostitutes any more than that they can "work" selling narcotics. The third idea is that prostitution is a form of *delinquency* or crime that needs to be deterred like other forms of unlawful conduct. Here we encounter problems in determining whether the crime is committed by the seller, the buyer or both. Here we also confront the anomaly that the act of prostitution *per se* is not criminal, an anomaly that tends to add legitimacy to the occupational

---

[21] *R. v. Downey*, [1992] 2 S.C.R. 10 at 47.

perspective. And finally, there is the idea that prostitution, especially juvenile prostitution, is a form of *sexual exploitation* of a vulnerable sector of society.

Nuisance, delinquency, occupation and exploitation are four very different ways of thinking about prostitution. None of these definitions of the situation is completely compelling. Each has different implications for how we conceive the alternative measures needed and how these measures would contribute to the issues of safety.

For most Canadians, prostitution is neither a job nor a nuisance. Despite the laws that fail to criminalize prostitution itself, many view it as offensive and would prefer to see it eradicated from our society. This is reflected in alternative measures designed to deter "johns." These operate at two levels — intimidating prospective customers via "Dear John" letters sent to the homes of men seen soliciting prostitutes, and shaming the "johns" by publishing their names in the media. Both Edmonton and Winnipeg have undertaken programs that attempt to "shame the johns." The Edmonton police strategy is designed to deter prospective customers from contacting street prostitutes by sending letters to the owners of vehicles observed cruising the strolls. The effect of these "Dear John" letters is unknown. Critics point out that the strategy could embarrass spouses and other family members who may see the letters. Edmonton police appear to employ such letters only to individuals who have already been charged under s. 213 of the *Criminal Code*.

In 1994, the Edmonton media were encouraged to carry the names of persons charged or convicted of communication for the purposes of prostitution. One case resulted in the suicide of a public school vice-principal whose involvement with a prostitute was exposed in the local media. The suicide was committed by a head-on car crash with a truck, and the driver of the truck subsequently died from injuries received in the accident.[22] In Winnipeg, the major newspapers have refused to publish names of persons charged, suggesting that the stories are of little public interest. A tabloid has been the only outlet for these announcements. When Winnipeg police released not only names but the employers of persons charged under s. 213, two men who were charged and employed by Revenue Canada indicated their intention to sue for damages. Again, the utility of this strategy is unknown. In 1994, when the Calgary Police Commission considered the issue of publishing the names of persons charged with communication for the purposes of prostitution, the police repudiated the logic completely: while punishment is the task of the court, it is not the task of the police. In other jurisdictions that simply release long lists of names of those convicted, there is concern that people with the same names as those involved will be mistakenly tarnished.

These campaigns against the "johns" address the safety of prostitutes only obliquely. They reflect the idea that the street trade is "dangerous and dehumanizing" and that life could be made safer for women by curbing demand and

---

[22] *Edmonton Journal* (17 and 18 May 1994).

reducing opportunities on the supply side. To the extent that these shaming strategies fail to suppress the street trade, it is inevitable that among the diminishing numbers of persons who ignore the informal measures, there would remain a core of men who may exhibit other anti-social tendencies, including a propensity for violence directed at prostitutes. This raises the question as to whether our society ought to be repressing communication for the purposes of prostitution for reasons of nuisance or suppressing prostitution itself. If communication sets the agenda, police strategies will probably be modest. If prostitution itself is the issue, more intrusive alternative measures may be required.

In the case of persons under age 18, the federal Parliament has already taken steps to target the prostitution *per se*, not only communication. The provisions of s. 212(4) of the *Code* were designed to protect adolescents from advances by adults. In contrast to the anti-communication law that stressed the equal liability of buyers and seller, s. 212(4) puts the liability entirely on the buyers. In the few cases that have been brought to court, judges have taken an extremely dim view of the conduct of such "johns" and have been prepared to impose significant penalties. This law would likely have the effect of dramatically reducing the numbers of casual buyers if it were widely enforced and potential buyers were apprised of its gravity, but this is difficult to enforce in practice as the police cannot usually overhear or record the communication between a juvenile prostitute and a customer.

The *Criminal Code* could again be amended to create a presumption of engagement of the juvenile for the purposes of prostitution for an adult who is in the company of an adolescent known to have communicated for the purposes of engaging in prostitution, thus placing an onus on the adult to establish that he was not procuring the adolescent's sexual services. This would allow the police to arrest a man who has approached a juvenile who had previously communicated with an undercover police officer for the purposes of engaging in prostitution, when the customer is later in her company (for example, in his car). The Supreme Court of Canada, in *R v. Downey*, upheld the constitutional validity of a similar "reverse onus" provision in s. 212(3) that requires a person "habitually in the presence of a prostitute" to prove that he is not "living on the avails of prostitution" (i.e., her pimp). The Court observed that "the pimp personifies abusive and exploitative malevolence" and justified the reverse onus provision as needed to attempt to "deal with a cruel and pervasive social evil."[23] Since the exploitation of juvenile prostitutes by adult customers is as much of a societal concern as the exploitation of adult prostitutes by pimps, this would suggest that such reverse onus provision for adult customers of juvenile prostitutes would be constitutionally valid.

Effective use of the criminal law to suppress the activities of adults who exploit juvenile prostitutes also requires a reorientation of police initiatives, along with community consensus and political will that such efforts are

---

[23] *R. v. Downey*, [1992] 2 S.C.R. 10 at 36.

justified. Public opinion appears to be shifting in that direction. Concerns in the Canadian public about child sexual exploitation and violent exploitation are beginning to redefine prostitution in terms of the victimization of the sellers, especially juvenile prostitutes. There is ample evidence to support the idea that sellers experience significant disadvantages in terms of education, personal security and family and community integration prior to prostitution.

In the area of social support for youth prostitutes, the community requires resources to provide emergency shelter, food, clothing and health care. For longer term needs, housing, employment, and educational opportunities are also essential. Such services are now available to some degree. However, they tend to be provided in institutional and quasi-institutional settings — and often only after the youth has been identified as "needy" by law enforcement officials (as in the case of Alberta's new *Act*). From the perspective of public policy, it is worth asking whether as a society we should limit investment in foster parenting to $20 per day while spending $250 a day for the same individual in institutional care. Institutional care may provide physical security, but it is limited in its capacity to provide the strong personal bonds that are needed to cultivate self-esteem and autonomy. Further, society tends to fold up the safety net for persons who may be looking for solutions after they have ceased to be "children," which in some provinces may be as young as 16, even though emotionally they may be quite immature. If public policy is going to be designed to terminate careers in prostitution — as the victimization perspective would propose — social supports will have to be open to "adult" prostitutes, i.e., young women 16-24 years of age and older.

The general objectives of the victimization perspective would be as follows. First, limit the dangers to prostitutes by reducing the opportunities for juvenile street prostitution through more effective prosecution of buyers. Second, limit the attraction of pimping similarly by reducing the opportunities to exploit the underground economy generated by the prostitution and narcotics income. And third, address the social disadvantages of young persons who are marginalized because of family conflict and early home leaving, and who are vulnerable to entrapment in the underground economy by designing broadly based social services, so displacing the reliance on corrections applied to people who only come to official attention following criminal activity. These objectives call for a radical reconstruction of the issues around prostitution, and such radical changes are unlikely to enjoy popular support without a major change in contemporary thinking.

Conclusion: Changing Societal Perceptions

Thirty years ago Canadian society experienced high levels of accidents caused by drunk drivers. A social movement arose that largely changed the public perception of "drunk driving." People have come to regard drunk driving as not merely a social impropriety or nuisance, but as an act that seriously endangers innocent lives. The legal system instituted strict minimum penalties to reinforce the growing public intolerance towards such misconduct. The images of children killed and maimed by drivers operating vehicles in a state of intoxication brought home the message that drunk drivers were a menace to the whole society. Anyone could be the victim of an irresponsible drunk.

Today, it may be possible to learn from this change in attitudes. The parents of young murder victims advise that "this can happen to anyone." Sensationalist media treatment of "teen hookers" is being replaced by accounts of "sexually procured adolescents." Victimization may overtake nuisance as a focus of public concern. There is greater public apprehension over the sexual exploitation of adolescent runaways today than ever before. There is also significant interest in urban and federal politics in dealing with prostitution in a meaningful way, suggesting a willingness to address this societal problem.

It must be acknowledged that addressing the problems of prostitution is a policy minefield, littered with the failures of previous attempts to find solutions. If we were to create a strategy for a long-term remedy for the dangers faced by adolescents and women in prostitution, the goal ought to be to eradicate prostitution itself. If we take the victimization perspective seriously, the exploitation of prostitutes is inherent in the institution itself. It comes from sexist attitudes that are contrary to mainstream Canadian values and that are increasingly offensive. In the short- to medium-term, a greater emphasis on crime control strategies to curb demand would reinforce the perception that prostitution needs dealing with. This is not because it is a minor irritant that can be dealt with by aggressive "stroll management" or by legalization, although both may play a short-term role in a longer-term strategy. Rather, prostitution needs "dealing with" because it is inherently demeaning and because it fosters an array of other destructive and self-destructive relationships.

In the medium- and longer-term, if the illicit market contracts, the social service side of a victimization strategy must reduce the numbers of youth at risk to work in the illicit economy. A strategy that combines increased efforts to prosecute buyers and pimps with the provision of social supports for prostitutes to help them avoid or give up this lifestyle may appeal to evolving community sentiments in terms of promoting values of equality and security, and the protection of youth and the vulnerable.

In the absence of a concerted effort to deal with prostitution in general, there remain special social issues related to juvenile prostitution. Further, the commitment that Canada has made in the *United Nations Convention on the Rights of the Child* requires that we effectively address the sexual exploitation of adolescents in all contexts, including in juvenile prostitution. This will require research into the effectiveness of new approaches, like Alberta's *Protection of Children in Prostitution Act*, to learn whether it is effective and should be replicated. In the meantime, we can expect the stress of conflicting goals and lack of resources to be a continuing reality for social workers, police, lawyers, and judges attempting to work on the frontlines with young prostitutes, their families and their communities.

6

Adoption

Theodore G. Giesbrecht[1]

The Social and Historical Context of Adoption

Adoption is the process by which the law creates a child-parent relationship and, by extension, brings the child into the kinship lines of the adoptive family, while at the same time terminating the child's legal relationships with the birth parents and family. The adoption process in Canada also results in the amendment of birth records, so that it appears that the adoptive parents gave birth to the child.[2] Adoption has profound social and psychological effects on adoptees, birth parents and adoptive parents. Adoption also results in a profound change in a child's legal status. Adoption is closely regulated by law in Canada, and is based on principles that place the child's best interests as paramount, but that also recognize the rights of biological parents.

Adoption is an age-old concept and references can be found in biblical writings and in Roman civil law. Under Roman Law, legal adoption was primarily used where an heir was required in order to preserve family wealth or position — a very different institution from modern adoption.

The English common law did not recognize adoption, because of concerns about maintaining bloodlines for inheritance purposes, though various arrangements were made by relatives, the church and later by the state to care for children whose parents died or abandoned them. While a wealthy orphan might have a legal guardian appointed to supervise property interests and provide care, the majority of orphaned children in nineteenth-century Canada were placed in orphanages, and "apprenticed out" at an early age to work on farms or in shops. Children without a parent or guardian were often exploited or abused, and suffered from high mortality rates.

Adoption is a matter of provincial jurisdiction under s. 92 of the *Constitution Act, 1867,* and the first adoption legislation that was enacted in Canada was in New Brunswick in 1873. In most provinces adoption laws were only enacted in the period during and after World War I, when a great increase in "illegitimacy" (children born to single mothers) gave rise to the need to find families to provide care for these children. At the same time, the growing middle class and the emergence of the "housewife" as an occupation meant that married women who were

---

[1] Theodore G. Giesbrecht is a lawyer in private practice and Adoption Licensee, Kitchener, Ontario.

[2] See e.g., Ontario *Child and Family Services Act,* s. 162(3).

unable to biologically bear children wanted to adopt children to have "as their own." Adoption was shrouded in secrecy; for the unwed mother there was the shame of having had an illegitimate child, and for the adoptive parents there was the stigma of illegitimacy. Children were often not told that they were adopted until well into life, and sometimes did not find out until after the deaths of their adoptive parents.

Until well past the middle of the twentieth century, there were more healthy newborn infants available for adoption in Canada than there were adoptive parents. Abortion was illegal; women who became pregnant out of wedlock faced social stigma, had very poor economic prospects, and would usually place their children for adoption. In the last decades of the twentieth century there were dramatic changes in the adoption field. Improved birth control and access to abortion meant that fewer children were being born to single mothers; social attitudes and supports for single mothers improved and more of these women chose to parent their children. At the same time, as more women postponed pregnancy, there was an increase in infertility. As a result, there is now a much greater demand in Canada for infants to adopt than there are children available. This has led to changes in adoption, such as more interest in international and inter-racial adoption, more adoptions of older children, and increased efforts to ensure that biological parents are involved in selecting adoptive parents.[3]

Historically in Canada, custom adoption was practised among the Aboriginal people. Custom adoption provided caregivers for children in situations where biological parents were dead, or had too many children to care for, and usually involved caregiving by biological relatives of the child. Under Aboriginal custom adoption, children are aware that their adoptive parents are not their biological parents and continue to have contact with biological relatives. Custom adoption recognizes the strength of extended families and does not only focus on the biological family but rather the community as a whole. Today custom adoption is recognized by statute in the Northwest Territories, Nunavut, and British Columbia, and has recognition at common law elsewhere. Interestingly, Aboriginal custom adoption is in some ways serving as a model for a new, more open approach that is being developed in the broader Canadian society.

The Legal Framework for Adoption

Today there is legislation in every province and territory in Canada[4] that regulates all aspects of domestic adoption within the jurisdictions, and in some cases provides guidance in relation to interprovincial adoptions. In Canada, children

---

[3] With changes in medical technology and increased infertility, there has also been an increase in the use of artificial reproductive technology, and society has had to confront such issues as the legal regulation of surrogate motherhood. Some of these issues involve adoption questions. A discussion of these complex issues, however, is beyond the scope of this chapter, as they do not involve child welfare agencies or the private adoption agencies that are involved in adoptions not involving reproductive technology.

[4] Ontario *Child and Family Services Act*, R.S.O. 1990, c. C. 11. Part VII, Adoption; Alberta *Child Welfare Act*, R.S.A. 2000, c. C-12. Part 6, Adoption; British Columbia *Adoption Act*, R.S.B.C. 1996, c. 5; Manitoba *Adoption Act*, C.C.S.M., c. A-2; New Brunswick *Family Services Act*, R.S.N.B., c. F-2.2. Part V, Adoption;

who are adopted from foreign countries are subject to the rules set out in the 1993 *Hague Convention on Intercountry Adoption*, which has been implemented in all provinces and territories in Canada.

While there is some variation within Canada in the details of adoption statutes, the legislative schemes share the same fundamental features, namely to:

- regulate adoption service providers, such as government child welfare agencies (like Ontario's Children's Aid Societies) and private adoption licensees;
- establish how children qualify for adoption, either by voluntary placement by their birth parents or by involuntary placement through state intervention in cases where children are neglected or in need or protection;
- define who qualifies as a legal "parent" of the child for the purposes of identifying those persons whose consent to adoption is required, or alternatively, whose consent must be dispensed with before an adoption order can be made;
- specify rules surrounding the giving of consent to adoption;
- set out the requirements for prospective adoptive parents;
- provide authority for a judge to make an adoption order and provide the basis for making such an order;
- provide for the changing of the name and birth registration particulars of the child;
- emphasize the need to help Aboriginal children preserve their cultural identity;
- provide rules relating to the maintenance of confidential records;
- implement proper procedures for disclosure of identifying information for adoptees and birth parents who wish to reunite;
- define offences and provide penalties for those who breach the legislation; and
- list exceptions to the regular adoption process in cases of step-parent or relative adoptions.

In addition to the provincial statutes which regulate the adoption process, case law precedents at all court levels, including the Supreme Court of Canada, have interpreted these statutes and helped to define adoption law. The main issues that these cases deal with are:

- the best interests of a child and the weighing of the various factors to be considered when determining whether or not an adoption order should be made;

Newfoundland and Labrador *Adoption of Children Act*, R.S.N.L. 1990, c. A-3; repealed by Adoption Act, S.N.L. 1999, c. A-2.1 (not in force; to be proclaimed); Northwest Territories *Aboriginal Custom Adoption Recognition Act*, S.N.W.T. 1994, c. 26. *Adoption Act*, S.N.W.T. 1998, c. 6; Nova Scotia *Children and Family Services Act*, S.N.S. 1990, c. 5, ss. 57-87; Nunavut *Aboriginal Custom Adoption Recognition Act*, S.N.W.T. 1994, c. 26. *Adoption Act*, S.N.W.T. 1998, c. 6; Prince Edward Island *Adoption Act*, c. A-4.1 (S.P.E.I., 1992, c. 1); Quebec *Civil Code of Quebec*, Book II: The Family, Title II, Filiation, Chapter II, Adoption; Saskatchewan *Adoption Act*, S.S. 1989-90, c. A-5.1; and Yukon *Children's Act*, R.S.Y, c. 22, Part 3.

- the definition of who is a legal "parent" of a child whose consent to adoption must be obtained or dispersed with; and

- constitutional issues regarding equal treatment of birth fathers in relation to consent issues and birth registration issues.

In addition to statutory provisions and case law precedents, child welfare agencies and private adoption licensees, in conjunction with their supervising provincial child welfare ministries, produce manuals setting out standards and guidelines that reflect evolving adoption practice.[5]

During the last decade, adoption practices have evolved towards more openness among the parties involved, including a call by adoptees and birth parents for more and earlier disclosure of identifying information and the opening of original birth registration records.

Best Interests of the Child

The most basic principle of adoption is that this institution is intended to promote the best interests of the child. While the interests of the biological and adoptive parents are subordinate to the interests of the child, in some contexts the law gives priority to the rights of birth parents and to maintaining a relationship between biological relatives and a child, but this is done with the objective of promoting the best interests of the child. Section 136(2) of Ontario's *Child and Family Services Act* is representative of the considerations in making decisions about adoption that are set out in legislation in other jurisdictions in Canada:

> Where a person is directed in this Part to make an order or determination in the best interests of a child, the person shall take into consideration those of the following circumstances of the case that he or she considers relevant:
>
> (a) The child's physical, mental and emotional needs, and the appropriate care or treatment to meet those needs.
>
> (b) The child's physical, mental and emotional level of development.
>
> (c) The child's cultural background.
>
> (d) The religious faith, if any, in which the child is being raised.
>
> (e) The importance for the child's development of a positive relationship with a parent and a secure place as a member of a family.
>
> (f) The child's relationships by blood or through an adoption order.
>
> (g) The importance of continuity in the child's care and the possible effect on the child of disruption of that continuity.
>
> (h) The child's views and wishes, if they can be reasonably ascertained.
>
> (i) The effects on the child of delay in the disposition of the case.
>
> (j) Any other relevant circumstance.

---

[5] See e.g., *Standards and Guidelines for Licensees in Private Practice under the Child and Family Services Act* and Ontario Regulation 70, (R.R.O. 1990, Reg. 70, as amended).

In addition to the above-noted criteria, most jurisdictions, including Ontario, have provisions that direct decision makers in the adoption process to consider the importance of preserving a child's cultural identity where that child is Aboriginal.[6]

Many cases dealing with determining the best interests of a child in relation to adoption focus on balancing the benefits of placing a child in a stable two parent family against the loss of breaking ties with the child's biological family. The balancing task becomes increasingly more difficult with the passage of time as the child is generally forming ever-strengthening psychological attachments with his or her caregivers, and to break this attachment would cause serious emotional trauma. Therefore, it is always preferable that decisions regarding the long-term placement of children be dealt with at the earliest opportunity.

Justice L'Heureux Dubé recognized the effects of delay in *Catholic C.A.S. of Metropolitan Toronto v. M.(C.),*[7] where the case of a young child wound its way through the court system for almost five years. During that long period of time, the biological mother sought to regain custody but the child became increasingly emotionally attached to the foster parents who wanted to adopt her.

> That the length of these proceedings may have been one of the factors which has contributed to the attachment of [the girl] S.M. for her foster family, and thus increased the emotional harm that would result from her removal from them, is a fact that is inescapable. The passage of time in matters of child custody and welfare over extended periods may, unfortunately, carry a heavy burden for all concerned. This is recognized by the Act in that a number of provisions mandate the timely resolution of cases and impose time limits on Children's Aid Society involvement with a family....

> I share [the concerns of one of the lower court judges]...with regard to the importance of reaching a speedy resolution of matters affecting children. The Act requires it and common sense dictates it. A few months in the life of a child, as compared to that of adults, may acquire great significance. Years go by crystallizing situations that become irreversible. This is exactly what happened here. The first time that S.M. was removed from the care of her birth mother she was one month old. The situation could have been easily remedied had the birth mother then been in a position to care for her daughter adequately. This did not happen. Now, over seven years later, the situation has drastically changed and, although the argument raised by the [mother] in relation to delay is well taken, looking at the totality of the evidence and circumstances of the child, it has become inevitable that it is in S.M.'s best interests to be made a [permanent] ward of the...society, with a view to her adoption by her foster family.

In most jurisdictions, in cases of involuntary relinquishment of children, children who are to be placed for adoption by a child welfare agency must be permanent wards without access to their biological parents. The traditional view has been that to sever the child's ties to the biological family is in the best interests of the child for many reasons, including the freedom of the adoptive parents to raise the child without intervention or contact from the child's birth family.

---

[6] See e.g. *Adoption Act*, R.S.B.C. 1996, c. 6 section 3(2).
[7] *Catholic Children's Aid Society of Metropolitan Toronto v. M.(C.),* [1994] 2 S.C.R. 165.

Recently the idea of the automatic severance of all links between the biological parents and an adopted child has been challenged. Although in most adoptions this severance will continue to occur, in some cases it may be in the best
interests of the child to have both the permanency of adoption and a continued
tie to biological parents. For example, in the 2002 Yukon case of *Re R.A.*,[8] Chief
Judge Stuart held that s. 7 of the *Charter of Rights* requires that courts must, in
appropriate cases, have the flexibility to allow adoption with continued access to
the biological parents, if this is in the best interests of the child before the court.
Even though this is not permitted by legislation, Stuart C.J. concluded that the
child's *Charter*-based right to be treated "in accordance with the principles of
fundamental justice" requires that courts have the flexibility to allow such
continued contact. The judge concluded that it was in the best interests of this
particular special needs child to be a permanent ward with a view to adoption,
but to have continued visits from her Aboriginal mother. The mother loved the
child and had continued to have visits with the child, who clearly benefited from
them, but she was unable to care for the child as she suffered from fetal alcohol
effect. The prospective adoptive parents welcomed the continued visits with the
biological mother. It is interesting that in this case, involving an Aboriginal
child, the judge used the *Charter of Rights* to develop a legal response that is in
some ways similar to the traditional Aboriginal custom adoption.

Across Canada, there are developments intended to make adoption a more
flexible and diverse institution. These developments, based on a concern about
promoting the best interests of the child, are resulting in an evolution of
adoption that includes:

- more openness in relationships between adoptees, their biological families
  and their adoptive families;

- confirmation of the link between adoptees and their biological parents by
  acknowledging the original birth record details and making them available
  to adoptees; and

- the preservation of Aboriginal culture in cases where the child has Aboriginal ancestry.

Types of Adoption

There are two basic types of adoption in Canada:

- familial adoptions where the adoptive parents are related to the child by
  blood or marriage and arrange the adoption privately; and

- adoptions where there is no prior relationship between the adoptive parents and the child, and the adoption is arranged with the involvement of an
  intermediary.

---

[8] *Re R.A.*, [2002] Y. J. No. 48 (Terr. Ct.).

In the category of adoptions where the parties are not biologically related or connected to the child through marriage, adoptions involve either voluntary or involuntary placements. *Voluntary placements* occur when birth parents plan for the adoption of their children, consent to the adoption, and engage a government child welfare agency or a private adoption licensee to facilitate the adoption. *Involuntary adoption placements* occur when a child is removed by court order from the care of the birth parents because the child has been neglected, abused or abandoned, and the child is made a permanent ward, usually without the parents having access rights, thereby putting the agency in the position of being able to place the child for adoption without the consent of the biological parents.

Familial adoptions, where the parties are related to each other or are connected through marriage, are either relative adoptions or step-parent adoptions. Familial adoptions are subject to less onerous regulations as the parties are known to each other and can assist in addressing the child's best interests. Often in familial adoptions the children involved are already living with the adoptive parents, and the adoption is intended to make permanent the legal tie between children and parents.

Involuntary Adoption Placements

Provincial child welfare statutes are premised on the view that it is generally in the best interests of children to preserve ties between a child and the biological parents, and that intervention should be the least disruptive course of action to achieve this goal. In severe cases of abuse or neglect, however, the best interests of the child may require permanent removal of the child from the birth family. Ultimately, the decision about whether to terminate the relationship between the birth parents and a child is based on a judicial assessment of the best interests of the child under child protection law.

If a court has determined that a child is to be a permanent ward, the child welfare agency has a duty to make a plan for the permanent care of the child. Indeed, an initial tentative plan will usually be developed before the agency comes to court seeking permanent wardship and will be presented to the court as part of the case for permanent wardship. If parental access rights are terminated under the child protection statute (and in some jurisdictions even if the parents have access rights[9]), the agency's plans for permanent care are likely to include an adoption plan. Adoption is often considered the best option for a child, as it offers the prospect of the permanent benefit of belonging to a family and enjoying a stable, positive child-parent relationship.

Child welfare agencies recruit and screen potential adoptive parents, and are likely to have on file many prospective adoptive families who have been

---

[9] For example, in Ontario under s. 160(1) of the *Child and Family Services Act,* access rights terminate with the adoption order. In British Columbia under s. 32 of the *Adoption Act,* a court may permit access to continue after an adoption order if it is in the best interests of the child. As further discussed below, even in Ontario, in "exceptional cases" the courts may use general custody and access statutes like the *Children's Law Reform Act* to permit a biological parent to have access rights after adoption.

investigated and approved after an agency home study process. Government child welfare agencies have the mandate to match a child in accordance with the child's physical, mental, and emotional needs; the child's cultural, racial, and ethnic background; the child's religious faith; and, where ascertainable, the birth parents' wishes. Racial, cultural, ethnic, and religious congruence between the child and the prospective adoptive family, and placement of a child with previously placed siblings, are factors that will normally be heavily weighted when the agency is considering a potential match, though none is determinative. While there is now a preference in child welfare agencies in Canada for intra-racial adoption, the reality in Canada is that there are relatively few non-Caucasian prospective adoptive parents and a relatively large number of visible minority and Aboriginal children who are permanent wards, and interracial adoption is not uncommon.

There are today in Canada many more couples who want to adopt healthy infants than there are such children available for adoption, and with these children the agency will usually not have difficulty making a match. Often, however, the children who become available for adoption through involuntary placements are older, and may have experienced abuse or neglect at the hands of their parents. Some of these children may have special needs and may, for example, be suffering from the effects of maternal alcohol or drug abuse during pregnancy. Local agencies sometimes have to contact other agencies to find suitable adoptive parents for children with special needs. Agencies may be more willing to consider single persons and gay or lesbian partners for these "hard-to-place" children, as many "traditional adoptive parents" (heterosexual married couples) are unwilling to consider this type of child.

In involuntary placements, it is not uncommon for a child to be in foster care for an extended period of time before a permanent wardship order is made. If the foster family is among the pool of prospective adoptive families under consideration, weight is usually given to the degree of attachment that has developed between the child and the foster family. Typically, the longer the child has been in the care of the foster family the greater the degree of attachment, and therefore, the greater the risk of emotional harm if the child is removed from the foster home and the greater the likely value of adoption. Indeed, the fact that a child has been in the care of a foster family for a significant period and wants to be adopted by the foster parents may be a reason for terminating the right of access of the biological parents, especially if they lack in parenting abilities and are unlikely to ever resume care of the child.[10] In most jurisdictions in Canada there are also programs to allow subsidies to be paid to adoptive parents who undertake the care of special needs children; the payment of subsidy may also make a long-term foster parent more willing to adopt a special needs child, as otherwise adoption may result in a significant loss of income.

[10] *C.A.S. of Sudbury and Manitoulin v. C.T.*, [2003] O.J. 3041 (Ont. Sup. Ct.).

The child welfare agency is solely responsible for selecting prospective adoptive parents for children who have been made permanent wards. Foster parents who take in children and want to adopt have "at risk" pre-adoptive placements, and adoption will only occur if the child is made a permanent ward and parents lose their rights to the child. Further, once a child is made a permanent ward without the parents having access, the child welfare agency is the legal guardian of the child and has the responsibility to find an adoptive placement that best meets the needs of the child. While in practice foster parents who want to adopt a child whom they have cared for will usually be given priority, the agency is not obliged to allow them to adopt and will have the right to place the child with another family for adoption.[11]

Voluntary Adoption Placements

Birth parents, for varying reasons, may decide to place their children for adoption. Such voluntary adoption placements almost always involve newborns or very young infants, usually born to parents who are not married or cohabiting with one another. The decision to place a child for adoption is often wrenching and emotional. The decision may involve consideration of the life plans of the parents, and their ability and interest in caring for children. Birth parents, in deciding to place their child for adoption, usually want to ensure the best possible future for their child. As discussed further below, those who arrange adoptions have an obligation to counsel biological parents before they consent to adoption and their children are placed for adoption. The adoption process is regulated to attempt to ensure that any decision that a parent makes is carefully considered and voluntary. No payment may be made to a biological parent in exchange for the consent to an adoption; the decision to place a child must be voluntary and it is an offence for a parent to receive any compensation for agreeing to the adoption of their child.

In all provinces and territories, child welfare agencies are authorized to undertake voluntary adoption placements, which typically involve the newborn children of unwed mothers who contact the agency, usually before the child is born. In some cases when an unwed mother contacts a child welfare agency and indicates that she wants to place her child for adoption, the agency will decide to apply to the court to have the child made a permanent ward without access, with the plan being adoption. The mother will be notified of the application and may consent to it, which will make the hearing a formality. This process is in many practical ways similar to a voluntary placement adoption with a child welfare agency, but may give the agency more flexibility about changing the plans for the child after the initial involvement of the mother is over.

---

[11] See e.g., *K.J. v. Catholic C.A.S. of Toronto*, [2003] O.J. 5058 (Ont. Div. Ct.); and *C.K. v. British Columbia (Ministry of Children and Family Development)*, [2003] B.C.J. 1165 (B.C.S.C.). As discussed in Chapter 3, there are situations in which foster parents may prevent the removal by the agency of a child for whom they have fostered for a significant period of time, but foster parents cannot require the child welfare agency to allow them to adopt the child.

Many of the mothers who voluntarily place their children for adoption were (or are) themselves wards of child welfare agencies, and prefer not to deal with that agency for the adoption of their child. Most Canadian jurisdictions also permit private adoption agencies and professionals to act as adoption licensees to provide adoption services, providing birth parents and adoptive parents with an alternative to the public adoption system. While public agencies charge no fees to adoptive parents, a private domestic adoption can cost $6,000 to $10,000 or more, but adoptive parents who are able to pay these fees may have an adoption arranged in a shorter period than through a public agency as licensees typically have shorter "waiting lists," and may have more children available for placement than public agencies.

The voluntary placement process also differs from the involuntary placement process in that the consent of the birth parents is required before an adoption order can be made. The subject of parental consent is discussed in detail below.

In a voluntary placement, the sharing of the social and medical history of the child's birth family is usually more complete than with an involuntary adoption because birth parents who voluntarily place their children for adoption are more likely to be willing to provide detailed information. Further, it is a common practice with private adoptions in Canada today for the birth parents to be involved in selecting the prospective adoptive parents.[12] This is done by the agency or licensee providing the birth parents with non-identifying written and pictorial profiles of prospective adoptive parents and allowing them to select the parents whom they prefer. It is also becoming more common to share identifying information once a match is made since birth and adoptive parents often wish to develop an open adoption plan, which may provide for the regular exchange of letters, pictures, and visits. In voluntary placements, an open adoption may be available as an option for consideration by the birth and adoptive parents, if they all feel comfortable with this type of arrangement.

The steps for finalizing a voluntary placement adoption are similar to those in an involuntary placement, in that an application is made to the court for a final adoption order. In a voluntary placement, however, the child's "parents" must consent to the adoption, though as further discussed below some biological fathers may not be legally regarded as "parents" and hence their consent will not be required, or a court may dispense with the consent of a biological parent to an adoption.[13]

Familial Adoptions

Most adoption legislative schemes in Canada[14] provide for a substantial relaxation of the statutory requirements for children who will be adopted by family members, as all of the adults involved know each other before the adoption

---

[12] See e.g., *Re Baby K.* (1988), 13 R.F.L. (3d) 209 (Ont. Sup. Ct.).

[13] See e.g., s. 137(1) of Ontario's *Child and Family Services Act*.

[14] Prince Edward Island does not provide for relaxed requirements for relative adoptions.

occurs. The difference in approach is intended to facilitate this type of adoption, on the premise that when biological parents cannot care for their children, familial adoption is likely to promote the child's interests by allowing the child to remain in the care of blood relatives and maintain his or her cultural heritage.

Outside of the context of adoption of a child by a close relative, biological parents cannot place their children for adoption; only a child welfare agency or a licensee can make such placements, as these intermediaries are trained and supervised to promote the best interests of the child. However, when biological parents, usually single mothers, decide to place a child with close relatives, they can do so without the involvement of a child welfare agency, adoption agency or licensee. There is no need for a home study, criminal records check or medical reports before a familial placement occurs, because birth parents are presumed to be able to satisfy themselves as to the prospective adoptive parents' suitability. Further, there is no requirement for a probationary period prior to obtaining an adoption order. Adoptive applicants will, however, be required to obtain the consents of the child's birth mother and any other legal "parent" of the child. The child's consent will also be required if the child has attained the statutory age threshold.[15]

The various statutes in Canada define the term "relative" with varying degrees of breadth. In Ontario, s. 136(1) of the *Child and Family Services Act* is quite narrow, providing that for adoption purposes a "relative" is "defined as the child's grandparent, great-uncle, great-aunt, uncle or aunt, whether by blood, marriage or adoption." By way of comparison, in Quebec, "relative" is defined more broadly, as a person related up to the "third degree," which, for example, allows a cousin to adopt a child under the relative adoption provisions.[16] In Ontario, first cousins and siblings of a child are excluded from relative adoptions, and adoptions by such persons requires the involvement of a child welfare agency or licensee, with all of the attendant legal requirements.

In a relative adoption, an adoption order re-orders the relationship of the child to its birth and adoptive relatives. For example, if the birth mother's mother adopts the child, the biological grandmother of the child becomes the adoptive mother, and the biological mother becomes the adoptive sister of the child.

Step-Parent Adoptions

Just as in relative adoptions, and for similar reasons, the various statutes regulating adoptions relax the requirements for the adoption of children by the spouse of their custodial parent. While the consent of every legal "parent" (discussed below) is required for a step-parent adoption, there are no requirements for home studies, probationary periods, or involvement of child welfare agencies or licensees.

---

[15] In Ontario a child who has attained the age of seven years must provide a consent. In all other jurisdictions the child must have attained the age of twelve years.

[16] Each "degree" of relationship is a link in a family tree, so that a parent or sibling is a relative in the first degree, a grandparent, aunt, or uncle is a relative in the second degree, and a first cousin is a relative in the third degree.

Most step-parent adoptions arise in situations where the biological father has little or no relationship with his child and the child has developed a close relationship with the stepfather. In such cases the stepfather must apply to the court for an adoption order, usually on the strength of his affidavit evidence establishing that he is a suitable parent and the filing of the consents of the child's birth parents or any other legal parent and the child, if the child is old enough. As is discussed more fully below, in cases where the birth father will not consent, an application can be brought to dispense with his consent.

Once the issues of consent are resolved, if the judge is satisfied that the stepfather is a suitable parent and that the adoption would be in the best interests of the child, an adoption order will be made. For legal purposes, the child joins the adoptive father's kinship line and is no longer part of the birth father's family. The child's relationship with the birth mother and her family remains intact. At the time of the order the child's name is usually changed and birth registration particulars are re-registered naming the adoptive father as the biological father of record.

Generally, in Canada, the definition of "spouse" for adoption purposes means a married or common law partner. This definition causes problems when a birth parent dies and the step-parent wants to adopt the child; the step-parent was a "spouse" prior to the death, but at the time of the adoption application is not a "spouse" and, therefore, does not qualify for the less onerous step-parent adoption process. Even though the child may have lived with the step-parent for many years, or even since birth, the adoption must be under the more stringent procedure that governs adoption by persons who are not relatives. Further, by losing the ability to use the step-parent adoption process, the child also loses legal ties to the family of the deceased birth parent, as well as losing legal ties to the other birth parent and family.

Until recently, the definition of "spouse" also made it difficult for the same-sex partners of biological parents to adopt. In many same-sex adoption cases, the children are conceived by artificial insemination and live their entire lives with the biological parent and the same-sex step-parent. In the 1995 Ontario case of *Re K.*,[17] Justice Nevins dealt with a constitutional challenge by a number of same-sex partners of biological parents who wanted to have step-parent adoptions. Interestingly, this case was decided before any of the major cases in which Canadian courts granted same-sex partners "spousal" status or the right to marry. In ruling on the exclusion of same-sex partners from the step-parent adoption provisions of Ontario's *Child and Family Services Act*, the judge considered that this was both discrimination on the basis of sexual orientation and contrary to the best interests of the children involved.

A number of provinces including Alberta, British Columbia, Manitoba, Newfoundland and Nova Scotia have amended adoption legislation to specifically allow adoption by same-sex partners under the "step-parent adoption"

---

[17] *Re K.* (1995), 15 R.F.L. (4th) 129 (Ont. Prov. Ct.).

route. In other provinces, the statutes have still not been amended, but case law like *Re K.* makes clear that it is unconstitutional to deny a same-sex partner of a biological parent the same rights as an opposite-sex partner to adopt as a step-parent, and these adoptions occur despite the absence of explicit legislation.

Regulation of Adoption Service Providers

In all jurisdictions in Canada, government child welfare agencies are authorized to carry out adoptions, and in most provinces private adoption licensees may also place children for adoption.[18] It is an offence for any other individual or agency to process adoptions. The purpose of restricting involvement in adoption is to ensure that the best possible placements are made for children, and that all of those involved in the adoption process receive appropriate services and support.[19] The legislation provides avenues to hold service providers accountable. This type of regulation reduces the risk of unscrupulous persons wishing to profit from the marketing of children or from persons trying to effect adoptions through the bypassing of legislative requirements.

The ultimate authority to regulate adoption rests with each provincial and territorial government, as domestic adoption is not within federal jurisdiction. In each jurisdiction, adoption is regulated by the ministry charged with child welfare responsibilities. That ministry appoints an officer, sometimes referred to as a "director," who oversees the provision of adoption services by authorized government child welfare agencies, private adoption agencies and licensed individuals.

All aspects of the activities of public child welfare agencies, including their adoption work, are subject to direct government control, and governments are responsible for the policies and work of these agencies.

In the case of private adoption agencies or licensed individuals, the ministry uses a licensing process to regulate entry into the adoption field. A licence will only be provided to an applicant if the ministry is satisfied that the agency or individual has sufficient skill, knowledge, and access to counsellors and medical services, to properly effect an adoption. In Ontario, once a private agency or individual is licensed, the licence remains in effect for one year. Annually, the licensee must report to the ministry and request a renewal of the licence.

Some of the private adoptive agencies are non-profit, religion-based agencies, and most of the professionals (usually social workers or lawyers) who act as private licensees are competent, reputable professionals. There are, however, concerns that with private adoptions there is the potential for the profit motive or personal prejudices to affect decisions, and private adoptions are subject to more legal controls than adoptions arranged by public child welfare

---

[18] Newfoundland, New Brunswick, and Prince Edward Island do not allow private adoption.

[19] Alberta's new *Child Welfare Amendment Act*, S.A. 2003, c. C-16.5, likely to come into force in the autumn of 2004, will allow for direct private placements without requirements for prior screening, home study, or counselling for any of the parties.

agencies. This regulation is intended to ensure accountability and to maintain a focus on the needs of children.

The Ontario case of *H.(R.) v. B.(T.)*, where a private licensee was contacted by a single mother who planned to place her newborn child for adoption, is a rare example of a problem that arose in private adoption. The mother of a newborn child wanted the child adopted by strangers and contacted the licensee to arrange this. The biological father told the licensee that he wanted his sister and brother-in-law to adopt the child, but the licensee ignored his requests. The licensee acceded to the mother's wishes and placed the child with a couple who did not know the parents. The failure of the licensee to fairly consider placement with the father's sister and brother-in-law meant that the licensee was disregarding the statutory provisions which make the "blood ties" between the child and adoptive parents a significant factor in assessing the child's best interests.[20] After litigation began with the father's relatives seeking custody, the couple with whom the licensee had placed the child decided to place the child with the brother's sister and brother-in-law to allow them to adopt the child. The judge dealing with the litigation was very critical of the conduct of the licensee and ordered her to pay a significant portion of the legal costs incurred by the father and his sister and brother-in-law, with Judge Nevins commenting:[21]

> ...because of the serious nature of an adoption proceeding it being the ultimate intrusion into the life of a child which can never be varied or set aside in the future, the obligation of a licensee is unique.... Implicit in the duty of a licensee is the requirement that she act neutrally and impartially at all times, in the best interests of the child. The conduct of a licensee, especially in those critical periods immediately before and after birth can have significant and long-lasting if not permanent, ramifications. The licensee to a degree is assuming a function normally reserved to a court, that is, to assess what may be in the best interests of a child.... [T]he natural parents leave the ultimate placement decision to her, the director relies on her recommendation, and the adoptive parents seek her approval.
>
> The licensee's conduct at all times must be, and be seen to be, impartial and fair and directed only towards the best interests of the child. The licensee can never allow this obligation to be compromised or interfered with, even though it may involve disappointing the adoptive parents or disagreeing with the natural parents. The licensee can never allow herself to side with a parent, either natural or adoptive.

In most jurisdictions, all financial transactions between the licensee and the prospective adoptive parents must be recorded by the licensee, held in a trust account, and be reported to the licensing ministry on an annual basis. The ministry must renew licences on an annual basis, and will only do so after reviewing the financial transactions and information regarding the files processed by the licensee in the preceding year.

---

[20] Ontario *Child and Family Services Act*, s. 136(2)6.

[21] (1991), 36 R.F.L. (3d) 208 (Prov. Ct.), per Nevins Prov. J. at para. 46-47; see also e.g., P.K. Strom Amlung, "Conflicts of Interest in Independent Adoptions: Pitfalls for the Unwary" (1990), 59 *University of Cincinnati Law Review* 169-189.

Eligibility to Adopt

Age and Residency of Adoptive Parents and Child

Most provinces require the adoptive parents to be at least 18 years of age and be resident in that province at the time the application is made. For example, Ontario's legislation only allows a court to make an adoption order if both the child and the prospective adoptive parent are residents of the province.[22]

Assessment of the Potential Adoptive Parent

Except for familial adoptions, there must be a home study assessment before a child is placed for adoption. Home study assessments are essentially investigations by a social worker into an individual's fitness to adopt and may be undertaken only by social workers approved by the provincial government for that purpose. Assessing the suitability and circumstances of a person wishing to adopt a child is the central task of the home assessment process.

In Manitoba, for example, individuals apply to an adoption agency, which in turn ascertains the person's suitability as a potential adopting parent. If suitability is established, the agency forwards relevant details to the provincial director, who enters the names and particulars on a central adoption registry. An agency with a child available for adoption may then recommend that applicants be entered in the central registry be permitted to adopt a particular child. If the director approves, the agency may then place a child with the applicant. Other provinces, such as Ontario, do not maintain a central register of applicants but allow approved adoption agencies to establish their own lists of approved applicants. The agencies often consult one another to suitably match a child with an adopting family.

The central question for professional staff selecting a potential adoptive parent is whether the person can create and sustain a positive parent-child relationship. The following tangible parental characteristics are typically identified in legislation or policies:

- ability to financially maintain and educate the child;
- a sufficient age gap between the prospective adopter and the child to effectively establish a genuine parent-child relationship; and
- if the adoption will result in the single parenthood of the child, it is generally necessary to establish special circumstances to justify the placement, such as that the child has special needs and a suitable two-parent home cannot be found.

More difficult qualities to assess are the intangibles, the most significant of which include the individual's understanding of and commitment to the uniqueness of the adoptive parenting role. It requires an assessment of the prospective adopting parent's ability and commitment to accept the child's reality, and to

---

[22] Ontario *Child and Family Services Act*, s. 146(5).

explain the adoption with an understanding of the child's ability and need to understand it at various stages of maturity.

Selection of Adoptive Parents

The process that ultimately leads to the selection of an appropriate adoptive family for a child is complex. It involves matching the parents' fitness to assume parenting responsibilities for a child not born to them with the child's suitability for such parenting. It is, in a sense, simulating a role usually reserved for nature. It is an awesome responsibility.

It is essential to dispel any myths that the prospective adoptive parents may bring to the process and to ensure that they understand and appreciate both the short- and, more importantly, the long-term consequences of adopting a child. In particular, prospective adopters need to know that:

- children who cease to be the legal offspring of their biological families at the date of the adoption order may nonetheless keep an emotional attachment to their biological families, especially with the increasing acceptance of open adoption relationships;
- provincial adoption legislation may preserve the cultural rights of children, particularly the right of Aboriginal children to enjoy the benefits of Aboriginal status;
- children gain a right to inherit from and through the adoptive parents and their kindred, unless specifically excluded by the terms of their last will;
- the secrecy of the child's pre-adoptive identity may dissolve when the child reaches adulthood or through the development of an adoption plan that features openness;
- the prospect of reunification through provincial disclosure mechanisms that have emerged in the last two decades may also attract other family members wishing to seek out the adoptee; and
- adoption does not rework life; despite the law's presumptuous pronouncement of rebirth, which for example includes listing the adoptive mother and father on the child's birth certificate as if they physically created the child, the child will continue to have a complex and sometimes subtle link to the biological family.

The Placement Process

Adoption Placement

Placement of a child for adoption can involve a "deemed" or an "actual" placement. A "deemed" placement refers to the crystallization of a decision that a child will be adopted after having been initially placed in a home on a different understanding.[23] This occurs when foster parents receive approval to adopt a

---

[23] See *Catholic Children's Aid Society of Metropolitan Toronto v. T.S. et al.* (1989), 20 R.F.L. (3d) 337 (Ont. C.A.).

child already in their home on foster placement. The placement process is usually acknowledged by the signing of a written document by adoptive applicants and witnessed by the placing agency or licensee.

With an "actual" placement the agency with responsibility for the child reviews the applicants and selects the parents who are considered most likely to provide stability and support; to some extent, the length of time that the applicants have been in the queue will be a factor, but a placement decision is never based solely on "waiting in line." It is now common practice for agencies and licensees to give birth parents a role in selecting among suitable applicants, usually by providing them with non-identifying information about different prospective adoptive parents. In theory, it is the agency who must make the final decision, but in practice, especially with private placement adoption, very significant weight is given to the views of the birth parents, whose consent is needed for any voluntary placement adoption.

Once the agency selects a prospective adoptive family, the agency will prepare the family for the placement by providing them with non-identifying social and medical information about the child and birth family to the extent that it is known. In involuntary placement adoptions, often this information is lacking detail because the birth parents are not co-operative and, therefore, do not provide family information freely.

After specific approved applicants are selected and confirm their interest, and the ministry has approved the placement, the child is placed in their home and the adoption probationary period begins.

Adoption legislation provides that a private agency or licensee may not place a child for adoption without the approval of a provincial director, which in most jurisdictions will only be given after a review by the director, if:

- the home study that has been prepared by a social worker;

- the supporting documentation establishing the suitability of the prospective adoptive parents to care for the child;

- evidence proving that the adoptive parents have reviewed the social and medical histories of the birth parents and are prepared to accept the risks attendant with adopting the child;

- the social and medical history of the child and birth family;

- a memorandum from the birth parents' social worker outlining the counselling received and the decision making process used by the birth parents in relation to their adoption plan;

- a memorandum from the licensee outlining the circumstances surrounding the matching of the child to the prospective adoptive parents; and

- a memorandum from each of the birth parents and adoptive parents confirming that they understand the roles of the ministry, licensee and social workers who are facilitating the adoption.

Unlike private licensees, a government child welfare agency is not required to seek the approval of a provincial official in order to place the child for adoption, since the agency provides the appropriate overview.

Adoption Probationary Period

Once the child is placed with the prospective adoptive parents, the agency or licensee monitors the placement for a probationary period, usually six months, in order to confirm that the child is satisfactorily adjusting to the placement and that the prospective adoptive parents are performing their duties appropriately.

Adoption probation is the process following the child's placement with the selected family. The central goal of adoption probation is the attachment of the child to the adoptive parents and other family members, and the bonding of the adoptive parent to the child. Thus, adoption probation prohibits making an adoption order when the child is initially placed for adoption. In the case of a child placed with strangers, it is the law's most outwardly visible acknowledgement that the security for the child intended by the placement has a fragility that can gain strength only with careful and committed nurturing, and that needs to monitored.

The usual time for the adoption probation is six months, but the period may be lengthened or shortened by court order to meet the particular circumstances of the child and family.[24] If, for example, the child is being adopted by the foster parents, adoption probation may be waived altogether, since there is already a basis upon which to measure the extent to which the child and prospective adopters have bonded. On the other hand, it is not unusual for adoption probation to extend to a full year in the case of an older child who is being adopted by strangers, if the child needs the additional time to work through emotional issues that have been carried from pre-adoptive life.

Adoption probation is generally supervised by a social worker designated by the provincial child welfare authority to monitor and support the new family unit. That social worker will ultimately prepare a report for the court outlining the child's adjustment to the adoptive family and the family's adjustment to the child. Ontario's legislation, for example, requires a formal written report recommending whether the court should finalize the adoption in any case where the child is less than 16 years of age and is not being adopted by a relative or step-parent.

The factors that are assessed during the probationary period depend on the particular circumstances of each case. Typically the social worker considers the characteristics of both the child and the adoptive parents, and addresses those factors that will provide the court with information to satisfy it that finalization of the adoption is in the child's best interests. The factors that are usually considered in an assessment of probation are:

---

[24] See e.g., Ontario *Child and Family Services Act*, ss. 149 and 154.

- the extent to which the prospective adoptive parents are meeting the child's physical, mental and emotional needs;
- the extent to which the parents recognize and accept the child's physical, mental and emotional levels of development;
- the extent to which the child is developing a positive relationship with the adopting parents, siblings and extended family, and establishing a secure place as a member of the adoptive family;
- the extent to which the child has been able to let go of prior relationships;
- the extent to which the adoptive family is providing the child with continuity of care;
- the extent to which the child's cultural background and religious faith is respected and nurtured within the adoptive family;
- the child's views and wishes about the adoption, in whatever verbal or non-verbal manner that they are communicated;
- the extent to which the child is ready to have the adoption finalized; and
- the extent to which the adoptive parents show themselves able to accept the child as an individual in his or her own right, not made in their image or there to satisfy their needs.

When the probationary period has expired and the social work report on the placement has been prepared, the agency or licensee will apply to the court on behalf of the parents for a final adoption order.

If the child is being adopted by a relative or a step-parent, legislation in most provinces does not require a probationary period, on the reasoning that the child is already a part of the adoptive family. However, if at the time that the relative or step-parent seeks the adoption order the court has concerns about the child's adjustment to the adoptive relationship, the court may adjourn the application and order an investigation and assessment of the child's situation by the provincial child welfare authority. The report prepared for the court as a result of this investigation assists the presiding judge in determining whether the adoption is in the child's best interests.

A Manitoba court considered the appropriateness of permitting a child welfare agency to intervene in a private adoption proceeding in which the court was being asked by the applicants to ignore the agency's home study report disapproving of the biological mother's choice of adoptive parents for her child.[25] The agency's request for intervenor status was opposed by both the prospective adoptive parents and the mother. The court permitted the agency to intervene in the court proceeding on the basis that the agency might be able to assist the court in a way that the parties might not. The court felt that it was unreasonable to expect the applicants to call evidence which, by its nature, might be detrimental to their case. The court also determined that the intervenor would not delay the litigation.

---

[25] *D.D.W. & D.D.W. v. V.M.* (1988), 17 R.F.L. (3d) 292 (Man. Q.B. — Fam. Div.).

Guardianship of the Child during Placement: Interim Guardianship

Legislative provisions specifying who has the legal right and responsibility for decisions related to the child during the adoption probation period vary between the provinces. In Ontario, until the completion of the adoption, legal rights and responsibilities for the child remain with the placing agency or licensee, once all parental consents to the child's adoption are signed and the 21-day period for cancellation has passed without incident. The adoptive parents do not have the legal right to make major decisions related to the child during the adoption probationary period, except insofar as the agency or licensee with guardianship responsibility delegates authority to them (e.g., the adoptive parents may be authorized to take the child on short trips but will need permission to take the child on an international vacation).

Interim guardianship orders are sometimes granted to prospective adoptive parents if the prospective adoptive parents wish to secure the child's custody from others during the adoption probationary period, but the court considering an adoption application is not satisfied that the adoption should be finalized at that particular point in time.

Consent to Adoption

Given the permanent and profound life-changing effects of adoption, a key aspect of the adoption process is the requirement for the consent of every legal "parent" to the adoption, unless there are strong reasons for a court to dispense with those consents. Further, legislation requires that children who are regarded as having sufficient capacity are also required to consent to the adoption.

A birth parent must be an adult, 18 years of age in most provinces, to be able to consent to an adoption without the involvement of a guardian or other adult. In Ontario, if a biological parent is under 18 years of age, the Children's Lawyer must provide legal advice before the parent can sign a consent.

A written consent must be witnessed either by a child welfare agency worker or an independent legal advisor. The witness or independent legal advisor must attest to the fact that the person consenting understands:

- the nature and effect of an adoption under the law of the province or territory;
- the nature and effect of the consent;
- the circumstances under which the consent may be withdrawn;
- the nature and operation of the jurisdiction's disclosure registry; and
- their right to counselling.

In addition the consent must identify when and where a consent revocation must be made and set out that the consent was given freely without threat or inducement.

A consent given by a person who is incapable of understanding the nature of the consent or who was tricked or misinformed may later be found to be invalid. In a 1973 British Columbia case the judge stated: [26]

> A consent, induced as this one was by fraud and undue influence, is neither free nor voluntary and is not binding. It is no consent at all. Equally it is plain that the mother, in the induced belief that the adoption of the child would not hinder her right to see the child at will or to regain the child upon reconciliation with her husband, had little or no understanding of the effect of adoption and of her consent thereto.

> It is true that the misrepresentation of the husband was as to his intention but it was nevertheless a representation that the alleged intention did indeed exist and, as it was untrue, there was a clear misrepresentation.... The misrepresentation was clearly intended to and did in fact cause the mother to sign the form of consent. It brought about in her mind a misunderstanding which induced her to act as she did. The misrepresentation was clearly fraudulent as there was, admittedly, a complete absence of honest belief in the husband's mind that there was any possibility of reconciliation or of regaining the child in a united home.

All jurisdictions in Canada prevent a parent from signing a consent before a child is born, and establish a time period in which to revoke the consent if parents wish to change their mind. These provisions are intended to ensure that the parent has an adequate opportunity to consider a very significant and irreversible decision. The decision to consent to an adoption should only be finalized after parents have experienced the birth of their children and have had an opportunity to spend some time with them.

In Ontario the child must be at least seven days old before the birth parents can sign a consent.[27] In Alberta there is no waiting period once the child is born, but it is common practice to wait until the second or third day before the consent is signed. Once the consent is signed the person consenting has the right for a limited period of time to withdraw or revoke the consent without giving reasons. In Ontario, the withdrawal must occur within 21 days of the signing of the consent,[28] while in Alberta the consent may be withdrawn within ten days of the signing of the consent.[29] It should be noted that in Ontario there is an exception to the 21-day limitation to withdraw a consent; if the child has not been placed for adoption with prospective adoptive parents before the expiration of the 21-day revocation period, the person who wishes to withdraw their consent may apply to a court for an order permitting the late withdrawal of the consent, which a court may allow if satisfied that this is in the best interests of the child.[30]

If birth parents live outside the province where the adoption order is being sought, the consent is deemed to be valid in the province granting the order, provided the requirements of the jurisdiction where the consent was signed have been followed.[31]

---

[26] *Re Adoption No. 71-09-013131* (1973), 9 R.F.L. 196 (B.C.S.C.), per Harvey L.J.S.C.

[27] Ontario *Child and Family Services Act*, s. 137(3).

[28] Ontario *Child and Family Services Act*, s. 137(8).

[29] Alberta *Child Welfare Act*, s. 61(1).

[30] Ontario *Child and Family Services Act*, s. 139(1)

[31] Ontario *Child and Family Services Act*, s. 137(13).

Dispensing with the Consent of a Parent

Where a parent, whose consent to an adoption is required, is unable, unwilling or unavailable to consent, all jurisdictions in Canada allow for an application to be made to the court dealing with the adoption to dispense with that consent. The application to dispense with consent is usually made on the basis of affidavits (sworn written statements), but the issues of dispensation to consent may result in a full trial with witnesses called to testify and to be cross-examined.

In some cases a birth mother is able to plan for the adoption of her child and completes all of the steps except the signing of the consent. In such a case a court may dispense with the consent of the mother, but will generally only do so if she has notice of the application. If the applicant can establish that significant efforts have been made to personally serve the mother but she cannot be located, the court may allow substituted service by leaving notice of the application with a relative or advertising in the newspaper. When a public child welfare agency is involved in an adoption but there has been a failure to obtain a signed consent before the mother loses contact with the agency, the agency may apply to have the child made a permanent ward without any parental right to access, and then proceed with the adoption without notifying the parents.

In the case of a birth father not providing a consent to an adoption, there are two mutually exclusive routes to be considered before proceeding with an application for adoption. If the birth father does not fit within the legal definition of a "parent" in the adoption statute (discussed below), his consent is not required and a motion may be brought for a finding that no consent other than the birth mother's is required for the adoption.

Alternatively, if the birth father does fit within the definition of a legally qualifying "parent," a motion can be brought for an order dispensing with his consent, based on the argument that doing so will promote the best interests of the child. In some cases, the father is not willing to sign the consent form, but has been notified of the proposed adoption and is not actively opposing the application; these cases can usually be quickly dealt with by the courts, though the applicant must set out the grounds for dispensation, typically focussing on the father's lack of involvement in the child's life and the best interests of the child.

Most of the contested applications to dispense with the consent of a father to the adoption of his child arise out of step-parent adoptions. The applicants, the biological mother and her new partner, have the onus of establishing that it is in the "best interests" of the child to dispense with the father's consent. If the father has been seeing the child with any degree of regularity, this application is not likely to be granted. However, if the father's visitation has been sporadic or stopped altogether, the court is likely to grant the application unless it can be shown that the mother was persistently thwarting the father's efforts to contact the child, for example by moving away without notice to the father and without leaving any contact information.[32]

Where the birth father is a legal "parent" and his whereabouts are unknown, prior to bringing a motion to dispense with his consent, a motion for substituted service, for example, by newspaper advertisement, must be obtained; an order for substituted service will only be granted if real efforts have been made to locate the father.[33] Courts prefer to have the direct input of the birth father who qualifies as a parent and this necessitates giving the birth father notice of the hearing. If the birth father is notified and chooses not to come forward, the court can draw the inference that he does not object to his consent being dispensed with.

Courts are loathe to dispense with a birth father's consent or to make a finding that he is not a parent whose consent is required without notice to the birth father. Judge Wolder of the Ontario Court of Justice (Provincial Division) in the case of *S.P. v. Z.S.*[34] explained:

> Unlike custody orders or even Crown wardship orders, adoption orders, once made are final and permanently terminate a parent's rights as a parent....
>
> Therefore, natural justice mandates that such order should not be made unless the parent who would be adversely affected by the adoption order has received actual notice of such application. Therefore, it is incumbent on the applicants to use their best efforts to make such parent aware of the application. The Act requires the applicants to make nothing less than a reasonable effort. Allowing the applicants to obtain an order terminating such parent's rights without making any effort to give notice therefore to such parent on the belief that providing notice may be difficult is contrary to the principle of natural justice....
>
> In the circumstances of this case and based on the minimum evidence before me, I cannot speculate what would constitute a reasonable effort to give such notice. A reasonable effort to give notice should be by personal service. If that is not successful, the applicant could seek an order for substitutional service of the proposed adoption application and of the motion to dispense with the biological father's consent by publication in a newspaper having national circulation in Poland or perhaps by personal service upon a relative, acquaintance or other person with whom the respondent is believed to maintain contact.

Since the application to dispense with notice affects the fundamental rights of both parent and child to enjoy a relationship with one another, and the application is by its very nature unopposed (an *ex parte* application), there is an obligation on the party seeking the dispensation with notice to provide "full and frank" disclosure to the court about all efforts to locate the parent. Lawyers, licensees or social workers who are not candid with the court about these applications may find themselves castigated by the judge, and their reputations with the court will suffer.[35]

---

[32] *L.(M.) v. M.(S.)*, [1989] O.J. 3 (Ont. U.F.C.).

[33] *S.P. v. Z.S.*, [1995] O.J. No. 826 (Ont. Ct. J. — Prov. Div.).

[34] *Ibid.*

[35] See *Re N.P.*, [2001] O.J. 441 (Sup. Ct.).

In a step-parent adoption, the court will expect the mother to be fully candid with the court about disclosing information about the identity and location of the father. However, when an agency or licensee is arranging the adoption, there may be cases in which the mother clearly wants the child placed for adoption, but is unwilling to identify and involve the father, perhaps saying: "I only know his first name and that he lives in Toronto."[36] In these cases, the courts may be somewhat more sympathetic to dispensing with notice to the father or making a ruling that he is not legally a "parent," since there is no effective way to compel the birth mother to disclose information.

Statutory Definition of "Parent"

In adoption cases, which usually involve children born out of wedlock, there has long been controversy about when a biological father is to be legally defined as a "parent" for adoption purposes. Historically, only if a woman was married was the consent of the father, who was presumed to be her husband, required for an adoption. There has been a gradual extension of the legal concept of "parent," and Canadian law now recognizes that a biological father who has taken sufficient steps as set out in the legislation should have the right to be involved in the decision to place the child for adoption. There are, however, also cases in which fathers may be difficult or even impossible to identify, and the law does not require the infinite delay of the adoption of a child to attempt to locate a man who has taken no steps to identify himself.

There is at present some variation between the provinces in terms of the definition of "parent." Ontario has one of the broader definitions of "parent" for the purposes of adoption, with s. 137(1) of the *Child and Family Services Act* providing:

> ..."parent" [for the purposes of adoption consent]...means each of,
>
> (a) the child's mother;
>
> (b) an individual described in one of paragraphs 1 to 6 of subsection 8(1) of the *Children's Law Reform Act* [which creates presumptions of paternity] unless it is proved on a balance of probabilities that he is not the child's natural father;
>
> (c) the individual having lawful custody of the child;
>
> (d) an individual who, during the twelve months before the child is placed for adoption...has demonstrated a settled intention to treat the child as a child of his or her family, or has acknowledged parentage of the child and provided for the child's support;
>
> (e) an individual who, under a written agreement or a court order, is required to provide for the child, has custody of the child or has a right of access to the child; and
>
> (f) an individual who has acknowledged parentage of the child in writing under section 12 of the *Children's Law Reform Act*.

---

[36] See e.g., *Re L.J.J.*, [2003] A.J. 1611 and 1612 (Q.B.).

In s. 137(1)(a) there is reference to s. 8 of the *Children's Law Reform Act,*[37] which creates presumptions of paternity where a man has been married to or cohabited with the mother of a child or has registered the birth of the child or has been found by a court to be the father of the child.

> S. 8(1) Unless the contrary is proven on a balance of probabilities, there is a presumption that a male person is, and he shall be recognized in law to be, the father of a child in any one of the following circumstances:
>
> 1. The person is married to the mother of the child at the time of the birth of the child.
>
> 2. The person was married to the mother of the child by a marriage that was terminated by death or judgement of nullity within 300 days before the birth of the child or by divorce where the decree nisi was granted within 300 days before the birth of the child.
>
> 3. The person marries the mother of the child after the birth of the child and acknowledges that he is the natural father.
>
> 4. The person was cohabiting with the mother of the child in a relationship of some permanence at the time of the birth of the child or the child is born within 300 days after they ceased to cohabit.
>
> 5. The person has certified the child's birth, as the child's father, under the *Vital Statistics Act* or a similar Act in another jurisdiction in Canada.
>
> 6. The person has been found or recognized in his lifetime by a court of competent jurisdiction in Canada to be the father of the child.

Further, and significantly, s. 12 of Ontario's *Children's Law Reform Act* allows any man who believes that he is the father of a child to file a statutory declaration with the Registrar General, which will entitle him to notice of any court application for adoption, but will also recognize the relationship for purposes of child support if the child is not adopted.

If there is a dispute about whether a man who is presumed to be the father of a child or has registered as the father is in fact the biological father, the issue of biological paternity may be resolved by a court, which will almost always decide this issue by means of DNA testing. Conversely, s. 137(1)(d) provides that individuals who are not biological parents may nevertheless be legal "parents" if they have demonstrated a settled intention to treat that child as a child of their own, or acknowledged parentage and provided for the child's support. Such psychological parents will have the right to consent to (or oppose) any adoption, but they will also have child support obligations.

Constitutional Challenges to the Definition of "Parent"

Historically, adoption legislation gave no rights to men who were not married to mothers of children being placed for adoption, even if they acknowledged paternity and lived with the mothers and children for significant periods of time. Not long after the *Charter of Rights* came into effect, the courts ruled that

---

[37] *Children's Law Reform Act*, R.S.O. 1990, c. C. 12.

legislation giving no rights to any fathers of children born out of wedlock violated the *Charter* guarantees against discrimination based on gender.[38] The courts, however, also recognized that there are constitutionally valid reasons for differential treatment of fathers and mothers. In the 1989 Ontario decision in *Ontario (Attorney-General) v. Nevins*, the court observed:[39]

> ...it is an erroneous oversimplification to say that the mother and a father who does not fall within the statutory definition of "parent" are similarly situated. The mother because of physical necessity has shown responsibility to the child. She carried and gave birth to it. The casual fornicator who has not demonstrated any interest in whether he did cause a pregnancy or demonstrate even the minimum responsibility to the child...cannot be said to be similarly situated to the mother. The statute recognizes as a parent a father who demonstrates the minimum interest in the consequences of his sexual activity. Most fathers are defined as parents. Only those who do not demonstrate some responsibility to the child are not. It is thus apparent to us that the different statutory treatment of the two persons is based upon their respective demonstrated responsibility to the child, not upon their different sexes....

In its June 2003 decision in *Trociuk v. British Columbia*, the Supreme Court of Canada considered the extent to which differential treatment of fathers was constitutionally permissible. The case involved the question of whether it is a violation of the s. 15 *Charter* rights of the father of a child born out of wedlock to leave it totally to the mother to decide whether his name appears on the birth certificate and whether to give him an opportunity to register his paternity. This case arose out of a challenge to British Columbia birth registration legislation brought by the biological father of triplets who had lived with their mother at the time of birth, and subsequently separated from her. A paternity test proved that he was the biological father, and he had court ordered access as well as the obligation to pay child support. The legislation in British Columbia (unlike Ontario) made no provision for a man in this situation to be registered on the birth certificate as the child's father. In striking down the statute, Justice Deschamps wrote for the unanimous Supreme Court:[40]

> Parents have a significant interest in meaningfully participating in the lives of their children. "The relations of affection between an individual and his family and his assumption of duties and responsibilities towards them are central to the individual's sense of self and of his place in the world." Including one's particulars on a birth registration is an important means of participating in the life of a child.... Contribution to the process of determining a child's surname is another significant mode of participation in the life of a child. For many in our society, the act of naming a child holds great significance.

There are still provinces in Canada, such as Alberta, which do not make provision to allow a father of a child born to a single mother to take steps to register his claim for paternity, thereby assuming obligations of child support but also gaining the right to notice and involvement in any adoption proceeding.

---

[38] See e.g., *MacVicar v. British Columbia Superintendent of Family and Child Services* (1986), 34 D.L.R. (4th) 488 (B.C.S.C.).

[39] *Ontario (Attorney General) v. Nevins* (1988), 13 R.F.L. (3d) 113 at 115-120 (Ont. Div. Ct).

[40] *Trociuk v. British Columbia (Attorney General)*, [2003] S.C.J. 32 at paras. 15-21.

Legislation in provinces such as Alberta may be vulnerable to challenge based on *Trociuk* for failing to allow for fathers of children born out of wedlock to take steps to declare their interest and be notified of any court hearings.[41]

The *Trociuk* decision makes clear that a man who is aware that he is the father of a child and wants to attempt to establish a relationship with the child cannot have a permanent termination of his relationship through wardship or adoption without the right to qualifying for notice and a hearing. That case arose in British Columbia and involved legislation which had a relatively narrow definition of who has the rights of a "father." It is significant to note that, in Ontario s. 12 of the *Children's Law Reform Act* allows a man who believes that he is the father of a child to file an affirmation of paternity with the Registrar of Vital Statistics, which then entitles him to notice of any child protection or adoption proceedings.[42] In one recent Ontario adoption case the court, of its own motion, raised the question of whether a man who knows that he is the biological father of a child but has not lived with the mother or the child and has taken no steps to register his status or assume support obligations should be entitled to the rights of a "parent" and be required to consent to the adoption. In *C.(D.) v. A.(W.)*, Justice Wolder distinguished *Trociuk* since in Ontario a man in this position has a "simple and effective method to become defined as a 'parent,'" namely by registration.[43]

The judge in *C.(D.) v. A.(W.)* nevertheless concluded that the man should be given notice of the application for the motion at which an order was being sought for a declaration that he was not a "parent," a conclusion that may be problematic. The Supreme Court in *Trociuk* clearly focused on the "arbitrary" denial of rights to a man who knows that he is a father and wants to exercise rights. The Court also accepted that there are cases in which there may be "good reasons" for a mother to assert that a man should have no rights, such as if the pregnancy was a result of rape or incest.[44] Further, the biological reality is that if a woman gives birth to a child and the father has not registered, it is not possible to force her to identify him.[45] It is submitted that given this reality, the Ontario legislature is justified in limiting rights to men who have either actually lived with the mother or child, or taken steps to formally identify themselves by registration (acquiring rights, but also assuming obligations of child support). While in rare cases this might result in some men losing rights that they might want to exercise without even being aware that they are fathers, the alternative is a scheme that would require the co-operation (or coercion) of women into identifying men whom they may not want to identify (or may not be able to identify).

---

[41] See e.g., *J.F.P. v. V.P.* [2003] A.J. 1588 (Alta Q.B.).

[42] See Ontario C.F.S.A. s. 37(1) and 137(1)(f). *Trociuk* may have some implications for the provisions of the *Vital Statistics Act*, R.S.O. 1990, c. V 4 that deal with the naming of children born out of wedlock, and perhaps some revisiting of the jurisprudence dealing with naming of children, such as *Kreklewetz v. Scopel*, [2003] O.J. 2364 (C.A.), leave to appeal to SCC dismissed [2002] S.C.C.A. No. 378.

[43] [2003] O.J. 5119 (Ont. Ct J.); see also *Re Adoption of Natalie Y.*, [2003] O.J. 2636 (Ont. Ct.J.).

[44] [2003] S.C.J. 32 at para. 25.

[45] See e.g., *J.F.P. v. V.P.*, [2003] A.J. 1588 (Alta Q.B.).

Such a scheme would ultimately be unworkable, and could indefinitely delay adoptions and hence would be contrary to the interests of children. If men want to have parental rights (and in the case of children born to single mothers the reality is that the vast majority of men want to avoid any obligations), they have to take the responsibility to know whether the women with whom they have had intercourse have had a child, and then take some steps to formally recognize the relationship with the child.

Timing of Qualification as a Parent

Adoption practitioners involved in voluntary placements for non-familial adoptions must be aware of issues relating to when an individual first qualifies as a "parent." An adoption placement becomes a legally protected placement once:

- a director approves the placement;
- all the required consents have been given and are not revocable; and
- the child is physically in the care of the prospective parents.

Adoption placements are to be protected from outside interference during the non-judicial phase or probationary period to allow the new family to form attachments. If a birth father does not fit within the statutory definition of a "parent" before the adoption placement, but he later becomes a "parent" (for example, by registering), he will have no opportunity to be involved until the judicial phase of the adoption process. The judicial phase typically does not start until seven or eight months after the birth of the child as the six-month probationary supervision period must pass. Because of the passage of time, in these cases a court may find that it is in the best interests of the child to dispense with the birth father's consent as the child has become attached to the prospective adoptive parents.

In the case of *B.B. v. C.S.*[46] Judge Kurkurin discusses the concept of the non-judicial and judicial phases of the adoption process.

> ...the determination of who is a "parent" for purposes of parental consent to adoption must be made at the time of the application for adoption, not at the time of placement.

> However, another determination, a non-judicial one, has to be made first. The...*Act* contemplates a process whereby a child will be placed with prospective adoptive parents by a licensee, in the case of a private adoption. Subsection 137(5) provides for a transfer of the rights and responsibilities of the child's parents with respect to the child's custody, care and control to the licensee when certain matters have been attended to. One of these matters is the securing of the written consent of every parent under subsection 137(2). Accordingly, the licensee is in a position of making a determination of whose consent is necessary by virtue of being a "parent" as defined in subsection 137(1). This determination may and usually does precede the judicial determination by several months....

> In the present case, the licensee rightly did not seek out the father's consent prior to placing the child. The father was not, at that time, a "parent" whose consent was

---

[46] *B.B. v. C.S.*, [1995] O.J. No. 4230 (Ont. Ct. — Prov. Div.), Kurkurin, J.

necessary.... Only on 7 July 1995, when he signed the statement of live birth at the licensee's office and, if not there and then, certainly when he signed a declaration affirming parentage on 31 July 1995 did he become a "parent."

During the non-judicial stage of the adoption, there is no obligation on the part of a child welfare agency or a licensee to seek out a non-qualifying father or to advise him of the birth of the child. The onus is on the father to make enquiries of the birth mother as to whether or not a pregnancy has resulted from their union. This, however, does not relieve adoption practitioners from the need to carefully analyse the status of fathers as it is a requirement to divulge this information to a Director prior to obtaining an approval to place and is necessary to establish that all required consents are in fact obtained prior to a placement being a legal adoption placement with its attendant protection of non-interference.

The Child's Consent to Adoption

If the adoptee is over the age of seven in Ontario, or over the age of twelve in other provinces and territories, the child's consent is required before an adoption order will be made. There are, however, legislative provisions to dispense with the child's consent if the provision of the consent would cause emotional harm or if the child is not able to consent because of a developmental handicap.[47]

In order to maximize the child's opportunity to make a choice about something that is already understood by the child, it is usual to wait until some time late in the adoption probationary period before formally discussing the issue with the child. Good social work practice requires that prior to any placement for adoption, the prospective adoption should be discussed with the child, in a manner that is consistent with the child's capacity to appreciate the circumstances and communicate.

In Ontario, a child's consent must be witnessed by a Children's Lawyer. The role of the Children's Lawyer is to ensure that the child:

- is able to understand and appreciate the consequences of the adoption;
- gives the consent freely, without fear of punishment or promise of reward; and
- has sufficient information, explained in appropriate language, to weigh the alternatives that are available.

Dispensing with the Child's Consent

All provinces provide a statutory mechanism to dispense with the child's consent to the adoption. The test varies from province to province, but typically focuses on the appropriateness of such exclusion of the child from participation in the adoption process when the statute gives him or her that specific right.

---

[47] See e.g. Ontario *Child and Family Services Act*, s. 137(9).

An Ontario court ruled that the right of a 12-year-old boy to know his true origins gives rise to a substantial onus on the applicants to show why that right should be withheld from him.[48] In that case, the reason advanced for by the applicants in a step-parent adoption for dispensing with the child's consent was that the child believed that the adoptive applicant (the mother's spouse) was his birth father. The mother had withheld from him the true facts of his paternity, and he would discover this fact if his consent was sought. The court considered the importance of evidence attesting to a child's particular sensitivity and vulnerabilities and was not prepared to rely solely on the parent's opinion that the child was not ready for the information about his true origins. Judge Nasmith did, however, dispense with the child's consent as

1. The parents [had] convinced [the court] through affidavit evidence and subsequently through viva voce evidence that they sincerely believed that the child [was] particularly sensitive and vulnerable at [that] time and would be devastated if he learned the truth about his natural father; and

2. The correct information if given would be that the psychological father is not the natural father and it would not be possible to identify the natural father or to make constructive use of the information.[49]

Finalization: The Adoption Order

The process of termination of the legal tie to the birth family and acquisition of new legal ties to the adoptive family come together in the application that is made to the court at the conclusion of the adoption probationary period to finalize the adoption. Each provincial adoption statute specifies which level of court has authority to finalize adoptions. In most provinces, the court with jurisdiction over child protection matters also has responsibility for adoption. The hearing, which will result in the presentation of a new status binding on the world, is a private one.

The course of the proceeding depends on the type of adoption. In particular, if the child is being adopted by applicants who are, and are intended to remain, unknown to the birth family, the legal process ensures that the identity of the birth family is protected and that court records cannot be used to identify the adoptive family of any child. The documents relating to the adoption application that reveal the child's biological parentage are kept confidential (in a sealed envelope in court files, for example) and cannot be disclosed without a court order. In cases where the birth identity is known to the adoptive applicants and the birth family is actively involved in the adoption (e.g., adoption by a relative or step-parent), such secrecy is meaningless for those involved in the process.

The judge will usually finalize the adoption in Chambers (i.e., the judge's office) by reviewing the documents filed in support of the adoption order. In most jurisdictions it is not necessary to have a formal hearing if the application is not opposed and the supporting documents are in order.[50]

---

[48] *Re the Adoption of "A,"* (1980), 3 F.L.R.R. 47 (Ont. Prov. Ct. Fam. Div.), Nasmith P.C.J.

[49] *Ibid.*

[50] *Re M.L.A. and three other applications* (1979), 25 O.R. (2d) 779 (Ont. Prov. Ct. — Fam. Div.), Beaulieu P.C.J.

The Test for Finalization: Making the Adoption Order

The first duty of the presiding judge is to be satisfied that all of the statutory requirements for adoption (e.g., those pertaining to residence and age of the prospective adopters) have been met. The next duty is to be satisfied that the adoption order is in the child's best interests.

The judge dealing with the adoption application must also examine the relinquishing documents to be satisfied that the interests of the child's birth parents were properly protected and that those persons who signed consent to the child's adoption understood the nature and effect of it. The report on the child's adjustment to the adoptive family that is prepared by the social worker designated to monitor the probationary period is a critical (although not necessarily determining) piece of evidence considered by the court.

While the burden of satisfying the court that the adoption furthers the best interests is on those who seek the adoption order, if the application is not opposed and all of the documents are in order and any required social work reports are favourable, the order is very likely to be granted.

Appeal and Annulments

The rights of appeal in the case of an adoption are strictly circumscribed by the provincial statute. For example, s. 156 of Ontario's *Child and Family Services Act* provides the right to appeal a decision granting or refusing an adoption order, but requires it to be launched within 30 days of the original decision. As with most other types of appeals, an appeal is not a rehearing of the case, but instead a review of the record that was before the judge who made the decision. The essential task of the appeal court is to determine whether the lower court judge made an error in law. The appeal court in an adoption case will be most reluctant to overturn the decision of a trial judge who had the opportunity to see all of the participants in person, and will only overturn the decision if there clearly was an error in the lower court's application of the relevant law.

In addition to the possibility of appealing a decision in regard to adoption, some provinces permit application for an annulment, or revocation, of an adoption order. An annulment is a declaration from a court that the original order is invalid because there was a fatal defect in making the original order. Arguably, in some situations an application for annulment can be made at any time, though some statutes specifically limit the time for making such an application. It appears that courts might have an inherent power to grant an annulment, for example, if parental consent to an adoption was obtained through fraud or duress.

In an Alberta case, the Court of Appeal set aside an adoption order of a five-year-old child on application by the child's putative birth father, because the child's mother and her new husband had not given complete information to the social worker who had prepared a report for the court in support of the adoption.[51] They had not disclosed the real history and extent of the relationship between the child's mother and father, had not told the worker that a court order had given him access and that he had abided by its terms when allowed to do so, and had misled the court by not informing it that the biological father had stopped his support payments because he had been advised in writing by provincial Social Services that the mother's marriage meant that he was no longer responsible for maintenance of the child.

It must be recognized that while adoption often works in the best interests of children and meets the needs of adoptive parents, the rate of breakdown in parent-child relationships is higher in adoptive families than it is in biological families. Problems in the adoptive relationship may develop long after the adoption is finalized, often in adolescence. In some cases this may be due to subtle neurological problems, such as fetal alcohol effects, that may not have been diagnosed early in life. In some cases, the child's adoptive status may contribute to an identity crisis and the breakdown in the relationship of parent and child. Once the adoption is completed, however, adoptive parents have full legal responsibility for the child and have no right to seek to revoke the adoption. If the relationship breaks down, the adoptive parents may contact their local child welfare agency, regardless of whether that agency arranged the adoption, and the agency may take the child into care, just as it would any other child with a troubled relationship with parents, but the adoptive parents will be obliged to provide financial support until the child reaches adulthood.

Unless there are grounds for an appeal or annulment, an adoption order, once made, cannot be rescinded. In *Re Chappell and the Superintendent of Child Welfare*,[52] a 22-year-old man sought to have an adoption order made when he was 4 years old rescinded. The adoption placement was not successful, and at the age of ten years, he moved out of his adoptive home and began a series of placements in the care of the child welfare authorities and in training schools. At the age of 20 he located his biological mother, resumed a relationship with her, and began to use her surname. The young man, the birth mother, the adoptive parents, and the child welfare authorities all agreed that it would be in the young man's best interests to have the initial order rescinded, but the court simply found that it lacked the jurisdiction to do so.

Effects of Adoption

Changing the Child's Name

The general rule is that the child assumes the surname of the adopting parents unless the court orders otherwise. Some provinces give the child no statutory say in changing either his or her given name or surname at the time of the adoption order. In Ontario and Alberta, at the time of adoption the court may

---

[51] *H.J.L. v. L.A. & R.D.A.* (1986), 1 R.F.L. (3d) 395 at 399 (Alta. C.A.).

[52] (1977), 81 D.L.R. (3d) 643 (B.C.S.C.).

change the given (first) name of a child 12 years of age or over only with that child's consent. In New Brunswick, the court must be satisfied that the change in a child's name is being made with the child's knowledge and agreement, insofar as the child's wishes can be ascertained.

Changing the Child's Status

For almost all purposes adoption creates a new status for the adoptee and adoptive parents. The effect of an adoption order is to terminate both the rights of birth parents to custody of their child and their duty to support their child, while at the same time giving the adoptive parents the right of custody and the responsibility of support.

In any will or other document, a reference to a person or group of persons shall be deemed to include a person who has acquired status by adoption, unless such an inference is expressly excluded. Thus, if a man in his will leaves his estate to "my nephews," this includes the adopted son of the man's brother. Also, adopted children acquire all of the rights to inherit property upon intestacy (if a person dies without a will), which they would have if they were biologically related children.

The Development of a More "Open" Attitude towards Adoption

Traditionally, adoption meant the severance of all legal ties and contact between adopted children and their biological families. In the past two decades, however, there have been a variety of developments that have resulted in more "open" approaches to adoption, with a range of innovations that recognize a role for both adoptive families and biological families in the lives of children. While there is variation between provinces in terms of legislative policy, it is now widely accepted that adopted children should have non-identifying information about their biological families, and that when they reach adulthood there should be the possibility of obtaining identifying information and perhaps having contact. It is becoming increasingly common to have voluntary adoption "openness agreements" with provisions for post-adoption exchanges of information and possibly for visits between children and their birth relatives. Further, in "exceptional cases," courts will order that there is to be access between adopted children and their biological parents or siblings.

Prior to the 1980s, it was rare for adoptive parents to ever meet a birth parent, though some agencies and licensees did sometimes arrange such meetings if the adoptive parents were willing and no identifying information was disclosed. Adoption has changed dramatically and many voluntary placement adoptions, especially those arranged by private agencies or licensees, now involve the parties meeting before the child's birth. These meetings often initially are on a first name basis only, and are intended to give the parties an opportunity to meet each other and discuss how they would like the adoption plan to unfold. These meetings may progress to the stage where the parties identify themselves and decide to have a continuing involvement with each other and the child. Visits may be planned after the birth of a child so that the linkage between the child and the biological family can be supported. Through openness in adoption a true relationship can be maintained between the adoptee and the birth parents, and a relationship may be established between the adoptive parents and the birth parents. This approach may satisfy the often profound need of adopted children to know about their heritage, as well as satisfying the longing of birth parents to see their children grow up while allowing adoptive parents to ensure that their children's best interests are being served. It is also often the case that normalizing the reality of the child's biological family links, instead of hiding it, allows for an honest portrayal of the relationship between adoptees and adoptive parents. Adoption should not be described in terms of ownership, but in terms of relationship. It is important to recognize that an adopted child has both biological relationships and adoptive relationships. This reality is more accurately reflected in open adoption cases.

Some cautions must, however, be kept in mind in relation to open adoptions. Parties must be suitable for an open adoption. In cases where children have been removed from the care of their parents because of protection issues, caution is necessary to protect the child and the adoptive family from harm. Some birth parents may suffer from mental or emotional disturbances, or may feel anger or resentment towards the adoptive parents, and openness may not be appropriate.

Before entering into an open adoption, all parties must be properly counselled to ensure that there is a clear understanding of what is meant by an open adoption. It is essential that proper boundaries be defined between the parties to ensure a positive and respectful relationship for all concerned.

Instead of agreeing to visits, the parties may decide to share letters and pictures periodically after the child's birth and often continuing until the child's eighteenth birthday. Judges now accept that they have the jurisdiction to make it a term of an adoption order that the adoptive parents are to annually provide a photograph and narrative account of the child's progress to the biological family.[53] A judge in one Alberta case concluded that this type of information-providing order was in the "best interests" of a four-year-old child who was being adopted by his foster family, as it might help the boy "understand his roots and himself better in the future." Such court orders are not common, however, as it is usually felt that these arrangements should be strictly voluntary, and it was significant in that case that the child was relatively old when the adoption occurred, and would likely continue to have some memories of his biological family.

In a number of provinces, including British Columbia and Manitoba, the *Adoption Act* now expressly allows an "openness agreement" to be made between prospective adoptive parents, the birth parents and, if the child is Aboriginal, members of the child's band. These agreements are intended for the purpose of "facilitating communication or maintaining relationships" between

---

[53] See e.g., *Re Adoption 46534*, [2002] A.J. 499 (Q.B.).

the child, the birth family and, for Aboriginal children, the child's community.[54] These agreements can only be signed after the birth parents have signed a consent to an adoption, as the birth parents should not be a position to threaten not to allow the child to be placed for adoption unless they can gain very extensive access rights. The agreements may provide for a dispute resolution mechanism if there are difficulties, such as through mediation. Even in jurisdictions without explicit legislation provision, those involved in adoptions are making agreements as part of the adoption process. It is expected that the parties to these agreements will usually voluntarily honour their terms, but it seems likely that if the parties do not voluntarily comply, the courts will be prepared to enforce the terms of these agreements, provided that it is in the best interests of the children involved.[55]

Post-Adoption Contact

While most adoptions that involve post-adoption visits between a child and biological parents are based on voluntary arrangements, it is now accepted that in "exceptional cases" a court can order that there are to be visits between a child and biological relatives after adoption.

In its 1998 decision in *New Brunswick (Minister of Health and Community Services) v. L.(M.)*, the Supreme Court of Canada recognized that there is a legal authority to make an adoption order conditional upon access, though indicated that this is to be done only in "exceptional cases":[56]

> ... there is no inconsistency in principle between a permanent guardianship order [or adoption] and an access order, [but] access is the exception and not the rule...the principle of preserving family ties cannot come into play in respect of granting access unless it is in the best interests of the child to do so, having regard to all the other relevant factors...an adoption, which is in the best interests of the child, must not be hampered by the existence of a right of access...access should not be granted if its exercise would have negative effects on the physical or psychological health of the child...adoption is more important than access for the welfare of the child and would be jeopardized if a right of access were exercised, access should not be granted.... In other words, the courts must not allow the parents to "sabotage" an adoption that would be beneficial for the child....

While accepting that in principle there can be post-adoption access between biological parents and children, in this case the Supreme Court (upholding the trial judge) felt that access was not appropriate, as access could have jeopardized the adoption of the children by the foster family, which was considered to be the most desirable plan for the children in that case. The evidence revealed further that the father was manipulative and unable to control his emotions, and the mother was emotionally stressed and unable to face up to the ordeal of the visits.

---

[54] See e.g., Manitoba, *The Adoption Act*, C.C.S.M. c A2, s. 33.

[55] See e.g., *S.R. v. M.R*, [1998] O.J. 5127 (C.A.).

[56] [1998] 2 S.C.R. 534 at paras. 39-50.

Most of the visits, even though brief, were disturbing and upsetting to the children, and maintaining the emotional tie with the biological parents was not consistent with the girls' psychological stability and best interests.

When a very young infant is being adopted by persons unknown to the biological parents in an adoption arranged by a licensee or an agency, it is easy to appreciate that allowing the biological parents access to the child could be disruptive and is not likely to be in the child's best interests. On the other hand, in the case of adoption by a step-parent or relative, allowing a biological parent access might sometimes be appropriate.

In *S.R. v. M.R.*, the Ontario Court of Appeal concluded that it was in the best interests of a child who had been adopted by her aunt and her husband to have continued access with the biological mother, relying in part on the fact that the parties agreed to this when the adoption order was made, and also on expert evidence from a psychologist which revealed that the child had a "healthy comfortable" relationship with the biological mother.[57] The court emphasized that "access in the context of a 'relative adoption' is very different from access in the context of a stranger adoption."

In *P. (M.A.R.) v. Catholic C.A.S. of Metro Toronto*, the Ontario courts ruled that an adolescent boy who was a permanent ward of a child welfare agency could have visits with his younger half-sister, who had been adopted by a single woman. The two children had been raised together in an orphanage in Mexico and brought to Canada by the woman who initially planned to adopt both children, but in the end only wanted to adopt the girl. In a decision affirmed by the Court of Appeal, Judge Nevins found that the two children had close emotional ties. He observed that there is a "very strong presumption against [court ordered] contact or 'interference' by the birth family following adoption, especially in those cases in which the child...was the subject of wardship proceedings and the birth parents" have had an ample opportunity to convince the court that it is in the best interests of their child not to be made a permanent ward.[58] This case, however, did not give rise to any concerns about the adopted child feeling "loyalty conflicts," and the court was prepared to order sibling access.

Disclosure of Information

Some of the most controversial issues in the adoption field concern the disclosure of information and, if identifying information is obtained, the possibility of meetings between adoptees and biological relatives.

---

[57] *S.R. v. M.R.* [1998] O.J. 5127 (C.A.).

[58] [1994] O.J. 3245 (Prov. Ct.) at para. 41, affd [1995] O.J. 2277 (C.A.), leave to appeal dismissed, [1995] S.C.C.A 453. Tragically, while this boy eventually got a court order for access, the adoptive mother was able to thwart his access rights and he spent a troubled adolescence in agency care; see "One way ticket out of the only nation he knows," *Globe and Mail* (15 July 2003).

There are two kinds of information that participants in the adoption process may be interested in: identifying and non-identifying. Identifying information includes names, addresses or other information that could permit the identification of a person involved in the process. Non-identifying information that an adoptee might want would include the reasons that the adoption occurred, a medical history of the birth parents, and some general information about the background of the biological family. Birth parents may also be interested in such non-identifying information as learning about the child's progress in school, sports or a career; birth parents may want periodic updates of this type of information. In general the laws governing disclosure of identifying information are much stricter than those governing disclosure of non-identifying information.

There has been an increasing effort over the years to provide more non-identifying information to the adults involved in an adoption at the time of the placement, in particular giving the adoptive parents as complete as possible a medical history of the birth parents and child. If after the adoption a child or adolescent adoptee wants more non-identifying information than was provided to the adoptive parents, such as information relating to the reasons for the adoption, the agency or licensee can be contacted by the adoptive parents and asked to provide this information. Once the adoptee reaches adulthood, the adoptee can directly contact the agency or licensee and ask for such non-identifying information without involving the adoptive parents, though the desired information may not be available.

The release of identifying information is governed by a strict set of statutory controls designed to ensure that the rights of privacy are respected for those participants to the adoption who wish to remain unidentified. Thus, in Canada as a general rule, identifying information is released from adoption records only if all persons to be identified agree in writing that it ought to happen.

The movement towards increased disclosure of information between adoptee and birth parents has been the subject of much political controversy in many countries. Although some adult adoptees do not want to know about their birth families, many adoptees have for years been claiming the "right" to know the identities of their birth parents, wanting this information for psychological and, in some cases, medical reasons. Many birth parents also want to find out what has become of the children whom they placed for adoption, though some birth parents prefer to "put the past behind them," and may even not have told their present families about a previous "illegitimate" child.

Some jurisdictions, like Scotland, have long had open access for adult adoptees to full information about their birth parents. Most North American jurisdictions, however, were slow to introduce legislation to permit the disclosure of identifying information, in part because of a desire to protect the privacy of birth parents, but also because some adoptive parents and many social service agencies were concerned that the prospect of the release of this information might strain bonds between child and adolescent adoptees and their adoptive parents.

In 1978 the Ontario Legislature introduced one of the first schemes in Canada to allow limited disclosure on identifying information, establishing what is now referred to as a "passive voluntary disclosure registry." The original Ontario scheme permitted release of identifying information only if a birth parent and an adult adoptee both contacted the Register and entered their names on the Adoption Disclosure Register and there was a "match." Further, under the original scheme, the consent of the adoptive parents was also required for the disclosure of identifying information, even though the adoptee had reached adulthood. The requirement for the consent of adoptive parents was a significant hurdle for some adoptees; while if asked very few adoptive parents refused to consent, many adoptees were reluctant to seek their adoptive parents' consent because they did not want their search to be interpreted as rejection of the adoptive family.

After considerable debate, in 1988 the Ontario legislation removed the requirement for the consent of adoptive parents, leaving the disclosure of identifying information essentially an issue between the adoptee and birth family members. The present scheme still provides that there ordinarily will only be a release of identifying information if an adult adoptee and a birth parent (or a birth grandparent or sibling) register and there is a "match," but the Disclosure Register is now "active"; if an adult adoptee registers, but the birth parent has not, the staff of the Register are to conduct a "discrete and reasonable search" to contact the birth parent and ask whether the birth parents will consent to having their identity revealed.[59] Unfortunately, the Register has limited resources, and it can take quite a while for a search to be conducted.

The present Ontario legislation also permits release of identifying information without the consent of birth parents, if, in the opinion of the Registrar of the Adoption Disclosure Register, the health, safety or welfare of a person requires such disclosure; this provision is occasionally used to deal with serious health needs, for example, if an adoptee needs a human tissue and a biological relative would be a likely suitable donor. Further, the disclosure of identifying information may be refused by the Registrar if it is believed that this might "result in serious physical or emotional harm to any person," though the refusal may be appealed to an independent Board.

Once identifying information is disclosed, the parties are free to arrange a meeting, though child welfare agencies have the responsibility of providing counselling to all involved before the information is disclosed. There have been repeated efforts to broaden the scope of the Ontario legislation, but to this point the provincial government has resisted these efforts.

Adult adoptees in Ontario have also tried to use *Charter*-based litigation to require the government to give them access to identifying information, but the courts have rejected these claims. For example, in 1983, the Ontario Court of Appeal refused the *Charter*-based claim of a 55-year-old woman to inspect

---

[59] Ontario *Child and Family Services Act*, s. 167.

documents related to her adoption. The court held that her interests in learning about her origins were not important enough either to outweigh the rights of the other parties to the adoption to confidentiality, or to jeopardize the province's interest in maintaining the integrity of its adoption system by preventing such access, except through the mechanism of the provincial Adoption Disclosure Register.[60]

While the courts and legislature in Ontario have resisted the advocacy of adoptees and birth parents for a further expansion of the right to identifying information, legislatures in a number of other provinces and countries have been more receptive to providing greater access of information to adoptees and birth parents. British Columbia, for example, now has a register that operates on the presumption that once an adoptee reaches adulthood (19 years of age in that province), both the adoptee and the birth parents should have access to identifying information, which will typically allow them to get in contact with each other if they wish. Either an adoptee or a birth parent, however, can file a "disclosure veto," which prevents the disclosure of identifying information, or a "no-contact declaration," which allows for the disclosure of identifying information but makes it an offence to attempt to contact the person who has filed the declaration.

The moves to allow for greater access to information for adult adoptees and birth parents address deep emotional needs that are felt by many adoptees to know more about their biological relatives. Even when not permitted by law, many birth parents and adoptees become involved in searches using various internet sites or services like Parent Finders that make use of the non-identifying information that has been provided and various public records to attempt to make connections.

Most of those who get identifying information will want to have a meeting and attempt to establish a relationship. As it is not uncommon for adoptees and their birth relatives to have unrealistic expectations, those who are going through this process should have counselling and support. While some of these meetings are quite disappointing for some or all involved, many of these meetings are positive experiences. Adult adoptees can establish very important relationships with their newly discovered biological relatives, though rarely does this result in any weakening of the ties to the adoptive family. While many adoptees have a strong desire to learn more about their heritage and have contact with biological relatives, most of them remain much more closely attached to their adoptive families.

---

[60] *Ferguson v. Director of Child Welfare, Minister of Community and Social Services* (1984), 36 R.F.L. (2d) 405 (Ont. S.C.A.D.). See also *Re Adoption of B.A.* (1981), 17 R.F.L. (2d) 140 (Man. Co. Ct.); and *Tyler v. District Court of Ontario* (1986), 1 R.F.L. (3d) 140 (Ont. Dist. Ct.).

International Adoptions

With the decline in the number of healthy young infants available for adoption in Canada, prospective adoptive parents have increasingly become involved in international adoptions, seeking to adopt children from orphanages in poorer countries.[61] There are now approximately 2,000 foreign children per year adopted by Canadian citizens.[62] While international adoption is relatively expensive, with total costs running in the range of $10,000 to $25,000 or more, the wait for an adoption is usually shorter than for a domestic adoption as so many children are available. Further, adoptive parents who might have difficulty being selected as the "best" match for the relatively few infants available domestically, such as older couples or single persons, may be able to adopt young infants internationally. There are also some individuals who specifically want to adopt internationally out of a sense of commitment to the developing world and to its many needy children.

Until recently, there was little legal regulation of international adoption, and protections against fraud, abuse, and "baby selling" were lacking. International adoptions are now regulated by the *Hague Convention on Protection of Children and Co-operation in Respect of Intercountry Adoption (Hague Convention)*, and by provincial and territorial implementing legislation. In Ontario, the implementing legislation is the *Intercountry Adoption Act*.[63]

The *Hague Convention* and the Canadian legislation attempt to prevent abuse and fraud in the adoption of children from abroad, protect the rights of biological parents, and ensure that adoptions serve the best interests of the children involved. The *Hague Convention* establishes a system of rules to coordinate efforts between the various jurisdictions and to ensure proper supervision of the adoption process by "central authorities" in each jurisdiction. In Canada, in each province the unit of the social services ministry that is responsible for adoption is the "central authority," and is required to ensure that:

- the agencies in Canada that arrange these adoptions are licensed and have qualified staff;

- there is appropriate screening of prospective adoptive parents who will be bringing the child into the province;

- there is post-placement assessment and report prepared by an approved social worker; and

- there is appropriate liaison with immigration authorities prior to immigration visas being granted for the child.

---

[61] See generally M. Eade, "Inter-country Adoption: International, National and Cultural Concerns" (1993), 57 *Saskatchewan Law Review* 381-395.

[62] *International Adoption and the Immigration Process* (Ottawa: Citizenship and Immigration Canada, 2000) at 3.

[63] S.O. 1998, c. 29. Every jurisdiction in Canada now has enacted legislation to implement the *Hague Convention* except Quebec, which has implemented the *Convention* by administrative regulation.

It is illegal for a child to be adopted from a foreign country without the involvement of a central authority and Immigration Canada if the child is a resident of a *Hague Convention* ratifying country.

The central authorities are responsible for ensuring that prospective adoptive parents meet minimum standards, which is done by reviewing home studies prepared by social workers in private practice who are approved by the provincial government. Once the central authority is satisfied that the parents are qualified, they provide Immigration authorities with a letter of non-objection as required by statute.[64]

International adoptions can only be facilitated by not-for-profit agencies that meet the provincial requirements. These agencies typically specialize in arranging adoptions from one country or region of the world through their contacts in those countries. The agencies also assist in arranging home studies in Canada, travel, and immigration. While they are non-profit agencies, they charge significant fees for the services that they provide, as well as government fees, travel expenses, and fees in the country of the child.

Once a home study has been completed and the prospective adoptive applicant is assessed by the central authority as qualified, an application can be made to Immigration Canada for approval as a sponsor of the child as a "Family Class Relative." A child is not permitted to enter Canada until the immigration visa is issued and care should be exercised before traveling to a foreign jurisdiction to escort a child into Canada.

Before a visa will be issued, the child must pass a medical test conducted in the foreign jurisdiction by a doctor who is approved by the Canadian government. Also, the prospective adoptive parents must have an income that exceeds a stipulated minimum.

The actual adoption is normally carried out in the jurisdiction where the child was born, in accordance with the processes and laws of that jurisdiction. This means that the adoptive parents will travel to that country and spend a few weeks there while the adoption is finalized, bringing all the appropriate documentation from Canada with them. Generally, the Canadian agencies and orphanages in the sending countries are reputable, and ensure that the adoptive parents are not exploited and that the adoption meets the needs of the child. While adoptive parents can generally complete an international adoption more quickly than if they use a domestic agency, the process can take a year or longer and is often frustrating for the adoptive parents, especially when dealing with the child welfare agency and legal system in the country of the child's origin. Differences in language and culture, and in some cases the potential for corruption within the justice system, can cause difficulties. In some cases prospective adoptive parents can spend large sums of money and not secure a child to adopt.

There are many complex social and political issues associated with international adoptions. One concern that adoptive parents may have is that a child may

---

[64] *Immigration and Refugee Protection Regulations,* SOR/2002-227, s. 117(1)(g).

have physical, neurological or emotional problems that they may not be aware of when adopting the child.[65] Once they have adopted the child, they are legally and morally responsible for the child, at least until adulthood. If an international adoption placement breaks down, the child may face even greater difficulties than when a domestic adoption breaks down, as the child may be suffering from cultural dislocation and have no hope of gaining any contact with biological relatives.[66]

Most international adoptions are transracial and intercultural adoptions. Many adoptive parents want to try to help their children maintain a knowledge of their culture and country of origin, and in some cases even contact with their biological relatives. Once an international adoption is finalized, however, the child's legal relationships with the biological family are severed, and accordingly, the child cannot sponsor members of his or her biological family for entry into Canada as relatives. Issues of disclosure of information and any possible meetings with biological relatives are governed by the laws of the country of the child's origin.

While there continue to be controversies about international adoption, and there is still only limited research into the long-term effects of international adoption, the research that has been done generally suggests that outcomes are at least as positive as domestic adoption.[67]

Conclusion

Adoption is an evolving institution. In adoptions during the time of the Roman Empire, adoption was a legal fiction used to provide heirs in order to preserve family wealth and power. Around the start of the twentieth century, the child welfare system in Canada began to use adoption to provide for children who were orphaned or born out of wedlock in a process that was shrouded in great secrecy. Starting in the 1970s the institution of adoption has been challenged to more accurately reflect the reality of the parties involved with a view to discarding the fiction that children are born of their adoptive parents, and to reject the view that birth parent involvement in the life of the adopted child will necessarily be harmful.

Long-standing fears of adoptive parents that their relationships with their children will be impaired if their children know their birth parents are dissolving

---

[65] See e.g., M.T. Stein, "International Adoption: A Four-year-old Child with Unusual Behaviors Adopted at Six Months of Age" (2003), 24 *Journal of Developmental & Behavioral Pediatrics* 1, at 69; and V. Groza, "Institutionalization, Behavior and International Adoption: Predictors of Behavior Problems" (2003), 5(1) *Journal of Immigrant Health* 5-17.

[66] See e.g., "One way ticket out of the only nation he knows," *Globe and Mail* (15 July 2003).

[67] See e.g., J. Swize, "Transracial Adoption and the Unblinkable Difference: Racial Dissimilarity Serving the Interests of Adopted Children" (2002), 88 *Virginia Law Review* at 1079; R.J. Simon and H. Altstein, *Adoption, Race & Identity: From Infancy to Young Adulthood*, 2nd ed. (New Brunswick, NJ, US: Transaction Publishers, 2002); and C. Bradley and C.G. Hawkins-Leon, "The Transracial Adoption Debate: Counseling and Legal Implications" (2002), 80 *Journal of Counseling & Development* 433-440.

as more literature is being published about open adoption,[68] and more adult adoptees and birth parents are having their voices heard. Adoption is normalized and destigmatized when children can have their questions relating to their origins answered openly and truthfully. Similarly, when birth parents can satisfy themselves as to how their children are faring, their pain and fear in placing their children for adoption can be diminished. Adoptive parents who receive early training regarding openness in adoption come to recognize that this can be a benefit for their child and, accordingly, they can incorporate mutually agreeable terms into their adoption plans.

The movement towards greater disclosure of identifying information has been partially achieved in British Columbia, and is being considered in other jurisdictions like Ontario. Achieving openness of records for adult adoptees and their biological relatives will further remove the secrecy surrounding adoption. Perhaps with the removal of the last vestages of secrecy, adoption will be recognized for what it really is, namely a way to provide a child, whose birth family is not in a position to provide parenting, with the best long-term care plan available. Greater openness should always honour both the actual ongoing biological linkage of children to their birth families and simultaneously honour the lifelong commitment of adoptive parents to their children.

Adoption is also becoming a more diverse institution. At one time, almost all adoptions involved agencies placing infant children born to single mothers with infertile couples of the same race. Today fewer single mothers are placing their children for adoption but, with the rise in divorce rates, step-parent adoptions are more common. International and transracial adoptions are also becoming common. Adoptive parents may be gay or lesbian couples or single parents, as well as married opposite-sex couples. Not only does adoption involve healthy newborn infants, but older and special needs children are now finding adoptive homes. This greater diversity in adoption means that professionals and courts involved in the adoption process need a greater range of knowledge and skills, and means that the law must be more flexible to respond to the demands of different situations.

---

[68] See e.g., A. Douglas and T. Philpot (Eds.), *Adoption: Changing Families, Changing Times* (New York: Routledge, 2003); D.H. Siegel, "Open Adoption of Infants: Adoptive Parents' Feelings Seven Years Later" (2003), 48(3) *Social Work* 409-419; H. Grotevant, "What Works in Open Adoption," in M.P. Kluger and G. Alexander (Eds.), *What Works in Child Welfare* (Washington, DC, US: Child Welfare League of America, Inc, 2000), 235-242; J. House, "The Changing Face of Adoption: The Challenge of Open and Custom Adoption" (1996), 13 *Canadian Family Law Quarterly* 333; and M. Bernstein, D. Caldwell, G.B. Clark, and R. Zisman, "Adoption with Access or 'Open Adoption'" (1992), 8 *Canadian Family Law Quarterly* 283-300.

7

Aboriginal Child Welfare

Murray Sinclair, Nicholas Bala, Heino Lilles,
and Cindy Blackstock[1]

For well over one hundred years, the policies of Canadian governments towards Aboriginal[2] children were a major factor in the deterioration of Aboriginal cultures in Canada, and often resulted in the suffering and abuse of Aboriginal children. Aboriginal people have a justified concern about the deterioration of their families, communities, values and customs as a result of the policies that were adopted by Canadian governments, first in the residential schools and later in the child welfare system. Recently there has been significant recognition of the harm caused by previous policies and practices. Laws and policies have been introduced that are more sensitive to the needs of Aboriginal children, families and communities, and Aboriginal child welfare agencies have been established in many places in Canada. Past government policies, however, continue to have intergenerational effects, and many Aboriginal parents and communities now face great challenges in caring adequately for their children.

An obvious and important indicator of the deterioration in Aboriginal cultures and communities is that Aboriginal children are taken into the child welfare system in disproportionately large numbers — at least five times greater than the rate of non-Aboriginal children.[3] In some jurisdictions and in all of the territories, the majority of child apprehensions involve Aboriginal children. The problem for Aboriginal communities is magnified by the fact that children make up over half of the current Aboriginal population and that the Aboriginal population continues to increase at a much faster rate than the non-Aboriginal population of Canada.[4]

---

[1] Murray Sinclair is Justice, Court of Queen's Bench of Manitoba. (Justice Sinclair's contribution to this chapter was made to the first edition of this book.) Nicholas Bala is Professor of Law, Queen's University, Kingston, Ontario. Heino Lilles is Chief Judge, Territorial Court of Yukon, Whitehorse, Yukon. Cindy Blackstock is Executive Director, First Nations Child and Family Services Caring Society of Canada.

[2] In this chapter, the term "Aboriginal" includes Status and Non-Status Indians, Inuit, and Métis peoples. The term "First Nations" is used to refer to Aboriginal communities that have an organized political structure and are exercising some governmental functions.

[3] N. Trocmé, K. Della, and C. Blackstock, "Pathways to the overrepresentation of Aboriginal children in Canada's child welfare system" (Centre for Excellence for Child Welfare, University of Toronto, 2003) report that about 5% of all children in Canada are Aboriginal, but an estimated 40% of children and youth placed in out-of-home care in Canada are Aboriginal. They also report a 71.5% increase in the number of Aboriginal children in care in the 1995 to 2001 period.

[4] Statistics Canada, 2001 *Census*. In the 2001 census, Aboriginal people were 3.3% of Canada's total population, but because of a high birth rate, 5.6% of all children are Aboriginal.

Aboriginal children who become involved with the child welfare system at an early age often spend time in multiple foster placements, and later in young offender institutions, and then in the adult correctional system. Although this "life path" is often followed by non-Aboriginal children, the adverse consequences of child welfare involvement are exacerbated when children are moved from their community and culture to a distant location as a result of child welfare involvement, as often happens with Aboriginal children. Aboriginal groups have expressed deep concerns that the pattern of apprehensions inhibits the development of these children as future contributing members of Aboriginal communities; it also has negative implications for Canadian society in general. One Aboriginal group asks:[5] "Is the system conditioning our young for lives in institutions and not in society?"

The cost of Canada's policies towards Aboriginal children and families, in both human and financial terms, is becoming clear. Public awareness of the financial expense related to institutionalizing Aboriginal people has increased. Canadian society and Aboriginal communities are starting to address the problems created or exacerbated for Aboriginal people by child welfare agencies that were at worst racist in their attitudes and at best culturally insensitive. The changes in Aboriginal child welfare are part of a broader change in government policies and public attitudes towards the relationship between Aboriginal peoples and the rest of Canadian society. This change in approach was both reflected in, and reinforced by, the inclusion in the 1982 repatriation of Canada's *Constitution Act*. The *Constitution Act* now contains provisions that recognize the unique constitutional and political status of Aboriginal peoples, who have inherent Aboriginal rights as well as treaty and statutory rights.[6] Canadian governments and First Nations have been dealing with a wide range of issues including land claims, unresolved treaty issues and claims for Aboriginal sovereignty or at least a greater degree of self-government.

In recent years, provincial child welfare legislation has given greater recognition to the special needs and status of Aboriginal children. In some places, child welfare agencies have been established that are controlled by Aboriginal peoples, albeit generally operating within the framework of provincial child welfare statutes. In other places, Aboriginal voluntary agencies are working with provincially mandated child welfare agencies to provide services to Aboriginal children and families. Although many Aboriginal communities have made significant strides in gaining more control over the future of their children and communities, they have yet to obtain full control free from federal and provincial government involvement. Further, there remain many Aboriginal children who receive child welfare services that are provided without any direct involvement of Aboriginal agencies.

---

[5] Swampy Cree submission to the *Public Inquiry into the Administration of Justice and Aboriginal People of Manitoba*, The Pas, Manitoba, (17 January 1989) at 14.

[6] *Constitution Act, 1982*, ss. 25 and 35.

There is no doubt that the history of racist and insensitive government policies towards Aboriginal children and families has played an important role in contributing to the overrepresentation of Aboriginal children in Canada's child welfare system. But it must also be recognized that many Aboriginal communities now suffer from a range of social and economic problems that are linked to high rates of child neglect and abuse, such as high rates of family violence, poverty, alcoholism and drug use.[7] While increasing the degree of control and involvement of Aboriginal communities in the provision of child welfare services is having positive effects, the transfer of responsibility is a complex and contentious process, and will not be a panacea for the problems of Aboriginal child welfare.

All of those who work in the child protection system, whether in an urban, rural or reserve environment, will encounter cases involving Aboriginal children. Social workers, lawyers and judges who are not informed of the Aboriginal communities' struggle for control of child welfare services, or of the cultural, social, legal and historical dynamics involved, will be unable to adequately provide for the needs of the children, let alone for their families and communities.

In an attempt to offer some basic information on problems of Aboriginal child welfare, this chapter begins with a review of historical developments in the treatment of Aboriginal children and then considers current cultural and legal issues. The chapter only provides an introduction to the many complex social, legal and political issues that arise in Aboriginal child welfare. A discussion of these issues is challenging because this is an evolving field, and there is a great range of issues and responses, not only between provinces and territories, but also within jurisdictions. Many issues are highly contentious, with fundamental disagreements not only between Canadian governments and First Nations, but also within Aboriginal communities. Further, there has not been a great deal of social science research or writing in this area, and much of what there is tends to be descriptive, or written from a policy advocacy perspective.

Historical Background

Assimilation

Since the earliest contact between Canada's Aboriginal people and European colonists, there have been conflicting values about many fundamental issues, including family relationships and child-rearing. Initially, however, there was little social interaction between the colonists and Aboriginal peoples, and these differences in values and behaviours had little impact on the lives of Aboriginal peoples. However, as the number of settlers increased and the colonists began to

---

[7] Trocmé, Della, and Blackstock, *supra*, note 3, conclude that the rates of child welfare involvement are the same for Aboriginal and non-Aboriginal children, *controlling* for such factors as higher levels of parental poverty, alcohol abuse, criminal activity and single parenthood. They also report that parental neglect is a disproportionately large problem compared to abuse.

exert their military and political power over Aboriginal peoples, the European colonists began to attempt to impose their values, beliefs, and practices on the original inhabitants of North America.

When European powers began to colonize North America, they formed trade and military alliances with Aboriginal peoples, and religious proselytizing of the "savages" began. The religious missionaries were the first to attempt to fundamentally change Canada's Aboriginal population, seeking to convert them to Christianity.[8]

Initially, much of the interaction between colonists and Aboriginal peoples was mutually beneficial, and in many ways the Aboriginal people controlled their own cultural and economic development. However, there was a gradual and growing emphasis on assimilation by missionaries and settlers. This shift in attitudes had devastating effects on Aboriginal cultures:[9]

> Part of the reason for this change in attitude lay...in the Indians' diminishing utility as Indians. As the nineteenth century progressed, Indians were becoming less valued for their original cultural attributes, whether as partners in the fur trade or as military allies. Settlement assumed priority. This new paternalistic, one-sided relationship received its legal justification in the *British North America Act,* which...took away Indians' independent status by making them wards of the federal government. As consolidated in the *Indian Acts* of 1876 and 1880, Indian self-government was abolished, and finance and all social services, including education, were placed under federal control. Lands reserved for Indians' use were to be managed on their behalf until such time as individual Indians enfranchised themselves or became sufficiently "civilized" to be allowed a measure of self-government.

The commitment to assimilation was reflected in the policies initiated in the nineteenth century by Canadian governments to "educate" Aboriginal children in the ways of the "white man." Many of the treaty negotiations that occurred after Confederation contain references by the government treaty commissioners to promote this objective. The residential school system which was established in the late nineteenth century was premised on the belief of governments and the dominant Canadian society that assimilation through education of young Aboriginal children was necessary and was to be achieved by removing the children from the influence of their parents and their communities.

In many parts of Canada, especially in the North and West, Aboriginal children were required pursuant to the *Indian Act* to attend these residential schools, often located far from their homes, removing them from the influences of their traditional culture and way of life, as well as from the emotional and social support of their parents and communities. The federal government funded these schools, but almost all of the schools were operated by religious groups affiliated with various Christian churches. In residential schools the children

---

[8] The history of missionary activity is recounted in J.W. Grant, *Moon of Wintertime: Missionaries and the Indians of Canada in Encounter Since 1534* (Toronto: University of Toronto Press, 1984).

[9] J. Barman, Y. Hebert, and D. McCaskill (Eds.), *Indian Education in Canada: The Legacy,* Vol. 1 (Vancouver: University of British Columbia Press, 1986) at 4. *The British North America Act of 1867,* which established Canada and divided jurisdiction over various issues between the federal and provincial governments, was renamed the *Constitution Act, 1867,* in 1982.

were forbidden to speak their own languages or practice any of their customs which were considered to be "uncivilized." Children were brutally punished for speaking to their friends and siblings in their native language, and traditional religious practices were not tolerated. In these residential schools,[10]

> all aspects of life, from dress to use of English language to behaviour, [were]...carefully regulated. Curriculum was...limited to basic education combined with half-day practical training in agriculture, the crafts, or household duties in order to prepare pupils for their expected future existence on the lower fringes of the dominant society.

Many Aboriginal parents appeared to co-operate with the placing of their children in residential schools, believing that it was beneficial to have their children educated in non-Aboriginal schools. Indeed, available evidence suggests that with some of the treaties, the "schoolhouse" clauses were requested by the Indians and not simply imposed by the government negotiators. While Aboriginal parents were saddened at the absence of their children, at least some of them believed that the benefits of obtaining a "white man's" education justified this separation.

Indian children, understandably, did not always co-operate with their removal from their homes and communities. In order to facilitate the return of children who ran away from residential schools, regulations were enacted that required Indian children to attend these schools and that removed the authority of Indian parents over their children while they were in residential schools. Indian parents were often required to seek and obtain passes from their local Indian Agent to leave the reserve, although no law was ever enacted to support the practice. Passes were not easily obtained, and if parents wished to travel from their reserve to see their child at one of the residential schools, passes were often denied, especially if the visit was not taking place during an established school holiday.

Conditions in these schools were often deplorable. One report from the early twentieth century focused on the extremely high rate of tuberculosis among the Indian children in the residential schools in Western Canada:[11]

> Insufficient care was exercised in the admission of children to the schools. The well-known predisposition of Indians to tuberculosis resulted in a very large percentage of deaths among the pupils. They were housed in buildings not carefully designed for school purposes, and these buildings became infected and dangerous to the inmates. It is quite within the mark to say that fifty percent of the children who passed through these schools did not live to benefit from the education which they had received therein.

This prompted *Saturday Night Magazine* to comment in 1907 that "even war seldom shows as large a percentage of fatalities as does the education system that we have imposed on our Indian wards."[12]

---

[10] *Ibid.* at 6.

[11] D.C. Scott, writing in 1920, quoted in D. Purich, *Our Land: Native Rights in Canada* (Toronto: James Lorimer, 1986) at 134.

[12] Quoted in Union of British Columbia Indian Chiefs, *Calling Forth Our Future: Options for the Exercise of Indigenous Peoples' Authority in Child Welfare* (2002) at 10.

While by the middle of the twentieth century health conditions at residential schools had improved, it is now clear that the removal of children from their families and communities was a highly destructive emotional experience for Aboriginal children. As well, the devaluation of the children's culture and heritage that occurred in these institutions had very damaging effects on their self-esteem.

Further, at many residential schools there were devastating patterns of physical and sexual abuse. While it is clear that the government was receiving reports of abuse and neglect, little was done to prevent the abuse of Aboriginal children in these schools. The extent of abuse in these schools was not publicly known at the time that it was occurring, with the assumption being that the religious groups that operated the schools were providing appropriate care. It is now clear, however, that many abusive adults took jobs as teachers in these schools and were able to exploit and abuse a very vulnerable population of children. The tragic reality of abuse in these schools only came to the public consciousness in the last years of the twentieth century as adult Aboriginal survivors of residential schools began to disclose to the public and report to the police and other authorities the stories of their childhood abuse.[13] There have been a number of criminal prosecutions coming out of the abuse in residential schools, although many of the abusers are now elderly and some are dead. Thousands of adult survivors have begun civil suits to seek financial damage awards for the abuse that they suffered, and the federal government has established a non-court based alternative dispute resolution scheme that offers limited compensation.[14] No financial award can begin to compensate for the emotional suffering that these victims have experienced, and the awards that most victims have received have not been huge. Further, the intergenerational effects of residential school abuse on the families and communities of the immediate victims are beyond the ability of a legal system to redress.

The federal government began to phase out residential schools in the 1950s, although the last of these schools was only closed in the 1990s. Day schools have been established on or near most reserves. Children from reserves began to be integrated into the public school system, although some Aboriginal children from remote communities still have to board with other families while attending school, especially high school. While there are no longer any residential schools, the intergenerational legacy of these institutions is still present. Due to

---

[13] For descriptions of the residential school system, see e.g., A.C. Hamilton and C.M. Sinclair, *The Justice System and Aboriginal People: Report of the Aboriginal Justice Inquiry in Manitoba* (1996), Vol. 1, 509-520; Royal Commission on Aboriginal Peoples, *Looking Forward: Looking Back* (1996), Vol. 1; and J. Milloy, *The National Crime: The Canadian Government and the Residential School System 1879 to 1986* (Winnipeg: University of Manitoba Press, 1999).

[14] See Indian Residential Schools Resolution Canada: http://www.irsr.gc.ca/english/dispute_resolution.html. Awards in the courts and from the alternate dispute resolution process for severe abuse in residential schools have generally been in the range of $150,000 to $300,000. These monetary awards can be problematic; an adult survivor of the residential school system who has a serious drug or alcohol abuse problem and receives a non-structured lump award may spend it unwisely, perhaps on alcohol and drugs, and may be worse off as a result.

an absence of parenting role models, children who grew up in residential schools often have great difficulty in effectively parenting their own children. As is common with survivors of childhood abuse, drug and alcohol addiction, depression and patterns of family violence are endemic among those who attended residential schools. Further, the experience of many Aboriginal parents in residential schools has meant that some do little to encourage their own children to attend school, contributing to very high drop out rates among Aboriginal students, and hence to the poverty and unemployment of a new generation of Aboriginal peoples.

Also during the 1950s, there was an increase in the number of Aboriginal families moving from reserves to urban centres in order to find employment and pursue educational opportunities. These families were faced with the stresses of entering a foreign, urban culture as well as a loss of community support. Many Aboriginal children in urban settings were, and still are, considered by child welfare authorities to be neglected.[15]

> Life for a child on a Reserve or in a native community is described as one of safety, love, adventure, and freedom. A child feels, and is welcome in any home and may join any family for a meal. A mother is not concerned if a child does not return home for a meal or even to sleep. The mother knows that some family is willingly providing for the child. This pattern is one that causes native parents grief when they move into urban centers because the reality is that urban life is different and dangerous. A mother who does not immediately report her child as missing is viewed as neglectful by the urban agencies.

More than half of all Aboriginal people now live off reserve, many in urban settings, and the child welfare concerns of this population raise especially challenging social and jurisdictional issues.

The "60s Scoop"[16]

Since the establishment of Canada in 1867, under the *Constitution Act*, legislation regarding Aboriginal people has been the responsibility of the federal Parliament, while child welfare matters have fallen under provincial jurisdiction. Prior to the 1950s, it was rare for provincial child welfare services to be offered on Indian reserves. Children considered to be in need of protection were apprehended by Indian Agents and either placed with another family on the reserve or sent to residential schools.[17]

While s. 91(24) of the *Constitution Act* gives the federal government legislative authority over "Indians and lands reserved for Indians,"[18] the federal government is not obligated to provide services under s. 91(24) of the *Constitution Act*

---

[15] E.C. Kimelman, *No Quiet Place: Review Committee on Indian and Métis Adoption and Placements* (Manitoba: Manitoba Community Services, 1985) at 163.

[16] The term "60's scoop" was coined by Patrick Johnston, but it is now widely used: P. Johnson, *Native Children and the Child Welfare System* (Toronto: Canadian Council on Social Development / James Lorimer & Co., 1983).

[17] J.A. MacDonald, "The Spallumcheen Indian Band By-Law and its Potential Impact on Native Indian Child Welfare Policy in British Columbia" (1983), 1 *Canadian Journal of Family Law* 75 at 77.

[18] *Constitution Act, 1982*, being Schedule B. of the *Canada Act 1982* (U.K.), 1982, c. 11, s. 91(24).

or the *Indian Act*. Although Parliament has the jurisdiction to enact legislation in regard to Aboriginal child welfare, it has chosen not to do so.

In 1951, the federal government amended the *Indian Act* to include a provision clarifying the extent to which provincial legislation applies to Aboriginal people. Section 88 states:[19]

> Subject to the terms of any treaty and any other Act of the Parliament of Canada, all laws of general application...in force in any province are applicable to...Indians in that province, except to the extent that such laws are inconsistent with this Act and except to the extent that such laws make provision for any matter for which provision is made...under this Act.

Because the *Indian Act* contains no reference to child welfare, this section implicitly requires that provincial child protection laws and services extend to Aboriginal children, both on- and off-reserve. However, in the 1950s and 1960s, there was little federal effort to provide financial assistance to the provinces to pay for Aboriginal child welfare services, and provincial governments were reluctant to extend provincial services to Indian reserves, primarily for financial reasons.

The result of this prolonged jurisdictional dispute was that the quantity and quality of child welfare services provided to Aboriginal children on reserves across Canada varied considerably. In several provinces, especially in western Canada, child welfare services were provided to Aboriginal children living on reserves only in "life-or-death" situations. The result was that many Aboriginal families in need of family support services were not provided with even basic services, and difficult situations worsened until they became life-threatening and children had to be removed from parental care.

In the 1960s and early 1970s, as residential schools began to close and child welfare agencies were growing and starting to take responsibility for Aboriginal children, there were massive increases in the number of Aboriginal children taken into agency care. In British Columbia, for example, in 1955 there were just 29 Indian children in the care of the provincial Child Welfare Branch, under 1% of the children in care in the province; by 1964 the number had risen to 1,446, more than 34% of the number of children in care.

The Aboriginal children who were removed from parental care in the 1960s and 1970s were usually placed in non-Aboriginal foster or group homes, or were adopted by Caucasian families. Some of them were placed for adoption in, the United States or Europe. Aboriginal parents rarely had access to lawyers, and these apprehensions and adoptions were invariably rushed through the courts without any type of meaningful judicial review. On some reserves, as many as one third of all children were taken into care and permanently removed by child welfare agencies. This is an event that is now known as the "60s

---

[19] R.S.C. 1985, C. I–5, s. 88.

scoop."[20] While child welfare laws and policies have changed since then, this massive intervention created an atmosphere of mistrust and resentment of child welfare authorities that exists to this day.

The result of the "60s scoop" was that even though the residential school system started to fade away in the 1960s, Aboriginal people continued to be dominated by the push towards assimilation. In fact, many Aboriginal people came to view the child welfare system as a vehicle for "cultural genocide," since it typically gave "little weight to the values, lifestyle and laws" of the Aboriginal people in Canada, and because it has imposed on them the "standards, cultural values, laws and systems" of the dominant society.[21]

Cultural Issues

Philosophy of Life

Many Aboriginal people are working to gain control of the child welfare programs that affect their lives. This struggle is more than just a legal or jurisdictional dispute. Aboriginal child welfare is grounded in an understanding of the world that is very different from the dominant European perspective. To understand the movement towards Aboriginal child welfare and the complexity of the cultural issues involved, one must consider elements of the world view common to many Aboriginal cultures. Fundamental to this world view is the interrelationship of all living things (including the physical environment as a living conscious entity).[22] Children are gifts from the Creator and are nurtured within flexible and extensive extended family systems. Aboriginal healers work with concepts of balance, holism, harmony, and relationships to promote growth and connectedness.[23] Models for this work are often expressed using a circle or Medicine Wheel framework.[24]

---

[20] *Supra*, note 16.

[21] B. Morse, "Native Indian and Métis Children in Canada: Victims of the Child Welfare System" in G.K. Verma and C. Bagley (Eds.), *Race Relations and Cultural Differences* (London: Croom Helm, 1984) at 31; see also P. Monture, "A Vicious Circle: Child Welfare and the First Nations" (1988), 3 *Canadian Journal of Women and Law* 1.

[22] See V. Morrissette, B. McKenzie, and L. Morrissette, "Towards an Aboriginal Model of Social Work Practice" (1993), 10(10) *Canadian Social Work Review*, 91-108; M.K. Zapf, "Location and Knowledge-Building: Exploring the Fit of Western Social Work with Traditional Knowledge" (1999), 2(1) *Native Social Work Journal* 138-152.

[23] See M.A. Hart, *Seeking Mino-Pimatisiwin: An Aboriginal Approach to Helping* (Halifax: Fernwood Publishing, 2002); B. McKenzie and V. Morrissette, "Social Work Practice with Canadians of Aboriginal Background: Guidelines for Respectful Social Work" in A. Al-Krenawi and J.R. Graham (Eds.), *Multicultural Social Work in Canada* (Toronto: Oxford University Press, 2003), 251-282; J. Proulx and S. Perrault (Eds.), *No Place for Violence: Canadian Aboriginal Alternative* (Halifax: Fernwood Publishing and Research & Education for Solutions to Violence and Abuse, 2000); B. Wharf and B. McKenzie, "Policy-Making in Aboriginal Child and Family Services," in B. Wharf and B. McKenzie, *Connecting Policy to Practice in the Human Service*, 2nd ed. (Toronto: Oxford University Press, 2004), 114-127.

[24] See G. Bruyere, "The Decolonization Wheel: An Aboriginal Perspective on Social Work Practice with Aboriginal Peoples" in R. Delaney, K. Brownlee, and M. Sellick (Eds.), *Social Work with Rural and Northern Communities* (Thunder Bay: Lakehead Centre for Northern Studies, 1999), 170-181; J. Carriere-Laboucane, "Kinship Care: A Community Alternative to Foster Care," (1997), 1(1) *Native Social Work Journal* 43-53; E. Connors and F. Maidman, "A Circle of Healing: Family Wellness in Aboriginal Communities" in

Aboriginal peoples also place great emphasis on the well-being and survival of the community, with a focus on individual identity within the context of a community rather than individual rights. Notions of private property ownership are not part of Aboriginal traditions, and even today land on reserves is not privately owned. Individuals are expected to share their good fortune with their extended family and their community. When disputes arise in an Aboriginal community, the focus is on finding a consensual resolution that restores harmony in the community, not on punishment of the offender or on vindication of individual rights.

Many non-Aboriginal people erroneously believe that the traditions, values, and beliefs of Indian cultures have completely disappeared, at least amongst those Aboriginal people who no longer speak an Aboriginal language or do not live on a reserve. Although Aboriginal cultures have undergone significant changes, Aboriginal peoples continue to have distinct cultures that are fundamental to their identities. Like all contemporary cultures, Aboriginal cultures are no longer the cultures of isolated, pre-literate peoples. Modern Aboriginal cultures are rooted in Aboriginal traditions, but they are no longer the Aboriginal cultures of a bygone era:[25]

> Many earlier sources of economic existence are gone (although traditional economic pursuits such as hunting, fishing, and trapping are still viable ways of earning a living in many northern Indian communities). Much is being lost because of the assimilation pressures of government policy and the innovations of modern technology. Some Indian languages are on the verge of extinction. Many Indians have adopted Christianity and no longer practice their [traditional Aboriginal] sacred ways. As well many institutions of larger society have replaced Aboriginal institutions. In dress, housing, employment, and other external aspects of culture, Indian peoples are becoming almost indistinguishable from other Canadians.

> But to conclude, as did the authors of the cultural assimilationist educational policy, that Indians would eventually disappear as a distinctive cultural group would be a serious mistake. Indians have not assimilated. Their identity as separate people — with a vision of reality and destiny and of themselves and their world — remains an essential feature of their lives.

In many Canadian jurisdictions, over half of the Aboriginal population live off reserves, many in large cities where there may be better employment and education prospects. Many Aboriginal people, especially those who are younger and live in cities, no longer speak their Aboriginal language; their culture and heritage, however, remain integral to their self-identity. The courts and child welfare agencies generally now recognize that Aboriginal heritage is an important factor, even in cases where families are living in urban areas and do not speak an Aboriginal language. This was, for example, recognized in *Winnipeg*

I. Prilleltensky, G. Nelson, and L. Pierson (Eds.), *Promoting Wellness and Preventing Child Maltreatment* (University of Toronto Press, 2001), 349-416); F.J. Graveline, *Circle Works: Transforming Eurocentric Consciousness* (Halifax: Fernwood Publishing, 1998); J. Stevenson, "The Circle of Healing" (1999), 2(1) *Native Social Work Journal* 8-20.

[25] J. Barman, Y. Hebert, and D. McCaskill (Eds.), *Indian Education in Canada: The Challenge*, Vol. 2 (Vancouver: University of British Columbia Press, 1986) at 156.

(Child and Family Services) v. M.S.N. where the child welfare agency was seeking permanent wardship of a three-and-a-half year old Aboriginal child, who had been living with Caucasian foster parents for two years as a result of the poor care provided by his mother. The grandparents, who lived in Winnipeg, were seeking custody. The grandparents were practicing Christians, spoke English and admitted that they only occasionally attended Aboriginal cultural events. In awarding custody to the grandparents, McCawley J. placed significant emphasis on the importance of maintaining the child's cultural heritage and noted that if the child remained an agency ward, the agency's plan for the child was adoption, and it was probable that this would not be in an Aboriginal home. The judge remarked:[26]

> Both R.M.F. and A.J.F. [the grandparents] candidly admitted that they do not attend a lot of Aboriginal cultural events. Although…they…attend pow wows once or twice a year…they are not members of any cultural organizations and do not otherwise participate. R.M.F. said they did not have a lot of time because of their work and family commitments.
>
> I do not accept this as an indication that the F.s do not value their Aboriginal culture. It is apparent they place considerable importance on their race and Aboriginal heritage and have a strong desire to see their grandson raised within their immediate and extended Aboriginal family. I found their evidence on this point to be refreshingly honest and practical.…
>
> In assessing the merits of the two plans proposed for the future care and wellbeing of K.B.N., I am persuaded that his best interests are served by allowing him to live with his paternal grandparents. They, in my view, are capable of providing him with a loving parent-child relationship and will be able to meet his mental, emotional, physical and educational needs adequately within their immediate and extended family. In addition, they are his blood, his race and Aboriginal heritage and, although they have assimilated many aspects of white urban culture into their lives, they will, as they said several times in this trial, teach K.B.N. "who he is."

This judgement illustrates that Aboriginal cultural heritage is a factor in making decisions in child welfare cases even for children and families who are living in urban settings.

Child-Rearing

While there are many different Aboriginal peoples in Canada, each with a distinctive language and culture, there are striking similarities, including similar philosophies and practices regarding children. The Aboriginal philosophy that humans are a part of, and must sustain, the delicate balance with nature is different from the dominant Euro-Canadian view that humans are superior to all other forms of life. The fundamentally different world views of Aboriginal and non-Aboriginal peoples have resulted in cultural conflict. These differing philosophies are, for example, reflected in fundamental differences between Aboriginal and Euro-Canadian child-rearing practices.

---

[26] [2002] M.J. 154 (Man. Q.B. — Fam Div.) at para. 35-40.

There are critical differences between the traditional child-rearing practices of Aboriginal peoples and those who are of European background.[27] One difference is that, generally, Aboriginal parents respect their child's individuality and allow the child greater freedom to develop naturally, whereas non-Aboriginal parents tend to direct and control their children. Another is that Aboriginal children are socialized in a different way than non-Aboriginal children, learning through example to display feelings only at appropriate times and in private, for the public display of emotion is considered to be a source of discomfort to the viewer. This emotional self-control is often mistaken for indifference by non-Aboriginal people.

An Aboriginal child may be cared for by several households of an extended family with the natural parents' understanding that the child is receiving the same love and care that they would provide while in the care of relatives. This contrasts with the non-Aboriginal emphasis on the nuclear family as the basic unit of child care provision.

An important difference in discipline is the use of humour and teasing in many tribal groups to shame and humour a child into good behaviour. This may be interpreted as emotional abuse by those unfamiliar with Aboriginal ways. Also, since Aboriginal children are considered by their Elders to be at one with nature, they are allowed great freedom to search for their enlightenment. The directive approach of non-Aboriginal schools conflicts with this nondirective approach, and many Aboriginal children have difficulty achieving goals set in the formal Canadian classroom, causing them to become discouraged with school. Children caught between Aboriginal and non-Aboriginal customs and expectations such as these are often confused and find it extremely difficult to conform to either.

When viewed by social workers not knowledgeable of and sensitive to the child rearing practices of Aboriginal people, Aboriginal approaches to child care could be construed as neglectful, or even emotionally abusive, and as reasons for intervention.

The Importance of Cultural Heritage to Aboriginal Children

Historically, the implicit objective of many government policies was to destroy Aboriginal culture; this was most obvious in the residential schools policy, which was intended to change the language and culture of Aboriginal children. The child welfare policies of the 1960s may not have been intended to attack Aboriginal families and communities, but they clearly had this effect. It is now recognized that an attack on a child's cultural heritage is a violation of the rights of the child and of the Aboriginal community, and it can have highly destructive psychological effects on the child.

---

[27] R. Andres, "The Apprehension of Native Children" (April 1981), 4 *Ontario Indian.*

Child welfare laws and policies in Canada now give a preference to placement of Aboriginal children within their own community and culture. This is, in part, based on the recognition that all children have the right to maintain their cultural heritage, as recognized in Article 20 of the *United Nations Convention on the Rights of the Child*, which provides that "due regard shall be paid to the desirability of continuity in a child's upbringing and to the child's ethnic, religious, cultural and linguistic background." This right is especially important in Canada, where Aboriginal peoples have a unique constitutional status, and where individual Aboriginal persons may have special legal rights and status.

The claim for a preference for placements of Aboriginal children within Aboriginal communities is also made by First Nation communities, as they recognize that their children are their future, and that the transmission of their culture and heritage to future generations is central to their survival as distinct communities. Aboriginal advocates have charged that the high rates of apprehension by child welfare agencies and placement of Aboriginal children in non-Aboriginal homes has constituted "cultural genocide."[28]

In addition to these essentially political and rights-based arguments about the importance of cultural heritage, there is a growing recognition that the placement of Aboriginal children in non-Aboriginal homes has often been emotionally damaging to these children. The confusion and identity crises that are often experienced by Aboriginal children and adolescents who were apprehended by child welfare agencies and placed in non-Aboriginal foster homes and adoption placements is now widely documented. The separation of Aboriginal children from their families and communities results in cultural separation and has often had profound long-term psychological consequences. Aboriginal children in care of non-Aboriginal caregivers often grow up in a state of dislocation in terms of their culture, family and community, lacking any clear sense of their identity.[29] There are studies that document how Aboriginal foster children who, overcome by the loss and grief of repeated foster care transfer, have difficulty expressing any feelings.[30]

The literature on transracial adoption, for example, for Afro-American children adopted by Caucasian parents, generally reveals that children who are transracially adopted have similar outcomes in terms of psychological well-being, educational attainment and most other measures which are not

[28] P.A. Monture, "A Vicious Circle: Child Welfare and the First Nations" (1988), 3 *Canadian Journal of Women and the Law* 1 at 3; S. Bull, "The Special Case of the Native Child" (1989), 47 *The Advocate* 523, at 525; T. Sullivan, "Native Children in Treatment: Clinical, Social and Cultural Issues" (1983), 1(4) *Journal of Child Care* 75 at 81; and M. Kline, "'Best Interests of the Child' Ideology and First Nations" (1992), 30 *Osgoode Hall Law Journal* 375.

[29] See e.g., Government of British Columbia, *Tenth Report of the Royal Commission on Family and Children's Law* (Vancouver, 1975); Kimelman, *supra*, note 15; and S. Watts, "Voluntary Adoptions Under the Indian Child Welfare Act of 1978: Balancing the Interests of Children, Families, and Tribes" (1989), 63 *Southern California Law Review* 213.

[30] See e.g., A.S. Pellatt, *An International Review of Child Welfare Policy and Practice in Relation to Aboriginal People* (Calgary: Canadian Research Institute for Law and the Family, 1991) at 16.

dissimilar to those for intra-racial adoptions.[31] Compared to other types of transracial placement, however, the rate of breakdown for adoptions and foster placement of Aboriginal children by Caucasians in Canada has been relatively high.[32] The reasons for the relatively high rates of breakdown for placements of Aboriginal children in non-Aboriginal homes are not fully understood. While fetal alcohol syndrome may play a role in some of these cases, it also seems likely that there are cultural and emotional issues that Aboriginal children and adolescents face that are not present in other transracial adoptions. Aboriginal culture in North America is uniquely devalued, with negative stereotypes of Aboriginal peoples in popular culture and in the history books that are used in many schools.

While many Aboriginal children have had positive experiences after placement for adoption or foster care with Caucasian families, there are sound reasons for generally preferring the placement in Aboriginal homes of Aboriginal children who cannot be adequately cared for by their own parents. There is a tragic history of emotional disturbance, despair and high suicide rates among Aboriginal adolescents who have been taken into child welfare agency care. Placement of Aboriginal children in Aboriginal homes not only protects the rights of Aboriginal children to their cultural heritage, it also tends to promote the development of a positive self-identity and emotional well-being.

Aboriginal Customary Adoption

Until recently, the legal system failed to recognize the importance of Aboriginal customary law and traditions. Of particular importance is the idea that the child is a member of a total community, not just a member of a single nuclear family. A number of Aboriginal customs, such as extended family parenting, stem from this. Many Aboriginal people think that the courts still do not give enough recognition to specific customs and laws such as these.

Aboriginal customary adoption was one of the first Aboriginal practices to receive recognition by Canadian courts. For such civil law purposes as inheritance or pursuing monetary claims for fatal injuries, since the 1960s the courts have accepted that the legal relationship of parent and child can be established by Aboriginal persons who were not so related biologically, if they have followed the customary practices of their tribe to establish the parent-child relationship.[33]

---

[31] See e.g., E. Bartholet, "Transracial Adoption Race Separatism in the Family: More on the Transracial Adoption Debate" (1995), 2 *Duke Journal of Gender, Law & Policy* 99; and J. Swize, "Transracial Adoption and the Unblinkable Difference: Racial Dissimilarity Serving the Interests of Adopted Children" (2002), 88 *Virginia Law Review* 1079.

[32] See Kimelman, *supra*, note 15; and Tae Mee Park, "In The Best Interests of the Aboriginal Child" (2003), 16 *Windsor Review of Legal and Social Issues* 43 at 56.

[33] See *Re Katie's Adoption Petition* (1962), 38 W.W.R. 100 (N.W.T. Terr. Ct.); *Re Beaulieu's Petition* (1969), 67 W.W.R. 669 (N.W.T.); and *Re M.R.B.*,[2002] 2 C.N.L.R. 169 (Que Ct.). See also B. Lomax, "Hlugwit'y, Hluuxw'y — My Family, My Child: The Survival of Customary Adoption in British Columbia" (1997), 14 *Canadian Journal of Family Law* 197-216.

The court in *Re Tagornak*[34] held that customary adoption is recognized not only on the basis of case law, but also as a right under s. 35(1) of the *Constitution Act, 1982*, which provides: "The existing Aboriginal and treaty rights of the Aboriginal peoples of Canada are hereby recognized and affirmed."

Traditionally, when Aboriginal parents were unable to care for their children, those children were taken in and cared for by relatives or others in their communities. In some cases the parents were dead, while in other cases the parents might have more children than they could adequately care for. In some cases, one sibling might give one or more children to another infertile sibling to care for. One aspect of Aboriginal customary adoption is that there is no secrecy. If the biological parents are alive, the children will usually have contact with them. As Judge Kimelman stated:[35]

> The raising of children is seen as a communal responsibility with the immediate and extended family carrying the primary responsibility for a specific child. In addition to the input of grandparents, aunts, uncles, and older siblings, the parents...may select a specific person to assume a special role in a child's life. This person will oversee the child's development, teach necessary skills, and maintain a lifelong relationship with the child.

> Adoption in native communities does not only apply to children. A family may adopt a grandparent. A child may adopt an uncle or an aunt. A man may adopt another as a brother and each will assume all the rights and responsibilities of a natural brother to each other's wife, children, and relatives.

In one 1985 Ontario case, the court recognized the importance of customary Aboriginal adoption and decided to place two sisters with relatives on the Grassy Narrows reserve where the natural mother also lived; this was contrary to the protection agency's plan that the children be adopted by a family on another reserve.[36] In making the decision to place the children on the same reserve as their mother, Judge Andrews observed:[37]

> [this placement]...will be in accord with the tribal tradition of "custom adoption" by reason of blood relationship. There is no evidence to indicate whether or not a subsequent legal adoption will offer any particular benefit to the children.

This case is significant because it reflects the legislation in Ontario and a number of other jurisdictions that requires consideration of cultural factors when courts are making placement decisions concerning Aboriginal children in child protection and adoption cases.

For many Aboriginal people, customary Aboriginal adoption is preferable to statutory adoption schemes as it permits the natural parents to know where their child has been placed, and it emphasizes and recognizes the importance of maintaining the child's cultural ties.

---

[34] (1983), 50 A.R. 237 (N.W.T.S.C.).

[35] Kimelman, *supra*, note 15 at 163.

[36] See, e.g., *Child and Family Services Act*, R.S.O. 1990, c C-11, s. 37(4), which specifically requires courts to consider "the importance...of the uniqueness of Indian and native culture, heritage and traditions, of preserving the child's cultural identity," as a factor in a child's "best interests"; see also s. 208 that recognizes "customary care."

[37] *Re D.L.S. and D.M.S. v. Kenora-Patricia C.F.S.*, [1985] W.D.F.L. 934 (Ont. Prov. Ct. — Fam. Div.).

It is interesting to note that many of the recent developments in adoption law in Canada and other countries have been in the direction of a more open adoption process, moves which have brought statutory adoption closer to the traditional Aboriginal custom, for example, by allowing biological parents to have a role in the selection of adoptive parents and maintaining post-adoption contact between their biological parents and their children.[38]

Standard of Care

It has been argued that Aboriginal people should decide what constitutes neglect and inadequate parenting within their own community,[39] and that the evaluation of Aboriginal parenting by non-Aboriginal professionals and judges usually does not take into account the different value systems, customs and community characteristics. A disproportionately large number of Aboriginal child welfare cases are based on allegations of neglect as opposed to other forms of child maltreatment such as physical or sexual abuse.[40] A finding of neglect by a child welfare worker or a court may implicitly suggest that the parents have the capacity to meet their children's needs. However, there has been insufficient study of how to redress the systemic risk factors, such as poverty and lack of community support services, that may lie outside the caregivers sphere of influence. Many Aboriginal peoples express concern that there has been inadequate research and dialogue on the interrelationship between poverty and the disproportionate reported incidence of neglect in Aboriginal families. Allegations of neglect by a non-Aboriginal child protection worker may reflect a worker's middle-class world view of both the standard of living and Aboriginal parenting style rather than constituting a pattern of behaviour that presents a real harm to the child.

Though the concept of neglect has not yet been defined by Aboriginal people for Aboriginal people, a number of more sensitive court decisions in Canada have ruled that different standards of care may be applied to parents in poor Aboriginal communities than those that are applied to non-Aboriginal middle-class communities.

In *Re E.C.D.M.* the court held that it should apply "different" expectations and "standards of parenting" for parents of Aboriginal ancestry living in remote, impoverished communities than it had for middle-class parents living in urban areas.[41] In this case, a 24-year-old single mother residing in a rural Cree community in northern Saskatchewan opposed a permanent wardship application for her 2-year-old child. Judge Moxley outlined some community differences to be taken into account. These included cultural differences such as an extended

---

[38] See Chapter 6 for discussion of developments in adoption.

[39] T. Sullivan, "Native Children in Treatment: Clinical, Social and Cultural Issues" (1983), 1 *Journal of Child Care* 75 at 87.

[40] See Trocmé, Della and Blackstock (2003), *supra*, note 3.

[41] (1980), 17 R.F.L. (2d) 274 (Sask. Prov. Ct.).

family concept and non-intervention in child-rearing, acquired community habits such as widespread drinking, and conditions forced on the community such as a high level of unemployment and dependence upon government assistance, and a lack of social support services. These differences formed the basis of a "different" standard which the court applied to the case, though ultimately concluding that the children should be made permanent wards since even by the standards of her community, the mother lacked the ability to care adequately for her child and the grandmother was not willing to take them in.

In another Saskatchewan case, an Aboriginal mother was successful in appealing an order for the permanent wardship of her three-year-old child on the basis that the trial judge had not taken appropriate account of the Aboriginal context. After the child was initially found to be in need of protection, the mother successfully completed treatment for her alcohol addiction and established another home separate from the people with whom she had previously associated. Judge Johnson considered the community standards of care:[42]

> What is basic in this kind of problem is the right and need of the child to be raised, if possible, by its natural mother in its natural environment and its own cultural surroundings. Although the standard of living provided by that mother and the care given to the child may not be considered acceptable by others, nevertheless if those standards conform to those considered average in the particular...group to which the parent(s) belong, the court ought not to interfere.

The issue of the community standard of care was also considered in *Director of Child Welfare of Manitoba v. B.B.*, where the trial judge, in considering whether two Aboriginal siblings were in need of protection, took account of the standards of care and resources available in the children's Aboriginal community. The trial judge held the 18-month-old twins were no longer in need of protection and were to be returned to their mother. The mother had never had custody of these children. She was living in a four-room house with another 5-year-old child, her 65-year-old mother, her sister, and her sister's two young children. The three adults received social assistance, and all were Non-Status Indians living on the outskirts of a reserve community. Alcohol abuse was evident in the home. In deciding the twins were not in need of protection, Judge Martin stated:[43]

> I have carefully reviewed the evidence and while I find that the...condition[s], and I refer to the extended family at Easterville, deplorable by standards which I take to be the norm for middle class white society, I cannot find proof, on balance, of the kind required that would allow me to say that B.B. should be denied the return of her children.

> I find that none of the incidents referred to or the living conditions reported are so far out of the ordinary, for Easterville, that I can say that the children would probably be at risk if returned to the mother.

---

[42] *Mooswa et al., v. Minister of Social Services for the Province of Saskatchewan* (1976), 30 R.F.L. 101 at 102 (Sask. Q.B.).

[43] *Director of Child Welfare v. B.B.* (1988), 14 R.F.L. (3d) 113 at 115 (Man. C.A.).

The trial decision was appealed by the protection agency, and overturned by the Manitoba Court of Appeal, with Justice Monnin stating:[44]

> That there is poverty in the area is not denied but poverty and the customs of the inhabitants of Easterville are not the issue. The sole issue is what is in the best interests of the twins....
>
> I do not accept as sound the principle enunciated by the trial judge that there are certain standards or norms which are acceptable for Easterville but unacceptable for the rest of the province. Economic conditions may differ but there is only one standard of care to be considered and applied whether the infants reside or whether the household is situated in Easterville, The Pas, Churchill, Brandon, Crescentwood, Tuxedo, West Kildonan or the Core area. In my opinion, the type of household in the case before us cannot provide the simple and essential elements of life since all three adults have shown themselves to be irresponsible where the other children are concerned and regularly over-indulge in alcohol.

The decision of the Manitoba Court of Appeal was appealed to the Supreme Court of Canada. The Supreme Court rejected the approach of the Court of Appeal to the issue of the appropriate standard of care and ordered a new trial. Justice Sopinka in the Supreme Court wrote a very brief decision, stating:[45]

> Although we do not agree with the test applied by the majority of the Court of Appeal, we agree with their conclusion that the children are in need of protection.... We are of the opinion, however, that the Court of Appeal failed to adequately consider the alternatives in s. 38 of the Act, and in addition, we have been told of evidence that indicates a change of circumstances have occurred. Accordingly, we would refer the matter back to the trial judge to consider what order is now appropriate under s. 38 [supervision, temporary wardship or permanent wardship].

This case is a good example of the child welfare dilemma faced by Aboriginal people. It is encouraging that the Supreme Court of Canada appears to recognize the inappropriateness of automatically applying the standards of the dominant society to Aboriginal peoples. Increasingly, Aboriginal communities are demanding that their own values and standards be applied when decisions are made concerning their children.

Jurisdictional Responsibility for Child Welfare

Court Decisions Recognize Provincial Jurisdiction

As discussed above, until the 1950s provincial governments generally did not provide child welfare or other services to Status Indians, viewing this as a matter of federal responsibility. The historical position of the provincial governments was that Indians were the legal and fiscal responsibility of the federal government and that the provinces had no responsibility to provide services to Aboriginal people living on reserves. The provincial justification was based partly on

---

[44] *Ibid.* at 114.
[45] [1989] 2 S.C.R. 291.

the provincial interpretation of s. 91(24) of the *Constitution Act*, which gives jurisdiction over Indians to the federal government, as well as appearing responsive to the concerns of some Aboriginal leaders who had stated that they were opposed to provincial interference in their affairs. In the absence of federal authorization and funding, provincial governments would not extend the same social and child welfare services to Indians that it provided to other citizens.

Even after the enactment of s. 88 of the *Indian Act* in 1951, there was some doubt as to whether child welfare statutes were "laws of general application" and most child welfare agencies were only willing to intervene in "life-and-death" situations, where the usual agency response was to apprehend the children and place them in non-Aboriginal homes and institutions. The agencies generally refrained from providing supportive services to Aboriginal families living on reserves, such as counselling and referral. These preventive and less intrusive services were regularly available to non-Aboriginal families for the purpose of assisting them in their crises, preventing family breakups and helping parents regain the custody of their children.

In 1975 the Supreme Court of Canada addressed the question of whether Indians were subject to the provisions of provincial child welfare legislation in *Natural Parents v. Superintendent of Child Welfare.*[46] It was argued by the parents of an Indian child being placed under care by the provincial Superintendent of Child Welfare of British Columbia that the provincial legislation was not applicable to them for several reasons, including the argument that they were subject to federal jurisdiction and not provincial child welfare laws. The Supreme Court ruled that under s. 88 of the *Indian Act*, provincial child protection legislation is a law of "general application" that governs Indian and other Aboriginal children, whether on reserve or not.

Even after the Supreme Court decision in 1975 in *Natural Parents*, some provincial governments were reluctant to provide a full range of child welfare services on reserves, claiming that the federal government should fund these services. In 1978 Judge Graeme Garson of the Manitoba Provincial Court was confronted with a case that arose directly from this provincial policy. An Aboriginal mother living on a reserve was known to be experiencing considerable coping problems that often resulted in her children being neglected. Evidence showed that counselling and other forms of assistance were needed, but were not provided to her because of the provincial policy. Although he granted a permanent order of guardianship, Judge Garson condemned the Manitoba government's failure to provide preventive support services to residents of Indian reserves.[47]

> The stark reality of the present situation [on this reserve]...is that the treaty Indian is caught in a political, financial and legal limbo, with both senior governments attempting to disclaim responsibility for the delivery of social and child welfare

---

[46] (1975), 60 D.L.R. (3d) 148 (S.C.C.).

[47] *Director of Child Welfare v. B.*, [1979] 6 W.W.R. 229 at 237 (Man. Prov. Ct).

services, with the not unsurprising result that the treaty Indian fails to get the services except in life-threatening situations.... The treaty Indian in Little Grand Rapids is being denied those services that all other Manitobans receive or are entitled to receive as of right and as a matter of course. Such a denial of services, for whatever reasons, can only be termed discriminatory to the treaty Indian.

The judge concluded that under s. 88 of the *Indian Act*, provincial legislation of general application applied to Indians and that child welfare services should be provided to Status Indians on the same basis and criteria as to other residents of the province.

This decision and similar cases elsewhere in Canada prompted a response by governments and child welfare agencies. The courts were indicating that denial of a full range of child welfare services to Indian children would not be tolerated. The initial response was the grudging extension of child welfare services by provincial governments to Aboriginal peoples. Provincial governments were, however, also expecting federal financial support, and in many places Aboriginal groups were also demanding involvement or control over the provision of child welfare services.

Contemporary Aboriginal Child Welfare

Political and Cultural Context

Before discussing contemporary Aboriginal child welfare issues, it is useful to provide an overview of the complex political status and cultural heritage of Canada's Aboriginal peoples.[48]

Canada's Aboriginal peoples have 52 different languages, which can be classified in 11 basic groups. Members of each language group, or tribe, also have a distinct history, culture and heritage.

There are over six hundred Indian reserves in Canada. These are areas of land that were reserved or set aside by the government for the exclusive use of Aboriginal peoples. Most of these reserves were established pursuant to a treaty between an Indian community and the Crown (originally the British government, later the federal government). Indians who are recognized as having "status" (or rights) under the *Indian Act* and other legislation are almost all members of a particular "band." A band is a political unit, though its members share a common Aboriginal culture, and often have close family ties. Generally, one band is responsible for each reserve, though in some cases two or more reserves are joined into a single band. Bands range in size from under a hundred members to over twenty thousand members, but most have between five hundred and two thousand members. Many band members live on-reserve, but

---

[48] Information in this section is mainly from *The Canadian Encyclopedia* (Toronto: Historical Foundation of Canada, 2003). See also Statistics Canada, *Registered Indian Population by Sex and Residence 2001* (Ottawa, 2002); on-line <http://www.ainc-inac.gc.ca/pr/sts/rip/rip_e.pdf>.

band members may live off-reserve, for example in an urban area, and still retain some of the rights of band membership.

Under the terms of the *Indian Act*, bands are governed by an elected band council and chief. Land and housing on a reserve is owned by the band, not by individuals. Bands may choose to rent out land or housing to non-members. Bands do not tax their members, but receive funding from the federal government. Many bands are also involved in a range of economic activities that provide employment and generate revenue for the band. Band councils are responsible for providing a range of services to band members, though other services, such as health care, may be provided directly by the federal government.

Members of a band who live off-reserve continue to have at least some of the rights of band members, and as discussed below, bands may continue to be involved in child welfare proceedings concerning children who live off-reserve.

Band councils have a great deal of power over the lives of members, who may be dependent on the band for employment, housing and other services. While many bands are fairly governed, there are concerns that some bands are not well governed. In particular, Aboriginal women's groups sometimes express concerns about the impact of political interference on services provided to women and children by male-dominated First Nations governments, including allegations that friends and relatives of those with political power are not held accountable for sexual or physical abuse.[49]

As discussed below in some detail, there is a growing movement to involve bands in child welfare proceedings that are going through the courts. There is also a growing number of child welfare agencies in Canada that are controlled by Aboriginal peoples, though operating within the framework of provincial child welfare legislation and under government supervision.

There are several hundred thousand Canadians who have an Aboriginal heritage but who do not have a formal "status" or legal recognition under the *Indian Act*. Many of these "Non-Status" individuals are "Métis," the term historically applied to individuals of mixed Aboriginal and French ancestry who settled in Manitoba and other parts of Western Canada, but is now used more loosely to refer to those of mixed Aboriginal and white ancestry. The Métis were not legally regarded as "Status Indians" governed by the *Indian Act*. Biologically and culturally the Métis share some of the characteristics of Indians, but they have a unique culture, with distinctive social, economic, and political institutions.

It is significant that when the *Canadian Charter of Rights and Freedoms* came into force in 1982, s. 35 explicitly recognized that the "Aboriginal peoples of Canada includes the...Métis" and "recognized and affirmed" their "existing

---

[49] See e.g., B. McKenzie, E. Seidel, and N. Bone, "Child Welfare Standards in First Nations: A Community-Based Study," chapter 5 in J. Hudson and B. Galaway (Eds.), *Child Welfare in Canada: Research and Policy Implications* (Toronto: Thompson Educational Publishing, 1995) at 55.

Aboriginal rights." It is, however, unclear exactly what rights the Métis peoples have, and this will have to be resolved through political negotiations or by the courts. In 2003 the Supreme Court of Canada in *R. v. Powley*[50] ruled that where communities of individuals with mixed ancestry have maintained a recognizable group identity living together in a geographical area, they could assert rights under the Constitution. The *Powley* case dealt with the recognition of hunting rights; its implications for child welfare are less clear.

In terms of child welfare, provincial governments historically treated Métis and other Non-Status Indians as part of the general population. There are, for example, no statistics on the number of Métis and Non-Status Indian children in care of the protection authorities, and very few studies have been done of their special problems. It is, however, clear that Métis children and families have faced problems similar to those of other Aboriginal groups. They have been disproportionately taken into care and have often not received appropriate services. The plight of Métis children received national attention following the 1984 death of Richard Cardinal, a Métis youth who moved through many foster placements. He committed suicide in a state of despair but left behind a moving journal of his experiences.[51]

Métis organizations have been advocating the establishment of their own child welfare agencies to deal with children and families in their communities. Governments are slowly beginning to recognize the needs and rights of the Métis. Child welfare programs and agencies for Métis children and families have been established in Manitoba, Alberta, Saskatchewan, and British Columbia, within the framework of provincial child welfare legislation, with government funding and community involvement.

The Inuit who live in northern Canada are not governed by the *Indian Act*, and are not organized into bands, but they have the same inherent constitutional rights as Aboriginal peoples and have access to many of the programs that are afforded to Status Indians. There are many Inuit in leadership positions in municipal and territorial governments in northern Canada, and there are Inuit political and social organizations that have an interest in child welfare issues. Child welfare services are provided for Inuit by territorial governments (and in Labrador by the provincial government).

There are also a number of Aboriginal organizations that have an important role in the development of child welfare policy. These include regional or provincially based political organizations, such as the Federation of Saskatchewan Indian Nations (FSIN), and the national Assembly of First Nations (AFN). Some of the regional groups are organized on the basis of cultural heritage and are referred to as Tribal Councils. These national and regional organizations are voluntary associations that are delegated to act on behalf of bands and other

---

[50] 2003 S.C.C. 43.

[51] *Richard Cardinal: Cry from a Diary of a Métis Child* (1986) is a documentary movie by the National Film Board that can be viewed at <http://cmm.nfb.ca/E/titleinfo/index.epl?id=16327&recherche=simple&coll=onf>.

local Aboriginal communities. They have important advocacy and educational roles and may provide some types of services. They get financial support from the member First Nations communities and may also receive funding from federal or provincial governments for core activities or specific projects, but they do not have any powers of taxation or direct governing powers.

The First Nations Child and Family Caring Society of Canada is a national non-profit organization that works with over one hundred local Aboriginal child and family service agencies that provide statutory child welfare services. The Society has an educational, research and advocacy role on a national level in the Aboriginal child welfare field.

Aboriginal Child Welfare in Canada

Although there is considerable variation across Canada in how governments and First Nations are responding to child welfare issues for Aboriginal children, there are a number of related developments that have substantially changed the laws and institutional structures over the past two decades. The major developments are:

- establishment of Aboriginal child welfare agencies, operating within the framework of provincial and territorial law; some of these agencies have a full legal mandate, while others are voluntary agencies;
- notification and involvement of bands in child welfare proceedings;
- development of community-based dispute resolution models for child welfare cases involving Aboriginal children;
- recognition of the importance of culture and heritage as factors in determining the best interests of the child; and
- introduction of laws and policies giving preference to placement of Aboriginal children in Aboriginal families and communities.

These developments are discussed separately here, though there are interrelationships between them.

Aboriginal Child Welfare Agencies

Perhaps the most significant development in Aboriginal child welfare in Canada in the past two decades has been the gradual establishment of a large number of agencies that are operated under the direction of Aboriginal peoples to provide services to Aboriginal children and families.[52] At present in Canada,

---

[52] Much of the material about Aboriginal child welfare agencies in this chapter is from R. McDonald, P. Ladd et al., *First Nations Child and Family Services: Joint National Policy Review* (Assembly of First Nations and Department of Indian and Northern Affairs, Ottawa, 2000); and D. Durst, J. McDonald, and C. Rich, "Aboriginal Child Welfare Services: Hobson's Choice?" chapter 4 in J. Hudson and B. Galaway (Eds.), *Child Welfare in Canada: Research and Policy Implications* (Toronto: Thompson Educational Publishing, 1995) at 55. One of the most influential reports to document problems and recommend changes in the field of Aboriginal child welfare was A.C. Hamilton and C.M. Sinclair, *The Justice System and Aboriginal People: Report of the Aboriginal Justice Inquiry in Manitoba*, Vol. 1 (1996), 509-548.

many, but far from all, Aboriginal children and families are receiving at least some child welfare services from agencies which are controlled to a significant degree by Aboriginal communities. These agencies do not exist everywhere in Canada, and there is great variation in the role, structure and functioning of these agencies.

The most common model of Aboriginal child welfare agency in Canada is what is termed the "delegated model," where First Nations or other Aboriginal communities receive authority from the provincial or territorial child welfare statute to provide either a full range of child protection services (full delegation), or family support and guardianship services (partial delegation). There is also a group of agencies, primarily located in Ontario, which provide a range of child welfare support services outside of the child welfare statute, but under licence to the province — these are known as "pre-mandated agencies." The federal government provides funding only for child welfare for on-reserve residents pursuant to a national funding formula known as Directive 20-1. Provincial (and territorial) governments fund child welfare services to Aboriginal peoples living off reserves.

Most importantly, with one notable exception — the Spallumcheen Band in British Columbia (discussed later in this chapter) — these Aboriginal child welfare agencies operate within the framework of provincial child welfare legislation and are subject to a degree of provincial supervision.

There are essentially two types of Aboriginal-controlled agencies that provide child welfare services:

- agencies delegated by provincial governments that carry out statutory duties in regard to child protection and adoption; and

- agencies that are not delegated to carry out statutory child welfare functions, and provide services that supplement the statutory child welfare agency.

Generally the delegated agencies operate on reserves, and the voluntary agencies operate to serve off-reserve populations, especially in cities.

Delegated Aboriginal Child Welfare Agencies: Directive 20-1

By the 1970s there was an awareness in the federal and provincial governments that the traditional approaches to child welfare for Aboriginal children were totally inadequate, and that there was a need to address both the jurisdictional issues and the demands of Aboriginal communities for control of their child welfare services. In the 1970s the federal government, the province of Alberta and one band in that province negotiated the first "tripartite agreement." The Blackfoot Social Services Agreement is the oldest tripartite child care agreement in Canada, negotiated between the band, the provincial Department of Family and Social Services, and the federal Department of Indian and Northern Affairs. It required the federal government to reimburse the band for the costs related to the provision of child welfare services to band members, and the provincial government to provide an employee (at the band's cost) authorized to invoke the statutory provisions of the province's *Child Welfare Act*. In the following years a number of similar agreements were negotiated in other provinces, but there was not a clear policy about child welfare policy for Aboriginal communities, and, as discussed below, in the 1980s the federal government also seemed willing to support a model that gave Aboriginal communities greater direct control over child welfare, when it accepted the Spallumcheen Child Welfare Bylaw.

In 1991, the federal government established a framework policy, known as Directive 20-1 for the provision of child welfare services to Aboriginal communities. This policy is intended to support "the creation of Indian designed, controlled and managed services" and provides federal funding for the provision of child welfare services to Aboriginal communities. A key part of the policy is that any child welfare agencies that are established are to operate within provincial (or territorial) child welfare statutes, and that legal proceedings are to be dealt with in the established provincial court systems.

Tripartite agreements have become the common method of addressing jurisdictional disputes over the provision of Indian child welfare services. These tripartite agreements between the Indian, provincial and federal governments are established under existing provincial child welfare legislation. Under these agreements the province delegates authority for child welfare for a specific population of Aboriginal children to a First Nations Child and Family Service Agency. In many cases provinces and territories will also spell out terms and conditions for the exercise of the delegated authority (i.e., requirement to follow provincial standards). The federal government provides full or partial financial assistance for these agencies pursuant to the Directive, or in Ontario, pursuant to a separate funding agreement. Under a tripartite agreement, the provincial laws governing child welfare services are followed both on and off the reserves. Aboriginal people may be given authority to administer the laws, but this is generally restricted to on-reserve geographic locations. Under the delegated model, Aboriginal peoples do not have the jurisdiction to enforce their own laws or customs, and the adoption of this model by First Nations is generally viewed by them as an interim capacity building measure pending recognition of self-government. Until tribal laws are recognized, the delegated model does afford Aboriginal communities an opportunity to put their own interpretation on the provincial laws, thereby incorporating some Aboriginal values, beliefs and customs in the provision of child welfare services to Aboriginal children.

Since the implementation of Directive 20-1, over one hundred First Nations Child and Family Services have been established that provide services to more than two-thirds of Canada's reserves, as well as providing some services to off-reserve Status Indians. Some of these agencies are very small, with as few as three employees and serve only one reserve, while others are quite large with over one hundred employees and responsibility for provision of services over a large geographical area that covers several reserves.

In each of these agencies the responsibility for the provision of child welfare services and decision making about individual cases rests with professional staff, but there is an accountability to the broader Aboriginal community. There is, however, substantial variation in organizational structures. Some of these agencies, especially those that serve just a single band, are directly accountable to the chief and band. Other agencies may be responsible for providing child welfare services to a number of bands and may be accountable to a Tribal Council made up of band chiefs. Other Aboriginal child welfare agencies, for example, those in Ontario, are non-profit corporations responsible to boards of directors that are elected or selected by their communities. In Quebec, the provision of child welfare services is generally provided as part of a larger social service program administered directly by the band. Despite the variation in structures, all of the tripartite agreements require that, in theory, there is to be a clear separation between the staff, who are responsible for individual cases, and the board, band or chiefs, who set policy. In the vast majority of cases these requirements are observed, but there have been reports that in some cases political leaders influenced how individual cases were managed. Tripartite agreements should include means of redressing cases of political interference in case management, whether they arise in Aboriginal child welfare agencies or in the provincial child welfare systems themselves.

When the first Aboriginal child welfare agencies were established in the 1980s, some of them aggressively pursued policies of "repatriation," taking Aboriginal children who had been in long-term foster care in non-Aboriginal settings and returning them to their reserves and to a native culture that was alien to them. This was sometimes done in a way that disregarded the rights and wishes of these children,[53] and sometimes caused them harm.

A particularly tragic example of "repatriation" was *Doe v. Awasis Agency of Northern Manitoba*,[54] a case that eventually received national media attention. When she was about a year old, in 1973, this status Indian girl needed medical treatment that was not available in her remote community and was removed from her isolated reserve in northern Manitoba and sent to a hospital in a northern mining community. After her release from hospital she was placed with a non-Aboriginal foster family, who later moved with her to Alberta, where they eventually adopted her. By the time that she was 14 years old, an Aboriginal child welfare agency had been established to serve her reserve. The agency located the girl, and had the adoption order set aside because the biological parents had not been notified of the adoption proceedings. While the girl had

---

[53] See e.g., *N.P.P. v. Regional Children's Guardian* (1988), 14 R.F.L. (3d) 55 (Alta. Q.B.). The child welfare agency planned to move a five-year-old native child from the non-native foster home where she resided for over three years into the care of relatives on her mother's reserve. Justice D.C. McDonald of the Alberta Court of Queen's Bench quashed the original decision, in part relying on the fact that it violated the *child's rights* under s. 7 of the *Charter*, and ordered that a hearing should be held "in accordance with the principles of fundamental justice" to determine whether the foster parents could become the child's private guardians.

[54] [1990] M.J. 402 (Q.B.).

clearly come to view the foster parents as her psychological parents, her prior removal from her native family had violated fundamental rights.

Against her wishes, the girl was taken from her father's family in Alberta by the Aboriginal agency and returned to her reserve and family of origin. The girl did not speak the Dene language that was spoken on the reserve, and most people on the reserve, including her parents, did not speak much English, so communication was difficult. Life on the reserve was very foreign to the girl, and she was treated as an outcast. She was repeatedly, forcibly confined and raped by male residents of the community, and contracted venereal disease as a result of the sexual assaults. She wrote in despair to her foster parents, who contacted the agency about the situation, but nothing was done. Eventually the girl was flown out of the reserve by a doctor, and she was hospitalized suffering from depression. The agency wanted her to return to her community, but a court ordered that she was to return to her foster parents in Alberta. She suffered enormous trauma from her experiences and twice attempted suicide while again living with her foster family. The girl received counselling and support and launched a court action against the Aboriginal agency for its negligence. The action was settled without trial for $75,000. The judge, who had to approve the settlement as the girl was still a minor, considered the settlement low, but accepted it as she was still too vulnerable to withstand the stress of a trial.

Since the early cases of repatriation, there has been more support for children who are being repatriated, development of Aboriginal repatriation programs that reflect past learnings and closer supervision from provincial governments, but these cases continue to cause controversy and pose difficult questions of balancing concerns about a child's emotional attachment against cultural heritage and Aboriginal community interests. Non-Aboriginal foster parents continue to seek hearings in the courts before Aboriginal children in their long-term care are removed and returned to their communities of origin, arguing both that this is contrary to wishes, rights and needs of these children, who have become closely attached to their foster parents.[55] There are no easy solutions to these cases, but it must be appreciated that *preventing removal* of Aboriginal children from their communities by having suitable Aboriginal placements is quite different from *forcing their return* after long periods in care. In the Canadian legal system, the courts focus on the needs and interests of the child, not the interests or rights of the community.

Aboriginal child welfare agencies are invariably more closely connected to their communities than traditional agencies. Often the agency staff are members of the community who are at least acquainted with the parents and extended family before they are professionally involved. Aboriginal agencies often make an effort to involve volunteers from their communities, and may call upon community

---

[55] A 2001 Saskatchewan case *Re R.M.S.* [2001] S.J. 724 (Sask Q.B.) involved litigation between the child welfare authorities, the biological mother, the foster parents, and the children's Aboriginal tribal council. The judge expressed a concern that the child's interests might not be fully presented to the court, and ordered separate legal representation for the child.

Elders to provide advice about policy or to help deal with specific cases. Aboriginal agencies also make an effort to have staff who are themselves native persons, if not members of the communities that they are serving. While these agencies recognize the need to have qualified staff and foster parents, and are required to meet provincial standards, they may be more flexible than traditional agencies about making use of para-professionals and in supporting their staff to improve their qualifications, for example, by taking distance education courses.

Aboriginal agencies, however, face real challenges in hiring and retaining qualified staff and foster parents. Relatively few Aboriginal persons have degrees in social work or psychology. Further, with the history of distrust of the child welfare system that exists in Aboriginal communities, qualified Aboriginal social workers are reluctant to enter the child welfare field, even in the employ of an Aboriginal agency. As a result, many Aboriginal child welfare agencies have significant numbers of non-Aboriginal staff, though these staff receive more training about Aboriginal issues and exposure to Aboriginal culture than staff in traditional agencies. New programs are developing to offer professional training for Aboriginal students in their home communities. For example, a Learning Circle model developed by the University of Calgary in collaboration with Aboriginal communities in Alberta offers credit BSW courses in modular format at nine rural delivery sites across the province.[56] Large numbers of Aboriginal child welfare workers have been able to achieve their professional degrees without leaving their home communities or employment.

While Aboriginal agencies (like traditional agencies) give priority to placement of children who have been apprehended with members of their extended family, and failing that in foster homes in their community, frequently it is not possible to arrange an Aboriginal placement. It is difficult to recruit foster parents from reserves who meet provincial standards as, for example, many families on reserves live in substandard homes or may have a member who has a criminal record. Further, with the poverty and housing shortages on many reserves, some families simply do not have the resources to care for another child. As a result, some Aboriginal child welfare agencies make quite extensive use of non-Aboriginal foster and group homes, though efforts are made to keep children in these placements in contact with their culture. Some placements made by Aboriginal agencies, however, may be quite far from the child's home on a reserve, and these children may experience significant culture shock, especially if taken from a relatively remote reserve and placed in southern Canada.

The establishment of Aboriginal child welfare agencies has resulted in the provision of services to Aboriginal children in a more sensitive and culturally appropriate fashion, but there remain very significant challenges in the transition to new institutions and service delivery arrangements. The establishment of

---

[56] M.K. Zapf, W. Pelech, B. Bastien, R. Bodor, J. Carriere, and G. Zuk, "The Learning Circle: U of Calgary Provides a New Model for Social Work Education" (2003), 15(2) *Tribal College Journal* 52-58.

these agencies has not ended the substantial overrepresentation of Aboriginal children in care. Since the mid-1990s, well over half of the Aboriginal children in the care of child welfare agencies in Canada have been in the care of Aboriginal agencies. And as the number of Aboriginal agencies has increased, the percentage of Aboriginal children in the care of traditional agencies has been steadily shrinking.[57] In the late 1990s and early years of the new millennium the total number of children in the care of child welfare agencies was rapidly increasing across Canada for a variety of reasons; the rate of increase for Aboriginal children was faster than for the general population, despite the increasing number of Aboriginal child welfare agencies.[58] The Aboriginal child welfare agencies are certainly not responsible for this increase, but rather are responding to changing social, legal and economic circumstances. This pattern does, however, make clear that merely transferring responsibility for child welfare services to Aboriginal-controlled child welfare agencies is not a panacea for the problem of overrepresentation of Aboriginal children in the child welfare system. Other initiatives that promote healthier communities are necessary if any real reduction is to be achieved.

Lori Sanderstrom-Smith, a government lawyer in Saskatchewan whose responsibilities include representing child welfare agencies, expresses concerns about the lack of adequate supervision by provincial child welfare authorities of Aboriginal agencies, as well as such issues as "information sharing [within the community], conflicts of interest, political interference, [and] lack of funding for preventative services."[59] She notes that Aboriginal parents and children who are dissatisfied with how they are being treated may feel powerless within their own communities, at the same time as having a profound sense of distrust of the courts and other institutions of non-Aboriginal society. She advocates the establishment of an Aboriginal Ombudsman, Child Advocate or Council of Elders for First Nations who would have responsibility for investigating complaints from parents, children or community members about the treatment of Aboriginal children in their communities or in the child welfare system. She envisages an office that would both share the traditional values of Aboriginal people and be independent of all three levels of government (federal, provincial and First Nations).

Although the establishment of mandated Aboriginal-controlled child welfare agencies and the tripartite agreements begin to address the jurisdictional difficulties and have helped alleviate some of the problems, they do not permit Aboriginal people to fully define how their lives and the lives of their children

---

[57] R. McDonald, P. Ladd et al., *First Nations Child and Family Services: Joint National Policy Review* (Assembly of First Nations and Department of Indian and Northern Affairs, Ottawa, 2000) at 89.

[58] The Centre of Excellence for Child Welfare at the University of Toronto reported on 10 December 2003 that, since the mid-1990s, the five-year rate of increase for children being removed from their homes by child welfare agencies was: 38% in British Columbia; 59% in Alberta; 60% in Ontario; and 71% in First Nations communities.

[59] L. Sandstrom-Smith, *Devolution of Child Protection Services in Saskatchewan and the Need for An Aboriginal Advocate for Children* (Ottawa: National Judicial Institute, 2002).

are to be governed. While the federal and provincial governments have delegated some of their powers to Aboriginal communities, ultimate financial and legal control rests with the federal and provincial governments. There are significant concerns within these agencies about the lack of adequate funding, especially for preventative and supportive programs.[60] It is essential that any transfer of responsibility to Aboriginal agencies is accompanied by provision of adequate resources. Aboriginal communities that are eager to take control of child welfare services may be pressured by governments into taking responsibility for child welfare services without getting adequate resources.

Beyond the important resource issues, many in Aboriginal communities have a fundamental concern about the lack of legal control of their child welfare services and of the continuing jurisdiction of the Canadian courts over Aboriginal children. Some Aboriginal people view the tripartite approach as a transitional step on the way to full Aboriginal control of child welfare services for their communities.[61]

Voluntary Aboriginal Organizations

The majority of reserves now have an Aboriginal controlled child welfare agency, and the number of these agencies is gradually increasing. However, there remain many reserves that do not have such services. In some cases the Aboriginal community may lack the financial and human resources or the political will to seek to establish such a service, while in other cases the Aboriginal community has been unable to reach an agreement with the federal and provincial (or territorial) governments about the service. Further, pursuant to Directive 20-1, First Nations with less than 251 Status Indian children resident on reserve are ineligible for child and family service funding.

For off-reserve Aboriginal peoples, provincial governments have been more reluctant to mandate Aboriginal agencies, and the provincial and federal governments have been less willing to provide funding support, so that off-reserve children and families generally receive statutory child welfare services from non-Aboriginal agencies. Manitoba has gone the farthest in establishing Aboriginal child welfare agencies with jurisdiction over off-reserve families and children.[62]

Increasingly, however, where the statutory child welfare agency is not controlled by the Aboriginal community, there are various other social service agencies that are operated by the Aboriginal community that may be able to

---

[60] See R. McDonald, P. Ladd et al., *First Nations Child and Family Services: Joint National Policy Review* (Assembly of First Nations and Department of Indian and Northern Affairs, Ottawa 2000), which documents the inequitable funding support provided to First Nations child welfare agencies compared to other agencies, reporting (at 94) that "DIAND expenditures per child are the fourth lowest of the provinces listed and $9,970 or 22% lower than the average province listed."

[61] See e.g., Union of British Columbia Indian Chiefs, *Calling Forth Our Future: Options for the Exercise of Indigenous Peoples' Authority in Child Welfare* (2002).

[62] See "New Manitoba child welfare law said 'unprecedented in Canada,'" *Lawyers Weekly* (9 January 2004); and *The Child and Family Services Authorities Act*, S.M. 2002, c. 35.

voluntarily provide culturally appropriate services to the parents and children. These voluntary Aboriginal agencies include Friendship Centers and other social service agencies. They may get funding from the federal, provincial or municipal governments, or may get support from the United Way. These non-mandated agencies may, for example, provide counselling or support to parents or children, or operate group homes that can provide care for Aboriginal children who are child welfare agency wards on a contract basis. A number of these non-mandated agencies operate in medium sized and large cities.

It is important for mandated child welfare agencies to be receptive to working with non-mandated Aboriginal agencies. It is now common for mandated agencies to work with non-mandated agencies, for example, to arrange for a culturally appropriate foster care or group home placement for an Aboriginal child who has been made a ward.[63] It is also common for a non-Aboriginal child welfare agency that apprehends a child, for example, in an urban area where the child was living with a parent, to arrange for a voluntary transfer of the case to the mandated Aboriginal agency that provides service to the parent's band.[64]

The Ontario case of *C.A.S. of Timiskaming v. J.C.* is an example of a situation in which the mandated agency failed to respect the contribution that a non-mandated Aboriginal agency made. Three Aboriginal children were living with their mother, who had alcohol addiction problems, a series of relationships with abusive men and a "transient lifestyle." At one point while she was living off-reserve, the local non-Aboriginal child welfare agency decided to apprehend the children, a decision that was justified at that time by her "erratic parenting." After the children were taken into care, the mother made contact with a local non-mandated native child and family service agency. The mother established a good relationship with an Aboriginal counsellor who helped the mother deal with her alcohol and spouse abuse issues, as well as supporting the mother's enrollment in a parenting program. The mandated agency, however, was not willing to co-operate with the native agency and had little contact with them. The child welfare agency came to court seeking an order for permanent wardship with a plan for the adoption of the three children. The agency's evidence to support its case was based principally on the agency records of the mother's condition prior to the apprehension of the children. The mother called a number of witnesses to testify about her rehabilitation, mainly workers from native-oriented agencies who had recent experience with her. The judge ordered that two of the children were to be returned to the mother's care under agency supervision, while ordering that the third child, who was the most emotionally traumatized, remain in agency care but with the mother having access. The judge expressed concern about the failure of the workers from the mandated agency to "understand Aboriginal issues," commenting that "it is difficult to understand how the [mandated child protection agency]...was not more aware

---

[63] See e.g., *Re A.B.*, [2003] B.C.J. 1722 (Prov. Ct.), involving a Métis child whose long-term placement was to be arranged by the Métis Family Services of British Columbia.

[64] See e.g., *Tikinagan Child and Family Services v. P.P.*, [2002] O.J. 1895 (Ont. Ct. J.).

of the importance of culturally appropriate agencies on a native person having alcohol and abuse issues."[65] These comments underscore the importance of cross-cultural training for workers in mandated and non-mandated agencies.

While mandated non-Aboriginal child welfare agencies must respect the contribution that can be made by non-mandated Aboriginal agencies, the mandated workers must continue to exercise their statutory responsibilities. In some cases, the non-mandated Aboriginal and professionals may place a much greater weight on the importance of culture than the mandated agency, or may be unduly optimistic about the capacities of their Aboriginal clients to care for their children. These differences can be minimized by maintaining open lines of communication between agencies and by holding regular interagency meetings where common issues and specific cases can be discussed. If differences cannot be resolved, it is for the courts to decide what will happen to the children. Provided that the child welfare workers have been open to the non-mandated agency, the courts may well support the position of the mandated agency.[66]

Band Involvement in Child Welfare Proceedings

Aboriginal children are not only considered to be members of their families but also members of their First Nations. Accordingly, if a child's parents are unable to provide suitable care, the band of which the child is a member may have an interest in finding them suitable care in their communities. Legislation in several provinces, including Alberta, Manitoba and Ontario,[67] requires that a child welfare agency that is commencing child protection or adoption proceedings concerning an Aboriginal child give notice to the band. Notification will allow the band to participate in the proceedings and, if appropriate, to put forward a plan for the care of the child by members of their community. In Nova Scotia, notice of the proceedings anywhere in the province involving an Aboriginal child must be given to Mi'kmaq Family and Children's Services, which will usually notify the child's band of the proceedings. In jurisdictions where there is no statutory provision giving a band the right to notification of the proceedings and standing to participate, the courts have held that they have the jurisdiction to allow a child's band to intervene in child welfare proceedings.[68]

While some Aboriginal parents welcome the involvement, and in some cases the support, of their band in their litigation against a child welfare agency, other parents may resent the intrusion into their lives and privacy that occurs from band involvement. Regardless of parental feelings, if a child is living on reserve at the time of apprehension, members of the band will know the child, and may be in a position to put forward a plan that will allow the child to remain in his or

---

[65] [2002] O.J. 1646 (Ct of J.), per Guay J.

[66] See e.g., *C.A.S of Sudbury v. D.D.*, [2003] O.J. 2455 (Ont. Ct.J.), per Lalande J.

[67] See e.g., Ontario *Child and Family Services Act*, R.S.O. 1990, c. C-11, s. 39(1) 4.

[68] See e.g., *Pitzel and Pitzel v. Children's Aid Society of Winnipeg*, [1984] 4 C.N.L.R. 41, [1984] 5 W.W.R. 474 (Man. Q.B.) (decided prior to the enactment of statute dealing with band involvement in child welfare proceedings); and *Re N.Q.*, [2003] Y.J. 38 (Terr. Ct.) per Faulkner Terr. Ct. J.

her Aboriginal community and continue to receive care from members of that community.

More difficult issues may arise when a child with Aboriginal status who has been living off-reserve is apprehended; in some of these cases one of the parents may be non-Aboriginal, and one or both of the parents may object to the involvement of the band in their litigation. In some of these cases the children were born and lived off-reserve, and there will usually be real questions as to whether the band has the resources to put forward a plan of care that will meet the best interests of the child. The general tendency of the courts in these cases is to allow the band to participate in the proceedings, even if not required by legislation, and to give consideration to the child's heritage when assessing the child's best interests.[69] However, when dealing with the future of a child, a judge may well prefer placement with a parent or relative off-reserve, even if that person is not Aboriginal, though there may be an expectation that the parent or relative will make efforts to maintain contact with the child's Aboriginal community.[70]

While Aboriginal agencies generally have closer ties to the Aboriginal community than non-Aboriginal agencies, the mandate and approach of Aboriginal child welfare agencies to cases may be quite different from those of the band councils within the areas that they operate. It is not unheard of for an Aboriginal child welfare agency to want to remove a child from the care of parents and from a reserve while the band council is opposing this step, leaving it for the court to determine what will happen to a child. In some cases, relations between an Aboriginal child welfare agency and a band may be quite adversarial.[71]

Alternative Dispute Resolution in Aboriginal Communities

As discussed in a number of places in this book,[72] there is an increasing use of "alternate dispute resolution" in child welfare cases, seeking alternatives to the conventional adversarial trial that occurs in the Canadian courts. There is, for example, a growing use of mediation to attempt to resolve family disputes, whether between two parents who have separated or between a child welfare agency and parents. Mediation is a non-adversarial method of dispute resolution that attempts to facilitate the negotiation of a settlement that is acceptable to all concerned, and may be especially useful in family disputes where the parties are likely going to continue to have an ongoing relationship, and there is great value in trying to avoid the emotional and financial bitterness that will result from a trial.

---

[69] See e.g., *Re C.K.W.*, [2002] Y.J. 3 (Terr. Ct.), per Lilles Terr. Ct. J.

[70] See e.g., *Nova Scotia v. R.L.F.*, [2001] N.S.J. 435 (N.S.S.C. — Fam. Div.).

[71] See e.g., *Abinoojii Family Services v. N.M.*, [2000] O.J. 3988 (Ont Ct. J.) where band was refusing to allow Aboriginal agency workers to supervise cases on reserve. The judge was highly critical of the "political stance" of the band, and ordered it to pay legal costs of the agency and the Children's Lawyer.

[72] See e.g., Chapters 3 and 15.

In some places in Canada, professional mediators, who are generally lawyers, social workers, or psychologists with special training, facilitate dispute resolution in a broad range of cases, including a growing number of child welfare cases. Alternative dispute resolution may, for example, result in more child welfare cases being resolved by some type of agreement to have an open adoption; in these cases the biological parents would accept that they cannot care for their children and that new permanent caregivers should care for them, while the agency and adoptive parents agree that there will be some limited form of contact between the biological family and the children. Alternative dispute resolution may involve extended family and community members, as well as parents and children.

Alternate dispute resolution may be especially valuable in Aboriginal communities where there are long traditions of consensus-based dispute resolution that are intended to preserve relationships within the community and develop harmonious outcomes to disputes. The growing use of circle sentencing and community justice projects to deal with the sentencing of adult and youth Aboriginal offenders is another type of alternative dispute resolution that attempts to involve the community in developing appropriate plans to deal with the causes of offending.

In Aboriginal communities, respected Elders may have an important role in attempting to mediate or resolve a dispute about the care of children. In *Re J.D.*, a Saskatchewan case,[73] the parties and judge decided to make use of an Opikinawasowin (a Cree term for a council of Elders) to attempt to resolve a dispute between two estranged parents and the child welfare agency about the care of their five children. The mother was Cree and a member of the Onion Lake First Nation where the family lived, and the father was a Métis. The judge decided that the three members of the Opikinawasowin were to include at least one Métis and at least one Cree but no one who was a member of the Onion Lake First Nation. The judge directed the Department of Justice to organize the logistics for holding the meeting, and pay for such expenses as translators. It was expected by the court that the meeting would begin with traditional prayers and ceremony, and members of the extended family, professionals and others concerned with the case, would attend and participate.

The judge expected that the Opikinawasowin would result in a resolution that was acceptable to all of the parties, or a recommendation from the Elders to the court about how to resolve the case. The traditional Opikinawasowin was modified in some important ways, for example by allowing the lawyers for the parties to attend and participate, and by requiring that the Elders were to receive information about the provincial child welfare legislation before the meeting. The judge also expected that "the recommendations made by them for resolution [would]...fall within [the]...framework" of that provincial statute.

---

[73] [2003] S.J. 453 (Sask.Q.B.).

There are a number of places in Canada where special alternative dispute resolution programs are being established for resolving child welfare disputes involving Aboriginal children. There undoubtedly will be more use of various forms of alternative dispute resolution methods in Aboriginal communities for dealing with a range of different types of cases, including child welfare cases. Not unlike the current court-based systems, alternative forms of dispute resolution demand time and energy from all involved, and resources to arrange and support the process. There are issues about alternative dispute resolution that need to be addressed, such as confidentiality and potential conflict of interest. The relationship between resolutions coming from these community-based methods and the Canadian courts will also need to be further addressed. However, this type of community-based method of dispute resolution holds promise for giving Aboriginal communities greater involvement in dealing with their child welfare problems, and in developing culturally sensitive responses to them.

Aboriginal Heritage as a Best Interests Factor

Legislatures, courts and child welfare agencies now recognize that cultural heritage is an important factor in determining what is in a child's best interests, and in particular that Aboriginal heritage is an important factor in making placement decisions for Aboriginal children. There is now widespread agreement that if the parents of an Aboriginal child cannot adequately care for the child, there should be a preference for placing the child with members of the child's extended family or with other members of the child's community. When decisions are being made about individual children and in formulating policies, however, there are still contentious questions about how much weight to place on a child's Aboriginal heritage when determining what is in the best interests of a child.

One of the first cases to reach the Supreme Court that dealt with the importance of a child's Aboriginal heritage was *Racine v. Woods*, decided in 1983. The case involved an Aboriginal child who was apprehended at the age of 6 weeks due to her mother's inability to care for the child due to the mother's alcohol abuse, and the child was placed with foster parents. After a period in the care of foster parents, the mother regained custody of the child for a couple of weeks, but then voluntarily returned the child to the foster parents, who by this time had become closely attached to the child. When the child was five years old, the mother sought the return of the child, while the foster parents made an adoption application. The trial judge made the adoption order, dispensing with the mother's consent to the adoption because of the mother's previous "abandonment" of the child. The adoption was later set aside by the Manitoba Court of Appeal, which expressed concern that adoption would have greatly affected the child's exposure to her heritage, and ruled that the trial judge had erred in concluding the baby had been abandoned. By the time the case got to the Supreme Court of Canada, the child had been in the care of the prospective adoptive parents for more than six years, and had had only very limited contact with the mother. The Supreme Court overturned the Manitoba Court of Appeal and allowed the child to be adopted by the foster parents. Madame Justice Wilson wrote:[74]

> When the test to be met is the best interests of the child, the significance of cultural background and heritage as opposed to bonding abates over time. The closer the bond that develops with the prospective adoptive parents the less important the racial element becomes.... Much was made in this case of the inter-racial aspect of the adoption. I believe that inter-racial adoption, like inter-racial marriage, is now an accepted phenomenon in our pluralistic society. The implications of it may have been overly dramatized by the [mother]...in this case.

This decision was very controversial, with commentators expressing particular concerns about the insensitivity of the judgement to the importance of Aboriginal heritage.[75] One can sympathize with the court's position that stability and continuity of care are very important for children's emotional well-being and with the proposition that the more closely children are bonded to foster parents, the more reluctant the courts should be to uproot them.[76] However, the making of an adoption order in this case had the effect of totally severing the child's link to her biological family. Further the comparison of interracial marriage to adoption of Aboriginal children outside of their Aboriginal community is very problematic. This is the type of case for which the flexibility of open adoption, which is now possible in Manitoba,[77] might be appropriate, as this is an arrangement that would allow the long-term caregivers their legal status of "parents," while assuring the biological members or other band members that they can maintain a degree of involvement in the child's life so that she can develop an understanding of her heritage and, if she wishes, later in life assume a role as a member of her Aboriginal community.

Since *Racine v. Woods* was decided, every jurisdiction in Canada has enacted child welfare legislation that specifically requires judges and child welfare agencies to consider a child's culture and heritage when making a decision about placement or adoption. In most provinces there is also specific reference to the importance of Aboriginal heritage.

Ontario's *Child and Family Services Act* has the most explicit provincial legislative provisions for the recognition of Aboriginal heritage in making decisions about children. The Declaration of Principles of Ontario's *Child and*

---

[74] [1983] 2 S.C.R. 173, 36 R.F.L (2d) 1 (S.C.C.) at 13-14. For an earlier decision that took a similar approach, see *Natural Parents v. Superintendent of Child Welfare* (1975), 60 D.L.R. (3d) 148 (S.C.C.).

[75] For a critique of *Racine v. Woods* and a provocative discussion of some of the issues in this chapter, see P. Monture, "A Vicious Circle: Child Welfare and the First Nations" (1989), 3 *Canadian Journal of Welfare Law* 1-17; see also E.F. Carasco, "Canadian Native Children: Have Child Welfare Laws Broken the Circle?" (1986) 5 *Canadian Journal of Family Law* 109; and Tae Mee Park, "In The Best Interests of the Aboriginal Child" (2003), 16 *Windsor Review of Legislation and Social Issues* 43. For a supportive view of the approach of the Supreme Court see C. Davies, "Native Children and the Child Welfare System in Canada" (1992), 30 *Alberta Law Review* 1200.

[76] The delay inherent in the court system as the case goes through the appeal process contributes to the problem and suggests that other methods of resolving these kinds of disputes should be explored.

[77] *Adoption Act*, S.M. 1997, c. 47, Chap A-2, s. 33(1).

Family Services Act states "as long as [measures taken]...are consistent with the best interests, protection and well being of children," it is the intent of the *Act*[78]

> to recognize that Indian and native people should be entitled to provide, wherever possible, their own child and family services, and that all services to Indian and native children and families should be provided in a manner that recognizes their culture, heritage and traditions and the concept of the extended family.

There are also specific provisions that require that a child welfare agency or court making a determination about the "best interests" of any child in a protection or adoption proceeding take into consideration the importance of preserving the child's heritage and cultural identity.[79] If a protection or adoption application involves an Aboriginal child, the decision maker "shall take into consideration the importance, in recognition of the uniqueness of Indian and native culture, heritage and culture, of preserving the child's cultural identity."[80]

To help operationalize these general statements, there are also provisions in the Ontario statute for notification and involvement of the band of an Indian child in protection proceedings.[81] If a child welfare agency is planning to place an Aboriginal child for adoption, the agency must give prior notification to the child's band or native community.[82] This is to allow Aboriginal communities to have input in the decision making about the adoption of their children, and make representations about culturally appropriate placements.

When an Ontario court is considering what type of order to make in regard to a child who has been found to be in need of protection, unless there is a "substantial reason for placing the child elsewhere," under s. 57(5) of the *Child and Family Services Act* the judge is required to consider placements for the child in the following order: (a) with a member of the child's extended family; (b) with a member of the child's band or native community; or (c) with another Indian or native family.[83]

With the enactment of this type of legislation, the courts are starting to give more weight to Aboriginal heritage when making decisions about Aboriginal children, as illustrated by a 1992 Ontario case, *Weechi-it-te-win Child and Family Services v. A.M.*[84] The two young children, one just five weeks old and the other three years of age, were taken into care because of their mother's inability to care for them due to alcohol and solvent abuse, and her violence towards others, and placed by the agency in the care of non-Aboriginal foster parents. After a year, the case had been transferred to a newly established Aboriginal child welfare agency, which wanted the children returned to their

---

[78] R.S.O. 1990, c. C-11, (as amended, S.O. 1999, c. 6) s. 1(2)5.
[79] Ss. 37(3) 3 and 136(2)3.
[80] Ss. 37(4) and 136(3).
[81] S. 39(1)4.
[82] S. 140(3).
[83] S. 57(5).
[84] [1993] 1 C.N.L.R. 169 (Ont. Prov. Div), per Little J.

reserve to live with a woman on the reserve under agency supervision. The Children's Lawyer supported the plan of the foster parents to continue to care for the children, to whom they had become closely attached. The judge noted:

> Weechi-it-te-win Family Services and the people of [the] Wabaseemoong [First Nation] are struggling with important child care issues. There is a political desire not to lose children from their reserve. At the same time, decisions in cases such as this must be made having regard to the individual circumstances and plans proposed for the specific children before the court. There also appears to be a shortage of competent homes which are available to provide alternate care for children....

The judge recognized that the foster parents would provide a "good home" and that they had a "sincere regard for the children" and a close psychological tie. The judge, however, was concerned that the children would lose contact with their native language and culture from such a placement, and decided that the children should be returned to a home on their reserve:

> I am satisfied that this disposition is in the best interests of the children because it is more likely that they will ultimately then be placed in a home which will safeguard their cultural and language roots.

The 1999 case of *D.H. v. H.M.* gave the Supreme Court another opportunity to consider the importance of Aboriginal heritage in a child-related dispute. The case involved a boy who was the son of a Canadian-born Aboriginal mother and an African American father. His Aboriginal mother had been born in Manitoba and adopted at the age of four by a Caucasian couple who then lived in Montreal but soon after the adoption moved with her to Connecticut, where she grew to adolescence. She had many problems in adolescence, including self-destructive behaviour, and may have been suffering from fetal alcohol syndrome, though this was not diagnosed at the time. When she was in her twenties, the mother became pregnant; the African American father had nothing to do with her or the child after the birth. In the child's first months of life the mother lived with her adoptive parents, but the mother would disappear for weeks at a time. As a result of these absences, the adoptive grandparents, in their words, "went from being...grandparents to effectively being...parents and...primary care-givers."

At about this time the mother, assisted by her adoptive parents, made contact with her birth parents who were residing separately in Vancouver, and she went to visit them for a couple of months, leaving the child in the care of the adoptive grandparents. When the boy was about eight months old, the mother returned to Connecticut and took her son with her to return to British Columbia. In British Columbia, the child welfare authorities apprehended the child, though he was soon placed in the care of his biological grandfather and his wife, with the mother having limited supervised access. The adoptive grandparents then came from Connecticut to British Columbia to seek custody of the boy from the biological Aboriginal grandfather and his wife.

By the time of trial the boy was about two years old and had been living with the biological grandfather and his family for about eight months. The biological grandfather had spent much of his childhood in a residential school and had history that included alcohol abuse and a criminal record, but had a stable family history for the past 15 years, and was raising a teenaged daughter. He was a concerned and loving father to that girl, though the court observed that he had a "laissez-faire" attitude to parenting. Though not involved in Aboriginal cultural activities, he was "very proud of his Aboriginal heritage." He was not employed at the time of trial, and was seriously considering returning to his reserve in Manitoba.

The trial judge awarded custody to the adoptive grandparents, who were considerably older than the grandfather, but also more affluent. The trial judge observed:[85]

> Of course, [the boy's]...Aboriginal heritage and the ability of his biological grandfather to preserve and enhance it are important considerations, but we must not overlook the obvious fact that Ishmael has an African-American background and American citizenship. That heritage is also of importance and it is equally deserving of preservation and nurturing. This is not a case of taking an Aboriginal child and placing him with a non-Aboriginal family in complete disregard for his culture and heritage.... [His] ties of blood to [his grandfather] are counter-balanced by his ties of adoption to...[his adoptive grandparents].

The British Columbia Court of Appeal overturned the trial decision and ordered that custody was to be given to the biological grandfather as the trial judge had placed too much emphasis on the economic advantages that the adoptive grandparents could offer, and had "underemphasized ties of blood and culture."[86] Both the trial judge and the Court of Appeal referred to the child welfare legislation in British Columbia which states that:[87] "If the child is an Aboriginal child, the importance of preserving the child's cultural identity must be considered in determining the child's best interests." The Supreme Court of Canada overturned the appeal decision in a very brief decision summarily concluding "that in fact the trial judge had given careful attention to the Aboriginal ancestry...together with all the other factors relevant to...best interests, and that there was no error in his decision, which was reached after five days of evidence and two weeks of reflection."[88]

While decisions of trial judges are entitled to significant deference, the Supreme Court decision in *D.H. v. H.M.* is at very least disappointing for its brevity. By the time that the case reached the Supreme Court of Canada, the boy was four years of age and had been living with the grandfather for almost three years, and they were living together in Manitoba in their Aboriginal community. In this case, unlike many similar cases, psychological bonding concerns were reinforcing the arguments based on preservation of Aboriginal heritage.

---

[85] [1997] B.C.J. 2144 (S.C.), per Bauman J. at para. 46-47.

[86] BCCA decision, paras. 13 and 20.

[87] *Child, Family and Community Service Act*, R.S.B.C. 1996, c. 46, s. 4(2).

[88] [1999] 1 S.C.R. 328, further reasons at 761. For another adoption decision that gave little weight to Aboriginal heritage, *Sawan v. Tearoe* (1993), 48 R.F.L. (3d) 392 (B.C.C.A.); for a critical commentary on the approach of the court in *Sawan*, see Mosikatsana, "Case Comment on *Sawan v. Tearoe*" (1994), 11 *Canadian Family Law Quarterly* at 89; see also Westad, *The God-Sent Child: The Bitter Adoption of Baby David* (Toronto: Penguin Books, 1994).

In the past few years, the courts have made statements in child protection cases recognizing the importance of Aboriginal heritage. However, if Aboriginal parents are not able to care adequately for their children and cannot deal with problems such as alcohol abuse within the period for temporary wardship (set by legislation, in Ontario at one year for children under the age of 6), the courts are prepared to uphold agency requests for termination of access to young children to allow for adoption by non-Aboriginal persons.[89]

In a 2001 Ontario case a child welfare agency apprehended a three-month-old Aboriginal child from his mother who had severe alcohol problems. The agency was unable to find an Aboriginal foster home that it considered suitable, and placed the child with non-Aboriginal foster parents who bonded with the infant and wanted to adopt him. The agency brought an application to terminate access rights with a view to having the child adopted, likely by the foster parents. The band intervened and suggested foster care by an Aboriginal family who were members of the child's band. The agency had some concerns about the suitability of the proposed Aboriginal foster parents, though the proposed foster mother had a university degree and experience in working with children. The court approved the agency plan and made the child a permanent ward with a view to adoption by the non-Aboriginal foster parents, with the judge rejecting the position of an Aboriginal social worker employed by the band who "categorically stated that Native people know better how to look after Native children" than non-Natives. The judge concluded that while s. 57(5) of Ontario's *Child and Family Services Act* gives a preference to placement of Aboriginal children with Aboriginal caregivers, it is not "paramount." Rather, Aboriginal heritage is one factor for a court to take into account in making a decision about what is in the child's "best interests."[90]

Although there is now more judicial recognition of the importance of Aboriginal children's cultural identity, many Aboriginal commentators believe this factor has not been weighed heavily enough by the courts when Aboriginal parents or communities are seeking custody of their children from child welfare agencies, or seeking to prevent the adoption of their children by non-Aboriginal persons.

It is clear from the case law that judges are still prepared to accept claims by child welfare agencies that the best interests of an Aboriginal child requires adoption and severance of the tie to Aboriginal parents and their community. Increasingly, however, child welfare agencies, both Aboriginal and traditional, are putting forward plans of care that involve long-term foster care by a non-Aboriginal foster parent, but allow for continuing visits with parents or other relatives and contact with members of their community. While the courts

---

[89] See e.g., *Catholic C.A.S. v. A.V.W.*, [2002] O.J. 1512 (C.A.); and *Alberta (Director of Child Welfare) v. G.N.*, [2002] A.J. 1609 (Q.B.).

[90] *Kenora Patricia Child and Family Services v. D.O.*, [2001] 4 C.N.L.R. 103 (Ont. Ct. J.), per Bishop J.; see also *Algonquins of Pikwakanagan v. C.A.S. of Toronto*, [2004] O.J. 1740, per Mesbur J.

have generally accepted these plans,[91] in a Manitoba case, the failure of the agency to seek adoption was the subject of adverse comment by the judge.

In *Winnipeg Child and Family Services v. M.A.* the court was dealing with a case where a child was apprehended at two months of age from the care of his 15-year-old mother and his grandmother. The mother and grandmother both had serious alcohol abuse problems, and the mother was associating with gang members. The child was in foster care for two years but had to be moved as the foster parents were unable to continue to care for the child. Agency workers concluded that adoption would be best for the child, as it would give the child an assurance of permanency, but the agency could not find an Aboriginal adoptive home and had a policy of not placing Aboriginal children for adoption in non-Aboriginal homes. The mother and grandmother were still not able to care for the child, and because the maximum two-year period for temporary wardship had expired, the agency was seeking permanent wardship. The judge granted the permanent wardship order, but expressed "frustration" that she did not have the power to direct that the child should be adopted by a non-Aboriginal family if a suitable Aboriginal family could not be found. Justice Beard commented:[92]

> This is a case about an Aboriginal child who is being denied her right to a permanent, secure family because the…agency…vetoed any such placement. The reason for the veto arises from a desire to stop the removal of Aboriginal children from their cultural heritage. While a laudable goal, its dogmatic application is counterproductive and unfair. The tragedy in this case is that the best plan for the child, which would see her placed with a permanent family, has been rejected for historical and political reasons that have nothing to do with her case…. While non-Aboriginal children are offered a permanent adoptive family, Aboriginal children continue to be offered the lesser option of a foster family, which lacks the permanence and security that would come with an adoption.
>
> It is important to point out that this is not a case about the non-Aboriginal child welfare system preferring a non-Aboriginal family over an Aboriginal family, because…[an] Aboriginal placement is not an option, in any form, so the child is left to be raised by one or more non-Aboriginal foster families, which is clearly not the best available option for her. The end result is that the child is being held hostage by a child welfare system that has put its own political interests and expediencies ahead of her best interests. Surely this is unfair to her.

The judge noted that Manitoba has gone further than most provinces in making statutory provision for "open adoption"[93] that would allow the band and birth parents to have a role in the selection of a suitable non-Aboriginal adoptive family and to sign an agreement with them that would allow for some contact. This would, in the judge's view, permit the child to have the "security of being a permanent member of an adoptive family and also ensure that she maintained her contact with her culture and birth family."

---

[91] See e.g., *Re A.J.A.*, [1999] S.J. 367 (Q.B.); *Alberta (Director of Child Welfare) v. Y.*, [2002] 1 C.N.L.R. 11 (Prov. Ct.); and *Kenora-Paricia C.F.S v. L.P.*, [2001] 4 C.N.L.R. 114 (Ont Ct. J.).

[92] [2002] M.J. 307 (Q.B.), per Beard J. at para. 1-2.

[93] *Adoption Act*, S.M. 1997, c: 47, Chap A-2, s. 33(1).

The Spallumcheen Band Child Welfare Bylaw

There is one band in Canada that has gone further than any other in gaining legal control over its child welfare services — the Spallumcheen Band in British Columbia.[94] This band has used its bylaw power under the *Indian Act* to enact a child welfare bylaw, setting out a framework for the provision of child welfare services for its members, without the requirement for provincial supervision.

In 1980 the then newly enacted *Family and Child Services Act* of British Columbia contained a clause which required the court to serve the band of which the child is a member with Notice of the Hearing before dealing with the child, though it gave no special legal status to bands. In October 1980, the Spallumcheen Band, in the interior of B.C., took direct action against the Ministry of Human Resources. Between 1960 and 1980, 150 children had been removed from their reserve. All of those children had been placed in non-Indian off-reserve homes. Since the band population was 300, the removal of 150 children had a devastating effect on the community's population and sense of future.

On Thanksgiving Day 1980, Chief Wayne Christian of the Spallumcheen Band organized an "Indian Child Caravan," which converged on the home of the provincial Minister of Human Resources. Prior to that date, the band had enacted its own Child Care Bylaw that had been presented to the Minister. Following the protest, the Minister of Human Resources signed an agreement with the band, recognizing the band's bylaw and agreeing to work with the band for the return of band children to the reserve. The federal government later signed an agreement to provide funding to support these services, and also agreed to authorize the bylaw. The bylaw only applies to residents on reserve, though the protocol agreement with the provincial government allows the band to provide some child welfare services to Spallumcheen Band members off-reserve but outside of the bylaw authority.

The Child Welfare Bylaw gives the Spallumcheen Band exclusive jurisdiction over child welfare issues and the removal of a child from the care of a band family due to concerns over abuse or neglect. The Chief and Council and any person authorized by them are empowered to remove the child from the home if there are concerns about the welfare of a child. As legal guardians, the Chief and Council are then responsible for the child's placement in a suitable home. Their decision is guided by "Indian customs" and, in the case of an older child, the child's wishes, but "the deciding consideration" in all cases is to be the "best interests of the child." The bylaw provides: "Whenever possible help should be given to rebuild the family of the Indian child." If the child is removed from parental care, there is a preference for placement with members of the extended family living on-reserve, and if that is not possible, placement with members of the extended family living elsewhere or to another Indian person. The bylaw

---

[94] See J.A. MacDonald, "The Spallumcheen Indian Band By-Law and its Potential Impact on Native Indian Child Welfare Policy in British Columbia" (1983) 1 *Canadian Journal of Family Law* 75 at 77.

states that "only as a last resort shall the child be placed in the home of a non-Indian living off-reserve." The band in some cases has continued to make use of non-Aboriginal off-reserve foster care placements, though returning the children to the reserve when placements become available on-reserve.[95] For a child to be placed in the home of a non-Indan living off the reserve it must be the only alternative, with the best interests of the child as the deciding factor in every case.

The band council's decision can be reviewed by the entire band, if requested by a band member, a parent, an Aboriginal guardian or a member of the child's extended family. The child, child's parent, Indian guardian or an extended family member may apply to the band council for the child's return or transfer to the home of another Indian guardian, with the decision reviewable by the entire band.

This collective model of decision making and lack of confidentiality that are central to the Spallumcheen Child Welfare Bylaw are very different from the policies at conventional child welfare agencies. The Chief and Band Council are given very significant responsibility and power over the lives of children and families. There is a concern with this type of model of child welfare that there is a potential for power to be misused, but this model reflects the confidence that the band has in its leaders and in collective decision making, with the final decision being made by the full band membership.

The authority of the Spallumcheen Band for introducing its Child Welfare Bylaw is s. 81 of the *Indian Act*, which allows a band council to make bylaws for a number of purposes, including "to provide for the health of residents on the reserve." Indian band bylaws, properly enacted, would clearly supplant provincial child welfare legislation because of s. 88 of the *Indian Act*. However, the Minister of Indian Affairs has the power to disallow any band bylaws,[96] and the federal government has indicated that it will not permit any more bands to enact such bylaws.

As a result of the bylaw, the Spallumcheen Band and the provincial government have entered into a protocol for the provision of child welfare services for children who are members of the band. The courts have accepted the legality of the bylaw and jurisdiction of the band, including the right of the band to take back to the reserve a child who was placed in a non-Indian off-reserve foster home without the supervision of the courts.[97]

The present federal government policy is to not permit any other bands to enact child welfare bylaws, so the Spallumcheen Bylaw has limited immediate applicability elsewhere in Canada. The Spallumcheen Bylaw may, however, serve as an important model as First Nations move to take direct control over child welfare services. It may be especially useful as a model in British

---

[95] See *S.(E.G.) v. Spallumcheen Band Council*, [1999] 2 C.N.L.R. 318 (B.C. Sup. Ct.).

[96] *Indian Act* s. 82.

[97] *S.(E.G.) v. Spallumcheen Band Council*, [1999] 2 C.N.L.R. 306 (B.C. Prov. Ct.).

Columbia and the Yukon where treaties are being negotiated, such as the Nisga's Treaty, which affirmed First Nations authority to make laws regarding child and family services on their lands.[98]

The United States: Tribal Agencies and Courts

In the United States, the federal government has taken more of a leadership role in enacting legislation that recognizes the special needs and rights of indigenous children and communities than has occurred in Canada. In the *Indian Child Welfare Act (ICWA)*, the United States government has recognized the importance of providing culturally appropriate child welfare services and has given Tribal Courts very significant jurisdiction over child welfare cases for children who are registered with the Bureau of Indian Affairs.[99]

The American *ICWA* recognizes shortcomings in the dominant society's system for dealing with Aboriginal children, and the deleterious effects of its imposition on Aboriginal people. Its enactment reflected the following:

- an alarmingly high percentage of Indian families were devastated by their children's removal and placement in non-Indian homes;
- state child welfare agencies often failed to recognize cultural and social standards prevailing in Indian communities and families; and
- the federal Bureau of Indian Affairs often failed to fulfill its responsibility to Aboriginal tribes by failing to advocate effectively with state governments and with non-native child welfare agencies and by failing to seek funding necessary for Indian tribes to fulfill effectively their responsibilities to their children.

Under this *Act*, American tribes are vested with jurisdiction in child protection proceedings involving Indian children living on reserves. Aboriginal people and tribal courts have the authority to decide whether an Aboriginal child will be removed from his or her family and community; American state courts and governments are required to respect these decisions.

Further, tribes in the United States have the power to intervene in cases in the state courts dealing with Indian children living off-reservation who may be subject to foster care placements or termination of parental rights. In the state courts there is also a preference for placement with the extended family or in an Aboriginal community. Funds for services and the administration of tribal courts are provided by the federal Bureau of Indian Affairs.

---

[98] See e.g., *Yukon First Nations Self-Government Act*, S.C. 1994, c. 35, Schedule III, Part II, para. 7, s. 11 and *Nisga's Final Agreement*, S.C. 2000, c. 7, para. 91.

[99] (1978), 25 U.S.C. para. 1901 *et seq*. For a description, see e.g., Davies, "Implementing the *Indian Child Welfare Act*," [July 1982] *Clearing House Review* at 179; S. Watts, "Voluntary Adoptions Under the *Indian Child Welfare Act of 1978*: Balancing the Interests of Children, Families, and Tribes" (1989), 63 *Southern California Law Review* 213; J.H. Hollinger, "Beyond the Best Interests of the Tribes: The *Indian Child Welfare Act* and the Adoption of Indian Children" (1988-89), 66 *University of Detroit Law Review* 451.

The constitutional, political and social context is in some respects different in the United States from that in Canada. Indian reservations in the United States typically have a substantially larger population and greater resources than the typical Canadian reserve. There may, however, be important lessons for Canada and its Aboriginal population from the models for provision of child welfare service for indigenous peoples that are being developed in the United States.[100]

Conclusion

The dominant non-Aboriginal society in Canada has not responded adequately to the problems of Aboriginal children and communities. Assimilationist and culturally insensitive policies have often harmed these children and their communities. While child welfare laws, institutions and policies have become more sensitive to the needs of Aboriginal children and communities, Canada's Aboriginal peoples now face enormous problems with their children and families. Poverty, alcoholism, spousal violence, fetal alcohol syndrome, neglect of children and child sexual abuse are very serious problems in many Aboriginal families and communities, and must be addressed by the communities themselves. Addressing these problems requires a significant investment in education, health and social services over an extended period of time.[101] Many Aboriginal adults were themselves brought up in residential schools or child welfare institutions and may lack appropriate role models for being nurturing parents. Some of these survivors are now functioning effectively as parents and community leaders despite histories of substance abuse, domestic violence or other criminal behaviours. Many survivors of residential school are fragile and vulnerable to relapse. As a result there are many parenting challenges in these communities.

The problems of providing appropriate child welfare services for Aboriginal children will defy a single, quick solution. Different First Nations have different strengths and problems. The challenges facing isolated northern communities, where Aboriginal languages are still spoken, are different from those faced by Aboriginal people who have moved to large urban areas in southern Canada.

An important step is for non-Aboriginal professionals who work with Aboriginal children and families to be better-trained and more sensitive to the culture, heritage and values of Canada's Aboriginal people, and to recognize their unique strengths and challenges. The professionals involved include social workers, child care workers, teachers, doctors, nurses, psychologists, police officers, lawyers and judges. As much as possible, the education should be

---

[100] There are similar issues in other countries, such as Australia: see e.g., P. Lynch, "Keeping Them Home: The Best Interests of Indigenous Children and Communities in Canada and Australia" (2001), 23 *Sydney Law Review* at 501.

[101] For example, simply rebuilding the troubled Labrador Inuit village of Davis Inlet in a different location at a cost of $150 million and changing its name will not, according to a former Chief, "miraculously wash away the problems that plagued her people for generations." See *Globe and Mail* (26 December 2003) at A14.

provided by Aboriginal people to others about the problems faced by Aboriginal families and children and the resources in Aboriginal communities.

Another important measure will be the increased recruitment and training of Aboriginal people to work with their communities and help them solve their problems. This process must involve the school system, as well as post-secondary institutions. In particular, various professional schools and colleges must be more aggressive in their recruitment of Aboriginal individuals, and more sensitive to them once enrolled. Agencies and institutions must also change their hiring and employment practices. While some services should be provided by professionals and paraprofessionals, there is also an important place for Aboriginal volunteers and lay persons in Aboriginal communities to serve in such roles as counsellors, foster parents, support persons and youth leaders.

There must also be changes in our policies and laws, and in the manner in which services are provided to Aboriginal communities. Such changes have been occurring and Aboriginal people are slowly gaining control over services provided to their communities, though it is apparent that some communities are more willing and able to do so than others. It is important that as responsibility has increased, legislation has been also been amended to be more responsive to the needs of Aboriginal children, and tripartite agreements have also given many Aboriginal communities more control over child welfare matters.

Many Aboriginal people, however, feel that these measures are not adequate. They feel that it is not sufficient that the federal and provincial governments should be delegating responsibilities to Aboriginal communities, but rather believe that they should have responsibility for their own children and should enact their own child welfare codes. The federal Parliament clearly has the constitutional authority to permit Indian bands to enact their own child welfare laws, but it has thus far failed to act. Some Aboriginal groups are advocating such action or asserting that responsibility for the provision of child welfare services should be granted to Aboriginal communities as part of broader moves towards recognition of Aboriginal self-government and sovereignty.

The reform of laws and changes in institutional structures to better meet the needs of Aboriginal children and communities is a process that will go on for many years. In the interim, it is essential that non-Aboriginal agencies and professionals are educated and sensitized to Aboriginal child welfare issues, and that larger numbers of Aboriginal professionals are educated, recruited and retained in the child welfare field. There is great potential for dialogue to the mutual benefit of both systems. Powerful concepts such as holism, balance, connections, and spiritual unity from the Aboriginal tradition could have profound impact on the child welfare system of the dominant non-Aboriginal society.

8

The Lawyer's Role

Over the past two decades there has been a great increase in the nature and volume of child welfare litigation in Canada. Child welfare statutes and rules of court have become increasingly complex, and judges and lawyers have come to play a greater role in the handling of child welfare cases. Although the protection of children remains paramount, respect for the rights of children and parents is also very important. Respect for individual rights and the autonomy of the family was reinforced by the enactment of the *Canadian Charter of Rights and Freedoms* in 1982, which resulted in the courts having a greater role in the protection of individual rights.

Today, Legal Aid plans generally provide low-income parents with access to legal representation in child welfare cases, and when the plans have failed to do so, the courts may be prepared to invoke the *Charter* to ensure that indigent parents have access to counsel. The role of counsel for parents in child welfare cases is challenging and emotionally draining.

Increasingly in Canada, lawyers are being appointed to represent children involved in child welfare proceedings, as well as in other types of cases. Representing children presents some unique issues in terms of ethics and professional role.

Child welfare agencies have become more complex, with larger bureaucracies, more professional staff, and more complicated policies and procedures. Legal advice is required in the formulation of policies and procedures which govern virtually every aspect of agency work, as well as in the presentation of cases in court. Lawyers for child welfare agencies have special obligations to the courts and to clients of the agencies, which can also make their role demanding.

While child protection work can be a very rewarding type of legal practice, it can also be heartbreaking. This chapter explores the special challenges and rewards that lawyers have in child welfare proceedings, with separate treatment for counsel for children, parents, and agencies.

A: REPRESENTING CHILDREN

Dan L. Goldberg[1]

Across Canada the practice of providing legal representation to children in child protection proceedings has evolved considerably over the past two

---

[1] Dan L. Goldberg is Senior Counsel, Office of the Children's Lawyer, Ministry of the Attorney General, Toronto, Ontario.

decades. Ontario's Child Representation Program, implemented through the Office of the Children's Lawyer (formerly the Office of the Official Guardian), which is a part of the Ministry of the Attorney General, is the most comprehensive system in the country for the provision of legal services to minor children. Most of the provinces and territories either have already introduced, or are in the process of introducing, some form of legal representation for children who are the subjects of child welfare proceedings.

In 1991 Canada ratified the *United Nations Convention on the Rights of the Child*.[2] This agreement recognized in international law the rights of children. Pursuant to Article 12 of the *Convention*, a child who can form views in a matter affecting him or her can either directly or through a representative or an appropriate body have those views placed before any judicial or administrative proceeding. While the *Convention* does not have the force of law in Canada, it can be used to help interpret the *Charter of Rights* and legislation. The *Convention* provides at least symbolic support for ensuring that the views of children are put before courts dealing with child protection cases.

Child Representation in Ontario

In 1973 the Ontario Law Reform Commission recommended that in child welfare proceedings a child would benefit from, and should have, separate legal representation:

> It seems to us inconsistent...that so far in the development of the law in this Province the right of a child to the protection of his own counsel in proceedings relating to his upbringing has not been established in any more than isolated instances. We believe that decisions concerning a child's physical and emotional welfare are as worthy of the state's special interest as those concerning his property rights, and that courts may be in the most informed position only when there has been an objective evaluation of a child's best interests by a person with legal qualifications who may present the child's case to a court.[3]

Less than one year later, in 1974, the Law Reform Commission of Canada also recommended the provision of independent legal representation for children who are the subject of family law proceedings. The Commission stated:

> Where the right or interest of a child will be directly or indirectly affected by a court proceeding, the Commission recommends that consideration be given to the appointment of independent legal counsel to represent the child. The Commission recognizes that, in many instances, there will be no conflict of interest among the parties or, on the other hand, the agreement between the adult parties will provide as adequately as is possible for the child's welfare. However, the interests of a child may require separate legal representation, particularly in matters of contested custody, contested adoption, and child neglect, and, occasionally, in maintenance proceed-

---

[2] UN GA DOC. A/RES/44/25 (1989).
[3] Ontario Law Reform Commission, *Report on Family Law, Part III, Children* (1973) at 124.

ings. It is not good enough to rely upon the judge, the parents or the parents' counsel, to act as an advocate for the child in such matters.[4]

In 1977 and 1978, the Attorney General's Committee on the Representation of Children issued two reports that formed the basis of amending the *Child Welfare Act* to allow the court to order counsel for a child.[5] This provision is now found in s. 38 of Ontario's *Child and Family Services Act.*[6]

A child may have legal representation at any stage of child protection proceedings. The court must, as soon as practicable after the commencement of the proceeding, determine whether legal representation is desirable to protect the "child's interests." The court may determine this issue again at a subsequent stage in the proceeding. If the court does determine that legal representation is desirable to protect a child's interests, it shall direct that legal representation be provided for that child.

Section 38 establishes criteria for the court to consider in determining whether or not an order for child's counsel should be made. In certain circumstances, legal representation is deemed to be desirable to protect the child's interests, unless the court is satisfied, having regard to the child's views and wishes, that the child's interests are otherwise adequately protected. Specifically, these circumstances are:

- where there is a difference between the views of the child and a parent or a Children's Aid Society and the Children's Aid Society proposes that the child be removed from a person's care or be made a ward;
- where the child is not permitted to attend the hearing;
- where the child is in the Children's Aid Society's care and no parent appears before the court; or
- where the child is in the Children's Aid Society's care and it is alleged that the child is in need of protection within the meaning of certain provisions of the Act (i.e., has suffered from physical harm, sexual molestation, emotional harm or a mental, emotional or developmental condition that if not remedied could seriously impair the child's development).

If a child asks the court to appoint counsel, usually through the Children's Aid Society worker or their parent(s), then it is likely that an order directing legal representation will be made. In addition, if the Children's Aid Society, a parent or an interested party requests that the court make an order providing a lawyer for a child, then an order will generally be made.

Once an order for child representation has been made by a court, it is mandatory for the Office of the Children's Lawyer to assign a lawyer to act as the child's counsel.

---

[4] Law Reform Commission of Canada, *Working Paper No. 1, The Family Court* (1974) at 40.

[5] Ontario Ministry of the Attorney General, *Report of the Committee on the Representation of Children in the Provincial Court (Family Division)* (1977), 7 R.F.L. (2d) 1; and *Second Report of the Attorney General's Committee on the Representation of Children* (1978).

[6] R.S.O. 1990 c. C.11, as amended.

In Ontario, child's counsel is appointed in a significant and increasing number of cases. In 1996-1997, there were 1,471 orders made by courts appointing child's counsel in child protection proceedings. By 2002-2003 this number had more than doubled to 3,223 orders.[7] This increase is likely, in part, a reflection of the increase in child protection cases in Ontario stemming from amendments to the *Child and Family Services Act* in 2000, which placed less importance on maintaining the integrity of the family unit and more emphasis on focusing on the safety of the child. This has resulted in more children being apprehended from parents in cases of suspected abuse or neglect.

The Office of the Children's Lawyer delivers legal services in child protection cases (and custody/access cases) to children throughout Ontario through its staff counsel, and through a specially trained and regularly supervised panel of over 400 lawyers who are private practitioners. The program is funded through the Ministry of the Attorney General, and there is no charge for parents or children if counsel is appointed to represent a child.

The Role of Child's Counsel

There are three different roles that lawyers for children can assume: the *amicus curiae*, the guardian *ad litem*, and the advocate.

A lawyer who acts as an *amicus curiae* or "friend of the court" is a neutral officer of the court, and an intermediary between the child and the court. The lawyer informs, assists, and advises the child about court procedures, the facts and the law, including the possible dispositions that the court may make. The lawyer will ensure that the child's views and preferences are placed before the court, along with all other relevant evidence, from a neutral position and does not advocate any particular position.

The second possible role of the lawyer is that of guardian *ad litem*, who is also appointed to protect and promote the interests of the child. The guardian *ad litem* does not fulfill a neutral function and will present recommendations to the court regarding what the lawyer believes to be in the child's best interests, without being bound by the child's stated views and preferences.

The third possible role of the lawyer is that of the traditional advocate, who acts within the context of the adversarial system. In this role the lawyer represents the child's wishes and owes a duty of confidentiality to the child in the same manner as would a lawyer who represents an adult client. The lawyer provides legal services including safeguarding procedural rights, adducing evidence and arguing relevant law, in order to support the child client's position. The lawyer acting in this role does not put forward his or her own personal views to the court regarding the best interests of the child.

In May 1981, the Professional Conduct Committee of the Law Society of Upper Canada adopted the recommendations of its Sub-Committee on the Legal

---

[7] Ontario Office of the Children's Lawyer, Official Statistics (2003).

Representation of Children. The main recommendation was that lawyers representing children in child welfare proceedings should be guided not by a guardian *ad litem* or *amicus curiae* approach, but rather by the same principles as are ordinarily intrinsic to the traditional solicitor-client relationship.[8]

The Law Society report stated that where a child has capacity to give instructions, the child's counsel is duty bound to represent those instructions. A decision regarding the capacity of a child to properly instruct their lawyer is to be determined by that counsel in the particular circumstances. Where a child may lack the capacity to give instructions, the lawyer is no longer under a duty to follow the instructions and must advise the court that, in their view, the child is incapable of providing instructions.

Whether or not the child has the capacity to instruct, the Law Society report provided that counsel should not be arguing what they consider to be in the best interests of their child client. This perspective was also put forward in *Re W.*, in which Judge Abella held that there is no distinction in the role of child's counsel from that of a lawyer for any other party, both of whom are to carry out their client's instructions and protect their interests:

> Where…the child has expressed definite views, these views, rather than those of the child's lawyer, should determine what is conveyed to the Court. The child's advocate is the legal architect who constructs a case based on the client's views.
>
> In many cases it is almost impossible to unerringly assess what is best for a child. Given this epistemological gap, why should the lawyer substitute his or her own opinion for that of the child?[9]

In *C.C.A.S. of Metropolitan Toronto v. M.(C)*, Justice Macdonald similarly suggested that child's counsel should not play a different role from other lawyers:

> The role of counsel in the courtroom should never vary, and all counsel are to be on an equal footing. Counsel is to be an advocate, and his or her personal beliefs or statements regarding the best interests of the child should be disregarded. In my view, this is especially true where counsel for the child is representing an interest that is adverse to that of the natural parent.[10]

In contrast, in *Re C.*, Judge Karswick interpreted the role of child's counsel to be quite different from that of the traditional advocate. He held that children's counsel should put forward both the children's wishes, and make submissions, in his or her professional view and as supported by the evidence, about what disposition would be in the best interests of the children. Judge Karswick stated:

> It can be acknowledged that the views and preferences of a child are not necessarily the determining factor in deciding the issue of custody but simply one important element among a number of others that have to be considered in resolving the crucial issue. When

---

[8] *Report of the Law Society of Upper Canada Subcommittee on Representation of Children*, adopted by Convocation May 15, 1981. The Law Society of Upper Canada is the professional governing body for lawyers in Ontario.

[9] (1980), 27 O.R. (2d) 314 at 316-317 (Ont. Prov. Ct., Fam. Div.).

[10] (1993), 99 D.L.R. (4th) 77 at 101 (Ont. Ct., Gen. Div.).

one considers the fundamental importance of this issue of custody for both the family and the community I do not think that the court can...direct the child's counsel to take a strict adversarial role and act as a "mouthpiece," blindly advocating a view, preference or instructions which confound or shock his professional opinion of what is in the best interest of the child. It makes eminently good sense to have counsel take an active, real and positive role in the social context of the family court and, as officers of this court, assume the obligation to adduce all relevant and material evidence on the issue of what is in the best interest of the child and, when called upon, to express a professional and responsible view of what that disposition should be.[11]

In *Strobridge v. Strobridge*, the Ontario Court of Appeal stated, in the context of a custody and access case, that unless there is consent to do so, counsel cannot be both an advocate and, effectively, a witness by conveying to the court what the children stated to be their preferences. The Court of Appeal went on to say that children's counsel could not make submissions regarding their own views as to what constitutes their clients' "best interests." Mr. Justice Osborne stated:

Counsel retained by the Official Guardian is entitled to file or call evidence and make submissions on all of the evidence. In my view, counsel is not entitled to express his or her personal opinion on any issue, including the children's best interests. Nor is counsel entitled to become a witness and advise the court what the children's access-related preferences are. If those preferences should be before the court, resort must be had to the appropriate evidentiary means.... The Official Guardian, through counsel, will see that evidence going to the issue of the children's best interests is before the courts.[12]

In *C.A.S. of the County of Bruce v. J.V.*, the Ontario Superior Court of Justice, on appeal, drew no distinction regarding the role of child's counsel in a child protection proceeding from that in a dispute between parents.[13]

There is still a range of judicial opinion about the role of child's counsel. In the 2000 case *Zamanchuk v. Baldwin*, a dispute between two separated parents over custody and access, the court held that children's counsel could and should present not only the child's wishes but also that lawyer's view of what was in the child's best interests. Justice Fleury stated:

Obviously wherever the Children's Lawyer is involved, his or her opinion concerning the best interests of the child...should be given considerable weight. Why is this? Because, firstly, the Children's Lawyer is appointed by the Court.... Secondly, because he or she may be the only independent advocate before the court putting forward the best interests of the child.[14]

As child representation has evolved since 1980, it has become increasingly clear to judges, lawyers, and mental health professionals that children represent a specialized, vulnerable client group. As such, traditional approaches to strictly advocating the instructions of a client have changed to take into account a child's age, cognitive development, emotional and other circumstances.

---

[11] (1980), 14 R.F.L. (2d) 21 at 25-26 (Ont. Prov. Ct. – Fam. Div.).

[12] (1994), 4 R.F.L. (4th) 169 at 180 (Ont. C.A.).

[13] [2001] O.J. No. 3392 at para. 39 (Ont. Sup. Ct.).

[14] [2000] O.J. No. 1323 at para. 10 (Ont. Sup. Ct.).

With the benefit of over two decades of experience representing many thousands of children in child protection cases, Ontario's Office of the Children's Lawyer has developed and published a *Role of Child's Counsel Policy Statement*. Of particular note, the *Policy Statement* states that:

- Child's counsel obtains the child's views and preferences, if any, the child is able to express;
- Child's counsel does not *represent* the "best interests" of the child, this being the issue to be decided by the court;
- Child's counsel is the "legal representative" of the child and is not a "litigation guardian" or *amicus curiae*; and
- The relationship between child's counsel and the child is a "solicitor-client" relationship.[15]

Paragraph 7 of the *Policy Statement* indicates that child's counsel must ensure that evidence is presented to the court to support the position taken on behalf of the child client:

Contested Hearing

If it is necessary for the court or a tribunal to determine the outstanding disputed issues counsel will advocate a position on behalf of the child and ensure that evidence of:

   (a)   the child's views and preferences,

   (b)   the circumstances surrounding those views and preferences, and

   (c)   all other relevant evidence about the child's interests, is before the tribunal.[16]

If a child is able to articulate views and preferences to the lawyer, then counsel must ensure that they are placed before the court. Counsel is, however, also to present other relevant evidence, including the circumstances surrounding influences on the child's views and preferences. While counsel for the child will often advocate a position based on the wishes of a child who is expressing clear views, counsel may decide not to advocate a position based on the child's wishes.

If a child is unable to articulate preferences, then counsel will ensure that all relevant evidence pertaining to the child's interests is adduced. The position taken will be based on the evidence and is not a reflection of counsel's personal opinion as to what may constitute the best disposition for the child.

Views and Preferences of a Child

In arriving at a position on behalf of a child who is able to communicate wishes to counsel, Paragraph 5 of the *Role of Child's Counsel Policy Statement* of the Ontario Office of the Children's Lawyer provides guidance:

---

[15] Office of the Children's Lawyer, *Policy Statement, Role of Child's Counsel*, published April 3, 1995; revised January 18, 2001 at 2.

[16] *Ibid.* at 3.

Position on Behalf of the Child

In taking a position on behalf of the child, child's counsel will ascertain the views
and preferences of the child, if any, and will consider:

   (a)   the independence, strength, and consistency of the child's views and
         preferences,

   (b)   the circumstances surrounding the child's views and preferences, and

   (c)   all other relevant evidence about the child's interests....[17]

The strength and consistency of a child's wishes are important for child's
counsel to understand. Sometimes a child will be adamant about returning to the
home from which the child was apprehended. Some children may be content to
remain in the care of the Children's Aid Society at a foster or group home. Still
other children may not hold strong views and may vacillate as to their wishes in
different meetings with their lawyers. Understandably, in this latter circumstance, counsel may have to rely largely upon other relevant evidence than the
child's statements to arrive at a position on behalf of the child.

Of great significance and frequent controversy in child representation are
situations when a child's views and preferences may not be independently
formed. Rather, a child may be expressing wishes that are a function of a parent
exerting excessive influence or pressure upon the child. It is usually not difficult
for child's counsel to determine when their client has been so influenced. These
children often speak in age-inappropriate language, are not able to provide
sensible reasons supporting their position and are very polarized in how they see
and present their options.

In *Boukema v. Boukema*, Justice Macdonald addressed this issue in the
context of a custody dispute between parents. Evidence had been put forward at
trial about how this 11-year-old girl had been influenced by her mother and
pressured to advise her lawyer that she wanted to live with her mother and move
from Toronto to New Jersey. In arriving at his position in the litigation, child's
counsel from the Office of the Children's Lawyer did not advocate the child's
"tainted" preferences; rather, child's counsel presented these preferences, but
also adduced evidence to provide the context regarding the surrounding circumstances. The judge commented:

> Amanda's stated wishes are a factor. I have been cautioned…about placing emphasis
> on Amanda's stated wishes to the exclusion of all other considerations. I have also
> been cautioned…that it is not the function of the Office of the Children's Lawyer
> merely to "parrot" the child's stated wishes. This is particularly so when it is appar-
> ent that the child's stated wishes have been influenced by one or the other parent....
>
> Amanda's views were not arrived at independently and it is for this reason that the
> Children's Lawyer declined to advocate Amanda's views without putting before the
> court detailed evidence of all of the factors that may have influenced these views....
>
> …I have considered Amanda's wishes but inasmuch as they have been greatly influ-
> enced by the mother, I have attached less weight to them than I otherwise would.[18]

---

[17] *Ibid.* at 3.

[18] (1998), 31 R.F.L. (4th) 329 at 348-349 (Ont. Ct. — Gen. Div.).

Where there is clear evidence that a child's stated wishes are a product of parental influence (and not simply those of a child being aligned with that parent), child's counsel must be vigilant not to be placed in a situation where counsel is advocating a position based solely on those wishes without adducing relevant evidence of the surrounding circumstances. The *Role of Child's Counsel Policy Statement* of the Ontario Children's Lawyer reflects this perspective. To do otherwise would do a disservice to the child and would jeopardize the independence and credibility of child representation.

The Independent Role of Child's Counsel

As mentioned earlier, in the 1970s the Law Reform Commissions of both Canada and Ontario recommended that children in family law proceedings should, in certain circumstances, have their own counsel. Both reports affirmed the importance of the independent role of child's counsel.

In *C.C.A.S. of Metropolitan Toronto and N.*, counsel for the mother sought to have child's counsel disqualified and removed because mother's counsel wanted to cross-examine child's counsel. The Office of the Children's Lawyer contended that its counsel was not a necessary witness, and that mother's counsel brought this motion as a strategic manoeuvre to disqualify the child's lawyer who took positions that were adverse to the mother's position. In dismissing the motion, Mr. Justice Zuker stated:

> Courts also must consider any motion to disqualify in the context of motivation behind the motion. One should minimize the use of the removal of a counsel who other counsel may wish to call as a witness. To consider the use of any determination as to whether it is a tactical weapon by adversary counsel, the Court must therefore balance the rights and the Court's interests.[19]

The court's decision was an acknowledgement of the importance of the independence of child's counsel.

Child's counsel, being independent of the parties, has the important responsibility of making independent enquiries of significant people regarding the circumstances of their child client. For example, if a parenting capacity assessment has been done, child's counsel needs to communicate *directly* with the psychologist who conducted the assessment rather than relying on the child welfare agency's interpretation of any communication or report from that assessor.

One of the unique aspects of child representation flows from the independent role that counsel has. Child welfare agencies have to enforce child protection legislation and are often considered by parents as hostile to their own interests and those of their child. Parents can be angry at, mistrustful of and unable to work with child protection workers who may have entered that parent's home, possibly with the assistance of police officers, to apprehend their child.

---

[19] [2000] O.J. 5093 (Ct. J.). See also *C.R. v. C.A.S. of Hamilton*, [2004] O.J. 1251 (S.C.).

As child's counsel is independent of the child welfare agency, a parent can sometimes be more receptive to their position and supporting reasons even if they are similar or identical to those of the agency. As such, child's counsel can often be instrumental in helping to narrow the issues or settle the case.

Confidentiality and Reporting Obligation of Child's Counsel

All Canadian provinces have laws imposing a duty on those who have reasonable grounds to suspect child abuse or neglect to report these suspicions to a child protection authority. This obligation extends to professionals such as a family physician or a therapist who may have confidential or privileged information. Most of these reporting laws, however, preserve solicitor-client privilege by overriding the duty to report by a child's counsel.

Counsel for children can often find themselves in the difficult position of having received privileged information from their client that indicates that their child client may be at risk of harm. An example is that of a teenage girl who wishes to return home and advises her lawyer that her stepfather is sexually assaulting her and that her mother does not protect her. Counsel will, assuredly, advise the child not to return home. However, if the child persists in her desire to return home, then in Ontario, the Law Society of Upper Canada's *Rules of Professional Conduct* would allow, but not compel, counsel to breach the privilege, as this is a case where there is "imminent risk of death, serious bodily harm, or serious psychological harm that substantially interferes" with the child's health or well-being.[20] However, if the child's counsel reports to a child protection agency the solicitor-client relationship may be damaged and the child may no longer trust their lawyer. It is for this reason that child's counsel would encourage the child to disclose to a child protection agency worker, or may suggest disclosure to another professional who would not be exempted from the duty to report. A child in these circumstances requires considerable assistance and support. Child's counsel may well be in the position of initiating the process of getting their client needed counselling and other support services.

Leaving aside situations where a child discloses information to a lawyer that reveals a serious risk to the child client, a lawyer for the child will only reveal what the child has said with the permission of the child. A lawyer will generally not share information received from the child with other professionals without the child's permission.

Counsel for the Child Withdrawing from a Case

As indicated earlier, child's counsel is appointed to provide legal representation to children in protection proceedings under s. 38 of Ontario's *Child and*

---

[20] Rule 2.03, The Law Society of Upper Canada, *Rules of Professional Conduct*, June 22, 2000, Consolidated with Amendments, Nov. 2002.

Family Services Act. The continued involvement of child's counsel is subject to review during the course of the proceedings.

The standard order appointing the child's counsel in protection cases in Ontario states that the Children's Lawyer has the right to apply to the court to have the order for legal representation set aside. The circumstances of each case will be evaluated by the Children's Lawyer before a decision to withdraw is made. The decision to seek to withdraw may be made if any of the following circumstances exist:

- The criteria in s. 38 of the *Child and Family Services Act* are no longer present;
- Given the child's young age, it is not possible to reasonably ascertain their views and preferences and all material and relevant evidence regarding the child's interests will be before the court even without the involvement of counsel for the child;
- The matter is proceeding on consent in a manner consistent with the child's interests, for example, at the status review stage;
- The matter will be contested and the position of the Children's Lawyer on behalf of the child is identical to the position of one of the parties and all material and relevant evidence regarding the child's interests will be before the court even without involvement of counsel for the child;
- Over a significant period of time the child client cannot be located by his/her lawyer to express views and preferences to counsel; or
- It is the view of the Office of the Children's Lawyer that, in the circumstances in which it seeks to withdraw, their counsel can no longer add meaningful input to the proceeding.[21]

Child Representation across Canada

Although Ontario has the most comprehensive child representation program in Canada, there are various forms of legal representation for children in the other provinces and territories.

British Columbia

In British Columbia, s. 39(4) of the *Child, Family and Community Service Act*[22] provides that the court may allow a child to be made a party to a child welfare proceeding, particularly if the child's views do not correspond with the views of the parent(s) or the Director of Child Welfare. If the child is made a party, the Attorney General will appoint counsel from the private bar who have been retained for the purpose of representing children. Where a child is 12 years of age or over or has been made a party, before a consent order is made, a court

---

[21] Ontario Office of the Children's Lawyer, Policy Statement, *Circumstances in Which the Office of the Children's Lawyer will Withdraw from Child Protection Proceedings*, April 2001.

[22] R.S.B.C. 1996, c. C. 46; also see sections 54.1 and 60.

must be satisfied that the child has been advised of the right to consult with independent legal counsel prior to consenting to the order. The British Columbia Legal Services Society and the Ministry of Children and Families have an agreement which has established a province-wide roster of lawyers to provide independent legal advice to children 12 years of age or over when their consent is required for a court-ordered plan of care. The Ministry of Children and Families funds this service.[23]

Where the Director seeks to permanently place a child with a person other than the child's parent, ten day's notice of the hearing must be given to a child 12 years of age or over.

Alberta

Under s. 112 of the Alberta *Child Welfare Act*,[24] the court may direct that the child be represented by a lawyer in any child protection proceeding. The court may make such a direction if the child, his or her guardian or a Director of Child Welfare requests the court to do so and the court is satisfied that the interests or views of the child would not be otherwise adequately represented. If such an order for child representation is made, the court shall refer the child to the Legal Aid Society of Alberta or to the Ministry of the Attorney General if no legal aid assistance is available to the child. In this latter instance a staff lawyer or a lawyer from private practice will be appointed to represent the child.[25]

Saskatchewan

In Saskatchewan, there may be circumstances during a child protection proceeding where the court will want to hear from the child. Section 29 of the *Child and Family Services Act*[26] provides that the court may, if it is in the best interests of the child, serve notice of hearing on the child and permit the child to be present at the hearing to present his or her views. Section 29(2) specifically states that notwithstanding the ability of the court to hear from the child, the child shall not be considered a party to the protection hearing. The Department of Social Services is obliged to bring all the information before the court from the perspective of the child's best interest and this is viewed in this province as eliminating the need for children to be represented by separate counsel.[27]

Manitoba

Under s. 34(2) of the *Child and Family Services Act*,[28] the court may order that counsel is to be appointed to represent the interests of the child. If the child is 12 years of age or older, the court may order that the child have the right to instruct counsel. The *Act* provides a non-exhaustive list of factors for the court to

---

[23] Communication with Legal Services Branch, B.C. Ministry of the Attorney General.

[24] R.S.A. 2000, c. C. 12.

[25] Communication with the Legal Aid Society of Alberta.

[26] S.S. 1989-90 c. C-7.2 as amended.

[27] Communication with the Saskatchewan Department of Justice.

[28] C.C.S.M. 1985, c. C. 80.

consider in making an appointment for separate representation, including: the child's views; the child's wishes regarding separate representation; and any differences in the views or the interests of the child and the views or interests of the other parties.[29]

Quebec

Pursuant to s. 5 of the *Youth Protection Act*,[30] the child protection agency must inform children as fully as possible of their rights under the *Act* and, in particular, of the right to consult an advocate. Section 6 of the *Act* requires that the child be given an opportunity to be heard by the court. The *Civil Code of Quebec*[31] also provides that children are to have an opportunity to be heard if their age and power of discernment permit it, in every application brought before the court affecting the interests of a child.

Section 78 of the *Youth Protection Act* provides that the court must inform the child and the parents of their right to be represented by counsel. Section 80 provides for independent legal representation for any child where the interests of that child are opposed to those of his or her parents. The Quebec Legal Aid program has staff lawyers with expertise in the representation of children in protection cases.

New Brunswick

Under s. 6 of the *Family Services Act*,[32] the court may advise the Minister to ensure that the interests of the child are properly represented separate from those of any other person by appointing counsel. In cases where the Minister is a party to the proceeding, the court may advise the Attorney General that in its opinion, counsel should be made available to represent the child's interests and concerns.[33] Legal representatives are drawn from a roster of lawyers with experience and or an expressed interest in the representation of children.[34]

Nova Scotia

Under s. 37(1)(2) of the *Children and Family Services Act*,[35] a child may have legal representation where a child is 12 years of age or older and requests being made a party and to have counsel, if the court determines that such status and representation is desirable to protect the child's interests.

Section 37(3) of the *Act* also provides for a guardian *ad litem* to be appointed for the child where the child is not a party, if the court determines that such a guardian is desirable to protect the child's interests, or where the child is 12 years of age or older and the child is not capable of instructing counsel.

---

[29] *Ibid.*, section 34(3).
[30] R.S.Q. 1977, c. P-43.1, as amended.
[31] S.Q. 1991, c. 64, as amended.
[32] R.S.N.B. 1980, c. F.-2.2.
[33] *Ibid.*, section 6.
[34] Communication with Legal Aid Manitoba.
[35] S.N.S. 1990, c. 5, as amended.

Section 37(4) of the *Act* provides for the payment by the Minister of reasonable fees and disbursements of the counsel or guardian, including the reasonable fees and disbursements of counsel for the guardian.

Prince Edward Island

Under s. 34 of the *Child Protection Act*[36] when the Director of Child Welfare has made an application to the court for an order pertaining to a child in need of protection and the child is at least 12 years old and apparently capable of understanding the circumstances, the court may order that the child is to be represented by counsel at the expense of the Director.

Newfoundland and Labrador

Under the *Child, Youth and Family Services Act*[37] there is no specific provision for a child to receive legal representation. However, the *Act* is to be interpreted in accordance with several principles, including one which states that there is a presumption that a child who is 12 years of age or older is capable of forming and expressing an opinion regarding his or her care and custody.[38] Section 7(h) of the *Act* also provides that one of the factors in the court's determination of a child's best interests is the child's views and wishes. Section 58(1)(a) states that even where a parent consents to an order under the *Act*, a judge must also be satisfied that the wishes of the child have been considered. Under s. 53, where a child requests that his or her views be known at a hearing, a judge shall meet with the child with or without the other parties and their counsel, permit the child to testify, consider any written material submitted by the child, or allow the child to express his or her views in some other way.

In this province, the Unified Family Court has jurisdiction to hear child protection cases. Under s. 15 of the *Rules of the Unified Family Court*, where the court is satisfied that the interests of a minor are involved in a proceeding, it may give such directions for the representation of the minor as the court considers proper.[39]

Northwest Territories

Under s. 86 of the *Child and Family Services Act*,[40] the court shall ensure that a child is represented by a lawyer who is independent of his or her parents where it appears to the court that the child's and parents' interests are in conflict, or that it would be in the child's best interests to be represented by his or her own counsel. This provision permits a judge to order that counsel be appointed for a child who is the subject of a child protection hearing.

The *Act* gives the court the authority to require parents, if they have the means, to pay the fees and expenses of child's counsel. The Department of

---

[36] S.P.E.I. 2003, C-5.1.

[37] S.N. 1998, c. C-12.1, as amended.

[38] *Ibid.*, section 7(h).

[39] 1979, Nfld. Reg. 99/79.

[40] S.N.W.T. 1997, c. 13.

Health and Social Services has an arrangement with the Legal Aid program by which the department, when serving as the guardian of a child, can pay for the provision of legal representation.[41]

Nunavut

The *Child and Family Services Act (Nunavut)*[42] is identical to the legislation in the Northwest Territories and allows a judge of the Nunavut Court of Justice to order the appointment of child's counsel.

Yukon

Under s. 168 of the *Children's Act*,[43] the Official Guardian has the exclusive right to determine whether any child who is in the care of the Director of Family and Children's Services or alleged to be in need of protection, requires separate representation by a lawyer or any other person. In determining the need for separate representation, the Official Guardian must consider the advice or recommendations of the judge and any party to the proceeding. The Official Guardian shall also consider the ability of the child to understand the proceeding, the nature, if any, of the conflict between the interests of the child and of any party, and whether the parties will adduce relevant evidence regarding the interests of the child. The Official Guardian may also appoint a person who is not a lawyer to provide separate representation.

Rights of Children in Child Protection Cases to Notice and Counsel

While the Supreme Court judgement in *New Brunswick (Minister of Health) v. G.(J.)* focused on the constitutional rights of *parents* to enjoy a relationship with children free from undue interference by the state, the Court also recognized that *children* have their own constitutional right to "liberty and security of the person" which may be affected by the child protection process.[44] As a child's rights and interests are not the same as those of a parent, some American decisions have recognized that when a child is "old enough to understand the nature of the guardianship proceeding and its effect on him, to have formed considered views about it, and to express those views," then "due process" requires that the child "be given the opportunity to be heard in a meaningful way."[45]

While a number of provinces, like Ontario, have statutory schemes that provide for individualized assessments to determine the appropriateness of notification and counsel for children in child protection cases, some jurisdictions do not. As a child's right to "liberty and security of the person" is affected by a protection proceeding, a *child with capacity* to understand the nature of the

---

[41] Communication with Newfoundland Legal Aid Commission.

[42] R.S.N.W.T. 1997, c. 13.

[43] R.S.Y. 2002, c. 31.

[44] There is also scope for children and adolescents to raise "liberty" interest-based challenges to legislation that may arise in their confinement for "treatment" purposes. See *Alberta v. K.B.* [2000] A.J. 1570 (Alta. Q.B.).

[45] In *re Adoption No. 6Z97003 for Montgomery County*, 731 A. 2d 467 (Md. Ct. Spec. App. 1999).

proceeding should have notice of the proceeding. In cases where the child has a position different from the parents or agency, there is arguably a constitutional right to independent counsel to advance the child's views, and there have been cases in which Canadian judges have invoked the *Charter* to order that a child is to have legal representation.[46]

Further, in some Canadian cases, in the absence of legislative provisions, judges have used the *Charter* to appoint counsel to represent the rights and *interests* of children who lack the capacity to communicate their views and preferences to counsel. This seems especially likely to occur in cases in which the child welfare agency for policy or legislative reasons, is unwilling to explore all of the alternatives that might promote the best interests of the children. For a superior court judge, invoking the *parens patriae* power may be an easier procedural route to achieve this remedy, since there is no need for notice to the Attorney General of a constitutional question being raised.[47]

Conclusion

The role of child's counsel takes on different forms across Canada and remains complex and evolving. One legal author's insightful observations in 1980 about the confusion and needed flexibility regarding the role of child's counsel in protection cases still continues to aptly describe the complexity in determining a proper role for counsel for a child:

> ...a major factor in the role confusion often experienced by counsel representing children is the tacit expectation that a single role should cover all aspects of their duties. The lawyer's proper role as representative of the child involves in fact a variety of roles. While the desire for a single, invariable role is understandable, the unique nature of litigation involving children does not allow exclusive adherence to any one...orientation...if the child's best interests are to be realized. Different roles will be appropriate at different times and in different cases. Determination of the proper role in a given case is achieved only after considering the kind of proceeding, the stage of proceeding, the needs of the child represented and the capacity of the child to express his own wishes to counsel.[48]

Lawyers who represent children require multidisciplinary training on issues such as the developmental stages of children, how to properly conduct an interview with a child, and an understanding of their important role in ensuring that their client's legal interests are properly advocated in the legal system.

Child protection agencies across Canada have limited resources to carry out their legislatively mandated functions. One of the many roles child's counsel can perform is to ensure that these agencies are properly serving children's

---

[46] This argument was accepted in *Re R.A.M.*; *Children's Aid Society of Winnipeg v. A.M.* (1983), 37 R.F.L. (2d) 113, reversed on other grounds 39 R.F.L., (2d) 239 (Man. C.A.).

[47] See e.g., *Re T.L.F.*, [2001] S.J. 353 (Sask. Q.B.), per Ryan-Froslie J.; *Re R.M.S.*, [2001] S.J. 724 (Sask. Q.B.) per Smith J.; and *P.W.S. v. British Columbia (Director of Child and Family Services)*, [2000] B.C.J. 2656 (B.C.S.C.).

[48] M.J.J. McHale, "The Proper Role of the Lawyer as Legal Representative of the Child" (1980), 18(2) *Alberta Law Review* 216 at 220.

interests and that there is not excessive delay in the final disposition of the case so that a permanent plan for a child can be implemented. This is especially true for a very young child.

Representing children can be a very challenging task, but it also can be an extremely rewarding professional experience to assist a child caught in difficult personal and family circumstances. Child representation has attracted more attention in recent years, and most family law courses offered in law schools include some components of children's law. Several law schools in Canada now offer entire courses on children's law. It is hoped that despite relatively low rates of remuneration, more law students and lawyers will view child representation as an important and meaningful contribution that they can make to children, in particular, and to society, in general, which will reflect their commitment to the core values of the legal profession.

B: REPRESENTING PARENTS

Mary Jane Hatton, Nicholas Bala, and Carole Curtis[49]

Child protection cases are different from most cases that lawyers handle. They do not deal in such matters as the sale of property or the enforcement of contracts. They deal with the most intimate and important aspects of people's lives. They also involve the complex interaction of some of the most fundamental values of our society — the power of the state, parental autonomy, the needs and rights of individuals within the family unit, and the rights, protection and nurturing of society's children.

Representation of parents in child protection proceedings is an especially challenging role for a lawyer. The lawyer's role will go beyond simply appearing in court to serve as the "mouthpiece" of the parents. The parent's lawyer may have to investigate a case, counsel clients about important life decisions, and arrange for various social supports, as well as engage in traditional legal advocacy. Unlike most litigation, which focuses on past events, child protection cases have a prospective orientation, and counsel for parents can have an important role in helping parents to develop a plan for the future that will allow them to care more effectively for their children. Child protection cases are also dynamic, with new developments and changing relationships, which can pose special challenges for counsel representing parents.

Before discussing some of the challenges that lawyers for parents face in understanding and effectively representing parents involved in child protection cases, it is important to be aware of the constitutional right that parents have to representation by a lawyer.

---

[49] Mary Jane Hatton is a Justice of the Ontario Family Court, Durham Region. (Justice Hatton's contribution to this chapter was prepared for the first edition of this book prior to her appointment to the Bench, and thus reflects her views as a privately practicing lawyer.) Nicholas Bala is Professor of Law, Queen's University, Kingston, Ontario. Carole Curtis is a lawyer in private practice, Toronto, Ontario.

The Constitutional Right of Parents to Legal Representation

Parents involved in child protection cases are often on social assistance or have poorly paid jobs, and they can rarely afford to pay for a lawyer. It is now accepted in Canada that indigent parents whose children have been apprehended by a child protection agency have the constitutional right to have a lawyer paid by the state.

Historically parents without the resources to hire a lawyer generally were unable to effectively challenge the decision of a child welfare agency to remove their children from their home and to terminate their rights. In the 1970s legal aid plans were established which were intended to ensure that indigent parents involved in child protection cases could have legal representation. In the 1990s, however, along with other deficit cutting measures, there were cuts to government funding for legal aid plans. New Brunswick was a province that made especially deep cuts to its legal aid scheme by restricting coverage to child protection cases involving permanent wardship, expecting parents who faced temporary wardship applications to represent themselves.

The situation in New Brunswick resulted in a case going to the Supreme Court of Canada which established the principle that parents involved in child protection proceedings have the constitutional right to be treated "in accordance with the principles of fundamental justice," including the right to legal representation. A single mother on social assistance had her three children removed from her care on the grounds of neglect; an initial order was made at a hearing at which she was only assisted by a friend who had no legal training. The agency then wanted the order extended for another six months, and the mother was again unable to afford a lawyer or obtain representation through legal aid. A lawyer in private practice was, however, prepared to represent her on a *pro bono* basis[50] at the status review hearing, both to argue that the mother should be provided with counsel paid by the government and for the purpose of contesting the extension of the temporary wardship. At that status review hearing, the agency introduced evidence from 15 witnesses, including expert psychological reports, and the children and father each had counsel, as did the agency. Clearly the mother would have been severely disadvantaged in having her position put before the court without a lawyer. While the wardship was extended for a further six months, the children were returned at the end of that time to the mother's care. The question of whether the mother had a constitutional right to

---

[50] *Pro bono* is from the Latin expression *pro bono publico*, meaning "For the public good." In this case the lawyer provided representation to the mother without being paid by her — i.e., *pro bono* — though as a result of successfully arguing the case to the Supreme Court he did ultimately get payment of fees and expenses for the case. It is a tradition of the legal profession that lawyers have a duty to represent those who have a just legal cause, even if they cannot afford to pay. Law firms, law schools, and professional organizations support this tradition of *pro bono* unpaid service to community groups and needy individuals, though there are limits to how much work any professional can reasonably be expected to do without being paid. It is now expected, and constitutionally required, that the state will ensure that representation is provided to indigent individuals facing a threat to "life, liberty and security of the person," rather than being forced to rely on the professional generosity of an individual lawyer.

representation paid by the state was dealt with separately, and eventually reached the Supreme Court of Canada.

In *New Brunswick (Minister of Health) v. G.(J.),*[51] the Supreme Court of Canada sent a strong message that parents have a vital, constitutionally protected interest in their relationship with their children, and that this relationship can only be severed by the state if there is a fair court process, which may require the state to pay for a lawyer for a parent who lacks the means to pay for a lawyer. The Court based its decision on s. 7 of the *Charter of Rights*, which provides that no person shall be deprived by the state of "life, liberty or security of the person…except in accordance with the principles of fundamental justice." The Court concluded that a single mother on social assistance whose children had been apprehended by a child welfare agency had the constitutional right under s. 7 of the *Charter* to be represented by counsel paid by the government to ensure that the temporary wardship proceedings were "in accordance with the principles of fundamental justice." The Court held that "security of the person" includes the right to enjoy a parent-child relationship, and that this right is very much affected by a child protection proceeding. Chief Justice Lamer wrote:[52]

> [T]he interests of fundamental justice in child protection proceedings are both substantive and procedural. The state may only relieve a parent of custody when it is necessary to protect the *best interests* of the child, provided that there is a fair procedure for making this determination….
>
> The interests at stake in the custody [child protection] hearing are unquestionably of the highest order. Few state actions can have a more profound effect on the lives of both parent and child. Not only is the parent's right to security of the person at stake, *the child's is as well. Since the best interests of the child are presumed to lie with the parent*, the child's psychological integrity and well-being may be seriously affected by the interference with the parent-child relationship….
>
> In light of these factors, I find that the [mother]…needed to be represented by counsel for there to have been a fair determination of the children's best interests.

While the court recognized that in this case it was not dealing with a permanent termination of the parent-child relationship but only with an extension of temporary wardship, the court nevertheless concluded that the parent's constitutional rights were clearly affected:[53]

> A six-month separation of a parent from three young children is a significant period of time. It is even more significant when considered in light of the fact that…[she]

---

[51] [1999] 3 S.C.R. 46, 50 R.F.L. (4th) 63. In a concurring opinion, Justice L'Heureux-Dubé agreed in the result with Lamer C.J.C., though arguing that the Equality Provisions of s. 15 of the *Charter* were also raised in this situation, since the parents affected by child protection proceedings are disproportionately low income, single mothers, and Aboriginal or members of various other minority groups.

[52] At para. 70 and 76. Emphasis added. The decision in *G.(J.)* is very important for child welfare law in general, though some of the analysis is a little confusing, with the Court failing to clearly distinguish between the constitutional rights of parents and the rights of their children. The lack of a clear analysis allowed the entire court to agree about the outcome of the case, though later constitutional cases revealed that there are actually sharp divisions on the Court about how to apply the *Charter* to child welfare cases; see e.g., *Winnipeg Child and Family Services v. K.L.W.*, [2000] 2 S.C.R. 519. See N. Bala, "The *Charter of Rights* and Family Law in Canada: A New Era" (2001), 18(3) *Canadian Family Law Quarterly* 373-428.

[53] At para. 77.

had already been separated from her children for over a year and that generally speaking, the longer the separation of parent from child, the less likely it is that the parent will ever regain custody....

A judge considering a request for counsel must assess the circumstances and complexity of the case. In this particular case, Chief Justice Lamer commented:[54]

> At issue in this appeal is whether the custody hearing would have been sufficiently complex...that the assistance of a lawyer would have been necessary to ensure her right to a fair hearing. I believe that it would have been. Although perhaps more administrative in nature than criminal proceedings, child custody [protection] proceedings are effectively adversarial proceedings which occur in a court of law. The parties are responsible for planning and presenting their cases. While the rules of evidence are somewhat relaxed, difficult evidentiary issues are frequently raised....

> In proceedings as serious and complex as these, an unrepresented parent will ordinarily need to possess superior intelligence or education, communication skills, composure, and familiarity with the legal system in order to effectively present his or her case.... Without the benefit of counsel, [she] would not have been able to participate effectively at the hearing, creating an unacceptable risk of error in determining the children's best interests and thereby threatening to violate both the appellant's and her children's rights....

As indicated in *G.(J.)*, an indigent parent does not have an absolute right to state-paid counsel in a child protection proceeding. However, as a result of the complexity and importance of most contested wardship applications, and the limited education and sophistication of most parents involved in these cases, there are likely to be few cases in which indigent parents will face the possibility of even temporary removal of a child from their care where a trial judge would be likely to find that there is no right to representation.

Following the 1999 decision of the Supreme Court in *G.(J.)*, provincial legal aid schemes have recognized that representation must be provided to indigent parents involved in child protection cases, but there remain real concerns about the nature of representation and the level of funding provided for individual cases. One limitation on the right to legal aid is that only those who are "indigent" are eligible.[55] Parents who are on social assistance or unemployed are usually eligible, but lower income parents who are employed may not be eligible for legal aid, even though they may be unable to afford the cost of hiring a lawyer to litigate against a state-funded child welfare agency. The proceedings are often long and complex, and the legal fees and expenses are costly.

In some places in Canada, legal aid clinics with staff lawyers have been established to provide representation for indigent parents. The staff lawyers at these clinics are generally dedicated and experienced in dealing with child protection cases, though some of these staff lawyers are just starting their careers. Some parents may be suspicious of legal aid clinics; even though the clinics are institutionally separate from government, parents who are embroiled in a dispute with

---

[54] At para. 78-81.
[55] See *F. & C.S. of Guelph and Wellington City. v. K.F.*, [2001] O.J. 4548 (Ont. Ct. J.), per Caspers J.

a government agency may lack confidence in a clinic or with the staff lawyer "assigned" to them. Some clinics can make arrangements for a parent to have representation by a lawyer in private practice if a parent has a high level of distrust of the clinic lawyer, or if the clinic has a conflict of interest, for example because the clinic is representing one parent and the parents have separated and each should have independent representation.

In many places in Canada legal aid representation for parents is provided by lawyers in private practice. A parent who is eligible for legal aid can then choose to be represented by any lawyer who is prepared to accept the client at the rate that legal aid will fund. Lawyers in private practice are concerned that legal aid offers low hourly rates, and often puts a "cap" on the hours that are billable so that the lawyer may not be paid for the full amount of time that is needed to adequately represent a parent. Many experienced lawyers are unwilling to accept legal aid clients, or restrict the number of such clients that they will serve. Some lawyers who accept legal aid clients may have difficulty in giving their cases the time that these cases deserve because of the funding limits that are imposed.

The courts have made clear that the constitutional right to representation involves more than simply the right to have a lawyer in court, it includes the right to *effective* legal representation. In a British Columbia case, *Walton v. Simpson*, a lawyer in private practice agreed to represent an indigent mother in a complex child protection case, but was concerned about the amount of preparation time that legal aid was prepared to fund. The lawyer brought a preliminary court application, arguing that the mother's constitutional right to effective representation was threatened by the limits on legal aid funding. Justice Meiklem accepted that in principle he had jurisdiction under s. 7 of the *Charter* to make an order concerning the level of legal aid funding, but felt that counsel had not established through "any independent or expert opinions" that the legal aid cap would not allow adequate preparation. After discussing the Supreme Court decision in *G.(J.)*, the judge wrote:[56]

> I do not accept the argument advanced by the Attorney General that, as a matter of principle, if there is legal aid coverage, and therefore counsel available, that is the end of the inquiry. *There is obviously some minimum threshold level of funding required to make the provision of counsel meaningful and effective to ensure the fairness of the hearing.* For example, if there was no funding for preparation in a case which required extensive preparation, providing counsel at the hearing alone would be perfunctory and probably would not ensure fairness....

On the evidence presented, the court dismissed the application for an order for an extension of the amount of preparation time that legal aid was prepared to fund. *Walton v. Simpson* establishes that the courts have a role in ensuring that representation for an indigent parent is adequate. But it also illustrates that judges will be cautious and require evidence to support requests to overturn a

---

[56] *Walton v. Simpson,* 2000 BCSC 758 (S.C.) at para. 14. Emphasis added.

decision by legal aid or government officials about how representation is to be provided.[57]

In another British Columbia child protection case, the Court of Appeal ruled that if counsel provides a parent with representation that is clearly ineffective, a new trial may be ordered. In *D.B. v. British Columbia (Director of Child, Family and Community Services)* an Aboriginal grandmother was seeking the return of children who had been in her care since their birth until their apprehension by a child welfare agency. An important issue in the case was the quality of the grandmother's care of her own children. Agency workers testified that the grandmother had been an abusive mother. The grandmother denied this and wanted to testify to rebut the agency evidence, but her lawyer pressured her not to:[58]

> [The lawyer's] version of events is that he had several conversations with [D.B., the grandmother] regarding the advisability of her giving evidence both before and during the hearing.... He said that he advised her that, in his opinion, it would not help her case to take the stand and be subjected to cross-examination. Further, he said that he advised her that if she insisted on giving evidence, he would have her sign a statement that doing so was contrary to his advice or, alternatively, he would put it on the record during the hearing that she was taking the stand against his advice. He described this as his usual practice. Undoubtedly, however, [the lawyer] made it abundantly clear to [D.B.] that she should not give evidence and that, to do so, would be contrary to his advice. The prospect that he would have potentially prejudiced her by telling [the judge] that she was giving evidence contrary to his advice, would, or should, have been enough to discourage her in any event.

The grandmother did not testify and the trial judge rejected her application for the return of the children from agency care. The grandmother then retained another lawyer and appealed, arguing that the lawyer at trial failed to provide effective representation thereby violating her rights under s. 7 of the *Charter.* The appeal court summarized the trial lawyer's role in this case:[59]

> Essentially, [the lawyer] believed and accepted the evidence against his client and concluded that her best hope was to work on addressing her many problems with a view to subsequently applying to get the children back. Having come to the conclusion that [D.B.'s] family was, in fact, dysfunctional, and from drawing on his own education, training and life experience from his own family, he was of the view that "history repeats itself," particularly for those that are not prepared to utilize available resources. Thus, in his view, had he put [D.B.] and members of her family in the witness box, and it was demonstrated through cross-examination that they were lying, her chance of ever being successful in subsequently applying to get her grandchildren back after the making of a continuing custody order would have been much diminished. [The lawyer] did not explain this strategy to [D.B.] or other members of

---

[57] In a 2002 Ontario child welfare case, a mother was unable to obtain a lawyer with her legal aid certificate because of the refusal of local counsel to accept the legal aid tariff rate of $88 per hour. Justice Cosgrove of the Ontario Superior Court invoked the *Charter* and ordered that counsel was to be paid at the rate of $125 per hour, a rate at which counsel was willing to provide representation. Decision of Cosgrove J., August 28, 2002, as reported in "Judge gives $37 over legal aid rate: Brockville lawyer appointed to defend child welfare case at $125 per hour," *Law Times* (9 September 2002) at 1.

[58] [2002] B.C.J. 253 (C.A.) at para. 14.

[59] [2002] B.C.J. 253 (C.A.) at para. 16.

her family or, if he did, it was not explained in a sufficiently straightforward manner that any of them could appreciate why he was not calling them as witnesses.

In ordering a new trial, Justice Rowles concluded:[60]

> trial counsel's method of discouraging the [grandmother] from giving evidence in this case was tantamount to denying [her]…the assistance of counsel. In other words, I would characterize this aspect of the ineffective representation by trial counsel as a constructive denial of the assistance of counsel, thereby calling into question the fairness of the adjudicative process that led to the order granting continuing custody of the children to the Director.

The decision in *D.B.* emphasized that it is not the role of counsel to assess the credibility of their clients or their suitability as parents. That is the role of the judge. If a lawyer feels unable to present the case that the client wants put before the court, the lawyer may attempt to withdraw their representation. If the lawyer is prepared to represent the client, the lawyer must follow the client's instructions. Although the lawyer has responsibility for making decisions about tactics, such as how to cross-examine particular witnesses, the client must make the major decisions, such as whether to seek custody and whether to testify. While the lawyer should provide the client with advice about these major decisions, the client has the final responsibility for making these major decisions.

Who Are the Parents Involved with Child Protection Agencies?

Parents who come into contact with child protection agencies are often from a different socioeconomic group than their lawyers, with different values and very different life experiences. Most lawyers will have had little or no previous contact with the background and life experiences of parents involved in child protection cases. The differences between the lawyer and the parent-client in education, standard of living, value systems, family history, and ethnic or cultural background can create barriers between the lawyer and client; their ability to communicate and understand each other is potentially compromised.

In general, parents involved with the child protection system fall into one of the following two categories:

- those whose parenting is called into question due to allegations concerning their own *active* behaviour (child abusers, alcoholics, drug addicts, those involved in crime, those with mental illnesses and those openly at war with the protection agency); or

- those whose parenting is called into question due to allegations concerning their own *passive* behaviour (those unable or unwilling to perform what seem like simple tasks, those with marginal parenting skills, those with limited cognitive abilities, and those with passive or dependant personalities).

---

[60] [2002] B.C.J. 253 (C.A.) at para. 64.

Each set of behavioral patterns presents unique problems requiring different skills by the lawyer. In addition, there are almost always major socioeconomic factors that exert a powerful impact on parents and their children, thereby contributing to their problems. These factors are outlined here.

Poverty: It is hard to overestimate the overwhelming impact of poverty on the lives of families. Many parents involved in the child protection system live in poverty. Some families live in serious deprivation, lacking the basic necessities for a healthy life (e.g., clothing, food, shelter and fuel). Some families live on the edge of a subsistence level, where life and health are maintained at a minimum standard, but the family lives with chronic insecurity and uncertainty about its ability to keep everyone clothed, housed, etc. Some parents are part of the working poor, earning too much to access societal safety net benefits, but not enough to provide adequately for their families. Poverty limits alternatives for parents, children, and those attempting to represent them.

Transience: Many families involved with child protection agencies move frequently and have a high level of instability in housing. However, parents should not lose their children simply due to an inability to find or maintain adequate housing. Often such instability arises from a series of income-related problems. A client who is constantly moving also poses challenges for a lawyer in terms of maintaining contact.

Isolation: Many parents involved in the child protection system are extremely isolated, with limited or no support networks of family, peers, or community. This may mean that the parents lean on the lawyer more than other clients. It may also mean that the parents lean on the child protection agency and other social agencies for help, and may even develop a network of social workers from different agencies that they turn to for help and emotional support. For these clients, the child protection agency whom they are litigating against may be part of their support system, and the agency worker may be one of their most supportive "friends." The lawyer faces a special challenge in attempting to manage or control a parent client's contact and interaction with "the other side."

Cultural bias: Changing immigration patterns in Canadian society have resulted in immigrant populations in the larger cities coming into contact with the child protection system. Aboriginal parents also disproportionately encounter the child protection system in urban and rural settings. Parenting always has a cultural context, with different cultures and communities following their own values, practices, and standards. Many notions regarding family (extended family, household size, space requirements, discipline, sleeping arrangements and gender roles) may differ from the dominant society.

Powerlessness: Many parents involved in the child protection system have very limited social and economic resources, and have very limited control over the world around them. To the parents, authority figures may seem like one amorphous mass, whom parents often resent, resist, become hostile towards or too passively accept. At times, parents may even see their own lawyer as part of "the system" that tries to control them.

A Lawyer's Personal Framework for Representing Parents

A lawyer representing parents in a child protection proceeding must not only cope with the legal aspects of a case, but must also be prepared to deal with clients who are likely to be very different from themselves and may also be very difficult to deal with. The demands made by a parent on their lawyer's personal and professional resources are sometimes onerous. Many lawyers avoid representing parents in child protection proceedings. Some find this area of work disturbing, as one must deal with cases involving physical abuse, sexual abuse, parental neglect and traumatized children. Not only do lawyers find these matters distressing, but they may be unable or unwilling to deal with parents who come from problematic backgrounds.

Lawyers acting for parents in child protection cases must develop personal frameworks to approach this work, in psychological, ethical and advocacy terms. First, in the majority of child protection proceedings there is a degree of systemic bias against parents by other participants in the process. There may be an assumption by some professionals that if the protection agency has become involved in a family's life, there must be good reason. The assumption implies that these parents cannot properly care for their children without some form of state intervention. The lawyer for the parents should start each case with the viewpoint that state intervention is not required in a family's life, unless proven on credible evidence after every reasonable opportunity has been given to the parents to care for their children without state and court involvement.

Second, most parents in child protection cases face overwhelming obstacles in their day-to-day lives that affect their personalities and the lifestyle choices they make. The parents' lawyer needs to identify and recognize the parents' strengths, as well as deal with those aspects of their lifestyles and personalities that might seem sordid or distasteful. A lawyer should identify their client's limits and attempt to help the client to address them.

Third, the lawyer must remember that the removal of a child from their care is one of the most devastating experiences a parent can ever face. The lawyer's role is to make certain that state intervention is absolutely necessary and that all alternatives to state care are explored, including the possibility of care by relatives.

Child protection cases are demanding of a lawyer's skills as an advocate. They also challenge a lawyer's personal resources for compassion and understanding. It is very important for the lawyer acting for parents to maintain an appropriately professional and suitably distant relationship with the parents. Lawyers who have unrealistic expectations of the parents' ability (or willingness) to change or perform the tasks necessary to have their children returned to them may be disappointed. A lawyer's unrealistic expectations can exacerbate a client's already desperate situation. A lawyer should have expectations of a client that are realistic and achievable.

There is a widely accepted social and professional ethic for criminal lawyers who represent those who are charged with criminal offences and may in fact be "guilty." Compared to the criminal defence bar, there has been relatively little attention to ethical and professional challenges faced by counsel for parents alleged to have abused or neglected their children and are seeking to regain custody in a protection proceeding. Representing parents is a challenging and important professional role, however, and lawyers who experience a sense of conflict or confusion about their obligations to the parent-client should not be doing this type of work. The lawyer must always remember that the parents are the lawyer's client, not the child. There are other professionals and agencies whose job it is to ensure that the child's best interests are protected (the protection agency lawyer, the social worker, the judge, the child's lawyer), but only the parents' lawyer is there to advocate on behalf of the parents.

Investigation of the Agency's Case

The first task for the parents' lawyer is a thorough investigation of the agency's case as early as possible in the proceeding. There are numerous advantages to conducting a thorough investigation. First, the parents' lawyer becomes fully apprised of the concerns of the agency and can discuss these issues in detail with the parents. Second, if certain facts can be agreed upon, the lawyer can focus on the contentious issues. Third, counsel who is aware of the agency's case can assess its weaknesses and more constructively advocate the parents' position.

The information required by the lawyer includes:

- copies of court documents and the chronology of the legal proceedings, the history of the agency's involvement with the family including the source and reason for the initial referral and the frequency, purpose and outcome of all contacts by agency personnel with the parent and the child;
- a list of the resources within the agency or in the community with which the parent or child has had contact and which may be available to help the parents address the protection concerns;
- copies of assessments, reports, home studies, case conference notes, records and other relevant documents in the possession of the agency;
- information regarding similar documents available from other agencies or persons;
- the allegations and concerns of the agency with respect to the parents' care of the child;
- information regarding any concurrent criminal proceedings;
- the criminal record of the parent and any other members of their household who may be proposed as caregivers in any plan of care being proposed by the parent; and
- the recommendations of the agency about the case.

Much of this information can be obtained from the agency worker or the agency lawyer. The easiest way for the parents' lawyer to obtain disclosure of this information is to get a copy of the agency file or to arrange a meeting with the agency worker or lawyer. The parents' lawyer will want to review the workers' notes and recordings on the case and to interview the agency representatives. The file may contain information about the parents that is quite positive, as well the negative material that the agency may be emphasizing in its court application.

If voluntary disclosure is not forthcoming, the parents' lawyer can ask for a court order for disclosure, and request that the agency disclose the material facts and evidence upon which it will rely at the hearing. It is also necessary for the lawyer to obtain disclosure from any other parties, such as guardians or relatives.[61]

Conducting an Independent Investigation

In some instances, it is necessary for the parents' lawyer to have an investigation or assessment conducted independent from those conducted by the agency. The difficulty for the parents' lawyer is that the parents usually do not have the financial resources to allow the lawyer to independently conduct a thorough investigation. If a parent is assisted through legal aid, it is often difficult for the lawyer to obtain the necessary authorization from the legal aid authorities to pay for an independent investigation or psychological assessment.

There are situations that demand further investigation by the parents and their lawyer. This occurs if the lawyer believes that the agency's investigation is incomplete or seriously flawed, and the agency is unwilling to reopen it. For example, individuals such as relatives, babysitters and other caretakers may not have been interviewed, and their input may be crucial to counteract allegations against the parents. In sexual or physical abuse cases, the agency often obtains a medical or psychiatric assessment; the diagnosis can be unfair, unduly biased against a parent, or simply incomplete. It may be incumbent on the parents' lawyer to attempt to arrange for a second opinion and for any further consultations with medical or mental health personnel that are required.

In situations where further investigation is required, or obvious discrepancies and inaccuracies appear in the agency's investigation, counsel for a parent is obligated to attempt to rectify the shortcomings in appropriate ways. The parents' lawyer can advise the agency of the problems and request that the agency utilize its resources to remedy the situation. For tactical reasons, particularly in cases where a trial seems inevitable, the parents' lawyer may not want to advise the agency of the deficiencies of its case. For example, if the agency's position can be successfully challenged and weakened at trial, then the parents' case may be strengthened. However, in many cases a settlement on terms favourable to the parents may be effected earlier if there is full disclosure by parents' counsel at the outset as to the incompleteness and weaknesses of the agency's

---

[61] See also discussion in Chapter 2 about the agency's obligation to disclose information. While in some jurisdictions children may be considered parties to a protection proceeding, the child's lawyer is not obliged to disclose the child's case prior to or during a hearing.

position. Much will depend on what the agency is seeking and what strategies best serve the parents' goals.

If the agency is unable or unwilling to reopen the investigation, a separate assessment should be arranged if at all possible. The following approaches may be considered by the parents' lawyer:

- Retain or ask the court to appoint an expert to conduct an assessment. This could include hiring a social worker to conduct a study in the parents' home, having a team of professionals assess the family members and their interactions, or obtaining an independent psychiatric evaluation of a parent with alleged mental health problems.

- Interview and/or secure the records of those persons previously omitted from the agency investigation, such as access supervisors, daycare providers, school teachers, relatives or friends. The evidence of professionals who have worked with the parents but are not employed by the child welfare agency, such as a family doctor or a teacher, may be helpful to the parents' case.

- In physical abuse or neglect cases, obtain all medical information regarding the family. This includes speaking to the family doctor and specialists who have examined the parents or children, and obtaining copies of all hospital records to note the observations of nurses, social workers and other hospital personnel. A second medical opinion should be obtained with respect to any injuries and their cause. The lawyer should also explore differing medical opinions, and perhaps arrange to meet the doctors to review their findings.

- In sexual abuse cases, the lawyer may refer the parent for psychological and other relevant testing. An expert's interpretation of a child's statement or a contradictory statement made by the child to other persons may be obtained. If there are serious concerns about the child's credibility, the lawyer may also arrange a psychiatric consultation.

- All community resources that have assisted the parent or child should be contacted for their observations with respect to parenting issues.

Developing the Parents' Plan

After investigating the agency's case and obtaining other information about the case, the lawyer for the parents must respond to the allegations of the child protection agency, and help to develop a realistic plan for the parents and children. The development of a plan can be most difficult for the lawyer. The lawyer may fall into the trap of sitting in the office and formulating an exhaustive but unrealistic list of tasks for the parent to perform in order to obtain the return of a child. Every player in the child protection system has views of what parents should or should not do.

The lawyer acting for parents in child protection cases must be realistic in setting expectations for the clients. Often these parents are unable (or unwilling) to perform in ways the lawyer may see as essential to success in the case (e.g., failing to find housing, not showing up for visits, behaving in ways that hurt their case during visits, saying things to the social worker that hurt their case, refusing to co-operate with the protection agency, refusing to follow conditions set out in court orders for supervision, or missing scheduled appointments with medical professionals).

The lawyer acting for the parents must set the goals in achievable increments, setting those goals out clearly for the parents (in writing, where appropriate), and being clear with the parents about the potential result of any failure to meet these goals (i.e., the children may not be returned to them). The lawyer should make the goals reasonable and reachable. It is better to set up consecutive short-term plans and goals, and approach them one at a time. It is tempting for the lawyer to try to come up with a life plan to transform the parents' lives. Lawyers for parents in child protection cases must guard against the "rescuer fantasy" (the Messianic approach to legal representation).

The lawyer must be clear-sighted about the parents' abilities and limitations, and must work with the parents to formulate a realistic plan. Many parents do not have the personal resources needed as they cope with difficulties such as health problems, mental instability, emotional fragility, poverty and cultural adjustment stress. The parents' lawyer must avoid the belief that the parents can be saved from all adversities.

Many lawyers have little experience with the cultural and socioeconomic problems of parents involved with the child protection system. Many of the parents are transient, isolated within their communities or experience feelings of powerlessness and hopelessness. Some have psychological or social problems, such as drug addiction, mental illness, or developmental handicaps. Some parents may themselves have been abused or neglected as children and were agency wards; they may have difficulty in trusting agency workers and may not appreciate their own maladaptive responses to their childhood histories. Some parents are intellectually limited, and may be unable to follow even simple instructions or fulfill reasonable expectations. These problems have the potential to alienate the parents from the lawyer or the lawyer from the parents, as each has different expectations of what can or should be done.

The lawyer must tread carefully with the parents in formulating a parenting plan. The lawyer must remain sympathetic to the parents' plight and, at the same time, point out valid concerns of the agency and the legal issues to be faced in the court proceeding. The lawyer must confront the parents with parenting problems, while offering support, strategies and encouragement to help the parents overcome them. In many cases the parents will find it difficult to trust an authority figure, including their own lawyer. The parent may see the lawyer as part of the overall system. If the lawyer is unduly harsh or judgemental, the parents will lose confidence in the lawyer and may even be unable to see the lawyer as an ally and advocate. However, if the lawyer minimizes concerns or fails to discuss detrimental evidence, the parent will not make necessary changes or be sufficiently apprised of the seriousness of the case, and will not be adequately prepared for the confrontation with the agency that will occur in court.

The best approach is to advise the parent in a factual manner of the evidence and of findings of fact a judge will likely make. The lawyer should explore with parents their version of events and allegations, including positive aspects of the evidence. Even if the evidence is fairly overwhelming against the parents, it is important to suggest changes in their behaviour that could counteract the agency's concerns.

It is difficult for a lawyer when parents refuse to acknowledge parenting problems or minimize the impact of their behaviour on a child. The parent who continually denies wrongdoing or inadequacies is usually not open to counselling, assessment or suggestions of different ways to parent. In these situations, the lawyer should point out the strengths of the agency's case and advise the parents of the likely result if certain problems are not addressed. Of course, there are also cases in which the parents are justified in denying the agency's allegations, and the lawyer's role is to effectively challenge the allegations.

Many parents will make promises to do things differently if the child is returned home. Past experience may have demonstrated that such good intentions are not likely to be realized.[62] The lawyer should encourage the parents to be realistic about what can be accomplished and to set goals that are not recipes for failure. The plan should be simple but sufficiently detailed and comprehensive so that all agency concerns are addressed in some way.

The plan of the parents should typically address the following issues:

- If the parent is seeking the child's return, all aspects of day-to-day care should be considered. This includes information about accommodations, amenities available in the neighbourhood, the availability of schools, the parents' employment, child care and babysitting arrangements, the availability of relatives and friends as caretakers, and information about a spouse or partner with whom the parent is living.

- In those cases where there are valid concerns about a parent, specific proposals must be provided for alleviating or eliminating those problems. For example, if a parent is alcoholic or abusing drugs, the parents should attend a self-help group, counselling or a specialized treatment program for addicts. Similarly, if mental health issues are raised, the parent should begin a program of therapy recommended by a competent professional. The parent should enroll in these programs at the earliest possible time and be able to provide evidence of progress at the trial.

- If the issue is that the child needs treatment, the parent must propose a plan whereby treatment will be provided.

---

[62] R. Groves, "Lawyers, Psychologists and Psychological Evidence in Protection Hearings" (1980), 5 *Queen's Law Journal* 241 at 252-254.

- Sometimes the dispute centres on the question of a parent's access to a child. The parent's proposed plan of access should propose the frequency, duration and location of the visits, the transportation arrangements and the degree and method of supervision, if any. If the contact is to take place in the parent's home, the parent should propose specific routines and activities, and describe how they will benefit the child.

- The parent should focus on short- and long-term goals with respect to the child. For example, a parent may not be ready to have a child returned home because the parent has unsuitable accommodation. In this case, the parent should propose a schedule of regular, frequent visits with the child over a specified period and the return of the child when accommodation has been secured.

- It is crucial that the lawyer connect the parents with community resources and supports. These are often community agencies with a different mandate and function from the protection authorities. The community agencies may have more supportive relationships with the parents. As previously stated, many parents are simply overwhelmed by numerous problems. Some of these problems can be addressed through the use of other resources, such as after-school programs for the children, babysitters to provide relief for a single parent, or supportive groups in the community.

Child protection proceedings are a massive invasion by the state into the most private and intimate aspects of a person's life. Most parents resent this invasion and have trouble coping with the multiple demands of the many people involved in a child welfare proceeding, including social workers, lawyers, assessors and community agency staff. All plans formulated by the parent in conjunction with the lawyer should balance the state's mandate to safeguard the well-being of a child with preserving the parents' sense of privacy. A plan that does not recognize the need of a parent for dignity and self-respect may be doomed to failure.

Advocating the Parents' Position

Vigorously advocating and defending the parents' position is not confined to the trial; it is also an integral part of the pre-trial process. Obtaining instructions from the parents can be problematic. In some cases, the parents will want to present a position that the lawyer knows will not be accepted by the court, and that may make the parents seem unreasonable and hence harm their standing in the eyes of the court. As set out above in the discussion of *D.B. v. British Columbia*, although the lawyer may attempt to influence or modify those instructions, it is ultimately the parents' case, not the lawyer's, and the parents must make the major decisions about the presentation of their case in court.

Advocating the parents' position involves protecting the parents' interests at all stages of the proceedings. For example, if there is an ongoing conflict between a parent and an agency case worker, the lawyer may request that all further communication between the two be through the lawyer. This curtails the ability of the agency to gather further negative evidence against the parents. However, this stance should only be taken when absolutely necessary as it will often backfire on the parent, if the parent is seen as unco-operative, evasive, and uncommunicative. In addition, the agency may not be able to fully assess the parents' plan. The lawyer must keep the parents apprised of the evidence as it is collected and discuss with the parents ways to counteract negative evidence and bring out positive evidence.

Good advocacy includes attempting to obtain a reasonable settlement of the case without protracted litigation. A meeting of all the parties and their counsel should take place early in the case. The purpose of a settlement meeting is to clarify each party's position and to explore possible areas of agreement and compromise. In less serious cases, it may be possible for parents' counsel to negotiate a voluntary service agreement between the parent and the agency, on the condition that the court case is to be withdrawn. Even when agreement cannot be reached on all the contentious issues, the areas of disagreement can be more clearly delineated and the trial shortened and simplified.

An independent assessment can also be a useful tool to help acheive a settlement. If the parties can agree to have a professional assessment done by a particular expert, they should also define in advance the issues to be addressed in the assessment, the background information to be provided to the assessor, the persons to be interviewed and the scope of the assessment. The recommendations of the assessor may be instrumental in achieving a settlement among the parties or, if the case goes to trial, may be highly influential in the litigation.

However, an assessment is not always helpful to the parents' position. If the lawyer has misgivings about the benefits of an assessment, the lawyer should advise the parents of those misgivings. For example, if the parents are determined to go to trial in the face of overwhelming evidence against them, an assessment may only add greater weight to the agency's position and will be unlikely to lead to a settlement.

In some cases, the agency is seeking a termination of the relationship between parents and children with the objective of having the children placed for adoption. Even if the agency case seems overwhelming, it may not be psychologically possible for the parents to accept this, and it may be necessary to have a trial.[63] In these cases, parents' counsel should not attempt to pressure parents into giving up their case and must take the seemingly hopeless case to trial, challenging the agency's evidence at trial in whatever way seems possible. Even if the parents lose their children, they may feel some satisfaction at having "given it their all."

Mediation is increasingly used in child protection matters. Under the guidance of a mediator, the parties, including the agency, try to effect a

---

[63] As discussed in Chapter 3, in some of these situations the agency may make a motion for summary judgement which, if successful, will obviate the need for a trial.

settlement. The mediator's role is to act as a neutral facilitator to help the parties settle the case, helping to explore whether there is an acceptable plan that would address the concerns of all of the parties. A lawyer acting for parents might consider mediation if the mediator is knowledgeable about child protection and skilled in redressing any power imbalances between the parties. However, the agency is unlikely to agree to mediation if they have significant concerns about the risk to the child of having a continuing relationship with the parents.

In many jurisdictions, before a case goes to trial there may be one or more judicially supervised conferences or meetings. A conference may be able to help the parties to narrow the issues and hence shorten the trial, or may even help to settle the case. At a conference, each party will summarize its case and advise the presiding judge of the witnesses and other evidence to be called.

In some cases, if the judge is not the judge who will preside at trial, the judge at the pre-trial conference facilitates settlement by playing an evaluative role, expressing a view of how a court may assess the position of each party ("Of course I have only heard a summary of the case, but if I were the trial judge, I would be likely to..."). This judicial evaluation may help the parties to settle the case. These conferences can be particularly useful for the parents' lawyer. A conference may help persuade the agency of the merits of the parents' case and help to settle on terms acceptable to the parents. Alternatively, it may be important for the parents to hear from a judge how difficult it will be for them to succeed at trial in the claim that they are making, and hence help to persuade the parents to settle on terms acceptable to the agency.

The trial itself presents a number of strategic challenges for the parents' lawyer. The tactical approach taken by the lawyer depends on the parents' position, the strengths and weaknesses of each party's case, the credibility of the parent as a witness, the availability of corroborating witnesses, and the strategies of the other lawyers. Often in a child protection proceeding, parents' counsel will be focusing on two broad issues: the parents' past conduct and the parents' future plans. One aspect of the parents' case may be the denial or minimization of the allegations of abuse or neglect. The other major aspect of the case will be demonstrating that the parents have a realistic plan that will meet the child's needs.

At the commencement of the trial, the parents' lawyer will generally state the parents' position. This brief opening statement should summarize which of the allegations are admitted, the issues in dispute and the parents' plan. This strategy directs the judge's attention to the contentious areas; the judge will also be aware of the parents' plan to address the agency's concerns as the agency evidence unfolds.

The parents' counsel will normally cross-examine the witnesses called by the agency and by any other parties. There are a number of different approaches to cross-examination, depending on the nature of the case and the evidence of a particular witness. Cross-examining counsel may test the reliability of observations, suggest other possible explanations for the events described, point out evidence that contradicts the witness's testimony, or attempt to attack a witness's credibility by drawing out biases or preconceptions. Another approach on cross-examination is to question the thoroughness of the social worker's investigation, the even-handedness of the worker's approach with the parent, or the range of services offered to the parents.

In some cases, it may be unlikely that the impact of a witness's testimony can be lessened on cross-examination. In these situations, it is better not to cross-examine the agency's witness but, rather, the lawyer for the parents will attempt to rebut the witness's evidence through the parents' testimony or with the evidence of other witnesses called on behalf of the parent.

The lawyer may be concerned that if the parents testify, they will present poorly and on cross-examination could become angry and hostile, undermining any claims that they may have. Unlike in a criminal trial, however, where the accused person quite frequently does not testify, it is very rare for a parent in a child protection case not to testify. Not having the parents testify in a protection case poses significant litigation risks, as the judge will not have the opportunity to directly assess the parents' character, credibility and sincerity, nor will the judge be able to hear the details of their plan for the child directly from the parents. Further, in some situations in a civil case, as a matter of law, a negative inference may be drawn about a factual issue that is in dispute from the parents' failure to testify (e.g., in failing to explain an injury to a child). And in any case involving a child, a judge will be most reluctant to entrust the child to the care of a person who does not personally present his or her position to the court. As discussed earlier, the decision about whether to testify is one that ultimately must be made by a client, not the lawyer.

At the conclusion of the hearing, the parents' lawyer should make submissions emphasizing those aspects of the parents' plan that address the agency's protection concerns. The lawyer's goal is to persuade the court that the parents' position is a reasonable and realistic response to the identified problems and that the agency's recommendations are unnecessarily intrusive.

Conclusion

In a decision-making process that so profoundly affects the lives of children and families, it is reassuring to see parents being represented by a diligent, energetic and committed lawyer. The representation of parents in child protection proceedings is one of the most demanding yet potentially rewarding areas of family law. The "odds" are usually against the parents. The parents may be difficult clients, defensive and emotionally demanding. There will often be very significant social, cultural and educational differences between the parents and their lawyer. In some cases the alleged behaviour of the parents towards the child may be repulsive to the lawyer; in other cases the invasive actions of the state may offend the lawyer's notions of family autonomy and personal privacy and integrity.

The challenge of representing parents in child protection cases lies in balancing all these considerations, while remaining mindful of the primary function — that is, in helping to develop and then advocating the parents' position.

C: REPRESENTING THE AGENCY

Gordon R. Kelly[64]

Child welfare legislation attempts to strike a balance between preservation of the integrity of the family and protection of children from harm or risk of harm. The role of the child protection agency is to investigate reports that children may be in need of protective services, to provide preventive and remedial services to families for the protection of children and to provide temporary and permanent care for children who cannot be adequately protected within the family structure. The legislation mandates that the agency protect children, with modern legislation directing a remedial and supportive role in all but the most serious cases. The legislative philosophy presumes that the family is the best social structure for meeting the needs of children, while maintaining the paramount objective of the protection of children. Counsel representing child protection agencies must not only understand the legislation from a legal perspective, but also must be cognizant of the philosophy embodied in the legislation and of the societal goals sought to be achieved. The legislation does not exist in a legal vacuum, but rather is a statement by society as to how its children are to be protected from harm and the assistance to be provided to families. It is within this context that counsel representing child protection agencies render their services.

The critical intersection where child protection services and legal services meet is usually when an agency decides to apply to the court to determine whether a child is in need of protective services. Until the last decades of the twentieth century it was common for child protection agencies to be represented in court by an experienced social worker. Although not extinct, representation by a "court worker" is generally limited to uncontested or administrative proceedings. Child welfare proceedings have become lengthier and more complex. Legislative reform, the *Canadian Charter of Rights and Freedoms*,[65] the higher profile of child protection in the community and the entitlement to counsel by parents/guardians[66] and children[67] involved in child welfare proceedings have all resulted in greater utilization of counsel by agencies. The statutory

---

[64] Gordon R. Kelly is a senior partner with the firm of Blois, Nickerson & Bryson, Halifax, Nova Scotia. Mr. Kelly has extensive experience as counsel for child welfare agencies.

[65] *Canadian Charter of Rights and Freedoms*, Part I of the *Constitution Act, 1982*, being Schedule B to the *Canada Act 1982* (U.K.), 1982, c. 11, s. 7.

[66] *New Brunswick (Minister of Health & Community Services) v. G.(J.)*, [1999] 3 S.C.R. 46.

[67] *Child Welfare Act*, R.S.A. 2000, c. C-12 at s. 3, s. 112; *Child, Youth and Family Advocacy Act*, R.S.B.C. 1996, c. 47; *Child and Family Services Act*, R.S.O. 1990, c. 11 at s. 38; *Child and Family Services Act*, S.M. 1985-86, c. 8 at s. 34; *Children's Act*, R.S.Y. 2002, c. 31 at s. 167, *Children and Family Services Act*, S.N.S. 1990, c. 5 at s. 37. See discussion in chapter 8A above.

framework, rules of procedure and case law have created substantive and procedural complexities which necessitate that agencies retain the services of lawyers for dealing with contested, or potentially contested, cases.

Provision of Legal Services

The quality of legal representation is an important issue for child protection agencies as it can impact on practice, policy and procedure. Child welfare law is becoming a specialized area of legal practice with subspecialties focused on the needs and interests of particular groups: the parents/guardians, the children and the agency.

A child welfare proceeding can be a multi-faceted, protracted and costly undertaking. The legal process associated with child welfare proceedings, including the substantive and procedural requisites, ordinarily requires that child protection agencies obtain the services of a lawyer. The cost of the legal services associated with an application will vary depending on the jurisdiction and will increase with the complexity and length of the proceeding.

A number of legal service delivery models for child protection agencies exist. The choice of model may depend upon the geography and demographics of the particular jurisdiction, the availability of specialized lawyers, government policies, caseloads, substantive and procedural control by government and historical delivery systems.

The provision of legal services to child protection agencies can be broadly described as either by retainer or employment. Acquiring legal services by retainer means that the agency retains a lawyer in private practice to advise and represent the agency on a case-by-case basis or on a standing basis. Providing legal services by employment means the agency is represented by a staff lawyer or government lawyer. An agency may employ a lawyer as part of the staff of the agency, generally referred to as "in-house" counsel. Alternatively, an agency may access legal services through a lawyer employed by government, either in the department responsible for child protection services or the department which provides legal services to government. The distinction between in-house counsel and a government lawyer is significant, as there are differences in terms of accountability and control. The sharpest distinction, however, is between the retained lawyer and the employed lawyer. An employee takes direction from the employer, is accountable to the employer, and owes specific duties to the employer. In the case of an employed lawyer, the lawyer has duties as an employee, though there is also a solicitor-client relationship, and the lawyer continues to have ethical and professional duties as a member of the bar.

Legal service delivery models are not utilized exclusively. Within jurisdictions and even within some agencies a combination of the models may be used, for example, having both staff lawyers and retaining counsel for some cases.

The delivery of legal services to child protection agencies should focus on the following criteria: accessibility, accountability, assistance, autonomy and costs. Government restraint policies have been a driving force behind the trend towards employed lawyers as opposed to retained lawyers. The operating assumption is that the cost of legal services can be reduced by employing rather than retaining lawyers in private practice. Increasingly agencies have full-time staff lawyers. Often overlooked is the reality that support and administrative structures must also be duplicated. Office space, administrative support, paralegal support, office technology and legal research resources must be available to the employed lawyer and are part of the cost of the provision of legal services.

The financial constraints present in virtually every government department and government supported agency have resulted in the depletion of human resources. Accordingly, access to legal resources, experienced support staff and experienced counsel may not be present. Moreover, low salaries, increasing case loads, and lack of incentives among employees result in major difficulties retaining staff lawyers over extended periods of time.

A staff lawyer model tends to facilitate involvement of counsel in case management, training of social workers and development of agency policies. Staff lawyers may be more accessible to social workers than retained counsel. Having staff counsel may also allow for better control of costs. There are, however, significant costs to having staff counsel, in terms of administrative support. Further, staff and government lawyers may, in some cases, lack the independence to provide effective criticism or advice concerning agency policy or handling of a case.

Context of the Provision of Legal Services

Child welfare legislation requires that social workers respond to reports of abuse or neglect by investigating and, when the reports are substantiated, initiating some form of intervention inclusive of service provision. The circumstances may warrant court proceedings as part of the intervention.

The requirements for agencies to disclose information to parents are significant and, when combined with the short time frames provided in most child welfare statutes, the administrative burden is significant. The legal service provider must be able to marshal administrative and litigation support quickly and effectively.

Lawyers are accustomed to codes of conduct[68] that govern their profession. In the context of child welfare litigation, lawyers may be unfamiliar with the ethical standards imposed by governing bodies on social workers. Agency counsel should appreciate the ethical standards[69] that govern the professional conduct of social workers in their jurisdiction.

---

[68] The Canadian Bar Association, *Code of Professional Conduct* (Ottawa: Canadian Bar Association, 1998); on-line: The Canadian Bar Association <http://www.cba.org/CBA/Epiigram/february2002/codeeng.pdf> (date accessed: 26 June 2002).

[69] Canadian Association of Social Workers, *Social Work Code of Ethics* (Ottawa: Canadian Association of Social Workers, 1984); on-line: Canadian Association of Social Workers <www.casw-acts.ca/English/Library/Code of Ethics.htm> (date accessed: 26 June 2002).

Although the court proceeding may come to dominate the relationship between the agency and the parent/guardian, the professionals involved must not lose sight of the fact that the court proceeding is only part of an intervention strategy. The social work process must continue, and the social worker and family must find ways to work together to access services and problem solve in the context of active litigation. The role of the agency lawyer is to facilitate, not hinder this process.

Obligations/Duties of the Lawyer

Regardless of whether the agency is represented by a retained or employed lawyer, the question remains as to whom the lawyer owes a duty. The client is the agency, which acts through the instructing social worker.

Simplistically, lawyers are retained to represent the client to the best of their ability and to follow instructions. The traditional role of counsel is as an advocate. The lawyer's role is to advise, advocate and carry out the client's instructions. The lawyer advises the client as to the law, prepares the case for trial, confronts the evidence of adverse parties, and attempts to persuade the court to decide the issues in dispute in favour of the client. Is the role of the agency lawyer any different?

The lawyer's ethical duty when representing a private client in court is to "ask every question, raise every issue, advance every argument, however distasteful, that the advocate reasonably thinks will help the client's case," and to "endeavour to obtain for the client the benefit of any and every right, remedy and defence that is authorized by law."[70] Representation of a child welfare agency involves representing a public institution charged with achieving defined societal goals and thus places a public duty on the lawyer as well. This public duty is akin to the duty of a Crown prosecutor in a criminal case. The role of the Crown prosecutor has been summarized as follows:

> When engaged as prosecutor, the lawyer's primary duty is not to seek a conviction, but to present before the trial court all available credible evidence relevant to the alleged crime in order that justice may be done through a fair trial upon the merits. The prosecutor exercises a public function involving much discretion and power and must act fairly and dispassionately. The prosecutor...should make timely disclosure to the accused or defence counsel (or to the court if the accused is not represented) of all relevant facts and known witnesses, whether tending to show guilt or innocence, or that would affect the punishment of the accused.[71]

The role of the Crown prosecutor is a complex one that requires a consideration of many different values as well as a sense of justice. The Crown prosecutor's role differs substantially from the responsibilities of a lawyer representing

---

[70] See e.g., Nova Scotia Barrister's Society, *Legal Ethics and Professional Conduct Handbook* (Halifax: Nova Scotia Barrister's Society, 1990); on-line: Nova Scotia Barrister's Society <http://www.nsbs.ns.ca/handbook/handbk_> (date accessed: 26 June 2002) at Chapter 10.

[71] The Canadian Bar Association, *Code of Professional Conduct* (Ottawa: Canadian Bar Association, 1998); on-line: The Canadian Bar Association <http://www.cba.org/CBA/Epiigram/february2002/codeeng.pdf> (date accessed: 26 June 2002) at Chapter 9, Guiding Principle 9.

a private client. Duties are owed not only to the public, but also to the accused and the justice system. The overriding duty to the preservation of justice reinforces the importance of ensuring that an accused receives a fair trial including all of the fundamental rights mandated by law.

There is a similar public duty imposed on agency lawyers in child welfare proceedings. The agency lawyer's primary public duty is to ensure procedural fairness, to make full and timely disclosure of the allegations and relevant evidence, and to present the agency's case in an evenhanded manner that respects the participants and seeks an equitable determination of the best interests of the child.

Counsel for the agency must ensure that all the relevant evidence is before the court so that the judge can make a determination based on the best interests of the child. Collaborative and collective approaches to the development of a case should be encouraged among all parties involved, particularly the agency lawyer. Rather than approaching proceedings in a strictly adversarial manner, encouraging input and support from all the parties involved ensures that the child's best interests are being considered. Case conferences attended by all interested parties and involved professionals are an effective adjunct to the court process in this regard. Child welfare proceedings require counsel to pursue reasonable efforts and strategies to achieve the legislative goals and agency mandate. This may involve formal and informal strategies and procedures. Utilization of pre-trial procedures, particularly settlement pre-trial conferences, and consensually appointed court experts can promote resolution.

Agency counsel must also ensure that the legal rights and interests of children involved in child welfare proceedings are protected. This requires consideration of whether the child should be represented in the proceeding.

The public duty of counsel for the agency does not vitiate their duty as an advocate. Agency counsel are not impartial, although their role as counsel for the agency heightens their public responsibility. Their ethical duty is to advocate the agency's position.

Counsel are obligated to conduct themselves in a manner characterized by courtesy and good faith. Agency counsel should not adopt an overly technical approach and should accede to reasonable requests that do not prejudice the agency or the child.

When the agency seeks legal advice, counsel must provide a competent opinion based on an adequate knowledge of the relevant facts, a proper consideration of the applicable law, and the experience and expertise of counsel. Counsel must be candid when providing advice as to the merits of a case and the probable outcome. Counsel should advise as to the strengths and weaknesses of the agency's case and appropriate means to address areas of concern.

Lawyers representing agencies are faced with difficult tasks. In addition to determining and advocating for the agency's interests, there are many other relationships to foster and develop with individuals involved in the child welfare proceeding including: the parents/guardians, other interested relatives, the child, witnesses, court administration, and service providers. Regardless of role complexities and relationships involved, agency counsel should always be cognizant of the purposes of child protection services and the court proceedings.

Definition of Roles

The client is the agency and the lawyer generally receives instructions from the assigned social worker. Although this is a solicitor-client relationship, it functions more in the nature of a partnership. Each professional must understand and respect the role of the other. Each has special training and expertise, and neither have a self-interest in the proceeding. The social worker must assess the family circumstances, develop a case plan, and maintain an ongoing working relationship with the family. It is social work staff who decide whether to apprehend a child and whether to seek a supervisory order, or temporary or permanent wardship. The lawyer must act upon and advocate the agency position as instructed by the social worker, but also must consider the evidence and advise the agency on the application of the law to the facts of the case. It is extremely important that counsel know where the line is between practicing law and practicing social work. This is a professional relationship that requires each to understand and respect the role and professional obligations of the other. The lawyer should not attempt to practice social work, and the social worker should not attempt to practice law. The line is often obscured because of the nature of the working partnership. The line is crossed when advice becomes decision making outside of professional expertise.

The lawyer needs to be sensitive to the impact of the manner of representation on working relationships with parents/guardians, professionals, service providers and other lawyers. The conduct and attitude of agency counsel sets the tone both inside and outside the courtroom. Whether the lawyer adopts a fair, reasonable and collaborative approach or an overly adversarial and technical approach impacts significantly on how the agency is perceived by all involved in the process including the court.

Agency counsel is obliged to ensure that their representation promotes the ongoing development and maintenance of agency and social worker credibility. The credibility of the agency and social worker is critical to the functioning of the agency in the community and the courtroom. It can take years to build credibility and only moments to lose it.

Lawyer's Role in the Early Stages

The lawyer's role in the child welfare process is as advisor and advocate. Ideally, counsel on behalf of the agency should become involved once it appears that the agency's intervention plan with a family may involve the court process. Involvement at this early stage can assist the social worker in assessing the information available and developing strategies for further investigation. Further, advice can be provided with respect to evidentiary and procedural matters that may avoid problems with respect to admissibility of evidence should the matter ultimately proceed to trial. Counsel would be able to provide advice with respect to the statutory provisions and case law that affect the intervention plan and to assist the social worker in applying the law to the factual circumstances. Such advice would augment the decision-making process and help to identify the appropriate legal considerations.

Prevention is a concept applicable to both the social work and legal context. Too often consultations with counsel are sought only after a problem has been experienced. Involvement of counsel during the investigatory stage provides the opportunity for counsel to advise on alternatives to court intervention, the remedies available through the courts, and areas of legal concern with respect to the specific case. Counsel are also able to provide advice with respect to the proper procedures for gathering physical, documentary and demonstrative evidence to ensure compliance with the criteria for admissibility in court. Involvement of counsel in evaluating the sufficiency of the available evidence can operate as a safeguard for the agency and assist in the deliberations relative to contemplated court proceedings.

During the early stages of agency investigation and intervention, counsel should also be available to provide advice with respect to other related statutes, interpretation of court orders or family law agreements, and to provide assistance to the social worker in exploring resolution utilizing legal processes outside of the child welfare legislation. This is particularly relevant when intra-family conflict is the underlying cause of the protection concerns, or in circumstances where litigants in a private family matter may be attempting to co-opt the social worker or agency resources.

Alternative Dispute Resolution

Alternative dispute resolution strategies are increasingly being used in child welfare cases and, when properly utilized, can augment or avoid the court process. Agency counsel should be cognizant of alternative dispute resolution processes and provide advice with respect to engaging these strategies when appropriate.

Several child welfare statutes specifically provide for mediation.[72] The agency and the parent/guardian can agree to the appointment of a mediator to attempt to resolve matters relating to a child. Even where the governing statute does not provide for mediation, the process is not excluded. Mediation is a consensual process that does not specifically require enabling legislation. Mediators should have special training and be certified by their governing body.[73] Several provinces offer specialized training for mediators in child welfare

---

[72] See e.g., *Child, Youth and Family Services Act*, S.N. 1998, c. C-12.1, s. 13, s. 37; *The Child and Family Services Act*, S.S. 1989-90, c. C-7.2, s. 15, *Children's Act*, R.S.Y. 2002, c. 31, s. 42; *Children and Family Services Act*, S.N.S. 1990, c. 5, s. 21. See also discussion in Chapter 3.

[73] Family Mediation Canada; on-line: Family Mediation Canada <www.fmc.ca> (date accessed: 26 June 2002).

matters. Counsel does not directly participate in the mediation unless there is specific agreement for a defined purpose or reason.

Mediation allows the participants to retain a degree of control over the process of dispute resolution. Generally, in child welfare matters, mediation may be considered when the factual foundation of the child welfare concerns are not in dispute. Mediation focuses on commonality of interests using co-operative rather than adversarial strategies and to be effective, the participants must be prepared to communicate and work with each other.

Counsel on behalf of the agency should consider whether the presenting circumstances are appropriate for mediation before the commencement of the court process. Once the court process has been initiated, if there are issues for which mediation would be an appropriate process, then this alternative should be considered. The court may adjourn proceedings for a fixed period of time while mediation is pursued.

The Trial Process

Child welfare litigation has become lengthier and more involved over the last few years. It is the role of the lawyer representing the agency to be knowledgeable of the child welfare legislation and related statutes, the relevant case law, the procedural rules of the court, the rules of evidence, local practices and the evidence to be tendered.

Counsel on behalf of the agency must constantly keep in mind that they are representing a societal institution and that the adverse parties are individuals. There is a significant resource imbalance in a child welfare proceeding. An individual does not have access to, and cannot match, the resources of the state. This resource imbalance is partially responsible for the imposition of additional duties upon a lawyer representing an agency. The requirements of procedural fairness and expanded obligations of agency counsel help to maintain a level playing field. There are many practical and somewhat minor courtesies that counsel on behalf of the agency can extend in recognition of this imbalance, especially if there are unrepresented parties. Counsel on behalf of the agency can subpoena all proposed witnesses for a trial, attend to the production of documents and files for use in the proceeding by all parties, and take the lead with respect to pre-trial procedures and administrative issues. These are all means to help conserve the usually limited resources of the opposite parties that do not prejudice the agency's case.

Litigation is expensive and can impose significant financial hardship on the average person. Legal aid services generally provide for minimal preparation time and meager amounts for disbursements. To the extent possible, agency counsel should conduct the litigation in a manner designed to conserve the legal resources of the parent/guardian to allow a fair addressing of the substantive issues rather than drain resources on administrative and procedural matters.

Child welfare proceedings are not static litigation, but rather dynamic in the sense that the factual circumstances continue to evolve and change as the proceeding progresses, as services are accessed, and as understandings and positions change. Ordinarily litigation is conducted to adjudicate as to an historical event. Generally, litigation is retrospective whereas child welfare litigation is both retrospective and prospective in nature. It is the prospective aspect of child welfare legislation that mandates an ongoing evaluation of the factual underpinnings of the agency position and case plan. As part of the child welfare proceeding, often assessments are undertaken, expert opinions are sought, and services provided to remediate the identified issue or issues. The living circumstances of the parties can change as well as relationships. Throughout the entirety of the process the child continues to grow and develop. This dynamic and evolving nature of child welfare proceedings requires counsel to constantly reassess case plans.

Agency counsel also has a role with respect to the gathering and preservation of evidence. In many cases, relevant information is available from third party sources and counsel on behalf of the agency should actively pursue obtaining this information. Agency counsel should also ensure that relevant evidence is properly preserved for the benefit of all parties and the court.

It is the responsibility of agency counsel to ensure that the agency case is properly prepared for presentation at all stages of the proceeding. Agency counsel must ensure that both the statutory and procedural requisites have been satisfied, assess and clarify factual issues, and determine the evidence available to support the position of the agency. Competent preparation of the agency's case requires extensive pre-trial preparation. Counsel on behalf of the agency should, as part of their pre-trial preparation, prepare witnesses, particularly lay witnesses, for their attendance at court.

The presentation of the agency's case in court is the responsibility of counsel, and the agency workers and supervisors should defer to counsel with respect to decisions related to evidence presentation, examination and cross-examination of witnesses, and procedural matters. Counsel should be open with respect to decisions regarding the conduct of the case and responsive to agency questions.

It is essential that counsel is well organized, and have command and control over the file. Child welfare proceedings typically generate significant documentation and document management becomes critical. Proper document management can facilitate the administration of a file and case presentation; failure to properly manage documents wastes valuable resources including court time.

Counsel on behalf of the agency must aggressively pursue and ensure full disclosure to counsel for the parents and child. As part of this crucial process, evidentiary considerations arise. Social workers maintain recordings with respect to their files. The social work process is documented in the recordings, including consultations with counsel. These consultations are subject to solicitor-client privilege, and counsel on behalf of the agency should identify all matters over which solicitor-client privilege is being claimed.

Once a party is represented by counsel, opposing counsel cannot communicate directly with that individual. An important and practical issue arises in terms of communication between the social worker and counsel for the parent/guardian. Technically, opposing counsel should not communicate directly with the social worker except through agency counsel.[74] Strict adherence to this ethical guideline can be cumbersome. For example, if counsel on behalf of a parent/guardian wants to confirm access arrangements, it can be an unwieldy process for counsel to contact agency counsel who then contacts the social worker and subsequently provides the information to counsel for the parent/guardian. On matters that are of an administrative nature and not in issue in the proceeding, agency counsel should consider whether strict observance of this ethical guideline is a benefit or a burden. Agency counsel, however, should not directly communicate with parents who are represented, as there is a real power imbalance.

When disclosure is being provided, agency counsel needs to review all material to ensure that appropriate claims of "privilege," or exception from disclosure are advanced. An example of a possible privilege is disclosure of the identity of foster parents.[75] The agency is not obliged to disclose the identity of foster parents, and in some circumstances disclosure of this information may present safety concerns. Counsel on behalf of the agency must, in consultation with the agency, consider this issue. Similarly, whether the agency is going to advance the "confidential informant privilege" with respect to referral sources needs to be considered.[76] The confidential informant privilege has been extended to child welfare agencies for public policy reasons, to encourage the reporting of suspected child abuse.[77] In all circumstances, where information is provided by a third party source, agency counsel in consultation with the social worker needs to make a determination as to whether this privilege will be advanced. Often this will involve consideration of safety or relationship issues. If the decision is made to claim the privilege, then it should be asserted in very clear terms.

The court has discretion to award litigation costs in child welfare proceedings, but as a general rule, only exercises this discretion in exceptional circum-

---

[74] The Canadian Bar Association, *Code of Professional Conduct*, (Ottawa: Canadian Bar Association, 1998); on-line: Canadian Bar Association <http://www.cba.org/CBA/Epiigram/february2002/codeeng.pdf> (date accessed: 26 June 2002) at Chapter 16, Guiding Principle 8.

[75] *New Brunswick (Minister of Health and Community Services) v. C.(G.C.)*, [1998] 1 S.C.R. 1073.

[76] The "confidential informant privilege" was developed in the criminal law context. It means that the Crown is generally able to assert a privilege — refuse to disclose the identity — of an informant to the police if that person is not being called as a witness. The informant's identity is not relevant to the court proceeding, and disclosure might result in danger to that person, and make individuals reluctant to report to the authorities. See *R. v. Leipert*, [1997] 1 S.C.R. 281, and discussion in Chapter 2 about reporting child abuse.

[77] *D. v. National Society for the Prevention of Cruelty to Children*, [1977] 1 All E.R. 589 (H.L.); *Slavutych v. Baker*, [1976] 1 S.C.R. 254; *Payukaytano James and Hudson's Bay Family Services v. T.*, [1994] O.J. No. 921 (Gen. Div.).

stances.[78] Parents are, in practice, never required to pay the costs of the agency for child welfare litigation, and it is only in "exceptional circumstances" that the agency is required to pay a portion, or all, of the legal costs of a parent who is successful in court in a child welfare proceeding. Exceptional circumstances would include a lack of due diligence on the part of the agency, unreasonable or oppressive agency conduct, an abuse of process, or agency intervention without sufficient evidence or investigation. It is axiomatic to state that counsel for the agency should act to identify such conduct and assist the agency with remediation and prevention.

Administrative

Counsel on behalf of the agency should develop mechanisms to keep agency staff abreast of the current status of the law and any relevant statutory and case law developments. If possible, agency counsel should be actively involved in staff training so as to minimize the disconnect between training and the realities of the legal process. This would also familiarize the lawyer with the caseworkers' training and assist the lawyer in incorporating the training in case presentation. Lawyers can contribute to the training of social workers in the effective gathering and presentation of their evidence.

A lawyer's experience in child welfare practice may be such that their views on policy matters may be of benefit to the agency. In such circumstances the lawyer is not providing strictly legal advice, but offering the benefit of experience.

Conclusion

Child protection caseworkers practice in a defined legal context. The responsibilities and authority of child protection agencies and caseworkers is governed by the child welfare legislation. The legal context is the foundation for the social work process in child protection matters and the relationship of the agency with counsel. The lawyer and social worker, although coming from different professions, share a common purpose in child welfare matters. The partnership of lawyer and social worker is most effective when the training, skills and experience that each has to offer is recognized and utilized.

---

[78] *Winnipeg Children & Family Services (Northwest Area) v. H.(A.M.)* (2002), 24 R.F.L. (5th) 199 (Man. C.A.); *Children's Aid Society of Algoma v. M.(R.)* (2001), 18 R.F.L. (5th) 36 (Ont. Ct. Jus.); *Children's Aid Society of Brant v. D.M.C.*, [1997] O.J. No. 3145 (Prov. Div.). See discussion in Chapters 3 and 13.

9

Abuse and Neglect Allegations in the Context of Parental Separation

Nicholas Bala[1]

The High Conflict Parental Separation

Even without allegations of abuse or neglect, if parents separate, disputes over the care of their children are emotionally charged and difficult for the parents, children and any professionals involved. If there are allegations of parental abuse or neglect, the emotional tension, bitterness and complexity of a case are invariably heightened. The *Canadian Incidence Study of Reported Child Abuse and Neglect* reported that in over 10% of all child protection investigations, the child protection worker noted that there was an ongoing dispute between separated parents over the arrangements for the care of their children.[2] These cases are among the most challenging for all of the professionals involved: child protection workers, lawyers, judges, police, physicians and mental health professionals. Investigations in these cases tend to be complex, and court proceedings often result in bitterly contested trials.

While many abuse or neglect allegations made after parents have separated are founded, this is a context in which there is a relatively high proportion of allegations that are unfounded. In some cases of unfounded allegations of abuse, the accuser may be deliberately fabricating the allegation. However, it is more common for the accusing parents to honestly believe what they are alleging. Distrust or hostility may result in misunderstandings and unfounded allegations, especially in cases where the children involved are young and the allegations are reported through a parent. Some cases of unfounded allegations may be the product of the emotional disturbance of the accusing parent.

The prospect of a child being forced to live with or visit an abusive parent is understandably horrific, which may tend to make some professionals want to "err on the side of caution" if there is uncertainty about whether abuse has occurred. It must, however, be appreciated that children also suffer if an unfounded allegation is treated as valid by the child welfare authorities or the

---

[1] Nicholas Bala is Professor of Law, Queen's University, Kingston, Ontario. Parts of this chapter are substantially revised from the chapter in the first edition of this book by Mary-Jo Maur Raycroft.

[2] N. Trocmé, B. MacLaurin, B. Fallon, J. Daciuk, D. Billingsley, M. Tourigny, M. Mayer, J. Wright, K. Barter, G. Burford, J. Hornick, R. Sullivan, and B. McKenzie, *Canadian Incidence Study of Reported Child Abuse and Neglect: Final Report* (Ottawa, ON: Health Canada, 2001).

justice system. Not only does a false allegation profoundly affect the child's relationship with the wrongly accused parent, but it also results in an intrusive investigation. Further, not infrequently in a false allegation situation, the child may come to believe that abuse occurred, and consequently may suffer induced emotional trauma.

Understandably, parents who are falsely accused of abuse often have a hostile attitude to professionals who may have been involved in bringing forward unfounded allegations, even if the professionals acted in an appropriate fashion. Unfortunately, in some cases some of the professionals involved may not have acted in an acceptable fashion, becoming inappropriately allied with one parent and failing to conduct a fair and careful investigation or reach a fair decision.

It is often very difficult to conduct an investigation into allegations of abuse in the context of parental separation. While there are legitimate concerns about *the possibility* that accusing parents or children may be lying or mistaken in their allegations, those who have abused children *usually* falsely deny or minimize their abuse. Abusers are only likely to admit their wrongdoing if confronted by irrefutable evidence. In most cases there is no clear forensic evidence that can prove or disprove the allegation, and there may be a welter of conflicting claims.

Once the issue of abuse is raised, a number of agencies with differing mandates may become involved, such as police, child protection and assessment clinics. There may be a number of different mental health professionals and social workers involved in a case, with differing roles and levels of expertise, and with conflicting opinions about the case. While some of the professionals and investigators are highly skilled, there are also cases in which some of the professionals involved may lack skill and objectivity, contributing to the making of unfounded allegations.

One of the most challenging outcomes for child protection workers can be the "unverified but ongoing concerns" case. Not infrequently, especially if the children involved are young, there may not be sufficient evidence to convince the court that the child was abused or neglected, but the worker will have concerns, either that the allegations *might* be true, or that even if the original allegations are unfounded, there may be serious concerns about the child's welfare.

Before considering some of the challenging issues that arise in dealing with allegations of abuse or neglect in the context of parental separation, it will be useful to consider some of the broader issues that arise when parents separate.

The Resolution of Disputes between Separated Parents

If the parents of a child separate or divorce, or if the parents have never lived together, an arrangement must be made for the custody (or care) of the child. There will usually also be an arrangement for access or visitation, that is, visits between the child and the non-custodial parent. Custody and access issues may be the subject of an informal arrangement between the parents, a formal written separation agreement, or a court order that can be made with or without the consent of the parents. All Canadian provinces and territories have legislation governing custody applications, and the federal *Divorce Act* has similar provisions. These statutes stipulate that custody and access disputes are to be decided on the basis of the "best interests" of the child.[3]

In most cases parents can work out a mutually satisfactory set of arrangements about the care of children and visitation without too much acrimony. About one-fifth of all cases of separation are "high-conflict" situations, where the parents have continuing high levels of acrimony and difficulty in making arrangements about the children. Some of these high-conflict cases may be resolved with the assistance of a mediator or through negotiations by lawyers, but some must be resolved by a judge. Allegations of abuse or neglect often arise in cases that were already high-conflict situations. Even if it was not a high conflict situation before the allegation was made, there is likely to be a great deal of tension and difficulty in resolving a case once the allegation arises.

Resolving Parental Disputes: Terms and Concepts

It is useful to understand some of the terms and concepts commonly used in family law proceedings involving parents who are separated or divorced. The discussion that follows uses the terms and concepts that are applied at the time of writing, in particular the terms "custody," "access" and "joint custody."

The traditional concepts of "custody" and "access" have been criticized, and amendments to the *Divorce Act*[4] have been proposed. The amendments would make use of new concepts, such as the "parenting order," which would allow provision to be made for "parenting time" (where the child will live and how much time the child will spend with each parent), and for the division or sharing of decision-making responsibility. Any new legislation would retain the "best interests of the child" as the central decision-making test. New legal concepts, if enacted, would have an effect on many of the disputes between separated parents, encouraging more emphasis on shared parenting after separation. However, the new legislation would be unlikely to have any effect on the very high conflict cases that arise when there are allegations of abuse or neglect; a parent alleged to have abused or neglected the child would be unlikely to have unsupervised "parenting time" or any decision-making responsibilities until the allegations are resolved.

Custody and Access

A person having "sole custody" of a child has the right to make decisions regarding the child, including those related to the child's education, health, religion and day-to-day schedule, without having to obtain the consent of the other parent.

---

[3] *Divorce Act*, S.C. 1986, c. 4, s. 16(1). In Ontario, for example, *Children's Law Reform Act*, R.S.O. 1990, c. C.12, s. 21.

[4] Bill C-22, 2nd Reading February 25, 2003. Not enacted.

"Access" is the right to visit a child who is in the legal custody of another person. It means the non-custodial parent, or sometimes another relative such as a grandparent, may visit with the child, usually at regular intervals for specified periods of time. A typical access arrangement may allow visits every second weekend and half of holiday periods, though arrangements for more or less access are also common. If the parents are able to communicate effectively, access orders or agreements may simply provide for "reasonable access," meaning the parents arrange access visits suitable for themselves and the children, varying the arrangements according to their needs.

Access usually includes the right to receive information from the appropriate agencies about the education, health and welfare of the child. This means a person with access may contact professionals involved with a child, such as teachers and doctors, and is entitled to obtain the same reports from these professionals as the custodial parent.

In some situations, particularly those where abuse allegations are under investigation or have been substantiated, access may be supervised. Supervised access is usually pursuant to a court order, and means the visits between the person with access and the child must be supervised by some other person or organization. The supervising person may be another relative, such as a grandparent, or may even be the custodial parent. In an increasing number of communities, there are agencies with a specific mandate to supervise access.

Joint Custody (or Shared Parenting)

Joint custody (or shared parenting) refers to a range of different arrangements under which there will continue to be a high level of involvement by both parents in the lives of their children after separation. The parents or court may fashion any reasonable arrangement that involves sharing of parental responsibility. In some cases the child spends roughly equal amounts of time with each parent, and the parents will jointly decide about all issues relating to the child: this is known as "joint physical custody" and is relatively rare. More common is "joint legal custody," an arrangement under which the child will have a "primary residence" with one parent and frequent contact with the other parent, while the parents will both continue to jointly make major decisions about the child.

Joint custody is usually appropriate only when the parents are able to put aside other differences and concentrate on the children without any unnecessary argument. It is not appropriate in situations where there are abuse or neglect allegations, or in cases involving high conflict or spousal abuse.

Joint custody used to be arranged only with the parents' agreement, and traditionally judges were most reluctant to impose joint custody on separated or divorced parents. Now that more fathers participate in their children's upbringing, some judges are prepared to order joint custody despite the objections of either or both parents, but only if the judge thinks that there are good prospects that the parents will actually be able to co-operate in the care of their child.

Best Interests of the Child

The test used by a court to resolve custody or access disputes between parents is a determination of what will be in the "best interests of the child."[5] This "family law" approach requires an assessment of the needs of the individual child, and the strengths and weaknesses of each adult seeking custody or access. The test is vague, but it permits the court to come to a resolution that will suit each individual child. The "best interests" test gives a court broad discretion to consider any factor that will affect the welfare of the child. In general, the courts consider factors such as: the emotional ties a child has to each parent; the child's preferences; the length of time a child has been in one parent's custody; and the abilities of the competing adults to care for the child. Generally the courts will be reluctant to separate siblings, though this can happen. The parenting capacity of new partners must also be considered. The judge must listen to all of the evidence, then decide what is best for the child, not what will make the parents, or even the child, happy.

While in some cases the best interests test is difficult to apply, it is clear that if one parent is found by a court to have abused a child, it would not be in the child's best interests to reside with that parent, and a court is very likely to severely restrict or terminate that parent's contact with the child.

Interim and Final Custody Orders

In cases in which there is a higher level of conflict between the parents, the courts are likely to be involved in making decisions about the child.

At the time of initial separation one or both parents may make an application to the court for "interim custody." In other words, they ask the court to decide who will have care of the child until there can be a full trial or an agreement can be negotiated, a process that could go on for many months. Interim applications for custody, support and exclusive possession of the home are generally resolved relatively quickly, and oral evidence is seldom heard by the court at this interim stage. The judge's decision at the interim hearing is usually based on affidavits (sworn written statements) from the parents and other individuals whose evidence may be important. The crucial decision of interim custody is often made close to the time of separation.

While interim orders are made without much time for judicial consideration, they are often in practice determinative to the final outcome of a parental custody dispute. The parent who obtains interim custody will typically have a better opportunity to develop a strong relationship with the child and formulate a

---

[5] The term "best interests of the child" is also used in most child protection statutes. When used in the context of a dispute between parents, the court will decide what it considers to be "best" for the child. There is no onus on in favour of either parent. In the child protection context, however, if a child is found to be in need of protection, there is still a general presumption that the child should remain with the biological parents, under the supervision of the agency, and there is an onus on the agency to establish that it is in the "best interests" of a child to be removed from parental care and to justify the agency's intrusion into the family.

sound plan of the care for the child, and will have a good argument at trial about the need to maintain "stability" in the child's life.

The longer a child remains with one parent and has no major problems, the more likely that a judge will decide that the child should remain permanently in the care of that parent. Since the judge is usually loathe to disrupt a child's situation without good reasons, the decision at an interim hearing can have a tremendous impact upon the outcome of a final hearing. In practice, relatively few parental disputes actually result in trials, with many cases being settled by the parents on the basis of the interim arrangement.

Variation

An important feature of any legal order or agreement concerning the care of a child is that it is always subject to variation if it no longer serves the "best interests" of the child.

In cases where parents have a reasonably good relationship, it is not uncommon for them to informally vary the arrangements for the care of the child as the child's needs and circumstances change. One parent cannot unilaterally vary custody or access arrangements, and must seek the agreement of the other parent or apply to the court for variation of the earlier order. However, if there are serious abuse concerns a parent may temporarily suspend the previous arrangements in order to protect the child, provided that the parent brings an application to seek a speedy judicial confirmation of the fact that there are serious abuse concerns, and that this type of action is justified.

If a child protection worker has serious abuse concerns, this may justify apprehending the child or commencing a child protection application, in which case any action taken under child welfare legislation will supercede an existing order for custody or access.

Child Representation

As discussed in Chapter 8, it is common in some Canadian jurisdictions for the child to have independent legal representation in a contested child protection case. Though not occurring in as large a portion of the parental separation cases, in provinces such as Ontario and Quebec it is not uncommon for a child who is the subject of a contested dispute between parents to have a lawyer appointed to represent the interests of the child. This lawyer will almost always be paid by the government, and may be a staff lawyer or in private practice.

Assessments

When there is a dispute between parents concerning the care of their children, it is often useful to have an assessment conducted by a mental health professional to help to determine what is in the "best interests" of the children. Assessments may be prepared at the request of one party, who retains the assessor, or at the request of both parties, in which case they jointly select an assessor. An assessment may also be ordered by the court, in which case the assessment might be done by a court-affiliated clinic or by an assessor appointed by the judge, often acting with the consent of the parties.

These assessments and the resulting reports may be completed by psychiatrists, psychologists or social workers. The person who prepares the report may be called as a witness at an eventual trial, and subjected to examination in court. Assessments can be very useful, and frequently are the basis of a negotiated settlement between the parties. They are also influential if a case goes to trial, though the courts have indicated that they are not obliged to follow the recommendations in an assessment report.

In most disputes between parents, the assessment will focus on the arrangements for the care of the child that, in the assessor's opinion, is in the best interests of the child. However, as discussed below, if there is an allegation of abuse, the assessment process may be more complex and will tend to focus on the veracity of the allegation.

Professionals who prepare reports for disputes between parents will not infrequently also prepare assessment reports for child protection proceedings as well. The assessment process and reports are similar for these two types of cases, though in a dispute between parents there tends to be more emphasis on the wishes and views of the child, and an assessment for a child protection case is more likely to focus on the parent's capacity to meet minimal parenting standards.[6]

Separation Agreements and Parenting Plans

In many cases parents are able to make mutually satisfactory arrangements for the care of their children and to resolve other legal issues, such as the division of property and child support. These arrangements may, usually with the assistance of lawyers, be embodied in a formal legal document known as a separation agreement, which is signed by the parties and may be a legally enforceable domestic contract.

In some cases a mediator may meet with both parties to try to help them reach an agreement about the care of their children and other issues. The mediator is a neutral professional, who may be a person with a background in social work or law, with training in the facilitation of dispute resolution. The mediator is not representing either party, and if an agreement is reached, the parties should each be referred for independent legal advice before signing a separation agreement.

Increasingly, separated parents are formulating "parenting plans" as part of the process of negotiating a separation agreement. Parenting plans focus

---

[6] See e.g., American Psychological Assoc., Committee on Professional Practice and Standards, *Guidelines for Psychological Evaluation in Child Protection Matters* (Washington D.C., 1998); and K. Budd, "Assessing Parenting Competence in Child Protection Cases: A Clinical Practice Model" (2001), 4 *Clinical Child and Psychology Review* 1-18. See also N. Bala and A. Saunders, "Understanding the Family Law Context: Why the Law of Expert Evidence is Different in Family Law Cases" (2003), 20 *Canadian Family Law Quarterly* 277-338.

specifically on the needs and care of the child, and may, for example, deal with recreation, religion, education and health care, as well as contact with each parent. Parenting plans are intended to be varied over time as a child's needs and circumstances change. The process of discussion and the development of better communication skills that lead to the formulation of a parenting plan may be as important, or more important, than the document which is finally prepared. Mediators may be involved in the negotiation of a parenting plan, and there are also materials available to help parents formulate these plans.

In many centres there are programs that offer parents a few hours of lectures on the effects of separation on their children, and that provide some information about the legal issues that arise. These programs may, for example, be jointly taught by a lawyer and a social worker, and will explain such options as parenting plans and mediation.

The Role of the Child Protection Agency

If an allegation of abuse or neglect is made in the context of parental separation, it is likely the local child protection agency will become involved in the case. Indeed, there will usually be a legal obligation to report the suspected abuse or neglect to the agency for investigation.

The period following a separation is often one of tremendous instability for one or both parents. Investigations of allegations of abuse in the context of custody and access disputes can be extremely difficult, and may be rendered more difficult by the atmosphere of mistrust and hostility. Allegations and counter-allegations may be made, leaving the protection worker to decide whether the evidence supports or refutes those allegations.

In some cases a parent will report a very clear allegation of abuse or neglect to the agency, typically stating that the child made a disclosure to the reporting parent. In other cases, one parent may have suspicions that the other parent is abusing or neglecting based on a child's behaviour or vague statements from the child, but because of poor communication between the estranged parents is unable to determine the validity of these concerns, and will contact the agency to report the suspicions in the expectation that the agency may be able to determine what has happened.

The inherent difficulties of cases in which there is an allegation of abuse or neglect in the context of parental separation may make child protection workers reluctant to get involved, hoping that the parents may be able to resolve the situation without the agency having to "take sides." Child protection agencies, however, have a legal responsibility to investigate whenever there is an allegation of parental abuse or neglect. In some cases the agency may decide that it is appropriate to bring a child protection application, or to contact the police in order to initiate an investigation to determine whether a prosecution should be commenced. In other cases the agency might decide, after conducting an investigation, that it is not appropriate to commence child protection proceedings, though the worker may continue to monitor the situation and may be called upon to testify by one of the parties to a custody or access dispute between the parents.

Child protection legislation has a different purpose than the statutes that govern disputes between parents. The function of child protection agencies is to protect children from harm, and to interfere in the lives of parents and children only when the standard of parental care falls below the minimum acceptable standard in the community. Accordingly, child protection agencies are usually permitted to intervene only if the child has, in fact, been harmed, or if there is a substantial risk that such harm is likely to result if the child remains in the home.

The issues in a child protection case are, in theory, different from those that arise in disputes between parents. In a child protection case, the question is: Will this child be at serious risk of substantial harm if left in the care of the parent or parents? By contrast, in a contest between parents the question is: Where is it in the child's best interests to live? In child protection litigation, a court is largely restricted to choosing between a parent and the state with its appointed care-givers, though there may also be some flexibility to place a child in the care of another relative, like a grandparent, but under agency supervision.

If a parent has rights under an order that was made in litigation between the parents, and an order of a court is made through child protection proceedings, the child protection order will supercede the order determining rights between the parents, since the child protection court has an overriding duty to protect children.[7] Thus, for example, if one parent has the right to visit or have care of the child at specified times under an order made in litigation involving the other parent, that order may in effect be suspended or even terminated by a later child protection proceeding.

Parental Disputes Raising Abuse Issues

In the context of parental separation, there are relatively high rates of unfounded allegations of parental abuse or neglect. In many cases the unfounded allegations are made by an estranged former partner, though grand-parents and other relatives also make unfounded allegations. Some of the most difficult cases to investigate involve sexual abuse allegations, usually with the mother alleging that the father has abused the child during access visits, though often it is the father who is alleging that the mother, or more commonly her new partner, is abusing the child.[8]

In some cases of unfounded allegations of abuse in the context of parental separation, there is deliberate fabrication by the accusing parent, who may be seeking revenge or hoping for a tactical advantage in custody or access

---

[7] See e.g., *Re J.D.* (1978), 5 R.F.L. (2d) 209 (Ont. Prov. Ct.) where the court recognized that the "special supervisory jurisdiction" under child protection legislation may supercede or extinguish parental rights under ordinary custody or access orders.

[8] N. Bala and J. Schuman, "Allegations of Sexual Abuse When Parents Have Separated" (2000), 17 *Canadian Family Law Quarterly* 191-241.

litigation. Less commonly an adolescent child who is seeking to manipulate the situation or is angry towards a parent or step-parent may make a false allegation.

In most cases of unfounded allegations, however, the allegation is made in good faith, and the allegation is a result of a legitimate misunderstanding or some form of miscommunication. These are often cases in which the atmosphere of mistrust, a common element in many separations, results in one parent misinterpreting what may be innocent actions by the other parent, and alleging sexual abuse.

There is, for example, the potential for a young child's memories about what occurred during visits with the father to have been influenced by suggestive and repeated questions by a well-intentioned but unduly suspicious mother, asking the child about visits with the father. Young children may be pressured by a parent into supporting a false allegation, or may become confused as to what really occurred as a result of repeated or highly suggestive questioning by a parent. In some cases, an accusing parent may be suffering from a mental or emotional disturbance which may cause a false report.

It can be very difficult to conduct an investigation into allegations of sexual abuse in the context of parental separation. In most cases the allegations involve fondling rather than penetration, or occurred long before investigators are called in. As a result there is usually no clear forensic evidence that can prove or disprove the allegation, and there may a welter of conflicting claims.

Investigations of abuse allegations in this type of case are especially difficult because the alleged perpetrator will often have legitimate reasons for touching and being touched by a child. With young children, for example, a parent will have regular occasion to touch a chld's genitalia for purposes of washing or diapering. Even with older children, a parent will frequently be touching the child. The determination of whether a touching was "sexual" requires an assessment of intent; it may be very difficult for an investigator or judge to make that determination based on the evidence available. There is usually no conclusive physical evidence, nor is there a valid psychological test or profile that can conclusively determine whether an accuser, an accused or a child is telling the truth about an allegation.

Despite studies suggesting that there is a higher incidence of unfounded and deliberately false reports of abuse and neglect in the context of parental separation, it is wrong to dismiss an allegation simply because it arises in this context. Even in the context of parental separation, there are many true allegations.

In some cases, it is only after separation has occurred that a child will feel that incidents of abuse can be safely revealed, with the offending parent out of the home. In other cases, after separation, a parent (usually the father) without an adult sexual partner may feel especially lonely and needy, which may result in the sexual exploitation of the innocent physical affection of his child. The difficult job of investigators and the courts is to distinguish the true allegation from the false.

Interim Orders When Abuse Allegations Are Made

The decision about interim arrangements is always significant, but it is even more important in cases where a parent is alleged to have committed child sexual abuse. In these types of disputes between parents, at the interim hearing the lawyers will generally try to present at least a summary of all the available evidence in order to substantiate or discredit the allegation of abuse. If an allegation of abuse is made and a judge has reasonable grounds to believe it is true, it is likely that at the interim stage the accused parent will be denied contact with the child, or will only have supervised access.

If there are reasonable grounds to believe that a non-custodial parent has been abusing a child during access visits, a custodial parent has the right, and even the duty, to suspend access until the allegation can be investigated or the matter brought to court for at least an interim hearing. If a child protection agency is involved, the agency will often advise the immediate suspension of access pending full investigation.[9] If there is no order made by a judge in the family law proceedings that suspends or supervises access, and the accused parent is not willing to "voluntarily" agree to a suspension of visits, a protection application may be brought by the agency.

When there is an allegation of abuse, especially of sexual abuse, at the interim stage of the family law proceeding, many judges will tend to "err on the side of caution" after the allegation is made and pending a full trial.[10] Interim hearings are generally decided on the basis of affidavits from parents and from any investigators or others who have been involved in the case. It is often difficult for an alleged abuser to challenge the validity of an accusation at this stage.

There are, however, reported cases in which judges have decided even at the interim stage that the evidence to support the allegation is so weak that unsupervised access may continue.[11] Judges are most prepared to allow unsupervised interim access to continue if there has been an assessment by a competent independent assessor, or an investigation by child protection workers or the police, that indicates that the allegations are unfounded.[12]

---

[9] See e.g., *B.M. v. N.G.W.*, [1998] O.J. 297, 36 R.F.L. (4th) 249 (Ont. Gen. Div.); see also comments of L'Heureux-Dubé J. in *Young v. Young* (1993), 49 R.F.L. (3d) 117 (S.C.C.).

[10] See e.g., *S.S. v. A.S.*, [1987] W.D.F.L. 897 (Ont. S.C.) per M. Cork and Zarb, "Allegations of Sexual Abuse in Custody and Access Disputes" (1994), 12 *Canadian Journal of Family Law* 91 at 100; and J. Wilson, "The Ripple Effect of the Sexual Abuse Allegation and Representation of the Protecting Parent" (1987), 1 *Canadian Family Law Quarterly* 138 at 160.

[11] For examples of cases where the judge concluded at the interim stage that the allegation of sexual abuse was unfounded and allowed unsupervised access, see *Flanigan v. Murphy* (1985), 31 A.C.W.S. (2d) 448 (Ont. S.C.), per M. Cork; and *B.J.A.B. v. K.J.R.* (1996), 21 R.F.L. (4th) 401 (Ont. Gen. Div.) per Aston J.

[12] See e.g., *Ingles v. Watt* (2000), 13 R.F.L. (5th) 399 (Ont. Sup. Ct.), per Greer J; and *Huxtable v. Huxtable* (2001), 17 R.F.L. (5th) 82 (Ont. Sup. Ct.) per Mossip J.

The Investigation: Child Protection, Police and Assessments

A report to a child protection agency of abuse or neglect made in the context of parental separation should be treated with the same seriousness as any other allegation, though these cases may require an especially careful, thorough and unbiased investigation. The investigators need to consider not only the circumstances of the child and the accused parent, but also must consider the possibility that the accusing parent is acting out of spite, or that there has been an honest mistake or even that the accusing parent is suffering from a mental or emotional disturbance. The investigator also requires great sensitivity in interviewing the child.

If an allegation of abuse, sexual or otherwise, arises in the course of an ongoing dispute between parents, there may be a number of investigations carried out simultaneously. The child protection agency may initiate an investigation using one of its workers, the police may be investigating potential criminal charges, and one or both parents may have started investigating the problem using independently retained experts.

It can be confusing for the child and parents if there are several investigations proceeding simultaneously, and the child may find repeated interviews by different professionals to be very intrusive. In most communities there are now child abuse investigation protocols, which are guidelines for child protection workers, police investigators and other professionals on how to jointly investigate an allegation of abuse or neglect. These protocols are premised on the principles that the investigation is to be unbiased and that interviews with the child are to be conducted sensitively, and that those questioning the child should avoid asking leading or suggestive questions. These protocols emphasize the importance of minimizing the number of intrusive interviews to which a child is subjected.

Typically the protocols require that, whenever possible, a police officer and child protection worker will interview the child together. There is generally an expectation that investigative interviews with the child will be videotaped, so that the tape can be used in court and shared with other professionals so as to minimize the number of times that the child must be interviewed.

Usually the police will take the lead in the forensic investigation, and in particular they will want to be the first to conduct interviews with the accused parent. Police have training in conducting interviews with those suspected of criminal acts. The police are aware of the requirements of the criminal law for ensuring that the rights of the suspect are respected so that any confession that is made is admissible in a later criminal trial, and they also have training in applying a range of questioning techniques that are likely to induce a confession.

In some cases it may be relatively easy to demonstrate that the opinion of one "expert" should be discounted. For example, an opinion may be of little value if the assessor or investigator lacks expertise and experience with the special issues that arise with child sexual abuse allegations in the context of parental separation. Another reason to discount an opinion (especially in this type of case) is if the professional has been involved in a therapeutic relationship with one *parent*, and hence is not in a position to present an unbiased position about whether or not the *child* has been abused.[13]

In some cases an officially "independent" investigator, like a child protection worker, may become "allied" with one parent (often the accusing parent, who is usually the first person to get in contact with an investigator). A biased investigator may, for example, behave in an unfair or unprofessional manner with the other parent (often the accused parent).[14] In this situation, the evidence of an investigator is likely to be discounted.

When professionals demonstrate the most obvious and serious professional bias and incompetence, they may face civil liability and discipline from their profession for their negligence. More commonly, their involvement does not entail civil liability, but it causes needless anguish and expense to the family. If the agency workers are biased in the way that they conduct an investigation and then bring an unsuccessful protection application, the agency may be liable to pay the costs of the falsely accused parent. Even if no protection application is commenced, it is possible for a child protection agency to be held civilly liable for damages in negligence in carrying out an investigation that results in a parent being falsely accused of sexually abusing his or her child. However, such suits rarely succeed as it is necessary to demonstrate that the agency was both negligent *and* acting in bad faith when it was treating the parent unfairly.[15]

An assessor or other mental health professional who testifies in court cannot be sued in negligence or slander *for their testimony*. Testimony in court is generally viewed as "privileged" and cannot be the basis for a civil suit.[16] However, if the professional has acted in a professionally inappropriate fashion, discipline sanctions may result. There may also be situations in which an assessor or therapist is liable for slander if the professional inappropriately circulates unfounded reports of abuse in the community.[17]

In some cases a man accused of sexually abusing a child may volunteer to undergo phallometric testing (also called penile plethysmograph testing).

---

[13] See e.g., *M.K. v. P.M.*, [1996] O.J. 3212 (Gen. Div.).

[14] See e.g., *L.T.K. v. M.J.K.*, [1991] O.J. 1381 (Ont. Prov. Div.) where Pickett Prov. J. rejected the opinion of the staff at a hospital child abuse clinic that a two-and-a-half-year-old child had been sexually abused by her father during an access visit. A physical examination by the physicians did not produce evidence of abuse (though that is not unusual even if the child has been abused), and the only source of the "disclosure" was through the mother. The assessors never interviewed the father and the judge characterized the staff as "anything but fair and open-minded." They "grossly over-interpreted innocent behaviour" such as how the child played with anatomically correct dolls.

[15] *D.B. v. C.A.S. of Durham Region*, [1994] O.J. 643, varied (1996) 136 D.L.R. (4th) 297 (Ont. C.A.) is the only reported Canadian case where a falsely accused parent succeeded in such a suit, recovering $85,000 from the agency. The court was satisfied that the child protection worker had clearly allied herself with the mother who made the unfounded allegation and that the agency had treated the father unfairly in the course of the investigation.

[16] *Carnahan v. Coates* (1990), 27 R.F.L. (3d) 366 (B.C.S.C.).

[17] *R.G. v. Christison* (1996), 150 Sask. R. 1, 31 C.C.L.T. (2d) 263, 25 R.F.L. (4th) 51 (Sask. Q.B.), varied with respect to costs (1997), 153 Sask. R. 311 (Q.B.).

Phallometric testing is used to measure a man's sexual response to photographs of people, including children, in various sexual and non-sexual positions, by monitoring minute physiological responses of the penis through use of electrodes. While this type of testing may be of some value in assessing the effectiveness of treatment of known pedophiles, its reliability as a diagnostic tool is much more doubtful,[18] especially in cases of allegations of post-separation abuse where the suspected abuse is likely to be "situational" rather than a reflection of pedophilic sexual preferences.

In some cases of post-separation allegations of abuse, the accused parent will offer to take a polygraph ("lie detector") test.[19] Although polygraph results are clearly not admissible in a criminal case, in family law cases there is a less stringent approach to evidentiary issues. Some judges in family law cases are prepared to admit polygraph results as corroborative of other evidence, though other judges are not.[20] Even if not admissible in court, polygraph results (or even the offer to take a polygraph test) may affect how investigators and assessors view a case.

Concurrent Proceedings

It should be appreciated that even after a thorough investigation, a child protection worker, police officer or mental health professional may be uncertain about whether abuse truly occurred. The conclusion of an investigation may range from certainty that abuse occurred to certainty that it did not. Sometimes the findings will fall between the extremes, with investigators only having a probability-based belief, or even frankly acknowledging that the investigation is inconclusive.

With parental separation involving an abuse allegation, there is the potential for a criminal prosecution, a child protection application and family law litigation between the parents to be proceeding at the same time in different courts, adding to complexity and expense. In practice, however, criminal or child protection proceedings are most likely in cases where there is the clearest evidence of more serious abuse, in which case there is less likelihood of a parental family law dispute reaching the trial stage. On the other hand, cases where there is more uncertainty of whether abuse occurred are most likely to be resolved in family law proceedings.

Criminal prosecutions will generally be undertaken only in cases where there is a high degree of certainty that a child was abused or seriously neglected, and that the identity of the perpetrator can be established. If a criminal prosecution

---

[18] *R. v. J.J.*, [2000] 2 S.C.R. 600, [2000] S.C.J. No. 52, 2000 SCC 51 at para 25.

[19] S. Morris, "Abuse Allegations: A Child's Story, A Lawyer's Nightmare," [Summer 1996] *Compleat Lawyer* 20-25.

[20] *C.(R.M.) v. C.(J.R.)* (1995), 12 R.F.L. (4th) 440 (B.C.S.C.) Edwards J.; and *L.(C.M.) v. T.(R.)* (2000), 8 R.F.L. (4th) 288 (Sask. Q.B.), per McLellan J.admitted polygraph evidence in a family law case involving sexual abuse allegations, but this type of evidence was not admitted in *S.(B.) v. T.(R.)* (2002), 25 R.F.L. (5th) 185 (Nfld. U.F.C.). In a criminal prosecution, the results of a polygraph test results are clearly inadmissible *(R. v. Beland*, [1987] 2 S.C.R. 398.).

occurs, the Crown prosecutor will take the lead in presenting the case. While the accusing parent and child are likely to be witnesses in the criminal prosecution, the Crown prosecutor will decide whether and how the case is to be dealt with, and is not "representing" either the parent or the child in criminal court. A conviction will only be obtained in criminal court if there is proof established under the relatively narrow criminal evidence laws, beyond a reasonable doubt, that a particular person has perpetrated a crime.

Canadian data suggest that in cases in which child protection workers investigate an allegation by a custodial mother of suspected abuse by a non-custodial father during visits, the police were called to investigate in under one-third of the cases, and charges were laid in fewer than one case in ten.[21]

If criminal charges are laid, they will tend to "dominate" the resolution of any family law proceedings, at least until the criminal charges are resolved. A common condition of the release of the accused in the community on bail pending a criminal trial is the denial of contact with the alleged victim, or at least close supervision of visits. In some cases, the criminal court judge will release the accused on bail with a condition that there be no contact with the child unless that contact is permitted by the order of the family law judge.

If there are simultaneous criminal and family law proceedings, the person accused of abuse will often have separate lawyers for each proceeding, though it is highly desirable for these two lawyers to communicate and coordinate their efforts. Defence counsel in the criminal case will generally be very reluctant to allow a person charged with a criminal offence to testify in a civil case that deals with the same issues, and will generally want any civil proceedings to be adjourned until the criminal case is resolved. If the accused files an affidavit or testifies in the civil case, for example for an interim access application, the Crown prosecutor may use any inconsistencies between that affidavit and testimony in a later criminal trial to impeach the credibility of the accused. Similarly, if the accusing parent testifies in the criminal trial, any inconsistencies between that testimony and evidence in a later family law trial may be used to impeach the credibility of that person in the civil case.

If the accused is convicted of abuse in the criminal trial, a judge in a later family law trial is very likely to regard the criminal conviction as establishing the abuse occurred. If the accused is convicted of a child abuse related offence in a criminal trial, at a subsequent civil trial, considerations of public policy may be invoked to preclude further inquiry into the issue of whether abuse occurred.[22] In theory, the fact that a person abused a child is not determinative of whether it is in the "best interests" of the child to lose contact with the perpetrator. However,

---

[21] N. Trocmé, *Ontario Incidence Study of Reported Child Abuse and Neglect* (Toronto, ON: Institute for the Prevention of Child Abuse, 1994).

[22] *Toronto (City) v. C.U.P.E. Local 79* (2001), 55 O.R. (3d) 541 (C.A.) articulated the view that considerations of "public policy" ordinarily prevent a person who has been convicted in criminal proceedings of abusing a child from relitigating the issue of whether he in fact abused the child in later civil proceedings. The Court of Appeal emphasized the desirability of bringing finality to the issue, as well as concern about limiting the number of occasions on which a victim might be required to testify.

if there has been a criminal conviction for child abuse, this will significantly reduce the likelihood that there will be a family law hearing dealing with the care of the child, as the abuser is likely to be considered unfit to have contact with the child.

While a criminal conviction for child abuse will often result in the termination of contact with the child, a judge in a family law case must still consider whether it is in the "best interests" of a child to continue or resume contact. Children who have been sexually or physically abused by a parent will often feel an attachment to that parent, despite the abuse. A family law court may allow contact with a convicted abuser if it is satisfied that this is in the child's best interests. The judge should be satisfied that the child will not be at risk, which may require supervision (especially at first) and evidence of the abuser having undergone treatment that will reduce the likelihood of future abuse. The judge should be satisfied that the visits will actually promote the welfare of the child, and will not simply allow contact based on some notion of parental rights.[23]

The fact that an alleged abuser is not charged or is tried and acquitted in criminal court is not binding on a judge in a civil proceeding. It is not uncommon for an alleged abuser to be acquitted in criminal court and then have the issues of abuse relitigated in the context of a family law trial, where the rules of evidence and the standard of proof make it easier to prove that abuse occurred. Sometimes the criminal charges against the alleged abuser are dismissed due to a violation of his rights under the *Charter*; this type of dismissal does not prevent the judge in civil family law proceedings from considering the abuse allegation. Further, even if there is no judicial finding of abuse in either the criminal or the family law proceeding, there may be other concerns about the parenting capacity of a person acquitted in criminal court that lead to a denial of custody.[24]

If the Crown withdraws the criminal charges or the alleged abuser is acquitted in criminal court, there may be a tendency for some accusing parents or others involved in the case to accept this criminal finding for civil purposes as well. The alleged abuser will often feel a psychological boost from the criminal acquittal or the Crown's decision not to proceed with charges. Indeed in some family law cases the judge has granted interim access to an alleged abuser, taking account of the fact that the police decided not to lay charges.[25]

In light of the different types of proceedings, it seems inappropriate for a family law judge to place much weight on the mere decision of the police not to

---

[23] *M.R.P. v. P.P.* (1989), 19 R.F.L. (3d) 437 (N.S. City Ct.), a new trial was ordered when trial judge allowed unsupervised access to a father convicted of sexually abusing the children five years earlier and trial judge was satisfied that the father was rehabilitated and there was no risk to safety of children. The appeal court held that the trial judge should have not only considered the issue of risk of further abuse, but should have also required evidence that access was in the best interests of the children.

[24] *S.S. v. P.S.*, [1994] O.J. 995 (Prov. Ct.), Main J.

[25] *Stuart v. Stuart* (1985), 32 A.C.W.S. (2d) 53 (Ont. S.C.) per Cork M. In *Bartesko v. Bartesko* (1990), 31 R.F.L. (3d) 213 (B.C.C.A.), McEachern C.J.B.C. suggested that the fact that no charges were laid is "less than conclusive" but it "was at least a matter that the trial judge was entitled to comment upon."

charge or on a criminal court acquittal. However, if the police officers who investigate are experienced in conducting this type of investigation and conclude that it is likely that abuse did not occur, this may be significant evidence in the family law case.[26]

Child protection agencies only need to establish abuse or neglect on the civil standard of proof — the balance of probabilities. Protection agencies, however, may be reluctant to bring an application based on concerns about abuse if they are truly uncertain about what has occurred, and do not have clear evidence of abuse. A parental family law case, however, may proceed in the face of considerable uncertainty about whether abuse occurred, with the abuse allegations forming only part of the total case. The parents (generally acting through their counsel) have a responsibility to collect evidence and present it to the court in a family law proceeding.

Depending upon the outcome of the investigation, the child protection agency may need to decide whether to play a role in the court process. An agency may decide it is necessary to bring forward a protection application immediately. Alternatively, if the family law case seems to be proceeding in a manner that protects the child, the agency may decide it is not necessary to bring a protection application before the court.

It is also possible that the investigating child protection worker or police officer may be called to testify as a witness by one of the parents in the family law hearing;[27] this can occur whether or not a criminal prosecution or child protection application has been commenced.

In those cases where there are reasons for having a protection application as well as a family law application, in some jurisdictions it may be necessary for the proceedings to be dealt with separately. For example, if the parental family law dispute is being dealt with under the federal *Divorce Act*, it will be heard in a superior court by a federally appointed judge, whereas the child protection application may (depending on the jurisdiction) have to be resolved by a provincially appointed judge. On the other hand, if the family law proceeding is initiated under provincial legislation in the provincial Family Court,[28] it may be possible for the two applications to be heard at the same time, and some judges feel that in these cases there are valid reasons for resolving the two proceedings in a single court hearing.[29]

---

[26] *Re S.D.* (2001), 14 R.F.L. (5th) 414 (Ont. Sup. Ct.).

[27] It has been held that parents involved in litigation with each other have a right to have disclosure of the file of the child protection agency for use in their litigation: see e.g., *P.H. v. H.H.*, [1998] N.W.T.J. 81 (Sup. Ct) and *L.G. v. P.B.*, [1996] O.J. 1600 (Ont. Ct. J.) per Brownstone J.

[28] Increasingly in Canada, Unified Family Courts are being established that have jurisdiction over all family law and child welfare cases. The judges in these courts have a discretionary jurisdiction to resolve in a single hearing custody proceeding under the *Divorce Act* and child protection proceedings concerning the same child.

[29] See e.g., *Children's Aid Society of Belleville, Hastings & Trenton v. H.* (1984), 27 A.C.W.S. (2d) 158 (Ont. Fam. Ct.).

If a child protection application and the family law case are being dealt with separately, in some cases the agency will request that the family law case should be resolved first, indicating that whether or not it proceeds (or what type of order it seeks) will depend on the outcome of the family law case. An order made in a child protection proceeding will prevail over any family law order made in regard to the same child.[30]

In practice, the problem of multiple civil proceedings can often be resolved without the need for two trials. The focus in both proceedings remains on the child and the child's needs. Once an agency is involved, there will usually be discussions between the lawyers for each parent, the agency's lawyer, and the child's lawyer, if there is one. Both applications will proceed to a hearing only if no reasonable solution can be found. Often, as noted above, the agency will not proceed with a protection application if it is satisfied that the allegations of abuse will be explored in the parental custody or access trial. Quite frequently agency workers who have investigated the case will be called as witnesses to testify in the parental family law dispute, but the agency will not formally be a party to the parental dispute.

Family Law Court Orders

Disputes between separated parents over the care of their children can be highly adversarial, and if allegations of abuse have been made the tensions inherent in this type of case are compounded. Counsel for a parent accused of abuse may have a professional duty to exhaust every piece of potential evidence, no matter how distasteful or emotionally difficult this is. Counsel for the accused parent may, for example, be obliged to respond by arguing that it is the new partner of the accusing parent who is abusing the child, or by suggesting that the allegation is unfounded and a reflection of the unbalanced psychological state of the accusing parent. There is a great potential for these types of claims to permanently damage the relationship between the estranged parents or between a parent and child.

Judges have, perhaps, the most difficult task of all. In few of these cases are there independent witnesses to the alleged abuse. The child may have been subjected to repeated questioning by parents, child protection workers, police, and assessors, and it may be impossible to discover the validity of any reports coming from the child, especially if the child is young. Most of the cases involve allegations of fondling and there is no medical evidence to corroborate or refute the allegations. The various professionals may have only varying degrees of certainty about what occurred. The judge will be required to decide whether the abuse occurred and, if so, what should be done about it.

---

[30] This will be so even if the custody order is made by a superior court and the protection order by a provincial court. As a general rule, an order of a superior court on the same issue overrides that of a provincial court, but a custody hearing is not on the same issue as a child protection hearing because the legal tests are different and the litigation in each case proceeds under different statutes. The order placing the child under the protection of the state agency takes priority. See e.g., *Re J.D.* (1978), 5 R.F.L. (2d) 209 (Ont. Prov. Ct.).

Sometimes a judge will be unable to find that abuse has occurred, but nevertheless makes a determination, based on the "best interests" of the child, to deny the alleged abuser custody or even access. There may be cases in which the "suspicions" of the judge do not merit a finding of abuse, but nevertheless influence the final outcome.

There are cases where the judge determines that the allegation of sexual abuse was not proven on the balance of probabilities, and makes a final order for regular unsupervised access or even custody to the falsely accused parent.

If an unfounded allegation was made by a custodial parent in good faith, judges are generally careful not to deprive the accusing parent of custody for having taken steps in the honest belief that these things were necessary to protect the child. On the other hand, if the judge concludes that an unfounded allegation was made maliciously or as a result of the accusing parent's unbalanced emotional state, the judge may decide that the accusing parent should not have the responsibility for care of the child.

No matter how careful the investigation and assessment, there will be cases in which judges, professionals and parents will have to accept that there are *reasonable suspicions of abuse, but not sufficient proof to convince a court* that abuse has occurred. Learning to live with uncertainty may be a very challenging dimension of some of these cases. In some cases where the judge is uncertain about what occurred, an order may be made that will be in effect for a specified period, for example for supervised access, and require a further review by the court.

It is often possible to take steps to protect the child against the *possibility* of further abuse without completely terminating contact with a *suspected* abuser. This may be done, at least for a time, through supervision of access, first in a neutral setting and perhaps eventually in the home, provided that the supervisor is a person committed to the welfare of the child.[31]

In some cases concerns about physical or even sexual abuse may be a result of inappropriate parenting as opposed to a desire to exploit a child; in such cases the court may order counselling or education of the parent if appropriate.[32]

A long-term plan to ensure the safety of the child may include therapy for the child by a skilled neutral professional, who can both provide support for the child after the stresses of litigation and monitor for possible abuse.[33] In some cases, it may be possible to educate the child about inappropriate touching and the need to report any inappropriate touching, though in other cases this may not be realistic due to the child's young age or developmental delays.

---

[31] See M.S. Fahn, "Allegations of Child Sexual Abuse in Custody Disputes: Getting to the Truth of the Matter," (1991), 25 *Family Law Quarterly* 193 at 213-16; and D.C. Bross, "Assumptions About Child Sexual Abuse Allegations at or About the Time of Divorce" (1992), 1 *Journal of Child Sexual Abuse* 2, at 115. See *E.S. v. D.M.* (1996), 143 Nfld. & P.E.I.R. 192 (Nfld. U.F.C) where the court was concerned that there was a "significant possibility" that the father had sexually abused the child during access visits, and allowed supervised access at the father's home.

[32] *C.A.S. Waterloo v. B.D.*, [1991] O.J. 2398 (Prov. Ct.).

[33] See e.g., *N.(D.) v. K.(B.)* (1999), 48 R.F.L. (4th) 400 (Ont. Sup. Ct.) per Métivier J.

Cases of parental separation in which allegations of abuse or neglect are made can be among the most challenging cases that child protection workers, family lawyers or judges may have to deal with. If the professionals involved have appropriate knowledge, training and support, they can approach these cases in an unbiased fashion, with sensitivity to the needs of the children and concerns of parents, to achieve an outcome that promotes the best interests of the children involved.

10

Criminal Prosecutions for Abuse and Neglect

Shelley Hallett and Nicholas Bala[1]

Criminal Justice and Child Protection

Child abuse or neglect may result in prosecution under the *Criminal Code*.[2] It is, for example, a criminal offence to fail to provide a child with "necessities of life," to use force against a child which is not "reasonable" and for the "purposes of correction," or to sexually abuse a child.

A criminal prosecution is legally different from a child protection proceeding. While it is possible for both types of proceeding to move forward simultaneously, each will be heard in a different court and have distinctive legal rules, purposes, hearings and judges. There may, however, be a joint police-child protection investigation. Some witnesses may testify in both proceedings, and the outcome in one may affect the other.

A criminal prosecution is intended to identify and punish offenders. The criminal law is intended to hold offenders accountable for their misconduct, and the prosecution of perpetrators is intended to deter offending behaviour. Rehabilitation of offenders is an important but secondary objective of the criminal justice process. The child protection process, on the other hand, is intended to intervene in the lives of families to protect the child, removing the child from parental care if necessary and, if possible, assisting the parents to improve the quality of the parental care they provide. The focus of the child protection proceeding is the welfare of the child.

In a criminal case, the onus is on the prosecution to prove its case beyond a reasonable doubt; this constitutes the highest legal standard of proof. Criminal proceedings employ strict rules of evidence and provide the accused with a full set of procedural protections under the *Canadian Charter of Rights and Freedoms*.[3] For example, in a criminal case it is usually necessary for the child victim of alleged abuse to testify in court and to be available for cross-examination.

---

[1] Shelley Hallett is Senior Counsel with the Ontario Ministry of the Attorney General, Toronto, Ontario. Nicholas Bala is Professor of Law, Queen's University, Kingston, Ontario.

[2] R.S.C. 1985, c. C-46.

[3] Part I of the *Constitution Act, 1982*, being Schedule B of the *Canada Act 1982 (U.K.)*, 1982, c. 11 [hereinafter *Charter*].

A child protection proceeding (or litigation between parents who have separated) is civil. In a civil case it is legally easier to establish that a child has been abused or neglected. In a child protection hearing the agency is only obliged to prove its case according to the lower civil standard of proof, on the balance of probabilities. In civil cases, the rules of evidence are not as strict as in criminal court and the *Charter* has only limited applicability. As a result, there may be an acquittal in criminal court or no criminal prosecution at all, while a finding of abuse could be made in the protection case.

Police are responsible for criminal investigations, while the Crown prosecutor is responsible for presenting a criminal case in court. There are sometimes disagreements between the child protection agency on one hand, and the police and Crown prosecutor on the other, about how a child abuse incident should be handled. Sometimes the protection agency has a concern about the potential detrimental effect of a prosecution upon the parents, family and child, resulting in the agency's reluctance to support a criminal prosecution. In other cases, the police may be unwilling to press criminal charges while the child protection agency believes that a prosecution would be appropriate. There have been considerable efforts in Canada to improve the relationship between child protection agencies and those responsible for criminal prosecutions. Communication and coordination have been facilitated by the development of protocols to govern joint police-child welfare investigations.

Until recently, criminal prosecutions for abuse or neglect were relatively rare. However, these prosecutions are becoming more common, especially as more cases of sexual abuse are being reported. Many criminal prosecutions of child abuse involve parents or partners of parents, but others are charged as well. In Canada, a significant number of criminal cases have been prosecuted against teachers, priests and others for abusing their positions of trust by sexually exploiting children. Some of these extrafamilial cases involve protection issues, as the perpetrators may still be responsible for the care of children. Others are historic abuse cases, with adult survivors testifying about abuse that occurred in their childhood, which in some cases was decades ago.

Criminal prosecutions involving child witnesses have been facilitated by changes in procedural and evidentiary rules that are intended to accommodate child witnesses, recognizing that while children can give accurate and reliable testimony, they are not adults. Although it is important for the courts to ensure that child witnesses are treated with respect, it is always necessary to balance concerns about children with fair treatment for accused persons, and the presumption of innocence. The promotion of the "best interests" of children is a concept that runs through much of child welfare law, but it is not a principle at play in the criminal justice system.

It should be noted that the federal Parliament has jurisdiction for enacting criminal law and procedure (e.g., the *Criminal Code* is federal legislation) while child protection law is a provincial responsibility. Responsibility for police and the prosecution of criminal cases, such as those involving child abuse and neglect, also rests with the provincial governments.

Child protection hearings are discussed extensively elsewhere in this book. This chapter provides an introduction to criminal prosecutions in cases of child abuse and neglect,[4] and discusses the interrelationship between criminal prosecutions and child protection proceedings.

Commencing a Criminal Prosecution

A criminal prosecution is commenced by a person (the "informant") going before a justice of the peace (a lower-level judicial officer) with an "information," a document setting out the basic nature of the offence that is alleged to have been committed by the accused. The informant must appear before a justice of the peace to swear that he or she has reasonable grounds to believe that the material in the information is true and the accused person has committed the specified offence. The information will generally identify the "complainant" (the technical term used for the victim of an alleged offence), even if that person did not directly disclose the offence.

While in theory any person may swear an information to commence a prosecution, in practice an information charging a criminal offence is most commonly laid by a police officer. The officer must have reasonable grounds to believe that an offence has taken place. While this does not mean that the officer must have direct knowledge that an offence has been committed, the officer's reasons must go beyond mere speculation, and the officer must have a genuine belief in the truth of the allegations.

The police officer usually establishes the "reasonable grounds" to believe that an offence has been committed as a result of an investigation that occurs after a report by the alleged victim or a witness. In some cases the officer has directly observed the accused committing the offence (though this is very rare in child abuse cases).

Following a report, a police investigation may last several days or even months, though for simple matters the investigation may be very brief. Usually, the victim of the alleged offence will be one of the first persons to whom the officer will speak during the investigation. Items that may have been used in the course of the offence (e.g., weapons), or that otherwise support the story of the victim and other witnesses (e.g., blood-stained clothing or an item left at the scene by the accused), will be collected during the officer's investigation and kept as exhibits for later use at trial.

The requirement that an informant believe on reasonable grounds that an offence has been committed is sometimes problematic in the context of sexual offences against children. Many victims of such offences are very young; thus

---

[4] For a fuller discussion of criminal prosecutions for abuse and neglect, A. Maleszyk, *Crimes Against Children: Prosecution and Defence* (Toronto: Canada Law Book, 2002); and W. van Tongeren Harvey and P. Dauns, *Sexual Offences Against Children and the Criminal Process* (Markham: Lexis Nexis, 2001).

they are at a disadvantage in expressing themselves in a convincing way to an investigating police officer. Although most police officers are now aware of the need for special sensitivity while interviewing child victims of abuse, many still have not received extensive training in interviewing children. Further, the offences are rarely committed in the presence of other credible witnesses and physical evidence of sexual abuse often cannot be found. The younger the child in such circumstances, the more the investigating police officer may face a dilemma in deciding whether to proceed with a charge. Investigators in this situation should be particularly thorough, exploring all avenues that may disclose evidence supportive of the child victim's complaint. Such avenues generally include discussions with the child's parents or caregivers, the child's family doctor, experts in child development, and other children who are or have been in contact with the alleged offender. Officers also, however, need to be aware of the possibility that allegations may be fabricated by the child or by an adult who has consciously or unconsciously manipulated the child.

No investigation based solely upon an interview with the alleged child victim is complete. In cases involving allegations of abuse, the decision not to lay a charge can only be justified following a careful investigation.

An investigation generally includes speaking with the person suspected of the offence. Sometimes, an interview will occur prior to any charges being laid, and as a result of the interview, the police will decide not to lay a charge. No individual is obliged to answer questions from the police related to a suspected offence, though most individuals recognize that a refusal to co-operate with an investigation may raise the suspicions of the police. If the police have sufficient evidence to lay an information, they may decide to do this and then arrest the suspect before undertaking any questioning. Under the *Charter*, when the police interview an individual charged with an offence, they are obliged to ensure that the person is aware of the right to consult a lawyer prior to making a statement. An individual is under no obligation to make a statement to the police and has the right to remain silent, or to have a lawyer present during questioning by the police.

Judicial Interim Release (Bail) Hearings

When the police believe that someone has committed an offence, they have the authority to arrest that person, even before an information has been laid if necessary. An arrest involves taking the accused into custody and confining that person to the police station or another detention facility. A person who has been arrested and is being taken to the police station will ordinarily be handcuffed to ensure the security of the arresting officer and prevent the person from possibly destroying evidence.

For many offences, including those involving the abuse or neglect of children, the police have limited discretion to release the person shortly after arrest and without a court appearance, provided that the accused signs a written document promising to come to court on a specified date. The document in which the individual undertakes to appear may be an "appearance notice," a "promise to appear," or a "recognizance." However, the police cannot impose conditions on the accused as part of the release. For example, the police cannot require the accused to stay away from the alleged victim pending trial. A court may, however, impose conditions upon the accused who is held in detention and released following a bail hearing.

In cases involving an allegation of child abuse, the public interest usually requires arrest and detention of the accused until a bail hearing is held. Release by the police is rarely appropriate; the risk of the accused seeking out the child for the purpose of intimidation or repetition of the offence is too great, particularly as no conditions can be attached to the release that would serve to protect the child or other children who may be at risk from that offender.

When accused persons are arrested and detained by the police, they must be taken before a justice of the peace or provincial court judge within 24 hours, or as soon as possible thereafter, for a bail hearing. At a bail hearing the court must decide whether the accused should be released from custody before the trial and, if so, under what conditions.

The bail hearing usually takes place at a courthouse, though in some locales it may be at a police station and there are now provisions for bail hearings to be conducted by video conference. At the bail hearing the Crown prosecutor is required to "show cause" why the accused should be detained in custody until trial, or released into the community after conditions of release are set.[5] Often, at the bail hearing, the Crown prosecutor will read a summary of the allegations to the court. However, if the accused does not consent to the allegations being read to the court by the Crown prosecutor, or when the Crown prosecutor prefers to do so, witnesses for the Crown may be called to testify about the case. In this event, the police officer involved in the case is usually called by the Crown. In addition to the allegations pertaining to the offence, the Crown prosecutor generally provides details about the accused's address, employment, marital and family status, previous criminal convictions, current outstanding charges and previous bail releases.

The strict rules of evidence that apply at a trial do not apply at the bail hearing. Rather, the judge "...may receive and base his decision upon evidence considered credible or trustworthy by him in the circumstances of each case."[6] Thus, the police officer may give evidence not only as to what the officer personally observed during the investigation, but also about anticipated testimony in the case, including what a child or other witnesses have told the officer. This is preferable to calling the child to testify at the bail hearing, which would expose

---

[5] In most bail hearings, the onus is on the Crown to show that detention of the accused is justified. However, in specific situations (e.g., when the accused is charged with one indictable offence while already out on bail for another charge, or is charged with an offence relating to the failure to appear in court or to abide by bail conditions previously imposed) the onus shifts to the detained accused to show cause why he or she should not be detained. This reverse onus makes it more difficult for an accused to be released from custody. See *Criminal Code*, s. 515(6).

[6] *Criminal Code*, s. 518(1)(e).

the child to an unnecessary and undesirable courtroom appearance. The defence may also call witnesses at the bail hearing. The accused may testify, but is not required to do so, and may for example give evidence about plans for residence and employment pending the trial. At a bail hearing, unless the accused specifically chooses to testify about circumstances of the alleged offence, the accused may not be questioned about the charges.[7]

There are two main considerations for the judge deciding whether to grant bail. The first is whether it is necessary to detain the accused in order to ensure their attendance at trial to answer to the charges. If detention is not necessary on that basis, the court goes on to consider whether it is necessary to detain the accused in order to protect the public, including the victim, having regard to all circumstances surrounding the alleged offence and offender. This should include consideration of whether there is a "substantial likelihood" that the accused will commit another criminal offence or interfere with the administration of justice (e.g., by intimidating witnesses) upon being released.[8]

If the court decides it is not necessary for the accused to be detained, the accused will be released upon signing an undertaking or a recognizance to appear, with or without conditions. A recognizance is more onerous for the accused, as it requires an amount of money to be paid by an accused person who fails to appear for court or does not comply with a condition imposed by the court. The amount of money for which the accused may be liable is determined by the court at the time of release and appears on the face of the recognizance. In addition, the court may require that an accused have a "surety" before being released on a recognizance. A surety is a person, usually a friend or relative, who guarantees payment of the money if the accused does not come to court for the trial or breaches bail conditions. The court may also stipulate that the accused or the surety is required to deposit cash or pledge other valuable security (e.g., Canada Savings Bonds or a lien on property such as a house) as a condition of the accused's release.

In a criminal case involving an allegation of child abuse, where an accused is not detained at the bail hearing, a suitable form of release would typically be a recognizance in the form of a substantial amount of money with a surety and a prohibition from communicating with the child victim or visiting the place where the child is living or going to school. In cases of extrafamilial abuse, prudent conditions would be regularly reporting to the police, staying away from public playgrounds, schoolyards and swimming pools, and not associating with children under a certain age. Abstaining from alcohol may, for example, also be an appropriate condition if the accused has a history of offending while

---

[7] *Criminal Code*, s. 518(1)(b). Other defence witnesses, however, may be asked questions at the bail hearing relating to the offence, including the whereabouts of the accused at the time of its commission. The Crown prosecutor is entitled to cross-examine all witnesses whom the defence calls at the bail hearing, just as the accused or his or her lawyer may cross-examine all Crown witnesses.

[8] *Criminal Code*, s. 515(10). In some cases involving very grave offences, such as murder, the court may also consider the effect on the public's "confidence in the administration of justice" of release of the accused pending trial (s.515(10)(c)).

intoxicated.[9] In cases involving allegations of abuse of a child by a parent, if the child has not been apprehended by the child welfare agency, it will almost always be a condition of release that the accused is not to reside with the child or to have contact with child.

Guilty Plea

A guilty plea dispenses with the necessity of having a trial at which the witnesses would be required to testify. While in theory an accused may plead guilty at any stage of the proceeding, including the first appearance for a bail hearing, the judge will normally encourage an accused person, especially if the charges are serious such as those in an abuse case, to consult with counsel before pleading guilty.

When the accused indicates to the court the desire to plead guilty, the clerk of the court stands up and formally reads the charge from the information that the police officer has filed with the court (or "arraigns" the accused). During the arraignment, the clerk must ask the accused whether he or she pleads guilty or not guilty. Upon the accused's formal plea of guilty, the clerk records the plea on the information.

The Crown prosecutor is then called upon to read a factual summary of the case to the court, based on material that has been prepared by the investigating police officer. At this point the accused or his or her lawyer may wish to modify or qualify some of the facts alleged by the Crown.[10] If the accused denies an essential element of the offence (e.g., the intention to touch a child's genitals for a sexual purpose, claiming that the touching was accidental), the judge is obliged to strike the guilty plea and order a trial.

On most guilty pleas, the facts read into the record by the Crown prosecutor are accepted with little modification by the defence. The judge makes a formal finding of the accused's guilt. The trial stage of the criminal proceeding is then over and the sentence hearing takes place. Sentencing may occur on the same day as the finding of guilt or may be adjourned by the court to another day to allow a pre-sentence report to be prepared or witnesses to be called for the purpose of the sentencing hearing. If the case is serious, such as where there are allegations of child abuse, the case will usually be adjourned to allow for the

---

[9] The police officer who prepares the bail hearing documentation to be used by the Crown prosecutor should recommend to the Crown conditions to be followed by the accused in the event of his release on bail. These recommended conditions should be dictated by the circumstances disclosed by the case investigation, and are most likely to be effective in protecting the child if the officer consults with the protection worker on the case. Such recommendations may guide the Crown in making submissions and hence influence the court in setting the terms of release.

[10] The Crown prosecutor may agree to some modification of the facts read in support of the charge, particularly if they relate to less important features of the case. However, the Crown will generally not accede to a proposed variation of the factual summary if a disputed fact is likely to substantially affect the sentence that the court is likely to impose. If the Crown prosecutor declines to modify the summary, the accused may be allowed by the judge to change the plea to "not guilty" and the case is adjourned to a later date for trial. Alternatively, the case may be adjourned to another court day to enable the Crown to call evidence only to prove the disputed fact as it relates to sentencing.

preparation of a pre-sentence report and to allow counsel to prepare for the sentencing hearing.

Disclosure

The *Charter of Rights* requires that, in order to ensure a fair trial, an accused is entitled to obtain disclosure of the evidence that the police have gained during their investigation. The disclosure of the Crown's case is intended to allow the accused to properly prepare for trial, and to decide whether to enter a guilty plea, perhaps after discussions with the Crown.[11] Disclosure is usually provided to the accused's lawyer by the Crown prosecutor, with the release of written summaries of statements from every person interviewed in connection with the investigation, a copy of any statement the accused has given to the police and the results of any scientific analysis carried out for the police, such as a DNA analysis of clothing found at the scene of a sexual assault.

If the police investigation included videotaped interviews with children, these tapes will generally only be released if counsel for the accused undertakes not to release the tapes into the possession of the accused or other persons, as there have been cases of pedophiles accused of offences gaining personal access and misusing these tapes.

Many victims of abuse have highly sensitive personal records, for example, records concerning counselling or therapy that they may have received, or the victim may have a diary. In some cases, child welfare agency or adoption records may have material that the accused might consider useful. Counsel for a person accused of abuse will often want access to these records for the purpose of using them in cross-examination of the victim, often with the intent of showing that the victim was lying, confused or mentally unstable.

For a number of years there was a great deal of controversy and a considerable amount of litigation in Canada about when, if ever, an accused person should be permitted to have access to records and documents about complainants. Almost all the controversy arose in the context of cases with allegations of sexual assault or sexual exploitation.[12] Defence counsel argued that such documents could contain information vital to a fair trial, while advocates for victims argued that these documents often contain highly sensitive and personal information and that their release could be emotionally traumatic to victims. There was also concern that the release of these records may intimidate victims, and cause them to ask that any proceedings that were commenced be discontinued. In many cases, advocates for victims of the abuse questioned whether these documents had any relevance to the charges before the court.

In 1997 the government enacted amendments to the *Criminal Code* that deal with the disclosure of personal records related to alleged victims and witnesses

---

[11] *R. v. Stinchcombe*, [1991] 3 S.C.R. 326.
[12] See e.g., *R. v. O'Connor*, [1995] 4 S.C.R. 411.

in criminal cases.[13] These provisions require an accused who seeks access to these documents, whether they are in the possession of the police, the person to whom they related or a third party like a therapist, to make an application to the court for release of the records. The application about whether to release the documents is to be decided by the court at a hearing at which the public is excluded. Before deciding whether to disclose the documents, the judge may personally examine them; the judge is required to balance the right of privacy and deleterious effects of disclosure of the documents on the person to whom the documents relate against the rights of the accused to a fair trial. The judge is only to order the disclosure of the documents to the accused if satisfied that they are "likely to be relevant to an issue" at trial and that their production is "necessary in the interests of justice." The judge will normally impose conditions on the disclosure of any such sensitive documents to ensure that they are only used for the purposes of the criminal process, and not further duplicated or circulated.

Plea Bargaining

The vast majority of criminal charges do not end up in a trial, but rather are resolved by the accused pleading guilty or by the Crown dropping the charges. A resolution by way of a guilty plea or by the dropping of charges may occur at an early stage in the process, but not uncommonly this type of resolution only occurs after the case has been in the justice system for months, or even years. Not infrequently resolution of a case without a trial is a result of "plea bargaining" between the Crown prosecutor and counsel for the accused.

Saving the community the cost of a trial, and the witnesses the trauma or inconvenience of testifying, are factors recognized by judges as having the potential to reduce the sentence that would ordinarily be imposed after a full trial. Further, the Crown may believe that the accused is guilty of the offences charged, but may have a concern that it may not be possible to convince the court of this according to the strict criminal rules of evidence and to the high criminal standard of proof. Accordingly, it is not uncommon for the Crown to offer the accused some type of advantage if the accused pleads guilty to one or more of the offences charged.

An accused may wish to know whether the Crown prosecutor will agree to a variation of the offence synopsis to be read to the court on the basis that the brief prepared by the police contains some inaccurate information or allegations that could not be proven in a trial. The defence might also wish to know whether the Crown prosecutor will accept a guilty plea to one or two of several offences or to a less serious charge than the one faced by the accused.

These matters are commonly discussed out of court by the Crown prosecutor and the accused's lawyer. Such discussions are popularly termed "plea bargaining," but are more correctly referred to as "plea negotiations" or "plea

---

[13] S.C. 1997, c. 30, enacting ss. 278.1-278.9 of the *Criminal Code*. The interpretation and constitutional validity of these provisions are discussed in *R. v. Mills*, [1999] 3 S.C.R. 668.

discussions." Plea discussions play an essential and practical role in the criminal justice system. Often both lawyers will be able to agree that for an accused facing multiple charges, after a trial on the existing evidence the accused would likely be found guilty of a certain offence and not guilty of others, and the Crown will accept a guilty plea on one or more charges that an accused faces and drop the others. A common outcome of plea bargaining is an agreement that the accused will plead guilty only if the Crown supports a particular sentence (or a range of sentences); in this situation there will be a "joint submission" to the judge from Crown and defence counsel about the appropriate sentence. While the sentencing judge is not bound by the plea discussions, judges generally accept recommendations made jointly by lawyers for the accused and Crown after such discussions.

Plea discussions can result in tremendous savings of the time, effort and cost that normally would be expended on a criminal trial. The accused becomes certain of the charges upon which he or she will be convicted, knows the sentence that is likely to be imposed, and may also have the sentence reduced in consideration of the guilty plea. The Crown enjoys the benefit of a certain conviction. This is significant as every trial involves a risk of acquittal, which may present danger to the community as a guilty party goes free. Witnesses are spared the inconvenience and stress of testifying, which may be particularly important in cases involving children or intrafamilial abuse.

Sometimes plea bargaining will occur just before a trial is scheduled to commence. Thus a child and other witnesses may be at the court and ready to testify only to find that the case has been resolved. While spared the trauma of testifying and being cross-examined, these witnesses may still have experienced the stress of preparing for court and waiting anxiously for the proceedings to be concluded.

The decision about whether the Crown will make a plea bargain rests with the Crown prosecutor. Although some Crown prosecutors make a practice of consulting with the investigating officer, and perhaps victim, before making a plea bargain, the decision about whether to resolve a case in this way is a matter of professional judgement. Some victims will oppose a resolution by way of a plea bargain, but they may not be aware of all of the factors that the Crown prosecutor must consider; in some cases, for example, the Crown prosecutor may be concerned that the alleged victim will not be a very convincing witness, though the victim may not appreciate this. It is the accused, not his or her lawyer, who must decide whether or not to act on the Crown prosecutor's offer to accept a guilty plea in exchange for a joint submission or the dropping of some charges. Defence counsel, however, has an ethical duty to ensure that a client is only pleading guilty to a crime that he or she is, in fact, prepared to admit having committed. If an accused is denying guilt to his or her own counsel, the case should not be resolved by a guilty plea but should go to trial.[14]

---

[14] *R. v. K.(S.)* (1995), 24 O.R. (3d) 199 (C.A.). See also M. Proulx and D. Layton, *Ethics and Canadian Criminal Law* (Toronto: Irwin Law, 2001), c. 8.

The Preliminary Inquiry

When an accused faces an indictable offence,[15] the accused may elect (i.e., choose) a trial in a superior court rather than the provincial court. This entitles the accused to a preliminary inquiry, typically conducted by a judge in the provincial court, and the right to a jury trial.

The preliminary inquiry usually takes place within a few months of the laying of the information. The Crown must call evidence at this hearing to show that the case against the accused is "sufficient" to warrant putting the accused through a trial. The preliminary inquiry also serves the purpose of giving the accused more knowledge of the Crown's case and of helping to decide whether to enter a guilty plea without a trial. From the perspective of a witness, the preliminary inquiry is similar to a trial, with examination-in-chief and cross-examination; however, the defence rarely calls any witnesses at the preliminary inquiry.

Often after calling one or two witnesses, the Crown is able to satisfy the court that there is sufficient evidence for the case to go to trial, which results in the preliminary inquiry being much shorter than a trial. However, in most cases involving offences of physical and sexual abuse against children, it is necessary for the Crown to call the child victim to testify at the preliminary inquiry and make the child available for cross-examination by defence counsel. Thus, if a case goes to trial, a victim of abuse may have to testify twice.

If the test of sufficiency is met or the defence waives the right to a preliminary inquiry, the presiding judge will commit the case for trial in the superior court, often with a jury and in another building. The case may not come to trial for several months or even a year or more, depending on the pending caseload in the particular jurisdiction.[16] If the Crown's evidence does not meet the test of sufficiency at the preliminary inquiry, the accused is discharged and no longer faces the threat of prosecution.

Trial

The basic procedure followed in a trial is the same whether it is held before a jury or a judge sitting alone, though trials before a jury are more formal and may be more intimidating for witnesses, especially child witnesses, as they are, for example, conducted in larger rooms before a larger number of individuals who are strangers to the child.

---

[15] Offences are categorized as indictable, summary or hybrid. Indictable offences are more serious and have greater penalties. An accused person charged with an indictable offence is generally afforded extra procedural protections, such as the right to a preliminary inquiry and a jury trial. Summary offences are considered less serious, have lesser maximum penalties (typically a maximum of 6 to 18 months) and are resolved by a more expeditious procedure. Hybrid offences afford the Crown a choice (or election) as to whether to proceed summarily or by indictment. Most offences involving allegations of child abuse or neglect are hybrid.

[16] This illustrates another advantage of the preliminary inquiry to the defence: the time it affords the accused to put off the trial and commencement of the sentence. Some accused put this time to good use by engaging in a treatment program, finding a job, or giving up drugs or alcohol, all of which puts them in a better light at the time of sentence.

The trial commences with the accused being arraigned and advising the court of his "not guilty" plea. The lawyers usually start the case with an opening statement summarizing their position; there is a more elaborate "opening address" in a jury trial.

The Crown always calls its witnesses first. As questioning of each witness is completed by Crown counsel, the accused's counsel has the right to cross-examine that witness. When a witness is being "examined-in-chief," the lawyer who has called that witness is limited to asking "non-leading" questions. When counsel is cross-examining a witness, counsel may ask "leading questions"; that is, there is a broader scope for counsel to ask pointed, challenging questions. After all witnesses for the Crown have been examined and cross-examined, the Crown closes its case.

One of the most important functions of the Crown prosecutor is to introduce in court the evidence gathered by the police showing that an accused person has committed the offence with which he or she is charged. This must be done fairly and impartially. In a criminal trial the onus is always on the Crown to prove the guilt of the accused beyond a reasonable doubt. If it becomes clear that a charge against an accused cannot be proven because of insufficient evidence, the Crown prosecutor is duty-bound to withdraw that charge.[17]

When the Crown has called all of its witnesses, the defence must decide whether the accused will testify and whether to call other witnesses to testify. The accused is not required by law to testify or to call any other witnesses. If the accused decides to testify or the defence calls other witnesses on its behalf, the same questioning pattern is followed in reverse; that is, after each defence witness is questioned by the lawyer for the accused, Crown counsel is afforded the opportunity of cross-examining the witness. After the case for the defence is completed, the Crown may exercise the right to call more witnesses to "reply" to evidence called by the defence, though this evidence is confined to responding to issues raised by the witnesses for the defence.

When all of the witnesses have testified, counsel for the Crown and the defence summarize the evidence and present their arguments on the applicable law to the presiding judge. If there is a jury, both lawyers address their closing argument to the jury and, after hearing legal argument from counsel, the judge instructs the jury in the law. In a jury trial, the jurors are the ultimate "triers of fact," responsible for deciding whether to convict or acquit. Any verdict must be unanimous; if it is not there is said to be a "hung jury" and there will ordinarily have to be another trial. If there is no jury, the judge alone is responsible for deciding all issues of fact and law.

---

[17] An essential pre-trial duty of the Crown prosecutor is to advise the police whether the police have enough evidence to prove a proposed charge according to the highest standard of proof (beyond a reasonable doubt). Sometimes, after consultation with the Crown, police officers may decide not to lay a charge. This also explains why charges are sometimes withdrawn by the Crown prosecutor before a trial.

Evidence[18]

The process of giving testimony by witnesses through questioning by the Crown and defence counsel is governed by the laws of evidence that are applied by the judge throughout the trial. If one lawyer seeks to introduce evidence or ask a question that the other lawyer considers to be in violation of the laws of evidence, there may be an argument between the lawyers put before the judge about the admissibility of the evidence. This argument about the admissibility of evidence is known as a *voir dire*,[19] and in a jury trial this will usually be conducted only after the jury has been excused.

One source of the laws of evidence is legislation, in particular the federal *Canada Evidence Act*,[20] which applies to criminal trials. Evidence law also comes from precedents set by English and Canadian judges and developed over many years (and even centuries); this type of law is known as common law, as distinguished from statutory law, like the *Canada Evidence Act*. The *Charter of Rights* may also have a role in determining what evidence is admissible; evidence obtained in violation of the accused's rights under the *Charter* may be excluded if receiving it would "bring the administration of justice into disrepute."[21]

The laws of evidence are based on notions of fairness and are intended to ensure that an accused person receives a just trial, based on reliable evidence. For example, a person accused of sexually abusing a child may have a history that includes convictions for possession of child pornography. Although this type of history might be clinically significant, the rules of evidence ordinarily prohibit the introduction of examples of bad character as proof of a criminal charge. In law, such evidence is not considered trustworthy enough to show that the accused committed a certain offence on a specific date. Admission of such evidence could also be unfair; the judge or jury might find accused persons guilty simply because they are thought to be bad persons and had a history of sexual offending, not necessarily because they committed the offence charged.[22]

However, the courts have recognized that there are circumstances in which the probative value of evidence of prior similar acts exceeds any prejudice to the accused and will admit evidence of "similar" occurrences. This can be especially important in child sexual abuse cases where it may buttress the credibility of a child or rebut the suggestion that touching was "innocent in purpose."[23]

Similarly, the requirements of fairness and reliability explain why the rules of evidence generally exclude hearsay testimony from a criminal trial. Hearsay evidence is information that another person has told the witness. The

---

[18] Issues related to the laws of evidence are also discussed in Chapter 11 of this book.

[19] The term *voir dire* is a corruption of the Norman term "vrai dire" — to hear the truth.

[20] R.S.C. 1985, c. C-5.

[21] *Charter*, s. 24(2).

[22] See e.g., *R. v. Corbett*, [1988] 1 S.C.R. 670.

[23] See *R. v. L.E.D.*, [1989] 2 S.C.R. 111; *R. v. C.R.B.*, [1990] 1 S.C.R. 717; *R. v. Arp*, [1999] 3 S.C.R 339; and *R. v. Handy*, [2002] 2 S.C.R. 908.

introduction of hearsay does not permit the cross-examination of the person who made the statement and is therefore considered less reliable than a statement made in court. Because of the hearsay rule, it is generally necessary for a child who is the alleged victim of an offence to testify in court and be available for cross-examination, even if the child has made extensive out-of-court disclosures. However, as discussed below, there are situations in which a videotape of an interview can be admitted in a criminal trial in addition to a child testifying, and as further discussed in Chapter 12, there may be situations in which a child's out-of-court statements are considered sufficiently reliable, that they may be admitted in court in addition to the child testifying, or even in the place of the child testifying, if the child is not available or would be unduly traumatized by the experience of testifying.

Evidence law allows experts to be called to give opinions on subjects beyond the general knowledge of the trier of fact (the judge or jury), but the scope for the admission of this evidence is quite narrow in criminal cases. The Supreme Court of Canada established in *R. v. Mohan*[24] that the party seeking to call the expert must satisfy four criteria:

- relevance of the expert evidence;
- "necessity" in assisting the trier of fact; that is, the witness must provide information that is likely to be outside the knowledge and experience of a jury or judge; it is not sufficient that this evidence would be "helpful";
- a properly qualified expert; and
- the absence of any exclusionary rule that would preclude the admission of the expert evidence.

The party who is proposing to call an expert must establish to the judge's satisfaction that the witness has the proper credentials to qualify as an expert, and that the proposed evidence satisfies the "basic threshold of reliability." It is not sufficient that the expert is merely relying on personal views or clinical experience; in the context of a criminal case the expert must be testifying based on a body of scientific research. The courts are also concerned that jurors may be overly impressed by experts, and that trials may become "battles of the experts." Accordingly, in criminal cases, the courts have recently tended to exclude proposed expert evidence that would deal with the credibility of the child, or the consistency of the child's behaviour with abuse.[25]

Judges in criminal cases are generally not willing to admit evidence from a doctor, psychologist or social worker, even one with special training, that they believed the child's allegations or that the child's behaviour was consistent with having been abused. However, in a prosecution for child physical abuse, opinion evidence from a medical doctor with appropriate training in dealing with these cases is admissible to establish that the child's observed injuries are inconsistent

---

[24] [1994] 2 S.C.R. 9.
[25] *R. v. D.(D.)*, [2000] 2 S.C.R. 275.

with the statements of parents about how the injuries occurred; this type of testimony, related to physical injuries, is generally considered more reliable and hence is admissible in criminal cases.

As discussed further in Chapter 11, there is a broader scope for the admission of expert evidence in civil child protection proceedings than there is in criminal trials.

Accommodation of Child Witnesses in Criminal Court[26]

Prior to 1988, it was very difficult for children to testify in criminal court. In 1988 a number of amendments were enacted that were intended to make it less difficult for children to be witnesses, and to recognize that children have different needs and capacities from adult witnesses.

Section 16 of the *Canada Evidence Act* sets out the conditions under which children may give evidence in court. If the child understands the "nature of the oath," the child may testify under oath. If a child does not demonstrate an understanding of the nature of an oath, a child is now permitted to testify "upon promising to tell the truth," if the judge is satisfied that the child is "able to communicate" the evidence in court. This is a more realistic approach to child witnesses than that used prior to 1988, as the old approach tended to focus more on the arcane issue of the child's understanding of the "nature of the oath." It is, however, still a common practice for a child to be asked questions to demonstrate an understanding of the "promise to tell the truth." While even young children have an understanding of the concept of promising, preschool children may have difficulty in answering abstract questions about the meaning of such concepts as "truth," "lie," and "promise," and may be excluded from testifying.[27]

Section 486 of the *Criminal Code* allows a judge to clear a courtroom of members of the public if the judge considers this to be "in the interest of the proper administration of justice." The judge should consider the "interests of the child" in dealing with such an application, as well as the right of the accused to a public trial. Exclusion of the public may, for example, be justified in cases where a child may be intimidated by the presence of members of the public, including friends and relatives of the accused. This section of the *Code* also allows the court to permit a "support person," like a social worker, to sit near a child while the child testifies in order to provide reassurance to the child. The support person should not communicate with the child while the child testifies, and should ordinarily be a person who will not be a witness. Section 486 of the *Code* also requires the court to ban publication or broadcast of name or

---

[26] Issues related to the preparation of children for testifying in court and their experience in court are also discussed in Chapter 12 of this book.

[27] See N. Bala, K. Lee, R. Lindsay, and V. Talwar, "A Legal & Psychological Critique of the Present Approach to the Assessment of the Competence of Child Witnesses" (2000), 38(3) *Osgoode Hall Law Journal* 409-451; the federal government wanted to amend this legislation to make it easier for children to be found competent to testify, but this legislation did not get enacted: see Bill C-12, *An Act to Amend the Criminal Code (Protection of Children and Other Vulnerable Persons) and the Canada Evidence Act*, 3rd Sess., 37th Parl., not enacted.

information that could identify a victim or child witness in a sexual offence case, if such an order is requested; the Crown invariably asks the court to make such an order when children are involved in a case.

Since 1988, judges have been able to permit a child witness in sexual offence cases to testify in front of a screen that blocks the child's view of the accused.[28] Alternatively, a judge may allow the child victim to testify from outside the courtroom by means of closed-circuit television, provided the judge, jury and accused can see the child testifying and the accused can communicate with his lawyer while watching the testimony.[29] Before either of these methods can be employed the law requires that the judge make a finding that their use "is necessary to obtain a full and candid account" of the alleged offence from the victim. This is usually established by hearing evidence from someone who knows the child, perhaps a parent or social worker, concerning the child's inhibitions about testifying in court without these aids.

Section 715.1 of the *Criminal Code* now allows a videotape of an interview with a child witness describing an alleged sexual offence to be shown in court as evidence. The videotape must have been made within a "reasonable time" of the commission of the alleged offence. Even with a videotape, the child must still testify at the proceedings, and "adopt" the contents of the videotape while a witness and be available for cross-examination.

The criminal law now better accommodates child witnesses, and prosecutors and police are better trained in dealing with children and recognizing their needs. Specially trained victim-witness workers are available to support children at many criminal courts in Canada. The experience of coming to criminal court can still be very distressing for children, and there is no doubt that some children who have in fact been abused are unable to testify effectively resulting in the acquittal of the accused. While the law now permits use of videotapes, screens and closed-circuit television, too frequently these aids are not available, or justice system personnel are not trained in their use.[30]

Sentencing

The judge who presides at the trial will sentence a person who is found guilty. Prior to imposing the sentence, the judge hears submissions on behalf of the offender and the Crown as to what would be a fitting sentence.

Unlike in a trial, when the rules of evidence are strictly followed, there is generally significant flexibility in how evidence is presented at a sentencing hearing, with the court relying on written documents and statements from counsel that would not be admissible in a trial.[31]

---

[28] *Criminal Code*, s. 486(2.1).

[29] *Criminal Code*, s. 486(2.2).

[30] See N. Bala, R.C.L. Lindsay, and E. McNamara, "Testimonial Aids for Children: The Canadian Experience with Closed Circuit Television, Screens and Videotapes" (2001), 44 *Criminal Law Quarterly* 461-486.

[31] *R. v. Gardiner*, [1982] 2 S.C.R. 368.

Sentencing submissions on behalf of the offender generally inform the court about the person's age, marital and family status, employment and educational and social background. Defence counsel may wish to show that the offence was out of character for the offender by calling witnesses to testify about ordinarily good character and worthwhile activities in the community. The offender may wish to personally express remorse for the offence or to offer, through counsel, some explanation for it. The offender's lawyer will attempt to highlight those circumstances of the offence which mitigate its seriousness (e.g., refraining from violence or lack of premeditation). Medical or other professional reports may be tendered by the defence to show the steps towards rehabilitation taken by the offender since the commission of the offence (e.g., engaging in therapy or a drug treatment program).

At sentencing the Crown prosecutor formally introduces the criminal record of the offender. The Crown prosecutor expresses the community's views on the seriousness of the offence, highlighting aggravating features that may call for a severe sentence, often considered the best way to protect society. Especially in sexual offence cases, victims are usually asked if they wish to write out a victim impact statement, explaining how the offence has affected them and their families, or, if they wish, they may be called as a witness to testify about the effect that the offence has had upon them. When young children are victims, their parents may prepare the victim impact statement or testify at the sentencing hearing.

In some cases, especially those involving Aboriginal offenders, Canadian courts sometimes use some form of "circle sentencing," with the possibility that the offender, the victim, and various family members can hear from each other about the effect that the offence has had on everyone affected, and to permit the offender to personally express his or her remorse to the victim. This process should only be undertaken if the victim is willing and has appropriate support, and if it seems that an offender is genuinely remorseful. While the views that a victim or other members of the community have about an appropriate sentence are not binding on a court, they may be influential with a judge.

Generally in serious cases such as those involving child abuse, a probation officer will prepare a pre-sentence report for the court to provide information about the offender's background and prospects for rehabilitation. To prepare this report, the probation officer will meet with the offender, and will usually be in contact with various people who know the offender, including family members.

Legislation that creates offences, like the *Criminal Code*,[32] sets out a maximum statutory penalty, though the maximum penalty is very rarely

---

[32] For young offenders, those between the age of 12 and 18 years at the date of the offence, the *Youth Criminal Justice Act*, S.C. 2002, c. 1, establishes a maximum custodial sentence that is generally much less than the adult maximum, two or three years for most offences. That *Act* also has a sentencing philosophy that emphasizes rehabilitation and lesser accountability than for adult offenders. See N. Bala, *Youth Criminal Justice Law* (Toronto: Irwin Law, 2003), chapter 8.

imposed.[33] The sentencing judge is expected to impose a sentence that is propor-
tionate to the gravity of the offence, and that serves the purposes of denunciation
of unlawful conduct, deterrence of the offender and others, rehabilitation and a
promotion of a sense of responsibility of the offender and, where necessary,
separation of an offender from society by means of incarceration.[34] The
balancing of these principles in individual cases involves a degree of discretion,
though trial judges also receive considerable guidance from the appeal courts
about the appropriate range of sentences for typical cases.

Child abuse cases often involve a breach of trust, and there is a tendency to
impose a jail term, which may range from a few weeks to several years. Judges,
however, have considerable discretion in sentencing and there are abuse cases in
which a judge decides to impose a sentence of probation or a conditional
sentence (sometimes called "house arrest"), especially for first offenders and in
cases where the abuse was historic and the judge considers it unlikely that the
offender will reoffend.[35]

Many judges are concerned that offenders receive appropriate treatment and
they recognize that the possibilities for treatment in prison are limited, though
not non-existent. In abuse cases, a judge may impose a probation period, invariably with a condition that the abuser undergo treatment. A probation period may
be imposed, either instead of imprisonment, or to follow a prison sentence not
exceeding two years. If there was violence and there are multiple victims, a
court will almost always impose a jail term in a child sexual abuse case.

The court is more likely to impose a longer sentence if a sexual abuse case
involves a breach of trust (e.g., abuse by a teacher or parent), violence or threats
of violence, multiple victims, a repeat offender, abuse continuing over a long
period of time or more serious abuse (e.g., intercourse as opposed to fondling
through clothes). Amenability of an abuser to treatment and an expression of
remorse may also lead to a less severe sentence.[36]

One particularly difficult issue that sometimes arises in intrafamilial child
abuse cases is when the victim of abuse asks to testify at the sentencing hearing
to request leniency. This may reflect guilt or familial pressure, or might be a
genuine sentiment on the victim's part. Although judges are doubtless moved by
these appeals, the courts have indicated that the wishes of the victim cannot be
determinative. It is recognized that if the courts were to place much weight on

---

[33] It is generally said that the maximum penalty is "reserved for the most serious example of an offence
committed by the worst offender," a theoretical case situation rarely acknowledged in reality by any
sentencing judge.

[34] See *Criminal Code*, ss. 718, 718.1 and 718.2. See generally, A. Manson, *The Law of Sentencing* (Toronto:
Irwin Law, 2001).

[35] See e.g., *R. v. L.F.W.*, [2000] 1 S.C.R. 132.

[36] For cases establishing some of the principles of sentencing, see *R. v. Nye* (1988), 27 O.A.C. 136 (Ont. C.A.), in
which an abuser with a prior record of sex offences against children received six months of imprisonment
followed by three years of probation for fondling a 13-year-old girl. In *R. v. Owens* (1986), 33 C.C.C. (3d) 275
(Ont. C.A.), a male teacher received three months of imprisonment followed by two years of probation for
fondling young male students.

the views of the victim, there would be even more pressure on children to request leniency for abusive parents. As the Alberta Court of Appeal observed:[37]

> We cannot...save the denunciatory sentence only for cases where families are not to be restored...if we did so, the offender could hold the family hostage to feelings of pity or guilt...if we lighten the sentence because a child victim "forgives" her father, we are threatening the child that if she will not forgive her father we will condemn him to prison. This is not right.

While denunciation and deterrence are very important in abuse cases, if the court believes that an offender is amenable to rehabilitation and that the family unit can ultimately be restored, this is undoubtedly a mitigating factor and, for example, progress in counselling prior to sentencing may be taken into account.[38]

Conversely, cases where there is a pattern of reoffending, especially if it involves children, will result in longer sentences. There are provisions in the *Criminal Code* for the imposition of indeterminate sentences on those who repeatedly commit offences against children and are found to be "dangerous or long-term" offenders.[39] There are also provisions in the *Code* that allow conditions to be placed on sexual offenders who have been released into the community at the end of their sentence, such as staying away from parks or schools.[40] While only providing limited protection to children, the enactment of these provisions does signal that society is taking offending against children more seriously.

The Criminal Process and Child Protection Proceedings

In cases of alleged abuse by parents, there may be both a child protection proceeding and a criminal prosecution for abuse. The rules of evidence are generally more flexible in the civil child protection proceeding than in the criminal trial. If there has been a joint investigation, it will not be uncommon for the investigating officer to testify in the child protection proceeding, and the child protection workers involved may be called upon to testify in criminal court, though this is less common.

The child will usually have to testify in criminal court, but there is a broader scope for the admission of a child's hearsay statements (out-of-court disclosures) in the civil child protection case, especially if a videotape was made of the

---

[37] *R. v. T.; R. v. S.* (1983), 46 A.R. 87 at 91 (Alta C.A.). In this sentencing appeal, the court ordered a man imprisoned for two years less a day, followed by two years probation, despite his willingness to undergo treatment and his victim's request for leniency. The man was convicted of sexually abusing his daughter over a lengthy period of time, with numerous sexual acts, including intercourse. On the same occasion the Alberta Court of Appeal affirmed a suspended sentence for a man who fondled his daughter on a single incident, because the man expressed remorse and had undergone treatment.

[38] See e.g., *R. v. Shalley* (1983), 2 O.A.C. 398.

[39] See *Criminal Code*, ss. 752-761; and Chapter 12, A. Manson, *The Law of Sentencing* (Toronto: Irwin Law, 2001).

[40] See *Criminal Code*, s. 810.1.

investigative interview, which may mean that the child will not have to testify in the child protection case.

The legal issues, the rules of evidence and the standards of proof will be different in the two proceedings, but the central factual issue will be the same — did the parent abuse the child? If the civil child protection proceeding occurs first and the parent chooses to testify at the prior civil trial, invariably to deny the allegations, the Crown prosecutor may order a transcript of the parent's testimony. While the *Charter*-guaranteed "privilege against self incrimination" prevents direct use of the prior testimony against the parent in the criminal trial, if there are any significant discrepancies between the testimony at the two hearings, the Crown may use the prior testimony to discredit the credibility of the parent when the parent testifies in the criminal trial.[41] It is for this reason that the criminal defence counsel for a parent charged with abuse usually advises the parent against testifying in any prior civil proceeding, and advises the parent to attempt to have any child protection trial postponed until after the conclusion of the criminal case. If the criminal charges are serious, and there is, for example, a preliminary inquiry, it may take months or even years for the criminal proceeding to be resolved.

The parent may also argue that the resolution of the child protection proceeding should be postponed because the outcome of the criminal case may have an effect on the civil case. Because the standard of proof is higher in a criminal case, the fact that a person has been acquitted in a criminal trial is not proof in a civil child protection trial that the person did not abuse their child. However, if a person is convicted in criminal court of having abused a child, this will usually be accepted as conclusive proof of this fact in a later civil trial.[42] Further, if a parent is convicted in criminal court, any sentence that is imposed may affect their possibility of resuming care of the child or even visiting with their child, as the sentence may involve imprisonment or prohibit contact with the victim or other children.

The judge in the child protection case may exercise some discretion about whether to adjourn the case until the resolution of the criminal proceedings, either by adjourning the ongoing child protection case or by making an interim order rather than a permanent order. The jurisdiction of a court to delay a resolution of a child protection proceeding may be affected by legislation that limits the total amount of time that a case can be adjourned or a child can be in temporary care.[43] In dealing with a request to delay resolution of a child protection proceeding, the court may consider such factors as how long it is likely to take to resolve the criminal case, the age of the child, and the seriousness of the charges that the parent is facing. Even if only one parent has been criminally charged, the

---

[41] See e.g., *R. v. W.D.B.* (1987), 38 C.C.C. (3d) 12 (Sask. C.A.); and also discussion in *R. v. Noel* (2002), 5 C.R. (6th) 1 (S.C.C.).

[42] See e.g., *Toronto (City) v. Canadian Union of Public Employees, Local 791*, [2001] O.J. 3239 (C.A.).

[43] See e.g., Ontario *Child and Family Services Act*, R.S.O. 1990, c. C-11, ss. 52 and 70, and the discussion in Chapter 3.

child protection court may consider whether the other parent nevertheless has a degree of responsibility for failure to protect the child that should be considered in the child welfare proceeding. As noted by one Ontario judge in refusing to delay making a permanent wardship order while criminal proceedings were resolved, ultimately the "best interests [of the child may] call for a resolution" of the child protection proceeding without waiting for a resolution of the criminal proceeding, rather than allowing a "prolongation of the state of uncertainty about the child's future."[44]

---

[44] *R.A. v. Jewish Family and Child Services*, [2001] O.J. 47 (Sup. Ct.), per Lane J.

11

Rules of Evidence and Preparing for Court

D.A. Rollie Thompson[1]

The Courtroom from the Witness's Perspective

"What you see depends upon where you sit." That just about sums it up for participants in the trial process. The counsel sit at their respective tables, looking at the judge and, to one side, the witness. The judge sits up at the front, surveying the assembled parties and their lawyers, taking notes and swivelling towards the witness from time to time. Both perspectives are well discussed in the literature on child protection and in the chapters of this book.

But what if you are a witness? You are called in from the waiting room when your number comes up. As the courtroom door opens for you, the room generally falls silent. You walk to the witness stand, with all eyes on you. Bible in hand, you take the oath, swearing to "tell the truth, the whole truth and nothing but the truth, so help me God." You sit down, give your name (spelling it if it's anything but "Smith") and the questions begin. Lawyer's questions — times, dates, places, who did what when, and who said what — details, details, and more details, often beyond the perception or memory of the average Nobel Prize winner. Then cross-examination and more questions, only now delivered with an edge in the lawyer's voice, pushing, probing, pulling, twisting, making the simple complex and the complex simple. Then the judge questions you, the lawyers get one last kick, and at last you get out of that chair. Now you get to walk back to that courtroom door, only this time no one is watching. They're finished with you.

It may not quite be Franz Kafka, but neither is it a day at the beach. This chapter will focus on the witness's perspective of the proceedings — across the table in the lawyer's office before court, in the waiting room outside Family Court and from the witness stand in the courtroom.

First, I will address the rights and obligations of a witness in child protection proceedings. Second, I will set out the basics of witness preparation for court, primarily what you are entitled to expect from the lawyer calling you. Third, the fundamentals of witness examination in the courtroom are presented. Fourth, I will discuss the cardinal principles of evidence law. Fifth, I will isolate a few of

---

[1] D.A. Rollie Thompson is Professor of Law, Dalhousie University, Halifax, Nova Scotia.

the most important rules of evidence for a witness in protection proceedings: opinion evidence, hearsay, past parenting evidence and privilege. In conclusion, I will make a few observations on evidence law in protection cases. Throughout I will focus on the relationships between lawyers and witnesses, which reflect an odd mix of law, trial practice and etiquette.[2]

What to Do after the Subpoena Is Served: Your Rights and Obligations

Your career as a witness in any particular case will typically begin with a telephone call from one of the lawyers in the case. In this section, I will take you from that first call to the arrival of the subpoena, and your resulting obligations and rights as a witness.

Dealing with Lawyers

Except for agency workers, most witnesses will first come into contact with a lawyer in a protection case with a telephone call, more or less out of the blue, from one of the lawyers, whether agency counsel, counsel for one or both parents or counsel for the child. From the beginning of this first conversation, a witness is entitled to know the lawyer's name, his or her firm, whom the lawyer represents and the particular proceeding in question. If the lawyer shows the poor manners of not introducing these particulars, the prospective witness should insist upon obtaining these details before any discussion takes place.

Generally speaking, witnesses have no obligation to discuss the details of their potential evidence with any counsel. Subject to confidentiality requirements, a witness may talk or not talk to the lawyer or limit the matters discussed. The witness controls the agenda at this early stage — you can stop the conversation at any time, refuse to answer certain questions, limit your answers or postpone discussion.

A professional witness will invariably have to be concerned with confidentiality, according to either the canons of the profession or the policies of the institutions within which he or she works, or both. A written release from the professional's client may be necessary, although some will be satisfied with prior verbal approval from the client or simply a familiarity with the client's lawyer.

Agency workers may face a different set of obligations in dealing with counsel for the parents or child. Unlike other witnesses, the agency worker in my view bears a general obligation of disclosure to opposing counsel, subject to agency policies and statutory requirements. Like agency counsel, an agency worker should have an affirmative obligation to make full disclosure to counsel for other parties, subject to claims of privilege and accepted local procedures.

---

[2] Obviously, the agency worker will have a different relationship with agency counsel, one much more long term and complex in nature than that of a non-agency witness. At this point I will focus solely upon the role of the agency worker as witness, although even here there are some significant differences. In the text, I will distinguish between "agency workers" and "non-agency witnesses."

Technically, no counsel has property in a witness. The mere fact that one counsel has contacted a witness first or even subpoenaed a witness, does not mean that the witness is barred from speaking to counsel for other parties. Again, subject to confidentiality restrictions, you are free to talk as much or as little as you wish. However, it should be pointed out that if you are a professional person, your unjustified refusal to discuss a case with a lawyer may be brought out at trial as adversely affecting your credibility, especially if you only talked to the lawyer for one side.

In one case where I acted for the parents, a worker for a family support agency was subpoenaed to testify by the agency. Between the time I spoke to the witness and her subsequent testimony at trial, the worker had changed her views on the parents' amenability to supervision and rehabilitation. Unfortunately, the worker was under the false impression that she could not talk to me after she received her subpoena from the agency, causing both myself and my clients to be surprised at her change of heart on the stand. That worker was perfectly free to approach me, as parents' counsel, prior to court and tell me of her changed views.

Affidavits

It has become increasingly common for witnesses in protection proceedings to be required to file written "affidavits." An affidavit is a sworn statement, essentially providing the same information you would provide if you testified in person on the witness stand (only without the lawyer's questions). Like your sworn testimony on the witness stand, your affidavit is usually limited to your personal knowledge about the matters in issue. Local court rules sometimes permit you to include matters based upon "information and belief" (i.e., what another person told or *informed* you and which you *believe* to be true). The lawyer calling you as a witness will usually interview you, then prepare a draft affidavit for you to review and, after any revisions, the lawyer will require you to "swear" the affidavit (i.e., to attest that all the information in the affidavit is true to the best of your knowledge).

Remember that your affidavit is a written substitute for your oral testimony before the court. It is *your* affidavit, not the lawyer's. When the lawyer prepares a draft affidavit, you are free to make whatever changes you wish, to make sure the affidavit says what you intend to say, and in the words you wish to use. Often attached to affidavits will be "exhibits," such as notes made by the witness, correspondence with others, or reports prepared by the witness.

Just as a potential witness has no obligation to discuss the details of their potential testimony with a lawyer, so too there is no obligation to provide or swear an affidavit in advance of a hearing. Where a client has not waived confidentiality over conversations with the witness or where the witness wishes to claim confidentiality over information for other reasons, it may not be appropriate to provide an affidavit at all. The lawyer would then have to subpoena the witness to attend in court, where the judge can consider and decide any claims of confidentiality or privilege, discussed later in this chapter.

Getting to Court: A Subpoena

Some witnesses will be quite content to attend court without a subpoena. Most lawyers, however, will have a subpoena served upon you. There are a number of reasons for the use of subpoenas. First, if a witness has not been subpoenaed and does not attend as expected, the lawyer may be denied an adjournment to locate and call the witness. Second, many witnesses will require a subpoena to obtain time off work. Third, most professionals should and do require a subpoena, to protect themselves on matters of confidentiality. Fourth, some willing witnesses may want a subpoena, since it allows them to say to the parents, afterwards: "I had no option." Finally, some witnesses simply will not attend without a subpoena, and some will not attend even with a subpoena.

What is a subpoena? Briefly stated, a subpoena (or a summons in some jurisdictions) amounts to an order from the court requiring you to attend court to be a witness at a stated place and time. Failure to obey a properly served subpoena can result in the issuance of a warrant for the arrest, detention and delivery of the witness to the court by the police.

Generally, a subpoena must be served upon the witness personally, along with any required witness fees. Apart from some special situations, no particular advance notice that a subpoena will be served is required, although common courtesy and a desire for a happy witness generally ensures that lawyers will provide adequate advance notice.

The subpoena will specify the place, date, time and proceeding in which you are to testify. It may require only that you personally attend, or it may go further and require that you bring with you documents or files relevant to the proceeding. If the latter direction is found in the body of the subpoena, then you must attend along with those documents or files.

As a matter of courtesy, most lawyers will provide you with the details of the timing of your attendance. If you are concerned about scheduling, then you should bring this to the attention of the lawyer calling you. Professionals with busy schedules can often be called first thing in the morning or the afternoon to ensure minimum disruption. But, in the end, unless you have a specific understanding with the lawyer calling you about the time of your appearance, the subpoena rules and you must attend as directed, even if it forces you to rearrange your appointment book.

If you attend at court and the matter is adjourned, then you may be called into the courtroom and directed to return at a specified date, which has the same operative effect as the subpoena proper.

Talking about the Case: Exclusion Orders

Witnesses to protection proceedings may or may not be permitted to sit in the back of the courtroom, before or after their testimony, depending upon local rules governing publicity and attendance by members of the "public," including media reporters. Generally, witnesses are left outside in a waiting room until it is time to testify. A protection court may, and usually will, make a formal "exclusion order" governing the witnesses in the proceeding. An "exclusion order" excludes witnesses from sitting in the courtroom or hearing the evidence before they have testified. Where the courtroom is closed or no members of the public attend, formal exclusion orders are often not made, but everyone seems to assume the operation of the exclusion rules described below.

Exclusion orders serve a number of important purposes: to avoid collusion amongst witnesses; to prevent the possibility of perjury; to avoid the inevitable influence of one witness's testimony upon others, conscious or unconscious; and to deny witnesses the benefit of watching the cross-examination of other witnesses so that a witness cannot anticipate his or her own cross-examination.

Where witnesses are excluded, the judge or counsel should explain the effect of the order to witnesses to guide their conduct outside the courtroom. First, one witness is not allowed to talk to other witnesses about the contents of their prospective testimony. Second, a witness leaving the courtroom is not to disclose the testimony given or questions asked to other witnesses waiting outside. Third, only after a witness is off the stand and has been released from any possibility of being recalled can that witness converse about his or her evidence with another witness, and then only if that person is similarly finished. It is worth noting that lawyers are also bound by exclusion orders, once made, such that a lawyer may not disclose the substance of courtroom testimony to a prospective witness. Of course, prior to court, a witness is free to discuss the contents of his or her own prospective testimony with a lawyer, as part of the preparation process.

Generally, when a witness has finished testifying, counsel will indicate whether there is any further need for a witness to remain available to be recalled to the stand. If counsel fail to express any such need, but equally fail to release the witness from further attendance, the witness is entitled to request such a release from the judge and, if there is no objection from counsel, the witness will be free to go.

Preparing for Court: The Witness's Right to Adequate Preparation

The Witness's Right; The Lawyer's Obligation

The lawyer who calls you as a witness is expected to give you proper preparation for court, as a matter of professional courtesy and sound trial practice. Preparation practices vary considerably amongst lawyers, depending upon the time available, the courtroom experience of the witness and the importance of the witness to the case. Witnesses can, and should, insist upon proper preparation from the lawyer calling them. A lawyer's failure to do so doesn't excuse the witness from testifying, but it can certainly affect the quality and cogency of the testimony.

Even if time constraints are tight, as with interim hearings or last-minute arrangements, a witness is entitled to some minimum steps, even in the hallway outside the courtroom before the hearing begins. The "five-minute-manager" version of preparation should include the following basics from the lawyer: an explanation of what the hearing is about, what the major issues are, what your testimony needs to prove, and a very rough outline of the topics to be covered.

The Basics of Witness Preparation

Usually a witness will have had at least one meeting, if not more, with the lawyer who is calling the witness, including a review of any relevant documents or files. The witness preparation interview should take place before the hearing, well enough in advance to resolve any problems, but not so early that the witness may forget the instructions.

It is important for witnesses to appreciate that there is nothing wrong with reviewing their testimony with the lawyer calling them. It is an acknowledged and necessary part of trial preparation; judges and opposing lawyers know that it takes place. There is no reason to hide or to be embarrassed in the courtroom about prior consultations with the lawyer. If asked whether the lawyer calling you has discussed your testimony with you, the question should be answered with a simple "yes," if this occurred.

There are ethical rules governing a lawyer's preparation of a witness, but you should let the lawyer worry about those. Simply put, a lawyer preparing a witness is entitled to instruct the witness about the methods, techniques and proprieties of testifying, but is not permitted to tell the witness what to say. Preparation focuses on *how* to testify. As an example, I once had a witness in a case who was a retired member of the Canadian Navy, but when asked in my office what he had previously done for a living, he answered, "I was a member of the Canadian Armed Forces, Maritime Command." I told him, "No you weren't, you were in the Navy," to make the point that there was no need to use stilted, formal language and that his everyday way of speaking was good enough in court.

In preparing a witness, I generally begin with the minimum described above. First, it is essential that an individual witness appreciate what the case is about and what the central issues are, including the positions of the parties. Only then can a witness grasp why I am asking my questions and why opposing counsel will be pursuing their lines of cross-examination. Then I go on to explain the role played by this particular witness: what their testimony is intended to prove and how they fit into my theory of the case. Many lawyers fail to provide this sort of information, treating the witness as just a cog in the machine. In my opinion, a witness is entitled to this information, since the witness is more than just a receptacle of a fixed supply of testimony, and is, in fact, a participant in the process. Should a lawyer fail to supply this larger context, the witness should ask questions to elicit this information.

The witness preparation interview then proceeds to the nuts and bolts of direct examination, sometimes called examination-in-chief. During direct examination, the examining lawyer is generally not permitted to lead the witness; that is, ask questions which suggest the desired answer. This means the questions must be open-ended, in the form of "who, what, where, when, why, and how." It is thus essential that the witness understand the matters sought by these formal, studiously neutral questions. That understanding is obtained by the lawyer taking the witness through the complete direct examination, at least once, or more often if necessary.

On this dry run, the lawyer and the witness essentially negotiate the form and content of the witness's testimony. If the lawyer presents a question that is unclear, the witness should ask that the proposed question be reformulated. If the witness does not understand the rationale for any question, the lawyer should explain the point of the question. If matters are left out, then the witness should ask why and explain why he or she thinks it is sufficiently important to be included. In some areas, it may be necessary for the witness to indicate the limits of first-hand knowledge to settle whether a question and answer will serve any useful purpose. In matters of opinion, you may feel there are limits to the opinions you are prepared to express and those limits should be clearly defined for the lawyer. By the time this process is complete, the direct examination should flow smoothly, with comfortable transitions from one topic to another and questions that the witness understands and can answer.

While preparation is necessary, your direct examination should not appear stilted or rehearsed. To avoid this, I tend to vary the structure and sequence of my questioning on each run through the direct examination.

If exhibits are to be introduced through the witness, typically documents from the witness's file, I walk the witness through the formal process of proving or authenticating the exhibit as it will take place in the courtroom. It is vital that the witness have copies of any exhibits and read them carefully before the hearing date. If a witness intends to "refresh memory" from notes or a file, I take the witness through the rote questions required for the court to grant permission to do so. More on this later.

For expert witnesses giving opinion evidence, it is critical that the lawyer and the witness have a common understanding of the precise phrasing and scope of questions eliciting opinions. Here the expert witness must be much more active in the preparation process, firmly establishing the permissible parameters of the questions, and ensuring accurate and precise language.

Proper preparation should cover not only direct examination, but also the cross-examination by opposing counsel. All witnesses should be subjected to some sample cross-examination, for a couple of reasons. First, there are always weaknesses in direct testimony and the witness should be prepared to meet those weaknesses, which will be probed by opposing counsel. Second, cross-examining lawyers use a traditional collection of techniques. The lawyer calling you should, through a sample cross-examination, demonstrate those techniques and assist the witness in finding methods of responding to them. Some simple examples include attempting to turn a minor inconsistency into a major one, forcing the witness to qualify strong statements, confusing the witness, limiting the witness's ability to qualify answers and leading the witness into "traps."

The lawyer should also explain that, on occasion, one or other of the lawyers will object to a question or answer. Once a lawyer rises to object, the witness should immediately stop talking. The lawyers will then argue about whether a question is permissible or certain testimony is admissible and the judge will rule whether the question can or must be answered or the testimony continued. Once the judge has made a ruling, then the witness will be told whether or not to proceed with the answer. Whether an objection is sustained or overruled should not be taken by the witness as a reflection on the quality of the testimony — it's a matter of legalities, for the lawyers and the judge.

Lastly, the lawyer should give you some guidance on the basics of courtroom layout and practice, such as where the witness stand is, where the lawyers sit and how to address the judge. In this pre-hearing interview, it is vital that the witness raise any questions, fears or concerns about testifying or the testimony to be given. Once you take the stand, the lawyer calling you is no longer able to help you on these points.

Some Pointers for Witnesses

As part of witness preparation, most lawyers will run through a standard list of do's and don'ts. Some even put the list in writing for the prospective witness to review. Here is a sample of some of the instructions I offer to witnesses:

1. *Tell the truth.* Honesty is the best policy. Honesty means being accurate, not venturing beyond what you know and not backing off from what you do know.

2. *Listen to the question.* Answer the question that is asked. Answer that question and no more. If your lawyer wants more information from you, he or she will ask another question. If the other lawyers want more information from you, let them ask another question.

3. *Take your time.* Testifying is not a quiz show. Think before you answer. If you need more time to think, tell the court that you need a moment to think about the matter.

4. *Don't guess.* If you don't know, say "I don't know." If you can't remember, say "I can't remember." No one can know or remember everything — judges realize that too.

5. *If you don't understand the question, say so.* If you don't understand the question, especially in cross-examination, ask the lawyer to repeat or rephrase the question. It is up to the lawyers to ask understandable questions — you're just a witness.

6. *Speak up.* Answer questions clearly and firmly. Say "Yes" or "No," because the taping equipment can't record a nod or a shake of the head.

7. *Be as precise as you can be, but no more.* No one remembers every detail. If you can give an exact date, time or distance, fine. But if you can't, do your best while making clear that you are approximating.

8. *Never say never, never say always.* Beware of answering any question by saying "I never do this" or "I always do that." The other lawyer may well find some occasion when you did otherwise.

9. *If you make a mistake, admit it.* If you slip up while testifying, correct yourself as soon as possible. We all sometimes make mistakes.

10. *Be polite and serious.* Simple courtesy to others in the courtroom always makes a good impression. And the courtroom is no place for jokes and wisecracks.

11. *Don't argue with the other lawyer.* Just answer the questions in cross-examination. Don't argue with the other lawyer — the lawyer will always win the argument, not because he or she is smarter, but because the lawyers get to ask the questions.

12. *Don't lose your temper.* Opposing lawyers try to aggravate you. Don't give them the satisfaction of losing your temper. If you lose your temper, you may say dumb things that will come back to haunt you.

13. *Don't ramble or volunteer information.* In cross-examination, answer the question, then stop. Don't ramble on just to fill the silence in the courtroom. It's up to the other lawyer to think up the next question. Don't volunteer information.

14. *If you're certain, don't back down.* Cross-examining lawyers will try to make you qualify yourself. If you are sure of what you saw or heard, stick to your guns in cross-examination.

15. *When you want to make a point, look at the judge.* In the end, it is the judge who has to decide the case. That's the person you have to convince, so don't forget to look at the judge, rather than the lawyers asking you the questions.

Besides running you through these do's and don'ts, the lawyer should also address any particular problems that you have exhibited in your preparation interview. Each of us has annoying habits, tics or nervous behaviours which detract from our testimonial abilities — everything from pulling one ear to inappropriate smiling to fiddling with some article of clothing or whatever. It is better that the witness be embarrassed in the privacy of the lawyer's office than in the public forum of a courtroom.

The Basics of Witness Examination: A Primer for Witnesses

By definition, lawyers are comfortable with the formalities and rituals of courtrooms. After all, that's where litigation lawyers spend much of their lives. Not so for the witness, especially the inexperienced witness. In this section, I will outline the basics of the examination of a witness, providing some pointers along the way.

The Basic Structure of a Witness Examination

There is a well-defined pattern to the short (sometimes longer) life of a witness on the stand in the courtroom. After you are called to the front of the courtroom, the clerk will place the Bible in your right hand and recite the standard oath.[3] The precise form of the oath varies, depending upon local practice, but it will run something like this: "Do you swear that the evidence to be given by you to the court touching the matters in question between the parties shall be the truth, the whole truth and nothing but the truth, so help you God?" To which you reply, "I do."

With the oath out of the way, you take the witness chair. The lawyer who has called you will then begin the direct examination, usually with some basic identifying information: your name, address, occupation, position, and so on. If your name poses any difficulties at all, you will be asked to spell your name for the court record.

The direct examination by the lawyer will consist of non-leading or open-ended questions, as was reviewed in the preparation interview. Once the direct is complete, the examining lawyer will sit down. At this point, the judge will turn to the opposing lawyer (or one of them if there is more than one) and ask for cross-examination. Cross-examination consists of a series of leading questions or, better, leading statements. No longer will the questions take the form, "Where were you at five o'clock that day?" but instead, "At five o'clock, you were at the home of Mrs. Smith, weren't you?"

Once the cross-examining lawyer is finished, the lawyer calling you will be asked for any redirect (i.e., any further questions arising from the cross-examination). There may or may not be any redirect.

At this point, the judge may choose to ask you a number of questions, which may or may not be leading. After the judge is finished, he or she will afford the lawyers an opportunity to ask further questions, the lawyer calling you first and then the cross-examining lawyer(s). Now you're finished and the judge will tell you that you may leave the witness stand.

Direct Examination

With the benefit of proper preparation, your direct examination should be relatively straightforward, following the sequence of topics and questions now familiar from the earlier session(s) with the lawyer. By the time you take the stand, you should be comfortable with the awkward form of open-ended questions on direct. If an affidavit has been filed, the direct examination will be brief. The lawyer may require you to identify and verify your affidavit on the stand, followed by a few questions to correct or update any information in the affidavit.

---

[3] If for any reason you object to taking the oath on the Bible, or a similar Holy Book such as the Torah or Koran, you may choose to affirm; i.e., to give a solemn affirmation that you will tell the truth, in a form similar to the oath, but without reference to God.

The purpose of direct examination is to lay out for the court what the witness knows that is of relevance to the issues in the case. First, it is critical for the lawyer to create a record, to place into evidence that information which is necessary to the lawyer's theory of the case; that is, the intended argument as to why his or her client should succeed. Second, the testimony should be organized and elicited in a way which is as persuasive to the court as possible. To be persuasive, the testimony must be clearly and logically developed and the witness must be credible — the first of these is largely in the hands of the lawyer, but the second is largely determined by the background and demeanour of the witness.

During direct examination, opposing counsel may object to a question asked by examining counsel or to some part of your answer. Later in this chapter, I will deal in greater detail with objections based upon the most important rules of evidence: hearsay, opinion and privilege. Here I will only briefly recount the most common objections raised on direct examination.

1. *Improper leading.* A leading question can take one of two forms. Best known is a question which suggests the answer the questioner desires. Less common, but equally objectionable, is a question which provides factual detail which could and should originate from the witness.[4] In the first case, the concern is improper suggestion to the witness and, in the second, that of improper ratification by the witness. Both attempt to ensure that the court hears the evidence as told freely and in his or her own words by the witness.

   There is no absolute rule against leading questions. The rule only bars *improper* leading. It is permissible for counsel to lead in a variety of situations: introductory matters, matters not in dispute, authenticating or proving exhibits, sometimes where the material is extremely complicated, to contradict a specific statement of another witness, to elicit testimony from a witness of limited abilities, to supply detail omitted by the witness out of forgetfulness or impaired memory, or to correct obvious misstatements of a witness. Determining whether a question is leading or not, how much leading may take place and when it becomes characterized as "improper" leading are left to the discretion of the trial judge, usually brought into play by an objection from one of the lawyers.

   If a judge concludes that a question involves improper leading, then one of three steps can be taken: (a) most commonly, the question is disallowed and the lawyer is asked to rephrase the question; (b) counsel is admonished by the judge, typically where the leading is the product of incompetence or bad intent; or, (c) in rare cases, the judge will disallow the question and, because of the seriously suggestive nature of the question on important matters, not allow the question to be restated. Most importantly, any answer to a question after improper leading may

---

[4] On these and other issues of the form of questions on direct and cross-examination, see M.P. Denbeaux and D.M. Risinger, "Questioning Questions: Objections to Form in the Interrogation of Witnesses" (1979), 33 *Arkansas Law Review* 439.

be given less weight in the judge's later assessment of the witness's testimony.

For the witness, it is important to realize that improper leading is a sin committed by lawyers. The witness is a mere bystander in the fray, bearing no responsibility for the judge's anger or frustration. Your job is to wait until the fuss is over and answer the next question.

2.   *Hearsay.* Sometimes a question will explicitly seek hearsay and sometimes the witness will inadvertently introduce hearsay in the answer. The witness should be instructed in preparation about the hearsay rule to avoid objections of this kind. Hearsay is an out-of-court statement (usually by someone other than the witness on the stand) offered to prove the truth of the matters asserted in the statement. I will address the hearsay rule and its exceptions below.

3.   *Opinion.* If a witness is not qualified as an expert witness (and thus entitled to give opinion evidence), then there are limits upon the witness giving testimony in the form of opinions, as opposed to matters of fact. More on this later.

4.   *Unresponsive.* The witness is required to answer the questions put on direct and then stop. If the witness fails to answer the question directly or answers and then rambles, an objection may be made. In this case, it is the fault of the witness and the witness may even be instructed on how to answer questions, with varying degrees of restraint, by the presiding judge.

There is an endless variety of potential objections during direct examination, of which only the most common are listed above. The vast majority of objections on direct reflect poor preparation of the witness by counsel or poor self-preparation by counsel. Some objections reflect battles amongst lawyers over evidentiary matters of little direct concern to the witness.[5]

Refreshing Memory: Using Notes

Most professional witnesses will bring their notes or file concerning the child or parents to the stand. When you deal with many individuals in the course of your work, it is difficult, if not impossible, to testify to the details without aid of your notes. You should have discussed the use of your notes in advance with the lawyer calling you.

If you wish to consult your notes to testify, the lawyer will typically take you through a rote series of leading questions: "Do you have with you your notes concerning your meetings with Mrs. Smith? And were those notes made by you at or near the time of the matters noted? Do you wish to consult those notes in

---

[5] In some instances, as in matters of opinion or privilege, the lawyer calling you should be aware of the problem in advance and warn you of the impending battle, precisely to avoid misinterpretation by the witness.

giving your testimony today?"[6] At this point, the judge will generally look to the opposing lawyer and ask if he or she has any objections, after which the court will generally grant permission to employ the notes in testifying.

A few points about notes. First, it is not necessary to exhaust your memory before being permitted to look at your notes. It is sufficient that you can give a fuller and more accurate account of the facts with the aid of the notes.

Second, once you use the notes to refresh your memory, opposing counsel will generally be permitted to inspect *all* your notes or your *whole* file prior to cross-examination, not just the parts you relied upon in direct examination. In effect, this means that everything in your file or notes can conceivably become fair game for cross-examination. Accordingly, it is essential that the lawyer calling you be familiar with the full file (assuming no confidentiality problems) and, more important, that you as a witness review the full contents of your file or notes before taking the stand. In my experience, some professionals are surprised to learn that the opposing lawyer is free to root through the notes, especially as such notes in protection cases often contain damaging confidential information about the parties.

In taking notes, especially where a proceeding can reasonably be anticipated or is already under way, the professional should be aware of what can happen to those notes in the courtroom. Many such witnesses find themselves on the horns of a dilemma. If you take careful notes, then lawyers will pick through the details for those most useful to their case. Yet if you fail to keep adequate notes, your credibility will be attacked based upon your largely unaided memory. Moreover, it is in the nature of note taking to be selective — to note only the important or the unusual. For example, if the professional supervised a parental visit, an uneventful visit may only result in a note, "Parent visited today for two hours," while an eventful visit will cause much more detailed note taking, exposing the witness to allegations of bias or at least unfair selectivity. I believe it is a wise course for witnesses to attempt to maintain consistent note taking, with sufficient detail of all encounters, to avoid such allegations.

Once granted permission to use notes, it is vital that the witness not merely read the notes, but truly use them as intended, namely to trigger or refresh memory. The notes should be an aid, not a crutch. Further, care should be taken to recount all the circumstances of a given encounter as revealed in the notes. Opposing counsel is entitled to inspect the notes and any conscious or unconscious editing on the stand will offer a prime target for cross-examination.

Cross-Examination

The cross-examiner generally has three purposes: (a) to obtain statements, especially admissions, of fact useful to his or her case; (b) to test and discredit

---

[6] Despite the form of these rote questions, a witness may refresh his or her memory from notes made later or even made by another person, so long as the notes act "as a trigger for [the witness's] memory": *R. v. Bengert (No. 5)* (1978), 15 C.R. (3d) 21 (B.C.S.C.) at 23, affirmed (1980), 15 C.R. (3d) 114 (B.C.C.A.) at 160-63. This approach was approved by the Supreme Court of Canada in *R. v. Fliss* (2002), 49 C.R. (5th) 395 (S.C.C.).

the story of the witness by exposing inconsistencies, gaps or errors; and (c) to discredit or impeach the basic credibility of the witness. This is not an easy task for the lawyer, despite your recollections of old Perry Mason shows, as most witnesses do their best to tell the truth on direct and all witnesses are on their guard for cross-examination.

The cross-examining lawyer attempts to control the witness, to draw out from the witness only what the lawyer wants. Some lawyers seek to control the witness through bluster, raised voice and intimidation. Often the most effective lawyers are the quiet, courteous and determined ones, who control your answers through a steady stream of carefully planned questions that do not disclose their purpose.

The cross-examiner's major tool for control is the leading question or statement. Or, more particularly, a series of simple, clear statements to which you tend to reply "yes" or "no." For example, where an agency worker on direct characterizes a mother's behaviour with her child during a supervised visit at the agency as "uncertain," "distant," and "unemotional," the mother's counsel might pursue the following cross-examination:

Q.   This was the first visit for the mother since the apprehension, wasn't it?

A.   Yes.

Q.   In fact, wasn't it the first time she had ever been inside the agency offices?

A.   Yes.

Q.   You were present in the room throughout the visit?

A.   No, I would leave the room for a few minutes at a time.

Q.   For the first half-hour, you were in the room the whole time, isn't that correct?

A.   Yes.

Q.   And naturally you were watching both mother and child carefully, weren't you?

A.   Yes.

Q.   And Mrs. Smith knew you were watching her carefully, didn't she?

A.   I suppose so.

Q.   Yourself, you weren't sure what to expect on this visit, right?

A.   I had some idea, but no, I wasn't entirely sure.

Q.   You wanted to make sure things went smoothly, didn't you?

A.   Yes.

Q.   So you were very careful in what you said and what you did?

A.   Yes.

Q.   You remained calm and professional throughout, I assume?

A.   Yes, that's correct.

Note the form of the cross-examination questions — short, pointed statements, a little bit at a time, leaving little room for editorial comment. Also noteworthy is the cross-examiner's focus, not upon the mother, but upon the worker's own reactions. If continued in this vein, the cross-examination will succeed in conveying the tense, unfamiliar atmosphere, neutralizing the worker's statements on direct and laying the groundwork for a few comments in closing argument, all without ever once confronting the worker openly on the issues.

Fortunately or unfortunately, depending upon your perspective, skilful cross-examinations are relatively rare, especially in child protection cases. More common are the unskilled, repetitive, awkward, and ineffectual cross-examinations.

Improper Forms of Cross-Examination

Generally speaking, the lawyer who calls you as a witness is responsible for objecting to improper cross-examination. Accepting that objections must be made strategically to avoid an appearance of obstructionism, many lawyers subscribe to the "no objections" philosophy that it is best to let the witness fend for himself or herself, to show that they can manage on their own. Because cross-examination focuses, not only on the facts of the case, but also on the credibility of the testimony and the witness, the courts will generally give wide latitude to the cross-examiner in the form and content of cross-examination.

Cross-examination does have its limits, although not always policed with vigour by lawyers and judges, and often not apparent to the witness on the stand. Here I want to focus upon improper forms of questions in cross-examination, for two reasons: first, to prepare you for what will surely come your way in cross-examination; and, second, to assist you as a witness when the lawyers don't offer much help. In this list, I will identify the problems by the traditional phraseology of objections to improper questions.

1. *Too general.* A witness is entitled to proper notice of the intended subject matter of the question. In effect, you are entitled to a sufficiently specific question to know what the examiner is after. For example, if you are asked: "How would you describe your relationship with the child's mother?" it is perfectly proper for you to reply, "In what respect?" or "What particular aspect of the relationship are you asking about?"

2. *Irrelevant.* While a wider compass is permitted in cross-examination, clearly irrelevant questions are not permitted. In a protection case, if you were asked whether you were a member of the Socialist Social Workers Club, it is unlikely that your political views would possess any relevance to the facts in issue, including your credibility.[7] If there is any question as to the relevance of a cross-examination question, yet no objection is

---

[7] Just such a question of a witness, whether he was a Marxist-Leninist, was ruled irrelevant in a picket-line assault case in *R. v. Fields* (1986), 53 C.R. (3d) 260 (Ont. C.A.).

forthcoming from a lawyer, the witness may ask the judge whether the question is relevant and must be answered. The judge may require cross-examining counsel to explain the relevance of the question. But, if the judge rules the question relevant, you must answer the question. Should you continue to refuse to answer after the judge's ruling, you can be found in contempt of court.

3. *Seeking inadmissible evidence.* Just as during direct examination, a question asked in cross-examination may seek to elicit evidence that would contradict one of the rules of evidence, such as inadmissible hearsay, opinion or privileged information. Except for privilege, such problems should be left to the lawyers or the judge.

4. *Ambiguous.* The questions in cross-examination should be clear and reasonably specific. If you don't understand the question, you are entitled to say, "I don't understand the question," and then it is up to the lawyer to rephrase the question so that you can understand it. Some questions may appear intelligible, but the ambiguity comes with the answer. Consider this question to an eyewitness: "Are you sure there is no possibility you were mistaken?" A simple "Yes" might mean, "Yes, I am sure" or "Yes, there is a possibility I was mistaken."

5. *Compound question.* A compound or multiple question is one which contains more than one question. In cross-examination, such compounding is particularly dangerous because the witness is pressed to ratify, through a single answer, more than one leading statement. For example, the question "Did you then go to the home of the parents and interview both parents and the child?" contains five separate factual inquiries. A "Yes" answer ratifies them all, while a "No" answer could deny one or all of them. The witness is entitled to have questions asked one at a time.

6. *Misstates the evidence.* The cross-examiner may, intentionally or unintentionally, misstate the evidence of another witness or your own evidence. If this occurs with your evidence and the lawyer calling you does not object, you should be quick to correct the misstatement.

7. *False choice, misleading.* Some questions are truly trick questions, in that they contain a false choice or a false dichotomy between two non-exhaustive alternatives. Take the commonly used but undeniably offensive question, "Have you stopped beating your wife?" or if you prefer, "Have you ceased being an alcoholic?" Whether you answer "Yes" or "No," you implicitly ratify the underlying assumption and any reluctance to answer makes you appear less than frank.[8] Few witnesses will have the presence of mind to address and deny the hidden assumption by saying "I have never beaten my wife" or "I have never been an alcoholic."

---

[8] *Supra*, note 4 at 478-81, for an excellent analysis of trick questions.

8. *Are you saying another witness is lying?* A less obvious form of false choice arises from a particularly improper form of cross-examination, one roundly condemned by the courts (including the Supreme Court of Canada), but one still ever-present in courtrooms.[9] Where an inconsistency is revealed between an answer of one witness and the evidence of another witness, the lawyer then asks, "Are you suggesting that witness A is lying?" There are many possible explanations for differing accounts, only one of which is that one or the other must be lying — a classic false choice. Not dissimilar is another gambit, where a witness acknowledges an inconsistency between an answer in cross-examination and a previous answer (on direct or in some pre-hearing statement), namely the question: "Well, which one is the truth?" or "So were you telling the truth then or are you telling the truth now?" Again, this presumes that only one of the two statements is the truth and excludes any other possible explanation for the inconsistency.

9. *Argumentative.* These are usually rhetorical questions, not really intended to be answered, and represent little more than an attempt by the lawyer to make part of his or her closing argument during cross-examination. Akin to this form of impropriety is editorializing upon your answers by the cross-examining lawyer, a more subtle but effective means to the same end. Leave these complaints to the lawyers.

10. *Badgering.* The Americans have a nice objection to this, termed "asked and answered." A cross-examiner is allowed to be persistent, to come back at the same point in different ways, in the hope of dislodging the witness from a previous answer. At some stage, persistence passes to redundancy, then on to badgering or full-scale arguing with the witness. Somewhere between redundancy and badgering, the court usually loses patience and allows a well-timed objection.

11. *Let the witness finish the answer.* Believe it or not, the most common objection in cross-examination is the failure of examining counsel to allow the witness to answer the question. Cross-examination is a battle for control between lawyer and witness. Many lawyers attempt to exert control by cutting off an answer, after the desired "Yes" or "No" answer. Most judges, with or without objection, will allow the witness to finish the answer, as long as the witness has been reasonably pointed and brief in previous answers.

   . The natural tendency of most witnesses, including experts, is to respond to a leading question in cross-examination with "Yes, but...,"

---

[9] Such questions were first condemned by the Supreme Court of Canada in *R. v. Markadonis*, [1935] S.C.R. 657 and most recently in *R. v. Brown and Murphy* (1983), 21 C.C.C. (3d) 477 (S.C.C.), affirming (1983), 1 C.C.C. (3d) 107 (Alta. C.A.). Appeal courts in Alberta and B.C. have recently overturned criminal convictions for such improper questioning by Crown prosecutors: *R. v. Kusk* (1999), 22 C.R. (5th) 50 (Alta. C.A.) and *R. v. Ellard* (2003), 10 C.R. (6th) 189 (B.C.C.A.).

then moving on to the qualifications upon the "Yes" or "No." Any pause or breath between "Yes" and "but" will provide the opening for the skilled cross-examiner to ask the next question, without appearing discourteous or unfair. Witnesses should work at avoiding this natural tendency, and try to let their answers take the form of "Insofar as (qualifying remarks), yes," putting the qualification first and forcing the cross-examiner to wait for the "Yes" or "No" at the end.

Cross-Examination on Previous Inconsistent Statements

None of us are ever perfectly consistent over time in our statements about a set of events or conditions. Especially in protection cases, witnesses will often have a long association with a family and the children, through ups and downs, through periods of support and periods of criticism. This creates fertile ground for previous inconsistent statements, the fodder of cross-examiners.

What can a cross-examiner do with a previous inconsistent statement? The lawyer is permitted to question you about the general subject matter of the prior statement, without disclosing to you his or her intention to employ the statement. After extracting inconsistent statements from you on cross-examination, the lawyer may then direct you to your previous written or oral statement.

Once confronted with the inconsistent statement, as a witness, you have three choices. First, you can adopt the prior statement, admitting its correctness and acknowledging the error of your current testimony. Second, you can admit making the prior statement, but seek to explain away the inconsistency, either in cross-examination or later on redirect. For example, it may be that you were in error earlier and, after an opportunity to reflect, you have changed your mind. Third, you can deny having made the earlier statement. If you do, however, the cross-examining lawyer will be allowed to call evidence from some other witness to prove you made the earlier statement. The judge will then be left to decide whether the earlier statement was, in fact, made.

Lawyers use previous inconsistent statements to cast doubt on a witness's credibility. Such statements can be drawn from a variety of sources: other witnesses to whom you may have spoken earlier, letters, notes in your file, other documents authored by you, previous affidavits or testimony in this or another proceeding. For this reason, before testifying, you should review your file carefully, both on your own and with the lawyer calling you as a witness.

Redirect Examination

After cross-examination is over, the lawyer calling you will be permitted an opportunity to conduct a redirect examination. Redirect is limited to new matters arising from the cross-examination, either to clarify or to further develop answers given on cross. Where no damage has been done in cross-examination, lawyers will generally not conduct any redirect.

The Cardinal Principles of Evidence Law

From the witness chair, legal arguments over the admissibility of evidence appear to be arcane disputes, largely engaged in by lawyers to keep damaging or prejudicial evidence out of the record. In fact, the law of evidence starts from a basic premise of admissibility unless some clear rule of evidence requires exclusion of evidence. Further, there is a tendency for the parties, especially in a protection proceeding, to consent explicitly or implicitly to the admission of evidence that may be technically inadmissible. In such situations, judges rarely refuse to admit evidence that the parties are prepared to have admitted. When evidence objections are raised, however, the arguments focus upon the so-called "exclusionary rules." All relevant evidence is admissible. The exclusionary rules are a series of exceptions, by which the law excludes certain kinds of relevant evidence for various reasons. Here I will first outline some of the general precepts of evidence law, before discussing the most important exclusionary rules.[10]

All Relevant Evidence Is Admissible

The first principle of evidence law is that all relevant evidence is admissible. Relevant evidence means "evidence having any tendency to make the existence of any fact that is of consequence to the determination of the [proceeding] more probable or less probable than it would be without the evidence."[11]

There are two components to relevance. First, any evidence offered must bear upon a fact in issue; that is, a fact which is of consequence to the litigation, a fact that is *material*, to use the legal term. Whether a fact is in issue is determined by the substantive law in the field and, within that substantive law, by the matters in dispute between the particular parties. For example, if the parent in a protection case concedes that the child should remain in temporary or society wardship, then the facts remaining in issue will relate to access or, perhaps, the terms of the wardship order. The second component is the more familiar meaning of relevance: the probative value of the evidence offered in relation to some fact in issue. That relationship has little or nothing to do with law, but is simply a matter of logic, experience and common sense.

Ultimately, the issue of relevance is a matter for the trial judge to determine. Given the multiplicity of issues in protection cases and the vague standards for finding and disposition, the limits of relevance in protection cases tend to be widely drawn and sometimes difficult to discern.

---

[10] I have discussed the purposes of evidence law at greater length in a recent article, "Are There *Any* Rules of Evidence in Family Law?" (2003), 21 *Canadian Family Law Quarterly* 245. *This article also reviews issues of privilege, opinion, and hearsay in family law cases generally, including protection cases.*

[11] This definition is drawn from the American Federal Rules of Evidence, Rule 401, reproduced in J.W. Strong (Ed.), *McCormick on Evidence*, 4th ed. (St. Paul: West Publishing Co., 1992) at 774.

Direct and Circumstantial Evidence

A distinction is sometimes drawn between direct and circumstantial evidence, with some undertone that the latter is less weighty evidence. Direct evidence consists of the testimony of an eyewitness to a specific event, for example, a person sitting in the family home when a parent physically assaults a child. Circumstantial evidence consists of evidence of facts which provide the basis for an inference that the event occurred, for example, evidence of a doctor that a child had suffered repeated serious injuries consistent only with the intentional application of force.

One should not presume that direct evidence of necessity possesses greater value than circumstantial evidence. Staying with the abuse example, compare the cogency of the doctor's circumstantial evidence of abuse with a parent's direct evidence that the child suffered the injury by falling off a tricycle. The former circumstantial evidence will generally be preferred if the child's injuries are inconsistent with the parent's explanation. Circumstantial evidence from a credible witness is often more compelling than direct evidence from a witness whose credibility is in issue.

Exclusionary Rules: Hearsay, Opinion, and Privilege

Evidence law starts from the premise that relevant evidence is admissible; that is, it may be placed before the judge for consideration in reaching a decision. Over the years, evidence law has developed a variety of rules which serve to exclude evidence from consideration by the court. In protection proceedings, those most commonly employed would be the rule excluding hearsay, the rule limiting opinion evidence, the rules of privilege and rules respecting evidence of past parenting. Each of these will be explored in greater detail below. If the judge rules that an item of evidence offends against one of these rules, then the evidence will be excluded; that is, the judge will not hear the evidence and it cannot form the basis of the court's ultimate decision.

Admissibility and Weight

Most evidence arguments relate to admissibility (i.e., whether the judge can hear and consider the evidence at all). But even if evidence is ruled admissible during the trial, that is not the end of the matter. After all the evidence has been heard, the lawyers will argue in their closing submissions over the "weight" to be given to individual items of evidence.

When we speak of the weight of the evidence, we are merely talking about the probative value of the evidence. For example, a note made by a nurse on a hospital chart may be ruled admissible as hearsay that comes in under the exception for business records, but the note may be ambiguous. Without the live testimony of the nurse to explain her note in more detail, the court may then conclude that the note deserves little or no weight in proving the mother's treatment of the newborn child.

The weight accorded to any item of evidence is finally a matter for the trial judge, when he or she makes the necessary factual findings to determine the appropriate disposition or whether the child is in need of protection.

Credibility

A central issue in most cases, especially protection cases, is the credibility of the witnesses. In determining what weight to give to testimony heard during the trial, the judge will have to determine credibility (i.e., who to believe on any given issue). The credibility of a witness is a function of the court's assessment of a witness's testimonial factors (i.e., personal knowledge based on perception, ability to perceive the event testified about, experiential capacity, memory, ability to communicate verbally and honesty).[12]

The assessment of credibility is one of the most difficult tasks facing a trial judge, who must rely primarily upon what the witness said in testimony as well as how the witness said it. A judge may occasionally find a witness simply not credible at all. More commonly, the judge will be left to sift through the testimony, accepting bits and pieces, preferring the evidence of one witness over that of another on a specific issue or event. In protection cases, precisely because the issues concern human relationships and characteristics, credibility is crucial to the fact-finding process. For this reason, protection appeals are rarely successful; appeal courts defer to the immense advantage of the trial judge in seeing the witnesses in person and observing their demeanour on the stand.

Application of Evidence Rules in Protection Cases

Despite the fixed sound of the phrase "rules of evidence," evidence law is applied with varying degrees of rigour depending upon the legal setting. Any person who has attended both a criminal trial for sexual abuse of a child and a child protection hearing in Family Court devoted to the same incidents will notice the different approach.

The rules of evidence are applied most stringently in criminal prosecutions, largely out of a concern for fairness to the accused. The limits of relevance are more tightly drawn and the exclusionary rules policed with greater care. Rules of evidence are relaxed somewhat in civil proceedings, where the interests of the parties are more evenly balanced. Within the civil sphere, family law cases tend to display an even more relaxed attitude towards evidence rules, notably in cases involving children. Where children are involved, the inherent vagueness of the "best interests" test renders the limits of relevance even harder to draw and there are strong tendencies for judges to admit more hearsay and opinion.

Protection proceedings sit uncomfortably within this spectrum in the application of evidence rules. As such cases must fundamentally focus on the welfare of the child, there are strong pressures to relax the rules of evidence, as in private custody cases. But, at the same time, protection proceedings involve a clash

---

[12] S.A. Schiff, *Evidence in the Litigation Process*, Vol. 1, 3rd ed. (Toronto: Carswell, 1988) at 200-02.

between the state and the individual, much like criminal matters, with the state agency bringing the parents and child before the court and seeking court-sanctioned intervention in the family. An order of permanent wardship (i.e., a permanent severing of the parent-child tie) is amongst the most serious steps that a society can take outside the criminal sphere. The seriousness of the issues and the gravity of the consequences drive courts towards a special concern for accuracy in factfinding and for fairness to the parents and child.

These pressures upon protection courts have led to some inconsistency and uncertainty in evidence rulings, depending upon the individual judge's perception of the appropriate model to apply.[13] At this point, I want to caution the reader: beware, the evidence law described in some parts of this chapter may or may not reflect your own experience in the particular courtrooms in your jurisdiction.

Opinion Evidence

Facts and Opinions

Evidence law distinguishes between facts and opinions. Witnesses testify as to facts based upon their personal knowledge, leaving it up to the judge to draw inferences from those facts. Any inference or conclusion drawn from those observed facts is characterized as opinion. There are two broad exceptions to this rule.

First, in matters calling for special skill or knowledge, a properly qualified expert will be permitted to range beyond first-hand knowledge of facts and offer opinions, providing inferences that the judge is unable to draw on account of the technical nature of the facts. Second, because of the often difficult and artificial distinction between fact and opinion, a lay witness (i.e., one not qualified as an expert) may be permitted to testify in the form of an opinion if the witness is in this way able to express more accurately the facts perceived.

Protection cases pose many problems in the application of these opinion rules because of the inherently interpretive nature of most evidence of child-rearing, parent-child interaction, child behaviour and parental conduct. When does an observation of fact become opinion? How much expertise must a witness demonstrate before being allowed to venture more complex opinions? What are the boundaries of the varying forms of expertise of witnesses called in protection cases?[14]

---

[13] I have developed these points in greater detail in a recent article, "The Cheshire Cat, Or Just His Smile? Evidence Law in Child Protection" (2003), 21 *Canadian Family Law Quarterly* 319. Much of the remainder of this chapter draws heavily upon this recent article, as well as an older two-part article: "Taking Children and Facts Seriously: Evidence Law in Child Protection Proceedings — Part I" (1988), 7 *Canadian Journal of Family Law* 11 and "Part II" (1989), 7 *Canadian Journal of Family Law* 223. Those with a desire to read further on these matters — with the benefit of too many legal-beagle footnotes — can refer to these articles.

[14] For a helpful review on expert evidence and assessments in family law, see N. Bala and A. Saunders, "Understanding the Family Context: Why the Law of Expert Evidence is Different in Family Law Cases" (2003), 20 *Canadian Family Law Quarterly* 277.

Qualifying as an Expert

Before being allowed to give opinion evidence, an expert must first be qualified by reason of sufficient skill, knowledge and experience in the pertinent field. The witness's qualifications are established in an initial stage of testimony, technically called a *voir dire*, to determine the admissibility of the expert opinion evidence.

Like any other part of a direct examination, the lawyer calling the expert should have run through the intended questions on the *voir dire* with the witness in the preparation interview. At the hearing, the lawyer will pose a straightforward series of questions pertaining to the expert witness's education, training, professional designations, publications, work experience and previous instances of acceptance by other courts as an expert — in effect, your curriculum vitae. It is not only proper, but advisable, that the lawyer lead the witness through this information, in order to avoid the appearance that the expert is blowing his or her own horn. In fact, a simple and effective way of proving qualifications is for the lawyer to introduce the witness's curriculum vitae as an exhibit, followed by questioning to highlight the relevant portions.

After counsel has completed the direct examination regarding qualifications, opposing counsel will have the opportunity to cross-examine on qualifications. In many instances, opposing counsel will concede the expert's qualifications (i.e., the admissibility of the expert opinion). If there is a question as to the witness's qualifications or the scope of the witness's permissible opinions, then counsel will argue the issue and the judge will rule on the issues. A typical ruling might be: "I find Ms Jones qualified to give opinion evidence as an expert social worker" or, where more specialized issues are involved, the court might add: "...and, more particularly, on the basis of her extensive practical experience and specialized training, to give expert evidence in respect of sexual abuse of children." Once the judge has ruled, the remainder of the witness's direct examination will take place. Even if there has been no challenge to the admissibility of the expert's opinions, opposing counsel will later cross-examine with a view to attacking the weight to be given to the opinions subsequently expressed.

The test for expert qualification is skill or expertise, not how that skill has been acquired, whether by education, training or experience. Hence, a social worker with 15 years of front-line experience in the field of child protection may qualify just as does a younger social worker with less experience but extensive education and training. In my own experience, being practical people, judges are inclined to prefer experience over academic education.

An Ontario case, *Catholic Children's Aid Society of Hamilton-Wentworth v. J.C.S.*,[15] reveals some of the difficulties that can be encountered. The agency social worker had completed one year of a B.S.W. program, followed by a two-year diploma in social services from a community college. After two years as a family enrichment worker, she had spent eight months as a children's

---

[15] (1986), 9 C.P.C. (2d) 265 (Ont. Unif. Fam. Ct.).

services worker, with some brief job-oriented training courses during that time, characterized as "superficial" by the trial judge. The case in question was in fact one of her first, starting shortly after her employment with the agency. Agency counsel sought to qualify her as an expert witness to render opinions on the issues of the best interests of the child, the appropriate disposition and the mother's parenting skills.

Judge Steinberg described the skills required to express these opinions as "...assessment skills not unlike those normally attributed to experienced psychologists and psychiatrists and senior experienced social workers."[16] First, the judge noted the worker's training was practical rather than theoretical. Second, the worker did not display the requisite work experience. The worker's experience was "very limited" and some of her experience was acquired from this very case, one of the first assigned to her.

For purposes of expert evidence, the individual worker's inexperience was not saved by the fact that she worked within a team at the agency, nor by the outstanding rating she received from her supervisor. As the court pointed out, the worker's "first-class potential" would have to be realized through future experience before she would be allowed to give expert opinion evidence. Based on this ruling, admittedly more strict than those commonly found in protection decisions, cases handled by inexperienced workers would require the active involvement of more senior agency workers or others who would qualify as expert witnesses.

The second half of the qualification equation is concerned with the nature of the opinions to be expressed. The more complex and specialized the subject matter of the opinions, the more demanding the court will be as to the witness's qualifications.

The Benefits and Costs of Expert Evidence

Just because there is a qualified expert witness doesn't automatically mean the evidence that witness gives is always admissible. Until 1994, Canadian courts had applied a very relaxed, common-sense approach to expert evidence. If the evidence would be "helpful" to the court, it would be admitted. In 1994, the Supreme Court of Canada raised the bar for expert evidence in a criminal case called *R. v. Mohan*.[17] In *Mohan*, the court emphasized the need for the trial judge to act as "gatekeeper" in admitting expert evidence and the implications of the court's cautious new approach are still being worked out in protection courts.

According to *Mohan*, "helpful" set "too low a standard" for expert evidence and the court required the evidence to be "necessary in the sense that it provide information which is likely to be outside the experience and knowledge of a

---

[16] *Ibid.* at 270.

[17] *R. v. Mohan*, [1994] 2 S.C.R. 9. In two subsequent decisions, the court further developed its *Mohan* approach: *R. v. D.(D.)*, [2000] 2 S.C.R. 275; and *R. v. J.(J.-L.)*, [2000] 2 S.C.R. 600.

judge or jury." In considering whether the evidence is "necessary," the Supreme Court has repeatedly noted the dangers of expert evidence: the bias of the "professional expert witness"; their use of jargon; their resistance to cross-examination by non-expert lawyers; the absence of any framework to assess their evidence when only one expert testifies; their reliance on hearsay sources; the expense, delay and consumption of time; the degeneration into a contest of experts; and the tendency of a non-expert judge to defer to specialized expertise. After *Mohan*, courts must weigh the "benefits" of expert evidence (i.e., its reliability and probative value) against these "costs" or "dangers" before allowing the expert to testify in a particular field of expertise.

Thus, there are *two* potential issues to be considered on a *voir dire* by the court before hearing the expert's opinion evidence: (1) Is this expert qualified to give opinion evidence, based upon education, training or experience? and (2) Is this expert testifying about matters where opinion evidence is "necessary," in the sense that the benefits of the evidence outweigh the costs and dangers? The second issue usually comes up in new areas of expertise, where there is less general acceptance of the probative value of the opinion. In *Mohan*, a defence psychiatrist was not allowed to testify about the psychiatric profiles of doctors who sexually abuse their patients, because his research was insufficiently developed. In the later case of *R. v. J.(J.-L.)*, the court rejected the testimony of a psychiatrist who used the penile plethysmograph as a means of diagnosing or predicting sexual behaviour.

For the most part, expert evidence is still readily admitted in protection cases, mostly because the experts are testifying in conventional and generally accepted areas of expertise. The *Mohan* approach does mean that objections can be raised to novel or unfamiliar or anecdotal forms of expertise or opinion. Even in these more contentious areas, specialized protection court judges are often prepared to admit the evidence, trusting in their ability to determine its reliability and weight, while remaining alive to its dangers.

The Expert's Opinions

Once qualified, an expert is liberated from the strict requirements for most witnesses that their testimony is based upon and devoted solely to first-hand observations of fact. In arriving at an opinion, an expert need not be so confined. The expert witness can draw upon varied sources of information in forming the opinions, such as first-hand observation, interviews, institutional records, other expert reports, texts, scientific literature, personal research and past professional experience in the field. In addition to being entitled to draw upon such information, the expert must detail the information upon which his or her opinion is based.

Inevitably, a substantial portion of that information base will consist of hearsay (i.e., out-of-court statements made by others to the expert to prove the matters asserted). Although it may be hearsay, an expert is allowed to state it in court for the purpose of identifying the basis of the opinion. It will be up to the lawyer calling the expert to ensure that those facts that form the basis of the opinion are properly proved through other witnesses and properly admissible evidence in order to underpin and support the expert's opinion.

An expert witness is often asked to prepare a written report for use in the proceedings, summarizing the expert's qualifications, involvement in the case and opinions. The lawyer calling the expert must file the report with the court and provide copies to all the other parties in advance of the hearing (days or weeks in advance, depending upon provincial rules and local practices). If a report has been filed in advance, the expert will still have to attend court to testify, unless waived by the parties. The report will be made an exhibit and will become the basis for direct and cross-examination.

A few comments about testifying on direct and cross-examination for experts are relevant here. First, experts must employ sophisticated, sometimes arcane, language to express their opinions accurately. Once a technical term is used, it should be explained in non-technical, accessible language. Further, jargon should be avoided where humanly possible. I once had a psychiatrist describe my parent client as "an episodic recreational user of soft drugs," which he then explained, at my insistence, to mean: "That's like being a social drinker." Second, as mentioned earlier, in respect of direct examination, experts should be quite specific about the limits and content of the opinions they are prepared to express on the stand. In my experience, experts have a tendency to express broader opinions in a private interview, when they aren't thinking of testifying (unlike lawyers, who always think in such terms), opinions that go further than they are prepared to defend on the stand. Further, lawyers usually have in mind the opinion they want for purposes of their case and often try to push and pull the opinion into that desired box. The expert must resist and, to avoid difficulties on the stand, even negotiate the very phrasing of critical questions.

Expert witnesses should be aware of the cross-examining lawyer's techniques to attack opinions expressed on direct. First, the brave or foolhardy lawyer may attempt to take the expert head-on in his or her field of expertise, employing texts, articles and other opinions to challenge the very formation of the opinion. In this type of cross-examination the expert has the upper hand against all but the most disciplined and knowledgeable lawyers. The expert witness need only become more detailed and specific about his or her knowledge in the field and the cross-examiner will often be forced to back off.

Another approach is to probe the expert's methods and sources. In assessments, for example, the cross-examiner will delve into the length and quality of interviews, the detail of note-taking, the adequacy of information, the range and quality of third-party sources explored, alternative hypotheses considered and rejected, matters included and excluded from the expert's report and direct testimony. In an imperfect world, with limited time and resources, few experts will achieve the perfection sought by the cross-examiner, thus opening up possible lines of methodological attack.

Third, the cross-examiner can accept the factual assumptions of the expert and attempt to offer an alternative interpretation (more favourable to the lawyer's client) than that put forward by the expert. In doing so, the lawyer is given the considerable advantage of choosing the field of the debate and confining the expert to answering in those areas. The expert must review his or her opinions for such weaknesses of interpretation and canvass the possible alternatives, preferably in conjunction with preparation by the lawyer calling the expert.

Fourth, and most common and effective, the cross-examiner will draw out factual errors and omissions on the one hand and supply new or additional facts on the other. By this technique, the lawyer seeks to undermine the opinion at its factual base, a field of endeavour where lawyers feel more comfortable. Typically, a series of such cross-examination questions will conclude with "Had you been aware of fact X, would that have altered your opinion?"

Opinion from Non-Expert Witnesses

As mentioned above, there is a second exception to the opinion rule, that of lay or non-expert opinion. The mere fact that a witness is not qualified as an expert does not bar the witness from occasionally testifying in the form of opinion. In my experience, courts in protection cases are prepared to allow considerable leeway for opinions, given the highly interpretive nature of much factual evidence about child-rearing and human behaviour.

A non-expert witness may express an opinion on matters requiring no special skill, where the facts perceived by the witness and the inferences from them are so closely associated that the opinion amounts to no more than a compendious statement of facts. While this covers a fair bit of ground in protection cases, there remain some important limits upon this lay opinion exception.

First, the witness may only testify to personal observations of the parent and child. Unlike an expert, a lay witness may not draw upon second-hand or hearsay sources in forming or expressing an opinion.

Second, this exception is intended only to allow the witness more accurately to express the facts observed. It is not a licence to offer free-standing, expert-like opinions. The opinion must be tied specifically to observed events, to the more concrete, detailed and specific end of the opinion spectrum. Thus, the non-expert witness should not phrase an answer in general terms, such as: "Mrs. Smith fails to discipline her child in age-appropriate fashion," but in more concrete, factual terms, such as: "Mrs. Smith would slap her 10-month-old child for minor misbehaviour like picking up a dangerous object, rather than simply removing the object from the child and saying 'No' in a firm voice."

Third, precisely because these opinions require nothing more than ordinary experience and no specialized knowledge, no preference should be given to the opinion of a non-expert social worker or official than to that of any other ordinary person, like a neighbour. All adults with a modicum of life experience should be treated similarly in the area of lay opinion, with credibility determined not by expertise but by the usual testimonial qualifications for factual matters.

Some Expert Issues: Sexual Abuse, Polygraphs, and Plethysmographs

Before leaving the opinion rule, a few recurring issues from protection cases should be considered, issues where the law is sometimes unclear and the practice of individual judges can vary widely. Typically, these issues arise around the proof or disproof of allegations of child sexual abuse.

Most frequent are the expert issues surrounding the identification and under-standing of child sexual abuse. Later, I will address the child hearsay issues, or how the child's evidence gets into court. Expert evidence about child sexual abuse can be classified into a number of general categories:

(a) evidence about the dynamics of child sexual abuse disclosure, including delayed disclosure, accommodation and recantation;

(b) evidence of behavioural symptoms that can accompany sexual abuse;

(c) evidence of factors that affect the reliability of the child's disclosures; and

(d) evidence of whether this child is telling the truth.

Criminal courts have uniformly rejected category (d), doubted the admissibility of category (c), and usually, but not always, admitted evidence in categories (a) and (b).[18]

Protection courts have been willing to admit all four categories of expert evidence, although there may be disagreements over category (d). In most instances, the expert offering the opinion of the child's truthfulness is the same expert who has interviewed and assessed the child and, pursuant to the emerging child sexual abuse hearsay exception, has relayed the child's statements of abuse to the court. In effect, the court is relying upon the expert's assessment of the child's credibility, as the child may not be taking the stand, and hence an opinion on the child's credibility may be admissible in a civil protection proceeding.

In my opinion, experts and counsel calling them should do their best to elicit evidence as to the child's credibility in the more detailed, concrete form of category (c), rather than the bald and more objectionable category (d). So long as the parent denies the sexual abuse and expressly argues or implies that the child is coached, exaggerating, fabricating, or fantasizing, then categories (a), (b), and (c) are plainly admissible in protection proceedings, precisely to counter the impeachment of the child's credibility.

Next, what about polygraph evidence? Sometimes the alleged perpetrator will want to lead lie detector evidence, to support denials of abuse. In 1987, the Supreme Court of Canada ruled in a criminal case that "the polygraph has no

---

[18] These issues have been discussed in a series of Supreme Court decisions, most notably: *R. v. B.(G.)*, [1990] 2 S.C.R. 3; *R. v. Marquard*, [1993] 4 S.C.R. 223; *R. v. Burns*, [1994] 1 S.C.R. 656; *R. v. R.(D.)*, [1996] 2 S.C.R. 291; *R. v. D.(D.)*, [2000] 2 S.C.R. 275. Of these, the clearest statement of the law is found in *Marquard*, which was actually a case of alleged physical abuse.

place in the judicial process where it is employed as a tool to determine or to test the credibility of witnesses."[19] That holding was explicitly extended by a provincial court judge into protection proceedings to bar such evidence in a sexual abuse case: *Catholic Children's Aid Society of Metro Toronto v. S.(J.).*[20] Consistent with this holding, even though investigators may continue to use them, there should be no reference made at all in the courtroom to polygraphs, a parent's agreement or refusal to take such a test, or the results of any test.

More recently, parties have attempted to lead evidence of phallometric testing, using the penile plethysmograph, to show that a man does or doesn't have certain sexual tendencies. In the leading criminal case of *R. v. J.(J.-L.),* the Supreme Court of Canada ruled that the accused could not lead this expert evidence to disprove his sexual tendencies, to show that he was not the kind of person to commit such sexual offences. The court held that the plethysmograph was not reliable as a means of diagnosing or predicting sexual behaviour, whatever its merits as part of a therapeutic regime for treating known sex offenders.[21] As with the polygraph, the Supreme Court's decision should likely bar the use of plethysmograph evidence in protection courts too.[22]

The Hearsay Rule and Its Exceptions

What Is Hearsay?

You are a witness on the stand. In a perfectly natural, neutral answer to a question, you say something like: "I arrived at the hospital and nurse X told me that there was a ruckus on the seventh floor where some parents were trying to take their child out of the hospital contrary to doctor's orders." Somewhere after "nurse X told me...," depending upon reflexes and alertness, the opposing lawyer bounds to his or her feet uttering the dreaded words, "Objection, HEARSAY!" What is going on here, you may ask?

First, your answer may or may not constitute hearsay. To be hearsay, two elements are needed. First, an out-of-court statement. That is satisfied, as you are repeating what nurse X said — nurse X is not here on the stand testifying, you are. Second, the statement must be offered to prove the truth of the matters asserted. What is the matter asserted? Here it is everything after "nurse X told me." But is it being offered to prove that? That is the crux of the hearsay rule. If you are offering the statement only to explain why you in turn went immediately to the seventh floor, technically it is not hearsay. It would be hearsay if you were offering nurse X's statement to prove that the parents were in fact removing the child contrary to doctor's orders. In practice, most judges would prefer that the witness avoid any hearsay dangers, by simply testifying, "After I spoke to nurse

[19] *R. v. Beland,* [1987] 2 S.C.R. 398.

[20] [1988] O.J. No. 2383 (Ont. Prov. Ct.).

[21] *Supra,* note 17.

[22] In one case, with some hesitation, an Ontario court admitted such evidence at the instance of the agency: *C.A.S. for Region of Peel v. S.R.,* [2002] O.J. No. 3501 (Ont. C.J.). That decision is likely wrong, given the Supreme Court's holding that such evidence is unreliable.

X, I went immediately to the seventh floor," without disclosing the details of the nurse's statement.

A statement only infringes the hearsay rule when it is offered to prove the truth of the matter asserted. There are many occasions when a witness on the stand offers another person's statement for a non-hearsay purpose. The following would be relevant examples from protection cases that would not infringe the hearsay rule:

1. *"I asked Mrs. Smith to visit on Wednesday and she agreed to come that day."* Mrs. Smith's words are offered to prove her agreement, irrespective of truthfulness, and hence are admissible.

2. *"On Tuesday, Mrs. Smith telephoned and said she wouldn't be able to visit on Wednesday because of a doctor's appointment."* Again, no problem, as the statement is offered to prove it was made, not for its contents.

3. *"I received a call from Mrs. Smith's mother. She told me that her grandson had been beaten and I therefore attended at Mrs. Smith's home and apprehended the boy."* The grandmother's statement would be admissible to demonstrate the worker's reasonable and probable grounds for apprehension, but not to prove that the child had in fact been beaten.

4. *"Mrs. Smith called late Friday and said, 'Come quick. I need help. Billy's been hurt.'"* The telephone statement is admissible, as the words are offered to prove the request and her belief that the child had been harmed, rather than the assertion of any particular fact.

5. *"Mrs. Smith called late Friday and said, 'Come quick. I need help. My husband has beaten Billy up.'"* This would be hearsay if it was offered to prove that Mr. Smith in fact had abused Billy and, in most instances, like the earlier hospital example, most courts would not allow it to be introduced in the absence of some hearsay exception.

Critical to the determination of whether an out-of-court statement is hearsay is the purpose for which it is offered. If the statement is explicitly offered to prove the truth of the matter asserted, then it will be characterized as hearsay and therefore inadmissible unless it falls within an exception to the rule. Moreover, where a statement may be used for a hearsay or a non-hearsay purpose, courts will usually assess the importance of the non-hearsay purpose in determining its admissibility. In most instances, the court will admit the statement while noting its limited non-hearsay use, although occasionally the cautious judge will prefer to avoid hearing unnecessary hearsay on crucial matters in issue, as in example (5) above or the earlier hospital example.

Exceptions to the Hearsay Rule

The hearsay rule is another exclusionary rule. If an out-of-court statement is offered to prove the truth of the matters asserted, the rule is that this hearsay is inadmissible, unless the statement falls within one of the recognized hearsay exceptions. Traditionally, these exceptions were treated as "pigeonholes," categories of statements that in turn had to meet specific legal requirements, such as admissions by a party or business records or prior testimony. If a statement met the requirements of one of these exceptions, then it was admissible. So tagging an out-of-court statement as "hearsay" doesn't mean it will always be excluded, which can be confusing for witnesses — and even some lawyers and judges.

Starting in 1990, with the landmark decision in *R. v. Khan*,[23] the Supreme Court of Canada began to reform and reconstruct the hearsay rule and its exceptions, a process that is still underway more than a decade later. It's no surprise that the case that started the "hearsay revolution" was a child sexual abuse case, where the statement of a three-and-a-half-year-old girl to her mother was held admissible to prove that abuse in a criminal prosecution. I will discuss child abuse hearsay at greater length below. The Supreme Court was not just addressing child abuse hearsay, but the very structure of the hearsay rule and its exceptions. In *Khan* and a series of subsequent cases, the court adopted an approach of "principled flexibility" to hearsay, taking the law back to its basic principles — why hearsay is excluded or admitted in the first place.[24]

Why do we exclude hearsay? Evidence at trial is presented by the oral testimony of witnesses, witnesses who testify under oath, who can be observed on the stand, and who are subject to cross-examination by opposing counsel. By these methods, especially cross-examination, the parties and the court can assess the reliability of the testimony. Not so with a statement made by what lawyers call an "out-of-court declarant"(i.e., the person making the statement now repeated in the courtroom). That statement is made outside the solemnity of the courtroom, not under oath, with no direct opportunity to observe the declarant's demeanour, and with no opportunity to cross-examine at the time the statement was made. All of these safeguards are lost if a witness on the stand can repeat what someone else said, to prove the truth of the events asserted in that hearsay statement. Thus the hearsay rule is intended to further two important and related values in our judicial process: fairness, as parties should be afforded an opportunity to test evidence offered against them; and reliability, as courts should be able adequately to assess the probative value of the evidence which will be relied upon in reaching a decision.

Not surprisingly, then, exceptions to the hearsay rule are built around three requirements: necessity, reliability and fairness. Necessity means that, were it not for the exception, the evidence might be unavailable to the court. Faced with the choice between no evidence and less reliable hearsay evidence, the court will often admit the hearsay. A classic example would be statements of a person now deceased or otherwise unavailable to testify. Reliability means that there is some

---

[23] *R. v. Khan*, [1990] 2 S.C.R. 531.

[24] The most prominent cases would be: *R. v. Smith*, [1992] 2 S.C.R. 915; *R. v. B.(K.G.)*, [1993] 1 S.C.R. 740; *R. v. Starr*, [2000] 2 S.C.R. 144. For an account of the court's hearsay decisions up to 1995, see D.A.R. Thompson, "The Supreme Court Goes Hunting and Nearly Catches a Hearsay Woozle" (1995), 37 C.R. (4th) 2282.

alternative assurance, other than cross-examination in the courtroom, that the out-of-court statement will be reasonably reliable. A prime example would be the exception for regularly kept business records, where the methods of record-keeping and business reliance on records offer a substitute test of trust-worthiness. Finally, fairness incorporates concerns about adequate notice to the opposing party of the hearsay statements to be used and any other safeguards to permit that party to test and respond to the hearsay.

Historically, the traditional hearsay exceptions had developed around these three characteristics, as courts struggled to develop categories or kinds of state-ments that met these requirements — dying declarations, spontaneous state-ments, business records, etc. In a 1970 decision, the Supreme Court of Canada made it clear that judges could even modify or add to these traditional excep-tions.[25] What changed with the *Khan* case was the whole approach to admissible hearsay, as the court allowed judges to admit hearsay statements on a principled basis, even where the statement did not fall within a "pigeonhole" traditional exception. A court could openly consider necessity and reliability and fairness in admitting a single statement in a particular case. Since 1990, Canadian courts, including child protection courts, have been exercising this new-found flexi-bility, to avoid some of the technicalities of the old hearsay rule and to simplify the law.

Here I will only discuss the most important of the traditional hearsay excep-tions, those that arise most frequently in child protection cases. I will then consider statements by children and, more specifically, children's statements about abuse. Many provincial protection statutes include special evidence provi-sions, to admit evidence that might otherwise be inadmissible under the general law of evidence and which will provide a basis for some closing comments on hearsay.

Admissions by a Party

The single most important hearsay exception in protection cases is that of admissions by parents or other parties. To constitute hearsay admissible as an admission, the statement must be that of a party, typically a parent or guardian, and it must be offered by an opposing party *against* the party who made the statement.

Evidence scholars have long argued about the rationale for the admissions exception, as neither necessity (the party is usually available to testify) nor reli-ability (we don't care whether the party's statement is reliable) appear to ground this exception. Briefly stated, some notion of a party's responsibility for his or her statements within an adversary system of litigation seems to lie at the heart of this exception (i.e., "Anything you say may be used against you").

Invariably, the parents in a protection case will have spoken to and consulted with a variety of professionals and other officials, both before and during the

---

[25] *Ares v. Venner*, [1970] S.C.R. 608, a decision expanding the business records exception.

protection proceedings, such as agency social workers, social assistance workers, community health nurses, drug counsellors, police officers, doctors, hospital staff and psychiatrists. Anything said by a parent to a witness called by agency counsel may be treated as an admission. Despite the term "admission," this type of statement need not be an outright admission or confession of neglect or abuse. It is enough that counsel for the agency — the opposing party — offers the statement in its case in chief, for whatever purpose.

Suppose you are a hospital social worker, called by the agency to give evidence in a protection case. The statements made by a parent during interviews constitute hearsay (i.e., out-of-court statements offered to prove the truth of the matters asserted) but may be treated as admissions. For example, if a parent states that he or she was abused as a child, that statement can come in under this exception to prove that the parent was in fact abused as a child. Of course, the parent is free to take the stand later to deny, clarify or explain that statement, thus leaving it for the court to resolve any questions of credibility or interpretation.

Given the private, often unwitnessed nature of much abuse and neglect, parental admissions will often make up much of the agency's case — to establish facts admitted, to lay the factual basis for expert opinion evidence and to afford the grounds for cross-examination of the parent's current testimony.

Parental admissions are treated differently in criminal prosecutions, where much more stringent conditions are applied to statements made to "persons in authority," such as police officers. Before an accused parent's confession to such a person can be admitted in a criminal court, the Crown must first prove beyond a reasonable doubt the statement is "voluntary" (i.e., that it was made by a person with an operating mind, not in circumstances of oppression, and not induced by threats or promises or other police trickery).[26] Further, the court must also be satisfied that the accused's *Charter* rights were not breached by the authorities.[27] Where criminal prosecution is likely, the interviewing of the alleged perpetrator is best left to the police, who can ensure that these criminal rules are satisfied.[28]

Business Records

Most provincial evidence statutes explicitly provide for the admissibility of business records or, more accurately, regularly kept records. What constitutes a "business record"? First, the record must be of an act, transaction, occurrence or

---

[26] This law of confessions was recently restated by the Supreme Court in *R. v. Oickle*, [2000] 2 S.C.R. 3.

[27] The *Charter* law governing confessions has become quite complicated, but is clearly stated in a leading Canadian evidence text, D. Pacciocco and L. Stuesser, *The Law of Evidence*, 3rd ed. (Toronto: Irwin Law, 2002), Chapter 8.

[28] To some extent it will depend on the circumstances of a particular case to determine whether or not a child protection worker will be regarded as a "person in authority," and hence, in the context of a criminal prosecution, be required to satisfy the special rules to be able to testify about statements a parent made. However, if a criminal prosecution seems likely, it is usually best to leave the initial interview with a suspect to the police.

event. Second, the record must have been made at the time of or shortly after the event recorded. Third, the record must have been made in the usual and ordinary course of business. Provided that the records meet these requirements, they can be introduced by anyone who made the record, or even through a witness, such as a medical records librarian, who has official custody of the records.

This exception to the hearsay rule exists because many individuals within an institution, such as a hospital, record information over a period of time. The sheer cost and inconvenience of locating and calling all of them as witnesses generates the necessity to rely upon written records. As for reliability, institutions themselves rely upon these records for day-to-day operations and decision making, providing some assurance that minimum standards of reliability in record-keeping are maintained.

The term "business records" may be misleading, as "business" is broadly defined to include "every kind of business, profession, occupation, calling, operation or activity, whether carried on for profit or otherwise," according to the statutes. Included in this broad range are hospitals, health clinics, doctors, drug rehabilitation centres, social assistance authorities, public housing authorities, psychologists and therapists. The records of child protection agencies also qualify as "business records." The regularity with which the activities of the institution or individual are recorded provides the basis for the exception.

There are two important limits to the use of such records. First, records may not be used to prove opinions of the kind typically given by experts. For example, a hospital discharge summary, containing a doctor's diagnosis and opinion, may not be entered into evidence through this exception; the agency would have to call the doctor and subject his or her expert opinions to the rigours of cross-examination. Second, the statements entered in the records must be made by individuals operating under a "business duty." Records will often contain statements made by others and noted in the records by an agency worker or a hospital staff member. Not all such third-party statements will be admissible. Only those statements made by other persons who are themselves acting under a business duty to be careful about what they say are admissible, such as a statement made by one nurse to another nurse and recorded by the latter in the hospital records. By contrast, a statement made by a person outside of the institution's operations and thus not under any similar "business duty" to speak carefully would not be admissible, just because the statement is written down in a business record. To take an extreme but common example, an anonymous report to a child protection worker is not admissible to prove the matters reported. Or, a statement by a parent's relative and written down by a nurse or social worker cannot be admitted within the business records exception.[29]

Judges tend to treat business records as inherently reliable, perhaps reflecting the court's preference for documentary evidence, especially if such documents

---

[29] Protection courts have become increasingly careful about opinion and multiple hearsay found in business records, e.g., *Catholic Children's Aid Society of Toronto v. J.L.*, [2003] O.J. No. 1722 (Ont. C.J.) and *Re S.V.*, [2002] S.J. No. 714 (Sask. Q.B.F.L.D.).

were created before any court proceeding was anticipated. If a witness is subpoenaed to court with records, the records are usually entered as an exhibit, even though the witness subsequently uses the records to refresh his or her memory. In this case, the records themselves become evidence, along with the oral testimony of the witness. With increased record keeping by institutions, professionals and officials, protection proceedings have become increasingly dominated by mounds of paper and bulging files.

Prior Testimony

Protection cases often involve families that have previously appeared in court for matters involving either this child or another child in the parent's care. Most provincial protection laws explicitly provide for admissibility of transcripts of testimony from prior protection proceedings, whether they involved this child or a child previously in a parent's care. Many protection statutes go even further, to admit evidence from any civil or criminal proceeding.[30]

Consider the following example. Less than a year ago, a parent's first child was found in need of protection and was made a permanent ward based upon, say, a finding that the mother suffered from serious psychiatric disorders that interfered with her ability to parent. Now that parent has another child, who was apprehended shortly after birth for essentially the same reasons. The court hearing the second child's case may admit transcripts of the previous year's proceeding, in part or even in whole.

Admitting prior testimony under these statutory exceptions fits quite comfortably within the Supreme Court's new hearsay analysis. Prior sworn testimony is the most reliable kind of hearsay, as it is sworn, accurately recorded and usually tested by some form of cross-examination. Sometimes the prior testimony will be necessary because a witness is no longer available. As for fairness, the issues in the prior protection proceedings will often be the same or similar to those in the current proceeding. If necessary, the court can require the protection agency to recall a particular witness from the previous proceeding for further cross-examination, to ensure fairness.

Statements by Children

Before addressing the new child abuse hearsay exception in *Khan*, it is worth remembering the concluding comments of Justice McLachlin in *Khan*: "This does not make out-of-court statements by children generally admissible."[31] In order to be admitted into evidence, a child's out-of-court statements must fall within a traditional exception, or within the new child abuse hearsay exception, or as an individual statement that meets the principled requirements of necessity and reliability.

---

[30] British Columbia, Alberta, Saskatchewan, Ontario, and Newfoundland.

[31] *Supra*, note 25 at para. 33.

One of the traditional exceptions is that of statements concerning the physical, mental or emotional state of the person making the statement, whether a child or an adult. As we have no other way of knowing a person's feelings (necessity) and most such statements are spontaneous or made for treatment purposes (reliability), the statements are admissible under this older exception, as long as the statements describe a *current* or *contemporaneous* condition. A child may say, "My bum hurts" or "I'm sad" or "I'm afraid of Daddy," and all of these out-of-court statements are admissible to prove those feelings asserted. Under this exception, however, a person's statement cannot be used to prove the cause of their current feelings (e.g., a child's statement, "I'm afraid of Daddy because he hit Mommy last night").

It is under this older exception that courts can hear an adult repeat a child's wishes or preferences. If a child tells his mother or father or relative, "I want to live with Mommy," that statement is admissible to prove the child's contemporaneous mental or emotional state. Courts will often give little weight to a child's wishes expressed to a parent, but the wishes are admissible in evidence. Statements to more neutral individuals, including assessors, will also be admissible under this exception and will receive more weight.

The Child Abuse Hearsay Exception

The *Khan* decision stands as the beginning of the Supreme Court's revolution in hearsay law. But it also stands for what is often called "the *Khan* exception," what I prefer to call the child abuse hearsay exception. *Khan* was a criminal prosecution for sexual assault, where Dr. Khan was alleged to have placed his penis in the mouth of the three-and-a-half-year-old girl, who came to his office with her mother. Half an hour later, in a casual conversation about the doctor's office, the child disclosed the act to her mother. The trial judge refused to admit the statement, but both the Ontario Court of Appeal and the Supreme Court of Canada held the statement should have been admitted. In the Supreme Court, Justice McLachlin held that "the hearsay evidence of a child's statement on crimes committed against the child should be received, provided that the guarantees of necessity and reliability are met."[32]

In reaching her decision, Justice McLachlin relied upon a series of earlier decisions from Family Courts in protection and custody cases where such statements were admitted, as the cases "point the way in the correct direction."[33] In turn, the *Khan* decision has now generated an extensive case law identifying the factors governing the necessity and reliability to admit such statements, in both criminal and protection cases. The court will assess necessity and reliability during a *voir dire*, the hearing within the hearing during which the court decides the admissibility of the child's statement.

---

[32] *Id*. at para. 33.

[33] *Id*. at paras. 25-28. The three cases were: *D.R.H. v. Superintendent of Family and Child Services* (1984), 41 R.F.L. (2d) 337 (B.C.C.A.); *W.M. v. Director of Child Welfare of P.E.I.* (1986), 3 R.F.L. (3d) 181 (P.E.I.C.A.); and *F.(J.K.) v. F.(J.D.)*, [1988] B.C.J. No. 278 (B.C.C.A.).

"Necessity" means "reasonably necessary." A number of grounds can create necessity, even in criminal cases, where courts are more likely to make a child testify:

(a) "normal" unavailability, e.g., illness, absence from Canada, a refusal to be sworn or to testify;

(b) not competent to testify, on account of young age or lack of understanding;

(c) trauma or harm to the child, proved by expert evidence;

(d) unable to give meaningful evidence, as when the child "freezes";

(e) unable to give a full, frank, and accurate account; and

(f) the child recants on the stand.

"Necessity" is even further relaxed in protection cases, mostly by courts being less demanding on grounds of trauma or harm under (c) above. Protection statutes in British Columbia, Saskatchewan, and Nova Scotia specifically substitute a "best interests of the child" test for the necessity test and, in most cases, it will not be in a child's best interests to testify.[34]

As for "reliability," there is a well-developed case law on reliability factors, reflecting our increased learning about child abuse, especially child sexual abuse. The court will look at the circumstances surrounding the statement, the status of the adult in court reporting the statement, the child's abilities, the contents of the statement and child behaviours accompanying the statement.[35] At this point, the court is concerned only with "threshold reliability"(i.e., are the statements reliable enough to be considered by the court?). Once admitted, the court will then consider how much "weight" to give to the statements, in reaching its final decision on the merits, what is sometimes called "ultimate reliability." Just because a statement is admitted does not mean that it will constitute conclusive proof of abuse, although it may.

Children's statements have been accepted through doctors, psychologists, social workers, daycare workers, schoolteachers, teacher's aides, police officers, foster parents and even parents. In practice, child protection courts appear to employ a rule of preference as to the status of the in-court witness reporting the child's statements. The first choice would be a professional skilled in investigating and interviewing about child abuse, followed by other experts with some training in the field, then to professionals generally, followed by independent third parties and lastly to persons possibly biased by their connection to either party. Professionals are more likely to appreciate the need for careful questioning and proper recording. Ideally, the child's statements would be videotaped, providing a complete record of what was said, as well as the child's demeanour, or at least audio taped.

---

[34] Each one of these provisions maintains the requirement that the statement be reliable.

[35] One of the more comprehensive listings of factors affecting reliability can be found in the judgement of Robertson J. in *J.A.G. v. R.J.R.*, [1998] O.J. No. 1415 (Ont. Gen. Div.). For a careful consideration of admissibility of such statements, see *Children's Aid Society of Ottawa-Carleton v. L.L.*, [2001] O.J. No. 4587 (Ont. S.C.J.).

Broad Statutory Hearsay Exceptions

Four provinces have protection statutes that include broad hearsay exceptions, giving protection courts a general discretion to admit hearsay evidence — Ontario, Alberta, British Columbia, and Newfoundland.[36] Ontario has the longest history with such a provision, which dates back to 1978 and has most recently been amended in 1999. Ontario's provision appears to be still tied to "evidence of past parenting," although there is some dispute on this point, in light of some very confusing language in the 1999 amendments.[37]

The previous version of Ontario's s. 50(1) was once described by Judge Peter Nasmith as "this strange little section" and "this enigmatic section,"[38] and the 1999 amendments made it even stranger and more enigmatic. The current version of s. 50(1) reads:

> 50. (1) Despite anything in the *Evidence Act*, in any proceeding under this Part,
>
>   (a)   the court may consider the past conduct of a person toward any child if that person is caring for or has access to or may care for or have access to a child who is the subject of the proceeding; and
>
>   (b)   any oral or written statement or report that the court considers relevant to the proceeding, including a transcript, exhibit or finding or the reasons for a decision in an earlier civil or criminal proceeding, is admissible in evidence.

There has been disagreement amongst Ontario protection courts whether this section should be read broadly, as if the hearsay rule were wiped out, or more cautiously, as encouraging a hearsay approach similar to the principled flexibility developed by the Supreme Court of Canada. So far, the second, more cautious approach appears to predominate in reported decisions,[39] although the first, broader approach is simply applied quietly in practice in many courts.[40]

The broad language of Alberta's similar provision has been read cautiously, to maintain the Supreme Court's requirements of necessity and reliability.[41] No definitive decisions have been handed down yet for the B.C. and Newfoundland provisions, although both those provisions require that any hearsay be "reliable." More important than the language of the statutory section has been

---

[36] Ontario *Child and Family Services Act*, R.S.O. 1990, c. C.11, s. 50(1); Alberta *Child Welfare Act*, R.S.A. 2000, c. C-12, s. 108(4); British Columbia *Child, Family and Community Service Act*, R.S.B.C. 1996, c. 46, s. 68(2); Newfoundland and Labrador *Child Youth and Family Services Act*, S.N. 1998, c. C-12.1, s. 50(2).

[37] I have discussed these statutory provisions at length in "Cheshire Cat," *supra*, note 13. On Ontario's 1999 amendment, see also N. Bala, "Reforming Ontario's Child and Family Services Act: Is the Pendulum Swinging Back Too Far?" (1999), 17 *Canadian Family Law Quarterly* 121 at 158-162.

[38] *T.T. v. Catholic C.A.S. of Metropolitan Toronto* (1984), 42 R.F.L. (2d) 47 (Ont. Prov. Ct.) at 51-2.

[39] The leading examples of this approach would be: *C.A.S. of Districts of Sudbury and Manitoulin v. P.M.*, [2002] O.J. No. 1217 (Ont. C.J.); *C.A.S. of Toronto v. N.C.*, [2003] O.J. No. 1525 (Ont. C.J.); and *Catholic C.A.S. of Toronto v. J.L.*, [2003] O.J. No. 1722 (Ont. C.J.).

[40] The broad approach is best represented by two decisions: *C.A.S. of Regional Municipality of Waterloo v. S.J.M.F.*, [1994] O.J. No. 955 (Ont. Gen. Div.); and *C.A.S. of Niagara Region v. D.P.*, [2002] O.J. No. 4015 (Ont. S.C.J.F.C.).

[41] The leading decisions would be: *Re J.M.*, [1995] A.J. No. 170, 11 R.F.L. (4th) 166, 162 A.R. 321 (Alta. C.A.), reversing [1994] A.J. No. 198, 152 A.R. 208 (Alta. Q.B.) and upholding [1993] A.J. No. 704, 143 A.R. 321 (Alta. Prov. Ct.); and *Re N.L., T.L. and J.L.* (1986), 72 A.R. 241 (Alta. Prov. Ct.).

the judge's attitude towards the use of hearsay in child protection proceedings generally.

Judicial Attitudes Towards Hearsay in Protection Cases

In protection cases, there are strong tendencies to relax and even ignore the hearsay rule, with or without such statutory provisions. Some judges like to characterize protection proceedings not as adversarial, but as more in the nature of an "inquiry." In this "inquiry" model, the court is less concerned about fairness to the adult parties and more concerned about hearing all relevant evidence, including hearsay, whatever its reliability, if it might affect the child's future. These judges emphasize the child's "best interests" and downplay concerns about evidence law or procedure or the rights of the parties.

There are other judges who firmly believe that the traditional adversarial process offers the best guarantees of a fully developed and reliable body of evidence upon which to base the court's decision. Most of these judges refer to the very serious consequences that can flow from protection decisions and to the position of the parents *vis-a-vis* the state protection agency. On this view of the process, hearsay should be admitted with caution, much as in criminal trials.

In between lie the majority of judges, who want to relax the hearsay rules while maintaining basic fairness towards the parties in protection cases. This vision is harder to articulate and even harder to follow consistently in practice. The trial judge in a protection case has so much discretion to admit or exclude evidence that witnesses will find considerable variation amongst individual judges, even in adjacent courtrooms, in their approaches towards the hearsay rule.

Evidence of Past Parenting

Past parental behaviour towards *this* child, now the subject of a protection proceeding, is always admissible, even though it is often loosely and incorrectly described as "evidence of past parenting." Here I use the term in a technical and limited sense, namely, evidence of past child-rearing practices and conduct on the part of the same parent in respect of a child in his or her care *other than* the child who is the subject matter of the current protection proceeding in which the evidence is offered.

A classic example would be *Children's Aid Society of Winnipeg v. Forth.*[42] The parents' third child was apprehended at five months of age, after a series of unexplained minor injuries. The agency led evidence that the two older boys had been apprehended and made permanent wards three years earlier, after each boy had suffered serious injuries; one boy suffered remarkably similar injuries to the minor ones suffered by the third child. In effect, past parenting evidence was offered to prove not only intentional rather than accidental abuse, but also to

---

[42] (1978), 1 R.F.L. (2d) 46 (Man. Prov. Ct. — Fam. Div.).

demonstrate the probability of future abuse of the third child. The same principle holds in neglect cases, especially where the neglect flows from some underlying form of continuing parental incapacity, such as mental illness or mental disability.

Courts have consistently expressed a concern for "undue emphasis upon past parenting" or "front-end loading," especially in cases of apprehension immediately upon birth, where the past parenting evidence carries the full freight of the agency's case.[43] In admitting or considering evidence of past parenting, courts should and sometimes do consider a number of factors, such as the similarity of the grounds for intervention, the lapse of time, any change of partners by a parent, and the amenability of causal factors to short-term change.

Privilege

What Is Privilege?

The rules of privilege provide a special basis for exclusion of evidence from the courtroom. Unlike the hearsay or opinion rules, which are primarily concerned with the reliability of evidence, privilege rules serve to exclude highly reliable evidence on the basis that other social values, outside the judicial process, are more important than truth-finding inside a courtroom.

Consider the following example. Outside the courtroom you see two lawyers, the agency counsel and the parents' lawyer, engaged in deep and obviously animated conversation. Probably the parents' counsel says, "Look, we're prepared to admit to the finding, if you're ready to agree to a supervision order with some stringent conditions," and the agency lawyer replies, "Our case for permanent wardship isn't the strongest, but we have concerns that I don't think we can satisfy by supervision." No resolution is reached and both lawyers go back into the courtroom. Despite potentially telling admissions from both sides, neither lawyer is free to adduce evidence of that hallway discussion, as their respective statements are privileged, being "without prejudice" negotiations with a view to settlement.[44]

In my view, a sharp distinction can be made between two distinct kinds of privilege. First, there are a series of privileges that are carefully policed by the courts, most of which serve other important purposes within the legal process. This group would include: the privilege against self-incrimination of an accused person (i.e., the right to remain silent); the privilege of a witness not to have incriminating evidence used against him or her in later proceedings; solicitor-client privilege; the privilege for legal negotiations or efforts to settle; and the privilege for informers.

---

[43] Most frequently cited is *C.A.S. of Regional Municipality of Waterloo v. R.C.*, [1994] O.J. No. 2955 (Ont. C.J.), especially at paras. 14-21.

[44] For a short and clear statement of the privilege for settlement negotiations in a family law setting, see *Leonardis v. Leonardis*, [2003] A.J. No. 848, 2003 ABQB 577 (Alta. Q.B.).

The second category consists of a variety of privileges that are more frequently qualified or overridden in the interests of truth-finding, privileges that typically protect some social value or relationship extrinsic to legal processes: a variety of confidential and professional relationships; husband-wife privilege; and so-called Crown privilege or public interest immunity for such things as state secrets and Cabinet discussions.

In this short section, I will only discuss privileges of importance for witnesses on the stand in child protection cases: claims of privilege for professional and confidential communications, solicitor-client privilege, litigation privilege, and the privilege for informers.

Privilege for Professional and Confidential Communications

Generally speaking, apart from confidential communications with one's lawyer (solicitor-client privilege), there is no absolute or blanket privilege for confidential communications between professionals and their clients or patients. Particularly in child protection and criminal cases, claims to professional privilege have been uniformly rejected in the case of doctor-patient, therapist-client or priest-penitent. Like it or not, when subpoenaed to court and asked questions pertaining to intimate, confidential information divulged by a person, the professional in a protection case will likely have to answer the questions and disclose the information.

Many professionals, especially those dealing with families and children, are surprised to learn that they must generally respond to such questions. Mere confidentiality between professional and client is not sufficient to ground a privilege (i.e., a right to refuse to answer such questions). Confidentiality may be essential to the relationship and may be assiduously observed by the professional in dealings with other third parties, but that does not amount to a "privilege" not to answer or disclose in a courtroom.

In a 1991 criminal case, involving statements by an accused person to a pastor, the Supreme Court of Canada acknowledged that there might be some "case-by-case" or partial privilege, where a court could balance the need for the information using a four-part test:

(1) The communication must originate in confidence.

(2) This element of confidentiality must be essential to the full and satisfactory maintenance of the relation between the parties.

(3) The relation must be one which, in the opinion of the community, ought to be sedulously fostered.

(4) The injury that would inure to the relation by the disclosure of the communication must be greater than the benefit thereby gained for the correct disposal of the litigation.[45]

---

[45] The case was *R. v. Gruenke*, [1991] 3 S.C.R. 263. The pastor was required to testify about what the accused said and properly so, said the Supreme Court. The four conditions were those suggested by an evidence scholar, Professor John Henry Wigmore.

While many professional claims can meet the first three of these conditions, in the context of a child protection case, few claims are capable of passing the fourth, where the benefit to truth-finding is balanced against the injury to the professional relationship.

Consider an earlier example, in a criminal case involving charges of indecent assault, gross indecency and intercourse with a girl under fourteen. The accused claimed medical or therapist privilege for confidential communications with a family clinic psychiatrist during family therapy. The claim foundered on the fourth condition, as the Ontario Court of Appeal held, "the search for truth in the criminal process outweighs the need for family counselling, at least in cases of suspected child abuse." The court ruled that the detection and prevention of child abuse is more important than preserving the confidentiality of psychiatric counselling or encouraging patients to seek out therapy.[46]

The leading civil case on this emerging form of "partial privilege" is the Supreme Court's 1997 decision in *M.(A.) v. Ryan*.[47] In *Ryan*, the plaintiff patient was suing her former psychiatrist for sexual abuse and then went to another psychiatrist, Dr. Parfitt, for treatment. Dr. Parfitt was not going to be called as a witness at trial by the plaintiff, but the defendant wanted full disclosure of Dr. Parfitt's records. The B.C. courts only ordered parts of the records disclosed, and those disclosed were subject to stringent conditions, such as only one copy to be made, not to be disclosed to the defendant but only to his lawyer and his expert witnesses. The Supreme Court of Canada held that, if privilege were claimed in such circumstances, a judge should probably review the professional's file, on a document-by-document and page-by-page basis, to balance the need for the information against the privacy interests of the individual. Only some parts might need to be disclosed and the judge can attach special conditions upon disclosure and use of the parts disclosed.

In child protection cases, even applying *Ryan*, the courts will err on the side of disclosure in order to protect children from abuse and neglect. By definition, the records involved will usually engage both great privacy interests and great probative value, given the most intimate and personal issues involved in protection cases. Most likely *Ryan* will only exclude less probative material around the margins, on the borderline of relevance anyway.

If a witness, professional or otherwise, has been directed to answer a question or produce a document, however confidential, the witness must comply. In the face of any reticence from the witness, the trial judge will instruct the witness on the law of privilege, the court's ruling and the realities of contempt of court. The witness will be given another opportunity to answer the question or disclose the document. If the witness still refuses to comply, the court will find the witness in

---

[46] *R. v. S.(R.J.)* (1985), 45 C.R. (3d) 161 (Ont. C.A.). In this case, before *Gruenke*, the accused father argued that there was a general privilege for such communications, using Wigmore's four conditions, but the result would be the same today under a "case-by-case" or partial privilege analysis.

[47] [1997] 1 S.C.R. 157.

contempt of court and can then decide the sanction, which can range from a nominal fine to imprisonment.

Solicitor-Client Privilege; Litigation Privilege

Solicitor-client privilege is one of the oldest and most important privileges, afforded the greatest protection. The privilege attaches to communications between the lawyer and the client, for the purpose of giving or receiving legal advice, as part of our societal commitment to personal autonomy and access to justice. In protection cases, this privilege will protect from disclosure the communications between agency counsel and the agency social workers or between parents' counsel and the parents.

More important from a witness perspective is the related privilege known as "litigation privilege." Again, at the centre of the operation of this privilege is the lawyer, but this time the privilege facilitates the lawyer's investigation and preparation of the case. As part of that preparation, the lawyer must contact and retain expert witnesses. For this privilege to arise, litigation must be contemplated or actually underway. The "dominant purpose" for which the report is prepared must be to submit it to the lawyer for advice and use in that litigation, if the report and related communications are to be privileged from disclosure.[48]

When a lawyer intends to call an expert witness, most rules of court require the filing of an expert's report some time before trial and the provision of a copy to the other parties. A lawyer may ask for a report and, after receiving the report, decide not to call the expert. In that case, litigation privilege will protect that report from production by the lawyer or the expert witness to any other party to the litigation. If the expert is to be called as a witness at trial, then the expert's report will remain privileged from production only until that time when the report must be disclosed under the rules of court.

In practical terms, if the report is prepared on the specific request of counsel, after litigation has commenced, and is submitted directly to counsel, this "dominant purpose" test will be satisfied. Where there has been a pre-existing or ongoing therapeutic or counselling relationship, courts may find that there is more than one purpose for the expert's work and thus the report would have to be disclosed immediately. Similarly, any report prepared and submitted to a lawyer before litigation is contemplated will also not be privileged, and have to be disclosed. For those slated to testify as expert witnesses, care should be taken in obtaining instructions and submitting reports, with proper advance advice and direction from the lawyer, to ensure a clear understanding of the procedures desired by the lawyer. Many lawyers will ask that an expert's initial opinions be provided orally, before requesting the production of a written report.

---

[48] The leading Canadian case on litigation privilege, also containing an excellent review of solicitor-client privilege is the Ontario Court of Appeal decision in *General Accident Assurance Co. v. Chrusz* (1999), 38 C.P.C. (4th) 203 (Ont. C.A.). As of 2003, its analysis has been adopted by the appeal courts in Newfoundland, Nova Scotia, New Brunswick, Manitoba, and British Columbia.

Privilege for Informers

There is clear common law authority that a state agency or its witness may not be compelled to disclose the identity of a person who provides information giving rise to an investigation.[49] This privilege is rationalized by the public interest in effective implementation of child protection laws and in the free flow of information to those officials charged with preventing and detecting child abuse and neglect.

There may be one small exception to this privilege where the identity of the informer is material to the parent's defence. In that rare case, almost invariably the agency will call the informer as a witness, thus avoiding the privilege issue.

Coping with Evidence Law: A Lawyer's Plea to Witnesses

For those not confused by a law degree, the foregoing rules of evidence will appear to be a series of unduly technical obstructions to any intelligent process of truth-finding. In part, this reflects the undue emphasis of traditional evidence law upon rules of exclusion; that is, when evidence should *not* be heard by the judge. In large measure, however, this appearance of obstructionism flows from the conflicting purposes within the legal process that our evidence law is intended to serve: reliability, fairness to the parties, trial efficiency and social values extrinsic to the trial process.

Rules of evidence and procedure together constitute a variety of laws often characterized as "adjective" law as opposed to "substantive" law. Substantive law consists of the legal rules and standards applicable to the resolution of the courtroom dispute. In the field of child protection, statutes and relevant judicial interpretations set out the criteria to be used in determining whether a child is in need of protection and what form of disposition is appropriate. Other chapters in this volume are devoted to the legal intricacies and underlying policies of this substantive law. The process of reaching those decisions is regulated by adjective law, rules of procedure and evidence applicable to protection proceedings. As a subsidiary form of law, adjective law must serve the larger substantive ends of protection law, namely, protecting children from harm, while also attempting to protect the family from unwarranted state intrusion.

Not only must evidence law in this field serve the intermediate ends of reliability, efficiency, fairness and extrinsic social values, but it must be adjusted to serve the larger goals of child protection law. Not surprisingly, then, evidence law as applied in protection cases varies from that found in criminal prosecutions for abuse or neglect or from that governing private custody disputes, as I explained earlier.

---

[49] *D. v. National Society for the Prevention of Cruelty to Children*, [1977] 1 All E.R. 589 (H.L.), approved by the Supreme Court of Canada in *Solicitor Gen. (Can.) v. Royal Commission of Inquiry into Confidentiality of Health Records in Ont.* (1981), 128 D.L.R. (3d) 193 at 221-24 and 226 and followed in *Re Infant* (1981), 32 B.C.L.R. 20 at 22 (S.C.). On the mechanics of claiming and protecting this privilege, in the criminal context, see *R. v. Leipert*, [1997] 1 S.C.R. 281. See also discussion in Chapter 2.

Of necessity, evidence law in protection cases reflects the unique nature of these proceedings and the complex interests at stake, groping towards some middle ground between the stringent criminal approach and the very relaxed approach of private custody disputes. Also, because of the very broad language employed in the substantive law of child protection, judges trying such cases often find themselves navigating that middle ground without much clear guidance from the legislatures or the higher courts. Different judges will arrive at different accommodations of the competing purposes at play, leading to uncertain and inconsistent evidence rulings. In turn, this generates problems of predictability for lawyers preparing for trial and for witnesses prepared by those lawyers and testifying before those judges.

In effect, this amounts to a closing plea from a lawyer for tolerance and understanding from those who must, as witnesses, ultimately take the brunt of these legal difficulties. In this chapter, I have attempted to outline some of the basics of evidence law, recognizing that anyone who has been a witness will know that these rules are applied unevenly in real cases in real courtrooms. Some understanding of the rules should prove helpful, if only to know how far practice in this courtroom in front of this judge varies from the law as it is written.

For a witness, the best means of protection from the vagaries of evidence law and judicial interpretations thereof is proper and careful preparation in advance by the lawyer calling you. The first half of this chapter was therefore devoted to the rights of witnesses and the obligations of lawyers in that preparation process: dealing with lawyers, subpoenas, exclusion orders, the mechanics of preparation by lawyers, pointers for witnesses in testifying, the structure of witness examination and coping with cross-examination tactics.

Armed with this practical information and some basic appreciation of evidence law, a witness should be able to survive the experience of testifying in a child protection case, with a minimum of Kafkaesque trauma and some modicum of apparent (albeit misleading) assurance. It should then be possible for you as the witness to focus upon what you say in the courtroom, rather than whether you can say it (the rules of evidence) or how you say it (preparing for court).

12

Preparing Children for Testifying in Court

Wendy van Tongeren Harvey[1]

Reports of child abuse, particularly sexual abuse, have increased enormously in recent years, and children are more frequently called upon to be witnesses in court. In protection proceedings and parental custody or access disputes, judges usually make a finding that abuse has occurred based on the evidence of witnesses other than the child who is the subject of the proceeding.[2] However, in criminal cases involving allegations of sexual abuse, it is almost always necessary for the child to be a witness for there to be a successful prosecution.[3]

In 1988, the *Criminal Code* was amended to facilitate the giving of evidence by children. Since then, more *Code* amendments have been made and the courts have provided many judgements to assist the practitioner when dealing with children's evidence. It is now easier to have children found "competent to testify" than it was prior to 1988, and it is no longer necessary for children to demonstrate an understanding of the oath. However, it is very important that children, especially young children, be adequately prepared for testifying in court, so that they can communicate effectively and not be unduly traumatized by the experience.

Preparation of a child for the court experience is important whatever the nature of the proceeding, but it is especially crucial for the criminal prosecution where the child is the victim or has witnessed victimization to another. Most of the professional literature on the subject of preparing children to testify focuses on the criminal setting, because this is the forum in which they most frequently are witnesses.[4] Further, it is the most adversarial setting in which a child may appear, and the area in which there is the most potential for hostile or abusive questioning. This chapter is intended to serve as an introduction for those who may be involved in preparing child victims of abuse to testify in court.

---

[1] Wendy van Tongeren Harvey is Crown Counsel, Ministry of the Attorney General, Vancouver, British Columbia.

[2] See, e.g., *D.R.H. v. Superintendent of Family and Child Services* (1984), 41 R.F.L. (2d) 337 (B.C.C.A.). See also discussion in Chapter 11.

[3] Since *R. v. Khan*, [1990] 2 S.C.R. 531 (S.C.C.) the courts have demonstrated a flexible approach to examining hearsay evidence for purposes of determining admissibility where trustworthiness and necessity exist.

[4] See A. Maleszyk, *Crimes Against Children: Prosecution and Defence* (Toronto: Canada Law Book, 2002) chapter 2; W. van Tongeren Harvey and P. Dauns, *Sexual Offences Against Children and the Criminal Process* (Markham: Lexis Nexis, 2001), chapter 5; and P. Hurley, K. Scarth, and L. Stevens, *Children as Witnesses: Helping Young People Give Their Evidence in Court: Helping Courts Hear the Evidence of Children* (London, ON.: Centre for Children, Families and the Justice System, 2002).

Dynamics of the Child Sexual Assault Prosecution

More child witnesses are now testifying in criminal court than ever before. This is primarily due to the relatively recent awareness of child sexual assault and the growing number of reports of abuse. In most of these cases, there are only two people who actually witnessed the act: the perpetrator and the child victim. If there is a trial, the child and the adult may give very different versions of the events in question. Although other witnesses may testify during the criminal trial, it is often the child witness who stands between the accused and the door to freedom. This means the child is vulnerable to the attempts of defence counsel to discredit the child, either through cross-examination or by calling other witnesses. While the Crown prosecutor and judge have a role in protecting the child from improper questioning, it must be appreciated that in our society a central focus of a criminal trial is the protection of the legal rights of the accused, and the defence has considerable scope in how it conducts its case.

A child needs to be supported through the experience of testifying to encourage unfettered communication. Support means preparation before the testimony, accompanying the child to court for the testimony, and skilled questioning by the Crown prosecutor. There are now accommodations that can be made that must be canvassed in advance, such as the use of closed circuit television to help the child testify. Those who prepare children for court should understand the dynamics of a child sexual assault trial, and be able to anticipate the child's fears and questions. Some of the procedural and evidentiary features of the criminal courts that children have difficulty understanding are embedded in the very foundation of our judicial system.

Fundamental principles of criminal law are designed to guarantee freedom and justice in our society, and to protect the rights of the accused. However, the system sometimes appears to be stacked against child witnesses and the credibility of their statements. Using their own terms, children often express quizzical confusion about the following legal precepts:

- Why is the accused presumed innocent until proven guilty?
- Why must the Crown prove the case beyond a reasonable doubt?
- Why does the accused have the right to remain silent? In other words, why do the victims have to go through all the rigours of investigation and trial as if they are not believed, when it appears the accused doesn't have to say anything?

In our system many allegations of sexual assault go unprosecuted and many others that go to court result in acquittals, despite the allegations of the child. It is not uncommon for the trier of fact to find the accused not guilty, without the accused having to call evidence or testify. This is because the prosecution must prove the case beyond a reasonable doubt. If the defence can demonstrate weaknesses in the child's allegations, the prosecution has not fulfilled its onus and the accused must be acquitted.

If the Crown has difficulty in prosecuting its case, the defence may choose not to call evidence and the accused may decide not to testify; by not testifying, the accused avoids the risks of having his own credibility directly challenged, particularly if he has a criminal record of any sort.[5] In the event the accused does testify, it is not a contest between the accused and the child, because of the strict onus on the prosecution. If there are inadequacies in the accused's testimony or the accused is not believed in his denial, the accused must still be acquitted unless the evidence establishes beyond a reasonable doubt that the accused is guilty of the offence charged.

In 1988, Parliament enacted a number of reforms that were intended to make it easier for children to testify in criminal court, for example, abolishing the mandatory requirement for corroboration of a child's testimony. Since these amendments were enacted, the Supreme Court of Canada has provided some guidance to trial judges on the need to show some flexibility in assessing the evidence. While the evidence of the Crown must satisfy the trier of fact, beyond a reasonable doubt, of the guilt of the accused, it must also be appreciated that children do not have the same capacities as adults to recall or understand some of the details of what occurred, and their evidence should not be discounted for this reason.[6]

Until 1988, children under 14 years were presumed to be incompetent to testify. In 1988, amendments to the *Evidence Act* made it easier for children to testify, though they were still required to undergo an inquiry to satisfy the judge that they were legally "competent" to testify. This could involve a relatively intrusive inquiry into the child's understanding of abstract concepts like "truth" and "promise," as well as into the child's understanding of religious concepts surrounding the oath.[7] Despite these and other legislative changes that have made it significantly easier for children to testify in court, there are still significant challenges in persuading a court to convict an accused based on the testimony of a child.

---

[5] In this chapter, the accused will be referred to by the masculine pronoun, because although some child sexual abusers are female, the vast majority are male. For ease of presentation, victims will be referred to by the female pronoun, though a significant portion of victims of child sexual abuse are boys.

[6] "There is no longer an assumption that children's evidence is less reliable than the evidence of adults." McLachlin J. in *R. v. W.(R.)* (1992), 74 C.C.C. (3d) 134 (S.C.C.) at 143: "We should approach the evidence of children not from the prospective of rigid stereotypes but by taking account the strengths and weaknesses which characterise the evidence offered in the particular case." Wilson J. in *R. v. B.(G.)* (1990), 56 C.C.C. (3d) 200 at 219-220: "Since children experience the world differently from adults, it is hardly surprising that details important to adults, like time and place may be missing from their recollection." Wilson J. in *R. v. B.(G.)* (1990), 56 C.C.C. (3d) 200 at 219: "The repeal of provisions creating a legal requirement that children's evidence be corroborated does not prevent the judge or jury from treating a child's evidence with caution where such caution is merited in the circumstances of the case. But it does revoke the assumption formerly applied to all evidence of children, often unjustly, that children's evidence is always less reliable than adults."

[7] Amendmends to the provision governing the competency of children to testify were proposed but not enacted; Bill C-12, 3rd Session, 37 Parliament, Third Reading, May 13, 2004, not enacted by Senate. Under the proposals, all children were presumed to have the capacity to testify. Children would be permitted to testify if they were "able to understand and respond to questions." Although children were to be required to promise to tell the truth, they were not to be asked any questions regarding "their understanding of the nature of the promise" (s. 16.1(7)).

The criminal justice system is designed to guarantee the accused's rights, and not to provide children comfort in the courtroom. Only recently have significant attempts been made to enhance the accessibility of children to the criminal courts.[8]

There are common themes raised by the defence counsel to discredit a child's allegation of sexual abuse. In the course of the trial, the child is often asked extremely embarrassing and emotionally evocative questions, sometimes far beyond the coping ability of a child. A child may also be asked to describe concepts and answer abstract questions that have little to do with the merits of the case. Some recurrent themes raised by defence counsel include:

1. The complaint was made after a long delay from the time the event is said to have occurred, which suggests falsehood. The defence may argue that if this abuse occurred, one would anticipate early disclosure. That there were many people in the child's life that she loved and trusted, and to whom one would anticipate she would tell, adds weight to this position. That the child still associated with the accused during the period of alleged abuse, gave him gifts or acted affectionately towards him, may also add weight to the argument.[9]

2. The complainant (the victim of the alleged offence) made up this allegation for her own reasons (revenge, anger, seeking attention, to be able to move away, or confusion), and once the investigation started she felt compelled to stick to her story. Her therapists, the investigators, the prosecutor and other persons involved have contributed to her fabrication by continually supporting her rather than challenging her "lie."

3. Because the child's situation has improved since her complaint (e.g., moving to a new foster home with more material goods and more social supports), she is not prepared to recant the story.

4. The child is convinced by overzealous investigators and prosecutors that this happened. She starts by acting or saying something that makes people suspicious. The interviewers put words in her mind and mouth that sound like an allegation. They teach her the proper names of the sex organs and the names for sexual activity. In therapy the child is taught to hate the accused and that he is a bad man. The child is young and vulnerable and moves with the flow to please these new authoritarian and obliging persons in her life.

---

[8] For example: Toronto has a comprehensive victim witness support program where a team approach is employed to prepare children for court including several sessions at a "court school," but not without loud voices of criticism from defence counsel who argue that child advocates have gone too far towards a blueprint of the conviction of the accused.

[9] The Supreme Court of Canada has held that the Crown cannot call expert witnesses in a child sexual abuse prosecution to explain the delay in disclosure, though the court may be obliged to instruct the jury that they should not draw an inference that the child's evidence is inherently unreliable because of a delay in disclosure. *R. v. D.(D.)* (2000), 148 C.C.C. (3d) 41, 2000 SCC 43 (S.C.C.).

5. Once one child spoke of abuse, friends and schoolmates followed suit because they wanted the attention too or really thought hysterically that they were abused too. The investigators and parents contributed to the similarities in their complaints by not keeping them separate and by discussing details in their presence.

6. If there is a confession by the accused, it may be explained as simply an attempt to gain entry to the therapeutic system and avoid the criminal process, as the product of inappropriate coercion or guilt-inducing questioning by investigators, or in an intrafamilial case as prompted by a desire to satisfy a condition imposed by protection authorities as a term of access to the child.

It is, of course, possible, depending on the facts, that one of these defences is valid. However, these types of defences are also often raised when the accused is in fact guilty, and there is no real basis for this type of defence. Despite the lack of basis for such a defence in a case, counsel for the accused may raise these types of issues in the course of cross-examination of Crown witnesses, hoping to create a reasonable doubt of the guilt of the accused. For example, a child's therapist might be asked: "You say you saw the complainant ten times before trial and often spoke to her about her allegations. Isn't it true that during those times you suggested to her that the accused was a 'bad' person and that you suggested to her that it was 'good' that she came forward with these allegations?" And the child might be asked: "Isn't it true that you didn't remember the part about the threat from the accused until your therapist asked you about whether he made a threat?"

Although there are many avenues to challenge the child's allegations, an important focus for the defence counsel is typically through the cross-examination of the child. It is often not difficult for defence counsel to discredit a child witness. Children in many places in Canada are often testifying one to two years after the actual assault, about incidents evoking fear, confusion and misunderstanding. The court forum is not only foreign to them, but is not designed to accommodate their needs. Many of the adult participants are ignorant of child development issues and the dynamics of abuse or, alternatively, feel the fundamental principles of criminal law supercede consideration of these issues.

On the witness stand, once the child has narrated the allegation, the cross-examination by defence, although in theory designed to elicit truth from adults, often serves as a technique to confuse and intimidate the young child. For example, in intrafamilial abuse cases a child may be shown gifts and cards that she gave to the accused in the past, or asked about why her personal diary did not describe the allegations.

Whether intentionally confusing or not, during cross-examination defence counsel often ask long, convoluted questions that may be beyond the capacity of the child to answer. Children, however, are generally eager to try to answer questions posed by adult authority figures, and will often try to give an answer even if the question was not understood; the child is likely to guess at the response based on the parts of the question that were understood. As Dr. J. Yuille describes:[10]

> One only needs to witness a single instance of the cross-examination of a child witness to realize that the procedure is ill-suited to children. It is easy to confuse a young child with the use of age-inappropriate language, long and circuitous questions, and a confrontational style. The adversarial system creates as many problems as it solves in the area of child sexual abuse.

Dr. Yuille summarizes some of the literature on child witnesses:

> A number of studies have indicated that younger children are susceptible to suggestion, although the extent of this susceptibility has been debated. However, a recent review of procedures that prosecutors and defence lawyers can employ when examining and cross-examining children demonstrates that in the courtroom suggestibility is a real issue. Myers provides a number of examples of how children can be confused and misled by a defence attorney in order to cause doubt in the victim's testimony. For example, he suggests [that defence counsel may be deliberately] confusing the child by asking questions following more than one train of thought at a time and changing the temporal order of the events.

From what we know of the dynamics of child abuse and disclosure, a complaint by a child of sexual abuse is clearly not easy to make, it is difficult to assess, and within the context of the Canadian criminal justice system, it is often difficult to prove. The challenge is to accommodate child victims in our courts without harming them, and in a manner that allows a fair testing of their allegations. The challenge is to do this while providing the ultimate protection for the child, which is maintaining an objectivity that does not put the support process itself into suspicion and the weight of the complaint into jeopardy.

In this context, good standards of practice by those involved from the beginning in the investigation and prosecution, as well as in any concurrent child protection proceedings, can assist the child complainant to make her complaint from a strengthened position.

The child's position is strengthened if:

1. There is confirming evidence to the child's complaint, the most helpful being the confession of the accused, but also medical evidence or even physical evidence, like a semen sample or clothing. Indeed, if investigators are able to obtain convincing medical evidence or a legally admissible confession from the accused, it is likely that the accused will plead guilty and there will be no trial.

2. All those in contact with the child have been not only supportive and well intentioned, but also skilled and conscious of contamination issues.

3. The child herself is thoroughly but properly prepared to face the rigours of the criminal process by individuals who understand the system and are not afraid of it.

---

[10] J. Yuille, *Expert Evidence by Psychologists: Sometimes Problematic and Often Premature* (Vancouver, BC: 1989) at 190.

The Status of the Child Witness in Criminal Court

A person's status in the criminal courtroom determines the extent to which one can address the judge and be heard on matters that affect the unfolding of the prosecution. Both the prosecuting and defence lawyers have status to address the judge, with the Crown addressing matters on behalf of the state and the defence on behalf of the accused. If the accused is unrepresented, he still has status and may personally address the court and make applications on his behalf without prejudicing his right to remain silent (i.e., to not give evidence as a witness).

A witness generally does not have the legal status to address the court about the governing of the trial, except for such matters as requesting a drink of water or seeking a recess to go to the bathroom. A complainant (victim of the alleged offence) or a lawyer acting on her behalf, may also request a ban, under s. 486(3) of the *Criminal Code*,[11] on the publication of information that would identify her. However, the child has no status to ask the court to admit into evidence a videotape of a prior interview under s. 715.1 of the *Code*, or to permit the child to testify via closed circuit television under s. 486(2.1); such requests can only be made by the Crown prosecutor.

The accused and his interests are represented in court, but the child witness has no true representation. Practically speaking, in most instances it appears that the Crown prosecutor is representing the child and her interests, because the prosecution is better served if the child is well prepared and protected. However, there may be circumstances where the duty of the Crown prosecutor as an officer of the court overrides any practical benefit to protect the child. The Crown prosecutor is, for example, obliged to disclose to the lawyer for the accused prior to the trial all of the evidence that the prosecution will be putting before the court; the Crown must also disclose evidence the police have discovered that might support the acquittal of the accused, even if the Crown prosecutor considers this evidence unreliable and has no intention of introducing it in court. The accused has no comparable duty of disclosure.

The *Code of Conduct* of the Canadian Bar Association establishes the following duties for a prosecutor:

> When engaged as a prosecutor, the lawyer's prime duty is not to seek a conviction, but to present before the trial court all available credible evidence relevant to the alleged crime in order that justice may be done through a fair trial upon the merits. The prosecutor exercises a public function involving much discretion and power and must act fairly and dispassionately. The prosecutor should not do anything that might prevent the accused from being represented by counsel or communicating with counsel...and, to the extent required by law and accepted practice, should make timely disclosure to the accused or defence counsel of all relevant facts and known witnesses, whether tending to show guilt or innocence, or that would affect the punishment of the accused.[12]

---

[11] *Criminal Code*, R.S.C. 1985, c. C-46.

[12] *Code of Conduct* (Ottawa, ON: Canadian Bar Association, 1988) at 37.

Thus, even if the Crown prosecutor is sensitive and experienced in handling child sexual abuse cases, there will be times when it seems that the child is not directly represented in the court, whereas the accused may have an aggressive lawyer, consistently advocating and protecting his interests. These problems will be exacerbated if, as is sometimes the case, the Crown prosecutor lacks experience or sensitivity with this type of case, or has not had an opportunity to meet the child before court and adequately prepare for the trial.

Principles of Trial Preparation

Practitioners preparing children for court, whether police, social workers or lawyers, must understand the criminal trial process and must be aware of the effect that their contact with the child may have on the evaluation of the child's credibility. In other words, what may be innocent gestures — such as giving the child a candy to comfort her into testifying, going repeatedly over her disclosure or speaking disparagingly of the accused — may provide the ammunition required by the defence to build up the reasonable doubt theme described earlier in this chapter. Equally, those who prepare children must evaluate their own feelings about the effectiveness of the system because their fear, cynicism, dismay or intimidation may be unwittingly communicated to the child.

Those dealing with children who will be going to court should adopt a general attitude that balances the important principles of the system. This guides one's decision making concerning the daily routines.

First, professionals must recognize the need to maintain a balance between the importance of protecting the rights of the accused and those of the children. Such a balance sends messages and information to the child consistent with the likely outcomes. The system recognizes the balances and outcomes reflect this. Thus it is not helpful or appropriate to raise expectations that everything in the criminal process will succeed according to the needs and wants of the child.

Second, the practitioner should constantly balance three goals in preparing the child for court. By doing so, one can support the child through the process, while conducting oneself with integrity and skill. The following should be sought:

1. minimal repeated trauma to the child by the investigative and court process;
2. maximizing the child's recall and minimizing the possibility of contamination of the child's memory; and
3. maintaining the integrity of the preparation process.

Who Prepares the Child for Testifying in Court?

There are situations in which it is very important that a particular person is, or is not, involved in preparing a child for court. In some cases the defence will cast aspersions on a child's testimony because a particular person was involved in court preparation. There may be suggestions that the person preparing the child had improper motives or engaged in improper conduct. For example, if a case includes an allegation of abuse in the context of a parental custody dispute, it is inappropriate to have the non-offending parent involved in any way in preparing the child for court. On the other hand, as between several professionals, such as police, child protection workers or other social workers, it may not be significant that one or another is involved, as long as those preparing the child for court have sensitivity, understanding and knowledge.

There are a wide variety of agencies and individuals who may participate in the preparation and support of children who are witnesses in criminal court. The respective roles differ from province to province, city to city, and agency to agency. Children are prepared by police, social workers, therapists, Crown prosecutors, victim assistance workers, child care workers, volunteers, parents and others.

A preparation that consists of repeated discussion of the alleged events may be looked upon suspiciously by the courts. Some therapists, for example, spend hours of sessions going over and providing insights about the abuse with the child. Often, despite the validity of the complaint, this results in the child sounding like a psychology scholar by court day, which may negatively affect her credibility. To minimize these concerns, a therapist might consider not discussing the details of the alleged events with the child prior to court but, rather, might focus on other therapeutic issues such as self-esteem or relationships. Equally, documenting the process of questioning the child about the events would enable a therapist to defend the techniques used if suggestions of contamination are made. Having a videotape of the child's own description of the abuse, made prior to the commencement of therapy, may also serve to dispel arguments that the therapist improperly influenced the child.

Ideally for a prosecutor, the fewer people with whom the child has discussed the events before the trial, the better. An increased number of conversations increase the types of reaction to the child's allegations and therefore leaves room for suggestions of contamination.

If the Crown prosecutor is involved in an extensive review of the evidence with the child prior to court, it is preferable to have another person present during the interview. This may prevent the Crown prosecutor from being called as a witness to testify about pre-trial conversations, as the other person can be a witness, if this is necessary to dispel suggestions of inappropriate preparation or contamination. A person who is called as a witness cannot also be a prosecutor in the same case.

If individuals other than the Crown prosecutor are preparing the child for court, they should include the Crown as part of the preparation. The prosecutor will then be able to function better in court having assessed what helps a particular child communicate well in court and what the child is going to say. Crown prosecutors with experience in this area always want to meet with the child in advance, if only to establish a rapport, and often to review the evidence that the child will give. Most Crown prosecutors want to be the only ones to review the child's testimony with the child before the trial, though even these lawyers acknowledge the crucial role that others can play in terms of preparing the child for the experience of testifying and providing emotional support during and after court.

Developing a System for Child Witness Preparation

The criminal justice context demands a systemized approach to preparing children and their families for the court process and testifying. A systemized approach, properly developed and administered, encourages a consistency not always present if preparation is done on an *ad hoc* basis, even by well-intentioned individuals. Proper development of a system of preparation requires a consideration of many factors: cost effectiveness, standards, accountability, efficiency, training, continuing education, balancing the child's needs with the demands of the criminal justice system and with the demands of the individuals in it, the mandate of the organizations providing the service (e.g., advocacy or informing and supporting the child), and philosophy.

Preparation should be done by individuals who are familiar with current research relating to child witnesses and sexual abuse, legislation and significant judicial precedents, the demands of the criminal justice system, as well the needs of the child witness. A structured program for preparation will likely address efficiency and cost effectiveness issues. Efficiency is particularly important in preparing children in a rural community or in communities isolated from courthouses and current information.

Those involved in the trial process, such as the police and the judiciary, should be familiar with, and have confidence in, the preparation methods used. Even if defence lawyers attack the process, preparation of children for court must take place. It is important to familiarize all professionals involved in the criminal justice system with the process despite the turnover and differing attitudes and energy levels of persons involved.

The preparation program may be police, community, mental health, social services or prosecution-based, depending on the protocols, personality, needs and structure of a given community and its members. Increasingly in Canada, programs have been established with specially trained victim/witness workers with a background in social work or psychology having a central role in the preparation and support of children and other vulnerable witnesses. Although the Crown prosecutor plays an essential role in the preparation of a child, other professionals typically constitute the core of the non-testimony preparation.

A standardized approach may be administered at different degrees or levels. For example, individuals in a small community may draft a protocol designing the roles of different agencies and how they interrelate in the preparation process. However, the development of a curriculum that is available to any organization may be carried out for a larger geographic area.

A system of preparation should include the following:[13]

1. A step-by-step procedure for imparting information to children and other caregivers about:

    (a) the criminal justice system in general; and

    (b) what the child and family might expect of different stages in the process, including information about how long the process is likely to last.

2. A procedure for designing strategies around:

    (a) the child's needs related to court and the coping mechanisms that work best with different children;

    (b) liaison with the police and Crown prosecutor assigned to the case to encourage dovetailed preparation; and

    (c) the child's current and future support network and how it might be included in the preparation.

3. Materials for each child and caregiver, which might include:[14]

    (a) a record-keeping method for the child's preparation;

    (b) a list of strengths written by the child;

    (c) a children's book on the court process;

    (d) a parent's guide to the court process; and

    (e) videotapes for children and parents on the expected process.

The effectiveness of court preparation is enhanced with concurrent policies providing guidelines for police, child protection, Crown prosecutors, court services, and corrections.

Sample Preparation

It is generally preferable to have a series of preparation meetings with the child held over a number of days. The following topics could be included:

Day One: Introduction

*   Explain the purpose of preparation.
*   Outline the course content.

---

[13] See also, A. Maleszyk, *Crimes Against Children: Prosecution and Defence* (Toronto, ON: Canada Law Book, 2002), Chapter 2; W. van Tongeren Harvey, and P. Dauns, *Sexual Offences Against Children and the Criminal Process* (Markham, ON: Lexis Nexis, 2001), Chapter 5; and P. Hurley, K. Scarth, and L. Stevens, *Children as Witnesses: Helping Young People Give Their Evidence in Court; Helping Courts Hear the Evidence of Children* (London, ON: Ontario Centre for Children, Families and the Justice System, 2002) for discussion of the principles, legal and practical matters related to preparing children for testifying.

[14] There are materials that are appropriate for children and their caregivers that help to explain the court process. See, for example, *What's My Job in Court* (Toronto: Ministry of the Attorney General, 1989), which was written for professionals to read to children who will be going to court; see also <http://www.tcac.on.ca> for an on-line court preparation program and "Cory's Courthouse." This site is operated by the Toronto Child Abuse Centre, which also has available a set of puppets, print materials and video — *Court Orientation Kit for Child Witnesses— "My Court Kit."*

- Suggest that the child or parent keep a journal (in which they can write down any questions for the Crown and document the events of the course).
- Receive information of the child's existing impressions of court.
- Introduce the courtroom and its participants.
- Use audio-visual products to introduce the criminal process.
- Give the child or parent material for home reading.
- Invite the child or parent to write down questions for next day.
- Complete the questionnaire on scheduling preferences.

Day Two: More on Court
- Engage in, or see a video of a court role-play. For the role-play, use situations unrelated to the case at hand (e.g., Goldilocks story, stolen pop bottles, broken window, and so forth).

Day Three: Practical Matters

With the child, go through a checklist of the practical matters that should be addressed, including:
- Engage the child in an exercise to elicit recognized strengths (draw a tree with branches or flower with petals which symbolize strengths) and reframe those to identify how they apply to the task of testifying. Then ask what might get in the way of him or her testifying and without inducing fear in the child, hear what the child's fears and apprehensions are around testifying and respond to those fears. Use this session as a means to identify accommodations that may be required for the child.
- Make arrangements for the child to meet the prosecutor if it has not already been done. The prosecutor may attend this session or the worker may visit the Crown's office with the child. Develop a protocol for this that is consistent with the needs of the community.

Day Four: Preparing the Evidence

This can be done in stages and may take several visits. It should be done by the Crown prosecutor who is taking the case through court and may include the following:
- Have the child recount the event from memory.
- Give the child an opportunity to read or view previous testimony or statements.
- Discuss how these matters will be treated in court.
- Communicate to the child questions that will be asked and invite the child to find her own words to answer the questions.
- Demonstrate some techniques commonly used in court by lawyers in their questioning.
- Inform the child that there may be many questions not covered during the preparation and help the child develop coping mechanisms for any situation in court.

Preparing for Court Procedure

- Prepare the child for each stage of her testimony (e.g., what it means when the defence counsel picks up the typed version of the child's statement and asks her to identify it).
- Develop methods to deal with all contingencies (e.g., tears, if the child stops talking, objections, or going to the bathroom).
- Find out what the child's apprehensions are and offer legal solutions (e.g., the possibility of a screen, closed-circuit television or exclusion of the public from court).
- Go into the courtroom in advance and make sure everything is ready for the child as planned.
- Discuss with the child how to deal with questions that the child does not understand or cannot answer, emphasizing the importance of not guessing at the meaning of a question or an answer.

Day Five: After Court

- The witness often requires a debriefing session once court is over.
- The child should be prepared for the possibility of the acquittal of the accused. It should be emphasized, in terms appropriate to the child, that just because the accused was acquitted does not mean that the judge did not "believe" the child, but rather may be due to the other aspects of the Crown's case, or arise from the fact that guilt must be proven "beyond a reasonable doubt." Further, even if the abuser is not convicted, there may be some satisfaction arising from the fact that he was in some fashion held accountable for his acts through the court process.
- An acknowledgement letter or certificate of participation can go a long way in assisting the young child during this period of withdrawal and healing. For some children it may be appropriate to give a "hero badge" or some other symbol of participation.

Role of Crown Counsel in Court Preparation

There is a continuing discussion in Canada over the appropriate role of non-lawyers in preparing children for court, and there should always be consultation with the Crown prosecutor before establishing a protocol. It is the writer's opinion that the Crown prosecutor should always be the one who reviews the evidence with the child. Other issues that some think should be left to a lawyer are:

General

- right of the accused to a fair trial;
- presumption of innocence; and
- court jurisdiction.

Procedure

- charging the accused;
- purpose of a preliminary hearing;
- trial by jury and trial by judge alone;
- implications for the witnesses of trials in different settings; and
- cross-examination by defence counsel.

Court Preparation

- the role of Crown prosecutor;
- the role of the witnesses;
- the role of the defence lawyer;
- the role of the judge;
- where child waits before testifying;
- preparing for the competency assessment that is to be carried out before the child is permitted to testify;
- who will wait with the child;
- how the child will know when to come into the courtroom; and
- how to signal a desire to use the bathroom.

The main concern expressed by Crown prosecutors when non-lawyers prepare child witnesses for court is that legal information imparted to the witnesses may not be possible as described, or may be presented in a way that could later cast aspersion on the witnesses' credibility. Equally, the lawyer needs preparation with the child just as the child does with the lawyer. It is a mutual benefit. As stated above, individual communities are encouraged to benefit from the establishment of an interagency protocol on child witness preparation.

13

Liability for Child Welfare Workers: Weighing the Risks

Marvin M. Bernstein, Cheryl Regehr, and Karima Kanani[1]

Jordan Heikamp was born on May 18, 1997, at Northwestern General Hospital in Toronto. He died five weeks later of chronic starvation, weighing just 4 pounds, 2 ounces. His mother, then 19, was estranged from her family, lived in shelters and had no source of income. With the approval of their child protection worker, Jordan and his mother moved to a women's shelter, where he slowly starved to death. Both the baby's mother and the child protection worker who was responsible for the case were charged with criminal negligence causing death. After a seven-month preliminary hearing, the judge decided that there was not sufficient evidence for the case to go to trial. In her 1999 decision to discharge the child protection worker involved, Justice Mary Hogan of the Ontario Court of Justice found that the worker "had a reasonable belief that Jordan was being monitored" and that the shelter where the mother and child were staying "was appropriate for him."[2] The judge further indicated that, while the worker should have verified the mother's claims about the care of her child, there was no evidence that the worker's acts or omissions were a contributing cause of Jordan's death by chronic starvation, and accordingly ruled that the worker should not be found criminally liable for the child's death.

Two years later a coroner's inquest into Jordan's death highlighted problems in the child welfare system and ruled that the death was technically a "homicide," the death of one person caused by the acts or omissions of another. Media reports were negative towards the Children's Aid Society and the child protection worker in the case, and towards social workers as a group. One reporter concluded that the coroner's jury "proved if nothing else, that while you can fool all of the social workers some of the time and some of the social workers all of the time, you can't snow the ordinary joe."[3] Undoubtedly the worker felt great anguish at the death of a child on her caseload; added to this

---

[1] This chapter is a revised and updated version of an article under the same title that was first published in *Canadian Social Work* and is reprinted with permission of the Canadian Association of Social Workers [(Winter 2001), 3 *Canadian Social Work* 2]. Marvin M. Bernstein is Director of Policy Development and Legal Support for the Ontario Association of Children's Aid Societies in Toronto. Cheryl Regehr is Associate Professor, Faculty of Social Work, and Director of the Centre for Applied Social Research, University of Toronto. Karima Kanani is with the legal firm Miller Thomson LLP, Toronto.

[2] *R. v. Heikamp and Martin* (Dec. 3, 1999), Toronto, O.C.J. (judgement at preliminary inquiry) at 16.

[3] C. Blatchford, "She Should be Sterilized: My Four Extra Recommendations to Add to the Jurors," *National Post* (12 April 2001) at A1, A10.

was the stress of being dragged through the criminal court process. Although the agency paid her legal fees, if it had not, the process would also have been financially ruinous.

This case has caused considerable consternation among child protection workers regarding the risks of criminal responsibility and civil liability they face related to their work. Laws requiring the mandatory reporting of child abuse have been strengthened in many jurisdictions, and reporting of child abuse has risen at a dramatic rate, substantially increasing the caseloads of child welfare organizations. Meanwhile, the risk of liability has also increased for child protection workers who are forced to make critical decisions about apprehending children, often against the parents' wishes. When protection workers apprehend children, they can be faced with the threat of potential civil lawsuits from disgruntled parents claiming that there has been negligence or a violation of their rights for the improper removal of their children. Conversely, when children remain in the home and further abuse or fatalities occur, the workers can be held liable both civilly and criminally for the child's injury or death. Criminal and civil courts in the United States have found child protection workers liable in some cases for breaching family members' rights to remain together, and in other cases for failing to protect children at risk.[4]

The atmosphere of scrutiny and accountability is acutely felt by workers in the child welfare field. Following the criminal indictment of a child protection worker in Illinois for failing to apprehend a child at risk, a state attorney proclaimed that this would "send a message to all social workers that the state attorney's office will be reviewing their work to protect all the children of this county."[5] Meanwhile, lawyers in British Columbia have claimed that, following child welfare reform in that province, social workers use a strategy of apprehending first and asking questions later. One commentator claimed: "Social workers' intrusiveness constitutes an unlawful invasion of privacy," and suggested that legal action against child welfare social workers is British Columbia's only growth industry.[6]

The dilemma and challenges faced by child protection workers were recognized by Lord Nicholls in an English case involving an investigation of allegations of sexual abuse:[7]

> Cruelty and physical abuse are notoriously difficult to prove. The task of social workers is usually anxious and often thankless. They are criticized for not having taken action in response to warning signs which are obvious enough when seen in the clear light of hindsight. Or they are criticized for making applications based on

---

[4] R. Alexander, "The Legal Liability of Social Workers after Deshaney" (1993), 38(1) *Social Work* 64-68; R. Alexander, "Social Workers and Immunity from Civil Lawsuits" (1995), 40(5) *Social Work* 648-654; and R. Alexander and C. Alexander "Criminal Prosecution of Child Protection Workers" (1995), 49(6) *Social Work* 809-814.

[5] *Ibid*, at 813.

[6] R. Brunet, "BC's Only Growth Industry: Complaints Quadruple Against Aggressive Children and Families Ministry" (1998), 9(33) *British Columbia Report* 14-17 at 16.

[7] *Re H. (Minors)*, [1996] A.C. 563 at 592 (H.L.).

serious allegations which, in the event, are not established in court. Sometimes, whatever they do, they cannot do right.

This chapter reviews recent Canadian case law and legislation to help explore the risks of criminal prosecution and civil litigation that child welfare workers and agencies may face. The chapter concludes by offering suggestions about strategies for reducing the risk of liability not only to child welfare workers, but also to social work as a profession.

Sources of Liability for Child Welfare Workers

Civil Liability

There are many cases in which even after an initial report and investigation by a child protection agency, the children remain in the care of their parents, or are returned to them and suffer further maltreatment at the hands of their parents. In such cases, the caseworker might face civil or criminal liability for inadequately protecting the child by failing to accept a report for investigation, failing to conduct an adequate investigation, failing to remove a child from parental care or an abusive placement, or failing to adequately supervise the child after a return to parental care.[8] Civil lawsuits in this situation are generally based on the tort of negligence. Essentially this action is based on the fact that the agency and the worker owe a duty to the child to protect against further harm, with the allegation that the worker responded in a substandard fashion, and that as a result the child was abused or injured. In all of these cases, the victims also sue the perpetrators of the abuse; while there is never legal doubt that the perpetrator is primarily liable, that person is usually unable to satisfy a judgement and the significant issue is whether the agency or its staff are also liable.

Two cases in the Canadian courts dealing with the issue of the civil liability of a child protection worker have reached differing conclusions, due to differences in their facts. In the first, the child was left in parental care after an initial investigation and suffered further abuse. The child protection worker was not found to be liable, as the child did not tell her worker about the abuse until after she had left the dangerous situation.[9] The guardian who brought the suit on behalf of the child argued that the worker should have investigated the child's situation more fully, but the court accepted that the worker did what could reasonably be expected and that in light of the child's persistent denial of abuse, leaving the child in parental care was a reasonable course of action.

In the second case, *A.J. v. Cairnie*, the court ruled that the child protection worker breached a duty of care, and the worker and agency were liable to the child for the injuries suffered after the initial report of abuse. In this case the child had made a vague disclosure to her worker that her stepfather had sexually

---

[8] *Supra*, note 5.
[9] *D.(S.) v. S.(D.W.)* (1994), 160 A.R. 61 (Master).

abused her, but was left in the home.[10] The girl later phoned the worker crying and hysterical to give further details, but the worker apparently responded by saying: "Well your stepfather said that you're nothing but a lying bitch and I guess he was right." Thereafter the stepfather raped the girl and threatened that he would kill her if she made any further reports, and the girl did not make any further disclosures but suffered repeated and escalating abuse at his hands. It was only many years later that the victim disclosed the abuse and brought a suit against the worker and the agency. In the course of this civil suit it was learned that the worker had a serious drinking problem and that her supervisor had significant concerns about her work, though she was not fired. The court held that the worker had failed to do what a "reasonable worker" would have done in terms of investigation and handling of the case. The court concluded that this was not a "mere error of judgement" in handling a difficult case, but actual negligence on the part of the worker. The agency as her employer was also found to be "vicariously liable" to this survivor of abuse.[11]

Workers and agencies do not just face liability for failure to protect children; there is also the potential for liability for too aggressive intervention. While the provincial laws give child protection caseworkers the authority to intervene into the privacy of the family, the need to protect children from abuse or neglect is not a justification for unnecessarily violating or ignoring parental rights. Violations of parental rights for which social workers can be held civilly liable include slander due to unfounded destruction of a parent's reputation, damages for wrongful removal of children, and malicious prosecution.[12]

There have been four reported Canadian cases that have gone to trial in which agencies and child protection workers faced civil suits for violating parental rights. In each of these cases the allegations of abuse were ultimately shown to be unfounded. In two cases, social workers and their agencies were found to be not legally responsible.[13] In the other two cases, the social workers and their agencies were found to be liable to parents.[14] The cases in which judges found

---

[10] *A.J. v. Cairnie*, [1999] M.J. No. 176 (Q.B.).

[11] Vicarious liability is a doctrine of tort law that holds that an employer is liable for the negligent acts of an employee carried out in the course of his or her employment. The employer does not have to be negligent in the supervision of the employee to be found liable, as long as the employee was carrying out his or her duties. A contentious question is whether non-profit child serving organizations should be held vicariously liable for sexual abuse perpetrated by employees against children in the care of the organization. In *Bazley v. Curry*, [1999] 2 S.C.R. 534 the Supreme Court of Canada held that an agency that operated a group home should be liable for sexual abuse perpetrated by an employee on a child resident in the home, as the opportunity for intimate private control and the development of a parent-like relationship that could be exploited arose directly from the employment relationship. But in *Jacobi v. Griffiths*, [1999] 2 S.C.R. 570 the Supreme Court held that a recreation club was not liable for sexual abuse perpetrated by a staff member against a child as the abuse occurred away from the club, and was not directly initiated as a part of the club's activities, even though the staff was clearly exploiting a relationship that was established as a result of the child's involvement in the club.

[12] *Supra*, note 4; *supra*, note 6 at 14-17.

[13] *Supra*, note 9; and *Farchels v. British Columbia (Minister of Social Services and Housing)*, [1988] B.C.J. 493.

[14] *B.(D.) v. Children's Aid Society of Durham* (1996), 136 D.L.R. (4th) 297 (Ont. C.A.); and *W.(D.) v. W.(D.)*, [1998] OJ. No. 2927 (O.C.J.). See also *D.K. v. Miazga*, [2003] S.J. No. 830 (Q.B.) where a police officer and a

the workers and agencies liable were ones in which there was not only a finding that, in hindsight, the allegations were unfounded. The courts imposed liability because they considered that workers were lacking in "good faith" in conducting their investigation, in the sense that the workers did not treat the parents fairly, though in each case the workers were acting under the direction of their supervisors.

Another area that brings potential exposure to civil liability for child protection workers and agencies is negligence in the supervision of foster parents and placements for children in state care.

In a recent trilogy of cases originating in British Columbia, dealing with historical sexual and physical abuse, the Supreme Court of Canada offered some useful guidance in this area.[15] In two of these cases, *K.L.B. v. British Columbia* and *M.B. v. British Columbia*, the former wards, by the time of the law suits adult survivors, sued the government (which had been providing child welfare services) for harm suffered as a result of abuse inflicted by their former foster parents. Although the social workers responsible for the children in state care were not personally sued, it is conceivable that social workers could find themselves sued in similar, future cases.[16] These cases addressed the issues of direct negligence, vicarious liability, breaches of non-delegable duties and breaches of fiduciary duties.

In the *K.L.B.* case, the court considered all four of these possible causes of liability, and found that the government was liable to the former child-victims, but only on the basis of direct negligence, subject to applicable limitation period defences. In the *M.B.* decision, the court considered only the concepts of vicarious liability and breaches of non-delegable duty and found that no liability had been established on those grounds.

The Supreme Court of Canada, in this trilogy of cases, has established the following guiding principles:

- The standard for direct negligence for those exercising control over a child in state care is a high one and is that of "a prudent parent" caring for the welfare of his or her child. This standard does not make the government (or a child welfare agency) a guarantor against all harm, but this standard does hold the agency responsible for harm sustained by children in foster care, if judged by the standards of the day, it was reasonably foreseeable that the child welfare agency conduct would expose these children to the harm ultimately sustained. The agency is under an obligation to implement proper

---

therapist were found liable for malicious persecution as a result of a very poorly conducted investigation of allegations of sexual abuse against foster parents.

[15] *K.L.B. v. British Columbia*, [2003] SCC 51; *E.D.G. v. Hammer*, [2003] SCC 52; and *M.B. v. British Columbia*, [2003] SCC 53.

[16] See, for example, *C.H. v. British Columbia*, [2003] B.C.J. No. 1706 (July 11, 2003), where the B.C.S.C. found that the social workers responsible for a child's care were liable for the damages suffered by the child at the hands of his foster parent, where no social worker supervision or control was exercised, but because they were not named as defendants, the Ministry was held to be vicariously liable for the negligent conduct of its social workers, whose negligence clearly occurred within the scope of their employment.

procedures in order to screen prospective foster parents and to supervise homes with foster children effectively, so that any abusive acts can be quickly detected. The Court concluded that the standards of the time of the abuse in this case (the 1960s and 1970s), were less rigorous than contemporary standards, but even by those old standards the agency was required to conduct a proper assessment of any proposed foster parents and their ability to meet a foster child's needs; to discuss the acceptable limits of discipline with the foster parents; and to provide regular supervisory visits in foster homes, especially foster homes that were considered "overplaced" and had a documented history of inappropriate behaviour.

- A child welfare agency is not "vicariously liable" (or indirectly liable as an employer) for negligent or abusive acts committed by its foster parents against the children entrusted to them. Because of the independent and family-based structure of foster care, the agency cannot supervise the actions of its foster parents on an ongoing basis and does not have the vicarious liability that an employer has for employees acting in the course of their employment. The fact that foster parents must operate independently in managing the daily activities of foster children and in resolving the children's immediate problems, and the fact that they exercise full managerial responsibility over their own households are indications that they are not acting as employees or agents. Foster parents do not hold themselves out as representatives of the child welfare agency in the community, nor are they perceived in that manner: "Although foster parents are indeed acting in the service of a public goal, their actions are too far removed from the government [child welfare agency] for them to be reasonably perceived as acting 'on account of' the government in the sense necessary to justify vicarious liability."[17] In *K.L.B. v. British Columbia*, the court distinguished the circumstances involving foster parents from two cases it had earlier decided,[18] where it had concluded that vicarious liability is contingent upon both the existence of an employer-employee relationship and a close tie between the employee's misconduct and the risk that the employer's enterprise and assignment of employee responsibilities have placed in the community (e.g., where, as in *Bazley v. Curry*, a non-profit organization that operated two residential facilities for emotionally troubled children was found liable for the sexually abusive acts of one of its employees, who was given the tasks of bathing children and putting them to bed). It is important, then, that child welfare agencies carefully consider liability implications before agreeing to any arrangement that would confer employee status on its foster parents or group home operators.

- The relevant British Columbia child protection legislation does *not* create a general non-delegable duty (i.e., impose strict liability) to ensure that no

---

[17] At para. 25.
[18] *Bazley v. Curry*, [1999] 2 S.C.R. 534; *Jacobi v. Griffiths*, [1999] 2 S.C.R. 570.

harm would be sustained by children in state care because of the negligence or abuse of their foster parents. Instead, the legislation imposed various specific duties, including placing the child in such a place as best meets his or her needs and caring for the physical well being of the child before the child is placed in foster care. If a child welfare agency were to be held responsible for all the wrongs that might be experienced by children in foster care, it would be unnecessary to list the more specific duties with respect to placement and supervision. It would seem no Canadian jurisdiction has legislation that creates a general non-delegable duty towards children in care, but a detailed review of the particular child protection legislation in each jurisdiction is required before a determination can be made as to whether such a duty exists.[19]

- A child welfare agency does *not* hold a general fiduciary duty to promote the best interests of its foster children or protect them merely because it stands in a special relationship of trust to children. Instead, its fiduciary duty, as an "institutional parent," to its foster children is more limited and requires only the avoidance of certain harmful actions that constitute a betrayal of trust. The agency also has a duty of loyalty; in this context, "disloyalty" means "putting someone's interests ahead of the child's in a manner that abuses the child's trust."

One further domain that raises the question of potential civil liability for front-line child protection workers and agencies is the rarely used 300-year-old intentional tort of "abuse of public office," which was recently canvassed by the Supreme Court of Canada in the case of *Odhavji Estate v. Woodhouse*.[20] In this case, the parents of a deceased young adult who was shot by two police officers sued the two officers and another 20 officers who witnessed the shooting, for allegedly sabotaging the investigation by disobeying an order to remain segregated; failing to turn over their notes; and refusing to speak promptly with the investigators from the Special Investigations Unit. Using the tort of "abuse of public office," the Court ruled that the family could proceed with its lawsuit against the officers for failing to co-operate with the Special Investigations Unit and against the former police chief for failing to ensure their co-operation. The Supreme Court ruled that "the class of conduct at which the tort is targeted is not as narrow as the unlawful exercise of a particular statutory or prerogative power, but more based on the unlawful conduct in the exercise of public functions generally."

It would appear that the liability implications of the *Odhavji Estate* decision for front-line child protection workers and agencies are limited. There are, for instance, a number of components to the tort of abuse of public office that would make it rarely applicable to child welfare social workers and agencies. For one thing, the tort has not been committed unless there is evidence of an intention to

---

[19] See e.g., in Ontario *Child and Family Services Act*, R.S.O. 1990, c. C.11, ss. 15(3), 61-63.
[20] [2003] SCC 69.

do harm or to be reckless in the discharge of one's statutory duties or in the omission of such duties. In addition, the lack of ability to discharge statutory duties through good faith inadvertence or because of budgetary constraints (an ongoing issue in the child welfare sector) would provide a defence, as would perhaps the exercise of one's constitutional rights (e.g., where a social worker suspects that he or she could be criminally charged and wishes to claim a constitutional protection against self-incrimination in the case of a criminal investigation). The existence of the tort of breach of public duty does, however, remind child protection workers that they have a duty to treat parents fairly.

It should be noted that while it is common to sue both the agency and the worker involved, and often both are found liable, in practice the agency (or its insurance company) will be likely to satisfy any judgement. Agencies know that it would be unfair and extremely demoralizing to all its staff if a worker were forced to personally cover a damage award. A worker who is sued will inevitably feel great stress even though the worker is not likely to have to personally satisfy the judgement.

Criminal Liability

Even more chilling than the civil suits with potentially large monetary damages are the criminal charges which can, in some cases, such as criminal negligence causing death, carry the possibility of a lengthy prison term if a conviction is obtained. In two Canadian cases, criminal charges were laid against child welfare social workers. The case of the death of Jordan Heikamp, previously described, resulted in the social worker being discharged from further criminal prosecution.

Similarly, in 1982, the executive director, a social work supervisor and a child protection worker of the Brockville Children's Aid Society were acquitted on charges of child abandonment and exposure of a child to danger arising from a case where a boy was brutally beaten by his mother while under the supervision of the local child protection agency. In acquitting the agency staff, Judge Newton considered the background of the child and parents prior to agency involvement, the services offered, the necessity of weighing competing factors of child protection and family preservation, and the worker's competence and dedication. He concluded that the Crown had failed to prove beyond a reasonable doubt that the conduct of the worker was so negligent as to constitute a "reckless or callous disregard" for the safety of the child.[21] This case emphasized that the mere fact that a child is injured or killed while under agency supervision does not mean that the agency staff are criminally liable; criminal liability will only be imposed for a clear dereliction of duty.

---

[21] M. Bernstein, "The Brockville Case: Legal Analysis" (1983), 6 *Family Law Review* 92-113; *R. v. Leslie*, [unreported] 1982.

Other Types of Liability

Other less conspicuous risks for agencies and their staff include: liability for "costs"; being found in "contempt of court"; or a finding of "homicide" and further charges flowing out of a coroner's inquest.

In some child protection cases where the court concludes that the agency was clearly unjustified, or even acting in "bad faith" in removing a child from parental care, the court may order the agency to pay "the costs" of the parents. Such an order requires the agency to pay all, or a substantial portion, of the legal expenses incurred by the parents. At least one judge has noted that, while the correct agency action may appear obvious in hindsight, agency mistakes in judgement due to the lack of experience of staff do not justify the awarding of costs.[22] Agencies are only likely to be ordered to pay the parents' legal costs if it is apparent that the agency took a case without merit to trial, or that the agency was acting in an oppressive fashion. Judges have said that they will only require the agency to pay the costs of parents if the agency's conduct was "unfair," for example, because the agency failed to reveal the results of psychological assessments that it had prepared.[23]

A court can make a finding that a person is in "contempt of court" if the person has willfully failed to comply with a court order. The contempt power is intended to ensure compliance with court orders, that is to protect rights that have been recognized by a court, and to ensure respect for the administration of justice. A finding of contempt of court is most likely to result in a fine, though in cases of *blatant* or *persistent* refusal to comply with a court order it could result in a period of imprisonment. There have been a few cases in which child protection agencies have been threatened with being found in contempt for failure to comply with court orders, for example to comply with an order requiring an agency to allow a parent to visit with a child in agency care, or failure to return a child to parental care when required to do so.

In one Ontario case, after a five-day hearing based primarily on concerns of parental neglect, the judge decided to return a child who had been apprehended to his parents under agency supervision. The agency workers inspected the parent's home immediately after the hearing, and still had significant concerns about the child's safety, and so they did not return the child but purported to carry out a "technical [re] apprehension," and kept the child in care. The parents brought a motion for contempt of court, and the agency and one worker were

---

[22] *Catholic Children's Aid Society of Toronto v. V.(S.)* (June 30, 2000), Toronto, O.C.J. at 4, per Katarynych J. (leave to appeal dismissed, Oct. 16, 2000, Ont. Sup. Ct.); court file C4290/99 (Scarborough, Ont.).

[23] See e.g., *C.A.S. of Niagara v. W.D.*, [2004] O.J. 475 (Sup. Ct.) (leave to appeal being sought at the time of writing) where the agency was required to pay the costs of a step-parent who was seeking to get the care of two children even though he was not successful in the case, because the agency originally encouraged him to do so but changed its position in the middle of the case, and failed to disclose two assessments that were unfavourable to his claim.

found guilty of contempt and fined. The judge emphasized the importance of agency workers complying with orders, even when they disagreed with them:[24]

> The court is not omniscient and does not have a monopoly on wisdom when the time comes to decide what is in a child's best interests. A worker...may very well disagree with the court's decision. This disagreement may be in good faith and may be based on excellent reasons. But the court's decision must be complied with and obeyed nonetheless, because the community has chosen democratically to give the court the mandate to decide these matters...the child protection system...cannot work unless court orders are strictly complied with. It is an area particularly susceptible to social unravelling because of what is at stake in the decisions and the tremendous degree of emotion that all orders elicit in the participants. It is essential to this entire legislative system, and therefore essential to ensuring the best interests of the children who are subject to this system, that court orders be treated with the utmost respect...if a worker or a Society can disregard an order because she or it considers the order contrary to the child's interests, the entire system will become compromised.

Of course, the agency may also appeal an order and seek a stay of the order pending an appeal, but if it does not do so, the agency must comply with the order.[25]

An additional concern for workers and agencies is a coroner's inquest that may result from a child abuse death. Inquests are a form of public inquiry that are intended to help society understand how a person died, and to ascertain what steps can be taken to prevent the recurrence of a preventable death. These inquests are presided over by a doctor — the coroner — who sits with a jury; relatives of the deceased, agencies involved in a case and interested groups are likely to have lawyers who may participate in calling evidence and examining witnesses. The inquest is not technically a trial, and the rules of evidence and procedure differ from those which govern ordinary litigation.

In all Canadian jurisdictions, a jury at a coroner's inquest is required by legislation only to make findings of fact and recommendations for policy change, but not to make findings of legal liability. For example, the *Coroners Act*[26] prohibits the jury from making "any findings of legal responsibility" or expressing "any conclusions of law." Indeed, any such finding in Ontario is considered to be "improper" and not receivable by the presiding coroner under subsection 31(4) of the *Act*. It is therefore important to differentiate between a finding of "homicide" at an inquest, such as was made in the *Heikamp* inquest discussed above, and a finding of "homicide" under the *Criminal Code*. The definition of "homicide" used at an inquest is the *Oxford Dictionary* definition, which is "the action of one human being killing another human being." This finding in a coroner's inquest, therefore, is not meant to attribute *legal* fault or blame to any particular person, unlike a finding of "homicide" in a criminal proceeding.

---

[24] [Translation] *N.G. v. C.M. v. C.A.S. of Prescott-Russell*, (unreported) Jan. 16, 2004, Ont. Sup. Ct., per Charbonneau J., paras. 43 and 62. This decision was under appeal at the time of writing.

[25] See discussion in Chapter 3 on appeals.

[26] *Coroner's Act*, R.S.O. 1990, c. C.37, ss. 31 and 42.

It is unlikely that criminal charges will flow from an inquest for two reasons. First, to provide a climate of optimal candour for the witnesses, the presiding coroner will not usually agree to convene an inquest until there is some reasonable assurance from the police and the Crown prosecutor's office that future charges will not be laid. Second, in most Canadian jurisdictions, the statute governing inquests gives witnesses protection for the answers that they are compelled to give by providing that such answers cannot be used against them at a subsequent proceeding.

Even though there are no criminal or civil consequences flowing from a coroner's inquest, participating in an inquest is emotionally draining for workers and financially expensive for agencies. If there is a suggestion that the agency might have prevented a child's death, from the perspective of a worker or agency involved in an inquest, there may be a feeling that they are "on trial" in the inquest. It is not uncommon for the workers involved in a case that results in an inquest to either leave the child protection field or to be reassigned to a position that does not involve ongoing risk assessment, so that the worker's judgement cannot be second-guessed in the future.

Legal and Statutory Protection for Child Welfare Workers

It is widely recognized that it would be unfair to hold workers or agencies liable for every case that, in hindsight, was not properly handled. Imposition of strict liability could be highly destructive for agencies, and would make inherently stressful jobs even less appealing. There is a recognition that child protection work, by its very nature, deals with risk and uncertainty, and that strictly imposing liability would make agencies and their workers very reluctant to ever leave a child in a situation where there is any risk of physical harm, even if the consequences of removal would certainly be emotionally traumatic for the child. Provincial legislatures recognize the dilemma that workers and agencies face, and have enacted statutory protections to limit the civil liability of child protection workers. For example, s. 15(6) of Ontario's *Child and Family Services Act* provides:[27]

> No action shall be instituted against an officer or employee of a society for an act done in good faith in the execution or intended execution of the person's duty or for an alleged neglect or default in the execution in good faith of the person's duty.

This is referred to as an "immunity provision." The immunity from civil liability provided for child protection caseworkers by this provision is a form of "qualified immunity" sometimes called "good faith immunity." Good faith suggests that a worker acted on his or her best judgement and knowledge by seeking out the most positive outcome for all parties based on an honest belief that the action taken was necessary. Good faith immunity will protect workers

---

[27] *Child and Family Services Act*, R.S.O. 1990, c. C.11, s. 15(6).

and agencies from liability for "errors of judgement," but it will not protect practice that was biased, vengeful, indifferent or grossly negligent.[28]

The legislation thus provides significant protection to social workers while still holding them accountable for egregious malpractice. The effect of this protection is to substantially reduce the legal dilemma of civil liability. Given protection for decisions made in good faith for or against apprehension, workers should be able to focus on making professional decisions in good conscience instead of making decisions based on the risk of liability.

Strategies for Protection against Liability

There are a number of strategies that agencies and workers can adopt to minimize the legal risk of civil liability or criminal prosecution. Most of these strategies are also good social work practice.

Good Clinical Social Work Practice

Some authors have suggested that, as a result of concerns for liability, child welfare workers have felt pressure to practice "defensive social work," resulting in the needless removal of children from their homes.[29] It is contended that as a result of negative publicity and concerns about liability, workers are prompted to remove a child from parental care whenever there is the slightest concern, on the theory of "better safe than sorry."[30]

However, legislation providing for "good faith immunity" is intended to ensure that workers and agencies are only liable if they are not acting in good faith or are grossly negligent, so it is not necessary for workers to avoid making difficult judgement calls for fear of incurring possible liability if the "wrong" decision is made. Further, a strategy of apprehending without fair consideration of all of the circumstances of the case exposes the worker and agency to the risk of liability for violating the rights of the parents and children. In *Catholic Children's Aid Society of Toronto v. V.(S.)*, the court catalogued a number of factors that could raise concern as to a child protection agency's lack of good faith and might, for example, result in a costs award against an agency in a child protection case:[31]

- Refusal to take account of information that should be considered to inform decision making in a case if the agency is faithful to its statutory duties;

---

[28] *Supra*, note 14; and W. Holder, "Malpractice in Child Protective Services: An Overview of the Problem" in W. Holder and K. Hayes (Eds.), *Malpractice and Liability in Child Protective Services* (Colorado: Bookmakers Guild, Inc., 1984). See also *Finney v. Barreau du Québec*, [2004] S.C.J. 31

[29] R. Thomas, *A Critical Look at the Child Welfare System: Defensive Social Work* (1998); on-line <http://www.liftingtheveil.org/defensive.htm>.

[30] R. Horowitz, "Improving the Legal Bases in Child Protection Work: Let the Worker Beware," in W. Holder and K. Hayes (Eds.), *Malpractice and Liability in Child Protective Services* (Colorado: Bookmakers Guild, Inc., 1984).

[31] *Supra*, note 22 at 7.

- Rigid reliance on a parent's history as a basis for current protective intervention without any meaningful attempt to ascertain whether that past history is the parent's "present";
- A tenacious hold to a theory about a child's need for protection in the face of the facts, that as a matter of common sense and objectivity, should prompt a revisiting of that theory;
- Selective and biased representation of facts in court that may mislead a judge as to the nature and extent of the present risk to the child;
- Malice towards a parent or other party;
- Arbitrary alignment with one parent to the prejudice of another, and specifically, ignoring information that would have led a reasonable person to question the reliability of the parent with whom the alliance has been formed; and
- Defiance of the court's orders or directions in the case, including the filing, without further action, of a Notice of Appeal as a means of delaying implementation of an unwanted decision.

In making decisions about a case, social workers in child welfare must therefore exercise good clinical judgement based on accepted theories and standards of practice. Risk assessment tools can serve as useful guides for decision making, but are not intended to replace sound clinical judgement. While parents are entitled to support from a child welfare agency, workers must always remember that the primary client is the child. It is therefore important for workers to maintain a healthy skepticism about what parents may report about their own behaviour, and critically assess the information that they receive from different sources. In the *Jordan Heikamp Coroner's Inquest* the jury made specific recommendations about the role of child welfare agencies and their workers:[32]

> It should be made clear to all Child Protection Workers and their Child Protection Supervisors that their client is the child in need of protection, not the parent or the family. Rationale: The evidence shows that the focus in this case was primarily on the mother and not on the child. (Recommendation 1).

> All Children's Aid Societies [should] adopt a critical role as well as a supportive role for their social workers. Rationale: Evidence showed that the social worker played a supportive role or advocacy role for the mother of the child and a more critical role was required. (Recommendation 11).

Adherence to provincial statutes and policies regarding child protection, and to the *Code of Ethics* for social work practice, as developed by the Canadian Association of Social Workers, will also ensure that social workers are practising according to expected standards.[33] This *Code*, for example, requires that social workers fully inform parents about the nature of child welfare

---

[32] *Inquest Touching the Death of Jordan Desmond Heikamp* (April 11, 2001, Toronto, Ont.) Jury Verdict and Recommendations, 1, 11.

[33] Canadian Association of Social Workers (CASW) (1994). *Social Work Code of Ethics* (Ottawa: CASW).

interventions and the possible consequences that may ensue as a result of providing information to a child welfare worker.

Good Record Keeping

Careful documenting of involvement in a case allows child welfare workers to maintain a record of their clinical assessments and clinical interventions to assist with ongoing work in a case, and to communicate clearly their opinions, findings, and interventions to others within the agency and other professionals with whom they are working. Further, if a case goes to court, good records can be the key to proving that practice decisions were well considered and that adequate measures were taken to ensure the safety and well-being of clients and others in the face of possible legal action. The *Code of Ethics* of the Canadian Association of Social Workers makes the following statements regarding record keeping:[34]

> 5.10. The social worker shall record all relevant information, and keep all relevant documents in the (client) file.
>
> 5.11. The social worker shall not record in a client's file any characterization that is not based on clinical assessment or fact.

Social workers in all areas of practice must remain aware that court and client access to clinical records is increasingly common, and thus, workers must write records with the anticipation that they may be shared with others.[35] In addition, social workers should take care to maintain detailed documentation of all significant discussions and decisions, as well as the reasons for those decisions.

In the *Heikamp and Martin* decision, Madam Justice Hogan placed considerable reliance on the fact that the child welfare worker with responsibility for the case followed all agency policies and procedures, regularly consulted with her supervisor and acted in compliance with supervisory direction. Child protection workers would be well advised, in their records, to identify relevant policies and procedures that may be operating and to confirm the date and content of supervisory meetings, including any significant direction obtained.

Effective Communication and Verification of Information

Child welfare workers will be better protected from potential criminal or civil responsibility if they engage in effective communication with their clients, other team members, their supervisors, and, not least, other collaterals involved in the case.

There is also a need to verify important information, which, in turn, should be carefully documented. Both Madam Justice Hogan and the coroner's jury in the *Heikamp* case emphasized the importance of the clarification of roles and responsibilities with collaterals, either by confirming letter or agreement,

---

[34] *Ibid.*

[35] C. Regehr, G. Glancy, and A. Bryant, "Breaking Confidentiality: Legal Requirements for Canadian Social Workers" (1998), 8(1) *Journal of Law and Social Work* 115-129.

particularly where there is room for misunderstanding or where there is the possibility of antipathy between the different agencies and professionals providing services to the child and family. They also underscored the need to verify important information, such as follow-up medical appointments and weight gains for a premature infant, especially in high-risk situations, or where parents providing the information may be unreliable or manipulative.

Ensuring Financial Protection — Insurance

Although insurance cannot compensate for the emotional costs of being sued, it can provide vitally needed financial protection. Workers should find out whether their agencies carry insurance or have indemnification programs and the coverage areas and extent of protection. Coverage for civil matters is common but is not necessarily comprehensive.

The insurance policies of most child welfare agencies have limited or no coverage for legal expenses incurred in a criminal defence. Where such coverage exists, it is usually predicated upon an ultimate acquittal or a withdrawal of the charges against the worker. It is useful for a worker to know how the agency has handled these matters in the past and whether the agency will assume financial responsibility for all interim billings by criminal defence counsel until such time as a final acquittal verdict has been delivered. Depending on the agency coverage, the social worker may wish to consider obtaining liability insurance privately.

Advocating Social Change

The root of negative defensive strategies in social work lies in the power of the socio-political environment to ostracize child protection workers following the injury or death of a child under their supervision. By embracing the identity and expertise of the child welfare profession and making responsible decisions, even in the face of negative publicity, child protection workers can reflect to the public confidence in their practice and profession. As well, there must be public policies that protect the rights of children and promote safe home environments. Finally, there must be sufficient economic resources to enable the provision of quality service to clients through appropriate worker training, standards of practice, manageable case loads and accessible community services.

Conclusions

In recent years there have been a number of highly publicized investigations into the deaths of children receiving child welfare services in North America, Europe and Australia.[36] These inquiries have focused public anger on child welfare professionals and agencies. There has also been an increase in recent years in attempts to hold workers and agencies in child welfare responsible for

---

[36] C. Regehr, S. Chau, B. Leslie, and P. Howe, "Inquiries Into the Deaths of Children: Impacts on Child Welfare Workers and Their Organizations," (in press) *Child and Youth Services Review.*

the abuse and deaths of children through the criminal and civil courts.[37] Critics have suggested that the imposition of liability on child welfare workers and agencies is nothing more than an attempt to find a scapegoat for a child's death or attempts by prosecutors to gain publicity.[38] In this social climate, child welfare workers may feel under siege and perceive themselves to be at high risk of criminal prosecution and civil liability. The reality to date, however, is that child·welfare workers who follow accepted standards of practice and who in good faith make difficult judgements to the best of their ability, have not been found criminally culpable or civilly liable. It is encouraging that the legislatures and the courts have taken an approach to accountability that is positive towards child welfare work, not only by respecting the expertise that underlies discretionary decision making in general, but also by undertaking a contextual analysis that appreciates the dynamics of child protection practice. This point is reflected in Justice Hogan's judgement discharging the child protection worker in the *Heikamp* case:[39]

> I should emphasize here that having found that mistakes or errors in judgement were made does not, therefore, mean that there is evidence on any of the essential elements of criminal negligence. People make mistakes all the time, professionals make errors in judgement but this doesn't mean that these mistakes or errors constitute criminal negligence unless it can be proved that they were of such a nature as to satisfy the essential elements of the charge. In this case, I have found that they did not.

Consequently, social workers in child welfare who exercise reasonable caution and engage in good clinical social work practice, good record keeping, and effective communication and verification of information can continue to strive to offer high quality services to children and their families, as they have always done, without any serious fear of recrimination.

---

[37] *Supra*, note 4; *supra*, note 6 at 14-17.

[38] *Supra*, note 4.

[39] *Supra*, note 2 at 20.

14

Concluding Thoughts from Social Work

Michael Kim Zapf[1]

More than a dozen years have passed since publication of the first edition of *Canadian Child Welfare Law: Children, Families and the State.*[2] Although the preface to that first edition acknowledged that the material was written mostly from a legal perspective, the book was clearly intended as a resource for two identified groups: law students and lawyers "with less experience in the field," and professionals "from other disciplines who are required to function within the alien, confusing, and sometimes hostile environment of the Family Court."[3] Most Canadian child welfare services are delivered by government agencies employing staff with social work training.[4] These social workers, especially in child protection, have been acknowledged to have responsibilities that are very demanding, difficult and stressful due to the conflicting nature of the dual functions of support/ therapy and investigation/authority.[5] The first edition of this book, then, was directed in part towards those social workers who would need to understand the relevant legal frameworks, processes and perspectives in order to function effectively in the child welfare arena.

Much has been added to the dynamic knowledge base for child welfare in the Canadian social work literature in the years since the first edition of *Canadian Child Welfare Law* was published. Along with individual journal articles and book chapters, there have been several consolidated sets of readings published during that period, including: *Rethinking Child Welfare in Canada;*[6] *Child Welfare in Canada: Research and Policy Implications;*[7] *Changing the Child*

---

[1] Michael Kim Zapf is Professor of Social Work, University of Calgary, Alberta.

[2] N. Bala, J. Hornick, and R. Vogl (Eds.), *Canadian Child Welfare Law: Children, Families and the State* (Toronto: Thompson Educational Publishing, 1991).

[3] G. Thomson, "Preface" in N. Bala, J. Hornick, and R. Vogl (Eds.), *Canadian Child Welfare Law: Children, Families and the State* (Toronto: Thompson Educational Publishing, 1991) at xix.

[4] B. Fallon, B. MacLaurin, N. Trocmé, and C. Felstiner, "A National Profile of Child Protection Workers" in K. Kufeldt and B. McKenzie (Eds.), *Child Welfare: Connection Research, Policy, and Practice* (Waterloo: Wilfried Laurier University Press, 2003), 41-52.

[5] N. Bala, "An Introduction to Child Protection Problems" in N. Bala, J. Hornick, and R. Vogl (Eds.), *Canadian Child Welfare Law: Children, Families and the State* (Toronto: Thompson Educational Publishing, 1991), 1-16.

[6] B. Wharf (Ed.), *Rethinking Child Welfare in Canada* (Toronto: McClelland and Stewart, 1993).

[7] J. Hudson and B. Galaway (Eds.), *Child Welfare in Canada: Research and Policy Implications* (Toronto: Thompson Educational Publishing, 1995).

Welfare Agenda: Contributions from Canada;[8] *Community Work Approaches to Child Welfare;*[9] and *Child Welfare: Connecting Research, Policy, and Practice.*[10] While these social work collections contain more than one hundred articles on Canadian child welfare, it may be surprising to learn that they include only two references to the first edition of *Canadian Child Welfare Law.*[11]

Why might a comprehensive book on Canadian child welfare law have so little apparent influence on the developing social work knowledge base for child welfare services? Is it because legal issues are not relevant for social workers in child welfare? This seems unlikely, given the legal framework for much of child welfare practice and the social work attention to context. Are the professions of social work and law constrained in their disciplinary silos to the point where a well-intentioned attempt at multidisciplinary sharing is ignored or rejected? Again, the explanation seems unlikely. The fact that the original book had limited observable impact on social work theory does not necessarily mean that it was rejected in practice. After all, the first edition of *Canadian Child Welfare Law* sold out; clearly someone bought and used the book. The book has also been quoted by lawyers and judges, including in the Supreme Court of Canada.[12]

Questions remain, however, about factors inhibiting social work academics and practitioners from full access to a potentially valuable resource that originates outside their discipline. The material covered here explores some of these potential obstacles: different writing styles and different approaches to knowledge building in law and social work, perceived threats to social work's professional identity, constraints in social work education, gender issues, frustrations with a residual system, micro/macro practice perspectives, and calls for a paradigm shift. These are important questions to consider if this second edition of *Canadian Child Welfare Law* is to realize its potential impact on front-line child welfare service delivery.

A Matter of Style

Close examination of the sources identified above reveals very different writing styles in the disciplines of law and social work. The child welfare readings from social work contain a wealth of bibliographic references to debates, research results and conceptual pieces from the social work literature. It

---

[8] S. Scarth, B. Wharf and E. Tyrwhitt (Eds.), "Changing the Child Welfare Agenda: Contributions from Canada," (May/June, 1995), LXXIV Special Issue of *Child Welfare.*

[9] B. Wharf (Ed.), *Community Work Approaches to Child Welfare* (Peterborough: Broadview Press, 2002).

[10] K. Kufeldt and B. McKenzie (Eds.), *Child Welfare: Connecting Research, Policy, and Practice* (Waterloo: Wilfrid Laurier University Press, 2003), 331-342.

[11] K. Kufeldt and E. Theriault, "Child Welfare Experiences and Outcomes: Themes, Policy Implications and Research Agenda" in J. Hudson and B. Galaway (Eds.), *Child Welfare in Canada: Research and Policy Implications* (Toronto: Thompson Educational Publishing, 1995), 358-366; and L. Davies, K. Fox, J. Krane, and E. Shragge, "Community Child Welfare: Examples from Quebec" in B. Wharf (Ed.), *Community Work Approaches to Child Welfare* (Peterborough: Broadview Press, 2002), 63-82.

[12] *Winnipeg Child and Family Services vs. K.L.W.,* [2000] S.C.R. 519, cited by both the majority and the dissent.

is interesting that virtually no specific cases are referenced. On the other hand, the 1991 edition of *Canadian Child Welfare Law* offers comprehensive tables of cases and statutes and occasional citations from the *Canadian Journal of Family Law* or *Family Law Quarterly*, and evaluation reports from various commissions and government ministries. Virtually no connection is made to the practice literature (although the one exception to this pattern, which proves the rule, is the chapter in *Canadian Child Welfare Law* that was written by social workers and features over 30 references to the practice literature but no specific case citations).

Clearly, social work and law have different traditions for building and communicating knowledge, conventional patterns and assumptions, which might block either group from fully engaging with the resources and perspectives of the other. Social workers may find the case approach constraining in their pursuit of larger system change. Lawyers may find the social issue approach less than relevant for the complex demands of decision making in specific cases.

Professional Identity

Child welfare has been called the "defining field of practice for social work...the only field of practice consistently recognized as the domain of social work."[13] Social workers in other spheres generally work with professionals who have more status or authority in that setting (hospitals, corrections, addictions, schools, mental health clinics, etc.). If social work's identity as a profession is very closely connected to child welfare, then venturing into the legal side of that work could be experienced as a threat to professional identity.

Child welfare is a field where the state can take on parenting functions normally assumed to be the responsibility of parents within the family unit. The legal component focuses on issues such as statutory duties, responsibilities, obligations and rights. The social work component focuses on families, child development, resources, and community. Situations where the state can intervene in family life are defined by the law, as are the processes for formal transference of parental rights to the state. The law also establishes mechanisms for the reporting of complaints to a delegated authority. Social work's primary function in child welfare has become the assessment of the need for protection of children, and taking action to assure that protection when necessary.[14] Social work activities in child welfare are initiated within a legal framework, and are monitored or supervised to varying degrees by the courts.

---

[13] M. Callahan, "The Administration and Practice Context: Perspectives from the Front Line" in B. Wharf (Ed.), *Rethinking Child Welfare in Canada* (Toronto: McClelland and Stewart, 1993), 64 at 66.

[14] A. Armitage, "The Policy and Legislative Context" in B. Wharf (Ed.), *Rethinking Child Welfare in Canada* (Toronto: McClelland and Stewart, 1993), 37-63.

When child welfare is perceived as legal work, then the courtroom becomes another practice setting dominated by professionals from a different discipline (lawyers), a potential threat to the identity of the social work profession.

Social Work Education

Since so many social work graduates go on to work in child welfare, would it not make sense to incorporate more specific child welfare law content in the social work education curriculum?

The Bachelor of Social Work (BSW) degree is the preferred entry-level credential for child welfare work in most Canadian jurisdictions. As accredited by the Canadian Association of Schools of Social Work, the BSW is a four-year undergraduate degree. Typically, the first two years consist of general education courses to provide a liberal arts foundation for the two years of social work content to follow. The social work component of the degree must include a prescribed practicum period (approximately 700 hours) of supervised educational practice. All of these requirements mean that there is little more than one full year of social work academic content in the BSW degree (during which students take required core courses in such areas as research, policy, human behaviour and environments, interviewing skills, practice models and methods). There may be little room in the core BSW academic curriculum for comprehensive content related to child welfare (or any other specific field of practice).

A concern sometimes expressed by child welfare agencies is that new BSW graduates are not ready to assume the duties of a full caseload without further training specific to child welfare. Of course, the same concern is heard from agencies providing service in mental health, corrections, addictions and health care. The BSW experience cannot presume to prepare graduates for immediate field competence in every one of these diverse fields of practice. Students can learn general models, skills and perspectives, and may have opportunities to focus on specific fields of practice through elective courses and practicum field placements, but there can be no expectation that every BSW graduate will have comprehensive exposure to child welfare practices and issues. Much of this training will fall to the agency hiring BSW graduates.

Gender Stereotypes

In Western society, care of children has traditionally been viewed as a responsibility of women. Most of the direct service offered by child welfare agencies is provided by female social workers.[15] Caseloads in child protection work are largely comprised of women, the mothers whom society traditionally holds

---

[15] K. Barter, "Services for Vulnerable Children: A Conceptualization" in J.C. Turner and F.J. Turner (Eds.), *Canadian Social Welfare* 4th ed. (Toronto: Pearson Education Canada, 2001), 250-264; and K. Swift, "Missing Persons: Women in Child Welfare" in S. Scarth, B. Wharf and E. Tyrwhitt (Eds.), "Changing the Child Welfare Agenda: Contributions from Canada" (May/June 1995), LXXIV Special Issue of *Child Welfare* 486-502.

accountable for protection of their children. Just as childcare functions have historically been associated with women, it could be argued that legal processes have a long history as primarily a male domain. Obviously these are gross generalizations, and there are competent women and men practicing in both professions. Further, there are an increasing number of women who are lawyers and judges. Yet long-standing stereotypes, erroneous yet entrenched, of social work as women's work, and legal argument as men's work, may serve to explain some of the historic tendency for social work to view the law as an enemy or, at least, a more powerful and insensitive regulator. Commenting on patriarchal society, Callahan observed that "mothers often felt accountable to their male partners or fathers" for child care matters.[16] It is not a stretch to suggest that female child welfare workers may also feel accountable to, and resentful of, the authoritative supervision of the court with its adversarial and hierarchical processes.

Frustration with a Residual System

The mandate of Canadian child welfare has been described as narrow, limited and residual. The state only becomes involved when absolutely necessary, when parents have exhausted their resources and their ability or will to care for their children.[17] There is an assumption that provincial government departments are best able to provide the needed service by assigning individual cases to individual social workers. In the current system, there are no incentives or supports for increasing levels of citizen involvement in child welfare service delivery.[18] The focus of the work for social workers in child welfare has become the investigation of complaints, determination of neglect and abuse, and the assessment of the level of risk for such behaviours. Workers could be seen as technicians preoccupied with reactive assessment and documentation of conditions that justify state intrusion into the private realm of family life.

Thirty years ago, social work manuals tended to be small, portable and focused on the agency's mission or mandate. Workers could carry the manual in the car with them for reference when deciding upon a course of action. Most worker manuals today are massive office-bound volumes articulating standardized procedures and forms, and specific steps to be followed for various categories of investigative and assessment activities regardless of context. In a study of front-line child welfare workers in 1993, Callahan found that such standards and manuals contributed to workers' feelings of insecurity and vulnerability by

---

[16] *Supra*, note 13 at 83.

[17] Davies et al., *supra*, note 11; M.L. Lovell and A.H. Thompson, "Improving the Organization and Delivery of Child Welfare Services: Themes, Policy Implications, and Research Agenda" in J. Hudson and B. Galaway (Eds.), *Child Welfare in Canada: Research and Policy Implication* (Toronto: Thompson Educational Publishing, 1995), 91-98; and B. Wharf, "Preface" in B. Wharf (Ed.), *Rethinking Child Welfare in Canada* (Toronto: McClelland and Stewart, 1993), 7-10.

[18] J. Lafrance, "Bridging the Gap: An Exploration of Social Service Administrators' Perspectives on Citizen Involvement in Social Welfare Programs" in J. Hudson and B. Galaway (Eds.), *Child Welfare in Canada: Research and Policy Implications* (Toronto: Thompson Educational Publishing, 1995), 13-19.

emphasizing accountability rather than support.[19] When a case blows up in the media, workers' activities are judged by level of compliance with the written standards rather than less measurable factors such as relationship, context and professional judgement.

Child welfare work frames and labels problems in individual terms. Agency caseloads are lists of individual names assigned to individual social workers. Family court dockets are lists of individual names appearing before assigned judges. Agency case files and court records are identified by individual names. High caseloads and the crisis orientation of child welfare work reinforce a focus on individual behaviours, thereby hiding the larger environmental issues. Although the literature clearly calls for new paradigms and societal accountability, most child welfare reform efforts have concentrated on enhancement of existing services, restructuring, and improving communication and coordination.[20] This residual system with its reactive focus on individual blame and accountability continues to obscure the larger social issues affecting children, parents, and families in Canadian society.

Micro/Macro Practice Perspectives

As a profession, social work declares a simultaneous focus on micro and macro levels of practice. At the micro level, social workers are involved with the provision and evaluation of direct services to individuals, families, and small groups. At the macro level, social workers are involved with policy issues and system change with organizations, communities, and society as a whole. As described in the previous section, the residual nature of current child welfare practice forces almost an exclusive concentration at the micro practice level. Child welfare workers are responsible for managing huge caseloads of individuals and families identified by the system as problems. Challenging the macro level issues that create and maintain unhealthy environments for children typically is not part of the job description. The task of identifying macro issues and proposing frameworks for change has largely fallen to the academics and professional literature in social work.

What are some of these macro level concerns? There is widespread agreement in the social work literature that poverty is a major influence on the ability and capacity to parent. According to Kufeldt and Theriault, "adequate income is the most basic and powerful preventive measure."[21] Higher placement rates are reported when child welfare investigations find "neglect as the primary category of maltreatment, benefits or employment insurance as the primary source of income, or public rental as the type of housing accommodation."[22]

---

[19] *Supra*, note 13.

[20] Wharf, *supra*, note 17.

[21] Kufeldt and Theriault, *supra*, note 11 at 358.

[22] B. MacLaurin, N. Trocmé, and B. Fallon, "Characteristics of investigated Children and Families Referred for Out-of-Home Placement" in K. Kufeldt and B. McKenzie (Eds.), *Child Welfare: Connecting Research, Policy, and Practice* (Waterloo: Wilfrid Laurier University Press, 2003), 27 at 39.

Child poverty persists as a Canadian reality. In 1993, Wharf decried the complex web of societal factors and policies "that condemn one-sixth of Canada's children to live in poverty."[23] A full decade later, Lightman reported no real change[24] (although there may be the appearance of change through Statistics Canada's recent adoption of a new indicator — the MBM or market basket measure). Overall the situation is shameful, especially given the federal Parliament's 1989 resolution to eliminate child poverty in this country by the year 2000.[25]

Society, however, cannot be held accountable for economic conditions by a child welfare system that is oriented to individual and family problems. Parenting is viewed as a private family concern; differing parenting patterns are understood as a matter of learning and individual choices that are not influenced by available resources. This perspective "favours techniques, such as casework, but also psychologizing of all sorts, that pathologize the individual."[26] The current situation in which child welfare agencies provide services that disguise poverty and its oppressive consequences has been described as "not morally acceptable," yet it continues.[27]

Culture is another macro issue that "remains poorly understood as a concept" in both research and practice related to child welfare.[28] Court decisions may not always take into account concerns of cultural identity, worldview, or historical treatment. In the child welfare arena, reliance on the belief system of the dominant society can perpetuate potentially harmful practices. According to Bernard and Bernard,[29] these can include placing children outside of their own culture, applying contextually inappropriate risk criteria, not recognizing strengths and resources within the cultural community, or not actively recruiting culturally appropriate adoption and foster homes. Unquestioning acceptance of the dominant culture can render child welfare workers "blind, both to collective injuries, whether they be of gender, race, or class, and to the merits of other communities."[30]

---

[23] B. Wharf, "Rethinking Child Welfare" in B. Wharf (Ed.), *Rethinking Child Welfare in Canada* (Toronto: McClelland and Stewart, 1993), 210 at 211.

[24] E. Lightman, *Social Policy in Canada* (Don Mills: Oxford University Press, 2003).

[25] C. Hughes, "Child Poverty, Campaign 2000, and Child Welfare Practice: Working to End Child Poverty in Canada" in S. Scarth, B. Wharf and E. Tyrwhitt (Eds.), "Changing the Child Welfare Agenda: Contributions from Canada" (May/June1995), LXXIV Special Issue of *Child Welfare*, 779-794.

[26] V. Strong-Boag, "Getting to Now: Children in Distress in Canada's Past" in B. Wharf (Ed.), *Community Work Approaches to Child Welfare* (Peterborough: Broadview Press, 2002), 29 at 35.

[27] K. Barter, "Services for Vulnerable Children: A Conceptualization" in J.C. Turner and F.J. Turner (Eds.), *Canadian Social Welfare* 4th ed. (Toronto: Pearson Education Canada, 2001), 250 at 262.

[28] K. Swift and L. Longclaws, "Foster Care Programming: Themes, Policy Implications and Research Agenda" in J. Hudson and B. Galaway (Eds.), *Child Welfare in Canada: Research Policy Implications* (Toronto: Thompson Educational Publishing, 1995), 245 at 249.

[29] C. Bernard and W.T. Bernard, "Learning From the Past/Visions for the Future: The Black Community and Child Welfare in Nova Scotia" in B. Wharf (Ed.), *Community Work Approaches to Child Welfare* (Peterborough: Broadview Press, 2002), 116-129.

[30] *Supra*, note 26 at 35.

Child welfare matters take on additional complexity in First Nations communities.[31] First Nations children are dramatically overrepresented in child welfare caseloads and children in care. Blackstock explains how "each day, First Nations children experience first hand the impacts of over 100 years of colonial policies perpetuated by governments, the churches, and later by child welfare systems."[32] In First Nations communities, "children's welfare is never simply the issue."[33] State interventions affecting local families are instances of a larger jurisdictional dialogue with the dominant society. For First Nations communities, taking control of child welfare services is a key component of the movement towards self-government. Individual cases may affect local families and community healing, but legal decisions set precedents with implications for broader jurisdictional issues and sovereignty.[34] The vision was expressed effectively by Blackstock:

> First Nations child and family services providers work to heal the despair caused by the residential schools and other instruments of colonization. In this regard, community-based child and family services are involved in much more than assuring the immediate protection of children at risk. They are attempting to rebuild communities and families in order that they may care for their own children within a framework that incorporates traditional values and practices. These programs are also dedicated to bringing First Nations children who have been lost and damaged home.[35]

Paradigms

A decade ago, Wharf expressed a "profound sense of dissatisfaction with child welfare policy and practice in this country."[36] He called for a change in the mandate of child welfare away from the focus on investigation of neglect and abuse towards a model that would offer support to parents and advocate with them for necessary resources. His vision was of a situation where legislation and policy would support the primary interactional work of social workers and clients, rather than the other way around. Lovell and Thompson agreed with this

---

[31] See discussson in Chapter 7.

[32] C. Blackstock, "First Nations Child and Family Services: Restoring Peace and Harmony in First Nations Communities" in K. Kufeldt and B. McKenzie (Eds.), *Child Welfare: Connecting Research, Policy, and Practice* (Waterloo: Wilfrid Laurier University Press, 2003), 331-342.

[33] C. Brown and P. Morrow, "'A Resource Most Vital': Legal Interventions in Native Child Welfare" (Summer 2001), 23 *The Northern Review* 103-120.

[34] A. Armitage, "Family and Child Welfare in First Nation Communities" in B. Wharf (Ed.), *Rethinking Child Welfare in Canada* (Toronto: McClelland and Stewart, 1993), 131-171; *supra*, note 33; D. Durst, J. McDonald, and C. Rich, "Aboriginal Government of Child Welfare Services: Hobson's Choice?" in J. Hudson and B. Galaway (Eds.), *Child Welfare in Canada: Research and Policy Implications* (Toronto: Thompson Educational Publishing, 1995), 41-53; B. McKenzie, E. Seidl, and N. Bone, "Child Welfare Standards in First Nations: A Community-based Study" in J. Hudson and B. Galaway (Eds.), *Child Welfare in Canada: Research and Policy Implications* (Toronto: Thompson Educational Publishing, 1995), 54-65; J. Timpson, "Four Decades of Literature on Native Canadian Child Welfare: Changing Themes" in S. Scarth, B. Wharf, and E. Tyrwhitt (Eds.), "Changing the Child Welfare Agenda: Contributions from Canada" (May/June 1995), LXXIV(3) Special Issue of *Child Welfare* 525-546.

[35] *Supra*, note 32 at 342.

[36] Wharf, *supra*, note 17 at 7.

direction but concluded the practice reality is one where such "innovative practice strategies directed at developing families' competencies are commonly seen as peripheral to the investigation of maltreatment reports."[37]

In 2002, Wharf assessed developments since his earlier book and came to the conclusion that "the child welfare enterprise has steadily deteriorated."[38] Social workers are still prevented from supporting families by horrendous caseloads and the crisis nature of the work. Clients have been objectified by case management approaches and the "paradigm of risk" that currently dominates mainstream child welfare practice. The whole process of risk assessment builds upon the conventional practice of casework with individuals. As explained by Wharf:

> Risk assessments are focussed on the personal characteristics of parents and even more narrowly with identifying their deficits and weaknesses rather than their strengths and abilities. In its neglect of contextual social issues and networks of support, the risk paradigm presents a pathological view of those being served and reinforces an individualistic approach to practice. Such a view confirms prevailing impressions in the media and even among some practitioners that individuals coming to the attention of child welfare agencies are beset by personal problems like addiction, unstable relationships, and immaturity. While most live in poverty, in inadequate housing, and in unsafe neighbourhoods, the personal problems dominate and occupy the foreground while the public issues fade into the background.[39]

Wharf points out that the risk paradigm also serves to protect bureaucratic policy makers.[40] Risk assessments generated through standardized instruments are easy for managers to review. When something major goes wrong and the public demands accountability, it is convenient for the agency to blame individual caseworkers for faulty risk assessments. Wharf advocates a shift to a community paradigm, but he does not think this will happen soon because the risk paradigm has such benefits for senior policy makers and bureaucrats.

Houston and Griffiths also called attention to the need for a shift away from the risk paradigm now dominating child welfare.[41] As expressed by Barter,[42] "protection of children must move beyond just protection in their own families to include their protection from the social, economic, and political forces that affect families and communities." Hughes advocated for child welfare organizations to "cultivate a social justice culture within themselves."[43] Commenting on the recent emergence of a National Children's Agenda in Canada, Theriault called for a new philosophy or paradigm for child welfare "based on principles

---

[37] Lovell and Thompson, *supra*, note 17 at 91.

[38] *Supra*, note 9 at 9.

[39] B. Wharf, "Building a Case for Community Approaches to Child Welfare" in B. Wharf (Ed.), *Community Work Approaches to Child Welfare* (Peterborough: Broadview Press, 2002), 181 at 183.

[40] *Ibid.*

[41] S. Houston and H. Griffiths, "Reflections on Risk in Child Protection: Is it Time for a Shift in Paradigms?" (2000), 5 *Child and Family Social Work* 1-10.

[42] Barter, *supra*, note 15 at 258.

[43] *Supra*, note 25 at 790.

of *child development* whereas Canadian child welfare legislation is based on a philosophy of *child protection*."[44]

Law may be perceived by social workers as re-enforcing the status quo residual nature of child welfare rather than as a force towards a desired shift in paradigms. Offering remedies after-the-fact to settle disputes or correct proven violations, the courts are seen as reactive, as "restorative rather than transformative,"[45] as a mechanism for maintaining rather than challenging the current paradigm.

Implications

This discussion has examined a number of issues that might block social workers from taking full advantage of a book on child welfare law written primarily by lawyers and judges. The two disciplines display obvious differences in the ways they build and communicate the knowledge base for their work. The defining identity for social work as a profession may be threatened in the increasingly litigious arena of child welfare. Social workers do not want to be technicians in someone else's process. Undergraduate social work education programs have little room for core course content on the specifics of child welfare law. Frustrated with the residual nature of the current child welfare system (where society takes no responsibility for the social, economic, and political environment in which parents must operate), social workers may at times perceive the law as maintaining that unjust system. As an expression of these frustrations, the social work literature on child welfare features critical analysis and calls for new paradigms and operations more consistent with child development and a community social work orientation.

What is the cumulative effect of these various obstacles? How can this book on Canadian child welfare law be useful and acceptable to social work practitioners in the field?

In her analysis of feminist approaches to child welfare, Callahan suggested that "the true aim of child welfare should be to ensure that mothers become citizens with the rights and responsibilities of citizenship."[46] Yet she emphasized that such a radical paradigm shift "does not exclude the use of civil and criminal actions to redress crimes against children and women. In fact, it encourages them."[47] This understanding is key. Paradigm shifts advocated by social workers in child welfare do not necessarily involve abandonment of potentially useful alternatives available through the court system. Along with active concerns for

---

[44] E. Theriault, "Child Welfare Research and Development in a National Context" in K. Kufeldt and B. McKenzie (Eds.), *Child Welfare: Connecting Research, Policy, and Practice* (Waterloo: Wilfrid Laurier University Press, 2003), 1 at 7.

[45] D. Turner, "Legal Issues" in F.J. Turner (Ed.), *Social Work Practice: A Canadian Perspective* (Scarborough: Prentice-Hall Canada, 1999), 319 at 323.

[46] M. Callahan, "Feminist Approaches: Women Recreate Child Welfare" in B. Wharf (Ed.), *Rethinking Child Welfare in Canada* (Toronto: McClelland and Stewart, 1993), 172 at 208.

[47] *Ibid.*

healthy child and family development, child welfare work necessitates making very difficult choices that can have powerful and intrusive impacts on personal privacy and individual rights. A trial process that is transparent, accountable and documented for the public record is crucial for such decision making. There continues to be a key role for the Family Court to play in this endeavour, but Family Court cannot be the totality, or even the centrality, of society's approach to child welfare.

Society is becoming more litigious. We are witnessing an increasing role for law in all areas of health and welfare in Canada. In spite of the obstacles discussed in this chapter, however, law and social work are not enemies in the child welfare arena. Lawyers, judges, social workers, parents, and communities in child welfare want to see safe and healthy children developing in supportive family and cultural contexts. The common enemy is a political and economic system that devalues women and children, blames them individually for social and economic conditions beyond their control, and inadequately funds services that can only react to crises.

Social workers know that the law "shapes the context of much social work intervention."[48] For effective child welfare practice, it is crucial that social workers have an understanding of relevant legal principles and be able to communicate these clearly in order to "keep the focus on making reasonable treatment and care decisions."[49] In addition to a basic practical knowledge of the relevant law, social workers in child welfare must be able to anticipate and thereby avoid potential legal problems in their work. The material in this book can help social workers in child welfare to work effectively with their individual clients and families (micro level) while they seek to change the system (macro level).

---

[48] *Supra*, note 45 at 319.

[49] R. Solomon, *Social Service Professionals and the Law: Blaming the Helpers* (Handout from workshop presented to social workers and psychologists, Calgary, Alberta, November 5, 1999) at 24.

15

Child Protection Proceedings: Some Concluding Thoughts from the Bench

---

Judges play a key role in the child protection process. The expectation is that they will impartially decide the cases brought before them on the basis of the evidence presented and the governing legal principles. It is, however, clear that their beliefs, values, experiences and personalities affect how they perceive those who appear before them.

The attitude of the judge towards the child protection process will inevitably influence how procedural and substantive issues are resolved, as well as affecting the atmosphere in the courtroom. It is thus fitting to conclude this book with a collection of judicial perspectives on the child protection process.

A: THE PAUCITY OF RESOURCES

Justice Lynn King[1]

For over 15 years I have been sitting on child welfare cases. Increasingly I have asked myself why these most heartbreaking of cases ever have to land in court. Legally, of course, they must, but from a societal point of view it represents an obvious sign of failure to help both individuals and families early on, however difficult that may be.

Once a matter is in court the evidence, reams of it, of various attempts to assist the families is heard: the referrals to counselling, to child care facilities, to parenting programs, and on and on — what I will describe as the "clearinghouse" model.

These efforts, however, so often strike me as patchwork — as too little too late. Too little, because the resources to which agencies can refer mothers, fathers and children are fewer and fewer, with longer and longer waiting lists. And "referring" an under-functioning parent to a helping agency is often a recipe for failure from the start, because of the parents' lack of a phone, lack of competence or assertiveness in making appointments, lack of organizational abilities, or even lack of motivation. Too late, because the weakness of the

---

[1] Justice Lynn King, Ontario Court of Justice, Toronto.

parent, whether psychological, physical, emotional, or economic, has so often become entrenched that it could take a lifetime to change, especially from the child's perspective, if indeed change is possible.

At the same time that the resources are shrinking, the child protection net, both legally and practically, is widening. I remember cases from my earlier years on the bench where the state of a parent's housing was of concern to the child protection agency; now it is lack of housing, never mind the state of it. These days no housing or shelter at all is often the driving reason for the intervention of a child protection agency.

As the child protection net widens, and child protection resources shrink, child protection workers look more and more like frantic enforcement officers citing a litany of matters the parents have *not* attended to, such as acquiring adequate housing or arranging anger management counselling. The child protection workers so often seem to be working against the parent. I am sure much of this has to do with frustration at their own conditions of employment, which include limited resources and caseloads that seem too large.

Again, I recall cases from early on in my judicial career where workers actually went into the home to teach childcare — be it meal preparation, organization, housekeeping or child discipline. Workers helped to arrange, and even attended, appointments with parents. In other words, they worked *with* the parents and family. Now workers' time constraints or perhaps training, or philosophy, seem to prevent this.

I am not talking about the good old days of child welfare. Cases were as grim then as they are now. And there was probably less identification then of needy cases requiring child welfare intervention than there is now. Regardless of the changes that have been made to legislation and the rules of court, most of which have been for the good, the child welfare system today seems so often hopelessly defeated by the paucity of out-of-court resources, in a practical and in an imaginative and political sense. When there is inadequate housing, the child welfare system will be called on; where there are fewer social workers in the public schools, the child welfare system will be called on; where there are fewer active and free community centres, the child welfare system will be called on. Ironically, the very societal factors that lead to child welfare intervention also limit the ability of that system to help in a meaningful way.

B: THE FAILED PROMISES

Judge Patricia Kvill [2]

A girl, just apprehended, huddled in a social worker's car and sobbed into her teddy bear: "This should not be happening to me. I'm only 12." Her words of anger and indignation continue to haunt me. When I first read the account of this girl's despair in a court report, I thought her words referred to the abuse she had

---

[2] Judge Patricia Kvill, Family and Youth Division, Provincial Court of Alberta, Edmonton.

suffered at the hands of her parent. Then it occurred to me that her anguish might have been the result of being torn from her home and family by a stranger. From the perspective of this child, overwhelmed by a combination of events that were frightening and unfair, there was probably no distinction. But it defines the dilemma that judges and social workers must grapple with in every case.

Child protection cases are profoundly important and difficult. They challenge the adversarial model on which our judicial system is based. They are not about money or property, which in time can be replaced; or about criminal prosecution and defense, where liberty or reputation may be at stake temporarily; or even about custody, where parents argue which of two adequate homes can provide the best marginal advantages for their children. Child protection cases determine the very survival, both physical and emotional, of a child. A decision to leave a child in an abusive family may result in death, disability or devastating psychological harm. But removing the child may bring the same results. This is the dilemma that must be faced by every decision maker involved in child protection. We must balance the benefits to the child of remaining within the care of family against the consequences of removing the child, always keeping in mind the possibility of devastating harm no matter what choice is made. And what weighs so heavily on us is the recognition that the trauma suffered by a child or a family, as the result of a wrong decision, may not be correctible by the slow legal process. Once a decision is made, irreparable harm may be immediate.

Our decisions not only determine the fate of children and their families — they touch on the roots of society and the bedrock beliefs about human nature upon which our laws are written. Biologists suggest we have a primordial instinct, "a biological imperative," to pass on our genes through our children. Social scientists suggest we are socially conditioned to desire children and to help them develop physically, morally and socially. Whether we are founded upon genetics or conditioning, we believe that a child's best chance for survival is within the biological family, and that the greatest tragedy for a parent is the loss of a child. We recognize a special bond between parent and child. Children feel this bond. So strong is this connection that even after being removed from abusive homes, many children express a preference to be raised by an inadequate or violent parent. We are all too familiar with children who have fled from foster homes returning to their parents, hiding from social workers in closets and denying obvious abuse they have suffered, all in an effort to remain living with family.

Layered over family are the cultural ties that may bind children to a larger group. These ties are particularly strong in minority cultures, where an apprehension may result in the child's loss of both family and culture. In these cases, not only the children, but their whole communities feel a profound sense of loss. Each time we remove a child from family and culture we tear a tiny hole in our social fabric. In Canada this is particularly true for Aboriginal children who are, in numbers, disproportionately removed from their families.

Child protection laws are simply our choice of last resort, a backup system to ensure that these children will survive and develop into adulthood. Judges must determine whether to interfere in the natural order. In doing so, we are regretfully aware that we may unintentionally cause more harm than good. Before we take such drastic steps, we must have a fundamental understanding of the importance of family and culture to a particular child, and we must ensure that the family is given a reasonable opportunity to care for the child. But in the end, we also must be prepared to draw that line in the sand where further involvement with family will do more harm than good for a child.

It would be simple-minded for judges to accept foster care as a panacea for all children removed from family. Most foster parents and group home workers provide extraordinary, even saintly care. However, not all foster care is perfect; there are foster parents who have been rejected as adoptive parents, although the state has placed children in their care for years.

In youth justice court, judges are given a small and different window into the lives of some children in care. These children relate pitiful stories of moving from one foster placement to another, then graduating to group homes, hotels with one-on-one workers, and later to treatment or secure treatment facilities. Eventually, when the child protection system has been exhausted, these children move to youth emergency shelters and the street. Severely mistreated children with high needs may have great difficulty connecting with alternative care givers. They have lost any ability to trust. This lack of trust is perpetuated as the child drifts through the system, abandoned by one caregiver after another. Physically and sexually abused children may continue the cycle of abuse in homes where they have been placed. Hardly a day goes by without a case of violence in group homes being before the court. Sitting in youth justice court, judges come to believe that youths in group homes often participate in or witness violence by other youths or against group home workers. It is hard to imagine a more horrid situation than a child being removed from family due to neglect or physical abuse, only to be abused by another child in care, but we see these cases in youth justice court.

The child protection system fails where there is insufficient funding to provide damaged children with specialized care and treatment, or where damaged children continue to be subjected to abuse because of inadequate care. For these children, the system has not given the promised protection. These children are the worst legacies of this system as they never receive adequate treatment and little training in social skills or moral judgement. Not surprisingly, judges sitting in youth court see these children again and again as they graduate though the criminal system. It is never clear how we are to factor this knowledge into child protection decisions.

On the other side of this difficult equation, the evidence of abuse or neglect that children suffer at the hands of their parents is shocking, and often difficult to comprehend. In some cases the abuse is not deliberate. Children may have an illness or disability that requires specialized care beyond the capacity of ordinary parents. Or parents with chronic illnesses or disabilities may not ever be able, physically, mentally or emotionally, to raise their children, and may not even recognize or comprehend their own limitations. These are truly sad, impossible cases, but they are often the easiest decisions we are asked to make because lines are so sharply drawn.

However, the vast majority of child protection cases involve parents who are at times capable of adequate caregiving, but who on other occasions present a real danger. In particular, I am thinking of alcoholic or drug-addicted parents, or those who from time to time suffer from mental illness. These parents may be unwilling or unable to change their behaviour. One moment the child is physically, sexually or emotionally abused by the parent, who the next moment is loving and kind. These children must always be vigilant to protect themselves, their younger siblings, and sometimes their own parent. When taken into care, these children worry about the safety of their parents. Some of these children have developed strong, sometimes even pathological bonds with their parent. Placing these children in care, without successful therapy, may not break the bond, but may only serve to intensify the bond through selective memory. They remember the good times and forget the bad.

The state promises that all reasonable steps will be taken to promote the reunification of the family, but if that is not possible, there is an implicit understanding that loss of family and culture will be compensated by safety and security. Inherent in this promise is the assurance that further abuse of these children, while in the care of the state, will not be tolerated. For most families and children this promise is fulfilled. The failed promises linger in my mind.

At times, the slow court process exacerbates the suffering of children. They wait for parents who cannot be located to be served with documents. I often wonder: "Where are these parents?" Caring parents would have been searching for lost children. They would be banging at the door of social services to have them returned. But these absent parents are either oblivious to what has happened to their children or they have placed their heads in the sand and refuse to face facts. Days, even months pass while the children are in care and parents still cannot be located. It is frustrating to learn that social workers, who should be working with children, are forced, as a cost-saving measure, to become process servers. Once located, parents promise to visit and then fail to show up, leaving their children confused and distraught. Children wait for their parents to take the promised drug or alcohol treatment. Aware of a parent's failings, these children become obsessed with the need for treatment, encouraging, even badgering mother or father to take treatment. When the parent fails to follow through, the child suffers a further devastating loss. Worse yet, some parents, who fear the loss of their children's love, pass surreptitious messages to their children in an effort to turn them against their foster placement or social worker. All this occurs while children should be protected in the care of the state.

These children live in an emotional limbo — never sure where to place their trust. Unsure if they will be returned home, they cannot afford to turn their backs on their parents, nor can they place any confidence in what may turn out to be a temporary foster placement. Each time a parent is permitted to continue this kind of behaviour or the courts fail to move expeditiously to establish security for the child, it seems to me that we are guilty of complicity in the further emotional harm to the child.

Time measured by a child is quite different from time measured by an adult. While a parent's memory of a child may not be damaged by long periods of absence, for a young child, whose brain and memory are not fully developed, even a short passage of time may render parents as strangers. For this reason, we must be very careful in our decision making. It is disastrous if a judge's decision goes to appeal, particularly for a procedural failing, for these children must continue to live in limbo while courts move in slow, adult time, to determine their future.

Against this background, we must examine whether the best method to make decisions is an adversarial proceeding. Child protection trials almost inevitably are trials with reams of evidence about the past failures of parents. Parents who appear before us become intent upon denying past inadequacies or abuse. These trials become more like criminal trials where parents deny abuse, focusing on themselves rather than their children. A decision maker is often left with the feeling that these parents have decided that the best defence is a good offence. Proceedings become red-herring trials where parents focus on this or that improper action by a social worker, rather than on the needs of their child. It is frustrating to grind through this kind of case, because we often feel that the children's needs have been lost in the process.

Alternative dispute resolution can offer parents a faster and more satisfactory approach to the resolution of child protection cases. Parents, who would have spent days in trial defending themselves and their actions, may be able to turn their focus towards their children. I am convinced that most parents know their faults. If the focus of the discussion is not on the fault of the parent, as it invariably is in a trial, but rather on the needs of the child, then parents seem to be able to work towards the best interests of their child. Most parents truly love their own children, and want to ensure that they are given the best chance to survive and flourish. When this is the focus of the discussion, parents are often able to adopt quite a different perspective than the one forced on them by a re-examination of their own past failings. Parents seem to need the opportunity to tell the court, the social worker and sometimes their children, how hard they have tried to change and how difficult this decision is for them. And they need the comfort of knowing that a judge would have made the same decision had the matter gone to trial. In this less formal setting, parents have an easier time talking freely, and realistically examining issues. Parents often acknowledge in dispute resolution that a child must, for his or her survival, be placed in the care of someone other than family. This is critical because the chance of successful placement is then greatly increased because of the acceptance of the parents.

Child welfare work is messy, sometimes ugly. It requires rolling up sleeves and wading in, sometimes leaving formality on the sidelines. But, like raising children, it is always interesting. It is difficult to forget many of the parents and children I have met through these cases. I wonder what has become of them. Did I do the right thing? Are these children flourishing or will I hear their sad and sordid tales next week in youth court? This is very serious and important work — to my mind, the most important work I do as a judge. No decision I make demands greater intellectual and emotional effort, because the consequences are so serious. My decision will determine a child's future and may in some small way affect the society in which that child will live. I am often reminded of this by a framed *Successories* greeting card my younger sister gave to me on my appointment: "A hundred years from now it will not matter what my bank account was, the sort of house I lived in, or the kind of car I drove...but the world may be different because I was important in the life of a child."

C: REFLECTIONS ON CHILD PROTECTION — LOOKING FOR THE BEST AVAILABLE OUTCOMES

Judge Thomas J. Gove[3]

After almost three decades as a lawyer and judge working in the area of child protection, I believe that Canadian courts are at last initiating more child-focused procedures when dealing with issues that affect the lives of children. Judges have moved towards a deeper understanding of the need to include the child's voice when making decisions. With a change to a more child-centred approach to child protection, the courts can now include children and their views in a decision-making process that focuses on children's needs and frames their futures.

Child protection hearings are held to determine if children need protection from their families. Should children be removed and placed in another home or can the family of origin, under court-ordered supervision, provide a minimum standard of care? Judges' decisions are based on both the factual and expert evidence presented. A decision as to what specific evidence is to be included and how it is to be presented is usually left to the lawyer representing the child protection agency.

In my experience, the government's philosophy of the day has had great influence on both the orders sought by child welfare agencies and the content of and the way the evidence has been presented. Philosophies and policies in the child protection field have varied over the years — some say that the "pendulum" has swung back and forth between a child-centered focus on one end of the spectrum, and a priority for family preservation or reunification on the other. The debate rages on even today. These shifts in mindset influence the

---

[3] Judge Thomas J. Gove, Provincial Court of British Columbia.

training and instructions given to front-line social workers. It also impacts their lawyers and the evidence that is presented.

I question whose interests should be paramount under the label of child protection. Is the focus of the proceeding on the needs of the child, or is it on the abilities and rights of the parents? The parents have always been parties with the right to lawyers. If every viewpoint is to be considered, where is the voice of the child?

Background

During my years as a lawyer and judge since 1974, child protection proceedings have been conducted as trials. Child protection agencies make applications for orders that give social workers legal authority to control children's lives — either with their parents, under supervision, or in foster or institutional care. A formal trial is held, an adversarial contest where each side — the agency and the parents — compete for victory. The judge is asked to make a decision based on information limited by the evidence presented by the lawyers.

It is my sense that over time, at least in British Columbia, there has been a subtle shift from a purely adversarial trial model to one where judges are taking more of a lead in inquiring into the circumstances of the child. Practice has shifted the focus from the fault of the parents to the safety and well-being of the child. The rules of evidence have been relaxed to let this occur.

But the battle to "win" continues. The perpetuation of the adversarial process is not surprising, considering that most lawyers and judges are trained to conduct trials, not inquiries. Judges can only make decisions along the road that lawyers lead them. They cannot decide which road to take. The matter is further confused when social workers, who instruct their agency lawyers, are required to play a variety of roles: risk assessor and manager; maker of difficult decisions; accuser; witness; and then counsellor and rehabilitator of the family and, ultimately, guardian of the children. Those whom the process is supposed to be about, the children, play little if any role in choosing the evidence and directing the way it is presented. Historically, children have had little or no say in the picture presented and the work involved in determining an outcome.

In recent years, through a lot of media attention to child protection, the public's view of child protection intervention has changed. Media stories have criticized agencies for being both unduly intrusive in the lives of children and families and for not intervening to protect children. Although foster homes, for the most part, are safe and nurturing places, some may not be able to satisfy the deep-seated emotional needs of a particular child. Foster homes also have their own personal, and changing, needs that can lead to children being moved from home to home in a "foster home drift." Many disturbing cases have also come to light, portraying very negative experiences of children in foster or institutional care.[4] Communities have become more educated with regards to flaws in the child welfare system and are asking for changes.

Judges have traditionally thought that erring on the side of caution meant having children in the care of child welfare agencies, and that the agencies could and would make better decisions and choices for them than their parents, whose skills are being questioned. This assumption has been challenged on many occasions, which has led some of us to rethink how we decide on the future care of children. Although the removal of a child from a family is sometimes necessary to ensure a child's safety, foster and institutional care have not always provided the rosy panacea that was envisaged.

Are the Children Heard?

Even while working in a mediation or case conference model, I have often been troubled that children are not meaningful participants in the process or the decisions that profoundly affect them. Often judges do not hear children, or even learn their views.

Sometimes children's opinions, desires and needs are presented in reports by professionals or through the evidence of foster parents, social workers, or parents. No doubt each of these adult witnesses believes that what he or she is saying is accurate, but the evidence is unavoidably subject to the witness's interpretation.

Children, especially teenagers, can be called as witnesses. The question is, what is the most appropriate forum for them? Even if young people can articulate what would be best for them practically and emotionally, it may be unhealthy or even damaging to require them to present their feelings and needs in an adversarial environment.

Sometimes judges interview children and youth. I have done this on occasion, but I have found it to be unsettling. I am not only uncertain about what specific questions to ask, but also about the purpose for which I am seeing a child privately. The child ought not to be expected to take on the responsibility of deciding the future — that is for the adults and ultimately me as a judge to determine. I am also troubled by the effect on parents who are not present when a judge interviews their child. They may believe that a decision on the custody of their child has been made based on an interview that they did not hear; they may not even be aware of what their child said.

Children can also participate in proceedings through child advocates or, in provinces such as British Columbia, as full parties to the case. In BC, the child

---

[4] See for example: Canada — B. Walter, *In Need of Protection: Children and Youth in Alberta* (Edmonton: Child Welfare Review, 1993); T. Gove, *Gove Inquiry Into Child Protection in British Columbia* (Victoria: Queen's Printer, 1995); B. Raychaba, *Pain — Lots of Pain: Family Violence and Abuse in the Lives of Young People in Care* (Ottawa: National Youth in Care Network, 1993); United States — N. Bernstein, *The Lost Children of Wilder: The Epic Struggle to Change Foster Care* (Random House, 2001); United Kingdom — *Childhood Matters: The Report of the National Commission of Inquiry into the Prevention of Child Abuse* (London: The Stationery Office, 1996).

can fully participate through legal counsel. I have often required this, but have some concerns that parents may see themselves as defending against the child welfare agency as well as their own child.

Mediation

For some time I have had doubts as to whether we are doing the best for children, either through adversarial trials or judicial inquiry proceedings, not only in child protection cases, but also in other proceedings that affect their well-being. I began to look at the mediation model as a possible option.

Mediation, as a dispute resolution process, has become a credible alternative for conflict resolution outside of traditional litigation. Mediators in private practice, including some lawyers, have developed well-deserved reputations for inexpensive, speedy resolution of disputes. The business community has adopted this method as a viable alternative to expensive trials. In family disputes between separated parents, mediators have become an alternative to the court system for the resolution of custody and access disputes in family breakup, as well as in the settlement of financial maintenance and property division.

Mediation works well in commercial disputes where the litigants alone may decide what they consider to be an appropriate outcome. The state usually has little interest and, as long as the parties agree, a judge will seldom interfere. In family disputes not involving child protection, parents are generally free to decide on how they wish to arrange the raising of their children and their financial affairs. Private mediators or publicly funded Family Court counsellors are available to help with these cases. There are also a wide variety of programs across Canada that attempt to help parents reach a resolution without adversarial litigation. Judges in some provinces conduct some form of mediation with separated couples in judicially supervised settlement conferences.

In recent years I have found that a judge-mediated case conference can be an effective alternative to traditional approaches for deciding child protection cases. Although the term "mediation" is used to describe these proceedings, they are clearly different from the interest-based resolution process used in commercial mediation. Because a judge is not a mediator, but rather a judicial officer using mediation as a process to achieve an outcome, the judge still has a responsibility to intervene if the "resolution" does not respect the law protecting children. Any order of the court must be in a child's best interests and protect the child. With that understanding, mediation administered by judges has proven to be a positive change in how child protection cases are conducted. The process allows for frank, disciplined discussion between all the players in a child's life and, in my experience, a consensual resolution in most cases. Children and youth, whether formally made parties or not, can participate in the case conference. The extent of their involvement should depend on their age, maturity, and the resources that the adults make available to them.

Currently, my preferred procedure when there is an application by a child protection agency for an order of custody or supervision, and when parents or a child 12 years or older do not consent, is to order a judge-mediated case conference. Prior to the case conference I consider the ages of the children and, where appropriate, either make them parties with their own assigned lawyer or ask that they be invited to attend the conference. I ask the agency lawyers to file a case conference brief that sets out a summary of the relevant facts, including what is agreed to and what orders are sought. If I am presiding at a case conference, I attempt to read all of the legal documents that have been filed prior to the conference so that time is not wasted going over history. As the case conference should be outcome-oriented, I want to move directly to search for the best child-centered outcome.

Case conferences are not open to the public. In some cases, the judge may allow other people directly involved with the family to be present. In British Columbia, a child over the age of 12 is entitled to be present, and I expect an explanation if the child is not at the case conference. I usually inquire as to his or her maturity and interest and invite any child who is between ages 9 and 11 to be present. Children often are not in the room during the entire conference. Usually they can tell me what part they want to be present for, and what part they would rather miss.

Case conferences typically take 1½ to 2 hours to conduct. I try to hold them in a conference room with everyone sitting around a table. The seating arrangement is important. I usually have the children sit near to me, then the parents, social workers and lawyers. A lawyer's role in a case conference is to give legal advice to his or her clients, to assist me with the background information and, sometimes, to help parents or children articulate their views. I do not make an official record of the case conference proceedings, except when an agreement is reached and an order is made. It is understood that a judge who conducts a case conference will not preside over any future trial if a resolution is not reached.

The task of mediation at a judge-mediated case conference in a child protection case, in my opinion, is to work towards what is the *best available outcome* for the child. Hopefully, the outcome will be acceptable to the family. If the interests of both the child and the parents cannot be achieved, it is clear to me that the child's interests must take precedence. I try to allow those who are the most affected by the outcome to have the most input. I usually ask the parents and children to speak first, often asking them to tell me in their own words why they believe the social worker thinks the child should be in the care of child welfare authorities. I also ask what they believe needs to be done before the child can return to the care of his or her family. The answers often demonstrate why this forum allows us to more quickly "get to the issues." I have had answers from parents such as: "I am an alcoholic, but have stopped drinking... I just need to prove that to the social worker and then I think I can raise my kids." I recall one 11-year-old child saying, "I don't know if my dad can care for my brother and me...he misses most of the visits at my foster home and when he does come he looks hung over." After that comment, the father knew that his son had concisely stated what he had not been prepared or able to hear from the social worker.

Quite often a second case conference is required. Usually the parents, with help from the social worker, will be expected to have performed certain tasks or reached certain goals between case conferences. In the event that all of the issues cannot be resolved at case conferences, the time is not wasted. They are useful processes from which a judge is able to narrow the issues at a hearing — what in British Columbia we call a "mini-hearing."

Best Interest or *Best Available Outcome*?

In a perfect world, all children would live in circumstances that serve to promote their best interests. When I first started to work in the area of child protection, there was a belief — perhaps an illusion — that freeing a child up for adoption was almost a guarantee of a better life than with a biological family that had come to the attention of a child protection agency. Most of us with experience in the area now know that this is simply not always the case. Sometimes a family does have the potential to overcome shortcomings, change patterns and be the best place to suit a child's needs, given time and resources. Sometimes a combination of regular biological family interaction but placement in a foster home or other community setting is preferred by and needed for a child. In other cases, however, a plan that leads to a child temporarily experiencing a series of foster homes in the hope that it will be possible to achieve parental rehabilitation and achieve family reunification may be worse than making the hard decision to place a child permanently outside of the biological family. In our less than perfect society, perhaps all we can hope to do is look for the best plan or *best available outcome*, using the information we can secure at one point in time. That information should include the views of the child in some form.

Conclusion

Since the introduction of judge-mediated case conferences in the spring of 1996, my experience is that fewer cases have gone to trial. Parents, children and social workers together are often able to come to an agreement on the *best available outcome* for the children and family.

Care must be taken that case conferences do not become vehicles for "plea bargaining" to compensate for too few judges or too little court time. There is no doubt that mediation and case conferences are substantially less expensive than traditional litigation. However, inexpensive resolution should not compromise the safety and well-being of any child. Judge-mediated outcomes that address the best interests of the children involved will always be more desirable than trials. This is not just because they are less formal and expensive but because, in the end, those most affected have agreed on what is best for them.

There will, however, continue to be a place for trials in our child protection system. In some cases, parents may be unwilling or psychologically unable to accept that state intervention is necessary to protect their child. And in cases in which the child protection agency is seeking permanent removal of the child from parental care with a plan for adoption, there may be no "middle ground."

D: THE JUDICIAL ROLE IN CHILD PROTECTION PROCEEDINGS

Judge James C. Wilson[5]

The proliferation of child protection cases over the last ten years has profoundly affected the work of Family Court judges. It is not just the number and complexity of these cases that causes them to dominate dockets, but the requirement that they be heard and decided in a timely manner frequently pushes other cases to the sidelines.

Because child protection is state intervention in the family, the judge's role in interpreting legislation and exercising his or her very considerable discretion requires a careful balancing of public and private interests. The consequences for the individuals involved, particularly the children, are enormous. Persons who find their parenting challenged by the awesome power and resources of the state must be concerned, if not intimidated. The purpose of child protection legislation is to protect children from harm, and a judge's role is to ensure that the rights of all individuals are respected according to law. The judicial role requires not only a thorough understanding of the law, but a lot of common sense and wisdom.

While legislation provides a procedural framework and general principles for the court to consider in assessing risks and determining best interests, the application of these rules and principles to a given set of facts can be very challenging. The presenting problems may be similar, but every situation is unique because of the parties involved. The judicial role is often like that of a wise parent. Every good parent knows he or she must treat all their children fairly and equally. That does not mean they are all treated the same. Similarly, child protection cases require different judicial approaches. Some parties respond best to an authoritarian approach, while others are engaged by a different way. Some parties are compliant with services, others test the limits. As judges we are challenged in each case to find the best approach.

Child protection cases today reflect the complexities of modern life. The parties before the court include not only the biological parents, but frequently step-parents, grandparents, and the older children themselves. The sheer number of parties and the complicated parenting issues make for challenging litigation. Because problems range from physical and sexual abuse, neglect and poverty to a host of emotional issues, it is necessary to involve many experts. While the vast majority of cases are resolved short of protracted litigation, when it does occur litigation is often complicated and lengthy. These problems, when superimposed upon stringent time lines, challenge the resources of all participants, including the judiciary.

---

[5] Judge James C. Wilson, J.F.C., Family Court, Nova Scotia.

Even the most seasoned veterans of family litigation find it difficult to think of child protection cases without experiencing strong emotions. These cases, more than any others, invoke in me a full range of emotion — sadness, anger, frustration, outrage, disgust, admiration and sometimes hope. Just when you think you have seen or heard it all you pick up a new file and read again about the pain and challenges facing children and their parents. I often wonder, as a fellow human being, how the circumstances could have gotten so bad. Too frequently I believe the best interests of the child have been compromised in an attempt to preserve a dysfunctional family unit. It is rare in my experience for files to reach court without the need for services being obvious.

While my initial reaction to a file may be at the human or emotional level, by the time I enter the courtroom for the initial appearance I am firmly in the judicial role. My job is to apply the law to the facts properly before me. At this initial stage and throughout the process, the judicial role is to ensure that the competing interests are heard, and a final resolution is reached in a fair and timely manner consistent with the purpose of the legislation.

The judicial role in child protection differs from private custody and access disputes between parents. In the latter type of case, the court is asked to choose which of two or more plans of care is in the best interests of the children. The court is asked to arbitrate a private family dispute, and in most of these cases the children will maintain contact with both parents, regardless of the outcome of the litigation. In child protection the process is more like a criminal proceeding. The initial burden (civil) is on the state agency to satisfy the court that there is need for a protection order. The state agency must satisfy the court that the quality of parenting being provided is not good enough; and that there is a reasonable and credible risk the children will suffer harm if the status quo remains. In my experience there are very few cases where the state is not able to discharge its initial burden by showing a need for services. I frequently find that while respondents may not agree with all the facts alleged by an agency, and indeed differ sharply on many points, the respondents nevertheless admit a problem and are willing to acknowledge a need for services. The real issues are often around placement, services and compliance.

The role of the agency and its representation in child protection is unique. They are at one and the same time an investigator, the applicant before the court, and the provider of services. As service providers they are required to work in a close and supportive relationship with the families. There is frequently tension in this relationship because of the dual role undertaken by the agency.

In my experience the child protection workers today, who more often than not are young and relatively inexperienced, are case managers or brokers of services rather than actual providers. Services are frequently contracted out to community agencies. While this may reduce tension between workers and parent clients, it also means that workers are not always as knowledgeable about their clients as they once were. The court is required to closely monitor this relationship. It is common for workers and clients to remain locked in an adversarial relationship. When the working relationship is frustrated by personality problems, caseloads, or a lack of practical experience, the judicial role becomes even more demanding as the parties and the court work towards resolution.

Child protection litigation presents other challenges for the court because the resources available to the parties are so unequal. Agencies generally have the advantage of very experienced, often full-time counsel. In addition they have professional social workers and access to a wide range of expert services. By contrast the respondents are frequently unrepresented and often are among society's most marginalized members. Legal representation is sometimes inadequate and respondents generally have no means to access special services. This inequality in resources for litigation exerts great pressure on parents to cooperate with the agency. In some cases it is left to the court to ask critical questions. Sometimes a judge must suggest the appointment of a guardian to assist counsel acting on behalf of child parties or respondent parents with mental or emotional disabilities. While it is generally not appropriate for judges to ask questions during a hearing, beyond a request for an explanation or clarification of evidence, child protection litigation is an area where the judge is under a greater obligation to raise issues or concerns that bear directly on the issues in dispute. This means the judge must be vigilant to ensure that the process remains not only fair but also is focused on those issues relevant to protecting children and promoting their best interests.

The types of problems creating child protection concerns are as varied as society itself. The traditional concerns created by poverty and physical abuse are now complicated by sexual abuse concerns and serious neglect and emotional abuse issues. In part because the family structure in society has become less stable and more subject to change, complex psychological disorders appear to be on the rise. The high level of mobility in our society means that many families now find themselves in difficulty without the aid of traditional extended family. All these pressures lead to complex child protection issues.

Despite the complex problems, the options for addressing the concerns remain relatively few. Either services are offered in the context of the family unit or children are removed. If removed, the issue becomes what services and/or contact with the parents is appropriate. Child protection legislation requires that the court recognize the sanctity of the family and remove children from the day-to-day care of their parents only when services to the family unit cannot protect children from harm or adequately address the presenting problems. Complex issues arise when only one of the respondent parents will engage in services but children's attachment to the other, non-compliant parent remains strong. Devising creative solutions is a constant challenge.

The emphasis on services over the last ten years has presented its own problems. Agencies, because of the legislated mandates, have at times been unrealistic in their expectations of what services alone could accomplish. All those who work in this area, particularly service providers, remain optimistic that people can and will change with appropriate supports. Experience, however, teaches us that those who suffer from chronic deficits, whether they are severe addiction problems, personality traits that are resistant to change, or mental, physical or emotional disabilities, are statistically unlikely to respond positively to services. Too often parents who lack the fundamental commitment or capacity to parent have monopolized scarce resources with little gain. The law requires that we be reasonable, but not exhaustive, in the use of services. It is not in the best interests of children to be held in limbo while parents are given yet another opportunity to pursue unrealistic goals.

Frequent reference is made to the stringent time lines which govern child protection. These are premised on the recognition that time is a significant factor in a child's development. It is generally accepted that children function best in a stable and predictable environment. Where there is too much uncertainty, too much exposure to negative influences, positive development is compromised. For these reasons the courts have been directed to bring matters to a timely conclusion. There are nevertheless cases where the facts make strict compliance with time lines not in the best interests of children. Children should not be compromised by undue delay in getting them settled in a nurturing or stable environment, nor should they be cut off prematurely from their family of origin. Time management is a constant challenge in child protection cases.

Removal of children from their parents is likewise complicated, and perhaps more so, the older the child. Removal of children carries with it the risk of triggering various attachment problems. Even children who have been traumatized in the care of their parents experience deep loss when removed from their care. These concerns simply underline the inherent risk in child protection. There is risk in everything we do.

While judges bring to their child protection cases a knowledge of the law and their accumulated life experiences, the nature of today's problems necessitates a heavy reliance on expert opinion. It is imperative that judges keep an open and critical mind, and develop a facility to consider what weight to attach to expert testimony. Social science is ever expanding our knowledge and understanding of human behaviour. Yesterday's gospel truths are constantly being modified by new knowledge. Judges must work hard to stay current with respect to attachment issues and other critical child developmental information. Only through regular attendance at educational conferences can judges hope to properly utilize and understand the reports and testimony placed before us. We must never abdicate our decision-making responsibility to the expert of the day. Despite the heavy load of cases, judges can never be passive or we will fail the very children we are trying to help. As noted above, child protection cases are about risk management and it is imperative that we exercise our judicial responsibility to manage that risk.

The *Canadian Charter of Rights and Freedoms* has had a strong influence on both child protection case law and legislation over the last 20 years. While the prospect of state intervention in a family is still scary, today's procedures offer a much better opportunity to get a result that is in the child's best interests.

Legislation mandates court appearances open to the public, full disclosure and detailed plans for care, all within strict time lines. While these requirements add complexity and cost to the litigation, they should yield better results. Child protection litigation is no longer "welfare court," but sophisticated public litigation.

Because child protection is complex litigation, it requires aggressive judicial intervention. Legislation mandates that it be given priority on our dockets. Good judicial management also requires a firm judicial hand to ensure that the rules are complied with. Because resources, including judicial resources, are limited, judges must be aggressive at pre-trial conferences to ensure that only those cases absolutely requiring litigation make it to our dockets. Aggressive judicial intervention throughout the process can keep all parties focused on the proper issue at the proper time. It is essential that judges through pre-trial conferences and settlement conferences encourage parties to consider all options, including mediation, to resolve their issues.

There are limitations to the judicial role. At the end of the day it is not judges, but parents and child protection agencies who must provide the care for children and make the decisions that will affect their day-to-day lives. Judges nevertheless must recognize that this is an area of the law where they exercise enormous discretion. To do this wisely we need not only a thorough understanding of the law, but an open and critical mind. The judicial role is not to impose our personal beliefs but to ensure that legislation designed to protect children from harm does so within the context of today's values.

Table of Cases

Table of Statutes

Index